3000 800061

St. Louis Community College

Meramec Library
St. Louis Commu
11333 Big Bend Road
Kirkwood, MO 63122-5720
314-984-7797

D0083093

WITHDRAWN

Self-Esteem Issues and Answers

Self-Esteem Issues and Answers

A Sourcebook of Current Perspectives

Edited by
Michael H. Kernis

Psychology Press
Taylor & Francis Group
NEW YORK AND HOVE

Published in 2006
by Psychology Press
270 Madison Avenue
New York, NY 10016
www.psypress.com

Published in Great Britain
by Psychology Press
27 Church Road
Hove, East Sussex BN3 2FA
www.psypress.co.uk

Copyright © 2006 by Psychology Press

Psychology Press is an imprint of the Taylor & Francis Group, an informa business

Typeset by Macmillan India Ltd, Bangalore, India
Printed and bound in the USA by Sheridan Books, Inc., MI, on acid-free paper
Cover design by Design Deluxe

All rights reserved. No part of this book may be reprinted or reproduced or utilized in any form or by any elec-
tronic, mechanical, or other means, now known or hereafter invented, including photocopying and recording, or
in any information storage or retrieval system, without permission in writing from the publishers.

10 9 8 7 6 5 4 3 2 1

Library of Congress Cataloging in Publication Data

Self-esteem issues and answers : a sourcebook of current perspectives / edited by Michael H. Kernis.
   p. cm.
  Includes bibliographical references and index.
  ISBN-13: 978-1-84169-420-7 (hardback : alk. paper)
  ISBN-10: 1-84169-420-7 (hardback : alk. paper) 1. Self-esteem. I. Kernis, Michael
Howard, 1955–
  BF697.5.S46S47 2006
  155.2–dc22

                        2006005409

ISBN13: 978-1-84169-420-7

ISBN10: 1-84169-420-7

To the memory of Mary Anne Lahey, for the courage she displayed and the inspiration she provided to others.

Contents

About the Editor

Michael H. Kernis is professor of psychology and research fellow in the Institute for Behavioral Research at the University of Georgia. His research on self-esteem and authenticity appears in the field's top journals and edited series and he has been funded by multiple grants from the National Science Foundation and National Institute of Mental Health. Dr. Kernis is a fellow of the American Psychological Society and the Society of Personality and Social Psychology and he is a member of the International Society for Self and Identity. His previous books include *Efficacy, Agency, and Self-Esteem* (Editor) and *Selfhood: Identity, Esteem, and Regulation* (coauthor with Hoyle, Leary, and Baldwin).

Contributors

Danu B. Anthony
University of Waterloo

Robert Atkins
Rutgers University

Mark W. Baldwin
McGill University

Mia Bartoletti
Marywood University

Krista L. Beiswenger
Clark University

Kathy Berenson
Columbia University

Jennifer K. Bosson
University of South Florida

Nathaniel Branden
Independent Practice

Aafje C. Brandt
University of Nijmegen

Jonathon D. Brown
University of Washington

Kirk Warren Brown
University of Rochester

David M. Buss
University of Texas at Austin

W. Keith Campbell
University of Georgia

Martin V. Covington
University of California, Berkeley

Rhonda G. Craven
University of Western Sydney

Jennifer Crocker
University of Michigan

Edward L. Deci
University of Rochester

Tracy DeHart
Loyola University of Chicago

Geraldine Downey
Columbia University

David L. DuBois
University of Illinois at Chicago

Bruce J. Ellis
University of Arizona

Seymour Epstein
University of Massachusetts,
    Amherst

Walter F. Foddis
University of Waterloo

Joshua D. Foster
University of South Alabama

Ron Friedman
University of Rochester

Lowell Gaertner
University of Tennessee

Matthew Gailliot
Florida State University

Brian M. Goldman
Clayton State University

Wendy S. Grolnick
Clark University

Daniel Hart
Rutgers University

Susan Harter
Denver University

Sarah E. Hill
University of Texas at Austin

Caroline Ho
University of Toronto

Rick H. Hoyle
Duke University

Christian H. Jordan
Wilfrid Laurier University

Howard B. Kaplan
Texas A&M University

Andrew Karpinski
Temple University

Michael H. Kernis
University of Georgia

Lee A. Kirkpatrick
College of William & Mary

Shinobu Kitayama
University of Michigan

Erika J. Koch
St. Francis Xavier University

Richard Koestner
McGill University

Mark R. Leary
Wake Forest University

Jeffrey D. Leitzel
Bloomsburg University of
    Pennsylvania

Christine Logel
University of Waterloo

Geneviève A. Mageau
McGill University

Herbert W. Marsh
University of Western Sydney

Margaret A. Marshall
Seattle Pacific University

Andrew J. Martin
University of Western Sydney

Leonard L. Martin
University of Georgia

Alyson R. McDavitt
Purdue University

Arlen C. Moller
University of Rochester

Christopher J. Mruk
Bowling Green State University

Sandra L. Murray
State University of New York at
    Buffalo

John B. Nezlek
College of William & Mary

Edward J. O'Brien
Marywood University

Jean P. O'Brien
King's College

Timothy J. Owens
Purdue University

Tom Pyszczynski
University of Colorado at Colorado
    Springs

Frederick Rhodewalt
University of Utah

John E. Roberts
State University of New York at
    Buffalo

Richard M. Ryan
University of Rochester

Constantine Sedikides
University of Southampton

D. Conor Seyle
University of Texas at Austin

Carolin J. Showers
University of Oklahoma

Sheldon Solomon
Skidmore College

Steven J. Spencer
University of Waterloo

Jennifer A. Steinberg
Temple University

Jerry Suls
University of Iowa

William Swann, Jr.
University of Texas at Austin

Romin W. Tafarodi
University of Toronto

Howard Tennen
University of Connecticut Health
    Center

Abraham Tesser
University of Georgia

Heather D. Tevendale
University of California, Los Angeles

Dianne M. Tice
Florida State University

Natasha Tursi
Rutgers University

Jean M. Twenge
San Diego State University

Roos Vonk
University of Nijmegen

Joanne V. Wood
University of Waterloo

Mark P. Zanna
University of Waterloo

Virgil Zeigler-Hill
University of Southern Mississippi

Preface

Research and theory on self-esteem have flourished in recent years, resulting in multiple perspectives on a wide range of fundamental self-esteem issues. The purpose of this book is to provide a comprehensive picture of the current state of knowledge regarding the nature of self-esteem and its role in individual and interpersonal functioning. The contributors comprise an elite group of psychologists and sociologists who have made important contributions to our understanding of self-esteem. I asked each contributor to provide a brief answer to a given question using his or her own research and theoretical perspective as well as other relevant literature. I also asked each author to make a strong case for his or her position without being highly critical of other positions.

I hope that readers will share my great enthusiasm for the essays contained in this volume and come away with a deeper appreciation for the complex, but important, role that self-esteem plays in the human condition. I believe that the broad scope of the essays strongly attests to the current vitality of the field and bodes very well for the future of self-esteem research and theory. A perusal of both academic and lay publications reveals that self-esteem issues are pertinent to researchers, students, educators, parents, clinicians, policy makers, organizational consultants, human relations officers, and so forth. Thus, individuals from many occupations should find much of interest in this compendium of current self-esteem research and theory.

The book is organized into five major sections: (i) Conceptualizing and assessing self-esteem; (ii) Development and determinants of self-esteem; (iii) Self-esteem and psychological functioning; (iv) Self-esteem in social context; and (v) Future directions. Here I briefly describe the sets of essays that comprise each section. In the volume itself, I begin each set by presenting the question that authors answered and summarizing briefly the contents of each essay.

SECTION I: CONCEPTUALIZING AND ASSESSING SELF-ESTEEM

The essays in this section focus on fundamental issues pertaining to conceptualizing and measuring self-esteem. The book starts with two sets of essays that address the definition of self-esteem (Brown & Marshall; Mruk; Marsh, Craven, & Martin) and its convergent and divergent validity (O'Brien, Bartoletti, Leitzel, & O'Brien;

Suls; Nezlek). Following examination of these basic issues, essays then tackle the controversial concept of nonconscious self-esteem (Bosson; Jordan, Logel, Spencer, & Zanna; Epstein) and the assessment of stability of self-esteem and contingent self-esteem (Kernis & Goldman). Other sets of essays in this section examine critical issues pertaining to the use of self-report and nonreactive self-esteem measures (Bosson; Koestner & Mageau; Karpinski & Steinberg; Tafarodi & Ho), and how best to characterize optimal self-esteem (Crocker; Ryan & Brown; Goldman).

SECTION II: DEVELOPMENT AND DETERMINANTS OF SELF-ESTEEM

The essays in this section focus on change and development in self-esteem. As a group, they address a number of fundamental issues and present some practical solutions to cultivating healthy self-esteem among children and adolescents. The section begins with a set of essays that focuses on developmental processes associated with the emergence of self-esteem (Harter; Kaplan; Hart, Atkins, & Tursi). The next set of essays focuses on the efficacy of self-initiated efforts and structured intervention programs to modify self-esteem (Mruk; Tevendale & DuBois; Vonk). The remaining sets of essays in this section focus on the extent to which intrapersonal or interpersonal processes influence self-esteem (Moller, Friedman, & Deci; Leary; Swann & Seyle), the interplay of self-knowledge and self-esteem (Hoyle; Showers & Zeigler-Hill; Brandt & Vonk), and the roles of parents and teachers in cultivating optimal self-esteem among their charges (Grolnick & Beiswenger; Branden; Covington).

SECTION III: SELF-ESTEEM AND PSYCHOLOGICAL FUNCTIONING

The essays in this section are wide in scope and implications. The first set examines the degree to which self-esteem is central to psychological functioning and well-being (Solomon; Koch; Tesser & Martin), while the second set addresses the costs and benefits of possessing and striving for high self-esteem (Crocker; Rhodewalt; Wood, Anthony, & Foddis). The remaining two sets of essays examine the critical role that self-esteem plays in psychological disorders and therapeutic settings (Roberts; O'Brien, Bartoletti, & Leitzel; DeHart & Tennen), and the evolutionary significance of self-esteem (Hill & Buss; Kirkpatrick & Ellis; Campbell & Foster).

SECTION IV: SELF-ESTEEM IN SOCIAL CONTEXT

The essays in this section focus explicitly on the social and cultural implications of self-esteem. The first set of essays examines self-esteem dynamics within close relationships (Murray; Baldwin; Berenson & Downey). Others focus on the interface between self-esteem and culture (Kitayama; Sedikides & Gaertner; Twenge) and the role that self-esteem plays in society's ills and triumphs (Owens & McDavitt; Pyszczynski; Tice & Gailliot).

SECTION V: FUTURE DIRECTIONS

The essays in this section focus on the most pressing issues facing researchers, parents, teachers, and therapists (Leary; Harter; Branden). They are essential reading for those interested in critical issues facing researchers and practitioners.

ACKNOWLEDGMENTS

The success of a book of this scope typically requires the skills and efforts of a large number of people who contribute in various ways, and such was the case with this book. I want to thank Paul Dukes at Psychology Press for his unwavering support throughout the publication process. Without his patience and support this project would never have come to fruition. I am also grateful to Nicola Ravenscroft at Psychology Press for her patience and expertise in guiding the book throughout the entire production process. In addition, I would like to thank Pam Riddle for her heroic efforts doing the correspondence with contributors and publishers, proofing the manuscript, etc., and, especially, for keeping me organized and on track. I am very fortunate to have a secretary who was so devoted to the success of this project. I also want to thank my current graduate students (Chad, Whitney, Patti, and Ted) who worked especially hard to keep the lab running successfully during those times when I was working on this book. Thanks also are due to the National Science Foundation and to the Psychology Department and the Institute for Behavioral Research at the University of Georgia for providing funds and resources that greatly facilitated our self-esteem research and the completion of this book. Importantly, I thank all the contributors to this volume, every one of whom enthusiastically and in a timely manner completed their essays. I am very grateful that such a stellar group of scholars agreed to work on the project and that all readily focused their essays on the questions posed to them. On a more personal note, I am very grateful to my friends and family, especially David Kritt, Sandy Rizen, Linda Kerr, Evelyn Pressman, and Janet Sundquist for their love and support. Finally, but certainly not the least, I would like to thank my wife Vicki June, for her love, support, and encouragement. Her life was not easy for a number of reasons during the time I completed this book, but she approached each day with good humor and a zest for life that was contagious. I thank her for sharing her life space with me.

Michael Kernis
University of Georgia

Section I

Conceptualizing and Assessing Self-Esteem

Question 1

What is the nature of self-esteem? How should it be defined? Is it global or specific? State and/or trait? How does it relate to self-evaluations in specific domains?

*T*he first question in this section focuses on the nature of self-esteem, how it should be defined, and how it relates to self-evaluations. The contributors were selected to represent the wide range of views on these issues. No attempt was made to achieve consensus. Instead, the goal was to provide the reader with a sense of the complexities involved. Rather than a single, simple definition of self-esteem dominating research and theory, multiple, complex definitions persist despite calls for uniformity. The essays that open the volume well represent these disparate views.

Brown refers to people's self-appraisals of their attributes and abilities as self-evaluations and shows how they are linked by researchers and theorists to global self-esteem in either a "bottom-up" or "top-down" fashion. Brown himself views self-esteem as "a capacity to construe events in ways that promote, maintain, and protect feelings of self-worth." In this view, "People with high self-esteem have a strong, abiding love for themselves that leads them to focus on their positive qualities, and to interpret and react to events in ways that maintain positive feelings of self-worth."

While endorsing the importance of "worthiness" to the definition of self-esteem, Mruk argues that an exclusive focus on such internal feelings has led to serious problems, oversimplification being among them. In his view, self-esteem is a complex phenomenon that involves the dynamic relationship between competence and worthiness. From this perspective, while self-esteem involves worthiness, worthiness must be earned through competent action; likewise, competence involves "actions that are worthy, not meaningless successes or destructive activity."

Marsh emphasizes the importance of specific self-concept dimensions as components of a multifaceted self-concept system. At the same time, his discussion minimizes the distinction between self-concept and self-esteem and the importance of affect, including feelings of self-worth, to the construct of self-esteem. Marsh's viewpoint stands in stark contrast to those of the other two contributors who define self-esteem in more affective terms, reflecting the general tendency of most current researchers and theorists. However, as the essays by Brown and Mruk indicate, substantial differences remain among self-esteem scholars.

1

The Three Faces of Self-Esteem

JONATHON D. BROWN and MARGARET A. MARSHALL

W e will start with a riddle: "What does everyone want, yet no one is entirely sure what it is, what it does, or where it can be found?" Although there may be more than one answer to this question, "self-esteem" is surely a likely candidate. In the past 30 years, self-esteem has become deeply embedded in popular culture, championed as the royal road to happiness and personal fulfillment, and an antidote to a variety of social ills, including unemployment, gang violence, and teenage pregnancy. Despite its widespread usage within nonacademic circles, academic psychologists have been divided with respect to self-esteem's function and benefits. Whereas some argue that high self-esteem is essential to human functioning and imbues life with meaning (Pyszczynski, Greenberg, Solomon, Arndt, & Schimel, 2004), others assert that it is of little value and may actually be a liability (Baumeister, Campbell, Krueger, & Vohs, 2003; Baumeister, Smart, & Boden, 1996). Between these two extremes lie various positions of an intermediary nature.

THREE WAYS THE TERM SELF-ESTEEM IS USED

We believe that part of the confusion stems from a lack of agreement regarding the construct itself. As we see it, the term is used in at least three different ways.

Global Self-Esteem (aka Trait Self-Esteem)

Sometimes self-esteem is used to refer to a personality variable that represents the way people generally feel about themselves. Researchers call this form of self-esteem, *global* self-esteem or *trait* self-esteem, as it is relatively enduring across time and situations. Depictions of global self-esteem range widely. Some researchers take a cognitive approach, and assume that global self-esteem is a decision people make about their worth as a person (e.g., Coopersmith, 1967; Crocker & Park, 2004; Crocker & Wolfe, 2001), others emphasize emotional processes, and define global self-esteem as a feeling of affection for oneself that is not derived from rational, judgmental processes (Brown, 1993, 1998; Brown & Marshall, 2001, 2002). However defined, global self-esteem has been shown to be stable throughout adulthood, with a probable genetic component related to temperament and neuroticism (Neiss, Sedikides, & Stevenson, 2002).

Feelings of Self-Worth (aka State Self-Esteem)

Self-esteem is also used to refer to self-evaluative reactions to valenced events. This is what people mean when they talk about experiences that "threaten self-esteem" or "boost self-esteem." For example, a person might say her self-esteem was sky-high after getting a big promotion or a person might say his self-esteem plummeted after a divorce. Following James (1890), we refer to these self-evaluative emotional reactions as feelings of self-worth. Feeling proud or pleased with ourselves (on the positive side), or humiliated and ashamed of ourselves (on the negative side) are examples of what we mean by feelings of self-worth.

Many researchers use the term *state* self-esteem to refer to the emotions we are calling feelings of self-worth, and *trait* self-esteem to refer to the way people generally feel about themselves (e.g., Heatherton & Polivy, 1991; Leary, Tambor, Terdal, & Downs, 1995; McFarland & Ross, 1982; Pyszczynski & Cox, 2004). These terms connote an equivalency between the two constructs, implying that the essential difference is that global self-esteem persists while feelings of self-worth are temporary. Other researchers disagree, arguing that momentary emotional reactions to positive and negative events do not provide an appropriate analogue for how people generally feel about themselves (Brown, 1993, 1998; Brown & Dutton, 1995; Brown & Marshall, 2001, 2002).

Self-Evaluations (aka Domain Specific Self-Esteem)

Finally, self-esteem is used to refer to the way people evaluate their various abilities and attributes. For example, a person who doubts his ability in school may be said to have low *academic* self-esteem and a person who thinks she is good at sports may be said to have high *athletic* self-esteem. The terms self-confidence and self-efficacy have also been used to refer to these beliefs, and many people equate self-confidence with self-esteem. We prefer to call these beliefs *self-evaluations* or *self-appraisals*, as they refer to the way people evaluate or appraise their physical attributes, abilities, and personality characteristics. Not everyone makes this distinction, however. In fact, many scales that assess self-esteem include subscales that measure self-evaluations in multiple domains (Harter, 1986; Marsh, 1993; Shavelson, Hubner, & Stanton, 1976). From this perspective, people have different levels of self-esteem in different areas. One person could have high athletic self-esteem but low artistic self-esteem, while another person could have low math self-esteem but high social self-esteem.

RELATIONS AMONG THE THREE CONSTRUCTS

Although conceptually distinct, the three constructs we have distinguished are highly correlated. High self-esteem people evaluate themselves more positively and experience higher feelings of self-worth than do low self-esteem people (Brown, 1998). These associations have led researchers to consider how these constructs are related.

A Cognitive (Bottom-Up) Model of Self-Esteem

Most researchers in personality and social psychology assume that these constructs are related in a bottom-up fashion. As shown in Figure 1.1, the bottom-up model holds that evaluative feedback (e.g., success or failure, interpersonal acceptance or rejection), influences self-evaluations, and that self-evaluations determine feelings of self-worth and global self-esteem. We refer to this as a bottom-up model because it assumes that self-esteem is based on more elemental beliefs about one's particular qualities. IF you think you are attractive, and IF you think you are intelligent, and IF you think you are popular, THEN you will have high self-esteem.

A variant of this approach assumes that not all self-evaluations influence self-esteem. Self-evaluations in domains of high personal importance exert a strong effect on self-esteem, but self-evaluations in domains of low personal importance do not. For example, it has been suggested that some people (typically men) base their self-esteem on their perceived competence, whereas other people (usually women) base their self-esteem on their social skills (e.g., Josephs, Markus, & Tafarodi, 1992). To predict self-esteem, we first weight each self-evaluation by its importance and then sum the weighted values. A related model assumes that cultures specify attribute importance, and that self-esteem derives from the perception that one possesses an abundance of culturally-valued attributes (Pyszczynski et al., 2004).

The bottom-up model makes an additional assumption. Because it assumes that self-evaluations underlie global self-esteem, the model assumes that global self-esteem effects are due to underlying self-evaluations. For example, if we find that high self-esteem people persist longer after failure than do low self-esteem people, it must be because high self-esteem people have more confidence in their ability to succeed (Blaine & Crocker, 1993). Several important social psychological theories, including Tesser's self-evaluation maintenance model (Tesser, 1988) and Steele's self-affirmation theory (Steele, 1988) adopt this assumption. Some have even gone so far as to suggest that global self-esteem is of little value and that researchers should concentrate instead on self-evaluations (Crocker & Wolfe, 2001; Marsh, 1990).

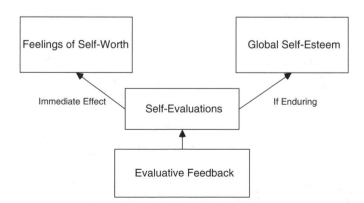

FIGURE 1.1   A cognitive (bottom-up) model of self-esteem formation and functioning.

An Affective (Top-Down) Model of Self-Esteem

Affective models offer an alternative way to think about the origins and function of self-esteem. According to this more top-down approach, self-esteem develops early in life in response to temperamental and relational factors and, once formed, influences self-evaluations and feelings of self-worth (Brown, 1993, 1998; Brown, Dutton, & Cook, 2001; Brown & Marshall, 2001, 2002; Deci & Ryan, 1995). Figure 1.2 depicts a schematic drawing of the model. The lack of an arrow between global self-esteem and evaluative feedback signifies that evaluative feedback does *not* influence global self-esteem. Instead, global self-esteem and evaluative feedback combine to influence self-evaluations and feelings of self-worth (see right hand side of Figure 1.2). This interactive effect is particularly pronounced when people confront negative feedback, such as failure in the achievement domain or interpersonal rejection. When low self-esteem people encounter negative feedback, their self-evaluations become more negative and their feelings of self-worth fall. When high self-esteem people encounter negative feedback, they maintain their high self-evaluations and protect or quickly restore their feelings of self-worth. In our view, this is the primary advantage of having high self-esteem: It allows you to *fail* without feeling bad about yourself.

Testing the Two Models

A study by Brown and Dutton (1995) tested the hypothesis that self-esteem regulates feelings of self-worth following success and failure. Participants completed two mood scales after receiving (bogus) feedback regarding their performance at an alleged test of their creativity and intelligence. One of the scales assessed very general emotional responses to success and failure (happy, sad, unhappy, glad), the other assessed feelings of self-worth (proud, pleased with myself, ashamed, and humiliated).

Self-esteem did not influence how happy or sad participants felt following success or failure, but it did influence how they felt *about themselves* after they succeeded or failed. Low self-esteem participants felt proud of themselves when

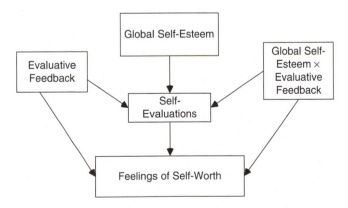

FIGURE 1.2   An affective (top-down) model of self-esteem formation and functioning.

they succeeded, but humiliated and ashamed of themselves when they failed. In contrast, high self-esteem participants' feelings of self-worth did not vary as a result of performance feedback (see also Brown & Marshall, 2001).

Cognitive models assume that self-evaluations explain these differences (e.g., Steele, 1988). From this perspective, low self-esteem people feel bad about themselves when they fail because they lack positive qualities. To test this hypothesis, Dutton and Brown (1997, Study 2) had participants complete a measure of global self-esteem, then indicate the extent to which 10 attributes described them (e.g., intelligent, attractive, incompetent, inconsiderate). Later, they performed an intellectual task and received success or failure feedback (determined by random assignment). Finally, they rated their feelings of self-worth.

Self-evaluations did not influence participants' emotional reactions to success and failure. Instead, low self-esteem participants who thought they had many positive qualities felt just as bad about themselves after they failed as did those who thought they had few positive qualities (and high self-esteem participants who believed they lacked many positive qualities felt no worse about themselves following failure than did high self-esteem participants who believed they had many positive qualities). Other analyses showed, however, that people's *cognitive* reactions to evaluative feedback (e.g., to what extent is your performance due to your ability?) did depend on self-evaluations, not self-esteem. Thus, self-esteem and self-evaluations seem to govern different aspects of psychological life (see also Bernichon, Cook, & Brown, 2003).

Concluding Remarks

The term self-esteem is used in different ways by different researchers. In this chapter, we have argued that the three terms are theoretically distinct, and have different developmental antecedents and consequences. Our point is not that one of these constructs is most important, only that they should not be used interchangeably. We base this recommendation on evidence that thinking you are good at things is not the same as having high self-esteem.

REFERENCES

Baumeister, R. F., Campbell, J. D., Krueger, J. I., & Vohs, K. D. (2003). Does high self-esteem cause better performance, interpersonal success, happiness, or healthier lifestyles? *Psychological Science, 4*, 1–44.

Baumeister, R. F., Smart, L., & Boden, J. M. (1996). Relation of threatened egotism to violence and aggression: The dark side of high self-esteem. *Psychological Review, 103*, 5–33.

Bernichon, T., Cook, K. E., & Brown, J. D. (2003). Seeking self-evaluative feedback: The interactive role of global self-esteem and specific self-views. *Journal of Personality and Social Psychology, 84*, 194–204.

Blaine, B., & Crocker, J. (1993). Self-esteem and self-serving biases in reactions to positive and negative events: An integrative review. In R. F. Baumeister (Ed.), *Self-esteem: The puzzle of low self-regard* (pp. 55–85). New York: Plenum Press.

Brown, J. D. (1993). Self-esteem and self-evaluation: Feeling is believing. In J. Suls (Ed.), *Psychological perspectives on the self* (Vol. 4, pp. 27–58). Hillsdale, NJ: Lawrence Erlbaum Associates.

Brown, J. D. (1998). *The self*. New York: McGraw-Hill.

Brown, J. D., & Dutton, K. A. (1995). The thrill of victory, the complexity of defeat: Self-esteem and people's emotional reactions to success and failure. *Journal of Personality and Social Psychology, 68*, 712–722.

Brown, J. D., Dutton, K. A., & Cook, K. E. (2001). From the top down: Self-esteem and self-evaluation. *Cognition and Emotion, 15*, 615–631.

Brown, J. D., & Marshall, M. A. (2001). Self-esteem and emotion: Some thoughts about feelings. *Personality and Social Psychology Bulletin, 27*, 575–584.

Brown, J. D., & Marshall, M. A. (2002). *Self-esteem: It's not what you think*. Unpublished manuscript, University of Washington, Seattle, WA.

Coopersmith, S. (1967). *The antecedents of self-esteem*. San Francisco: W. H. Freeman.

Crocker, J., & Park, L. E. (2004). The costly pursuit of self-esteem. *Psychological Bulletin, 130*, 392–414.

Crocker, J., & Wolfe, C. T. (2001). Contingencies of self-worth. *Psychological Review, 108*, 593–623.

Deci, E. L., & Ryan, R. M. (1995). Human autonomy: The basis for true self-esteem. In M. Kernis (Ed.), *Efficacy, agency, and self-esteem* (pp. 31–49). New York: Plenum.

Harter, S. (1986). Processes underlying the construction, maintenance, and enhancement of the self-concept in children. In J. Suls & A. G. Greenwald (Eds.), *Psychological perspectives on the self* (Vol. 3, pp. 137–181). Hillsdale, NJ: Lawrence Erlbaum Associates.

Heatherton, T. F., & Polivy, J. (1991). Development and validation of a scale for measuring state self-esteem. *Journal of Personality and Social Psychology, 60*, 895–910.

James, W. (1890). *The principles of psychology* (Vol. 1). New York: Holt.

Josephs, R. A., Markus, H. R, & Tafarodi, R. W. (1992). Gender and self-esteem. *Journal of Personality and Social Psychology, 63*, 391–402.

Leary, M. R., Tambor, E. S., Terdal, S. K., & Downs, D. L. (1995). Self-esteem as an interpersonal social monitor: The sociometer hypothesis. *Journal of Personality and Social Psychology, 68*, 518–530.

Marsh, H. W. (1990). A multidimensional, hierarchical model of self-concept: Theoretical and empirical justification. *Educational Psychology Review, 2*, 77–172.

Marsh, H. W. (1993). Academic self-concept: Theory, measurement, and research. In J. Suls (Ed.), *Psychological perspectives on the self* (Vol. 4, pp. 59–98). Hillsdale, NJ: Lawrence Erlbaum Associates.

McFarland, C., & Ross, M. (1982). The impact of causal attributions on affective reactions to success and failure. *Journal of Personality and Social Psychology, 43*, 937–946.

Neiss, M.B., Sedikides, C., & Stevenson, J. (2002). Self-esteem: A behavioural genetics perspective. *European Journal of Personality, 16*, 1–17.

Pyszczynski, T., & Cox, C. (2004). Can we really do without self-esteem? Comment on Crocker and Park (2004). *Psychological Bulletin, 130*, 425–429.

Pyszczynski, T., Greenberg, J., Solomon, S., Arndt, J., & Schimel, J. (2004). Why do people need self-esteem? A theoretical and empirical review. *Psychological Bulletin, 130*, 435–468.

Shavelson, R. J., Hubner, J. J., & Stanton, G. C. (1976). Self-concept: Validation of construct interpretations. *Review of Educational Research, 46*, 407–441.

Steele, C. M. (1988). The psychology of self-affirmation: Sustaining the integrity of the self. In L. Berkowitz (Ed.), *Advances in experimental social psychology* (Vol. 21, 261–302). New York: Academic Press.

Tesser, A. (1988). Toward a self-evaluation maintenance model of social behavior. In L. Berkowitz (Ed.), *Advances in experimental social psychology* (Vol. 21, pp. 181–227). New York: Academic Press.

2

Defining Self-Esteem: An Often Overlooked Issue with Crucial Implications

CHRISTOPHER J. MRUK

*T*he field of self-esteem consists of a body of work that focuses on research-ing this phenomenon by using an extremely wide range of qualitative and quantitative methods, theorizing about what is found, and using that infor-mation to help at the practical level. Accordingly, a good place to start when ask-ing specific questions is by defining how terms are being used and why they were selected, because operational definitions allow readers to follow and evaluate arguments more clearly. There are several additional reasons to begin in this fash-ion when thinking about self-esteem. First, social scientists define it in at least three very different ways, each of which has a long history of legitimate use in a field that is already over a century old. Second, each definition gives rise to a dif-ferent body of research findings, theories, and conclusions about self-esteem. This kind of situation can make it difficult to keep in mind which definition goes with what kind of work, thereby generating confusion in the field. Third, with at least three active definitions and an intermingling set of findings, it is surprising to find that relatively little attention is devoted to thinking about just how important defining self-esteem is in this field. In fact, it could be argued that this issue is so foundational that it should be necessary to begin by defining what one means by the words "self-esteem" whenever this subject is discussed.

One way to define self-esteem is to see it in terms of *worthiness*, or as Rosenberg (1965, p. 60) said, "Self-esteem, as noted, is a positive or negative atti-tude toward a particular object, namely, the self...High self-esteem...expresses the feeling that one is good enough." Understanding self-esteem in terms of worthiness has certain powerful advantages, especially in terms of designing research. Chief among them may be that such a one-dimensional approach makes researching self-esteem relatively easy to do. For example, defining self-esteem as a particular type of belief, attitude, or affect makes it possible to design a survey or scale that assess-es indications of worthiness (as well as the lack of it); administer the instrument to any number of people; and then to correlate responses with age, gender, race, and so forth. Indeed, defining self-esteem in terms of worthiness in the largest sense, which is to see it as a "favorable global evaluation of oneself," seems to be the most commonly used definition by far (Baumeister, Smart, & Boden, 1996).

Unfortunately, understanding self-esteem in terms of worthiness alone also leads to serious problems. One of the most important of them is that if we define self-esteem as only an "internal" phenomenon, i.e., as an attitude, belief, or feeling, then oversimplification can occur. This problem often leads to such things as designing self-esteem enhancement programs that merely focus on making people feel good about themselves. While there is nothing inherently wrong in helping people feel good about themselves, it does matter whether or not such self-perceptions are warranted: they must be connected to reality through corresponding forms of behavior. To feel good about oneself without earning it risks all kinds of problems, such as tolerating undesirable academic performance in school, facilitating the development of narcissism, or even risking an increase in the likelihood of violence (Baumeister et al., 1996; Damon, 1995). The California self-esteem movement of the 1980s, and much of the popular criticism that has come to self-esteem work since then (Johnson, 1998; Leo, 1990), can be seen in this light. It may even be possible to argue that the entire field of self-esteem came close to losing its credibility because of work that is based on defining self-esteem largely in terms of worthiness.

Fortunately, there are two other ways to define self-esteem that have achieved a place in the field. For example, it is well known that when William James first talked about self-esteem in 1890, he described it as a ratio or relationship between our achievements and our aspirations. However, what is not so well appreciated is that his definition points in a very distinct direction.

> So our self-feeling in this world depends entirely on what we back ourselves to be and do. It is determined by the ratio of our actualities to our supposed potentialities; a fraction of which our pretensions are the denominator and the numerator our success: thus,

$$\text{Self-esteem} = \frac{\text{Successes}}{\text{Pretensions}}.$$

> Such a fraction may be increased as well by diminishing the denominator as by increasing the numerator. (James, 1890/1983, p. 296)

This approach to self-esteem stresses a certain type of behavior rather than affect, attitude, or belief, because "backing oneself" requires action, especially effective action, or *competence*. Although much less common in the field these days, this view has considerable support, especially among those who approach self-esteem from a developmental context (Harter, 1993; Pope, McHale, & Craighead, 1988; White, 1963). Understanding self-esteem in terms of competence, which involves having goals, developing the skills to bring them into reality, and doing just that through one's own hard work, has its own advantages. One of them is that competence is tied to behavior, which is more readily observable than feelings, attitudes, or beliefs. Such things as problem-solving skills (or the lack of them) and achievements (or failures) can be seen and even measured. In addition, competence is a part of many important developmental processes that we already know about, such as mastering age-appropriate cognitive, academic, social, and occupational skills. This more behaviorally oriented approach to defining self-esteem makes it easier to focus on thinking about or researching connections between self-esteem and individual actions. At the very least, understanding self-esteem from this perspective reduces the merit of criticisms about work that focuses on simply making people feel good about themselves.

It must be said in all fairness that there are major problems with this approach as well. Perhaps the most important among them is that there are many kinds of behavior at which one can become quite good, but which are also so undesirable that they contradict the entire notion of self-esteem as a positive psychological phenomenon. For example, an individual could become highly skilled at lying, cheating, bullying, violating the rights of others, and so forth. Yet, such behavior is antithetical to the kinds of competencies associated with high, i.e., genuine or healthy, self-esteem. In addition, there are many people who suffer from low self-esteem, but who also happen to be quite competent in various areas, such as business, academia, athletics, and so forth, and who do *not* feel worthy enough to enjoy their success. These so-called overachievers, or those who are merely driven to succeed, may stand as an example of the limits of defining self-esteem in terms of competence. Similarly, most clinicians have known people who seem to have everything going for them in terms of career or marriage, but who then commit suicide, which certainly does not reflect high, positive, or healthy self-esteem.

The third and final major approach to defining self-esteem seems to avoid these pitfalls because it is based on a relationship between competence and worthiness. Seen in this way,

> Self-esteem has two interrelated aspects: it entails a sense of personal efficacy and a sense of personal worth. It is the integrated sum of self-confidence and self-respect. It is the conviction that one is *competent* to live and *worthy* of living. (Branden, 1969, p. 110)

The chief difference between this definition and the others is that it understands self-esteem as a more complex phenomenon consisting of three components instead of just one. Competence is one of them, which means that self-esteem is tied to, and reflected in, a particular class of behavior, namely, behavior that is effective or successful. Another is worthiness, which involves a sense of that which is in some sense "good" or meritorious and deserving of respect. The third component, expressed by the word *and*, may be the most important because it specifies that there is a connection between what the individual does in the world and how they feel about themselves. Since each component is as important as any other, their relationship is based on balance. On one hand, then, self-esteem involves worthiness, but worthiness must be earned, meaning that it depends upon behaving competently. On the other hand, in order for competence to result in feelings, attitudes, or beliefs of worthiness, such behavior must involve actions that are worthy, not meaningless successes or destructive activity. As we shall see, any significant imbalance between these crucial components is important because it creates various self-esteem related problems.

There are several advantages to understanding self-esteem as a dynamic relationship between competence and worthiness that support the value of this definition. For one thing, this approach does not fall prey to the dangers of thinking one-dimensionally that we saw earlier. Instead, we see that self-esteem is neither primarily internal (cognitive, attitudinal, or affective) nor merely external (behavior that is simply effective but not necessarily healthy or meritorious). In other words, self-esteem is seen as a "lived" phenomenon, which is to say that it involves thoughts, feelings, and behavior connected to each other as a unified form of experience and perception. Such experiences are meaningful because they are connected to one's identity as a person. Rather than ignoring this important dimension of self-esteem, research based on this definition tends to focus on examining real life experiences that enhance or lessen self-esteem. This type of work is usually more qualitative than surveys or experiments, but it involves an extremely rich and substantial source of data, which is much too valuable to ignore. For example, such research indicates very clearly that when people describe what happens for them in terms of their own self-esteem, they talk about competence and worthiness rather than either one alone (Epstein, 1979; Jackson, 1984; Mruk, 1983). Of course, more empirically oriented work also supports this position (Bartoletti & O'Brien, 2003; Hakim-Larson & Mruk, 1997; Tafarodi & Swann, 2001).

Second, understanding self-esteem in terms of competence and worthiness also lends itself to a natural typology of self-esteem and self-esteem problems. For example, it is possible to describe worthiness as a vertical axis that ranges from very low (feeling very unworthy) to very high (feeling very worthy) and competence as a horizontal axis ranging from very low (extremely ineffective) to very high (extremely effective). When the two are transposed into a diagram, we see the following type of configuration (see Figure 2.1).

Although it is not possible to go into detail here, it is important to realize that this approach to self-esteem shows just what the literature on the subject

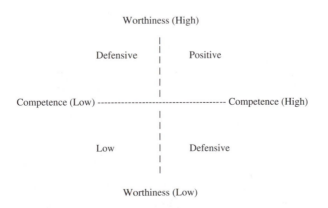

FIGURE 2.1   Self-esteem matrix (Mruk, 1999, 2006).

says we should see: that there are certain types of self-esteem. For example, the upper right quadrant of the matrix is nicely compatible with the position that positive, healthy or high self-esteem consists of competence and worthiness. Low self-esteem, by contrast, involves difficulties with feeling worthy and with being competent, so it is found in the opposite area. The diagram goes on to indicate that there are two other configurations characterized by an imbalance of competence and worthiness. Self-esteem literature terms such conditions "defensive self-esteem" (Coopersmith, 1967) because they involve a certain form of vulnerability, which must be defended against. People who live competence coupled with low worthiness must watch for and avoid a further erosion of worthiness, and people who live worthiness but with low competence must monitor and defend against additional losses concerning competence. In another work (Mruk, 1999, 2006), I show how working with competence and worthiness accommodates more research on self-esteem, such as the relationship between self-esteem and various forms of depression (low self-esteem), narcissism or aggression (defensive self-esteem), and coping ability (high self-esteem).

The third consequence of defining self-esteem in terms of competence and worthiness takes the form of opportunity. During the past three decades, various researchers have noted that, although self-esteem seems to be a very powerful concept, it is extremely difficult to establish statistically significant links between self-esteem and almost any form of specific behavior (Smelser, 1989; Wells & Marwell, 1976). Seeing self-esteem as a relationship between two components might help in this regard because a certain class of behavior is seen as a central part of the phenomenon from the beginning. Not all forms of competence are connected to self-esteem and some might even lessen it. Accordingly, there may be considerable value in researching what various behaviors and events *mean* to individuals in terms of their self-esteem. If such work finds that certain types of actions or circumstances are likely to have a positive or negative impact on self-esteem, then it may be more fruitful to look for statistically significant relationships in those areas. Finally, in addition to supporting such lines of research, there are also other possibilities to consider. For instance, if self-esteem is understood in terms of a relationship between competence and worthiness, and if most of the research in the field is based on only one component *or* the other, then many findings may need to be re-examined. In this case, we have an opportunity to view a very large amount of existing work in different light, a process that could also lead to new understandings. In short, it is clear that defining self-esteem is just as important today as it was a century ago and doing so in terms of competence and worthiness is rich with possibilities, even in a field that is as old as this one.

REFERENCES

Bartoletti, M., & O'Brien, E. J. (2003, August). *Self-esteem, coping and immunocompetence: A correlational study*. Poster session presented at the annual meeting of the American Psychological Association, Toronto, Canada.

Baumeister, R., Smart, L., & Boden, J. (1996). Relation of threatened egotism to violence and aggression: The dark side of self-esteem. *Psychological Review, 103*, 5–33.

Branden, N. (1969). *The psychology of self-esteem*. New York: Bantam.

Coopersmith, S. (1967). *The antecedents of self-esteem*. San Francisco: Freeman.

Damon, W. (1995). *Great expectations: Overcoming the culture of indulgence in our homes and schools*. New York: Free Press.

Epstein, S. (1979). The ecological study of emotions in humans. In K. Blankstein (Ed.), *Advances in the study of communications and affect* (pp. 47–83). New York: Plenum.

Hakim-Larson, J., & Mruk, C. (1997). Enhancing self-esteem in a community mental health setting. *American Journal of Orthopsychiatry, 67*, 655–659.

Harter, S. (1993). Causes and consequences of low self-esteem in children and adolescents. In R. Baumeister (Ed.), *Self-esteem: The puzzle of low self-regard* (pp. 87–111). New York: Plenum.

Jackson, M. (1984). *Self-esteem and meaning: A life historical investigation*. Albany: State University of New York Press.

James, W. (1983). *The principles of psychology*. Cambridge, MA: Harvard University Press. (Original work published 1890)

Johnson, K. (1998, May 5). Self-image is suffering from a lack of esteem. *New York Times*, p. F7.

Leo, J. (1990, April 2). *The trouble with self-esteem*. U.S. News and World Report, p. 16.

Mruk, C. (1983). Toward a phenomenology of self-esteem. In A. Giorgi, A. Barton, & C. Maes (Eds.), *Duquesne studies in phenomenological psychology* (Vol. 4, pp. 137–148). Pittsburgh: Duquesne University Press.

Mruk, C. (1999). *Self-esteem: Research, theory, and practice* (2nd ed.). New York: Springer.

Mruk, C. (2006). *Self-esteem research, theory, and practice: Toward a positive psychology of self-esteem* (3rd ed.). New York: Springer.

Pope, A., McHale, S., & Craighead, E. (1988). *Self-esteem enhancement with children and adolescents*. New York: Pergamon Press.

Rosenberg, M. (1965). *Society and the adolescent self-image*. Princeton, NJ: Princeton University Press.

Smelser, N. J. (1989). Self-esteem and social problems: An introduction. In A. M. Mecca, N. J. Smelser, & J. Vasconcellos (Eds.), *The social importance of self-esteem* (pp. 294–326). Berkeley: University of California Press.

Tafarodi, R. W., & Swann, W. B. Jr. (2001). Two-dimensional self-esteem: theory and measurement. *Personal and Individual Differences, 31*, 653–673.

Wells, E. L., & Marwell, G. (1976). *Self-esteem: Its conceptualization and measurement*. Beverly Hills, CA: Sage.

White, R. (1963). Ego and reality in psychoanalytic theory: A proposal regarding independent ego energies. *Psychological Issues, 3*, 125–150.

3

What is the Nature of Self-Esteem? Unidimensional and Multidimensional Perspectives

HERBERT W. MARSH, RHONDA G. CRAVEN,
and ANDREW J. MARTIN

S elf-concept researchers continue to debate about the relative usefulness of a *unidimensional perspective* that emphasizes a single, global
domain of self-concept, typically referred to as self-esteem, and a *multidimensional perspective* based on multiple, relatively distinct components of
self-concept with a weak hierarchical ordering (Marsh & Craven, in press).
Analogous debates reverberate across different psychological disciplines,
where researchers are increasingly recognizing the value of multidimensional perspectives (e.g., multiple intelligences vs. a global measure of IQ to characterize a
profile of intellectual abilities). The case for a multidimensional self-concept perspective is particularly strong because the multiple dimensions of self-concept
are so distinct that they cannot be explained in terms of a single global component and have dramatically different patterns of relations with different background variables, outcomes, and experimental manipulations. Hence, Marsh and
Craven (1997, p. 191) argued that: "If the role of self-concept research is to better
understand the complexity of self in different contexts, to predict a wide variety
of behaviors, to provide outcome measures for diverse interventions, and to
relate self-concept to other constructs, then the specific domains of self-concept
are more useful than a general domain." For example, from an educational perspective, if a child has a low reading self-concept and a high math self-concept
then a measure of global self-esteem is not a useful diagnostic tool. It also follows logically that if a child's reading self-concept needed enhancement, then
an intervention targeting reading self-concept would be far more useful than
one targeting global self-esteem (see Craven, Marsh, & Burnett, 2003).

THE NATURE OF SELF-ESTEEM RESPONSES: A STABLE TRAIT OR AN EPHEMERAL STATE?

What is the role of self-esteem? How is self-esteem related to specific components of self-concept? How do individuals integrate specific self-concept information to form self-esteem? These vexing questions have plagued self-concept researchers since the time of William James (1890/1963), who proposed that the best representation of a person's overall self-evaluation is an appropriately weighted average of self-evaluations in specific domains based on those that represent "the strongest, truest, deepest self" evaluated in relation to "what we back ourselves to be and do" (p. 310). Marsh (1986, 1990, 1993, 1995; Marsh & Craven, 1997; Marsh & Hattie, 1996) evaluated a variety of theoretical models of relations between global and specific components of self-concept that incorporate individual measures of the importance of each domain, standards of excellence or ideals for each domain, and the certainty of views about each domain. Here, however, we focus on self-esteem scales, whereby this global dimension of self-concept is inferred from responses to a relatively unidimensional self-concept scale comprised of characteristics such as self-confidence and self-competence that are superordinate, but not specific to, any particular content area. Self-esteem may be inferred from a stand-alone instrument or from one scale that is part of a multidimensional instrument designed to measure many facets as in the Self Description Questionnaire (SDQ) instruments that are the basis of much of our research.

Historically, self-concept measurement, theory, research, and application has been plagued by the poor quality of both theoretical models and self-concept measurement instruments (e.g., Shavelson, Hubner, & Stanton, 1976; Wells & Marwell, 1976; Wylie, 1974, 1979). In an attempt to remedy this situation, Shavelson et al. (1976) reviewed existing self-concept research and instruments, proposed a new theoretical model of self-concept, and provided a blueprint for the development of multidimensional self-concept instruments (see review by Marsh & Hattie, 1996). In the multidimensional, hierarchical model proposed by Shavelson et al., general self-concept at the apex of the model is divided into academic and nonacademic components of self-concept. The academic component is divided into self-concepts specific to general school subjects and nonacademic self-concept is divided into physical, social, and emotional components, which are further divided into more specific components.

Shavelson et al. (1976) hypothesized that global components of self-concept should be more stable than specific components of self-concept, but this was not supported by subsequent research (e.g., Marsh, 1990, 1993; Marsh & Craven, 1997; Marsh & Hattie, 1996). For example, Marsh, Richards, and Barnes (1986a, 1986b) evaluated the stability of the 12 specific scales and one global self-esteem scale from the SDQ III instrument over four occasions spanning an 18-month period. Self-esteem was one of the most reliable but least stable of the 13 scales over both long and short periods of time. In two studies of self-other agreement, Marsh and Byrne (1993) reported that despite the very substantial self-other agreement across all 13 SDQ scales (mean $r = .57$ and .56), self-other agreement on self-esteem (r of .41 and .42) was among the lowest. Thus, particularly when measurement error is taken into account, self-esteem is less stable over time and less predictable by significant others than by specific components of self-concept.

Pursuing this transitory aspect of self-esteem, Marsh and Yeung (1999) (see also Schwarz & Strack, 1991) proposed the *chameleon effect*. In forming self-esteem responses, it is implicitly assumed that respondents pursue the cognitively demanding task of subjectively evaluating themselves in a variety of specific domains, weighted perhaps by the saliency of each particular domain (Marsh & Hattie, 1996). However, Marsh and Yeung (1999) proposed that respondents simply base self-esteem responses on their immediate experience, mood, or on the contents of their short-term memory. In three different studies they embedded self-esteem items within a broadly based multidimensional self-concept instrument or within domain-specific instruments focusing specifically on academic, artistic, or physical self-concept. Factor analyses demonstrated that the same self-esteem items embedded in different instruments measured somewhat different constructs. Responses to the same self-esteem items were more "academic" when presented as part of an academic self-concept instrument, more "physical" when presented as part of a physical self-concept instrument, and more "artistic" when presented as part of a performing arts self-concept instrument. Hence, like the chameleon, self-esteem items took on a somewhat different character depending on the nature of the immediate context; they blended in with, assimilated with, and were more strongly related to academic, artistic, or physical items with which they were presented.

UNIDIMENSIONAL VS. MULTIDIMENSIONAL PERSPECTIVES IN DIFFERENT PSYCHOLOGICAL DISCIPLINES

A new generation of self-concept instruments stimulated by the Shavelson et al. (1976) model has provided overwhelming support for the multidimensionality of self-concept (Byrne, 1996b) that is increasingly being recognized in different psychological disciplines.

Educational psychology provides particularly compelling support for the multidimensional perspective (Marsh, 1993). Many important academic outcomes are substantially related to academic self-concept but are relatively unrelated to self-esteem and nonacademic components of self-concept (e.g., Byrne, 1996a; Marsh, 1993; Marsh, Trautwein, Lüdtke, Köller, & Baumert, 2006). For example, Marsh et al. (2006) demonstrated a predictable pattern of substantial relations between eight academic criterion variables (grades, test scores, and coursework selection in different school subjects) and corresponding academic self-concepts, whereas self-esteem was nearly uncorrelated with all these criteria ($r = -.03$ to .05). Similarly, Marsh (1992) established that relations between academic self-concepts in eight specific school subjects were substantially related to school grades in the matching school subjects ($r = .45$ to .70), offering support for the external validity of specific facets of academic self-concept. In contrast, self-esteem was nearly uncorrelated with school grades in all the school subjects, indicating that it had no validity in relation to this criterion.

Causal ordering studies based on longitudinal structural equation models demonstrate that academic self-concept influences subsequent academic achievement, coursework selection, and accomplishments, beyond which can be explained by prior academic achievement, whereas self-esteem has little or no influence. Thus, for example, research based on the reciprocal effects model demonstrates that academic self-concept is a cause as well as an effect of academic achievement (e.g., Marsh, Byrne, & Yeung, 1999) in that prior academic self-concept influences subsequent academic achievement beyond the effects of prior academic achievement. Marsh and Yeung (1997) also demonstrated that whereas self-concepts in school subjects and matching school grades were substantially correlated, the specific components of academic self-concept predicted subsequent coursework selection much better than did school grades or more general components of self-concept. These results provide empirical evidence calling into question the usefulness of a general self-esteem construct in educational psychology research, and offer strong support for the multidimensional perspective.

Developmental psychology research shows that children as young as five can reliably differentiate between multiple dimensions of self-concept with appropriately constructed self-concept instruments (Marsh, Craven, & Debus, 1991; Marsh, Ellis, & Craven, 2002; Marsh, Debus, & Bornholt, 2005) and that the different facets of self-concept become increasingly distinct with age (Marsh & Ayotte, 2003). Thus, for example, factor analysis of adolescent responses to a recent adaptation of the SDQ III clearly supported the 17 self-concept factors that the instrument was designed to measure (Marsh et al., 2006). The average correlation among the 17 self-concept factors, even after controlling for unreliability, was only .14, attesting to the distinctiveness of these factors. In hierarchical factor analyses the correlations between responses to the self-esteem scale and the highest-order self-concept factor are consistently greater than .9, thus supporting the construct validity of both these conceptualizations of global self-concept (see Marsh & Craven, 1997; Marsh, Parada, Craven, & Finger, 2004b). Obviously, however, neither the single higher-order factor nor the self-esteem factor is able to provide an adequate summary of such distinct factors that provide so much useful information beyond that provided by self-esteem.

In mental health research, Marsh, Parada, and Ayotte (2004a) (see also Marsh et al., 2004b) demonstrated that relations between 11 self-concept factors and seven mental health problems varied substantially ($+11$ to -83; mean $r = -35$) and formed an a priori multivariate pattern of relations that supported a multidimensional perspective. Support for the multidimensional perspective was particularly strong for the externalizing (e.g., delinquent and aggressive behaviors) mental health factor. It was modestly negatively correlated with self-esteem ($r = -34$), substantially negatively correlated with some specific components of self-concept (e.g., parent relations, $r = -70$), and nearly uncorrelated or even positively correlated with physical appearance, same-sex, and opposite-sex SDQ II self-concept factors. Self-esteem was able to uniquely explain only 3% of the covariation between mental health and self-concept factors, whereas specific components of self-concept explained 97% of this covariation. Based on higher-order factor analyses, Marsh et al. (2004a) noted that single higher-order factors could not explain relations among the self-concept factors, among the mental health factors, or between the self-concept and mental health factors; a unidimensional perspective was not viable.

In personality research, Marsh et al. (2006) demonstrated a well-defined multivariate pattern of relations between multiple dimensions of self-concept and personality (e.g., Big Five personality factors, positive and negative affect, life satisfaction). Seven higher-order factors resulted from the 25 first-order (17 self-concept, 8 personality) factors. Each Big Five personality factor loaded primarily on one higher-order factor, along with a distinct set of self-concept factors to which it was most logically related. Importantly, self-esteem contributed substantially to only one of the seven higher-order factors, and even for this one higher-order factor, self-esteem was not the highest loading self-concept factor. In this same study, academic outcomes were logically and substantially related to the academic self-concept factors, but nearly unrelated to self-esteem, other nonacademic components of self-concept, and the eight personality factors (except, perhaps, Openness). This highly differentiated multivariate pattern of relations argues against the unidimensional perspective of self-concept still prevalent in personality research.

In sports and exercise psychology, there is also broad acceptance of the multidimensional perspective of self-concept (Marsh, 1997, 2002). For example, Marsh and Peart (1988) reported that results of a physical fitness intervention, and physical fitness indicators, were substantially related to physical self-concept but nearly uncorrelated with nonphysical components of self-concept. Marsh (1997, 2002) demonstrated that objectively measured components of physical fitness are substantially correlated to the specific components of physical self-concept to which they are most logically related, but are substantially less correlated with self-esteem.

Gender studies also support the multidimensional perspective. Although gender differences in self-esteem are small (Wylie, 1979), there are modest differences favoring boys that grow larger through high school and then decline in adulthood (Kling, Hyde, Showers, & Buswell, 1999). However, these small gender differences in self-esteem mask larger, counter-balancing gender-stereotypic differences in specific components of self-concept (e.g., boys have high math, physical, and emotional self-concepts; girls have higher verbal, honesty/trustworthiness, and social self-concepts) and this pattern of gender differences is reasonably consistent from early childhood to adulthood (e.g., Crain, 1996; Eccles, Wigfield, Harold, & Blumenfeld, 1993; Marsh, 1989, 1993). This rich pattern of gender differences in multiple dimensions of self-concept could not be understood from a unidimensional perspective.

INTERVENTION STUDIES: A MULTIDIMENSIONAL PERSPECTIVE TO CONSTRUCT VALIDATION

Following from a multidimensional perspective, Marsh (1993; Marsh & Craven, 1997) argued for a construct validity approach to self-concept interventions in which the specific dimensions of self-concept most relevant to the intervention should be most affected, whilst less relevant dimensions should be less affected and should serve as a control for response biases. This approach was demonstrated in a series of studies based on the Outward Bound program. The Outward Bound standard course is a 26-day residential program based on physically and mentally demanding outdoor activities (Marsh et al., 1986a, 1986b). Consistent with the primarily nonacademic goals: (1) gains were significantly larger for the SDQ III scales predicted a priori to be most relevant to the goals of the program, compared to less relevant SDQ III scales; (2) the effect sizes were consistent across 27 different Outward Bound groups run by different instructors at different times and in different locations; and (3) the size and pattern of the gains were maintained over an 18-month follow-up period. In contrast, the Outward Bound bridging course is a 6-week residential program designed to produce significant gains in the academic domain for underachieving adolescent males through an integrated program of remedial teaching, normal schoolwork, and experiences likely to influence particularly academic self-concept (Marsh & Richards, 1988). Consistent with the primarily academic goals: (1) academic self-concept effects were substantial and significantly larger than nonacademic self-concept effects; and (2) there were also corresponding effects on reading and math achievement. If only self-esteem had been measured in these studies, the interventions would have been concluded to be much weaker and the richness of understanding the match between specific intended goals and actual outcomes would have been lost. The juxtaposition of these two interventions and their contrasting predictions provides a powerful demonstration of the importance of a multidimensional perspective of self-concept.

In a meta-analysis of self-concept intervention studies, Haney and Durlak (1998) found modest—but significantly positive—effect sizes. However, reflecting the prevailing unidimensional perspective in many studies included in their meta-analysis, they considered only one effect size per intervention—the mean effect size averaged across different self-concept dimensions if more than one was considered. In contrast, O'Mara, Marsh, Craven and Debus (in press) updated and extended this meta-analysis to embrace a multidimensional perspective, coding the nature of the self-concept outcomes in relation to the intervention. Consistent with our multidimensional perspective, effect sizes were substantially larger for specific components of self-concept logically related to the intended outcomes of the intervention than for self-esteem and other less relevant components of self-concept. Studies designed to enhance global self-esteem were not very successful compared to studies that focused on more specific components of self-concept that were most relevant to goals of the intervention. In summary, intervention research supports the usefulness of a multidimensional perspective of self-concept.

SUMMARY AND IMPLICATIONS

In our research we have integrated specific and global self-esteem dimensions of self-concept into a single multidimensional, hierarchical model, but we argue that appropriately selected specific domains of self-concept are more useful than self-esteem in many research settings. Clearly it follows that our multidimensional perspective, which incorporates specific components of self-concept and self-esteem, is more useful than a unidimensional perspective that relies solely on self-esteem. Self-esteem is ephemeral in that it is more affected by short-term response biases, situation-specific context effects, short-term mood fluctuations, and other short-term time-specific influences. Self-esteem apparently cannot adequately reflect the diversity of specific self-domains. Indeed, as emphasized by Marsh and Yeung (1999), it is worrisome that a construct so central to the self seems to be so easily influenced by apparently trivial laboratory manipulations, bogus feedback, and short-term mood fluctuations. Despite the overwhelming empirical support for a multidimensional perspective on self-concept, we are not arguing that researchers should abandon self-esteem measures that have been used so widely and we include self-esteem as one of the scales on the SDQ instruments that are the basis of much of our research. Rather, we contend that researchers should consider multiple dimensions of self-concept particularly relevant to the concerns of their research, supplemented, perhaps, by self-esteem responses.

REFERENCES

Byrne, B. M. (1996a). Academic self-concept: Its structure, measurement, and relation to academic achievement. In B. A. Bracken (Ed.), *Handbook of self-concept* (pp. 287–316). New York: Wiley.

Byrne, B. M. (1996b). *Measuring self-concept across the life span: Issues and instrumentation*. Washington, DC: American Psychological Association.

Crain, R. M. (1996). The influence of age, race, and gender on child and adolescent multidimensional self-concept. In B. A. Bracken (Ed.), *Handbook of self-concept: Developmental, social, and clinical considerations* (pp. 395–420). New York: Wiley.

Craven, R. G., Marsh, H. W., & Burnett, P. C. (2003). Cracking the self-concept enhancement conundrum: A call and blueprint for the next generation of self-concept enhancement research. In H. W. Marsh, R. G. Craven, & D. M. McInerney (Eds.), *International advances in self research* (Vol. 1, pp. 67–90). Greenwich, CT: Information Age.

Eccles, J., Wigfield, A., Harold, R. D., & Blumenfeld, P. (1993). Age and gender differences in children's self- and task perceptions during elementary school. *Child Development, 64*, 830–847.

Haney, P., & Durlak, J. A. (1998). Changing self-esteem in children and adolescents: A meta-analytic review. *Journal of Clinical Child Psychology, 27*, 423–433.

James, W. (1963). *The principles of psychology*. New York: Holt, Rinehart & Winston. (Original work published 1890)

Kling, K. C., Hyde, J. S., Showers, C. J., & Buswell, B. N. (1999). Gender differences in self-esteem: A meta-analysis. *Psychological Bulletin, 125*, 470–500.

Marsh, H. W. (1986). Global self esteem: Its relation to specific facets of self-concept and their importance. *Journal of Personality and Social Psychology, 51*, 1224–1236.

Marsh, H. W. (1989). Age and sex effects in multiple dimensions of self-concept: Preadolescence to early-adulthood. *Journal of Educational Psychology, 81*, 417–430.

Marsh, H. W. (1990). A multidimensional, hierarchical self-concept: Theoretical and empirical justification. *Educational Psychology Review, 2*, 77–172.

Marsh, H. W. (1992). The content specificity of relations between academic achievement and academic self-concept. *Journal of Educational Psychology*, 84, 43–50.

Marsh, H. W. (1993). Academic self-concept: Theory measurement and research. In J. Suls (Ed.), *Psychological perspectives on the self* (Vol. 4, pp. 59–98). Hillsdale, NJ: Lawrence Erlbaum Associates.

Marsh H. W. (1995). A Jamesian model of self-investment and self-esteem—comment. *Journal of Personality & Social Psychology*, 69, 1151–1160.

Marsh, H. W. (1997). The measurement of physical self-concept: A construct validation approach. In K. Fox (Ed.), *The physical self: From motivation to well-being* (pp. 27–58). Champaign, IL: Human Kinetics.

Marsh, H. W. (2002). A multidimensional physical self-concept: A construct validity approach to theory, measurement, and research. *Psychology: The Journal of the Hellenic Psychological Society*, 9, 459–493.

Marsh, H. W., & Ayotte, V. (2003). Do multiple dimensions of self-concept become more differentiated with age: The differential distinctiveness hypothesis. *Journal of Educational Psychology*, 95, 687–706.

Marsh, H. W., & Byrne, B. M. (1993). Do we see ourselves as others infer: A comparison of self-other agreement on multiple dimensions of self-concept from two continents. *Australian Journal of Psychology*, 45, 49–58.

Marsh, H. W., Byrne, B. M., & Yeung, A. S. (1999). Causal ordering of academic self-concept and achievement: Reanalysis of a pioneering study and revised recommendations. *Educational Psychologist*, 34, 155–167.

Marsh, H. W., & Craven, R. (1997). Academic self-concept: Beyond the dustbowl. In G. Phye (Ed.), *Handbook of classroom assessment: Learning, achievement, and adjustment* (pp. 131–198). Orlando, FL: Academic Press.

Marsh, H. W., & Craven, R. G. (in press). Reciprocal effects of self-concept and performance from a multidimensional perspective: Beyond seductive pleasure and unidimensional perspectives. *Perspective on Psychological Science*.

Marsh, H. W., Craven, R. G., & Debus, R. (1991). Self-concepts of young children aged 5 to 8: Their measurement and multidimensional structure. *Journal of Educational Psychology*, 83, 377–392.

Marsh, H. W., Debus, R., & Bornholt, L. (2005). Validating young children's self-concept responses: Methodological ways and means to understand their responses. In D. M. Teti (Ed.), *Handbook of research methods in developmental psychology* (pp. 138–160). Oxford, UK: Blackwell Publishers.

Marsh, H. W., Ellis, L., & Craven, R. G. (2002). How do preschool children feel about themselves? Unravelling measurement and multidimensional self-concept structure. *Developmental Psychology*, 38, 376–393.

Marsh, H. W., & Hattie, J. (1996). Theoretical perspectives on the structure of self-concept. In B. Bracken (Ed.), *Handbook of self-concept* (pp. 38–90). New York: Wiley.

Marsh, H. W., & Hau, K. T. (2004). Explaining paradoxical relations between academic self-concepts and achievements: Cross-cultural generalizability of the Internal-External Frame of Reference predictions across 26 countries. *Journal of Educational Psychology*, 96, 56–57.

Marsh, H. W., Parada, R. H., & Ayotte, V. (2004a). A multidimensional perspective of relations between self-concept (Self Description Questionnaire II) and adolescent mental health (Youth Self Report). *Psychological Assessment*, 16, 27–41.

Marsh, H. W., Parada, R. H., Craven, R. G., & Finger, L. (2004b). In the looking glass: A reciprocal effects model elucidating the complex nature of bullying, psychological determinants and the central role of self-concept. In C. S. Sanders & G. D. Phye (Eds.), *Bullying, implications for the classroom: What does the research say?* (pp. 63–106). Orlando, FL: Academic Press.

Marsh, H. W., & Peart, N. (1988). Competitive and cooperative physical fitness training programs for girls: Effects on physical fitness and on multidimensional self-concepts. *Journal of Sport and Exercise Psychology, 10,* 390–407.

Marsh, H. W., & Richards, G. (1988). The Outward Bound Bridging Course for low achieving high-school males: Effect on academic achievement and multidimensional self-concepts. *Australian Journal of Psychology, 40,* 281–298.

Marsh, H. W., Richards, G., & Barnes, J. (1986a). Multidimensional self-concepts: A long term follow-up of the effect of participation in an Outward Bound program. *Personality and Social Psychology Bulletin, 12,* 475–492.

Marsh, H. W., Richards, G., & Barnes, J. (1986b). Multidimensional self-concepts: The effect of participation in an Outward Bound program. *Journal of Personality and Social Psychology, 45,* 173–187.

Marsh, H. W., Trautwein, U., Lüdtke, O., Köller, O., & Baumert, J. (2006). Integration of multidimensional self-concept and core personality constructs: Construct validation and relations to well-being and achievement. *Journal of Personality, 74,* 403–455.

Marsh, H. W., & Yeung, A. S. (1997). Coursework selection: The effects of academic self-concept and achievement. *American Educational Research Journal, 34,* 691–720.

Marsh, H. W., & Yeung, A. S. (1999). The liability of psychological ratings: The chameleon effect in global self-esteem. *Personality and Social Psychology Bulletin, 25,* 49–64.

O'Mara, A. J., Marsh, H. W., Craven, R. G., & Debus, R. (in press). Do self-concept interventions make a difference? A synergistic blend of construct validation and meta-analysis. *Educational Psychologist.*

Schwarz, N., & Strack, F. (1991). Evaluating one's life: A judgment model of subjective well-being. In F. Strack, M. Argyle, & N. Schwarz (Eds.), *Subjective well-being* (pp. 27–47). New York: Pergamon.

Shavelson, R. J., Hubner, J. J., & Stanton, G. C. (1976). Validation of construct interpretations. *Review of Educational Research, 46,* 407–441.

Wells, L. E., & Marwell, G. (1976). *Self-esteem: Its conceptualization and measurement.* Beverly Hills, CA: Sage.

Wylie, R. C. (1974). *The self-concept* (Rev. ed., Vol. 1) Lincoln: University of Nebraska Press.

Wylie, R. C. (1979). *The self-concept* (Vol. 2) Lincoln: University of Nebraska Press.

Question 2

What is the state of affairs with respect to the divergent and convergent validity of self-esteem? For example, how much does it overlap with such constructs as depression, neuroticism, narcissism, and mood?

*T*his set of essays focuses on issues pertaining to the convergent and divergent validity of self-esteem. These are broad issues, so not surprisingly each contribution focuses on different aspects of them.

O'Brien, Bartoletti, Leitzel, and O'Brien review evidence showing clear limitations on the association between self-esteem and narrow bandwidth aspects of adaptive behavior (e.g., school performance, delinquency, drug and alcohol use). However, rather than taking the absence of strong relationships as evidence for the lack of self-esteem's importance (and its lack of predictive validity), they forcefully argue for the role of self-esteem as part of more complex, interactive models. O'Brien and colleagues also review evidence showing that while self-esteem generally converges with other broad bandwidth measures of adaptation, this is not true for a subset of individuals with unstable or defensive self-esteem (arguing for a multicomponent conceptualization of self-esteem).

Suls reviews findings on the interrelations among self-esteem, personality, and mood. In this research, associations between self-esteem, neuroticism, and negative affectivity (specifically depression) seem sufficiently strong to challenge the discriminant validity of self-esteem and to question whether self-esteem is a "free-standing individual difference construct." Suls also comments briefly on individual differences in stability of self-esteem and on how self-esteem is distinct from self-efficacy and narcissism.

Nezlek focuses his essay on issues pertaining to "state" self-esteem (i.e., feelings of self-worth that change across time and situation). His findings parallel those reported by Suls at the trait level—self-esteem relates strongly to depression, followed closely by general positive and negative affectivity. However, Nezlek also reports that self-esteem relates to daily events above and beyond these other constructs, attesting to its discriminant validity. Finally, Nezlek describes findings suggesting that individual differences in self-esteem stability may reflect a specific manifestation of a more general "instability" factor.

4

Global Self-Esteem: Divergent and Convergent Validity Issues

EDWARD J. O'BRIEN, MIA BARTOLETTI, JEFFREY D. LEITZEL, and JEAN P. O'BRIEN

*T*his chapter examines areas of behavior that are less closely related to overall or global self-esteem (divergent validity) and areas that are more closely related (convergent validity). Self-esteem is defined here as a hierarchical set of self-evaluations that vary from highly specific to global levels of worthiness. In this analysis we will consider self-esteem at the global level, since most research has focused on this definition (Kernis, 2003). Our analysis will examine self-esteem that is defined in a stable or trait-like manner rather than self-esteem defined as a state or as variability in self-esteem. Our analysis will focus primarily on Mruk's (1999) worthiness dimension while considering the importance of realistic vs. defensive self-esteem. Finally, we will consider the "downside" of high self-esteem involving defensiveness, narcissism, and unstable self-esteem that may have negative implications for adaptation (e.g., Baumeister, Heatherton, & Tice, 1993; Kernis, 2003; Morf & Rhodewalt, 2001).

The literature discussed here is primarily correlational in nature and our discussion will mainly be of patterns of association rather than causes and effects. Patterns of correlation can suggest possible underlying causal mechanisms, though studies that examine substantial changes in global self-esteem are difficult to conduct outside of the realms of psychotherapy, longitudinal research, or studies of major life changing events. Trait analyses of self-esteem provide information about the structure of self-evaluations and their associations with other markers of adaptation. Such structural analyses can help identify areas for process analyses that can further examine potential causal mechanisms. Trait levels of global self-esteem cannot be strongly manipulated in single-session experiments and thus most experimental research on self-esteem is more properly viewed as studying the effects of mild changes in state self-esteem that have rather limited implications for global self-esteem.

SELF-ESTEEM IS NOT EVERYTHING
(DIVERGENT ISSUES)

Recent research has convincingly shown that global self-esteem correlates only to a minimal or moderate degree with a number of adaptive behaviors such as school performance, adolescent drug and alcohol abuse, delinquency, aggression, and success in interpersonal relationships (Baumeister, Campbell, Krueger, & Vohs, 2003). Naïve assumptions about the ubiquity of simple and powerful links between self-esteem and many specific aspects of adaptive functioning (e.g., Mecca, Smelser, & Vasconcellos, 1989) have been shown by Baumeister et al. to have little empirical support. Of course, not many empirically oriented psychologists were ever part of the pop psychology "self-esteem movement," which made wild exaggerated claims about the impact of self-esteem on virtually every aspect of life. Most self-esteem researchers have simply reported the modest to moderate (.10–.40) correlations they observed between self-esteem and school performance and other specific markers of adaptation (e.g., Coopersmith, 1967, 1981; Harter, 1999; O'Brien & Epstein, 1988; Rosenberg, 1979). Correlations in the .10–.40 range suggest that self-esteem could only have, at most, a modest causal relationship with variables like school performance and/or that school performance could, at most, only modestly affect global self-esteem levels.

Rather than repeat the cogent conclusions of Baumeister et al. (2003), we will simply note that there are good reasons to not expect global self-esteem to strongly predict specific behaviors like school performance.[1] As noted by Baumeister et al., global self-esteem and school performance exist at very different levels of aggregation (Epstein & O'Brien, 1985; Fishbein & Ajzen, 1975; Rosenberg, Schooler, Schoenbach, & Rosenberg, 1995). As a narrow bandwidth aspect of experience, school performance may have varying implications for self-esteem in different individuals. Many of us know a star high school athlete or musician who has high self-esteem and only marginal academic performance because academic performance is of less importance for him or her. Likewise, some star students may have low self-esteem because from their own viewpoint academic achievements are less important than perceived failures in other areas (e.g., friendship problems, negative evaluation of appearance) (e.g., Harter, 1999; Harter & Whitesell, 2003). While there is controversy related to empirical support for this argument (e.g., Marsh & Hattie, 1996), James' (1892) insight into self-esteem involving the ratio between one's successes and pretensions is supported by considerable research (Harter, 1999).

The search for single predictors of complex specific behaviors such as school performance is clearly not justifiable today. Such specific behaviors are best understood as complex developmental interactions among multiple contextual influences (e.g., Bronfenbrenner, 1989; Lerner, 1991). There may be some specific situations in which school performance and self-esteem are more strongly associated. For example, some low self-esteem high school students with subclinical depression may set academic goals that represent underachievement, may have low frustration tolerance, overgeneralize from failures, and lack persistence in goal seeking (e.g., studies of "subclinical" depression groups with low self-esteem, Gotlib, Lewinsohn, & Seeley, 1995). Work with such "at risk" groups may be warranted even though there is no uniform or strong association between global self-esteem and academic performance across all levels of self-esteem. Self-esteem may have some relevance, some of the time, with some individuals, in interaction with other variables, in terms of predicting such things as school performance. Baumeister et al. (2003), Dawes (1994) and others have done a service by showing the folly of anyone still remaining in "the self-esteem movement" who would make the simple-minded argument that self-esteem ubiquitously and strongly predicts every specific aspect of adaptation for all individuals.

On the other hand, even small effects that are shown with some "at risk" individuals can have meaningful implications. For example, the physician's health study was discontinued when an effect size of .03 was discovered (3/100 of a standard deviation) in heart attack rates as a function of whether patients were taking aspirin or a placebo. It was concluded that the presence of such an effect would make it unethical to leave patients in the control group (Rosnow & Rosenthal, 1989). Even if self-esteem and academic achievement show only a modest association across all levels of self-esteem and achievement, it may still be important if interventions can achieve a 5–10% increase in self-esteem and academic performance (e.g., a half letter or one letter grade improvement) of low self-esteem/low performance "at-risk" adolescents by means of targeted interventions aimed at enhancing self-esteem and academic achievement. In addition, given the associations between self-esteem and other markers of emotional well-being (e.g., depression), it is important to consider the value of raising self-esteem in terms of the possibility of mental health implications per se as much as any value in enhanced academic achievement. High academic achievement, while an important goal, is certainly preferable in the context of emotional well-being rather than in the context of neuroticism, depression, and low or unstable self-esteem.

The limited number of clinical trials outcome studies in school-based interventions to increase self-esteem and academic achievement makes it problematic to draw firm cause-and-effect conclusions. We disagree with the somewhat favorable review offered by Baumeister et al. (2003) of the Scheirer and Kraut (1979) study of outcomes in changing self-esteem and achievement (the primary study cited by Baumeister et al., as providing cause-and-effect evidence in this area). Our review suggests that Scheirer and Kraut found little in the way of valid experimental research to evaluate the effects of self-esteem or educational achievement interventions. Most studies reviewed, and particularly those aimed at increasing self-esteem, employed rather minimalist interventions such as providing a "role model" teacher, providing activities in "open" rather than regular classrooms, or including sports activities in school programs. We agree with Scheirer and Kraut, who described most of these interventions as poorly defined with little coherent theoretical analysis of how interventions might affect self-esteem or achievement. Most studies were not experimental in design and often used untested or inappropriate measures of outcome as part of unpublished dissertations (Scheirer &

Kraut, 1979). We were struck by the poor quality of this research and the weak implementation of intervention programs. The work cited in Scheirer and Kraut is certainly not representative of contemporary methods of evaluating outcomes in psychoeducational interventions (e.g., Kazdin, 1998, 2003). Rather than providing evidence for the effects of self-esteem on achievement (or achievement on self-esteem), this article illustrates how poorly thought-out and even absurd some of the implementations of the "self-esteem movement" were. We still need to know whether self-esteem in students can be enhanced, and if so, whether such changes will affect academic achievement (or vice versa, i.e., can academic performance be experimentally enhanced, and, if so, does this lead to enhanced psychological adjustment or well-being?).

It would be interesting to see whether Mruk's (1999) self-esteem change program (based in large part on empirically validated aspects of cognitive behavioral and phenomenological therapies) would have effects on self-esteem and achievement in adolescents (e.g., as a psychoeducational program like those conducted by Lewinsohn and colleagues in successfully treating subclinical and clinically depressed high school students, e.g., Clarke, DeBar, & Lewinsohn, 2003). It should be expected that a successful self-esteem change intervention would have the strongest effect on other measures of psychological well-being (see the section that follows). Modest, but potentially valuable effects might also be seen in academic achievement if that were to be part of the focus of the self-esteem intervention (e.g., realistic increases in goal setting regarding school performance).

What is true regarding the modest correlations between academic achievement and self-esteem is equally true for other broad bandwidth markers of adjustment. Near zero to modest (.40 range) correlations are found between school performance and measures of depression, neuroticism, state/trait and test anxiety, explanatory style, global self-efficacy, optimism, constructive thinking, and learned helplessness (Diaz, Glass, Arnkoff, & Tanofsky-Kraff, 2001; Epstein & Meier, 1989; Hair & Graziano, 2003; Jeffreys et al., 1997; Leitzel, 2000; Martinez & Sewell, 2000; McKean, 1993; Petrie & Russell, 1995; Wang & Newlin, 2000). These correlations are in the "expected" direction, but show a modest magnitude similar to what Baumeister et al. (2003) found for self-esteem and suggest that none of these variables is a strong, single cause (or effect) of achievement behavior for general populations of students.

The principles at work here may be stated as follows: no global measure of adjustment (e.g., self-esteem, optimism, depression) shows promise as a strong single predictor or causal agent with regard to specific adaptive behaviors such as school performance. Complex interactive models are needed to account for such specific variables as school achievement. Simple, unidimensional models of how broad bandwidth adjustment variables can fully account for narrow bandwidth variables like school achievement are not tenable and such models should not be informing public policy or educational approaches. Likewise, interventions aimed at enhancing educational achievement cannot be justified by claims that they will lead to large increases in broad bandwidth variables such as global self-esteem or psychological adjustment.

SELF-ESTEEM IS RELATED TO CORE ISSUES OF ADJUSTMENT AND WELL-BEING (CONVERGENT ISSUES)

While self-esteem has been shown to have only modest correlations with narrow bandwidth behaviors such as school performance, moderate to strong relationships are typically found between self-esteem and other global measures of psychological adjustment. Judge and colleagues obtained moderate to strong correlations (.50–.85) among measures of self-esteem, self-efficacy, locus of control, and non-neuroticism (e.g., Judge & Bono, 2001; Judge, Erez, Bono, & Thoresen, 2002). These four measures, aggregated as an overall index of adjustment, were the strongest dispositional predictors of job satisfaction and performance (Judge & Bono, 2001). These four measures can be seen as a "superfactor" (Eysenck & Eysenck, 1985) that shows a coherent pattern of correlations with a number of criteria. Interestingly, correlations between these global markers and narrow bandwidth measures of job performance or satisfaction are typically in the .10–.40 range (Judge & Bono, 2001) that is typically found for self-esteem and school performance.

The overall measure of adjustment sought by Judge and his colleagues might also need to consider including other facets of adjustment such as optimism, ego resilience, coping, self-esteem stability, low depression, and anxiety. There may be value in seeking such a "super-trait" measure, but care needs to be taken as to what goes into such a measure since this will determine its eventual validity (e.g., Block, 1995). For now, there is strong evidence that self-esteem, generalized self-efficacy, locus of control, and non-neuroticism share a considerable amount of variance and that they show similar relationships with a number of criterion measures.

Correlations between self-esteem and the four other factors of the "Big Five" (John & Srivastava, 1999) (i.e., not including the neuroticism factor as it was discussed above) generally are lower in magnitude (divergence from self-esteem). Conscientiousness and extraversion show slightly higher correlations (typically in the. 30–.40 range) than agreeableness or openness (.10–.20 range) (Judge et al., 2002; Robins, Tracy, Trzesniewski, Potter, & Gosling, 2001). Other studies have found similar patterns of divergence between self-esteem and these four Big Five scales and moderate to strong convergence (correlations in the .45–.70 range) between global self-esteem and non-neuroticism (e.g., Farmer, Jarvis, Berent, & Corbett, 2001; Kling, Ryff, Love, & Essex, 2003; Watson, Suls, & Haig, 2002).

Self-esteem also produces moderate to strong correlations with measures of life satisfaction. Judge, Locke, Durham, and Kluger (1998; Judge et al., 2002) cited correlations between these two measures in the .30–.50 range. Diener and Diener (1995) found self-esteem to be correlated with life satisfaction (.47) across college samples from 31 different countries with correlations being higher in samples from individualist than from collectivist cultures. Sheldon, Elliot, Kim, and Kasser (2001) found that self-esteem was implicated as one of the four most salient aspects of highly satisfying life experiences, along with Deci and Ryan's (2000) needs for autonomy, competence, and relatedness.

Moderate to strong correlations are found between self-esteem and measures of depression and anxiety. Leitzel (2000) examined self-esteem in relation to the tripartite model (e.g., Laurent et al., 1999) and found that self-esteem showed stronger correlations with depression (low positive affect, $r = -.66$) and generalized distress (negative affect, $r = -.62$) than with anxiety (physiological hyperarousal, $-.40$) (see also Watson et al., 2002). Many measures of depression and anxiety are confounded by shared variance with general distress (negative affect) items that lead to high correlations between depression and anxiety scales. For example, Leitzel (2000) found equivalent correlations between self-esteem and trait measures of anxiety ($-.74$) and depression ($-.72$) that shared negative affect items (Spielberger, 1995).

Bartoletti (2003; Bartoletti & O'Brien, 2003) found strong correlations between self-esteem (O'Brien & Epstein, 1988) and optimistic explanatory style (Peterson, Semmel, von Baeyer, Abramson, Metalsky, & Seligman, 1982) ($r = .67$) and global constructive thinking inventory (CTI) (Epstein, 2001) ($r = .82$). These three measures showed moderately strong correlations (.61, .55, and .52) with a physiological measure of immunocompetence, level of Immunoglobulin A.

Studies have also examined the "downside" of high self-esteem in terms of links to defensive self-enhancement, narcissism, and unstable self-esteem. Raskin, Novacek, and Hogan (1991) found an average correlation of .35 between global self-esteem and defensive self-enhancement (social desirability bias). O'Brien and Epstein (1988) reported a correlation of .17 between global self-esteem and defensive self-enhancement. Rather than accepting self-esteem reports at face value, it is important to assess the extent to which such reports may be influenced by self-presentation biases and/or need for social approval (Mruk, 1999).

Raskin et al. (1991) found correlations between various measures of global self-esteem and narcissism in the .14–.59 range (with an average correlation between self-esteem and narcissism of .41). Interestingly, the lowest correlations (.14 and .20) between global self-esteem and narcissism found by Raskin et al. were for the Rosenberg Self-Esteem Scale. These low correlations are most likely due to the severe ceiling effect of the Rosenberg Scale (O'Brien & Leitzel, 2000). The ceiling effect of the Rosenberg Scale (at least with the four response alternative format) should lead to underestimates of the correlation between narcissism and self-esteem because narcissism is associated with high, but not low self-esteem (Baumeister et al., 2003) and the Rosenberg Scale reliably differentiates among individuals only up through moderately positive levels of self-esteem (O'Brien & Leitzel, 2000). High levels of narcissism have been more strongly associated with aggressive and problematic interpersonal behavior than having high levels of self-esteem (e.g., Bushman & Baumeister, 1998; Morf & Rhodewalt, 2001).

Instability and level of self-esteem have been shown to be related to level of anger and hostility (Kernis, Grannemann, & Barclay, 1989). Individuals with high and unstable self-esteem showed the highest levels of anger and hostility, whereas individuals with high and stable self-esteem showed the least anger and hostility. Low self-esteem individuals, regardless of self-esteem instability, showed intermediate levels of anger and hostility (Kernis et al., 1989).

SUMMARY

Research has found clear limits on the association between self-esteem and narrow bandwidth aspects of adaptive behavior (e.g., school performance, delinquency, drug and alcohol abuse). Simplistic analyses of self-esteem as the cause of such specific behaviors are no longer justified and should not continue (Baumeister et al., 2003). What is true for the limitations of self-esteem in predicting narrow bandwidth adaptive behavior such as school performance is equally true for other broad bandwidth markers of adjustment (e.g., optimism, depression, generalized self-efficacy). Analyses of self-esteem and psychological adjustment as they interact with other contextual factors involved in these specific behaviors may still lead to empirically valid analyses with practical implications. Likewise,we should avoid simplistic analyses that suggest direct and strong causal links between single specific adaptation markers (school performance, delinquency, drug and alcohol abuse) and global adjustment markers like self-esteem, optimism, and depression. Complex interactive models are needed to relate global and specific levels of adaptation to one another.

Self-esteem is a key variable in broad bandwidth measures of adaptation and well-being. In most cases, high self-esteem is associated with other measures of positive adaptation (e.g., lower neuroticism; lower depression, anxiety, and stress; more effective coping; higher life satisfaction, self-efficacy, and optimism). High self-esteem is, at least in some individuals, associated with maladaptive issues such as defensiveness, narcissism, and unstable or inauthentic self-esteem (e.g., Deci & Ryan, 2000; Kernis, 2003). Further work is needed to examine how and when self-esteem can have adaptive consequences in terms of high competence and high worthiness (Mruk, 1999) and maladaptive consequences in terms of defensive high self-esteem, narcissism, and unstable self-esteem (e.g., Mruk, 1999; Morf & Rhodewalt, 2001; Kernis, 2003).

NOTES

1. Due to space limitations we will limit our analysis to self-esteem and school performance because it is the most extensively studied issue reviewed by Baumeister et al. (2003).

REFERENCES

Bartoletti, M. (2003). *Self-esteem, coping and immunocompetence: A correlational study*. Unpublished Master's thesis, Marywood University, Scranton, PA.

Bartoletti, M., & O'Brien, E. J. (2003, August). *Self-esteem, coping and immunocompetence: A correlational study*. Poster session presented as part of Division 8 Program, American Psychological Association Convention, Toronto, Ontario, Canada.

Baumeister, R. F., Campbell, J. D., Krueger, J. I., & Vohs, K. D. (2003). Does self-esteem cause better performance, interpersonal success, happiness, or healthier lifestyles? *Psychological Science in the Public Interest, 4* (1), 1–44.

Baumeister, R. F., Heatherton, T. F., & Tice, D. M. (1993). When ego threat leads to self-regulation failure: Negative consequences of high self-esteem. *Journal of Personality and Social Psychology, 64* (1), 141–156.

Block, J. (1995). A contrarian view of the five-factor approach to personality description. *Psychological Bulletin, 117*, 187–215.

Bronfenbrenner, U. (1989). Ecological systems theory. In R. Vasta (Ed.), *Annals of child development: Vol. 6. Six theories of child development: Revised formulations and current issues.* Greenwich, CT: JAI Press.

Bushman, B. J., & Baumeister, R. F. (1998). Threatened egotism, narcissism, self-esteem, and direct and displaced aggression: Does self-love or self-hate lead to violence? *Journal of Personality and Social Psychology, 75*, 219–229.

Clarke, G. N., DeBar, L. L., & Lewinsohn, P. M. (2003). Cognitive-behavioral group treatment for adolescent depression. In A. E. Kazdin (Ed.), *Evidence-based psychotherapies for children and adolescents* (pp. 120–134). New York: Guilford Press.

Coopersmith, S. (1967). *The antecedents of self-esteem.* San Francisco: Freeman.

Coopersmith, S. (1981). *Self-esteem inventories.* Palo Alto, CA: Consulting Psychologists Press.

Dawes, R. M. (1994). *House of cards: Psychology and psychotherapy built on myth.* New York: Free Press.

Deci, E. L., & Ryan, R. M. (2000). The "what" and "why" of goal pursuits: Human needs and the self-determination of behavior. *Psychological Inquiry, 11* (4), 227–268.

Diaz, R. J., Glass, C. R., Arnkoff, D. B., & Tanofsky-Kraff, M. (2001). Cognition, anxiety, and prediction of performance in 1st-year law students. *Journal of Educational Psychology, 93* (2), 420–429.

Diener, E., & Diener, M. (1995). Cross-cultural correlates of life satisfaction and self-esteem. *Journal of Personality and Social Psychology, 68* (4), 653–663.

Epstein, S. (2001). *Constructive thinking inventory (CTI).* Odessa, FL: Psychological Assessment Resources, Inc.

Epstein, S., & Meier, P. (1989). Constructive thinking: A broad coping variable with specific components. *Journal of Personality and Social Psychology, 57* (2), 332–350.

Epstein, S., & O'Brien, E. J. (1985). The person-situation debate in historical and current perspective. *Psychological Bulletin, 98* (3), 513–537.

Eysenck, H. J., & Eysenck, M. W. (1985). *Personality and individual differences: A natural science approach.* New York: Plenum Press.

Farmer, R. F., Jarvis, L. L., Berent, M. K., & Corbett, A. (2001). Contributions to global self esteem: The role of importance attached to self concepts associated with the five-factor model. *Journal of Research in Personality, 35*, 483–499.

Fishbein, M., & Ajzen, I. (1975). *Belief, attitude, intention, and behavior.* Reading, MA: Addison-Wesley.

Gotlib, I. H., Lewinsohn, P. M., & Seeley, J. R. (1995). Symptoms versus a diagnosis of depression: Differences in psychosocial functioning. *Journal of Consulting and Clinical Psychology, 63* (1), 90–100.

Hair, E. C., & Graziano, W. G. (2003). Self-esteem, personality and achievement in high school: A prospective longitudinal study in Texas. *Journal of Personality, 71* (6), 971–994.

Harter, S. (1999). *The construction of self: A developmental perspective.* New York: Guilford Press.

Harter, S., & Whitesell, N. R. (2003). Beyond the debate: Why some adolescents report stable self-worth over time and situation, whereas others report changes in self-worth. *Journal of Personality, 71* (6), 1027–1058.

James, W. (1892). *Psychology: The briefer course*. New York: Holt.

Jeffreys, D. J., Leitzel, J. D., Cabral, G., Gumpert, J., Hartley, E., Lare, D., Nagy, N. M., O'Brien, E. J., Russo, T. J., Salvaterra, M., & Strobino, J. (1997). *Military adolescents: Their strengths and vulnerabilities*. Technical Report 97-4, Scranton, PA: Military Family Institute.

John, O. P., & Srivastava, S. (1999). The big five: History, measurement, and development. In L. A. Pervin & O. P. John (Eds.), *Handbook of personality: Theory and research* (pp. 102–138). New York: Guilford.

Judge, T. A., & Bono, J. E. (2001). Relationship of core self-evaluation traits—Self-esteem, generalized self-efficacy, locus of control, and emotional stability—with job satisfaction and job performance: A meta-analysis. *Journal of Applied Psychology, 86* (1), 80–92.

Judge, T. A., Erez, A., Bono, J. E., & Thoresen, C. J. (2002). Are measures of self-esteem, neuroticism, locus of control, and generalized self-efficacy indicators of a common core construct? *Journal of Personality and Social Psychology, 83* (3), 693–710.

Judge, T. A., Locke, E. A., Durham, C. C., & Kluger, A. N. (1998). Dispositional effects on job and life satisfaction: The role of core evaluations. *Journal of Applied Psychology, 83* (1), 17–34.

Kazdin, A. E. (Ed.) (1998). *Methodological issues and strategies in clinical research* (2nd ed.). Washington, DC: American Psychological Association.

Kazdin, A. E. (Ed.) (2003). *Evidence-based psychotherapies for children and adolescents*. New York: Guilford Press.

Kernis, M. H. (2003). Toward a conceptualization of optimal self-esteem. *Psychological Inquiry, 14* (1), 1–26.

Kernis, M. H., Grannemann, B. D., & Barclay, L. C. (1989). Stability and level of self-esteem as predictors of anger arousal and hostility. *Journal of Personality and Social Psychology, 56* (6), 1013–1022.

Kling, K. C., Ryff, C. D., Love, G., & Essex, M. (2003). Exploring the influence of personality on depressive symptoms and self-esteem across a significant life transition. *Journal of Personality and Social Psychology, 85*, 922–932.

Laurent, J., Catanzaro, S. J., Joiner, T. E., Jr., Rudolph, K. D., Potter, K. I., Lambert, S., Osborne, L., & Gathright, T. (1999). A measure of positive and negative affect for children: Scale development and preliminary validation. *Psychological Assessment, 11* (3), 326–338.

Leitzel, J. D. (2000). *A confirmatory factor analytic investigation of the tripartite model of depression and anxiety in high school adolescents*. Doctoral dissertation, Marywood University, Scranton, PA.

Lerner, R. M. (1991). Changing organism-context relations as the basic process of development: A developmental contextual perspective. *Developmental Psychology, 27* (1), 27–32.

Marsh, H. W., & Hattie, J. (1996). Theoretical perspectives on the structure of self-concept. In B. A. Bracken (Ed.), *Handbook of self-concept* (pp. 38–90). New York: Wiley.

Martinez, R., & Sewell, K. W. (2000). Explanatory style as a predictor of college performance in students with physical disabilities. *Journal of Rehabilitation, 66* (3), 30–36.

McKean, K. J. (1993). Using multiple risk factors to assess the behavioral, cognitive, and affective effects of learned helplessness. *The Journal of Psychology, 128* (2), 177–183.

Mecca, A. M., Smelser, N. J., & Vasconcellos, J. (Eds.) (1989). *The social importance of self-esteem*. Berkeley, CA: University of California Press.

Morf, C. C., & Rhodewalt, F. (2001). Unraveling the paradoxes of narcissism: A dynamic self-regulatory processing model. *Psychological Inquiry, 12* (4), 177–196.

Mruk, C. J. (1999). *Self-esteem: Research, theory and practice* (2nd ed.). New York: Springer Publishing Company.

O'Brien, E. J., & Epstein, S. (1988). *MSEI: The multidimensional self-esteem inventory.* Odessa, FL: Psychological Assessment Resources, Inc.

O'Brien, E. J., & Leitzel, J. (2000, August). Implications of ceiling effects in the measurement of self-esteem. Poster session presented as part of Division 8 Program, Personality and Social Psychology, American Psychological Association Convention, Washington, DC.

Peterson, C., Semmel, A., von Baeyer, C., Abramson, L. T., Metalsky, G. I., & Seligman, M. E. P. (1982). The attributional style questionnaire. *Cognitive Therapy and Research, 6,* 287–300.

Petrie, T. A., & Russell, R. K. (1995). Academic and psychosocial antecedents of academic performance for minority and non-minority college football players. *Journal of Counseling and Development, 73,* 615–620.

Raskin, R., Novacek, J., & Hogan, R. (1991). Narcissism, self-esteem, and defensive self-enhancement. *Journal of Personality, 59* (1), 21–38.

Robins, R. W., Tracy, J. L., Trzesniewski, K., Potter, J., & Gosling, S. D. (2001). Personality correlates of self-esteem. *Journal of Research in Personality, 35,* 463–482.

Rosenberg, M. (1979). *Conceiving the self.* New York: Basic Books.

Rosenberg, M., Schooler, C., Schoenbach, C., & Rosenberg, F. (1995). Global self-esteem and specific self-esteem: Different concepts, different outcomes. *American Sociological Review, 60,* 141–156.

Rosnow, R. L. & Rosenthal., R. (1989). Statistical procedures and the justification of knowledge in psychological science. *American Psychologist, 44* (10), 1276–1284.

Scheirer, M. A., & Kraut, R. E. (1979). Increasing educational achievement via self concept change. *Review of Educational Research, 49* (1), 131–150.

Sheldon, K. M., Elliot, A. J., Kim, Y., & Kasser, T. (2001). What is satisfying about satisfying events? Testing 10 candidate psychological needs. *Journal of Personality and Social Psychology, 80* (2), 325–339.

Spielberger, C. D. (1995). *Preliminary manual for the state-trait personality inventory (STPI).* Unpublished manuscript, University of South Florida, Tampa, FL.

Wang, A. Y., & Newlin, M. H. (2000). Characteristics of students who enroll and succeed in psychology web-based classes. *Journal of Educational Psychology, 92* (1), 137–143.

Watson, D., Suls, J., & Haig, J. (2002). Global self-esteem in relation to structural models of personality and affectivity. *Journal of Personality and Social Psychology, 83* (1), 185–197.

5

On the Divergent and Convergent Validity of Self-Esteem

JERRY SULS

Most classic and contemporary researchers use the term "self-esteem" to refer to the individual's global sense of personal worth. Global self-esteem can be logically differentiated from self-evaluations of specific domains (e.g., academic self-esteem, social self-esteem, physical attractiveness) (Marsh, 1986, 1993), often referred to as self-concept. One of the most frequently used measures of global self-esteem is Rosenberg's (1965) 10-item self-report questionnaire with items such as, "On the whole, I am satisfied with myself," and "I certainly feel useless at times" (reverse-scored). Theorists and researchers have debated about the relationship between global and specific self-views, with some arguing that global self-worth represents the sum total of specific assessments of particular skills and attributes (a "bottom-up" perspective) and others (e.g., Brown, 1993) that global feelings about the self influence specific views of personal attributes (a "top-down" perspective). (In the latter view, global feelings of self-worth have their origin in inherited differences in temperament and early socialization experiences.)

Although the importance of domain-specific self-assessments cannot be disputed, they should be differentiated from global favorability, especially in a discussion of convergent and divergent validity of self-esteem. Williams James (1890), who started this enterprise, maintained the same view. He proposed that self-esteem is a function of judgments about self-attributes (i.e., the famous self-esteem = success/pretensions ratio), *but* also acknowledged, "... there is a certain average tone of self-feeling ... which is independent of the objective reasons we may have for satisfaction and discontent" (James, 1890, p. 306). This second definition refers to global dispositional feelings of self-worth. By definition, if self-esteem refers to broad and relatively stable feelings then it should be logically related to personality and temperament. In fact, a large body of evidence finds evidence of substantial correlations between global self-esteem and personality and mood.

GLOBAL SELF-ESTEEM AND THE BIG FIVE

Conceptualization and measurement of personality has a long and controversial past; however, extensive analyses of the natural language of trait descriptors consistently reveal five broad factors: Neuroticism, Extraversion, Conscientiousness, Agreeableness, and Openness to Experience. This structure, commonly known as the "Big 5," consistently emerges from both self- and peer ratings (McCrae & Costa, 1987), in children and adults (Digman, 1987), and across languages and cultures (McCrae & Costa, 1997). This five-factor model is conceived as a hierarchical structure such that each of the Big 5 dimensions can be decomposed into a number of specific facet traits. For example, the facets of Neuroticism are anxiety, angry hostility, depression, self-consciousness, impulsiveness, and vulnerability. The Big 5 is commonly measured with self-report questionnaires; the NEO-PI-R (Costa & McCrae, 1985), Goldberg's (1993) lexical markers, and the Big Five Inventory (John, Donohue, & Kentle, 1991) are the most popular.

Many studies have assessed associations between neuroticism, extraversion, and global self-esteem, using the Rosenberg (1965) scale or the Coopersmith (1967) inventory, another popular measure. Results are quite consistent: global self-esteem relates negatively to neuroticism, with correlations typically exceeding $-.50$ (Judge, Erez, & Bono, 1998,) and relates positively to extraversion with correlations typically ranging between .30 and .50. The correlations of self-esteem with other dimensions of the Big 5 have been less extensively studied. In three recent studies (Watson, Suls, & Haig, 2002) that included all five dimensions, the previously noted associations with neuroticism and extraversion were replicated. In addition, conscientiousness, agreeableness, and openness to experience also were associated with self-esteem, but more modestly. For example, in our second study, the correlation with the Rosenberg (1965) scale was approximately $-.7$ with neuroticism and .4 with extraversion. Openness to Experience, Agreeableness, and Conscientiousness correlated with self-esteem at .31, .23, and .37, respectively (Watson et al., 2002). These results suggest that global feelings of self-worth are strongly associated with the standing on neuroticism, somewhat less so with extraversion and modestly with the other broad personality dimensions.

GLOBAL SELF-ESTEEM AND MOOD

As noted above, global self-esteem also should logically be related to individual differences in the experience of certain moods and emotions. Affective differences have been conceptualized in terms of two relatively independent dimensions: Negative Affectivity and Positive Affectivity (Watson & Tellegen, 1985). Negative Affect refers to the extent to which one experiences negative mood states such as fear, sadness, and anger. Positive Affect refers to the extent to which one experiences positive states such as joy, interest, and enthusiasm. Because negative affect tends to be strongly correlated with neuroticism ($r = .5$) and positive affect with extraversion ($r = .5$), it is not surprising that global self-esteem is positively associated with positive affectivity and negatively associated with negative affectivity ($r = -.50$). In sum, people who report feeling satisfied with themselves also tend to experience more positive moods and less negative moods in general. The magnitude of these correlations and those with neuroticism and (less so) extraversion is sufficiently large to inquire whether global self-esteem is a free-standing individual difference construct (which is the way it is conventionally researched) or better considered as a more specific facet of general structural models of personality and affect.

GLOBAL SELF-ESTEEM AND DEPRESSION

The association of self-esteem with negative affect may be rather specific. An affinity between self-esteem and depression has often been observed (e.g., Tarlow and Haaga, 1996) and cognitive theories of depression emphasize the etiologic importance of negative self-concept. Furthermore, feeling of worthlessness is a criterion for a major depressive episode. In contrast, negative self-concept and anxiety, a second aspect of negative affect, seem to be more tenuously connected.

To explore this specificity, in our research (Watson et al., 2002), the relationships among global self-esteem and symptoms of depression (e.g., anhedonia, absence of positive experience) and anxiety (e.g., somatic tension and arousal) were assessed. In two studies, global self-esteem was moderately related to anxiety ($r = .4$), but very strongly related to depression ($r = .8$). In a third study, a Big 5 measure that included lower-order facets (including depression) (Costa & McCrae, 1992) was also completed by participants. In support of specificity, Rosenberg scores were more strongly correlated with the depression facet ($r = .79$) than with any of the other facets. A structural equation model, which adjusted for measurement error and the reliability of the measures, indicated that depression was more strongly associated with global self-esteem ($r = -.86$) than with general neuroticism/negative affectivity ($r = -.73$), general extraversion/positive affectivity ($r = -.69$) or a specific negative affect, anxiety ($r = -.53$). The strong inverse association between self-esteem and depression suggests that they may be conceptualized as endpoints of a bipolar continuum.

Global self-esteem appears to be linked to general affective dispositions, but the results for depression suggest that self-esteem might be better viewed as a lower-order construct. Specifically, measures such as the Rosenberg and Coopersmith define one end of a bipolar continuum with indicators of depression marking the other.

In brief, the research suggests that global self-esteem shares significant overlap with measures of personality and affect. The magnitude of the correlation between self-esteem and depression is quite substantial and challenges the discriminant validity of the two constructs. However, this finding also has the potential to facilitate a synthesis of structural models of personality and affect social psychological research on self-esteem. For example, the recognition of the overlap and correlation among self-esteem and personality/affect measures should lead to research that includes relevant constructs to evaluate rival explanations. When an investigator finds a significant association between global self-esteem and performance or affect, it should be important to evaluate whether the association is significant after controlling for other related constructs, such as positive and negative affectivity. If the original association remains significant then the effects are likely to be due to self-esteem per se. Of course, measures may share variance with self-esteem but predict outcomes differently. This possibility also needs to be considered. With the accumulation of research that adopts this strategy, the field will have a better perspective on just how "free-standing" a construct self-esteem is.

STATE AND STABILITY IN SELF-ESTEEM

Most of my comments have been devoted to dispositional or trait self-esteem, but a few words about *state* self-esteem are warranted. Although people do experience relatively consistent feelings about the self, specific experiences, such as success or failure experiences, can increase or decrease these feelings at least temporarily (Heatherton & Polivy, 1991). Even the individual with extremely high or low self-esteem is likely to show some transitory shift as a result of such experiences.

However, Kernis has demonstrated that some people are predisposed to be more unstable in self-esteem than others and this tendency is independent of self-esteem level. Hence, there are individuals who score high in global self-esteem and are highly stable and others who are generally high but exhibit fluctuations. The same is the case for people who are moderate and low in self-esteem. Some are relatively stable in their self-feelings while others fluctuate.

Kernis, Grannemann and Barclay (1989) have reported that those who are unstable are more susceptible to social provocation and threats to the self (Kernis, Cornell, Sun, Berry, & Harlow, 1993); persons with stable self-esteem are less affected by minor stressors. The correlations between self-esteem, stability, and the Big 5 are informative (Kernis and Waschull, 1995). Among high SEs, instability is related to greater agreeableness and conscientiousness, while among low SEs, instability is related to lower agreeableness and conscientiousness. As Kernis and Waschull (1995) observe, "among low SE's instability is related to emotional and behavioral difficulties...among high SEs...instability is related to greater attempts to get along with others and to maintain control over the details of their lives" (pp. 130–131). Thus, differences in personality seem implicated in the instability in feelings of self-worth experienced by some individuals.

DIFFERENTIATING GLOBAL SELF-ESTEEM FROM SEEMINGLY RELATED CONSTRUCTS

Global Self-esteem and Specific Attributes

As noted earlier, global self-esteem can be logically distinguished from domain-specific self-esteem. Empirical studies show that self-evaluations of specific domains relate modestly to global self-esteem; some researchers find, however, that the correlations are larger when only attributes that are considered important by the individual are considered (Pelham, 1995; Pelham & Swann, 1989). However, these correlations still tend to be relatively small in magnitude (Marsh, 1995). This is not surprising; strong associations between general individual differences in personality/affectivity, from which global self-esteem appears to emerge, and specific skills or capabilities should not be expected.

Self-efficacy

A construct that is often mentioned in the same context as self-esteem is self-efficacy (Bandura, 1986). This refers to expectations about whether one can successfully execute the behavior to produce a successful outcome. Bandura defines self-efficacy with reference to specific tasks and skills. Because of its specificity, it should act more like domain-specific self-concept than global self-esteem. Indeed, empirical investigations find that self-efficacy with respect to particular domains is not strongly correlated with self-esteem (Bandura, 1986; Chen, Gully, & Eden, 2004). Typically, the correlations do not exceed .3 and are often smaller (Bandura, 1986; Marsh, 1992).

Narcissism

The final related construct to be discussed here is narcissism, a construct that originated in the psychiatric literature and refers to a personality disorder characterized by a lack of empathy, need for admiration and a pattern of grandiosity (American Psychiatric Association, 2000). However, research with normal samples focuses on subclinical levels—individuals with some of the attributes but not necessarily at levels that are psychopathological. One of the most commonly used assessment measures is the Narcissistic Personality Inventory (NPI) developed by Raskin and Hall (1979), a self-report scale consisting of several forced choice items, each containing two alternative statements, such as "I will be a success" (narcissistic) vs. "I am too concerned about success" (non-narcissist).

On a purely logical basis, narcissism should be related to global self-esteem; both narcissists and persons with high self-esteem report positive feelings about themselves. Indeed, a meta-analysis by Campbell (1999) (cited in Foster, Campbell, & Twenge, 2003) found an average correlation of .29 between Rosenberg scores and narcissism scores. However, the modest magnitude of this relationship suggests that these are not identical constructs. In fact, although narcissism is positively correlated with extraversion, and negatively correlated with neuroticism (like self-esteem), the association of narcissism with extraversion is stronger than with neuroticism; for self-esteem the pattern is reversed.

Campbell, Rudich, and Sedikides (2002) investigated whether narcissists (identified with the NPI) vs. persons with high self-esteem (measured with the RSE) are characterized by different kinds of "self-love." Participants rated themselves on a variety of scale dimensions relative to the average person and their romantic partners. Although narcissists and persons with high self-esteem both reported positive self-views, they diverged in significant ways. High self-esteem persons perceived themselves as more intelligent, extraverted, open, agreeable and moral than the average person. Narcissists saw themselves as better in intellectual skills and extraversion, but not in terms of agreeableness and morality. Interestingly, narcissists also rated themselves as better than their romantic partners; persons with high self-esteem did not. In sum, narcissists perceive themselves as having certain agentic traits and their orientation is egoistic. In contrast, high self-esteem is associated with perceiving oneself as both competent *and* moralistic. These differences in self-views provide at least one reason why self-esteem and narcissism are not more highly correlated.

Concluding Thoughts

In sum, a substantial aspect of global self-esteem seems to be rooted in broad differences in personality and affectivity, particularly neuroticism and extraversion. The different ways in which people generally behave and experience the social and physical world are mirrored in dispositional feelings of self-worth. Further, self-esteem, as measured by conventional measures, seems to define the opposite pole from a specific affect, depression. In contrast to its appreciable overlap with general dimensions of affectivity and personality, global self-esteem is distinct from specific self-concepts, narcissism, and self-efficacy.

In recent years, several implicit measures of self-esteem have been developed. Unlike self-report scales such as the Rosenberg (1965), these assessment techniques gauge implicit, nonconscious feelings about the self (Greenwald & Banaji, 1995) by using measures that measure automatic associations. Based on several empirical studies, the relationship between these implicit measures and explicit measures appears to be quite modest (e.g., Greenwald & Farnham, 2000), which suggests that the conscious self-esteem may be quite different from nonconscious self-esteem. Preliminary research in my laboratory, which has explored associations among implicit and explicit measures of self-esteem and the Big 5, reinforces this independence. However, more research will be required before any definitive conclusions about the relationship between implicit self-esteem and personality can be made.

REFERENCES

American Psychiatric Association. (2000). *Diagnostic and statistical manual* (4th ed., Text Revision.). Washington, DC.

Bandura, A. (1986). *Social foundations of thought and action: A social cognitive theory.* Englewood Cliffs, NJ: Prentice-Hall.

Brown, J. (1993). Self-esteem and self-evaluation: Feeling is believing. In J. Suls & A.G. Greenwald (Eds.), *Psychological perspectives on the self* (Vol. 4, pp. 27–58). Hillsdale, NJ: Lawrence Erlbaum Associates.

Campbell, W. K., Rudich, E., & Sedikides, C. (2002). Narcissism, self-esteem and the positivity of self-views: Two portraits of self-love. *Personality and Social Psychology Bulletin, 28*, 358–368.

Chen, G., Gully, S., & Eden, D. (2004). General self-efficacy and self-esteem: Toward theoretical and empirical distinction between correlated self-evaluations. *Journal of Organizational Behavior, 25*, 375–395.

Coopersmith, S. (1967). *The antecedents of self-esteem.* Palo Alto, CA: Consulting Psychologists Press.

Costa, A., & McCrae, R. (1985). *The NEO Personality Inventory manual.* Odessa, FL: Psychological Assessment Resources.

Digman, J. (1997). Higher order factors of the Big Five. *Journal of Personality and Social Psychology, 41,* 417–440.

Foster, J., Campbell, W. K., & Twenge, J. (2003). Individual differences in narcissism: Inflated self-views across the lifespan and around the world. *Journal of Research in Personality, 37,* 469–486.

Goldberg, L. (1993). The structure of phenotypic personality traits. *American Psychologist, 48,* 26–34.

Greenwald, A. G., & Banaji, M. (1995). Implicit social cognition: Attitudes, self-esteem, and stereotypes. *Psychological Review, 102,* 4–27.

Greenwald, A. G., & Farnham, S. (2000). Using the Implicit Association Test to measure self-esteem and self-concept. *Journal of Personality and Social Psychology, 79,* 1022–1038.

Heatherton, T., & Polivy, J. (1991). Development and validation of a scale for measuring state self-esteem. *Journal of Personality and Social Psychology, 60,* 895–910.

James, W. (1890). *The principles of psychology.* New York: Holt.

John, O., Donohue, E., & Kentle, R. (1991). *The Big Five Inventory—Versions 4a and 54.* Technical Report, Berkeley: Institute of Personality and Social Research, University of California.

Judge, T., Erez, A., & Bono, J. (1998). The power of being positive: The relation between positive self-concept and job performance. *Human Performance, 11,* 167–187.

Kernis, M., Cornell, D., Sun, C., Berry, A., & Harlow, T. (1993). There's more to self esteem than whether it is high or low: The importance of stability of self-esteem. *Journal of Personality and Social Psychology, 65,* 1190–1204.

Kernis, M., Grannemann, B., & Barclay, L. (1989). Stability and level of self-esteem as predictors of anger arousal and hostility. *Journal of Personality and Social Psychology, 56,* 1013–1023.

Kernis, M., & Waschull, S. (1995). The interactive roles of stability and level of self-esteem: Research and theory. In M. Zanna (Ed.), *Advances in experimental social psychology* (Vol. 27, pp. 93–141). Orlando, FL: Academic Press.

Marsh, H. (1986). Global self-esteem: Its relation to specific facets of self-concept and their importance. *Journal of Personality and Social Psychology, 51,* 1224–1236.

Marsh, H. (1992). The content specificity of relations between academic achievement and academic self-concept. *Journal of Educational Psychology, 84,* 43–50.

Marsh, H. (1993). Relations between global and specific domains of self: The importance of individual importance, certainty and ideals. *Journal of Personality and Social Psychology, 65,* 975–992.

Marsh H. W. (1995). A Jamesian model of self-investment and self-esteem—comment. *Journal of Personality & Social Psychology, 69,* 1151–1160.

McCrae, R., & Costa, P. (1987). Validation of a five-factor model of personality across instruments and observers. *Journal of Personality and Social Psychology, 52,* 81–90.

McCrae, R., & Costa, P. (1997). Personality trait structure as a human universal. *American Psychologist, 52,* 509–516.

Pelham, B. (1995). Self-investment and self-esteem: Evidence for a Jamesian model of self-worth. *Journal of Personality and Social Psychology, 69,* 1141–1150.

Pelham, B., & Swann, W. (1989). From self-conceptions to self-worth: On the sources and structure of global self-esteem. *Journal of Personality and Social Psychology, 57,* 672–680.

Raskin, R., & Hall, C. (1979). A narcissistic personality inventory. *Psychological Reports, 45,* 590.

Rosenberg, M. (1965). *Society and the adolescent self-image.* Princeton, NJ: Princeton University Press.

Tarlow, E., & Haaga, D. (1996). Negative self-concept: Specificity to depressive symptoms and relation to positive and negative affectivity. *Journal of Research in Personality, 30,* 120–127.

Watson, D., Suls, J., & Haig, J. (2002). Global self-esteem in relation to structural models of personality and affectivity. *Journal of Personality and Social Psychology, 83,* 185–197.

Watson, D., & Tellegen, A. (1985). Toward a consensual structure of mood. *Psychological Bulletin, 98,* 219–235.

6

Divergent and Convergent Validity of Self-Esteem: A State Perspective

JOHN B. NEZLEK

*T*he vast majority of research on self-esteem has considered it as a trait, an individual difference that is more or less enduring across time and situations. As attested by the richness of the research and ideas described in the chapters in this book, research conceptualizing self-esteem as a trait has been quite valuable. Nevertheless, there is a growing body of research suggesting that it is also useful to consider self-esteem as a state, a construct that is presumed to change across time and situations, and this chapter will focus on the validity of state self-esteem. Evaluating the validity of a construct requires a clear definition of that construct, and for present purposes, self-esteem is defined primarily in terms of a global self-evaluation of one's worth. Certainly, other definitions are possible, and the considerations discussed here can be applied to most any definition (or definitions) of self-esteem.

There are numerous ways to evaluate the validity of a construct, and this chapter focuses on convergent and divergent validity. Convergent validity exists when a measure of a construct is related to measures of other constructs to which the definitions of the constructs suggest it should be related. The convergent validity of state self-esteem was evaluated in terms of the strength of the relationships between measures of the state self-esteem and measures of other state constructs, such as depressive thinking, for which it was reasonable to expect self-esteem to be related. Divergent validity exists when a measure of a target construct is unrelated to measures of other constructs to which the definitions of constructs suggest it to be unrelated (the complement of convergent validity). Divergent validity also implies that a target construct predicts, or is related to, some outcome of interest above and beyond relationships between other measures and this outcome. The divergent validity of state self-esteem was evaluated in terms of both these criteria.

The choice of constructs used to evaluate the validity of a target construct or measure is critical, and choosing different constructs may lead to different conclusions about the validity of a measure. The validity of state self-esteem was evaluated in terms of the following constructs: psychological well-being (e.g., depression), affect, self-referential thinking, self-concept, and perceptions of control over the environment. These constructs were chosen on the basis of trait-level research that has consistently found relationships between trait measures of these constructs and the trait self-esteem. Although state- and trait-level relationships are mathematically independent and may represent different psychological processes (e.g., Nezlek, 2001; Tennen & Affleck, 1996), relationships among traits may represent good starting points for examining relationships among the same constructs considered as states.

The empirical basis for this examination was a series of studies in which participants provided data every day for 2–3 weeks. State-level constructs were measured with items taken from trait-level measures, reworded for daily administration. Daily self-esteem was measured, using an "uncharacteristic–characteristic of me" response scale, with four items from Rosenberg (1965), one of which was "Today, I had a positive attitude toward myself". Daily depressogenic adjustment was measured with three items based on Beck's (1967) triad, one of which was "How optimistic are you about how your life (in general) will be tomorrow?" Daily affect was measured using 20 items representing a circumplex model (e.g., Feldman Barrett & Russell, 1998). There were five items representing each of positive activated mood (e.g., happy), positive deactivated mood (e.g., relaxed), negative activated mood (e.g., nervous), and negative deactivated mood (e.g., sad). Self-referential thinking was defined in terms of the two dimensions of private self-consciousness suggested by Trapnell and Campbell (1999), reflection and rumination, and public self-consciousness (Fenigstein, Scheier, & Buss, 1975). For example, participants indicated "How much today did you ...," think about your attitudes and feelings (reflection), ruminate or dwell on things that happened to you (rumination), and think about what other people thought of you (public self-consciousness). Self-concept was measured with four items taken from the Self-Concept Clarity scale (Campbell, Trapnell, Heine, Katz, Lavallee, & Lehman, 1996), and participants indicated how much each statement applied to them that day, e.g., "My beliefs about myself often conflict with one another." Measures of perceived control over one's environment were based on Deci and Ryan's (1985) work on causality orientation. Based on analyses described in Nezlek and Gable (2001), perceived control was measured with four items, two items for control over the social and achievement domains. These items corresponded to Deci and Ryan's impersonal and autonomy dimensions. For example, "Thinking back on your day today in terms of the social events that occurred and the relationships you have with others, how much choice did you really have about what you did?" All measures used 1–7 scales.

Relationships between self-esteem and depressogenic adjustment, affect, self-referential thinking, self-consciousness, and perceived control were estimated from data described in Nezlek (2005). Sample sizes for these analyses ranged between 558 and 735 participants and between 8079 and 11,153 days. Relationships between self-esteem and self-concept clarity were estimated from data described in Nezlek and Plesko (2001). These data were analyzed with a series of multilevel models in which days were treated as nested within persons. Conceptually, a within-person regression equation describing the relationships between self-esteem and other measures was estimated for each person, and then the mean of these relationships was calculated. [See Nezlek (2001) for a more detailed description of, and rationale for, these analyses.]

The relationships between state self-esteem and other state constructs were in directions consistent with the definitions of the constructs. State self-esteem was positively related to depressogenic adjustment, both measures of positive affect, self-concept clarity, and perceived control, and it was negatively related to both measures of negative affect, rumination, and public self-consciousness. On days when people's self-esteem was higher, compared to days when their self-esteem was lower, people experienced more positive affect, their self-concept clarity was greater, etc., and they experienced less negative affect, ruminated less, etc.

Usually, validity coefficients are described in terms of correlations, and the estimated within-person correlations between self-esteem and other state-level constructs are presented in Table 6.1. Due to the nature of the multilevel analyses, these correlations were derived from shared variance estimates, and these shared variances are also presented in Table 6.1. This procedure is described in Nezlek (2001). These relationships are sufficiently strong (within-person correlations between .25 and .70) to demonstrate the convergent validity of the state self-esteem; however, they are not so strong to suggest that the state self-esteem cannot be differentiated from these constructs.

As can be seen from these data, these relationships varied in strength, with the relationship between self-esteem and depressogenic adjustment being the strongest. The fact that this relationship was the strongest of the group parallels research on trait-level relationships; however, it also needs to be considered in light of the fact that one of the depression items, "Overall, how positively did you feel about yourself today" is basically a measure of self-esteem. Most theories and explanations of depression posit that depression includes a diminished sense of self-worth, so the substantial overlap between the two constructs is not surprising.

TABLE 6.1   Shared Variances and Within-Person Correlations between State Self-Esteem and Other State Constructs

Construct	Shared Variance	Correlation
Depressogenic adjustment	0.51	.71
Positive activated affect	0.36	.60
Positive deactivated affect	0.36	.60
Negative activated affect	0.32	−.57
Negative deactivated affect	0.33	−.57
Reflection	0.09	.30
Rumination	0.13	−.36
Public self-consciousness	0.06	−.24
Self-concept clarity	0.25	.50
Control over events	0.11	.33

At the trait level, some have suggested that self-esteem can be represented by combinations of variables, such as affect (e.g., Watson, Suls, & Haig, 2002). Such a possibility was considered by predicting self-esteem from the four affect measures, and in a separate analysis from reflection, rumination, and public self-consciousness. The estimated within-person multiple R (based on changes in the error variance in self-esteem) when all four affect measures were included as predictors was .75, and when all three measures of self-referential thinking were included the reduction was .46. It is important to note that these correlations correspond to 56% and 21% shared variance between self-esteem and the two combinations of variables.

Simply demonstrating that the correlation between two measures is not 1.0 does not de facto indicate that the measures have divergent validity. Additional corroboration can come from demonstrating that the relationship between a target measure (i.e., self-esteem) and another, criterion measure does not overlap with the relationship between the criterion measure and a comparison measure (e.g., positive effect). The selection of "criterion" measures is not straightforward. Nevertheless, much of the research on within-person variability in psychological states has concerned relationships between such states and daily events, and so daily events were used as the criteria to evaluate the divergent validity of the state self-esteem. Is daily (state) self-esteem related to daily events above and beyond the relationship between daily events and other daily (state) measures?

In all of the studies described thus far, participants also described the events that occurred to them each day using a variant of the Daily Events schedule (Butler, Hokanson, & Flynn, 1994). These events represented four categories, combinations of positive vs. negative and social vs. achievement. Each event was rated on a 0 (did not happen) to 4 (happened and was very important) scale. Event ratings were averaged within each category to create an impact score. Impact scores were used for the analyses instead of frequency counts (i.e., how many events in each category occurred) because impact scores had more desirable psychometric properties (e.g., homogeneity of variance). It should be noted that relationships between frequency counts and daily measures of psychological states were functionally equivalent to the results discussed here. [See Nezlek & Gable (2001) for a brief discussion of impact scores and frequency counts.]

First, daily events (positive and negative, social and achievement) were regressed onto self-esteem. Self-esteem positively covaried with positive social and achievement events and negatively covaried with negative social and achievement events (all p values < .001). Moreover, separate analyses found that all of the validating constructs were also related to daily events (all p values < .001). These analyses are discussed in detail in Nezlek (2005) and in Nezlek and Plesko (2001). Next, validating constructs were entered as predictors, singly and in the groups described above (the four mood measures and the three self-referential thinking measures). In all cases, relationships between self-esteem and the event measures remained significant (all p values < .001) after taking into account within-person (daily) variability in the other measures.

Taken together, these two sets of results suggest that measures of global state self-esteem based on Rosenberg's trait measure have convergent and divergent validity. That is, state self-esteem was related to other states in ways that were consistent with the definitions of the constructs being considered. Equally important, state self-esteem was related to daily events above and beyond relationships between state self-esteem and other state-level constructs and the relationships between daily events and these other constructs, suggesting that state self-esteem has divergent validity.

In addition, relationships between state self-esteem and other states were generally weaker than relationships between the same constructs measured at the trait level. This difference may have been due to the fewer items used to measure each construct, although some research [unpublished analyses from Nezlek & Gable (2001) and Nezlek & Plesko (2001)] has found reasonable (.65 to .9) item-level reliabilities for the state-level constructs discussed here. Moreover, the multilevel analyses reported here take into account different types of unreliability.

Assuming that state relationships between self-esteem and other constructs are weaker than corresponding trait relationships suggests that state- and trait-level self-esteem constructs differ. The high correlations some have found between trait self-esteem and other measures may reflect the fact that responses to trait measures reflect some sort of general assessment of one's life more than state measures. Most trait measures either explicitly or implicitly ask people to make some sort of aggregate judgment. When people describe their typical mood (e.g., Watson, Suls, & Haig, 2002), they are implicitly aggregating across some unknown period of time and number of occasions, and they go through a similar process when describing their general self-worth. In contrast, and by definition, state measures reflect the immediate situation more than the past. State measures are time and/or situation bound.

Some think of trait measures as functionally equivalent to aggregates of state measures [see Fleeson (2001) for a discussion of this issue]. If this is the case, then aggregates of state measures of self-esteem may be more valid measures of self-esteem than trait measures because they may be less prone to selective recall and other biases and may have greater divergent validity. Although this either/or argument could be made, it is probably not the most productive to pursue. It is probably more productive to think of state and trait measures of self-esteem as measures of related, but distinct constructs. Such a position presents an interesting challenge of determining just what each of these measures truly represents.

CONCEPTUALIZING STATE VARIABILITY AS A TRAIT

The preceding discussion has examined how changes in state self-esteem correspond to changes in other state measures; however, a large body of research, pioneered by Kernis and colleagues, has treated changes in the state self-esteem as a trait variable, typically labeled "instability". Instability is defined in terms of within-in-person standard deviations, and this measure is treated like a trait. The logic of this approach can be extended to other states. For example, within-person standard deviations could be calculated for perceived control over the environment. Moreover, the within-person relationships between state self-esteem and other

states suggest that the instability of state self-esteem may be related to the instability of other states. That is, other states covary with state self-esteem, and it is
reasonable to expect that within-person changes in these measures would be
positively related to within-person changes in self-esteem. For example, the
more unstable a person is in terms of self-esteem, the more unstable he or she
will be in terms of perceived control. If the relationships among a set of measures
of instability are sufficiently strong, it is possible that they may form (or more
accurately, reflect) the existence of a some sort of a general "g" factor of instability. If this is the case, then unstable self-esteem may be an "s" (specific) factor of
this general factor.

The existence of "g" factor of instability was examined by Gable and Nezlek
(1998), who collected daily measures (for 3 weeks) of self-esteem, depressogenic
adjustment, perceived control over the environment (as described previously),
daily anxiety, and causal uncertainty (Weary & Edwards, 1994). They calculated
within-person means and standard deviations for each of these measures, and a
confirmatory factor analysis found that all five means loaded on one factor and all
five standard deviations loaded on another factor (an instability factor). Moreover,
the correlation between the two factors was $-.34$, very similar to the correlations
between mean self-esteem and self-esteem instability reported by Kernis and
colleagues (e.g., Kernis, Grannemann, & Mathis, 1991).

These results suggest that the instability of state self-esteem is a specific
manifestation of a more general factor of instability. This does not mean that the
instability of self-esteem is not a meaningful or worthwhile construct; rather, it
suggests that when thinking about the instability of self-esteem we need to be
mindful of the possible operation of a broader factor. Of course, simply demonstrating that the instability of self-esteem shares variance with the instability of
other states does not mean that the instability of self-esteem does not have divergent validity. The instability of self-esteem may be related to other measures
above and beyond relationships between these other measures and the instability of other states. That is, it might be useful to think more in terms of s-factors
than a g-factor of instability, much like the improvements that measuring facets
of the Five Factor Model (FFM) sometimes provides over measures of the
broader factors. Clearly, resolving this issue requires further research.

REFERENCES

Beck, A. T. (1967). *Depression: Clinical, experimental, and theoretical aspects*. New York:
    Harper & Row.
Butler, A. C., Hokanson, J. E., & Flynn, H. A. (1994). A comparison of self-esteem lability
    and low trait self-esteem as vulnerability factors for depression. *Journal of
    Personality and Social Psychology, 66*, 166–177.
Campbell, J. D., Trapnell, P. D., Heine, S. J., Katz, I. M., Lavallee, L. F., & Lehman, D. R.
    (1996). Self-concept clarity: Measurement, personality correlates, and cultural
    boundaries. *Journal of Personality and Social Psychology, 70*, 141–156.
Deci, E. L., & Ryan, R. M. (1985). The General Causality Orientations Scale: Self-determina-
    tion in personality. *Journal of Research in Personality, 19*, 109–134.

Feldman Barrett, L., & Russell, J. A. (1998). Independence and bipolarity in the structure of current affect. *Journal of Personality and Social Psychology, 74*, 967–984.

Feningstein, A., Scheier, M. F., & Buss, A. (1975). Public and private self-consciousness. *Journal of Consulting and Clinical Psychology, 43*, 522–527.

Fleeson, W. (2001). Toward a structure- and process-integrated view of personality: States as density distributions of traits. *Journal of Personality and Social Psychology, 80*, 1011–1027.

Gable, S. L., & Nezlek, J. B. (1998). Level and instability of day-to-day psychological well-being and risk for depression. *Journal of Personality and Social Psychology, 74*, 129–138.

Kernis, M. H., Grannemann, B. D., & Mathis, L. C. (1991). Stability of self-esteem as a moderator of the relation between level of self-esteem and depression. *Journal of Personality and Social Psychology, 61*, 80–84.

Nezlek, J. B. (2001). Multilevel random coefficient analyses of event and interval contingent data in social and personality psychology research. *Personality and Social Psychology Bulletin, 27*, 771–785.

Nezlek, J. B. (2005). Distinguishing affective and non-affective reactions to daily events. *Journal of Personality, 73*, 1539–1568.

Nezlek, J. B., & Gable, S. L. (2001). Depression as a moderator of relationships between positive daily events and day-to-day psychological adjustment. *Personality and Social Psychology Bulletin, 27*, 1692–11704.

Nezlek, J. B., & Plesko, R. M. (2001). Day-to-day relationships among self-concept clarity, self-esteem, daily events, and mood. *Personality and Social Psychology Bulletin, 27*, 201–211.

Rosenberg, M. (1965). *Society and the adolescent self-image*. Princeton, NJ: Princeton University Press.

Tennen, H., & Affleck, G. (1996). Daily processes in coping with chronic pain: Methods and analytic strategies. In M. Zeidner & N. Endler (Eds.), *Handbook of coping* (pp. 151–180). New York: Wiley.

Trapnell, P. D., & Campbell, J. D. (1999). Private self-consciousness and the five factor model of personality: Distinguishing rumination from reflection. *Journal of Personality and Social Psychology, 76*, 284–304.

Watson, D., Suls, J., & Haig, J. (2002). Global self-esteem in relation to structural models of personality and affectivity. *Journal of Personality and Social Psychology, 83*, 185–197.

Weary, G., & Edwards, J. A. (1994). Individual differences in causal uncertainty. *Journal of Personality and Social Psychology, 67*, 308–318.

Question 3

Does a nonconscious component to self-esteem exist? If so, how should it be conceptualized and measured? What role(s) does it play in psychological functioning? 3a: How should the self-esteem components of contingent self-esteem and stability of self-esteem be conceptualized and measured?

This next set of essays considers the issue of whether other self-esteem components exist besides level of self-esteem. Contributors to Question 3 were asked only to focus on whether a nonconscious self-esteem component exists and how best to conceptualize it. In response to a reviewer's suggestion, Brian Goldman and I contributed an essay on Question 3a after all other essays were completed.

All contributors to Question 3 suggest that a nonconscious self-esteem component does indeed exist, though they differ in specifics regarding how best to conceptualize and operationalize it.

Bosson presents a sophisticated analysis of what we "should" mean by nonconscious self-esteem. In her view, "…when discussing the nonconscious aspects of self-esteem, it seems that what is hidden from awareness is not the feeling evoked in response to the self, but the fact that the self served as the stimulus that elicited the feeling." In her view, nonconscious self-esteem can be conceptualized "…as a subjectively experienced, affective orientation toward the self that is elicited automatically by self-primes, and in the absence of conscious control, regulation, or interference by higher-order cognitive processes (such as rational decision-making, hypothesis-testing, logic, etc.)." Bosson discusses some important implications this conceptualization has for psychological functioning.

Jordan, Logel, Spencer, and Zanna suggest that people do possess highly efficient, automatic self-evaluations of which they are largely unaware. Jordan and colleagues suggest that these automatic self-evaluations (implicit self-esteem) are "preconscious" rather than unconscious. "Although people may be generally unaware of their implicit self-views, their implicit self-esteem may enter awareness in some situations, perhaps in the form of vague feelings associated with the self." The authors review evidence suggesting that whereas the combination of high explicit and low implicit self-esteem reflects heightened defensiveness (relative to "high-high"), the combination of low explicit and high implicit self-esteem (relative to "low-low") may reflect a "glimmer of hope" that buffers against psychological distress.

Epstein also focuses on the existence of preconscious self-esteem, as informed by cognitive experiential self-theory. Whereas self-esteem at the experiential (preconscious) level is "automatically derived from lived experience" and "manifested by a person's feelings and behavior," self-esteem at the rational (conscious) level is "derived from conscious inference" and "indicated by what a person consciously believes and can be assessed by what a person reports." Epstein also discusses the implications for psychological health and functioning of self-esteem as a "need" or "belief" within the rational and experiential systems, and he touches on ways to measure implicit or experiential self-esteem.

Kernis and Goldman describe methods by which researchers can assess stability of self-esteem and contingent self-esteem. In the most common method to assess self-esteem stability, respondents complete multiple assessments of current self-esteem (i.e., how they feel about themselves at that moment). At least two measures exist to assess contingent self-esteem. Whereas one measure focuses on overall differences in the degree of contingent self-esteem (Kernis & Paradise, 2002), the other measure focuses on specific domains on which self-esteem is contingent (Crocker, Luhtanen, Cooper, & Bouvrette, 2003).

7

Conceptualization, Measurement, and Functioning of Nonconscious Self-Esteem

JENNIFER K. BOSSON

There is an episode of *The Simpsons* in which a traumatized and desperate Ned Flanders asks Reverend Lovejoy if God is punishing him. Lovejoy promptly replies "Short answer: 'Yes' with an 'If,' long answer: 'No' with a 'But'" (Young & Anderson, 1997). For some reason, when I read the first of the three questions posed here ("Is there a nonconscious component to self-esteem?"), I thought of Reverend Lovejoy's words. I think it must be because whichever perspective (i.e., "Yes" vs. "No") one adopts regarding nonconscious self-esteem, there are bound to be several important "ifs" and "buts." So, I begin by discussing some of these qualifiers and explaining the roles they play in my thinking about nonconscious self-esteem. (Note that some of these qualifiers pertain to the second question regarding conceptualization and measurement, so my responses to the first two questions are inextricably linked.)

Is there a nonconscious component to self-esteem? *Qualifier #1: It depends on how you define "self-esteem."* As commonly conceptualized, self-esteem is a subjectively experienced, affective response to the self (e.g., Brown, 1993; Kernis, 2003; Leary, Tambor, Terdal, & Downs, 1995; Rosenberg, 1965). That is, self-esteem is experienced as a feeling-state, elicited in response to the attitude-object "the self," and ranging in valence from intensely negative/unpleasant to intensely positive/pleasant. If one accepts this as the basic definition of self-esteem, then it is difficult to conceive of a component of self-esteem that is nonconscious, i.e., inaccessible to conscious awareness. As Gregg (2003, p. 35) points out, "to feel *means* to subjectively experience," so if self-esteem is defined as a feeling one has about the self, then it makes little sense to speak of an aspect of self-esteem that can go un-felt.

On the other hand, if one conceptualizes self-esteem more broadly—as a generalized attitude (or perhaps schema) about the self that contains affective, cognitive, and behavioral components, all of which are linked to varying degrees, are organized in memory according to a particular structure, and reflect evaluative responses to the self—then it becomes easier to see how aspects of this generalized attitude may operate nonconsciously (Gregg, 2003). Consider, for example, an individual who, in walking past a store window, catches a quick glimpse of her reflection in the glass and is immediately flooded with negative emotions (cf. Bosson, Swann, & Pennebaker, 2000). Consider also that this individual is *not* consciously aware of having perceived her own reflection, but *is* consciously aware of being overtaken somewhat unexpectedly by unpleasant feelings. In this scenario, I would argue that a nonconscious aspect of self-esteem has produced this woman's sudden shift in mood—but, importantly, it is the automatic link between the self-prime and the evaluation that operates nonconsciously, not the feeling that becomes activated in response to the self-prime. Thus, if one conceptualizes self-esteem as a multifaceted and complex construct rather than merely as a feeling, then I believe it is safe to say that there are nonconscious components to self-esteem.

This point has of course been made before, so I make no claims of authorship here. In what has come to be regarded as a seminal treatise on implicit self-attitudes, Greenwald and Banaji (1995, p. 11) defined implicit self-esteem as "the introspectively unidentified (or inaccurately identified) *effect of* the self-attitude on evaluation of self-associated and self-dissociated objects" (italics added). Again, implicit (or nonconscious) self-esteem is not defined here as a *feeling* about the self that is hidden from awareness, but as a *link* between activation of the attitude-object "the self" and a resulting feeling (or evaluation, or affective state, etc.). Put another way, the aspect of self-esteem that is nonconscious is one that I would characterize as a "process" rather than as a "component." This brings me to Qualifier #2.

Qualifier #2: It depends on how you define "component." Is a "process" ("link," "effect," etc.) the same as a "component"? Not to put too fine a point on it, but I think this is a potentially important distinction. According to my *Webster Handy College Dictionary* (Morehead & Morehead, 1981), a "component" is "a constituent part" (p. 114) and a "process" is "a series of changes leading to some result" (p. 420). So, again, to the extent there are nonconscious aspects of self-esteem, I would argue that these aspects are not merely components—i.e., isolated thoughts or affective states—but instead are processes—i.e., specific concept-evaluation sequences that have been paired so frequently that they are chronically associated in memory and therefore can operate in the absence of conscious intention and/or reflection.

Qualifier #3: It also depends, of course, on how you define "nonconscious." Social-cognitive theorists recognize several key features of nonconscious processes including: automaticity and uncontrollability (e.g., Fazio, Sanbonmatsu, Powell, & Kardes, 1986; Murphy & Zajonc, 1993); processing efficiency (e.g., Bargh, 1994); unavailability for verbal articulation (e.g., Nisbett & Wilson, 1977); a tendency to operate in the absence of conscious reflection (e.g., Greenwald & Banaji, 1995; Koole, Dijksterhuis, & van Knippenberg, 2001); and a tendency to regulate primarily affective, intuitive, and implicit forms of information (e.g., Epstein, 1994). Note that none of these features implies something that cannot be felt or experienced subjectively. To the contrary, Epstein emphasizes the subjectively experienced, affective nature of implicit knowledge in his cognitive-experiential self-theory (CEST). According to CEST, nonconscious—i.e., "experiential"—self-knowledge is that which is acquired and processed automatically and intuitively, and is based on "synthesis of emotionally significant" self-relevant experiences (Teglasi & Epstein, 1998, p. 543). Thus, if one's thinking about nonconscious self-esteem is informed by CEST (as is mine), then one might conceptualize it as a subjectively experienced, affective orientation toward the self that is elicited automatically by self-primes, and in the absence of conscious control, regulation, or interference by higher-order cognitive processes (such as rational decision-making, hypothesis-testing, logic, etc.).

Again, when discussing the nonconscious aspects of self-esteem, it seems that what is hidden from awareness is not the feeling evoked in response to the self, but the fact that the self served as the stimulus that elicited this feeling. I am reminded here of one of the classes of introspective shortcomings identified by Nisbett and Wilson (1977, p. 247), who wrote "Even when people are completely cognizant of the existence of both stimulus and response, they appear to be unable to report correctly about the effect of the stimulus on the response." That is to say, an individual may be fully aware of a certain stimulus (such as the self) and of a certain response (such as negative affect), but be unaware that these two things are linked such that the stimulus automatically causes the response.

There are other details that I would add to this conceptualization of nonconscious self-esteem. For instance, I believe it is worthwhile to distinguish between state and trait nonconscious self-esteem. Whereas *state* nonconscious self-esteem would be the affective state that is automatically elicited in response to the self on any given measurement occasion, *trait* nonconscious self-esteem would be the average affective state that is automatically elicited in response to the self across several measurement occasions (see DeHart, Pelham, & Tennen, 2004). Moreover, given the complex and multifaceted nature of the self, there is reason to assume that different components of the self-concept, when primed, will automatically elicit different affective states. That is to say, there may be numerous types of nonconscious self-esteem that correspond to the numerous dimensions of the self. Having one's social self primed may automatically elicit one affective state, whereas having one's academic or intellectual self primed may elicit an altogether different affective state. Researchers are beginning to branch out and explore the full gamut of "nonconscious self-esteems" which, in my opinion, is a positive trend.

Having already used more than half of my allotted space to address the existence and conceptualization of nonconscious self-esteem, I now (speedily) address the issue of measurement. Here, I defer to experts in the measurement of implicit attitudes who note that three cognitive phenomena can be utilized to tap into people's automatic attitudes. First, people tend (without being aware) to assign value to objects that are closely associated with the self, such as their name initials and/or birthday numbers (Greenwald & Banaji, 1995; Koole et al., 2001; Koole & Pelham, 2003; Nuttin, 1985; Pelham, Mirenberg, & Jones, 2002). Thus, one way to tap into the automatic link between self and affective state would be to query people about their liking for self-associated stimuli. Second and third, people's evaluations of stimuli are activated automatically upon sight (e.g., Fazio et al., 1986), and activation of an affective state facilitates the subsequent processing of evaluatively similar information (e.g., Collins & Loftus, 1975). To measure the automatic link between self and affective state, then, researchers may (1) prime the concept of the self (either subliminally or supraliminally); and (2) assess the ease with which people can subsequently identify negative/unpleasant vs. positive/pleasant stimuli. Indeed, most nonconscious self-esteem measures of which I am aware are based on these cognitive phenomena, although there are some exceptions to this general rule (e.g., Aidman, 1999). With regard to how nonconscious self-esteem *should* be measured, however, I decline to comment here and instead refer interested readers to Bosson et al. (2000), Fazio and Olson (2003), and the other response pieces in this section.

What role(s) does nonconscious self-esteem play in psychological functioning? Recent findings suggest that the affect that is automatically linked to the self may play an important role in various self-regulatory processes. For example, to the extent that an individual has primarily positive affective reactions to the self, this positive affect may serve as a buffer against self-threats (e.g., Jones, Pelham, Mirenberg, & Hetts, 2002), perhaps even warding off self-threatening information before it enters the individual's consciousness (Hetts & Pelham, 2001). This may occur via the tendency for nonconscious self-esteem to influence how people encode, interpret, and/or recall ambiguous self-relevant feedback (e.g., Greenwald, 1980). Consider a scenario in which you telephone an acquaintance and, upon hearing your voice, she cryptically muses "I figured it was you" (Tafarodi, 1998). If self-primes elicit for you mostly positive affective states, then you are liable to interpret your acquaintance's ambiguous statement in a manner consistent with that affective state, i.e., as reflecting a favorable attitude toward you. Similarly, the nature of the affect automatically elicited by self-primes should influence people to recall ambiguous self-relevant information in a manner consistent with this affect (Story, 1998). In these ways, nonconscious aspects of self-esteem may function like "self-concept armor," imbuing ambiguous stimuli with positivity and thereby defusing their potential power to threaten consciously held, favorable self-views.

Of course, to the extent that an individual's automatic affective links to the self are primarily negative, the opposite should occur: The unpleasant affect elicited by self-primes should influence the individual to encode, interpret, and/or recall ambiguous self-relevant feedback in a negative manner. The point is that nonconscious aspects of self-esteem, whatever their valence, should influence the manner in which people make sense of their social worlds, guiding them to process ambiguous information in a manner that is consistent with these chronic, well-practiced evaluations of the self. Nonconscious self-esteem may thus be a mechanism through which people maintain feelings of self-consistency and coherence that are crucial for psychological health and well-being (Swann, 1990; Swann, Rentfrow, & Guinn, 2003).

Nonconscious aspects of self-esteem may also function to help people repair negative thoughts and feelings about the self following (or during) self-threats. To demonstrate, Jones et al. (2002) found that people high in self-esteem who were induced to consider an important personal shortcoming subsequently displayed more favorable automatic associations to the self. These and other findings (see Dodgson & Wood, 1998; Hetts, 1999) suggest that, in the face of a threatening experience, people with positive automatic associations to the self will (unintentionally) activate these associations as a way to self-enhance and thus preserve their favorable self-views. Consistent with this thinking, Pelham et al. (2002) argued that people engage in this form of nonconscious self-enhancement (or *implicit egotism*) during difficult—and thus potentially self-threatening—life decisions such as choice of career, spouse, and geographical residence. A tendency to heighten one's favorable assessment of self-associated stimuli during threat may thus explain the finding that people choose occupations, romantic partners, and hometowns that begin with their own name letters at a rate statistically higher than chance would predict (e.g., people named Edward are disproportionately likely to become engineers, mate with Ellens, and live in Everton, England). Of course, people with negative automatic associations to the self lack access to this protective resource—Jones et al.'s findings showed that, for people low in self-esteem, consideration of a shortcoming *decreased* the positivity of their subsequent automatic self-associations. Thus, an Edward with primarily negative automatic reactions to the self would, presumably, choose a career in engineering at a rate no different from, or perhaps even lower than, random chance.

In sum, evidence suggests that nonconscious aspects of self-esteem guide people's interpretations and memories of their worlds, shape their reactions to self-relevant stimuli, and help them regulate their cognitive and affective responses to real and potential self-threats (Greenwald & Banaji, 1995; Jones et al., 2002). Of course, people's consciously held evaluations of the self also contribute a great deal to psychological functioning, and recent findings suggest that conscious and nonconscious aspects of self-esteem may work together to predict various self-regulatory outcomes such as narcissistic responding, in-group favoritism, and unrealistic optimism (Bosson, Brown, Zeigler-Hill, & Swann, 2003; Jordan, Spencer, Zanna, Hoshino-Browne, & Correll, 2003). Thus, the manner in which nonconscious aspects of self-esteem impact people's psychological functioning may depend, in part, on how closely matched their conscious and nonconscious self-evaluations are. Clearly, there is much to be learned with regard to the links between nonconscious self-esteem and psychological functioning; the current findings are encouraging because they point to broad trends, but they also hint at a host of complexities, nuances, and moderating factors that have yet to be fully discerned. I am hopeful that research conducted over the next few years will lead to dramatic increases in our understanding of nonconscious aspects of self-esteem.

REFERENCES

Aidman, E. V. (1999). Measuring individual differences in implicit self-concept: Initial validation of the self-apperception test. *Personality and Individual Differences, 27,* 211–228.

Bargh, J. A. (1994). The four horsemen of automaticity: Awareness, intention, efficiency, and control in social cognition. In R. S. Wyer & T. K. Srull (Eds.), *Handbook of social cognition, Vol. 1: Basic processes; Vol. 2: Applications* (2nd ed., pp. 1–40). Hillsdale, NJ: Lawrence Erlbaum Associates.

Bosson, J. K., Brown, R. P., Zeigler-Hill, V., & Swann, W. B. Jr. (2003). Self-enhancement tendencies among people with high explicit self-esteem: The moderating role of implicit self-esteem. *Self and Identity, 2,* 169–187.

Bosson, J. K., Swann, W. B. Jr., & Pennebaker, J. W. (2000). Stalking the perfect measure of self-esteem: The blind men and the elephant revisited? *Journal of Personality and SocialPsychology, 79,* 631–643.

Brown, J. D. (1993). *Self-esteem and self-evaluation: Feeling is believing.* In J. M. Suls (Ed.), *Psychological perspectives on the self* (Vol. 4, pp. 27–58). Hillsdale, NJ: Lawrence Erlbaum Associates.

Collins, A. M., & Loftus, E. F. (1975). A spreading-activation theory of semantic processing. *Psychological Review, 82,* 407–428.

DeHart, T., Pelham, B. W., & Tennen, H. (2006). What lies beneath: Parenting style and implicit self-esteem. *Journal of Experimental Social Psychology, 42,* 1–17.

Dodgson, P. G., & Wood, J. V. (1998). Self-esteem and the cognitive accessibility of strengths and weaknesses after failure. *Journal of Personality & Social Psychology, 75,* 178–197.

Epstein, S. (1994). Integration of the cognitive and the psychodynamic unconscious. *American Psychologist, 49,* 709–724.

Fazio, R. H., & Olson, M. A. (2003). Implicit measures in social cognition research: Their meaning and use. *Annual Review of Psychology, 54,* 297–327.

Fazio, R. H., Sanbonmatsu, D. M., Powell, M. C., & Kardes, F. R. (1986). On the automatic activation of attitudes. *Journal of Personality & Social Psychology, 50,* 229–238.

Greenwald, A. G. (1980). The totalitarian ego: Fabrication and revision of personal history. *American Psychologist, 35,* 603–618.

Greenwald, A. G., & Banaji, M. R. (1995). Implicit social cognition: Attitudes, self-esteem, and stereotypes. *Psychological Review, 102,* 4–27.

Gregg, A. P. (2003). Optimally conceptualizing implicit self-esteem. *Psychological Inquiry, 14,* 35–38.

Hetts, J. J. (1999). *Self-evaluations under fire: Implicit self-regard and explicit self-esteem in the face of failure.* Unpublished doctoral dissertation, University of California, Los Angeles.

Hetts, J. J., & Pelham, W. B. (2001). A case for the nonconscious self-concept. In G. B. Moskowitz (Ed.), *Cognitive social psychology: The Princeton symposium on the legacy and future of social cognition* (pp. 105–123). Mahwah, NJ: Lawrence Erlbaum Associates.

Jones, J. T., Pelham, B. W., Mirenberg, M. C., & Hetts, J. J. (2002). Name letter preferences are not merely mere exposure: Implicit egotism as self-regulation. *Journal of Experimental Social Psychology, 38,* 170–177.

Jordan, C. H., Spencer, S. J., Zanna, M. P., Hoshino-Browne, E., & Correll, J. (2003). Secure and defensive high self-esteem. *Journal of Personality and Social Psychology, 85,* 969–978.

Kernis, M. H. (2003). Toward a conceptualization of optimal self-esteem. *Psychological Inquiry, 14,* 1–26.

Koole, S. L., Dijksterhuis, A., & van Knippenberg, A. (2001). What's in a name: Implicit self-esteem and the automatic self. *Journal of Personality and Social Psychology, 80,* 669–685.

Koole, S. L., & Pelham, B. W. (2003). On the nature of implicit self-esteem: The case of the name letter effect. In S. J. Spencer & S. Fein (Eds.), *Motivated social perception: The Ontario Symposium* (Vol. 9, pp. 93–116). Mahwah, NJ: Lawrence Erlbaum Associates.

Leary, M. R., Tambor, E. S., Terdal, S. K., & Downs, D. L. (1995). Self-esteem as an interpersonal monitor: The sociometer hypothesis. *Journal of Personality & Social Psychology, 68*, 518–530.

Morehead, P. D., & Morehead, A. T. (Eds.). (1981). *The new American Webster handy college dictionary.* New York: New American Library.

Murphy, S. T., & Zajonc, R. B. (1993). Affect, cognition, and awareness: Affective priming with optimal and suboptimal stimulus exposures. *Journal of Personality & Social Psychology, 64*, 723–739.

Nisbett, R. E., & Wilson, T. D. (1977). Telling more than we can know: Verbal reports on mental processes. *Psychological Review, 84*, 231–259.

Nuttin, M. J. Jr. (1985). Narcissism beyond Gestalt and awareness: The name letter effect. *European Journal of Social Psychology, 15*, 353–361.

Pelham, B. W., Mirenberg, M. C., & Jones, J. T. (2002). Why Susie sells seashells by the seashore: Implicit egotism and major life decisions. *Journal of Personality and Social Psychology, 82*, 469–487.

Rosenberg, M. (1965). *Society and the adolescent self-image.* Princeton, NJ: Princeton University Press.

Story, A. L. (1998). Self-esteem and memory for favorable and unfavorable personality feedback. *Personality & Social Psychology Bulletin, 24*, 51–64.

Swann, W. B. Jr. (1990). To be adored or to be known: The interplay of self-enhancement and self-verification. In R. M. Sorrentino & E. T. Higgins (Eds.), *Handbook of motivation and cognition* (Vol. 2, pp. 408–480). New York: Guilford Press.

Swann, W. B. Jr., Rentfrow, P. J., & Guinn, J. S. (2003). Self-verification: The search for coherence. In M. R. Leary & J. P. Tangney (Eds.), *Handbook of self and identity* (pp. 367–383). New York: Guilford Press.

Tafarodi, R. W. (1998). Paradoxical self-esteem and selectivity in the processing of social information. *Journal of Personality & Social Psychology, 74*, 1181–1196.

Teglasi, H., & Epstein, S. (1998). Temperament and personality theory: The perspective of cognitive-experiential self-theory. *School Psychology Review, 27*, 534–550.

Young, S. (Writer), & Anderson, B. (Director). (1997). Hurricane Neddy [Television series episode]. In B. Oakley & J. Weinstein (Executive Producers), *The Simpsons.* Beverly Hills, CA: Fox Broadcasting Company. Retrieved June 1, 2004, from http://www.snpp.com/episodes/4F07.html.

8

Nonconscious Self-Esteem: Is There Something You're Not Telling Yourself?

CHRISTIAN H. JORDAN, CHRISTINE LOGEL, STEVEN J. SPENCER, and MARK P. ZANNA

*M*ost people seem to have a good sense of their own self-esteem (SE). If you were to ask your hair stylist, bus driver, neighbor, or family doctor how they feel about themselves, each could probably give you a fairly quick and straightforward response. If you then, however, asked them whether they believe they have self-feelings of which they are not aware, you would probably be greeted by a polite smile and sheer bewilderment. We suspect that most people feel so well-attuned to their own inner experiences that they would strongly doubt that they possess any nonconscious self-feelings. Psychologists, on the other hand, are more divided on this point. In this chapter, we review evidence that people possess highly efficient self-evaluations of which they may be largely unaware, and which may affect their psychological functioning in significant ways. We note, however, that controversies persist around these issues and we strive to specify areas where clear evidence is lacking.

Although the existence of nonconscious self-feelings remains controversial, the fact that many (perhaps most) mental processes occur outside awareness is now almost universally accepted by psychologists. The psychodynamic view of the unconscious as that part of the mind where one's most primitive and irrational impulses reside has slowly given way to a "kinder, gentler" view of the cognitive unconscious (Kihlstrom, 1987, 1990). Rather than being maladaptive, nonconscious processes are now viewed as highly adaptive, freeing up scarce cognitive resources for other tasks (e.g., Bargh & Chartrand, 1999; Epstein, 1994). People certainly do not deliberate over every minor decision and action they make in their daily lives. Although some actions and reactions are clearly consciously controlled, others are triggered automatically by environmental stimuli (Bargh, 1994; Bargh & Chartrand, 1999; Wegner & Bargh, 1998). Learning and memory can apparently occur without awareness (see Holyoak & Spellman, 1993; Jacoby & Kelly, 1992;

Schacter, 1995). Patients with neurological deficits, moreover, provide dramatic evidence of nonconscious processes—retrograde amnesiacs are clearly capable of learning without awareness (see Schacter, 1992) and cortically blind patients can sometimes respond to visual stimuli (a phenomenon known as *blindsight*; e.g., Weiskrantz, 1986). In many contexts, it seems that affective processes can also occur without any awareness or conscious guidance (see Westen, 1998).

More generally, many theorists have posited the existence of two largely independent cognitive systems; one that is relatively slow, deliberative, effortful, and rule-based, and another that is relatively fast, unintentional, efficient, and associative (see Epstein, 1992; Smith & DeCoster, 2001; Wilson, Lindsey, & Schooler, 2000). The former system is believed to operate primarily through conscious, *controlled* processes whereas the latter is believed to operate primarily through nonconscious, *automatic* processes. Consistent with this possibility, many environmental objects trigger automatic affective reactions as well as eliciting the more controlled, deliberative evaluations normally associated with attitudes (Bargh, Chaiken, Raymond, & Hymes, 1996; Fazio, Sanbonmatsu, Powell, & Kardes, 1986). Intriguingly, the self may be one such object. That is, in addition to the deliberative self-evaluations normally associated with SE, people may possess highly efficient self-evaluations that occur unintentionally and perhaps outside awareness (e.g., Farnham, Greenwald, & Banaji, 1999; Greenwald & Banaji, 1995; Hetts & Pelham, 2002). These latter, more automatic self-evaluations have become known as *implicit* SE; the former as *explicit* SE.

Numerous measures of implicit SE have been devised (see Bosson, Swann, & Pennebaker, 2000), all of which share properties that are consistent with the view that they measure automatic self-feelings. Although explicit SE is measured by fairly transparent self-report scales, implicit SE is measured indirectly, often by reaction time tasks that require responses that are difficult to control. Thus, implicit SE appears to be quite efficient and unintentional, two hallmarks of automatic processes (Bargh, 1994). One common measure of implicit SE, the Implicit Association Test (IAT) (Greenwald & Farnham, 2000), focuses specifically on efficient cognitive associations that a person might have between the self-concept and positive and negative stimuli. That is, activation of the self-concept may lead quite directly to activation of positive or negative feelings. This focus on efficient cognitive associations suggests that the IAT may reflect the operation of automatic, associative processes (Smith & DeCoster, 2001). Given these characteristics of measures of implicit SE, it may be tempting to assume that implicit SE is also nonconscious, another common (though not universal) characteristic of automatic processes (Bargh, 1994). Yet, there is no inherent property of measures of implicit SE that guarantees that respondents are unaware of their evaluations (see Fazio & Olson, 2003; Jordan, Spencer, & Zanna, 2003a). The status of implicit SE as conscious or nonconscious is thus unclear. There is, however, ample evidence of the value in distinguishing between implicit and explicit SE.

Measures of implicit and explicit SE do not correlate with each other. Thus, individuals who report having high SE do not necessarily have high implicit SE (nor vice versa) (e.g., Bosson et al., 2000; Jordan et al., 2003a). In fact, many people show sizable discrepancies between their levels of explicit and implicit SE, suggesting that their implicit self-views are distinct from their explicit self-views. In addition, implicit SE can enhance prediction of self-relevant behavior beyond what is predicted by explicit measures. Measures of implicit SE have thus predicted persistence in the face of failure, experiences of positive and negative affect, and reactions to success and failure feedback independently of explicit SE (Bosson et al., 2000; Greenwald & Farnham, 2000; Jordan et al., 2003a). Implicit SE can also predict different behaviors than does explicit SE. Spalding and Hardin (1999) found that a measure of implicit SE predicted apparent nonverbal anxiety about an impending personal interview whereas explicit SE did not. In contrast, explicit SE predicted verbal reports of anxiety whereas implicit SE did not.

A full account of how self-views affect psychological functioning, moreover, may require consideration of both explicit and implicit SE together. Given the lack of correlation between the two, the degree of correspondence (or lack thereof) between explicit and implicit SE may define unique psychological states within individuals. Among people with high explicit SE, for instance, those with relatively low implicit SE may be characteristically defensive (e.g., Epstein & Morling, 1995; Jordan et al., 2003a; Jordan, Spencer, Zanna, Hoshino Browne, & Correll, 2003b; Kernis & Paradise, 2002). Consistent with this possibility, we found that individuals with high explicit but low implicit SE (measured with a modified IAT) were more narcissistic than individuals with any other combination of explicit and implicit SE (Jordan et al., 2003b, Study 1). The same pattern was also observed independently with a different measure of implicit SE (name-letter preferences; cited in Brown & Bosson, 2001). Notably, these findings support conceptualizations of narcissists as individuals who are defensive because their grandiose self-views mask deep-seated self-doubts and insecurities (Kohut, 1971; Morf & Rhodewalt, 2001).

We further explored whether implicit SE predicts defensive reactions among individuals with high explicit SE. We found that, for individuals with high explicit SE, those with relatively low implicit SE rationalized their decisions more, in such a way that they might appear to be more competent decision makers (Jordan et al., 2003b, Study 3). High explicit SE individuals with relatively low implicit SE also self-enhanced by allocating more rewards to an ingroup member than an outgroup member in a minimal group situation (Study 2). Extending this finding to existing (rather than minimal) social groups, we found that high explicit SE individuals were more likely to discriminate against an ethnic outgroup member, in the face of ego-threat, if they had relatively low implicit SE (Jordan, Spencer, & Zanna, 2005). Specifically, individuals with high explicit but low implicit SE who had their self-views threatened by failure feedback recommended a more severe punishment for a Native student who started a fistfight than for a White student who committed the same offense. Among individuals with high explicit SE, then, those with relatively low implicit SE appear to be more defensive, whereas those with relatively high implicit SE appear to be more secure.

Convergent evidence supports this conclusion. Individuals with high explicit but low implicit SE also self-enhance more by demonstrating more unrealistic optimism, more strongly preferring positive to negative personality descriptions, and reporting smaller self-ideal discrepancies than individuals with high explicit and implicit SE (Bosson, Brown, Zeigler-Hill, & Swann, 2003). In one study, individuals with high explicit but low implicit SE reacted to uncertainty about a personal relationship by defensively exaggerating their conviction about unrelated social issues (i.e., abortion and capital punishment) (McGregor & Marigold, 2003). These findings are particularly noteworthy because they reflect consistent patterns of results across two different measures of implicit SE (the IAT and name-letter preferences). A conceptually perplexing aspect of measures of implicit SE is that they do not correlate with each other, as they should if they measure the same construct (e.g., Bosson et al., 2000; Jordan et al., 2003a). Nevertheless, different measures often behave similarly and predict similar criteria, as is the case here. These different measures might thus reflect different aspects of the same underlying construct despite their lack of correlation with each other. Clearly, further research is needed to understand this issue better.

Discrepancies between high explicit and low implicit SE may thus be related to defensiveness. Notably, however, the opposite discrepancies—between low explicit and high implicit SE—do not show the same pattern. But might these discrepancies predict other aspects of psychological functioning? Some individuals who report having low SE do demonstrate relatively high levels of implicit SE. Could high implicit SE act as a buffer against psychological stress for such individuals? Consider, for example, that low SE is closely associated with depression (e.g., Battle, 1978; Tennen & Affleck, 1993). Deeply dysphoric individuals appear to automatically associate negative attributes with themselves (Bargh & Tota, 1988), suggesting that they may have low implicit SE as well as low explicit SE. In the light of this association, perhaps the obverse relation holds true too: among individuals with low explicit SE, perhaps high implicit SE buffers against depression. Some preliminary evidence supports this possibility.

We had students complete a standard measure of depression (the Beck Depression Inventory) three times over the course of an academic term (Logel, Jordan, Spencer, & Zanna, 2005). We also measured explicit and implicit SE (with the Rosenberg Self-Esteem Scale and modified IAT, respectively). At the beginning of the term, students who were low in both explicit and implicit SE were most depressed overall, significantly more so than individuals who were low in explicit but high in implicit SE. This pattern held for later depression as well. Perhaps most remarkably, whereas students with low explicit and low implicit SE reported becoming more depressed as the term progressed, those with low explicit but high implicit SE showed measurable improvement (see Figure 8.1). High implicit SE may thus help protect some low explicit SE individuals from falling into a depressive cycle. Other evidence similarly suggests that there are benefits associated with having high implicit SE for low explicit SE individuals. Among such individuals, those with relatively high implicit SE are more optimistic about their futures (Bosson et al., 2003) and less prone to self-handicapping (Spalding & Hardin 1999; for a more detailed discussion, see Spencer, Jordan, Logel, & Zanna, in press).

Distinguishing between explicit and implicit SE thus seems to be crucial for understanding how self-views affect behavior. As noted, however, it is unclear whether implicit SE is conscious or unconscious. We would actually suggest a third possibility: that implicit SE is preconscious. Although people may be generally unaware of their implicit self-views, their implicit SE may enter awareness in some

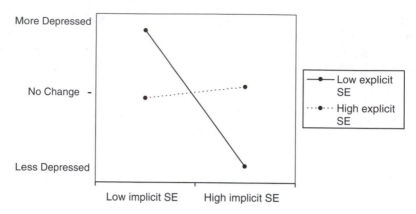

FIGURE 8.1   Change in depression as a function of explicit and implicit self-esteem.

situations, perhaps in the form of vague feelings associated with the self. For individuals who have congruent explicit and implicit SE, such experiences would not likely be consequential, because they would simply confirm their explicit self-views. For individuals with high explicit but low implicit SE, however, such experiences could be quite aversive. Negative implicit self-views, in this case, may be experienced as inexplicable insecurities, or nagging doubts about the self, which question their explicitly positive self-views. Such experiences might motivate defensive tendencies, as these individuals strive to confirm their explicitly positive self-feelings and deny their implicitly negative self-feelings. On the other hand, among individuals with low explicit SE, experiences of high implicit SE might be experienced as glimmers of hope that buffer against stress and enhance their optimism (Spencer et al., in press).

Some evidence does suggest that ego-threatening situations may cause high explicit SE individuals with low implicit SE to have self-doubts. Participants in one study rated how well various personality traits described themselves and also how much they believed the same traits contribute to leadership ability (Jordan & McKillop, 2005). We took the correlation between these ratings as an index of how much participants believed their own traits contribute to leadership ability (after Dunning, Perie, & Story, 1991). As can be seen in Figure 8.2, we found overall that the correlations were higher for high explicit SE individuals (replicating Beauregard & Dunning, 1998). They were, however, unrelated to implicit SE, except among high explicit SE individuals who had recalled a major personal failure. Participants with high explicit but low implicit SE, in this case, showed less consistency between their self-ratings and ratings of leadership ability. In contrast, those with high explicit and high implicit SE showed greater consistency. The self-ratings of high explicit SE individuals thus suggested that their self-assurance (or confidence that they had the traits needed to be a good leader, at least) was undermined if they had low implicit SE. These findings may suggest that high explicit SE individuals with low implicit SE had self-doubts, perhaps reflecting awareness of their low implicit SE.

Other evidence speaks more directly to whether people are aware of their implicit SE. Although implicit and explicit SE are typically uncorrelated, Koole,

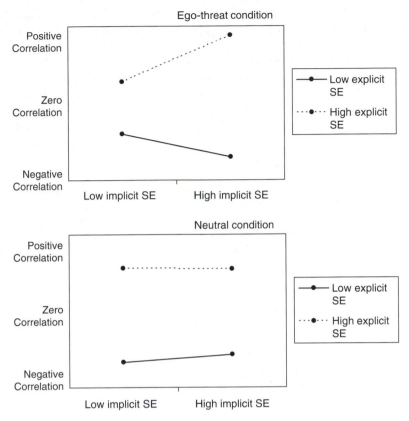

FIGURE 8.2 Correlations between self- and leader-ratings as a function of explicit and implicit self-esteem in both ego threat and neutral conditions.

Dijksterhuis, and van Knippenberg (2001) found that people who were taxed by cognitive busyness or time pressure constraints reported explicit self-views that were more consistent with their implicit SE, suggesting they had some awareness of their implicit self-views. In contrast, other evidence suggests that some aspects of implicit SE exist outside awareness. Baccus, Baldwin and Packer (2004) found that repeatedly pairing self-related words with pictures of smiling faces enhanced implicit SE but had no effect on explicit SE. This finding helps to substantiate the view that implicit SE involves the operation of automatic, associative processes (as it can be associatively conditioned), whereas explicit SE involves the operation of more controlled, rational processes (see Epstein, 1992; Smith & DeCoster, 2001). Somewhat more pertinently, using a subliminal evaluative conditioning procedure, Dijksterhuis (2004) similarly found that repeatedly pairing self-related pronouns with positive words enhanced implicit SE, as assessed by two different measures of implicit SE. Because this procedure was subliminal, participants could not have been aware of this source of their implicit self-views. There is thus evidence that people may sometimes be aware of their implicit SE, but also evidence that at least some aspects of its operation occur outside awareness. We believe that these findings are most consistent with the possibility that implicit SE is preconscious, although this point is certainly debatable.

In some ways, the controversy about the existence of nonconscious SE echoes a somewhat older controversy over the existence of perception without awareness. Two ways of assessing nonconscious experiences are used in that literature—subjective, self-report measures and a variety of more objective measures (e.g., forced-choice discriminations) (Merikle, 1992). It is unclear, however, whether any objective measure can truly separate conscious from nonconscious processes. Thus, whether one accepts the existence of some nonconscious processes—such as unconscious or preconscious SE—may ultimately depend on whether one is willing to trust people's reports of conscious experience. Certainly, researchers should continue to strive to settle the case for nonconscious SE more definitively. As Merikle (1992) noted, however, the real value in conceptualizing distinct conscious and nonconscious processes may lie in whether such "conscious and unconscious processes lead to qualitatively different consequences" (p. 794). In this regard, we would argue, implicit SE clearly fits the bill.

REFERENCES

Baccus, J. R., Baldwin, M. W., & Packer, D. J. (2004). Increasing implicit self-esteem through classical conditioning. *Psychological Science, 15,* 498–502.

Bargh, J. A. (1994). The four horsemen of automaticity: Awareness, efficiency, intention, and control in social cognition. In R. S. Wyer, Jr. & T. K. Srull (Eds.), *Handbook of social cognition* (2nd ed., pp. 1–40). Hillsdale, NJ: Lawrence Erlbaum Associates, Inc.

Bargh, J. A., Chaiken, S., Raymond, P., & Hymes, C. (1996). The automatic evaluation effect: Unconditional automatic attitude activation with a pronunciation task. *Journal of Experimental Social Psychology, 32,* 104–128.

Bargh, J. A., & Chartrand, T. L. (1999). The unbearable automaticity of being. *American Psychologist, 54,* 462–479.

Bargh, J. A., & Tota, M. E. (1988). Context-dependent automatic processing in depression: Accessibility of negative constructs with regard to self but not others. *Journal of Personality and Social Psychology, 54,* 925–939.

Battle, J. (1978). Relationship between self-esteem and depression. *Psychological Reports, 42,* 745–746.

Beauregard, K. S., & Dunning, D. (1998). Turning up the contrast: Self-enhancement motives prompt egocentric contrast effects in social judgments. *Journal of Personality and Social Psychology, 74,* 606–621.

Bosson, J. K., Brown, R. P., Zeigler-Hill, V., & Swann, W. B. (2003). Self-enhancement tendencies among people with high explicit self-esteem: The moderating role of implicit self-esteem. *Self & Identity, 2,* 169–187.

Bosson, J. K., Swann, W. B. Jr., & Pennebaker, J. (2000). Stalking the perfect measure of implicit self-esteem: The blind men and the elephant revisited? *Journal of Personality & Social Psychology, 79,* 631–643.

Brown, R. P., & Bosson, J. K. (2001). Narcissus meets Sisyphus: Self-love, self-loathing, and the never-ending pursuit of self-worth. *Psychological Inquiry, 12,* 210–213.

Dijksterhuis, A. (2004). I like myself but I don't know why: Enhancing implicit self-esteem by subliminal evaluative conditioning. *Journal of Personality and Social Psychology, 86,* 345–355.

Dunning, D., Perie, M., & Story, A. L. (1991). Self-serving stereotypes of social categories. *Journal of Personality and Social Psychology, 61,* 957–968.

Epstein, S. (1992). The cognitive self, the psychoanalytic self, and the forgotten selves. *Psychological Inquiry, 3,* 34–37.

Epstein, S. (1994). Integration of the cognitive and the psychodynamic unconscious. *American Psychologist, 49,* 709–724.

Epstein, S., & Morling, B. (1995). Is the self motivated to do more than enhance and/or verify itself? In M. Kernis (Ed.), *Efficacy, agency, and self-esteem* (pp. 9–29). New York: Plenum Press.

Farnham, S. D., Greenwald, A. G., & Banaji, M. R. (1999). Implicit self-esteem. In D. Abrams & M. A. Hogg (Eds.), *Social identity and social cognition* (pp. 230–248). Oxford: Blackwell Publishers Ltd.

Fazio, R. H., & Olson, M. A. (2003). Implicit measures in social cognition: Their meaning and use. *Annual Review of Psychology, 54,* 297–327.

Fazio, R. H., Sanbonmatsu, D. M., Powell, M. C., & Kardes, F. R. (1986). On the automatic activation of attitudes. *Journal of Personality and Social Psychology, 50,* 229–238.

Greenwald, A. G., & Banaji, M. R. (1995). Implicit social cognition: Attitudes, self-esteem, and stereotypes. *Psychological Review, 102,* 4–27.

Greenwald, A. G., & Farnham, S. D. (2000). Using the Implicit Association Test to measure self-esteem and self-concept. *Journal of Personality and Social Psychology, 79,* 1022–1038.

Hetts, J. J., & Pelham, B. W. (2002). Non-conscious aspects of the self-concept. In G. Moscowitz (Ed.), *Cognitive social psychology: The Princeton symposium.* Mahwah, NJ: Lawrence Erlbaum Associates, Inc.

Holyoak, K., & Spellman, B. (1993). Thinking. *Annual Review of Psychology, 44,* 265–315.

Jacoby, L., & Kelly, C. M. (1992). A process-dissociation framework for investigating unconscious influences: Freudian slips, projective tests, subliminal perception, and signal detection theory. *Current Directions in Psychological Science, 1,* 174–179.

Jordan, C. H., & McKillop, A. J. (2005). *Types of self-esteem and self-assurance: Explicit and implicit self-esteem moderate reactions to threat.* Paper presented at the annual meeting of the Society of Personality and Social Psychology, New Orleans.

Jordan, C. H., Spencer, S. J., & Zanna, M. P. (2003a). "I love me... I love me not": Implicit self-esteem, explicit self-esteem, and defensiveness. In S. J. Spencer, S. Fein, M. P. Zanna, & J. M. Olson (Eds.), *Motivated social cognition: The Ontario symposium* (Vol. 9, pp. 117–145). Mahwah, NJ: Lawrence Erlbaum Associates, Inc.

Jordan, C. H., Spencer, S. J., & Zanna, M. P. (2005). Types of high self-esteem and prejudice: How implicit self-esteem relates to ethnic discrimination among high explicit self-esteem individuals. *Personality and Social Psychology Bulletin, 31,* 693–702.

Jordan, C. H., Spencer, S. J., Zanna, M. P., Hoshino Browne, E., & Correll, J. (2003b). Secure and defensive high self-esteem. *Journal of Personality and Social Psychology, 85,* 969–978.

Kernis, M. H., & Paradise, A. W. (2002). Distinguishing between secure and fragile forms of high self-esteem. In E. L. Deci & R. M. Ryan (Eds.), *Handbook of self-determination research* (pp. 339–360). Rochester, NY: University of Rochester Press.

Kihlstrom, J. (1987). The cognitive unconscious. *Science, 237,* 1445–1452.

Kihlstrom, J. (1990). The psychological unconscious. In L. A. Pervin (Ed.), *Handbook of personality: Theory and research* (pp. 445–464). New York: Guilford Press.

Kohut, H. (1971). *The analysis of the self*. New York: International University Press.

Koole, S. L., Dijksterhuis, A., & van Knippenberg, A. (2001). What's in a name: Implicit self-esteem and the automatic self. *Journal of Personality and Social Psychology, 80*, 669–685.

Logel, C., Jordan, C. H., Spencer, S. J., & Zanna, M. P. (January 2005). *Implicit self-esteem and depression: A longitudinal study*. Paper presented at the annual meeting of the Society of Personality and Social Psychology, New Orleans.

McGregor, I., & Marigold, D. C. (2003). Defensive zeal and the uncertain self: What makes you so sure? *Journal of Personality and Social Psychology, 85*, 838–852.

Merikle, P. M. (1992). Perception without awareness: Critical issues. *American Psychologist, 47*, 792–795.

Morf, C. C., & Rhodewalt, F. (2001). Unraveling the paradoxes of narcissism: A dynamic self-regulatory processing model. *Psychological Inquiry, 12*, 177–196.

Schacter, D. L. (1992). Understanding implicit memory: A cognitive neuroscience approach. *American Psychologist, 47*, 559–569.

Schacter, D. L. (1995). Implicit memory: A new frontier for cognitive neuroscience. In M. Gazzaniga (Ed.), *The cognitive neurosciences* (pp. 815–824). Cambridge, MA: MIT Press.

Smith, E. R., & DeCoster, J. (2001). Dual-process models in social and cognitive psychology: Conceptual integration and links to underlying memory systems. *Personality and Social Psychology Review, 4*, 108–131.

Spalding, L. R., & Harding, C. D. (1999). Unconscious unease and self-handicapping: Behavioral consequences of individual differences in implicit and explicit self-esteem. *Psychological Science, 10*, 535–539.

Spencer, S. J., Jordan, C. H., Logel, C. & Zanna, M. P. (in press). Nagging doubts and a glimmer of hope: The role of implicit self-esteem in self-image maintenance. In A. Tesser, J. V. Wood, & D. A. Stapel (Eds.), *New perspectives on the self*. Philadelphia: Psychology Press.

Tennen, H., & Affleck, G. (1993). The puzzles of self-esteem: A clinical perspective. In R. F. Baumeister (Ed.), *Self-esteem: The puzzle of low self-regard* (pp. 241–262). New York: Plenum.

Wegner, D. M., & Bargh, J. A. (1998). Control and automaticity in social life. In D. Gilbert, S. Fiske, & G. Lindzey (Eds.), *Handbook of social psychology* (4th ed., pp. 446–496). Boston: McGraw-Hill.

Weiskrantz, L. (1986). *Blindsight: A case study and implications*. Oxford, England: Clarendon Press.

Westen, D. (1998). The scientific legacy of Sigmund Freud: Toward a psychodynamically informed psychological science. *Psychological Bulletin, 124*, 333–371.

Wilson, T. D., Lindsey, S., & Schooler, T. Y. (2000). A model of dual attitudes. *Psychological Review, 107*, 101–126.

Zajonc, R. B. (1980). Feeling and thinking: Preferences need no inferences. *American Psychologist, 35*, 151–175.

9

Conscious and Unconscious Self-Esteem from the Perspective of Cognitive-Experiential Self-Theory

SEYMOUR EPSTEIN

*T*his chapter begins with a brief review of selected aspects of cognitive-experiential self-theory (CEST) in order to provide the background for understanding self-esteem from the perspective of CEST. It is followed by a discussion of the operation of conscious and unconscious aspects of self-esteem. The chapter closes with a brief discussion of measurement issues.

COGNITIVE-EXPERIENTIAL SELF-THEORY

According to CEST, people process information in two systems, experiential and rational. The experiential system is an automatic learning system that is the same system with which non-human animals have adapted to their environments over millions of years of evolution. It operates in a manner that is preconscious, automatic, nonverbal, associative, rapid, effortless, concrete, holistic, and intimately associated with affect. It acquires its schemas, or implicit beliefs, from lived experience, hence its name. The rational system, in contrast, is a uniquely human system that solves problems by reasoning. It operates in a manner that is conscious, slow, primarily verbal, effortful, abstract, analytic, and affect free. It acquires its beliefs by logical inference. To be sure, it also learns from experience, but it does so by reasoning rather than by associative learning.

The two systems operate in parallel and are interactive. Behavior is determined by their combined influence, with their relative contribution varying according to situational requirements and individual preferences. In some situations, such as solving mathematics problems, behavior is primarily determined by the rational system, whereas in others, such as those involving interpersonal relationships, behavior is primarily determined by the experiential system. Despite such variation in situations and individuals, everyday behavior for every individual is primarily determined by the experiential system, i.e., primacy of the experiential system is the default condition.

According to CEST, individuals automatically construct an implicit theory of reality in their experiential system. An implicit theory of reality consists of a self-theory, a world-theory, and connections between the two. The schemas in an implicit theory of reality are hierarchically organized cognitive–affective networks. Influence in the hierarchy proceeds in both directions, bottom-up and top-down. Higher-order schemas provide the system with stability and generality and lower-order ones with flexibility and specificity. When a higher-order schema is invalidated it threatens the entire organization of the conceptual system.

There are four basic needs in the experiential system: obtain pleasure and avoid pain (the pleasure principle of Freud (1900/1965) and the reinforcement principle of learning theorists), maintain the stability and coherence of the conceptual system (e.g., Lecky, 1945/1969), establish and maintain relationships (e.g., Bowlby, 1973), and enhance self-esteem (e.g., Allport, 1927/1961). According to CEST, all the basic needs are equally important as each can dominate the others and the frustration of any one of these can have equally serious consequences. Behavior is determined by the combined influence of all of the needs that are activated at a particular moment in time. Associated with the four basic needs are four basic beliefs acquired in the course of fulfilling the four basic needs. Related to the basic need to maximize pleasure and minimize pain is the basic belief about the degree to which the world is a source of pleasure and security vs. pain and insecurity. Related to the basic need to maintain a coherent, stable conceptual system for accurately representing experience is the basic belief about the degree to which life is meaningful (including predictable, controllable, and just) vs. meaningless (including unpredictable, uncontrollable, and unjust). Related to the basic need for relatedness is the basic belief about the degree to which people are trustworthy, supportive, and a source of comfort vs. untrustworthy, threatening, and a source of distress. Related to the basic need for self-enhancement is the basic belief about the degree to which one is a worthy (including competent, good, and lovable) person vs. an unworthy person (including incompetent, bad, and unlovable).

The basic needs and beliefs are important not only because of their direct influence on feelings, conscious thoughts, and behavior, but also because of their interactions, including whether the different needs are fulfilled in a conflicted or a harmonious manner. Most often they are fulfilled in a way that produces compromises (Epstein & Morling, 1995; Morling & Epstein, 1997). Of particular importance is that they tend to operate in a manner that provides checks and balances against each other. When one need is fulfilled at the expense of the others, the other needs become more insistent, which moderates the fulfillment of the first need. A failure in such moderation can account for various forms of psychopathology (Epstein, 1998).

IMPLICATIONS OF CEST FOR THE CONCEPTUALIZATION OF SELF-ESTEEM

If there are two processing systems, experiential and rational, each operating by its own rules and each including its own schemas or beliefs, there must be two kinds of self-esteem, one based on self-assessments in the experiential system (automatically derived from lived experience) and the other on self-assessments in the rational system (derived from conscious inference). Self-esteem in the experiential system is manifested by a person's feelings and behavior and therefore can be assessed by examining these. Self-esteem in the rational system is indicated by what a person consciously believes and can be assessed by what a person reports.

There are two facets of self-esteem within each system, self-esteem as a belief and self-esteem as a need or motive. Self-esteem as a belief in the rational system corresponds to a person's conscious evaluation of the self. In addition to a global evaluation of the self, it comprises different attributes of the self, including the self as intelligent, competent, love-worthy, attractive, moral, and so on. Because the evaluations are conscious, they can readily be assessed by self-report instruments. An example of such an instrument is the Multidimensional Self-Esteem Inventory (O'Brien & Epstein, 1983), which provides a measure of Global Self-Esteem and the following components: Competence, Lovability, Likeability, Self-control, Personal Power, Moral Self-approval, Body Appearance, Body Functioning, Identity Integration, and Defensive Self-enhancement.

Self-esteem as a need in the rational system corresponds to a person's thoughts about why it is desirable to behave in a certain way. As a thought-driven rather than an affect-driven motive it lacks the automaticity and emotional intensity that is characteristic of motives in the experiential system. It is important to recognize that a person can be aware of and therefore report the existence of a need in the experiential system. Although awareness would change a need from implicit to explicit, it would not change a need in the experiential system to one in the rational system. It would simply mean that the person is aware in his rational system of a need in his experiential system. The central issue, according to CEST, is not whether a belief or need is explicit or implicit but whether it operates in the domain of the experiential or rational system. This is not to deny that awareness can make a difference in the influence and control of an experiential need.

Self-esteem as a belief in the experiential system corresponds to a cognitive–affective schema acquired from emotionally significant experience. As previously noted, such experientially derived schemas are considered in CEST to be far more influential in determining people's everyday feelings and behavior than the conscious beliefs in their rational system. I suspect that the main reason that conscious self-assessments predict anything at all besides other self-reports is because of their overlap with beliefs in the experiential system. That is, most people's experientially and rationally determined beliefs are mainly congruent, or else they would be in a continuous state of conflict and stress.

Self-esteem as a need in the experiential system refers to a motive to enhance self-esteem that is driven by the anticipated positive affect following elevations in self-esteem and the anticipated negative affect following decreases in self-esteem, which in turn are determined by the affective strength of relevant past experience. As one of only four basic needs in the experiential system, self-enhancement is among the most powerful of human motives. Like the other basic needs, it can dominate all the other basic needs. Relatedly, as one of only four basic beliefs, self-esteem as a belief is among the most important cognitive–affective schematic networks in a personal theory of reality. The importance of self-esteem both as a need and as a belief can be appreciated from a consideration of their developmental origin. In agreement with Mead (1934) and Sullivan (1953), I assume that the most fundamental source of self-esteem is the internalization of the evaluation of a person by significant others, particularly parental figures. Because of its importance, let us more carefully consider why and how this occurs.

A young child is dependent on a caretaker not only for survival but because the caretaker is the greatest source of the child's everyday pleasure and alleviation of distress. Thus, the worst fear a child can have is of abandonment. As a result, the child is strongly motivated to please the parent. A particularly effective way of accomplishing this is by adopting the parents' values. Once the child has internalized the values of the caretaker, it can then behave naturally in ways that are most likely to gain the caretaker's approval. From then on, whenever the child behaves consistently with its internalized values it feels comfortable, and when it behaves otherwise it feels distressed. The most important value that the child internalizes is the caretaker's evaluation of the child as love-worthy. This internalization is the child's most fundamental source of its self-esteem, which, operating as the nucleus of a regnant cognitive–affective schematic network, has a widespread influence on the child's feelings, behavior, and interpretation of events that influences the child's further development. As favorable self-evaluations produce good feelings (analogous to receiving love from a parent) and unfavorable self-evaluations produce bad feelings (analogous to rejection or disapproval by a parent) the child has also acquired an affect-driven motive to behave in ways that increase self-esteem and that avoid decreases in self-esteem.

THE ROLE OF SELF-ESTEEM IN PSYCHOLOGICAL FUNCTIONING

Self-esteem influences behavior, thoughts, and emotions in its capacity both as a basic schema and as a basic need. As a basic schema, a high level of self-esteem is normally associated with feelings of security, happiness, confidence, and general well-being (Coopersmith, 1967; Epstein, 1979; Rogers, 1959; O'Brien & Epstein, 1983). Such cognitive–affective schemas facilitate effective performance and serve as a buffer against adversity. With respect to self-esteem functioning as a basic need, anticipation of the positive affect associated with increases in self-esteem and the negative affect associated with decreases in self-esteem is a powerful motive for accomplishment.

There is also a negative side to self-esteem. A chronic low level of self-esteem is a direct source of sadness and depression and can result in giving up rather than striving to succeed. Most importantly, in a desperate attempt to defend their self-esteem, people of low self-esteem often engage in self-defeating behavior. For example, by faulting others rather than recognizing their own complicity in unfavorable outcomes, they may temporarily bolster their self-esteem at the cost of failing to learn from experience and of alienating others.

It is important to distinguish between two kinds of self-esteem, conditional and unconditional. Conditional self-esteem corresponds to William James' (1890) view of self-esteem as people's appraisal of their accomplishments relative to their aspirations. People with high conditional self-esteem regard themselves as highly competent and love-worthy and, as a result, generally feel good about themselves. However, should they fail to meet their performance standards or be rejected by someone they can be very disapproving of themselves. Alternatively, their high self-esteem can produce driven behavior for achievement that brings no lasting joy once the goal is obtained, for despite bringing fame, fortune, and admiration, it does not fulfill their need for unconditional love, the likely source of their lack of unconditional self-love.

In contrast, people with unconditional high self-esteem are self-accepting and feel good about themselves, no matter what their level of performance or acceptance by others. They may disapprove of their behavior and decide to work on improving it, but they do not disapprove of themselves. Unlike people with conditional self-esteem, they do not have to accomplish anything to justify their positive feelings about themselves; they simply have them. Such unconditional self-acceptance is analogous to unconditional love by a parent.

Self-esteem has important implications for mental disorders. Psychotic depression, schizophrenia, and paranoia are often instigated by events that threaten self-esteem. Pathological depression, as distinguished from reactive depression, is associated with an irrational decrease in self-esteem. The irrational reaction can be understood by recognizing that a decrease in self-esteem for an adult is similar to the perception by a child of loss of love of a parent. Some people have been more sensitized to such loss than others. An acute schizophrenic episode following a severe blow to self-esteem can be understood as the disorganization of a personal theory of reality following the deep frustration of the basic need for self-esteem and the invalidation of the basic belief that the self is love-worthy. Paranoia with delusions of grandeur can be understood as a desperate attempt to shore up self-esteem at the cost of sacrificing fulfillment of all the other basic needs. Paranoia with delusions of persecution can be understood as a defense against both disorganization and a threat to self-esteem. By focusing on an external threat and mobilizing all of the person's resources to combat it, the paranoid is able to achieve and maintain a high degree of cohesiveness. Delusions of persecution also serve to bolster self-esteem, as having antagonists of great power and influence implies that one is a person of considerable importance oneself.

The interaction of the basic needs is able to account for phenomena that might otherwise appear anomalous. For example, there has been considerable controversy about whether it is more adaptive to be unrealistically self-enhancing than to be completely realistic. Evidence suggests that most people are somewhat unrealistically self-enhancing. Why should this be? The explanation, according to

CEST, is that the unrealistic behavior represents a compromise between the basic needs to enhance self-esteem and to maintain a stable, coherent, accurate model of reality. The compromise is to be positively biased, but only within limits. That is, most people operate as strategic self-enhancers, being favorably biased under conditions in which they receive a greater gain in terms of feeling good than a loss in terms of feeling bad because of the outcome of being modestly unrealistic. When the cost of being unrealistic is increased, normal people become more realistic in contrast to subclinically depressed people, who become less realistic (Pacini, Muir, & Epstein, 1998).

THE MEASUREMENT OF SELF-ESTEEM

Since the experiential and rational systems both contain self-evaluative beliefs, it is necessary to measure both if one wishes to obtain a full picture of a person's self-esteem. The different kinds of relations that the two kinds of self-esteem establish with other variables are obviously important in their own right. Of special importance are incongruities between the two systems as they can be a source of maladjustment and defensiveness. Kernis, Abend, Goldman, Shira, Paradise, and Hampton (2004) obtained interesting findings using a procedure involving an experimental induction of discrepancies between the two systems. It would be interesting to further test discrepancies by examining the relation between natural-occurring discrepancies between the two systems and measures of defensiveness and adjustment.

Measuring self-esteem at the conscious, rational level can be readily accomplished with any of several self-report instruments. An important improvement would be to recognize the distinction between conditional and unconditional self-esteem and to construct separate scales for measuring them. It would be most interesting to compare the correlates of these two kinds of self-esteem.

The situation is much more complicated for measuring self-esteem at the preconscious experiential level, as people do not have direct access to the operation of their experiential systems. The Implicit Association Test (IAT; Greenwald & Farnham, 2000; Greenwald & Banaji, 1995) is a promising procedure for measuring self-esteem and the self-concept at the experiential level, as it is an associative test and the experiential system is an associative system. It would be interesting to include measures of individual differences in experiential and rational thinking styles, (e.g., Epstein et al., 1996; Pacini & Epstein, 1999; Pacini, Muir, & Epstein, 1998) and to examine the use of emotionally evocative images, as the experiential system consists primarily of cognitive-affective nonverbal networks (Epstein, 2003). There are several other approaches worth pursuing. One is to construct a self-report test in which people report behavior, thoughts and feelings from which inferences can be made about experiential schemas. This can be done by consulting the principles of experiential processing proposed in CEST (see Epstein, 2003) and by considering the kinds of behavior and feelings in situations that are likely to be differentially acknowledged by people of high and low experiential self-esteem, such as excessive pride, boastfulness, proneness to take offense, and sensitivity to disapproval compared to confidence, forgiveness, security, and ego-strength (Epstein, 2001).

Another approach worth trying is to construct projective tests, such as Thematic Apperception Tests (TATs), Word Association Tests, and Sentence Completion Tests specially designed to elicit responses relevant to self-esteem. In a series of studies with specially constructed TATs, McClelland and Weinberger and their associates (McClelland et al., 1989; Weinberger & McClelland, 1991) demonstrated that implicit motives inferred from TAT responses predicted behavior, whereas self-reported motives predicted only other self-reported responses. In the measurement of self-esteem with projective tests measurement it is important to include stimuli at various levels of strength for eliciting self-esteem relevant responses, analogous to including items at various levels of difficulty in ability tests.

An additional approach is to use procedures other than the IAT that have been used by social psychologists in research on implicit attitudes, such as sub-threshold, reaction-time, and priming procedures (see review by Bargh & Chartrand, 1999).

As the experiential system is normally the dominant mode in everyday behavior, another approach is to infer experiential schemas from repetitive patterns of behavior. This can be accomplished with the use of diary records, time sampling, and interviews (e.g., Losco & Epstein, 1978; O'Brien & Epstein, 1974). Despite some obvious disadvantages, interviews also have advantages over other self-report procedures, as they can be used to observe expressive behavior, note defensive reactions, and, most importantly, assess the emotional intensity which certain situations evoke. Emotions, according to CEST, are the royal road to the schemas in a person's experiential system (Epstein, 2003).

REFERENCES

Allport, G. W. (1927/1961). *Pattern and growth in personality*. New York: Holt, Rinehart & Winston.

Bargh, J. A., & Chartrand, T. L. (1999). The unbearable automaticity of being. *American Psychologist, 54*, 462–479.

Bowlby, J. (1973). *Attachment and loss: Vol. 2. Separation, anxiety, and anger*. New York: Basic Books.

Coopersmith, S. (1967). *The antecedents of self-esteem*. San Francisco: W. H. Freeman & Co.

Epstein, S. (1979). The ecological study of emotions in humans. In P. Pliner, K. R. Blankstein, & I. M. Spigel (Eds.), *Advances in the study of communication and affect, Vol. 5: Perception of emotions in self and others* (pp. 47–83). New York: Plenum.

Epstein, S. (1998). Emotions and psychopathology from the perspective of cognitive-experiential self-theory. In W. E. Flack & J. D. Laird (Eds.), *Emotions and psychopathology: Theory and research* (pp. 57–69). New York: Oxford University Press.

Epstein, S. (2001). *Manual for the Constructive Thinking Inventory*. Odessa, FL: Psychological Assessment Resources.

Epstein, S. (2003). Cognitive-experiential self-theory of personality. In T. Millon & M. J. Lerner (Eds.), *Comprehensive handbook of psychology* (Vol. 5, pp. 159–184), *Personality and social psychology*. Hoboken, NJ: Wiley.

Epstein, S., & Morling, B. (1995). Is the self motivated to more than enhance and verify itself? In M. H. Kernis (Ed.), *Efficacy, agency, and self-esteem* (pp. 9–29). New York: Plenum.

Epstein, S., Pacini, R., Denes–Raj, V., & Heier, H. (1996). Individual differences in intuitive–experiential and analytical–rational thinking styles. *Journal of Personality and Social Psychology, 71,* 390–405.

Freud, S., (1965). *The interpretation of dreams* (J. Strachey, Trans.). New York: Avon Books. (Original work published 1900)

Greenwald, A. G., & Banaji, M. R. (1995). Implicit attitudes: Attitudes, self-esteem, and stereotypes. *Psychological Review, 102,* 4–27.

Greenwald, A. G., & Farnham, S. D. (2000). Using the Implicit Association Test to measure self-esteem and the self-concept. *Journal of Personality and Social Psychology, 79,* 1022–1038.

James, W. (1890). *Principles of psychology* (Vol. 1). New York: Holt.

Kernis, M. H., Abend, T. A., Goldman, B. M., Shira, I., Paradise, A. N., & Hampton, C. (2005). Self-serving responses arising from discrepancies between the explicit and implicit self-esteem systems. *Self and Identity, 4,* 311–330.

Kohut, H. (1971). *The analysis of the self.* New York: International Universities Press.

Lecky, P. (1969). *Self-consistency: A theory of personality.* Garden City, NY: Anchor Books. (Original work published 1945)

Losco, J. P., & Epstein, S. (1978). *Reactions to favorable and unfavorable evaluations in everyday life as a function of level of self-esteem.* Paper presented at the Eastern Psychological Association Convention, Washington, DC.

McClelland, D. C., Koestner, R., & Weinberger, J. (1989). How do self-attributed and implicit motives differ? *Psychological Review, 96,* 690–702.

Mead, G. H. (1934). *Mind, self, and society.* Chicago: University of Chicago Press.

Morling, B., & Epstein, S. (1997). Compromises produced by the dialectic between self-verification and self-enhancement. *Journal of Personality and Social Psychology, 73,* 1268–1283.

O'Brien, E. J., & Epstein, S. (1974). *Naturally occurring changes in self-esteem.* Paper presented at the American Psychological Association Convention, New Orleans, LA.

O'Brien, E. J., & Epstein, S. (l983). *The Multi-dimensional Self-esteem Inventory.* Odessa, FL: Psychological Assessment Resources.

Pacini, R., & Epstein, S. (1999). The relation of rational and experiential information processing styles to personality, basic beliefs, and the ratio-bias phenomenon. *Journal of Personality and Social Psychology, 76,* 972–987.

Pacini, R., Muir, F., & Epstein, S. (1998) Depressive realism from the perspective of cognitive-experiential self-theory. *Journal of Personality and Social Psychology, 74,* 1056–1068.

Rogers, C. R. (1951). *Client-centered therapy.* Boston: Houghton Mifflin.

Snygg, D., & Combs, A. W. (1949). *Individual behavior.* New York: Harper & Row.

Sullivan, H. S. (1953). *The interpersonal theory of psychiatry.* New York: W. W. Norton.

Weinberger, J., & McClelland, D. C. (1991). Cognitive versus traditional motivational models: Irreconcilable or complementary? In R. Sorrentino & E. J. Higgins (Eds.), *Handbook of motivation and cognition* (Vol. 2, pp. 562–597). New York: Guilford Press.

10

Assessing Stability of Self-Esteem and Contingent Self-Esteem

MICHAEL H. KERNIS and BRIAN M. GOLDMAN

*H*istorically, most research and theory on the nature, antecedents, and consequences of self-esteem has focused on its level, that is, on whether it is low or high. Recently, it has become increasingly clear that a full understanding of self-esteem requires taking into consideration other self-esteem components, namely *stability*, *contingency*, and *implicit self-esteem* (Crocker, Luhtanen, Cooper, & Bouvrette, 2003b; Kernis, 2003, 2005; Kernis & Goldman, 2003). More researchers are incorporating measures assessing these components into their studies, oftentimes resulting in richer and more nuanced findings that underscore self-esteem's complexity. In this chapter, we focus on issues pertaining to the measurement of *fragile* forms of self-esteem, specifically self-esteem stability and contingent self-esteem.

STABILITY OF SELF-ESTEEM

Self-esteem variability (instability) has been conceptualized both in terms of short- and long-term fluctuations (Rosenberg, 1986). When viewed as long-term fluctuations, self-esteem instability reflects change that occurs gradually over an extended period. Rosenberg (1986) referred to this as change in one's *baseline* self-esteem. Most research and theory, however, have focused on self-esteem variability as reflected in short-term fluctuations in one's contextually based global self-esteem (for a review, see Kernis, 2005). Rosenberg (1986) referred to these short-term fluctuations as *barometric* instability. In his view, unstable self-esteem involves dramatic short-term shifts between feelings of worthiness and worthlessness. In fact, his Stability of Self Scale (Rosenberg, 1965) requires individuals with unstable self-esteem to endorse items such as "Some days I have a very good opinion of myself; other days I have a very poor opinion of myself."

Another perspective is that self-esteem instability may take numerous forms. As Rosenberg notes, some people may in fact experience dramatic shifts from feeling very positively to very negatively about themselves. Others, however, may primarily fluctuate in the *extent* to which they feel positively or negatively about themselves. The precise nature of these fluctuations is likely to depend upon a number of factors, including: (1) which self-aspects are salient; and (2) the valence of recently experienced self-relevant events (cf. Kernis & Johnson, 1990; Markus & Kunda, 1986). Kernis and his colleagues (Kernis, Cornell, Sun, Berry, & Harlow, 1993) argued that the essence of unstable self-esteem is the propensity to experience short-term fluctuations in contextually based feelings of self-worth that interacts with situation-based factors to produce specific patterns of fluctuations. These fluctuations may at times (or for certain people) be primarily unidirectional (e.g., within a relatively positive or negative range) or bidirectional (between positive and negative ranges) (for a relevant discussion of this issue, see Vallacher & Novak, 2000). The implications of various specific patterns of fluctuations have yet to be systematically examined (instead, researchers have focused only on the extent of fluctuations), but we suspect that in general they all will reflect an underlying fragility in feelings of self-worth.

The most common way to assess short-term fluctuations in self-esteem is to have respondents complete a self-esteem measure (Rosenberg's Self-Esteem Scale) once or twice daily over a 4–7 day period under instructions to base their responses on how they feel *at the moment they are completing each form* (Kernis, 2005). The standard deviation of each individual's total scores across these multiple assessments then is computed; the greater the standard deviation, the more unstable one's self-esteem. To measure self-esteem *level*, respondents complete the same self-esteem scale, but this time they base their responses on how they *typically or generally feel about themselves*. Generally, self-esteem level is assessed in small group settings prior to the time that individuals complete the multiple assessments of contextually based current self-esteem.

Correlations between level and stability of self-esteem generally range from the low teens to the low 30s, suggesting that they are relatively independent dimensions of self-esteem (for a summary of representative values, see Kernis & Waschull, 1995). Invariably, the direction of the correlation indicates that self-esteem that is more unstable is associated with lower levels of self-esteem. However, it is incorrect to presume that only low self-esteem individuals possess unstable self-esteem. In fact, researchers frequently find that self-esteem stability has effects among both high and low self-esteem individuals and sometimes this effect is stronger among individuals high, not low, in self-esteem (e.g., Kernis, Grannemann, & Barclay, 1989; Kernis, Lakey, & Heppner, 2005).

A potential alternative to obtaining multiple assessments of current self-esteem is to administer Rosenberg's five-item Stability of Self Scale (e.g., Kernis, Grannemann, & Barclay, 1992). However, it is unclear whether the two types of unstable self-esteem assessments are assessing precisely the same construct. First, Kernis et al. (1992) reported a nonsignificant correlation between scores on this scale and self-esteem stability as assessed through multiple assessments, but a high correlation between these scores and self-esteem level ($r = -.58$). Second, asking people to rate the extent to which their responses on Rosenberg's Self-Esteem Scale would change from day to day more strongly related to scores on Rosenberg's Stability of Self Scale than it did to observed self-esteem instability (Kernis et al., 1992). In our view, these data suggest that people are not fully aware of the degree to which their self-esteem is unstable. Consequently, we believe that asking them how much their self-esteem fluctuates cannot substitute for a measure of self-esteem stability that is based on repeated assessments obtained in naturalistic contexts (for an extended discussion, see Kernis et al., 1992).

Issues of Validity

The major virtue of obtaining multiple assessments of current self-esteem is that it provides for the measurement of self-esteem stability in the context of everyday events experienced by individuals. Along with this ecological validity, however, comes a relative lack of control over the data collection. Fortunately, our previous research indicates that the quality of data we obtain is very high. Almost all participants take the task seriously and complete the measures at or close to the times that we asked them to (as assessed in individual debriefing sessions). In our research, we drop from analyses a small number of people who do not complete at least 75% of the multiple assessments (typically 6 of 8). We endorse this practice because we feel that people who complete less than this probably are not very invested in the study.

Some might take what we refer to as unstable self-esteem as merely greater unreliability in responding. However, we think that this would be a mistake. First, it would mean ignoring the psychological significance of unstable self-esteem, as demonstrated in our previous research, as well as that of other researchers (for reviews, see Kernis, 2005; Kernis & Goldman, 2003; Kernis & Waschull, 1995). Second, when assessing stability of self-esteem, we explicitly ask people to base their responses on how they feel at the moment they are completing the form. Because people can legitimately fluctuate in their momentary self-feelings, there is ample justification for viewing self-esteem as reflecting primarily the true score component of responses rather than the error component (for a related discussion, see Tellegen, 1988).

CONTINGENT SELF-ESTEEM

As described by Deci and Ryan (1995), "Contingent self-esteem refers to feelings about oneself that result from—indeed, are dependent on—matching some standard of excellence or living up to some interpersonal or intrapsychic expectations" (p. 32). Individuals with contingent self-esteem are preoccupied with their standings on specific evaluative dimensions (e.g., How attractive am I?) and how they are viewed by others (Do people think I am smart?), and they continually engage in setting and meeting evaluative standards to validate their feelings of self-worth.

High self-esteem that is *contingent* is *fragile*, because it remains high only as long as one is successful at satisfying relevant criteria (Deci & Ryan, 1995). Moreover, the strong need for continual validation drives the person to seek more and more successes. Should these successes cease, the person's self-esteem likely will plummet (for extended discussion, see Deci & Ryan, 1995; Kernis & Paradise, 2002).

Paradise and Kernis (1999) reasoned that people with highly contingent self-esteem would be threatened by an insulting evaluation and, as a result, would become especially angry and hostile. We utilized a 15-item measure of contingent self-esteem (The Contingent Self-Esteem Scale; see appendix for scale) that focuses on the degree to which people's self-esteem depends upon their matching standards, performance outcomes, and evaluations by others. The scale is internally consistent ($\alpha = .85$) and shows considerable test–retest reliability ($r = .77$). Our findings strongly supported our hypothesis. Other researchers (e.g., Neighbors, Larimer, Geisner, & Knee, 2004; Patrick, Neighbors, & Knee, 2004) also have used this scale successfully.

Building upon Deci and Ryan's framework, Crocker et al. (2003b) provide evidence that individual differences exist in the specific criteria that people with contingent self-esteem attempt to satisfy to maintain their positive self-feelings. For some people, a domain such as academic competence is most critical, whereas for others, it is social acceptance. Other major categories of contingencies, each having its own criteria, include one's physical appearance, God's love, power, and virtue. Empirical efforts to assess individual differences in the strength of these various contingencies have been very encouraging (see Crocker et al., 2003b). For example, Crocker, Karpinski, Quinn, & Chase (2003a) found that, compared with baseline days on which undergraduate participants received no news regarding their graduate school application status, the current self-esteem of individuals whose self-esteem was contingent on academic competence was especially likely to rise with news of acceptance and decline with news of rejection.

Although research on contingent self-esteem is not as abundant as research on stability of self-esteem, that which exists offers encouraging initial support for the construct of contingent self-esteem and its implications for distinguishing between fragile and secure high self-esteem (Kernis, 2003). At least two measurement instruments are available (Kernis & Paradise's and Crocker et al.'s), both of which should provide valuable information in future research. Whereas the focus of the Kernis and Paradise measure is on assessing the overall degree to which the person's self-esteem is contingent, the focus of Crocker et al.'s measure is on assessing the specific domains of contingency on which the person's self-esteem depends. Each provides important information.

SUMMARY

Self-esteem involves a complex set of processes. Acknowledging that it is multi-faceted allows for a rich understanding of its role in psychological functioning and well-being. In this essay, we discussed measures and procedures to assess two important facets of self-esteem—stability and contingency. Assessing each of these facets in addition to self-esteem level often yields patterns of self-esteem relationships that would have been otherwise obscured (Kernis, 2003, 2005; Kernis et al., 2005). The same is true for assessing implicit self-esteem (see Bosson and Jordan's essays, this volume). We encourage researchers to incorporate these various self-esteem components into their research.

REFERENCES

Crocker, J., Karpinski, A., Quinn, D. M., & Chase, S. (2003a). When grades determine self-worth: Consequences of contingent self-worth for male and female engineering and psychology majors. *Journal of Personality and Social Psychology, 85,* 507–516.

Crocker, J., Luhtanen, R., Cooper, M. L., & Bouvrette, S. A. (2003b). Contingencies of self-worth in college students: Measurement and theory. *Journal of Personality and Social Psychology, 85,* 894–908.

Deci, E. L., & Ryan, R. M. (1995). Human agency: The basis for true self-esteem. In M. H. Kernis (Ed.), *Efficacy, agency, and self-esteem* (pp. 31–50). New York: Plenum.

Kernis, M. H. (2003). Toward a conceptualization of optimal self-esteem. *Psychological Inquiry, 14,* 1–26.

Kernis, M. H. (2005). Measuring self-esteem in context: The importance of stability of self-esteem in psychological functioning. *Journal of Personality* [Special Issue: Advances in Personality and Daily Experience], *6,* 1569–1606.

Kernis, M. H., Cornell, D. P., Sun, C. R., Berry, A., & Harlow, T. (1993). There's more to self-esteem than whether it's high or low: The importance of stability of self-esteem. *Journal of Personality and Social Psychology, 65,* 1190–1204.

Kernis, M. H., & Goldman, B. M. (2003). Stability and variability in self-concept and self-esteem. In M. R. Leary & J. P. Tangney (Eds.), *Handbook of self and identity* (pp. 106–127). New York: Guilford Press.

Kernis, M. H., Grannemann, B. D., & Barclay, L. C. (1989). Stability and level of self-esteem as predictors of anger arousal and hostility. *Journal of Personality and Social Psychology, 56,* 1013–1023.

Kernis, M. H., Grannemann, B. D., & Barclay, L. C. (1992). Stability of self-esteem: Assessment, correlates, and excuse making. *Journal of Personality, 60,* 621–644.

Kernis, M. H., & Johnson, E. K. (1990). Current and typical self-appraisals: Differential responsiveness to evaluative feedback and implications for emotions. *Journal of Research in Personality, 24,* 241–257.

Kernis, M. H., Lakey, C., & Heppner, W. (2005). Fragile self-esteem and verbal defensiveness. Manuscript in preparation.

Kernis, M. H., & Paradise, A. W. (2002). Distinguishing between secure and fragile forms of high self-esteem. In E. L. Deci & R. M. Ryan (Eds.), *Handbook of self-determination research* (pp. 330–360). Rochester, NY: University of Rochester Press.

Kernis, M. H., & Waschull, S. B. (1995). The interactive roles of stability and level of self-esteem: Research and theory. In M. Zanna (Ed.), *Advances in experimental social psychology.* San Diego: Academic Press.

Markus, H., & Kunda, Z. (1986). Stability and malleability of the self-concept. *Journal of Personality and Social Psychology, 51,* 858–866.

Neighbors, C., Larimer, M. E., Geisner, I. M., & Knee, C. R. (2004). Feeling controlled and drinking motives among college students: Contingent self-esteem as a mediator. *Self and Identity, 3,* 207–224.

Paradise, A. W., & Kernis, M. H. (1999). *Development of the contingent self-esteem scale.* Unpublished data, University of Georgia.

Patrick, H., Neighbors, C., & Knee, C.R. (2004). Appearance related social comparisons: The role of contingent self-esteem and self-perceptions of attractiveness. *Personality and Social Psychology Bulletin, 30,* 501–514.

Rosenberg, M. (1965). *Society and the adolescent self-image.* Princeton, NJ: Princeton University Press.

Rosenberg, M. (1986). Self-concept from middle childhood through adolescence. In J. Suls & A. G. Greenwald (Eds.), *Psychological perspective on the self* (Vol. 3, pp. 107–135). Hillsdale, NJ: Lawrence Erlbaum Associates, Inc.

Tellegen, A. (1988). The analysis of consistency in personality assessment. *Journal of Personality, 56,* 621–663.

Vallacher, R. R., & Novak, A. (2000). Landscapes of self-reflection: Mapping the peaks and valleys of personal assessment. In A. Tesser, R. B. Felson, & J. M. Suls (Eds.), *Psychological perspectives on self and identity.* Washington, DC: American Psychological Association.

APPENDIX

KERNIS AND PARADISE CONTINGENT SELF-ESTEEM SCALE

Listed below are a number of statements concerning personal attitudes and characteristics. Please read each statement carefully and consider the extent to which you think it is like you. Circle one number on the scale below each statement that best reflects your answer. There are no right or wrong answers, so please answer as honestly as you can. Thank you.

1. An important measure of my worth is how competently I perform.

1	2	3	4	5
Not at All Like Me		Neutral		Very Much Like Me

2. Even in the face of failure, my feelings of self-worth remain unaffected.

1	2	3	4	5
Not at All Like Me		Neutral		Very Much Like Me

3. A big determinant of how much I like myself is how well I perform up to the standards that I have set for myself.

1	2	3	4	5
Not at All Like Me		Neutral		Very Much Like Me

4. My overall feelings about myself are heavily influenced by how much other people like and accept me.

1	2	3	4	5
Not at All Like Me		Neutral		Very Much Like Me

5. If I get along well with somebody, I feel better about myself overall.

1	2	3	4	5
Not at All Like Me		Neutral		Very Much Like Me

6. An important measure of my worth is how physically attractive I am.

1	2	3	4	5
Not at All Like Me		Neutral		Very Much Like Me

7. My overall feelings about myself are heavily influenced by what I believe other people are saying or thinking about me.

1	2	3	4	5
Not at All Like Me		Neutral		Very Much Like Me

8. If I am told that I look good, I feel better about myself in general.

1	2	3	4	5
Not at All Like Me		Neutral		Very Much Like Me

9. My feelings of self-worth are basically unaffected when other people treat me badly.

1	2	3	4	5
Not at All Like Me		Neutral		Very Much Like Me

10. An important measure of my worth is how well I perform up to the standards that other people have set for me.

1	2	3	4	5
Not at All Like Me		Neutral		Very Much Like Me

11. If I know that someone likes me, I do not let it affect how I feel about myself.

1	2	3	4	5
Not at All Like Me		Neutral		Very Much Like Me

12. When my actions do not live up to my expectations, it makes me feel dissatisfied with myself.

1	2	3	4	5
Not at All Like Me		Neutral		Very Much Like Me

13. Even on a day when I don't look my best, my feelings of self-worth remain unaffected.

1	2	3	4	5
Not at All Like Me		Neutral		Very Much Like Me

14. My overall feelings about myself are heavily influenced by how good I look.

1	2	3	4	5
Not at All Like Me		Neutral		Very Much Like Me

15. Even in the face of rejection, my feelings of self-worth remain unaffected.

1	2	3	4	5
Not at All Like Me		Neutral		Very Much Like Me

Scoring Instructions:

1. Reverse responses to items 2, 9, 11, 13, and 15.
2. Add up responses to the remaining items and sum that with sum of responses to reversed items. Range = 15 to 75. Higher scores equal more contingent self-esteem.

Question 4

What are the strengths and drawbacks of the major self-report and available nonreactive measures? What steps can researchers take to accentuate their strengths and minimize their drawbacks?

*T*he essays in this section focus on issues pertaining to the use of self-report and nonreactive measures to assess self-esteem.

Bosson focuses on the strengths and weaknesses of available self-report and nonreactive measures, outlines some important issues and concerns associated with each, and offers some suggestions for maximizing their effectiveness. As she notes, nonreactive measures can potentially capture aspects of self-esteem not represented in self-report measures.

Koestner and Mageau apply key lessons from the motive literature to the measurement of implicit and explicit self-esteem. They note that criticisms of self-report measures, in particular Rosenberg's Self-esteem Scale, are at odds with their considerable face and construct validity. They suggest that a more reasonable conclusion would be that while self-reported self-esteem is generally useful as an indicator of a person's subjective sense of self-worth, it might be vulnerable to distortions. The authors then discuss vital lessons from the motive literature and offer suggestions for future research.

Karpinski and Steinberg suggest that measures of self-esteem comprise three types: direct, indirect, and association based. Direct self-report measures assess individuals' conscious feelings of self-worth. Association-based measures (such as the IAT) assess individuals' implicit, or relatively automatic, nonconscious self-evaluations. Indirect measures are hybrid measures that tap aspects of both implicit and explicit self-esteem. Karpinski and Steinberg present data from their lab that addresses the validity of this distinction.

Tafarodi and Ho offer a conceptual critique of the implicit/explicit distinction. In addition, they argue that most self-report measures are incomplete because they do not capture what they believe are two separate, but interrelated components of global self-esteem: self-liking and self-competence. They then review evidence pertaining to the use of the Self-Liking/Self-Competence Scale (Tafarodi & Swann, 1995, 2001) to assess these dual self-esteem components.

11

Assessing Self-Esteem via Self-Reports and Nonreactive Instruments: Issues and Recommendations

JENNIFER K. BOSSON

*T*hose of us interested in the role of self-esteem in people's overall functioning and adjustment may find ourselves simultaneously delighted and overwhelmed by the proliferation of measures available for capturing the self-esteem construct. Here, I attempt to provide some guidance by summarizing the major features of the available self-report and nonreactive self-esteem measures. In doing so, I outline what I perceive to be the most important issues and concerns associated with each type of measure, and offer suggestions for maximizing their effectiveness.

SELF-REPORT MEASURES OF SELF-ESTEEM

By far, most self-esteem research utilizes self-report measures (Blascovich & Tomaka, 1991). Not surprisingly, there are many available self-report scales from which to choose, reflecting a variety of theoretical perspectives. In their review of the available self-esteem scales, Blascovich and Tomaka identified several frequently used measures including Rosenberg's (1965) Self-Esteem Scale, Coopersmith's (1967) Self-Esteem Inventory, the Tennessee Self-Concept Scale (Roid & Fitts, 1988), Janis and Field's (1959) Feelings of Inadequacy Scale, and the Texas Social Behavior Inventory (Helmreich, Stapp, & Ervin, 1974). I would add to this list the Self-Liking and Self-Competence Scale (Tafarodi & Swann, 2001) and the State Self-Esteem Scale (Heatherton & Polivy, 1991).

Self-report measures of self-esteem can boast multiple strengths, not the least of which is their directness. Because such measures are high in face validity, respondents generally know what is being asked of them when they complete self-report scales. Such scales thus have the potential to tap personal knowledge that is unavailable to others (Hamilton, 1971), and reveal important information about people's self-theories. The high face validity of self-report measures also facilitates their interpretation by researchers. Despite some differing perspectives (e.g., Baumeister, Tice, & Hutton, 1989), self-esteem theorists generally concur that an individual's endorsement (or rejection) of the statement "I like myself" reflects something meaningful about his or her subjectively experienced evaluations of the self. Also in their favor, self-report measures of self-esteem demonstrate strong psychometric properties. They tend to be internally consistent and reliable across time, and they correlate as predicted with measures of other theoretically related constructs (Blascovich & Tomaka, 1991). Most importantly, self-reported self-esteem predicts a wide array of behaviors and outcomes including psychological well-being, academic achievement, relationship and life satisfaction, and physical health (Bednar & Peterson, 1995; DuBois & Tevendale, 1999; Mecca, Smelser, & Vasconcellos, 1989; Taylor & Brown, 1988). Indeed, most of our current knowledge of self-esteem and its correlates is based on people's self-reports. Finally, self-report measures of self-esteem are practical. From a researcher's perspective, self-report scales are inexpensive to reproduce, easy to administer, and simple to code, making them suitable for a wide range of measurement contexts and subject populations. From a respondent's perspective, self-report scales can be completed quickly and with little instruction, training, or effort. When time, space, finances, or human resources are limited, self-report measures of self-esteem may present an attractive option.

Not surprisingly, some of these strengths of self-report self-esteem scales also represent their greatest weaknesses. For instance, the directness of self-report self-esteem scales makes them easy to interpret, but it can also make their meaning transparent to respondents. Thus, people can easily manipulate the image they convey with their responses to such scales. Of particular concern to many researchers is the possibility that self-presentation motives will compel people to report unrealistically high self-esteem (Farnham, Greenwald, & Banaji, 1999; Paulhus, 1986), although it is also possible that people may downplay their feelings of self-worth. Either way, the directness of self-report scales allows respondents a high level of control over their scores, which raises the possibility that self-reported self-esteem does not reflect people's true feelings. On a related note, people may be unable to fully and/or accurately portray their self-esteem via self-reports. People may lack introspective access to their self-attitudes because they are motivated to avoid self-critical thoughts (Paulhus, 1986), or because aspects of their self-esteem operate in an implicit or "experiential" mode (Epstein & Morling, 1995). Moreover, self-report self-esteem scales are often limited in scope. Even scales designed to capture multiple dimensions of self-esteem do not assess all aspects of this multifaceted construct, such as its stability across time (Kernis, 1993), or its contingency on internal vs. external sources (Crocker, Luhtanen, Cooper, & Bouvrette, 2003). Despite their directness, then, self-reports may not tell the full story about respondents' self-esteem. Finally, the strong psychometric properties of self-report self-esteem scales may be offset by the numerous potential sources of measurement error inherent to such scales. Minor changes in the wording, context, and formatting of self-report items can undermine the validity and reliability of people's responses (Schwarz, 1999). In a powerful illustration of this fact, Marsh and Yeung (1999) showed that people provided substantially different answers to the same global self-esteem items when these items were embedded in instruments that tapped different self-concept domains.

I offer two recommendations for accentuating the strengths and minimizing the weaknesses of self-report self-esteem measures. First, researchers should remain attentive to features of the measurement context including the wording of items, the order in which items and scales are administered, and the broader environment in which self-esteem is assessed. Several writers (e.g., Schwarz, 1999) offer useful strategies for minimizing the measurement problems that plague self-report measures, and I direct interested readers to their works. Second, investigators might do well to supplement self-report scales with additional measurement techniques that can shed light on self-esteem (Wells & Marwell, 1976). Several studies show that the relations between self-reported self-esteem and other theoretically related variables are clarified when multiple measures of self-esteem or self-concept are utilized (Bosson, Brown, Zeigler-Hill, & Swann, 2003; Jordan, Spencer, Zanna, Hoshino-Browne, & Correll, 2003; Kernis, Cornell, Sun, Berry, & Harlow, 1993; Schneider & Turkat, 1975). As our understanding of the multifaceted nature of self-esteem grows, it becomes more apparent that a single self-report scale, administered once, may not suffice to capture the construct.

NONREACTIVE MEASURES OF SELF-ESTEEM

Nonreactive measures have long been used by psychologists to tap aspects of personality, but their popularity among researchers of the self has increased dramatically in recent years. In an exploration of nonreactive self-esteem measures, Bosson, Swann, and Pennebaker (2000) reviewed the Implicit Association Test (IAT; Greenwald, McGhee, & Schwartz, 1998), two cognitive priming tasks (Hetts, Sakuma, & Pelham, 1999; Spalding & Hardin, 1999), a word-completion task (Hetts et al., 1999), and people's preferences for their birthday numbers and name letters (Nuttin, 1985). Additional nonreactive measures include the Thematic Apperception Test (TAT; Murray, 1943), the Self-Apperception Test (Aidman, 1999), the Go/No-Go Association Task (Nosek & Banaji, 2001), and the extrinsic affective Simon task (De Houwer, 2003). Interested readers are referred to Fazio and Olson (2003) for a review of other implicit measures that may be modified to assess attitudes toward the self.

A primary strength of nonreactive self-esteem measures is, of course, their indirectness. Although nonreactive measures vary in the extent to which their purpose is apparent to respondents, they tend to be less obvious than self-report measures (Fazio & Olson, 2003). When completing nonreactive measures, respondents do not answer direct questions about their self-esteem. Instead, they reveal their self-evaluations via reaction-time tasks that utilize priming techniques, or projective tests in which they respond to ambiguous self-relevant stimuli. The meaning behind nonreactive measures is often masked by rapid, distorted, or subliminal presentation of stimuli, and respondents may work under time pressure or cognitive load. Thus, whether unaware of what is being measured or merely unable to control how they score, people cannot easily manipulate the image they convey on nonreactive measures. These measures may therefore capture self-evaluations that the bearer wishes to keep hidden. Also because of their indirectness, nonreactive measures may be well suited to tap people's automatic, spontaneous self-associations (often referred to as *implicit self-esteem*). This is an important asset, as implicit self-esteem is theorized to guide self-presentation and self-regulation behaviors, perceptual biases, and even major life decisions including choice of spouse, career, and residence (Greenwald & Banaji, 1995; Jones, Pelham, Mirenberg, & Hetts, 2002; Pelham, Mirenberg, & Jones, 2002). Of course, self-report scales may also capture elements of implicit self-esteem, just as responses to nonreactive measures may reflect explicit self-views (Gregg, 2003). Still, their indirectness should give nonreactive measures an advantage over self-reports when it comes to tapping automatic self-associations. If so, nonreactive measures may reveal aspects of self-esteem not captured by self-reports, as evidenced by recent findings (Aidman, 1999; Bosson et al., 2003; Jordan et al., 2003; Kitayama & Karasawa, 1997; Spalding & Hardin, 1999).

Despite their promise, however, a lack of clarity clouds the interpretation of several nonreactive self-esteem measures. For instance, because the self-esteem IAT (Greenwald & Farnham, 2000) measures the strength of automatic associations between the self and an evaluative dimension (e.g., good–bad), we can assume that an individual who categorizes self-relevant and pleasant words together particularly quickly on the IAT must associate the self with relatively strong, positive feelings. But does this mean that the individual necessarily *endorses* a favorable attitude toward the self (i.e., she believes personally, on some level, that the self is good), or can it merely suggest that the individual has learned, through prior exposure, to associate the concept "self" with the evaluation "good" (Karpinski & Hilton, 2001)? This interpretational nuance may be a subtle one, but it has nonetheless garnered a fair amount of empirical and theoretical attention (see Banaji, 2001; Karpinski & Hilton, 2001; Olson & Fazio, 2004). Similarly, whereas some argue that a preference for one's initials reflects high self-esteem, others suggest that people like their initials because of mere exposure (Jones et al., 2002). Until research clarifies the mechanisms that drive people's responses to nonreactive measures, interpretational ambiguities remain an issue of concern.

Furthermore, several of the available nonreactive measures have weak and/or inconsistent psychometric properties. Whereas the IAT and name-letter preferences demonstrate decent reliability and validity, other nonreactive measures tend to be unstable across time and measurement contexts, low in convergent validity, and limited in their predictive abilities (Bosson et al., 2000). Depending on which findings researchers review, their conclusions regarding the viability of nonreactive measures may thus differ dramatically. Contrast Koole and Pelham's (2003, p. 108) assertion that "name letter preferences...qualify as a valid marker for implicit self-esteem" with Schimmack and Diener's (2003, p. 105) conclusion that "there is no compelling empirical evidence to suggest a construct of implicit self-esteem that is revealed in preferences for initials." Considering that name-letter preferences are among the more reliable and valid of the nonreactive measures, these conflicting conclusions do not bode well for nonreactive measures as a whole. Finally, many of the available nonreactive self-esteem measures are costly, resource-wise. Multiple computers (and the laboratory space in which to house them) are needed if one is to collect response latency data efficiently, and nonreactive measures often take more time to administer and complete than self-report scales. The coding of nonreactive measures may be costly as well, requiring the training of independent coders or the writing of complex computer programs. Given the above-noted issues of reliability and validity, researchers may be (understandably) reluctant to devote the requisite resources to measures that cannot necessarily be counted on to "perform."

What can researchers do to accentuate the strengths and minimize the weaknesses of nonreactive measures? My first suggestion is simple: Keep abreast of the literature in this area. New nonreactive measures are published with regularity, and existing ones are continually being updated and refined. As an example, Greenwald and his colleagues recently published a new algorithm for scoring the IAT that yields stronger results compared to the original algorithm (Greenwald, Nosek, & Banaji, 2003). Second, researchers should strive to measure and, if desired, control contextual features when administering nonreactive measures. Even more than self-reports, people's responses to nonreactive measures may be highly influenced by factors such as previously administered questionnaires, recently primed concepts, affective states, and self-threats (Bosson et al., 2000; Gemar, Segal, Sagrati, & Kennedy, 2001; Jones et al., 2002; Karpinski & Hilton, 2001; Rudman, Ashmore, & Gary, 2001).

Finally, and perhaps most importantly, researchers hoping to accentuate the strengths of nonreactive self-esteem measures are advised to arm themselves with a strong theoretical model before designing studies and formulating hypotheses. Fazio and Towles-Schwen's (1999) Motivation and Opportunity as Determinants model (MODE), and Epstein's (1994) Cognitive Experiential Self Theory, may provide useful frameworks for understanding the nature of the processes tapped by the different nonreactive measures, as well as the conditions under which people's responses to nonreactive measures should correlate with (and deviate from) their self-reports and behaviors. As such, these and other dual-process theories have the potential to clarify some of the confusing issues that surround nonreactive measures. For example, the MODE proposes that people's responses to self-report and nonreactive measures should correlate to the extent that they lack either the motivation or the opportunity to control their responses. Moreover, motivation and/or opportunity may vary according to situational factors and individual differences, both of which can be measured and controlled. When viewed from the perspective of the MODE, the low predictive and convergent validity of several nonreactive measures (e.g., Bosson et al., 2000; Schimmack & Diener, 2003) may reflect features of the context in which these measures were administered rather than weaknesses of the measures themselves. Clearly, a richer theoretical understanding of nonreactive measures and the processes they tap should enhance researchers' capacity to make the most of such measures. After all, non-reactive measures can only be as strong as the theories that guide their use.

REFERENCES

Aidman, E. V. (1999). Measuring individual differences in implicit self-concept: Initial validation of the self-apperception test. *Personality and Individual Differences*, 27, 211–228.

Banaji, M. R. (2001). Implicit attitudes can be measured. In H. L. Roediger III, J. S. Nairne, I. Neath, & A. M. Surprenant (Eds.), *The nature of remembering: Essays in honor of Robert G. Crowder* (pp. 117–150). Washington, DC: American Psychological Association.

Baumeister, R. F., Tice, D. M., & Hutton, D. G. (1989). Self-presentational motivations and personality differences in self-esteem. *Journal of Personality*, 57, 547–579.

Bednar, R. L., & Peterson, S. R. (1995). *Self-esteem: Paradoxes and innovations in clinical theory and practice* (2nd ed.). Washington, DC: American Psychological Association.

Blascovich, J., & Tomaka, J. (1991). Measures of self-esteem. In J. P. Robinson & P. R. Shaver (Eds.), *Measures of personality and social psychological attitudes* (Vol. 1, pp. 115–160). San Diego, CA: Academic Press.

Bosson, J. K., Brown, R. P., Zeigler-Hill, V., & Swann, W. B. Jr. (2003). Self-enhancement tendencies among people with high explicit self-esteem: The moderating role of implicit self-esteem. *Self and Identity*, 2, 169–187.

Bosson, J. K., Swann, W. B. Jr., & Pennebaker, J. W. (2000). Stalking the perfect measure of self-esteem: The blind men and the elephant revisited? *Journal of Personality and Social Psychology*, 79, 631–643.

Coopersmith, S. (1967). *The antecedents of self-esteem*. San Francisco: Freeman.

Crocker, J., Luhtanen, R. K., Cooper, M. L., & Bouvrette, A. (2003). Contingencies of self-worth in college students: Theory and measurement. *Journal of Personality and Social Psychology*, 85, 894–908.

De Houwer, J. (2003). The extrinsic affective Simon task. *Experimental Psychology*, 50, 77–85.

DuBois, D., & Tevendale, H. D. (1999). Self-esteem in childhood and adolescence: Vaccine or epiphenomenon? *Applied and Preventive Psychology*, 8, 103–117.

Epstein, S. (1994). Integration of the cognitive and the psychodynamic unconscious. *American Psychologist*, 49, 709–724.

Epstein, S., & Morling, B. (1995). Is the self motivated to do more than enhance and/or verify itself? In M. H. Kernis (Ed.), *Efficacy, agency, and self-esteem* (pp. 9–30). New York: Plenum.

Farnham, S. D., Greenwald, A. G., & Banaji, M. R. (1999). Implicit self-esteem. In D. Abrams & M. A. Hogg (Eds.), *Social identity and social cognition* (pp. 230–248). Malden, MA: Blackwell Publishers.

Fazio, R. H., & Olson, M. A. (2003). Implicit measures in social cognition research: Their meaning and use. *Annual Review of Psychology*, 54, 297–327.

Fazio, R. H., & Towles-Schwen, T. (1990). The MODE model of attitude-behavior processes. In S. Chaiken & Y. Trope (Eds.), *Dual-process theories in social psychology* (pp. 97–116). New York: Guilford Press.

Gemar, M. C., Segal, Z. V., Sagrati, S., & Kennedy, S. J. (2001). Mood-induced changes in the Implicit Association Test in recovered depressed patients. *Journal of Abnormal Psychology, 110*, 282–289.

Greenwald, A. G., & Banaji, M. R. (1995). Implicit social cognition: Attitudes, self-esteem, and stereotypes. *Psychological Review, 102*, 4–27.

Greenwald, A. G., & Farnham, S. D. (2000). Using the Implicit Association Test to measure self-esteem and self-concept. *Journal of Personality and Social Psychology, 79*, 1022–1038.

Greenwald, A. G., McGhee, D. E., & Schwartz, J. L. K. (1998). Measuring individual differences in implicit cognition: The Implicit Association Test. *Journal of Personality and Social Psychology, 74*, 1464–1480.

Greenwald, A. G., Nosek, B. A., & Banaji, M. R. (2003). Understanding and using the Implicit Association Test: I. An improved scoring algorithm. *Journal of Personality and Social Psychology, 85*, 197–216.

Gregg, A. P. (2003). Optimally conceptualizing implicit self-esteem. *Psychological Inquiry, 14*, 35–38.

Hamilton, D. L. (1971). A comparative study of five methods of assessing self-esteem, dominance, and dogmatism. *Educational and Psychological Measurement, 31*, 441–452.

Heatherton, T. F., & Polivy, J. (1991). Development and validation of a scale for measuring state self-esteem. *Journal of Personality and Social Psychology, 60*, 895–910.

Helmreich, R., Stapp, J., & Ervin, C. (1974). The Texas Social Behavior Inventory (TSBI): An objective measure of self-esteem or social competence. *JSAS Catalog of Selected Documents in Psychology, 4*, 79.

Hetts, J., Sakuma, M., & Pelham, B. (1999). Two roads to positive self-regard: Implicit and explicit self-evaluation and culture. *Journal of Experimental Social Psychology, 35*, 512–559.

Janis, I. S., & Field, P. B. (1959). A behavioral assessment of persuasibility: Consistency of individual differences. In C. I. Hovland & I. L. Janis (Eds.), *Personality and persuasibility* (pp. 55–68). New Haven, CT: Yale University Press.

Jones, J. T., Pelham, B. W., Mirenberg, M. C., & Hetts, J. J. (2002). Name letter preferences are not merely mere exposure: Implicit egotism as self-regulation. *Journal of Experimental Social Psychology, 38*, 170–177.

Jordan, C. H., Spencer, S. J., Zanna, M. P., Hoshino-Browne, E., & Correll, J. (2003). Secure and defensive high self-esteem. *Journal of Personality and Social Psychology, 85*, 969–978.

Karpinski, A., & Hilton, J. L. (2001). Attitudes and the Implicit Association Test. *Journal of Personality and Social Psychology, 81*, 774–788.

Kernis, M. H. (1993). The roles of stability and level of self-esteem in psychological functioning. In R. F. Baumeister (Ed.), *Self-esteem: The puzzle of low self-regard* (pp. 167–182). New York: Plenum.

Kernis, M. H., Cornell, D. P., Sun, C. R., Berry, A. J., & Harlow, T. (1993). There's more to self-esteem than whether it is high or low: The importance of stability of self-esteem. *Journal of Personality and Social Psychology, 65*, 1190–1204.

Kitayama, S., & Karasawa, M. (1997). Implicit self-esteem in Japan: Name letters and birthday numbers. *Personality and Social Psychology Bulletin, 23*, 736–742.

Koole, S. L., & Pelham, B. W. (2003). On the nature of implicit self-esteem: The case of the name letter effect. In S. J. Spencer & S. Fein (Eds.), *Motivated social perception: The Ontario symposium* (Vol. 9, pp. 93–116). Mahwah, NJ: Lawrence Erlbaum Associates.

Marsh, H. W., & Yeung, A. S. (1999). The lability of psychological ratings: The chameleon effect in global self-esteem. *Personality and Social Psychology Bulletin, 25*, 49–64.

Mecca, A., Smelser, N., & Vasconcellos, J. (Eds.). (1989). *The social importance of self-esteem.* Berkeley, CA: University of California Press.

Murray, H. A. (1943). *Thematic Apperception test manual.* Cambridge: Harvard University Press.

Nosek, B. A., & Banaji, M. R. (2001). The Go/No-go Association Task. *Social Cognition, 19*, 625–666.

Nuttin, M. J. Jr. (1985). Narcissism beyond Gestalt and awareness: The name letter effect. *European Journal of Social Psychology, 15*, 353–361.

Olson, M. A., & Fazio, R. H. (2004). Reducing the influence of extrapersonal associations on the Implicit Association Test: Personalizing the IAT. *Journal of Personality and Social Psychology, 86*, 653–667.

Paulhus, D. L. (1986). Self-deception and impression management in test responses. In A. Angleitner & J. S. Wiggins (Eds.), *Personality assessment via questionnaire* (pp. 143–165). New York: Springer-Verlag.

Pelham, B. W., Mirenberg, M. C., & Jones, J. T. (2002). Why Susie sells seashells by the seashore: Implicit egotism and major life decisions. *Journal of Personality and Social Psychology, 82*, 469–487.

Roid, G. H., & Fitts, W. H. (1988). *Tennessee Self-Concept Scale* (Rev. manual). Los Angeles: Western Psychological Services.

Rosenberg, M. (1965). *Society and the adolescent self-image.* Princeton, NJ: Princeton University Press.

Rudman, L. A., Ashmore, R. D., & Gary, M. L. (2001). "Unlearning" automatic biases: The malleability of implicit prejudice and stereotypes. *Journal of Personality and Social Psychology, 81*, 856–868.

Schimmack, U., & Diener, E. (2003). Predictive validity of explicit and implicit self-esteem for subjective well-being. *Journal of Research in Personality, 37*, 100–106.

Schneider, D. J., & Turkat, D. (1975). Self-presentation following success or failure: Defensive self-esteem models. *Journal of Personality, 43*, 127–135.

Schwarz, N. (1999). Self-reports: How the questions shape the answers. *American Psychologist, 54*, 93–105.

Spalding, L. R., & Hardin, C. D. (1999). Unconscious unease and self-handicapping: Behavioral consequences of individual differences in implicit and explicit self-esteem. *Psychological Science, 10*, 535–539.

Tafarodi, R. W., & Swann, W. B. Jr. (2001). Two-dimensional self-esteem: Theory and measurement. *Personality and Individual Differences, 31*, 653–673.

Taylor, S. E., & Brown, J. D. (1988). Illusion and well-being: A social psychological perspective on mental health. *Psychological Bulletin, 103*, 193–210.

Wells, L. E., & Marwell, G. (1976). *Self-esteem: Its conceptualization and measurement.* Beverly Hills, CA: Sage.

12

The Assessment of Implicit and Explicit Self-Esteem: Lessons from Motive Research

RICHARD KOESTNER and GENEVIÈVE A. MAGEAU

C oming from outside of this research area, we have been struck by the almost universal suspicion that social and personality psychologists have recently voiced regarding self-report measures of self-esteem. The measures have been criticized as too global, too static, too culture-bound, too easily conflated with narcissism, too easily obscured by self-presentation and not really important to effective functioning. Other self-related personality variables, such as self-regulation, self-discrepancies, or self-determination have been put forward as alternative constructs that are more important to healthy functioning. Many researchers interested in self-esteem have shifted their attention to implicit measures such as the Implicit Association Test (Greenwald & Banaji, 1995) or the Initials Preference Task (Bosson, Swann, & Pennebaker, 2000). This field-wide consensus questioning the value of the traditional measurement of self-esteem led us to assume that there was probably little value in measuring people's self-esteem with self-report scales.

It was with surprise then that we found ourselves impressed when reading over the 10 items of the widely used Rosenberg's (1965) self-esteem scale. The items have an essential face validity that is disarming. They clearly capture the feelings of self-acceptance and self-worth that are central to a humanistic view of self-esteem (Rogers, 1951). Items such as "I feel that I am a person of worth" and "On the whole I am satisfied with myself" certainly seem to reflect the sentiments of someone with high self-esteem. One cannot but imagine that a parent or teacher would consider it important that their child or student reported positive responses to these items. Alternatively, a parent or teacher would be concerned if a child endorsed one of the reverse-scored items such as "I feel I do not have much to be proud of."

The psychometric qualities of the Rosenberg self-esteem scale (SES) also seem excellent, despite it being brief and easy to administer (Blascovich &

Tomaka, 1991). The scale is uni-factorial, with high internal consistency and good test–retest reliability. Its validity has been supported by correlations with peer reports and with other self-esteem related measures (Blascovich & Tomaka, 1991). Rosenberg self-esteem appears to function well as a marker of positive mental health. It is positively related to other well-being indicators such as life satisfaction and positive and negative affect, and it is negatively related to indicators of psychological distress (Schimmack & Diener, 2003). It has been shown to be unrelated to demographic factors such as gender, age, and marital status, and it is only moderately related to social desirability (Fleming & Courtney, 1984).

Why then is there such angst about self-report measures of self-esteem? One clear problem is that recent research has shown that some pretty disturbed individuals with rather serious personality problems, such as antisocial behavior and narcissism, often report very high levels of self-esteem (Bushman & Baumeister, 1998). Another problem is that there is evidence that people with high self-esteem sometimes behave in more maladaptive ways than those with low self-esteem. For example, after receiving ego-threatening negative feedback, people with high self-esteem have been shown to make risky and unwise choices about what level of challenge they can handle (Baumeister, Heatherton, & Tice, 1993). A third problem is that research has shown that self-esteem may serve a primarily defensive function rather than reflecting deep and stable feelings of self-worth. For example, there is evidence that when faced with mortality salience many people will inflate their estimates of self-esteem (Greenberg, Solomon, & Pyszczynski, 1997).

Despite these problems, one wonders why researchers have not concluded that self-reported self-esteem is a *generally* useful indicator of a person's subjective sense of worth and value but that it may be vulnerable to distortion in the face of extreme personality pathology or extreme situations. Such a conclusion would lead to the practical solution that in order to get a full picture of an individual's functioning, one would want to collect additional information—e.g., rule out narcissism, recent failure or mortality experiences, ensure stability over time, etc. Researchers have tended not to choose the route of supplementing self-report self-esteem measures with such ancillary measures, instead they have shifted their attention to nonreactive or implicit measures of self-esteem.

Implicit self-esteem has been defined as an automatic, over-learned, and nonconscious evaluation of the self that guides spontaneous reactions to self-relevant stimuli (Greenwald & Banaji, 1995). The most commonly used method to assess implicit self-esteem is the Implicit Association Test (IAT) (Greenwald & Farnham, 2000), which is a computerized categorization task that measures the ease with which an individual automatically associates pleasant and unpleasant words with the self (Greenwald, McGhee, & Schwartz, 1998). A tendency to quickly associate pleasant rather than unpleasant words with the self is thought to reflect high implicit self-esteem. The IAT self-esteem measure demonstrated superior reliability, stability, and predictive validity relative to other implicit measures of self-esteem (Bosson et al., 2000). Interestingly, the IAT was moderately positively correlated with the Rosenberg scale, and it mirrored the Rosenberg in predicting how raters would evaluate an essay writer's self-esteem and self-competence, whereas other implicit measures were unrelated to the Rosenberg and failed to predict raters' evaluations (Bosson et al., 2000).

The IAT self-esteem thus seems to be the most promising of the implicit self-esteem measures on psychometric grounds (there is ongoing debate regarding the IAT, cf. Karpinski, 2004), but there does seem to be general enthusiasm for response time measures of implicit self-esteem (Fazio & Olson, 2003). IAT self-esteem is marginally positively related to the Rosenberg self-esteem scale, and similarly predicts certain outcomes, but the two measures share only a small percentage of variance. The question that naturally arises then is how researchers should use these two relatively distinct measures of self-esteem. We would like to suggest that the history of work on implicit and explicit motives may serve as a useful guide for work on implicit and explicit self-esteem (Bosson et al., 2000). In the following section, we outline some insights derived from 50 years of motivation research on how to build a theory of implicit and explicit self-esteem.

Three distinct motives have received considerable attention over the previous 50 years: the need for achievement ("a recurrent concern with standards of excellence"), the need for power ("a recurrent concern with having impact or influence on others"), and the need for intimacy ("a recurrent concern with establishing warm, reciprocal relations with others"). From the earliest work in this area, researchers developed *both* implicit and self-report measures of each motive. Implicit measures were based on coding the thematic content of imaginative stories that participants told in response to ambiguous picture cues presenting achievement or social scenes. The coding systems were derived by arousing a particular motive (e.g., a convivial party for need for intimacy) and then comparing the stories written under aroused conditions with those written under neutral conditions (e.g., a classroom setting). The coding systems were objective and high levels of inter-rater reliability could be attained after a brief training period.

The early motive researchers did not expect the implicit and self-report measures of motives to be related to each other, or to predict similar outcomes. Indeed, McClelland (1951) conceptualized personality as consisting of three major systems, traits, motives, and schemas, and he believed that self-report measures of motives actually belonged in the category of a schema. That is, the self-report motive measures reflected how people thought about themselves rather than how they naturally and spontaneously organized their thoughts in relation to goals and incentives. A critical early study demonstrated that the implicit and explicit measures of achievement motivation were uncorrelated and predicted entirely different sets of outcomes (deCharms, Morrison, Reitman, & McClelland, 1955). Explicit achievement motivation was associated with being influenced by expert opinions whereas implicit achievement was associated with better performance on tasks that involved internalized standards of excellence. Many subsequent studies have confirmed that explicit and implicit motives predict different outcomes (Koestner, Weinberger, & McClelland, 1991; Woike, Gershkovich, Piorkowski, & Polo, 1999).

Despite the early evidence that implicit and explicit motives were independent and could both contribute to explaining behavior, motivation research became dominated by questions regarding the psychometric credentials of the implicit measures, repeated attempts to design valid self-report measures, and arguments about which type of measure displayed greater predictive validity.

This long-running implicit versus explicit debate was finally "resolved" in 1989 when McClelland restated his earlier view that it should be possible to build a more comprehensive theory of behavior by including *both* implicit and explicit measures of the three motives (McClelland, Koestner, & Weinberger, 1989). The following five central points were made:

1. Implicit and explicit motives represent different levels of personality and their measures will typically be uncorrelated with each other.
2. Implicit and explicit motives will each importantly influence behavior (and knowing about both of them is better than knowing about only one of them).
3. Implicit and explicit motives will predict different kinds of outcomes with implicit motives predicting spontaneous, self-initiated patterns of behavior over time whereas explicit motives predicting response tendencies in particular social situations.
4. Implicit and explicit motives are responsive to distinct sets of environmental stimuli (i.e., activity incentives such as challenge level for the implicit motive and social incentives such as whether a task is described as achievement-relevant for the explicit motive).
5. Implicit and explicit motives have distinct developmental histories with the key formative era for implicit motives being the first two years of life and the key era for explicit motives being middle childhood.

How is this history of implicit and explicit motives relevant to current work on self-esteem? We think there are three parallels for self-esteem research that have already become evident. First, one could have predicted that the implicit measures would come under attack because their psychometric qualities pale in comparison to those of self-report scales. (David McClelland was always dubious of the high reliability of self-report scales which he felt were based on asking redundant questions to participants who felt compelled to respond consistently.) Second, one could have predicted that many researchers would become discouraged by the fact that implicit and explicit measures were uncorrelated and predicted different outcomes. (The absence of a positive correlation between self-report and implicit measures of the achievement motive was central to Entwisle's (1972) influential critique of motive research.) Third, it could have been predicted that researchers would respond to this situation by spawning additional implicit and explicit measures.

What would someone schooled in the motive literature advise regarding future work on implicit and explicit self-esteem? The following four key points stand out:

1. Researchers should settle on the implicit measure that seems to have the best psychometric credentials (but recognize that no implicit measure will ever attain the same levels of reliability as explicit self-report scales).

2. Researchers should be untroubled by the lack of relation between implicit and explicit measures.
3. Researchers should work to identify the class of outcomes that are uniquely associated with implicit and explicit self-esteem.
4. Researchers should outline the distinctive situational and developmental factors that impact on implicit and explicit self-esteem.

Above all, self-esteem researchers would do well to avoid becoming mired in a debate regarding which type of measure is better. Instead, they should celebrate the fact that self-esteem can be assessed at both an implicit and explicit level and be inspired to build a complex, multilevel theory of self-esteem that can take its place amidst other recent comprehensive, multilevel conceptualizations of personality (McAdams, 1995, 2001; Sheldon, 2004).

REFERENCES

Baumeister, R. F., Heatherton, T. F., & Tice, D. M. (1993). When ego threats lead to self-regulation failure: Negative consequences of high self-esteem. *Journal of Personality & Social Psychology, 64*, 141–156.

Blascovich, J., & Tomaka, J. (1991). Measures of self esteem. In J. L. Robinson, P. R. Shaver, & L. S. Wrightsman (Eds.), *Measures of personality and social psychological attitudes* (Vol. 1, pp. 115–160). New York: Academic Press.

Bosson, J. K., Swann, W. B. Jr., & Pennebaker, J. W. (2000). Stalking the perfect measure of implicit self-esteem: The blind men and the elephant revisited? *Journal of Personality & Social Psychology, 79*, 631–643.

Bushman, B. J., & Baumeister, R. F. (1998). Threatened egotism, narcissism, self-esteem, and direct and displaced aggression: Does self-love or self-hate lead to violence? *Journal of Personality & Social Psychology, 75*, 219–229.

deCharms, R., Morrison, H. W., Reitman, W. R., & McClelland, D. C. (1955). Behavioral correlates of directly and indirectly measured achievement motivation. In D. C. McClelland (Ed.), *Studies in motivation* (pp. 414–423). New York: Appleton-Century-Crofts.

Entwisle, D. R. (1972). To dispel fantasies about fantasy-based measures of achievement motivation. *Psychological Bulletin, 77*, 377–391.

Fazio, R. H., & Olson, M. A. (2003). Implicit measures in social cognition research. Their meaning and uses. *Annual Review of Psychology, 54*, 297–327.

Fleming, J. S., & Courtney, B. E. (1984). The dimensionality of self-esteem. *Journal of Personality and Social Psychology, 39*, 921–929.

Greenberg, J., Solomon, S., & Pyszczynski, T. (1997). Terror management theory of self-esteem and cultural worldviews: Empirical assessments and conceptual refinements. *Advances in Experimental Social Psychology, 29*, 61–136.

Greenwald, A. G., & Banaji, M. R.(1995). Implicit social cognition: Attitudes, self-esteem, and stereotypes. *Psychological Review, 102*, 4–27.

Greenwald, A. G., & Farnham, S. D. (2000). Using the implicit association test to measure self-esteem and self-concept. *Journal of Personality and Social Psychology, 79*, 1022–1038.

Greenwald, A. G., McGhee, D. E., & Schwartz, J. L. K. (1998). Measuring individual differences in implicit cognition: The implicit association test. *Journal of Personality and Social Psychology, 74*, 1464–1480.

Karpinski, A. (2004). Measuring self-esteem using the Implicit Association Test: The role of the other. *Personality and Social Psychology Bulletin, 30*, 22–34.

Koestner, R., Weinberger, J., & McClelland, D. C. (1991). Task-intrinsic and social extrinsic sources of arousal for motives assessed in fantasy and self-report. *Journal of Personality, 59*, 57–82.

McAdams, Dan P. (1995). What do we know when we know a person? *Journal of Personality, 63*, 365–396.

McAdams, Dan P. (2001). *The person: An integrated introduction to personality psychology.* New York: Harcourt-Brace.

McClelland, D. C. (1951). *Personality.* New York: Sloane.

McClelland, D. C., Koestner, R., & Weinberger, J. (1989). How do self-attributed and implicit motives differ? *Psychological Review, 96*, 690–702.

Rogers, C. (1951). *Client-centered therapy.* Boston: Houghton-Mifflin.

Rosenberg, M. (1965). *Society and the adolescent self-image.* Princeton, NJ: Princeton University Press.

Schimmack, U., & Diener, E. (2003). Predictive validity of explicit and implicit self-esteem for subjective well being. *Journal of Research in Personality, 37*, 100–106.

Sheldon, K. M. (2004). *Optimal human being: An integrated multi-level perspective.* Mahwah, NJ: Laurence Erlbaum Associates.

Woike, B., Gershkovich, I., Piorkowski, R., & Polo, M. (1999). The role of motives in the content and structure of autobiographical memory. *Journal of Personality & Social Psychology, 76*, 600–612.

13

Implicit and Explicit Self-Esteem: Theoretical and Methodological Refinements

ANDREW KARPINSKI and JENNIFER A. STEINBERG

S elf-esteem has been an integral concept in social psychological research since the writings of William James in 1890. *Explicit self-esteem* has been conceptualized as a conscious, reasoned self-evaluation of global self-worth and has been assessed traditionally using direct, self-report procedures (see Coopersmith, 1967; Rosenberg, 1965; Taladori & Swann, 2001). Research relying on *direct measures of self-esteem* has been fruitful, and a large body of knowledge has accumulated regarding the nature, function, and conse-quences of explicit self-esteem (see Baumeister, 1998; Brown, 1998; Leary & Baumeister, 2000; Sedikides & Stroebe, 1997). These measures have several important strengths that contribute to their frequent use, including their ease of administration and their excellent psychometric properties (Rosenberg, 1979).

Increasingly, however, there has been a growing awareness of the limitations of direct measures of self-esteem, with a focus on two main weaknesses. First, direct measures of self-esteem are susceptible to self-report and self-presenta-tional biases. For example, explicit self-esteem, as assessed by direct measures, has been found to correlate with self-presentation, impression management, and self-deception (Lindeman & Verkasalo, 1995; Wells & Marwell, 1976). Second, because direct measures of self-esteem rely on a conscious, self-report of self-esteem, they are unable to capture aspects of individuals' self-beliefs that reside outside of conscious awareness (Greenwald & Banaji, 1995). This omis-sion is particularly problematic for clinical research, given that many of the dysfunctional self-attitudes and self-schemata thought to play a crucial role in the development of psychopathology are conceptualized as operating outside of conscious awareness (Beck, 1967; Clark, Beck, & Alfort, 1999; De Houwer, 2002).

ALTERNATIVE CONCEPTUALIZATIONS AND MEASURES OF SELF-ESTEEM

Researchers have hypothesized the existence of implicit self-esteem, or aspects of self-esteem that operate outside of conscious awareness and control (Greenwald & Banaji, 1995). Theoretically, there has been some ambiguity regarding the definition of implicit self-esteem, which has derived, in part, from differences among the measures developed to assess this construct. We define *implicit self-esteem* as the strength of evaluative self-associations, which operate in a relatively automatic fashion, outside of conscious awareness (see also Dijksterhuis, 2004). *Association-based measures of self-esteem* directly assess the strength of these evaluative self-associations or the associations that are automatically activated by the self.

The literature on self-esteem measurement has focused on the distinction between direct and association-based measures. However, there is a third class of self-esteem measures that does not fit the definition of either direct or association-based measures. These *indirect measures of self-esteem* do not directly ask an individual for a conscious, self-report of self-esteem, nor do they directly measure automatic, evaluative self-associations. Indirect measures of self-esteem are hybrid measures that may assess implicit self-esteem, explicit self-esteem, or some combination of the two.

The precise definitions of explicit and implicit self-esteem and the measures designed to assess them will allow for greater precision in hypothesis testing and will provide a framework for classifying the growing body of self-esteem measures (see Figure 13.1). For example, there has been debate about the relationship between implicit and explicit self-esteem. Are they distinct theoretical constructs or are they just separate definitions of the same underlying self-esteem construct? Our model allows for a relationship between explicit and implicit self-esteem, as it seems unlikely that one's conscious evaluation of global self-worth is completely independent from one's automatic evaluative self-associations (see also Cunningham, Preacher, & Banaji, 2001). However, as a result of poorly defined theoretical constructs, blurred boundaries between association-based and indirect measures, and the use of measures with poor psychometric properties, the relationship between implicit and explicit self-esteem remains elusive. In order to test

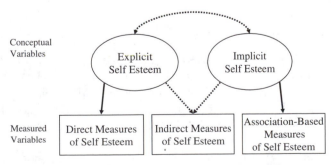

FIGURE 13.1   The relationship between conceptual and measured variables of self-esteem.

this and other theoretical research questions regarding implicit and explicit self-esteem, reliable and valid measures are necessary.

CURRENTLY USED ASSOCIATION-BASED AND INDIRECT MEASURES OF SELF-ESTEEM

Association-Based Measures

Social psychologists have developed a number of association-based measures of self-esteem, including variations of priming-based measures (Hetts, Sakuma, & Pelham, 1999; Spalding & Hardin, 2000) and the self-other Implicit Association Test (Greenwald & Farnham, 2000). These measures directly assess the automatic evaluative associations with the self.

Priming-based measures assess the evaluative information that is automatically activated by the self. In a typical priming paradigm, participants are presented with self-relevant stimuli (either subliminally or superliminally) followed by a positive or negative target word, which participants are instructed to categorize as quickly as possible. A priming-based measure of self-esteem assesses the extent to which self-stimuli facilitate or inhibit the identification of positive compared to negative stimuli. As is often the case with priming-based measures of attitudes, priming-based measures of self-esteem have typically displayed poor internal consistency and test–retest reliability (see Bosson, Swann, & Pennebaker, 2000). Poor psychometric properties and weak construct validity have likely contributed to the infrequent use of priming-based measures by self-esteem researchers.

The self-other IAT measures the relative strength of the positive and negative associations that a person has with the self compared with others. Among the association-based measures of self-esteem, only the self-other IAT has demonstrated adequate levels of reliability (Bosson et al., 2000). However, the self-other IAT is not a pure measure of *self*-associations; it assesses the relative strength of the positive and negative associations that a person has with the self *and* with others. A self-other IAT score reveals as much about the strength of one's other-associations as it does about one's self-associations (Karpinski, 2004a). Thus, there is a need for an association-based measure of self-esteem that assesses participants' *self*-associations, exclusively.

Indirect Measures

The most prominent indirect measure of self-esteem is the name-letter task, in which participants rate the degree that they like the letters of the alphabet. The name-letter effect measures the extent to which individuals like letters in their own name (particularly their initials) more than other people like those letters (Greenwald & Banaji, 1995; Koole, Dijksterhuis, & van Knippenberg, 2001; Nuttin, 1985, 1987). The tendency to prefer one's initials may be viewed as one instance of Thorndike's (1920) halo effect, in which the judgment of an attribute (in this case, initials) is influenced by the judgment of a seemingly irrelevant attribute (the self). Psychometrically, the name-letter effect has yielded respectable findings, with modest internal consistency and stability over one month (Bosson et al., 2000; Koole et al., 2001). Given that the name-letter task does not directly measure self-associations, nor provide a direct, self-report measure of self-esteem, it is an indirect measure of self-esteem. The available evidence suggests that the name-letter task captures aspects of both implicit and explicit self-esteem. In general, responses on the name-letter task correlate more strongly with direct measures than with implicit measures of self-esteem (Bosson et al., 2000; Jones, Pelham, Mirenberg, & Hetts, 2002), suggesting that the name-letter effect may capture aspects of the explicit self-esteem construct. At the same time, the name-letter effect is affected by cognitive processes outside of conscious awareness and control (Koole et al., 2001), suggesting that it may also capture aspects of the implicit self-esteem construct. Nevertheless, important questions remain regarding the name-letter effect. First, how can the name-letter effect be measured more reliably, on par with direct measures of self-esteem? Second, to what degree is the name-letter effect influenced by implicit self-esteem, relative to explicit self-esteem?

Although the name-letter effect has desirable qualities as an indirect measure of self-esteem, the model we have presented (see Figure 13.1) suggests that no one measure of self-esteem is completely adequate. Self-esteem is a multi-faceted construct that requires many types of measures to fully capture its complexity. In the following sections, we review two recently developed measures that assess different aspects of self-esteem. First, the Single Category Association Test (SCAT; Karpinski & Steinman, 2005) is a modified version of the IAT that measures the strength of positive and negative associations with a single attitude object (the self, in this case), providing an *association-based measure* of self-esteem. Second, the Breadth-based Adjective Rating Task (BART; Karpinski, Versek, & Steinberg, 2004) capitalizes on a linguistic bias to indirectly assess expectations regarding the self. This latter technique yields an *indirect measure* of self-esteem.

THE SELF-SCAT AS AN ASSOCIATION-BASED MEASURE OF SELF-ESTEEM

Based on the conceptual definitions provided, an association-based measure of self-esteem ought to measure automatic evaluative associations with the self. Thus far, none of the reliable, commonly used measures of self-esteem fit this definition. The self-other IAT comes closest to this ideal, but evidence suggests that other-associations contaminate its measurement of *self*-associations (Karpinski, 2004a). The self-SCAT is a modified version of the IAT that was developed to measure self-associations, exclusively.

The self-SCAT is a two-stage task. In each stage, participants categorize target words as being good, bad, or self-related. The self-words used for this task include the participant's first and last name, as well as personal pronouns (I, me, myself). In the first stage, good words and self-words are categorized on one response key and bad words on a different key (self + good). In the second stage, bad words and self-words are categorized on one response key and good words on a different key (self + bad). The mean response latency for all target words in the self + good block is subtracted from the mean response latency for all target words in the self + bad block, providing a measure of the strength of individuals' evaluative associations with the self (for additional details, see Karpinski & Steinman, 2005).

In order for the self-SCAT to be of use, it must be a reliable measure of implicit self-esteem. To examine its reliability, we had 34 female participants complete a self-SCAT. Twenty-seven participants returned one week later and completed the measure again. The self-SCAT displayed excellent levels of internal consistency ($\alpha = .75$). In addition, the test–retest reliability of the self-SCAT was acceptable, although somewhat low, $r (26) = .54$. These data provide some preliminary evidence for the reliability of the self-SCAT.

Karpinski and Steinman (2004; Study 2) examined the relationships between the self-SCAT, a self-other IAT, and explicit measures of self-esteem. Overall, participants had high self-esteem on the explicit measures (values of $d \geq 1.35$), on the self-SCAT ($d = 1.13$), and on the self-other IAT ($d = 1.84$). We have speculated that explicit and implicit self-esteem are, at least, modestly correlated. Following this reasoning, if the self-SCAT is an improved measure of implicit self-esteem over the self-other IAT, then it should evidence stronger correlations with measures of explicit self-esteem, when compared to the self-other IAT. As predicted, the self-SCAT correlated significantly and positively with the explicit measure of self-esteem, $r (42) = .33, p = .04$, whereas the self-other IAT failed to correlate with the explicit measure of self-esteem, $r (42) = .07, p = .67$. Interestingly, self-SCAT and self-other IAT scores were uncorrelated, $r (50) = .19, p = .18$, providing indirect empirical support for the contaminating effect of other-associations on self-other IAT scores.

The self-SCAT was designed to measure the self-associations that constitute implicit self-esteem. Empirically, these findings provide some initial evidence that the self-SCAT has the reliability and validity necessary to be considered a viable, association-based measure of self-esteem.

THE SELF-BART AS AN INDIRECT MEASURE OF SELF-ESTEEM

One approach to indirectly measuring explicit self-esteem is to take advantage of the overlap between one's conscious self-evaluations and one's self-expectations. A task that assesses an individual's expectations about the self could be used as an indirect measure of his or her explicit self-evaluation. The self-BART was developed to reveal the same information as explicit measures of self-esteem, while being less affected by self-presentational concerns.

People tend to describe expectancy consistent information at a higher level of abstraction than expectancy inconsistent information (Maass, Milesi, Zabbini, & Stahlberg, 1995; Wigboldus, Semin, & Spears, 2000). The breadth of a trait adjective provides a measure of linguistic abstraction by quantifying the number of behaviors subsumed by that adjective (Hampson, John, & Goldberg, 1987). In accordance with their tendency for positive self-expectations, high self-esteem individuals tend to describe themselves with broad positive and narrow negative traits. Conversely, low self-esteem individuals tend to describe themselves with narrow positive and broad negative traits (Karpinski, 2004b). The self-BART quantifies this expectancy bias. In this task, participants rate the degree to which 144 trait adjectives, known to vary by breadth and valence, are descriptive of them. An overall self-BART score is obtained by summing the ratings of the narrow positive and broad negative traits and subtracting this sum from the ratings of the broad positive and narrow negative traits (for additional details, see Karpinski et al., 2004). The self-BART provides an indirect measure of self-esteem by assessing the self-expectation revealed in participants' adjective use.

The results of the three studies provide initial support for the reliability and validity of the self-BART as an indirect measure of explicit self-esteem (Karpinski et al., 2004). First, the self-BART displayed reasonable levels of stability over time. Although the test–retest reliability of the self-BART over a 4-week interval ($r = .64$) was somewhat low in comparison to direct measures of explicit self-esteem, it was in the range of reliabilities typically observed for indirect and implicit measures of self-esteem (see Bosson et al., 2000). A second important indicator of the self-BART's validity is its relationship with direct measures of explicit self-esteem. As predicted, the self-BART correlated significantly and positively with a composite of three direct measures of self-esteem in two independent samples, $r (58) = .29$, $p = .02$ and $r (132) = .30$, $p < .01$. Third, an indirect measure of self-esteem ought to be less sensitive to self-presentational concerns than direct measures of explicit self-esteem. The Balanced Inventory of Desirable Responding (BIDR; Paulhus, 1991) was included to assess participants' tendencies to present themselves favorably. As expected, whereas the self-BART was unrelated to BIDR scores, $r (132) = 0.04$, $p = .87$, a relatively strong positive relationship was observed between explicit measures of self-esteem and BIDR scores, $r (132) = 0.32$, $p < .01$. Finally, numerous studies have found a negative relationship between current levels of explicit self-esteem and depression (for example, see Roberts & Monroe, 1994). Thus, the self-BART ought to correlate with measures of depression. Supporting its validity, the self-BART showed the expected correlation with the Beck Depression Inventory [Beck, Ward, Mendelson, Mock, & Erbaugh (1961); $r (131) = -.22$, $p = .01$].

The self-BART was developed as an indirect measure of self-esteem. Again, research on this measure is in the early stages and there are many questions about the self-BART that have not been addressed. However, the results from the three studies reviewed provide support for the reliability and validity of the self-BART as a measure of self-esteem.

CONCLUSIONS

Since the quintessential review by Greenwald and Banaji (1995), researchers have acknowledged the need for alternatives to direct measures of explicit self-esteem. We have presented a framework for dividing measures of self-esteem into three categories: direct, indirect, and association-based. Based on the data we have reviewed, we can conclude that the self-SCAT has considerable potential as an association-based measure of self-esteem, and the self-BART and name-letter task are promising indirect measures of self-esteem.

Our analysis suggests that different measures of self-esteem may assess different aspects of the self-esteem construct. Given that multiple measures are necessary to capture the complexity of self-esteem, it is vital for researchers to continue developing new measures like the self-SCAT and the self-BART. With multiple measures assessing different aspects of self-esteem, we will likely discover that different measures are more or less useful depending on the situation. It is vital to ensure that measures of self-esteem have a strong theoretical foundation and are as reliable and valid as possible. Only then can theoretical models about implicit and explicit self-esteem be tested.

REFERENCES

Baumeister, R. F. (1998). The self. In D. T. Gilbert, S. T. Fiske, & G. Lindzey (Eds.), *The handbook of social psychology* (4th ed., pp. 680–740). Boston: McGraw-Hill.

Beck, A. T. (1967). *Depression: Clinical, experimental, and theoretical aspects*. New York: Harper & Row.

Beck, A. T., Ward, C. H., Mendelson, M., Mock, J., & Erbaugh, J. (1961). An inventory for measuring depression. *Archives of General Psychiatry, 4*, 561–571.

Bosson, J. K., Swann, W. B., & Pennebaker, J. W. (2000). Stalking the perfect measure of implicit self-esteem: The blind men and the elephant revisited? *Journal of Personality and Social Psychology, 79*, 631–643.

Brown, J. D. (1998). *The self*. New York: McGraw-Hill.

Clark, D. A., Beck, A. T., & Alford, B. A. (1999). *Scientific foundations of cognitive theory and therapy of depression*. New York: Wiley.

Coopersmith, S. (1967). *The antecedents of self-esteem*. San Francisco: W. H. Freeman.

Cunningham, W. A., Preacher, K. J., & Banaji, M. R. (2001). Implicit attitude measures: Consistency, stability, and convergent validity. *Psychological Science, 12*, 163–170.

De Houwer, J. (2002). The Implicit Association Test as a tool for studying dysfunctional associations in psychopathology: Strengths and limitations. *Journal of Behavior Therapy, 33*, 115–133.

Dijksterhuis, A. (2004). I like myself but I don't know why: Enhancing implicit self-esteem by subliminal evaluative conditioning. *Journal of Personality and Social Psychology, 86*, 345–355.

Greenwald, A. G., & Banaji, M. R. (1995). Implicit social cognition: Attitudes, self-esteem, and stereotypes. *Psychological Review, 102*, 4–27.

Greenwald, A. G., & Farnham, S. D. (2000). Using the Implicit Association Test to measure self-esteem and self-concept. *Journal of Personality and Social Psychology, 79*, 1022–1038.

Hampson, S. E., John, O. P., & Goldberg, L. R. (1987). Category-breadth and social desirability values for 573 personality terms. *European Journal of Personality, 1*, 37–54.

Hetts, J. J., Sakuma, M., & Pelham, B. W. (1999). Two roads to positive self-regard: Implicit and explicit self-evaluation and culture. *Journal of Experimental Social Psychology, 35*, 512–559.

James, W. (1890). *The principles of psychology*. Cambridge, MA: Harvard University Press.

Jones, J. T., Pelham, B. W., Mirenberg, M. C., & Hetts, J. J. (2002). Name-letter preferences are not merely a matter of mere exposure: Implicit egotism as self-enhancement. *Journal of Experimental Social Psychology, 38*, 170–177.

Karpinski, A. (2004a). Measuring self-esteem using the Implicit Association Test: The role of the other. *Personality and Social Psychology Bulletin, 30*, 22–34.

Karpinski, A. (2004b). *The language of self-esteem: An adjective-based breadth-bias and its role in self-esteem maintenance.* Unpublished manuscript.

Karpinski, A. & Steinman, R. B. (2005). *The Single Category Association Test as a Measure of Implicit Attitudes.* Paper presented at the sixth annual conference of the Society for Personality and Social Psychology, New Orleans, LA.

Karpinski, A., Versek, B., & Steinberg, J. (2004). *The Breadth-based Adjective Rating Task (BART) as an indirect measure of self-esteem.* Paper presented at the fifth annual conference of the Society for Personality and Social Psychology, Austin, TX.

Koole, S. L., Dijksterhuis, A., & van Knippenberg, A. (2001). What's in a name: Implicit self-esteem and the automatic self. *Journal of Personality and Social Psychology, 80*, 669–685.

Leary, M. R., & Baumeister, R. F. (2000). The nature and function of self-esteem: Sociometer theory. In M. P. Zanna (Ed.), *Advances in experimental social psychology* (Vol. 32, pp. 1–62). New York: Academic Press.

Lindeman, M., & Verkasalo, M. (1995). Personality, situation, and positive-negative asymmetry in socially desirable responding. *European Journal of Personality, 9*, 125–134.

Maass, A., Milesi, A., Zabbini, S., & Stahlberg, D. (1995). Linguistic intergroup bias: Differential expectancies or in-group protection? *Journal of Personality and Social Psychology, 68*, 116–126.

Nuttin, J. M. (1985). Narcissism beyond Gestalt awareness: The name letter effect. *European Journal of Social Psychology, 15*, 353–361.

Nuttin, J. M. (1987). Affective consequences of mere ownership: The name-letter effect in twelve European languages. *European Journal of Social Psychology, 17*, 381–402.

Paulhus, D. L. (1991). Measurement and control of response bias. In J. P. Robinson, P. R. Shaver, & L. S. Wrightsman (Eds.), *Measures of personality and social psychological attitudes* (pp. 17–59). New York: Academic Press.

Rosenberg, M. (1965). *Society and the adolescent self-image.* Princeton, NJ: Princeton University Press.

Rosenberg, M. (1979). *Conceiving the self.* New York: Basic Books.

Sedikides, C., & Stroebe, M. J. (1997). Self-evaluation: To thine own self be good, to thine own self be sure, to thine own self be true, to thine own self be better. In M. P. Zanna (Ed.), *Advances in experimental social psychology* (Vol. 29, pp. 209–269). New York: Academic Press.

Spalding, L. R., & Hardin, C. D. (2000). Unconscious unease and self-handicapping: Behavioral consequences of individual differences in implicit and explicit self-esteem. *Psychological Science, 10*, 535–539.

Taladori, R. W., & Swann, W. B. (2001). Two-dimensional self-esteem: Theory and measurement. *Personality and Individual Differences, 31*, 653–673.

Thorndike, E. L. (1920). A constant error in psychological ratings. *Journal of Applied Psychology, 4*, 25–29.

Wells, L. E., & Marwell, G. (1976). *Self-esteem: Its conceptualization and measurement.* Beverly Hills, CA: Sage.

Wigboldus, D. H. J., Semin, G. R., & Spears, R. (2000). How do we communicate stereotypes? Linguistic biases and inferential consequences. *Journal of Personality and Social Psychology, 78*, 5–18.

14

Moral Value, Agency, and the Measurement of Self-Esteem

ROMIN W. TAFARODI and CAROLINE HO

When we ask others how much they value themselves, we are hoping to share a gaze in their private mental mirrors—the contents and color of their self-consciousness. Inferences about a person's self-esteem are therefore inferences about an intentional stance, or inner experience, that is expressed to us in the form of publicly observable behavior. To the canny observer, one's demeanor, preferences, decisions, written and spoken words, and other actions all betray a particular valuation of the self, although the connection is never certain. Measurement, or formal and theoretically grounded observation of self-esteem is no less inferential and no less contestable. Seen in this light, all measurement of self-esteem is *implicit*: The hidden subjectivity of another person is merely indicated or implied in their voluntary and involuntary behavior, be it utterances, scale ratings, response times, skin conductance, or cerebral blood flow. This recognition contrasts with the current penchant for describing as "implicit" only those measures that do not involve the person's awareness of the relation of the behavior to the attitude being measured (see Fazio & Olson, 2003).

The most direct indicators of self-esteem are avowals about oneself. The predicates that are linked to the symbolic representation of self in speech and writing, if sincere, give others a nuanced understanding of how we feel about ourselves. For example, when grunge musician Kurt Cobain described himself as a "miserable, self-destructive, death rocker" in his suicide note of 1994, he gave unequivocal voice to the self-loathing that both fueled his career and ensured its brevity. Heavyweight boxer Muhammad Ali's announcement to the world in 1962 of "I am the greatest!" left it equally clear how he felt about himself.

Measurement requires standardization, which is most easily accomplished in relation to avowals by relying on fixed questions rather than spontaneous statements. This has been the primary approach to self-esteem testing since the publication 58 years ago of the first self-esteem instrument (Raimy, 1948). Direct-question self-esteem measures require respondents to indicate the extent to which they agree with first- or second-person statements reflecting positive and negative valuative stances toward the self. Such statements may capture an overall stance (e.g., *I feel good about myself; You are unworthy*) or a more specific belief, attitude, or tendency assumed to be strongly associated with the overall stance (e.g., *You feel good about your appearance; I am an unworthy father; I really hate myself when I make mistakes at work*). Graded or categorical agreement is averaged across statements in a weighted or unweighted manner to form a single score or several domain-specific subscores (often hierarchically related). These scores are used as quantitative indices of self-esteem. Although scores created in this way are rarely if ever confirmed as anything more than ordinal in metric meaning, they are treated as interval scales for purposes of statistical analysis. Popular examples include Rosenberg's (1965) Self-Esteem Scale (SES), Coopersmith's (1967) Self-Esteem Inventory, and Janis and Field's (1959) Feelings of Inadequacy Scale. Of these, the SES has been the most widely used in psychology and it continues to be the instrument preferred by most self-esteem researchers. The factor structure of the SES, however, alerts us that there are in fact two distinct forms of personal value that we all experience. These two forms are best understood as the fundamental axes or dimensions of self-esteem.

TWO-DIMENSIONAL SELF-ESTEEM

Morris Rosenberg designed the 10-item SES as a unidimensional Guttman scale with "contrived" or combined responses yielding a final 7-point scale. This economy fit with his view of the individual's "global self-esteem" as "a generally favorable or unfavorable, positive or negative, pro or con feeling toward himself as a whole" (1979, p. 21). However, when researchers switched to using the SES items with standard 5- or 7-point Likert rating scales and simply summing the 10 ratings, it became evident that at least two factors commingled within the ostensibly unidimensional measure. A review of these structural analyses, and their mixed results and interpretations, is beyond the scope of this brief chapter (see Tafarodi & Milne, 2002, for a detailed discussion). Our own interpretation of the findings, one supported by confirmatory factor analyses and tests of divergent predictive validity (e.g., Tafarodi & Milne, 2002; Tafarodi & Swann, 1995), is that SES items such as *I take a positive attitude toward myself* reflect a different type of valuation than do items such as *I am able to do things as well as most other people*. The first is founded on consideration of one's own moral significance, the second on the experience of personal power or efficacy. Both types of valuation are integral to global self-esteem, which consists of nothing more or less than their composite.

The two-dimensional approach to understanding and measuring self-esteem is premised on the duality of persons as social objects and agents. As social objects, we hold moral significance to ourselves and others; as agents, we exert influence upon the world according to our plans, and sometimes in spite of them. Moral consideration pertains to character or disposition and trades on discriminations of good and bad, credit and blame, virtue and vice, attraction and repulsion. When each of us look into the mirror, we see reflected back a *person*, not a thing. Only persons can serve as proper moral objects. However much we may like or dislike a cat, dog, or horse, and feel satisfied or dissatisfied with it, we cannot exalt or condemn it in the way we do ourselves and others. In those instances where we appear to do so, we are merely engaging in anthropomorphic projection.

The ability to apprehend ourselves as moral objects follows from the internalization of the perspective of the other, a developmental transition that splits our consciousness and endows us with the reflexive awareness that is the signal feature of the human mind. This cognitive achievement provides the basis for pride and shame, righteousness and guilt, self-satisfaction and self-criticism—all these being expressions of a fully-fledged moral orientation toward oneself. To value ourselves means to take a moral stance toward ourselves and to see our attributes and actions as worthy or unworthy of the standards and ideals that we individually hold as good, right, and beautiful. What we are describing here is a thoroughly socialized conception of personal value. There is, however, more to self-esteem than that. We are more than mental microcosms of our societies. The difference lies in our agency, our capacity for willed action and the biologically rooted satisfaction that derives from it.

When we act upon the world with purpose, we do so out of desire. The ends of our desires are our goals, mundane and grandiose. At times, actions are their own goals, as is true for the child who idly flings stones into the sea with no target or particular consequence in mind. In such cases, the normal execution of the action carries its own reward—it is inherently gratifying. More typically, however, it is fulfillment of the intended goal that satisfies the desire and provides us with pleasure. Whether our intention was to scale Mount Everest, conquer the armies of a continent, or simply cross the street or stay awake at the wheel, the recognition that we did so is immediately satisfying. Of course, the pleasure may be too subtle and habitual to capture our attention in the case of especially mundane goals. The unmistakable joy of the youngster after her first bicycle ride without training wheels is as unmistakably absent in the 30-year-old bicycle courier who crisscrosses the city each day. This does not mean, however, that basic riding ability plays no role in sustaining the courier's normal sense of efficacy and competence. Take away these unremarkable and uncelebrated skills—through illness, accident, or old age—and the connection becomes painfully clear. How, then, does the subjective experience of agency relate to self-esteem?

Successful action or efficacy leaves a double imprint on self-consciousness. First, the primitive, visceral satisfaction of affecting the world according to one's intentions imbues our situational self-awareness with a positive tone that can be described variously as feeling strong, healthy, robust, effective, powerful, capable, and competent. The result is an immediate and relatively nonreflective inflation of the self. This initial inflation requires only a casual level of self-awareness, not a deeper consideration of the symbolic meaning of the action for one's identity. Upon further reflection, however, the moral significance of the action is taken into account, leaving a second, distinct imprint on self-consciousness in terms of the "goodness" or "badness" of the action and, by extension, the goodness or badness of oneself. This secondary elaboration, the moralization of the action, explains how the outcomes of our efforts come to directly influence that part of personal value that is rooted in consideration of our character and social significance.

The initial imprint, involving the reflexive gratification of what White (1959) called "effectance" and its diffusion into self-awareness, qualifies as a separate source and form of self-esteem. This is the valuative representation of one's own agency, which exists alongside the representation of one's own moral quality. Elsewhere, one of us has referred to the first as *self-competence* and the second as *self-liking*. Together, they constitute what it typically understood as global or general self-esteem. Each dimension, considered as a personality trait, represents the synthetic abstraction of a lifetime of experience and action. In this sense, self-competence and self-liking are the twin valuative themes in our ongoing personal narrative. They reflect how strong and able we believe we are and where we think we stand in relation to the good. Clearly, the two themes are highly interdependent and therefore highly correlated. Competence easily takes on moral significance and accepting oneself as a good and worthy person has profound consequences for one's engagement with the world and the development of abilities and skills. Even so, it is important to recognize and appreciate the essential duality of self-esteem. There are many instances of dissociation between the efficacy and moral significance of an act or a person. For example, the thrill of power that comes from successful wrongdoing is often followed by crushing regret and guilt, just as the inability to overcome a moral scruple when it is adaptive to do so may leave one feeling weak and inept yet pure of character. Similarly, we all know those who are conspicuous for their ability to adore themselves in spite of obvious and admitted incompetence, and those who despise themselves in spite of marvelous talents and achievements (Tafarodi, 1998; Tafarodi, Tam, & Milne, 2001).

MEASURING SELF-COMPETENCE AND SELF-LIKING

If we are to take seriously the above phenomenal analysis of personal value, we need to ensure that our instruments capture the duality of what we are aiming to measure. It is somewhat ironic that the most popular measure of global self-esteem, Rosenberg's SES, appears to betray the intentions of its author by pointing to this very duality. This highlights the need to formally and explicitly distinguish between self-competence and self-liking in our measures. The separation will allow us to examine the unique and interactive associations of the two dimensions with variables of interest. This strategy will lead to more refined models of how self-esteem emerges and develops as an aspect of self-consciousness and how it influences our behavior. A decade ago, one of us and Bill Swann published the 20-item Self-Liking/Self-Competence Scale (Tafarodi & Swann, 1995) as an alternative to unidimensional measures such as the SES. Now available as a revised, 16-item version with improved psychometric properties (SLCS-R; Tafarodi & Swann, 2001), this instrument consists of simple first-person statements reflecting high and low self-competence (e.g., *I am highly effective at the things I do; I wish I were more skillful in my activities*) and self-liking (e.g., *I am secure in my sense of self-worth; I do not have enough respect for myself*). Respondents indicate their agreement with the statements using a 5-point Likert rating scale. Ratings are then summed to produce separate self-competence and self-liking scores. The scores are moderately correlated ($r = .58$), consistent with the theoretical interdependence of the two dimensions. Despite this overlap, divergent patterns of *unique* relations have been found for the two dimensions in relation to memory (Tafarodi, Marshall, & Milne, 2003), negative life events (Tafarodi & Milne, 2002), word recognition (Tafarodi & Milne, 2002), and cultural comparisons (Tafarodi, Lang, & Smith, 1999; Tafarodi & Swann, 1996; Tafarodi & Walters, 1999). These findings illustrate the heuristic advantage of distinguishing self-competence and self-liking in theory and measurement. Notably, the two dimensions account for virtually all the true-score variance of the SES ($R^2 = .83$, uncorrected for reliability), *with each dimension independently accounting for a sizable share* (Tafarodi & Milne, 2002). This pattern reinforces our claim that the SES is measuring two different aspects of self-esteem.

One apparent drawback of the SLCS-R is its reliance on direct statements about competence and efficacy to index self-competence. Admittedly, the belief in one's ability to exercise control over the environment, referred to by Bandura (1989, 1992) as *self-efficacy*, is not itself an experience of personal value or self-esteem. In its generalized form, self-efficacy refers to "what we can do" on the whole, whereas self-esteem refers to "what we are" on the whole. However, the same successful efforts and outcomes that increase self-efficacy over time also amplify our sense of personal value by causing us to experience ourselves as strong and capable agents. Thus, self-efficacy and self-competence are best understood as psychologically distinct concomitants of willfully engaging with the world. That said, it is clear that many of the SLCS-R self-competence items refer to what one can do rather than what one is. The justifying assumption is that the correlation of generalized self-efficacy and self-competence is high enough to allow test indicators of the former to serve as indicators of the latter. This assumption is consistent with demonstrations of the high redundancy of the two types of indicators in the context of measurement (Bernard, Hutchison, Lavin, & Pennington, 1996; Stanley & Murphy, 1997).

We began by recognizing that all measures of self-esteem are at most implicit of the individual's private symbolic experience, which can only be inferred from observed behavior. Nonetheless, disenchantment with self-report methods has given sway over the past decade to both measures of self-esteem identified as "implicit" because they circumvent awareness of what is being measured and a new *construct* of personal value referred to as "implicit self-esteem." The latter was defined by Greenwald and Banaji (1995) as "the introspectively unidentified (or inaccurately identified) effect of the self-attitude on evaluation of self-associated and self-dissociated objects" (p. 11). Elsewhere, it is defined with greater economy as "the association of the concept of self with a valence attribute" (Greenwald, Banaji, Rudman, Farnham, Nosek, & Mellott, 2002, p. 5). These definitions are notable in that they divest self-esteem of its experiential content, reducing it to a semantic association or theoretical relation in a process model. To distinguish self-esteem as a conscious, reflexive stance from its implicit counterpart, Farnham, Greenwald, and Banaji (1999) describe the latter as a "construct of self-regard" that is "unavailable to introspection" (p. 244). Consistent with this separation, Greenwald and Farnham (2000) claim that measures of implicit self-esteem "define constructs that are distinct from, although correlated with, nominally the same constructs measured by self-report" (p. 1034). A fair discussion of the interpretive difficulties presented by these claims would lead us off the main path of this chapter. It is enough for the present purposes to point out that any argument for "implicit" self-competence or self-liking as holistic abstractions formed outside of conscious experience or sequestered beyond the reach of awareness is implausible in light of their theoretical origins. Both dimensions of self-esteem are the result of ongoing synthetic interpretation that renders complex configurations of evaluative thought and feeling meaningful within a unified narrative identity. Integrative self-symbolic activity of this sort can occur only within the field of self-consciousness. If we doubt the validity of people's responses to our questioning of what they see in the mirrors of their own minds, we should try convincing them to look closer and answer with greater care and honesty. Reinventing self-esteem as an alienated and unrecognizable ghost of the mind is not the solution.

REFERENCES

Bandura, A. (1989). Human agency in social cognitive theory. *American Psychologist, 44,* 1175–1184.

Bandura, A. (1992). Exercise of personal agency through the self-efficacy mechanism. In R. Schwarzer (Ed.), *Self-efficacy: Thought control of action* (pp. 3–38). Washington, DC: Hemisphere.

Bernard, L. C., Hutchison, S., Lavin, A., & Pennington, P. (1996). Ego-strength, hardiness, self-esteem, self-efficacy, optimism, and maladjustment: Health-related personality constructs and the "Big Five" model of personality. *Assessment, 3,* 115–131.

Coopersmith, S. (1967). *The antecedents of self-esteem.* San Francisco, CA: Freeman.

Farnham, S. D., Greenwald, A. G., & Banaji, M. R. (1999). Implicit self-esteem. In D. Abrams & M. A. Hogg (Eds.), *Social identity and social cognition* (pp. 230–248). Oxford, UK: Blackwell.

Fazio, R. H., & Olson, M. A. (2003). Implicit measures in social cognition research: Their meaning and use. *Annual Review of Psychology, 54,* 297–327.

Greenwald, A. G., & Banaji, M. R. (1995). Implicit social cognition: Attitudes, self-esteem, and stereotypes. *Psychological Review, 102,* 4–27.

Greenwald, A. G., Banaji, M. R., Rudman, L. A., Farnham, S. D., Nosek, B. A., & Mellott, D. S. (2002). A unified theory of implicit attitudes, stereotypes, self-esteem, and self-concept. *Psychological Review, 109,* 3–25.

Greenwald, A. G., & Farnham, S. D. (2000). Using the Implicit Association Test to measure self-esteem and self-concept. *Journal of Personality and Social Psychology, 79,* 1022–1038.

Janis, I. S., & Field, P. B. (1959). A behavioral assessment of persuasibility: Consistency of individual differences. In C. I. Hovland & I. L. Janis (Eds.), *Personality and persuasibility* (pp. 55–68). New Haven, CT: Yale University Press.

Raimy, V. C. (1948). Self reference in counseling interviews. *Journal of Consulting Psychology, 12,* 153–163.

Rosenberg, M. (1965). *Society and the adolescent self-image.* Princeton, NJ: Princeton University Press.

Rosenberg, M. (1979). *Conceiving the self.* New York: Basic Books.

Stanley, K. D., & Murphy, M. R. (1997). A comparison of general self-efficacy with self-esteem. *Genetic, Social, and General Psychology Monographs, 123,* 79–99.

Tafarodi, R. W. (1998). Paradoxical self-esteem and selectivity in the processing of social information. *Journal of Personality & Social Psychology, 74,* 1181–1196.

Tafarodi, R. W., Lang, J. M., & Smith, A. J. (1999). Self-esteem and the cultural trade-off: Evidence for the role of individualism-collectivism. *Journal of Cross-Cultural Psychology, 30,* 620–640.

Tafarodi, R. W., Marshall, T. C., & Milne, A. B. (2003). Self-esteem and memory. *Journal of Personality and Social Psychology, 84,* 29–45.

Tafarodi, R. W., & Milne, A. B. (2002). Decomposing global self-esteem. *Journal of Personality, 70,* 443–483.

Tafarodi, R. W., & Swann, W. B. Jr. (1995). Self-liking and self-competence as dimensions of global self-esteem: Initial validation of a measure. *Journal of Personality Assessment, 65,* 322–342.

Tafarodi, R. W., & Swann, W. B. Jr. (1996). Individualism–collectivism and global self-esteem: Evidence for a cultural trade-off. *Journal of Cross-Cultural Psychology, 27,* 651–672.

Tafarodi, R. W., & Swann, W. B. Jr. (2001). Two-dimensional self-esteem: Theory and measurement. *Personality & Individual Differences, 31,* 653–673.

Tafarodi, R. W., Tam, J., & Milne, A. B. (2001). Selective memory and the persistence of paradoxical self-esteem. *Personality and Social Psychology Bulletin, 27,* 1179–1189.

Tafarodi, R. W., & Walters, P. (1999). Individualism–collectivism, life events, and self-esteem: A test of two trade-offs. *European Journal of Social Psychology, 29,* 797–814.

White, R. W. (1959). Motivation reconsidered: The concept of competence. *Psychological Review, 66,* 297–333.

Question 5

How best to characterize optimal
self-esteem?
Of what relevance are components
other than self-esteem level
(e.g., contingencies, stability)?
What are some ways that people can
orient toward developing optimal
self-esteem without being trapped into
endorsing self-esteem development
as the prime directive?

*T*he essays in this section focus on the nature and determinants of optimal self-esteem. It is noteworthy that a great deal of convergence exists among them.

In her essay, Crocker suggests that self-esteem is optimal when it is not a concern and people are striving toward goals that are not only good for themselves, but that benefit others as well. She describes "optimal" features of academically related goals that foster learning over the appearance of being smart. Crocker notes that highly contingent self-esteem can undermine health and well-being, particularly when the domains of contingency are external (e.g., appearance) rather than internal (e.g., virtue). She concludes that not pursuing self-esteem, then, may be the clearest route to optimal self-esteem.

In their essay, Ryan and Brown, who open by distinguishing contingent from true self-esteem, echo this same theme of not pursuing self-esteem as a route to optimal self-esteem. In true self-esteem, one's sense of self-worth is taken as a given and is not beholden to specific accomplishments or accolades. Ryan and Brown suggest that a key to developing optimal self-esteem is to develop one's awareness, which they define as an authentic appraisal of one's inner experience and social context. The authors end with suggestions of ways to develop this awareness.

In his essay, Goldman begins by distinguishing fragile from secure forms of high self-esteem. As he notes, fragile high self-esteem is unstable, contingent, and discrepant with implicit self-esteem, whereas secure high self-esteem is stable, true, and congruent with implicit self-esteem. Goldman suggests that optimal self-esteem reflects the sum total of all the secure components of self-esteem. He then links optimal self-esteem to authentic functioning and introduces a multicomponent conceptualization of authenticity. In this conceptualization, breakdowns in specific components may promote aspects of fragile self-esteem.

15

What is Optimal Self-Esteem?

JENNIFER CROCKER

I dentifying the characteristics of optimal self-esteem requires asking, "For what?" What do we think optimal self-esteem leads to? What are we ultimately trying to achieve by having optimal self-esteem? For me, the aim is to be on the path of accomplishing our most cherished goals—goals that are both good for the self and good for others. Being on the path of accomplishing those goals requires motivation, commitment, even a sense of passion; it requires a vision of how to accomplish those goals, the steps along the path; it requires a true learning orientation, in which people are realistic about their strengths and weaknesses and about the obstacles they face, and are committed to addressing the weaknesses that interfere with accomplishing their goals.

With this aim in mind, what would be optimal in terms of self-esteem? I think self-esteem is optimal when it is not a concern. When people are preoccupied with their worth and value, they behave in ways that undermine the accomplishment of their most cherished goals. Self-esteem as a motivating force tends to interfere with learning, relatedness, autonomy, self-regulation, and mental and physical health (Crocker & Park, 2004). For example, students who believe their worth depends on being smart want to be smart, and are often concerned with "looking smart" in their classes or study groups. These students are often very eager to show what they know, but reluctant to ask for help, raise their hand to ask questions when they do not understand a point in lecture, or admit what they do not know in their study groups. Consequently, although these students may, in the short term, create the image of being smart and understanding everything, their reluctance to reveal their confusions actually can create a downward spiral in which they become more and more lost and confused, sometimes with disastrous results for performance. Furthermore, their behavior can create a climate that makes it unsafe for other students to reveal their confusions, or ask for clarification. In the long run, these students neither are smart nor look smart. More generally, when people are driven by their ego (i.e., by concerns about their worth and value), they tend to create the opposite of what they really want.

As this example illustrates, being driven by concerns about self-esteem can be counter-productive. The search for optimal self-esteem, then, could focus on identifying the type of self-esteem that is sufficiently secure that it is never, or rarely, an issue or concern in daily life. Self-esteem that is high and noncontingent (i.e., does not require that one be or do something to have worth and value as a person) is relatively impervious to daily setbacks and not easily threatened; this type of self-esteem might seem optimal (Crocker & Nuer, 2003; Kernis, 2003). However, the assumption that noncontingent high self-esteem is always optimal is, in my view, too simple and not very useful. It is too simple because high self-esteem is not always a good thing, and it is not very useful because there is no known recipe for creating high and noncontingent self-esteem.

IS HIGH SELF-ESTEEM OPTIMAL?

High self-esteem people tend to have positive and certain views of themselves; they are self-confident. High self-esteem people have unrealistically positive views of themselves and their abilities, and also have unrealistically positive views of their futures (Taylor & Brown, 1988). This is an asset in some situations, but a liability in others, when it leads to overconfidence and lack of preparation or failure to exercise appropriate caution. More important than self-confidence is being grounded in reality—both a realistic understanding of one's strengths and weaknesses, and a realistic understanding of the obstacles one faces. This realism does not come from having positive and certain self-views; it comes from having a learning orientation, in which one seeks out information about one's strengths and weaknesses, and works to improve on the weaknesses.

High self-esteem can interfere with learning from experience, including both successes and failures, which may be the most important ingredient for accomplishing one's goals. People who are high in self-esteem tend to take credit for their success, but minimize their responsibility for failure (for reviews see Blaine & Crocker, 1993; Bradley, 1978; Greenberg & Pyszczynski, 1985; Miller & Ross, 1975); this tendency can interfere with learning from experience. When people boost their self-esteem by taking full credit for success, they do not explore many other factors that may have contributed to the success, including the efforts of other people, changed circumstances, and so on. Consequently, they do not learn all they can about how to re-create success in the future. Similarly, when people discount, dismiss, or excuse their mistakes and failures, they are unable to appraise their flaws and shortcomings realistically, and identify what they need to learn or change to avoid that failure in the future. Even if the test is unfair, the evaluator is biased, or there is a good excuse for failure, there is often some important information or lesson to be learned from these negative experiences.

IS LOW SELF-ESTEEM OPTIMAL?

This discussion of how high self-esteem can interfere with being on the path of accomplishing one's most cherished goal may lead some people to leap to the conclusion that if high self-esteem is a problem, it's opposite—low self-esteem—must be the solution. But this is not the case. Just as high self-esteem people are unrealistically positive about themselves and their abilities and take too much credit for success, low self-esteem people can be excessively negative about themselves and their abilities, and take too much blame for failure. Indeed, the problems associated with low self-esteem have led many psychologists to assume that people need high self-esteem (e.g., Pyszczynski, Greenberg, Solomon, Arndt, & Schimel, 2004). Furthermore, low self-esteem people are often so lacking in self-confidence that they are unable to act or take risks of any sort.

WHAT IS THE OPTIMAL CONTINGENCY OF SELF-ESTEEM?

Self-esteem is a multifaceted construct—not only can it be high or low, but also people differ in their contingencies of self-worth, or what they believe they need to be and do to have worth and value as a person (Crocker & Wolfe, 2001). For some people, self-esteem depends on being attractive or admired, for others it depends on academic or professional success, for others it depends on adherence to moral standards. What contingencies of self-esteem are optimal? External contingencies of self-worth, such as basing self-esteem on appearance, approval, and regard from others, or success at academics or other accomplishments, are associated with more negative outcomes than relatively internal sources of self-worth (Crocker, 2002; Pyszczynski, Greenberg, & Goldenberg, 2002). A longitudinal study of college freshmen (Crocker, 2002; Crocker, Luhtanen, Cooper, & Bouvrette, 2003b; Crocker & Luhtanen, 2003; Lawrence & Crocker, 2002) found that external contingencies of self-worth such as appearance, others' approval, competition, and academic competence were associated with more problems during the freshman year, whereas internal contingencies, such as virtue or religious faith, were associated with lower levels of these problems (Crocker, 2002). For example, students who based their self-esteem on appearance partied more, used more alcohol and drugs, became more depressed over the freshman year, and were higher in symptoms of disordered eating, whereas students who based their self-esteem on virtue used less alcohol and drugs, had fewer symptoms of disordered eating, and even earned higher grades in college (Crocker & Luhtanen, 2003).

External sources of self-worth may have greater costs because outcomes in these domains are more at the mercy of people or events outside of one's control. The resulting belief that one's worth or value as a person depends on other people or events may increase stress, anxiety, and negative emotion. Furthermore, when self-esteem is staked on external sources, the result may be greater self-esteem instability, which is linked to both depression and narcissism (Kernis, Whisenhunt, Waschull, Greenier, Berry, Herlocker, & Anderson, 1998; Rhodewalt, Madrian, & Cheney, 1998). For example, a daily report study of college students showed that the more students based their self-esteem on academic performance, the more their self-esteem tended to drop on days they received a worse-than-expected grade on an exam or paper. This instability of self-esteem, in turn, predicted increases in depressive symptoms over the 3 weeks of the study, especially among students who were initially high in depressive symptoms (Crocker, Karpinski, Quinn, & Chase, 2003a).

Although internal contingencies of self-worth appear to be healthier than external contingencies, I hesitate to suggest that internal contingencies are optimal. Whether they pursue self-esteem through internal or external sources, people feel threatened by negative feedback or criticism in the domains in which their self-worth is contingent, and have difficulty appraising their strengths and weaknesses realistically. If self-worth is at stake, they will feel pressure to succeed in that domain, value success and self-esteem boosts ahead of learning, and will be preoccupied with themselves, rather than what other people need.

From this perspective, noncontingent self-esteem may be optimal. However, developing noncontingent self-esteem may be an unrealistic goal. College students rarely have none of the seven contingencies of self-worth measured by the Contingencies of Self-Worth Scale (Crocker et al., 2003b), and these students could have any of hundreds of less common contingencies not measured by the scale. Furthermore, it is not clear how one could acquire noncontingent self-esteem or create it in others.

HOW CAN PEOPLE ACHIEVE OPTIMAL SELF-ESTEEM?

Optimal self-esteem, in my view, is best characterized by the absence of a preoccupation with one's worth and value. There is no particular set of self-esteem ingredients—high or low self-esteem, contingent or noncontingent self-esteem that can reliably produce this lack of preoccupation, although noncontingent self-esteem probably fosters this lack of preoccupation better than any other ingredient.

Paradoxically, optimal self-esteem may best be achieved when people do not pursue self-esteem—when they are unconcerned with whether they have value and worth as a person, or what they need to be or do to have value and worth, and proving that they are those things. Rather than focusing on raising their level of self-esteem, people might be better served if, regardless of their level of self-esteem, they focused on adopting goals on which improvement is possible and progress can be made: goals that do not put them at the mercy of other people or events in their lives. Learning goals are always achievable, even when the outcome is failure at a task; hence, learning goals foster self-confidence and perhaps self-esteem grounded in realistic appraisal of one's strengths and weaknesses.

Optimal self-esteem may also be fostered by goals that are larger than the self, goals that are good for others as well as the self. These alternative goals need not be altruistic, or "good" goals in a moral sense. They simply need to include others or involve creating or contributing to something larger than the self. Goals that include others are more likely to satisfy fundamental human needs for autonomy, learning, and relatedness, and foster self-regulation and mental and physical health than the goal to raise self-esteem by satisfying contingencies of self-worth (Crocker & Park, 2004).

Paradoxically, it is only when we are willing to let go of the benefits of pursuing self-esteem and pursue goals that are larger than the self, without regard to whether self-esteem will increase as a result, that we unleash our potential and dare to create what we truly want in our lives. As British philosopher and business writer Charles Handy suggests, "I cannot live without others, but my life starts with me. I call it Proper Selfishness, the search for ourselves that, paradoxically, we often pursue best through our involvement with others. To be Properly Selfish is to accept a responsibility for making the most of oneself by, ultimately, finding a purpose beyond and bigger than oneself. It is the paradox of Epicureanism, that we best satisfy ourselves when we look beyond ourselves" (Handy, 1998).

REFERENCES

Blaine, B., & Crocker, J. (1993). Self-esteem and self-serving biases in reactions to positive and negative events: An integrative review. In R. F. Baumeister (Ed.), *Self-esteem: The puzzle of low self-regard* (pp. 55–85). Hillsdale, NJ: Lawrence Erlbaum Associates.

Bradley, G. W. (1978). Self-serving biases in the attribution process: A reexamination of the fact or fiction question. *Journal of Personality and Social Psychology*, *36*, 56–71.

Crocker, J. (2002). The costs of seeking self-esteem. *Journal of Social Issues*, *58*, 597–615.

Crocker, J., Karpinski, A., Quinn, D. M., & Chase, S. (2003a). When grades determine self-worth: Consequences of contingent self-worth for male and female engineering and psychology majors. *Journal of Personality and Social Psychology*, *85*, 507–516.

Crocker, J., & Luhtanen, R. K. (2003). Level of self-esteem and contingencies of self-worth: Unique effects on academic, social, and financial problems in college students. *Personality and Social Psychology Bulletin*, *29*, 701–712.

Crocker, J., Luhtanen, R., Cooper, M. L., & Bouvrette, S. A. (2003b). Contingencies of self-worth in college students: Measurement and theory. *Journal of Personality and Social Psychology*, *85*, 894–908.

Crocker, J., & Nuer, N. (2003). The relentless quest for self-esteem. *Psychological Inquiry*, *14*, 31–34.

Crocker, J., & Park, L. E. (2004). The costly pursuit of self-esteem. *Psychological Bulletin*, *130*, 392–414.

Crocker, J., & Wolfe, C. T. (2001). Contingencies of self-worth. *Psychological Review*, *108*, 593–623.

Greenberg, J., & Pyszczynski, T. (1985). Compensatory self-inflation: A response to the threat to self-regard of public failure. *Journal of Personality and Social Psychology*, *49*, 273–280.

Handy, C. (1998). *The hungry spirit: Beyond capitalism: A quest for purpose in the modern world*. New York: Broadway Books.

Kernis, M. H. (2003). Toward a conceptualization of optimal self-esteem. *Psychological Inquiry*, *14*, 1–26.

Kernis, M. H., Whisenhunt, C. R., Waschull, S. B., Greenier, K. D., Berry, A. J., Herlocker, C. E., & Anderson, C. A. (1998). Multiple facets of self-esteem and their relations to depressive symptoms. *Personality and Social Psychology Bulletin*, *24*, 657–668.

Miller, D. T., & Ross, M. (1975). Self-serving biases in attribution of causality: Fact or fiction? *Psychological Bulletin*, *82*, 213–225.

Pyszczynski, T., Greenberg, J., & Goldenberg, J. (2002). Freedom in the balance: On the defense, growth, and expansion of the self. In M. R. Leary & J. Tangney (Eds.), *Handbook of self and identity* (pp. 314–343). New York: Guilford.

Pyszczynski, T., Greenberg, J., Solomon, S., Arndt, J., & Schimel, J. (2004). Why do people need self-esteem? A theoretical and empirical review. *Psychological Bulletin, 130,* 435–468.

Rhodewalt, F., Madrian, J. C., & Cheney, S. (1998). Narcissism, self-knowledge organization, and emotional reactivity: The effect of daily experiences on self-esteem and affect. *Personality and Social Psychology Bulletin, 24,* 75–87.

Taylor, S. E., & Brown, J. D. (1988). Illusion and well-being: A social-psychological perspective on mental health. *Psychological Bulletin, 103,* 193–210.

16

What is Optimal Self-Esteem? The Cultivation and Consequences of Contingent vs. True Self-Esteem as Viewed from the Self-Determination Theory Perspective

RICHARD M. RYAN and KIRK WARREN BROWN

S elf-esteem is a concept that is treated ambivalently by psychologists. On the one hand, it is clear that a sense of worth and confidence, both aspects of self-esteem, can yield many benefits in terms of motivation and mental health. On the other hand, there is suspicion that too often self-esteem is misplaced, inaccurate, or vulnerable. Many people have an inflated sense of self-worth, mismatched with actual merits or accomplishment. Others, particularly narcissists, may well have high self-esteem, but nonetheless are insensitive, self-centered and often poorly regarding of others (Paulus & Williams, 2002). Finally, there is something disconcerting about people esteeming themselves—a concept that seems in principle to lack humility and grace.

This ambivalence is, in our view, well placed. Self-esteem can be an asset, but it can also be problematic, even when high. This is why the study of self-esteem has required a more differentiated approach; one that recognizes that the self-regard people manifest differs as a function of its antecedents or foundations, yielding different consequences for adjustment (Kernis, 2003; Ryan & Deci, 2004). In self-determination theory (SDT; Deci & Ryan, 2000; Ryan & Deci, 2000), we distinguish between two different types of self-esteem, each built on different grounds, and each motivating different types of behaviors. Specifically, we distinguish *contingent self-esteem* from *true self-esteem*; the latter being most easily characterized as "optimal" (Deci & Ryan, 1995).

Contingent self-esteem (CSE) is a sense of worth that is based on the introjection of externally defined standards. It is evident wherever a person's evaluations of self are based on meeting certain goals, comparing well with others, or gaining outside admiration or accolades. Examples include the student who feels herself to be worthy or lovable only when she gets A's, or the man who needs to surround himself with conspicuous material goods to feel important and successful. CSE is unstable and fragile, in the senses outlined by Kernis (2003), because should a setback occur, or external admiration not be forthcoming, the individual's self-esteem can plummet, or conversely, when success at these extrinsic outcomes occurs, self-inflation follows. Indeed, CSE describes a dynamic in which one's sense of self rises and falls in accord with the attainment of attributes that have come to be adopted as markers of worth. Moreover, because self-esteem fluctuation is painful, people with high levels of CSE are vulnerable to introjecting others' goals to gain admiration, and/or distorting events to maintain their fragile sense of worth. They are more self-conscious (Ryan & Kuczkowski, 1994), more prone to extrinsically focused lifestyles (Ryan, Sheldon, Kasser, & Deci, 1996), and more likely to conform to external controls than people whose self-esteem is less contingent (Deci & Ryan, 1995).

In contrast, true self-esteem is a sense of self as worthy, not by virtue of external trappings or specific accomplishments, but because one experiences one's worth as inherent or "given." Indeed, true self-esteem is a sense of worth that is noncontingent. It does not inflate when one succeeds, nor crumble when setbacks occur. This is not to say that successes do not yield positive feelings and failures disappointments, but the *worth of the self as a whole* is not implicated in each event. Moreover, because people with true self-esteem are not basing their worth on specific external outcomes, material successes, or others' contingent approval, they are less prone to introjection, and they behave with greater integrity and authenticity.

WHY THE DISTINCTION HAS BEEN NECESSARY

The need for a distinction between the more optimal or true self-esteem, and the less optimal CSE has become increasingly clear as research on self-esteem has burgeoned. The reason is that the same indicator, evaluations of self-worth, can be high for quite distinct reasons. When traditional self-report measures of self-esteem are completed, people with CSE may, depending on whether they are meeting the standards they perceive to determine their worthiness, report high scores. Those with true self-esteem are also likely to record high scores, because they would reflectively endorse the idea that they are worthy of both love and regard. Yet, despite that high score, those with true self-esteem are not ongoingly concerned with self-esteem because their sense of self-worth is not in question. Esteem is not a salient issue in everyday life. In contrast, those with CSE, whether high or low, are preoccupied with the question of self-worth. They desire esteem, worry when it is not forthcoming, and that desire and worry over esteem regulates and controls much of their behavior. For those with CSE, self-esteem becomes what Kernis (2003) called a "prime directive," motivating the person to pursue goals that are expected to garner admiration or avoid disapproval.

Because they experience an inherent sense of worth, the actions and goals of persons with true self-esteem are more likely to reflect abiding values and interests, rather than merely "what others might think." And while successes and failures may affect feelings and well-being, the self as a whole is not evaluated accordingly. This separates our view of CSE from that of Crocker, Luhtanen, Cooper, and Bouvrette (2003), who define contingent worth in terms of a person being affected by positive or negative events, internally or externally defined, in any domain. Our definition is more specific, because although we also believe that goal-related outcomes impact people, not all people use those events to gage their self-worth in general. Further, because CSE stems from contingent regard, it tends to be focused on externally defined standards such as appearance, popularity, wealth, or other publicly accessible markers of status, and SDT specifically predicts negative effects of this external focus, which is what Crocker et al. found. And because meeting or not meeting these external standards affects one's whole sense of self, people with CSE are more preoccupied, sometimes desperately so, with meeting those standards. The materialist must make more money, the socialite must be popular, and the fitness fanatic must stay lean. This reflects what we describe as the paradox of self-esteem: Those who need it, don't have it; those who have it, don't need it (Ryan & Brown, 2003; Ryan & Deci, 2004).

DEVELOPMENTAL AND SOCIETAL FOUNDATIONS OF CONTINGENT VS. TRUE SELF-ESTEEM

It is important to note here that some level of contingent self-esteem is modal for adults, and in fact, most of us experience CSE differentially across different life domains (Assor, Roth, & Deci, 2004). But individual differences in CSE are robust and impactful, both within and across domains. Moreover, we suggest that while CSE vulnerability can be domain-specific (e.g., an athlete who has hinged self-esteem completely on sport success), many people with high CSE experience it across extrinsic outcomes such as image, popularity, and materialism. For instance, people focused on image also tend to be hooked on related issues of popularity, appearance of success, materialism, etc. This is why some people are so susceptible to consumerism, conformity, fashions, and fakery. To the extent that individuals believe that they are only worthy if sufficiently attractive, successful, popular, smart, or any other externalized characteristic, they may be willing to twist themselves into a pretzel to gain an edge in these attributes. One becomes "ego-involved" (Ryan, 1982) concerning specific outcomes such as money, beauty, or performance, feeling as if these criteria are what confirm one's worth.

In SDT's formulation, the roots of CSE lie in contingent regard (Deci & Ryan, 2000). When parents, teachers, or other significant figures are invested in specific outcomes they often wittingly or unwittingly convey that their love, regard, or support is contingent on the child attaining that outcome. The child is lovable only if brave, smart, athletic, attractive, or whatever else the desired outcome might be. Often such contingent regard concerns precisely those standards the adult has accepted as a condition for their own worth, or areas where he or she feels the child's image or status may reflect the adult's social worth (Grolnick, 2003). In any case, when contingently regarded the child is prone to "introject" these conditions of worth, judging themselves in accord with these external signs of merit. For example, Gagné, Ryan, and Bargmann (2003) showed that athletes with unstable self-esteem were significantly more likely to report that their motivation for sport was either introjected or driven by external factors such as parental or coach approval. Assor et al. (2004) showed that persons with contingent self-esteem perceived their parents as withdrawing or withholding love after failures and lavishing it after successes, in essence teaching contingent self-worth. These investigators further showed that the parents who did this reported that their own parents treated them similarly, suggesting that CSE is a motivational dynamic whose grip may be multigenerational.

It is not just parents, coaches and teachers, however, who can foster CSE. Today's media saturated world attempts to prompt consumerism precisely through activating a sense of contingent self-esteem. Advertisements strategically foster a sense of insecurity and social comparison, and then promise a product to remedy the problem (Kasser, Ryan, Couchman, & Sheldon, 2003). In fact, much consumerism is driven by desires for products that will lead others to esteem us for our image, youth, and success. But of course, even if that promise were true, the esteem one would garner would be contingent. Peer groups and colleagues can further this dynamic, holding out approval for those who have or do what is fashionable, and disparaging those who do not conform to what has been popularly sanctioned.

Whereas the foundations of CSE lie in insecurity linked with the promise of contingent approval, the development of true self-esteem is understood within SDT as an outgrowth of supports for basic psychological needs. True self-esteem is developmentally facilitated by caregivers who convey caring and relatedness noncontingently, support the child's autonomy, and facilitate a sense of competence. A person who feels unconditional relatedness, autonomy, and competence in ongoing life "has" self-esteem, of a stable and persistent quality. Such individuals are neither preoccupied with the question of esteem, nor worried about retaining it. In this sense, they are less motivated by the search for esteem, and less likely to focus on others' regard as a primary basis for deciding what is important in life. For example, using longitudinal data, Kasser, Ryan, Zax, and Sameroff (1995) showed that mothers who were more supportive of their child's needs for autonomy and relatedness had teenagers who were less materialistic and better adjusted. These investigators suggested that thwarting needs for autonomy and relatedness sets up a desire for trappings of worth to stave off inner insecurity. In short, SDT posits that the basis of true self-esteem is the satisfaction of basic needs for relatedness, competence, and autonomy, and when these are fulfilled, self-esteem concerns evaporate (Ryan & Deci, 2004).

HOW CAN A PERSON MOVE TOWARD MORE OPTIMAL SELF-ESTEEM?

Given the dynamics of CSE it seems clear that, the more salient it is, the more one pays costs levied in terms of diminished growth, integrity, and well-being. It is also clear that there are many forces that work to keep CSE robust, from controlling parents and partners to creative marketers. Is there any antidote?

From the SDT perspective, a key to "unhooking" from CSE, and to living a fuller, more satisfying life, is the cultivation of *awareness*. We define awareness as authentic appraisal of what is going on both within oneself and in one's social context. In awareness a person holistically represents what is occurring, what drives actions, and what is truly satisfying and fulfilling. Awareness in this view is not self-consciousness (how one thinks one is viewed by others) but rather an open and nonjudgmental consciousness of self and environment (being in touch with what is occurring). Awareness is foundational in the process of regulation (Deci & Ryan, 1985), and helps a person sort out what is a genuine value or interest, and what is salient because of what others think or because of contingencies in the social environment. Awareness is what supports interest and volition, and identifies obstacles to it.

One operationalization of awareness is *mindfulness*, a state in which one openly perceives and processes what is occurring in the present (Brown & Ryan, 2003; in press). When mindful one witnesses the passing drama of feelings, social pressures, desires, and even of being esteemed or disparaged by others without getting "hooked" or attached. Open observation allows access to the inputs most important to congruent, integrated action, and to being able to resist the ongoing pressure of CSE to regulate action. In short, mindfulness supplies a better foundation for self-regulation than concern with what others esteem (Ryan & Brown, 2003).

There are many routes to greater awareness and mindfulness. Obvious, of course, is personal training in mindfulness, such as through meditation. Another route is psychotherapy which, when meaningful, helps people to gain perspective and reflectively consider one's motives, actions, and circumstances (Epstein, 1995). As Rogers (1963) noted, effective therapy, by creating an atmosphere that is unconditionally regarding, helps to clarify the phenomenal field. In turn, this facilitates a higher sense of vitality and better self-regulation (LaGuardia & Ryan, 2003). Relatedly, awareness is also facilitated in informal interpersonal contexts where one can share, symbolize and process events, and experience without being contingently regarded or controlled. In fact, it is with others who noncontingently value a person that honest and clear talk emerges, and from that greater awareness typically grows (Ryan, LaGuardia, Solky-Butzel, Chirkov, & Kim, 2005). There are other informal routes through which we can gain more awareness as well, such as through quality time spent in solitude, wherein one can authentically reflect and deepen one's understanding of self and others.

Finally, according to SDT, gaining optimal self-esteem comes about not by seeking esteem, but by actually leading a life that satisfies basic psychological needs. By cultivating awareness of one's basic needs for autonomy, competence and relatedness, and by seeking out relationships, vocations and interests in which those needs can be truly satisfied, a sense of self that is vital and well is nurtured, the self-esteem motive itself weakens and atrophies, and extrinsic goals become less salient. Those who find opportunities to satisfy needs and to increase their awareness of themselves and their surroundings thus find the whole phenomenon of self-esteem to be less and less important in life. And in the SDT view, the less salient self-esteem is, the more optimal is one's self-esteem.

REFERENCES

Assor, A., Roth, G., & Deci, E. L. (2004). The emotional costs of parents' conditional regard: A self-determination theory analysis. *Journal of Personality, 72,* 47–88.

Brown, K. W., & Ryan, R. M. (2003). The benefits of being present: Mindfulness and its role in psychological well-being. *Journal of Personality and Social Psychology, 84,* 822–848.

Brown, K. W., & Ryan, R. M. (in press). Fostering healthy self-regulation from within and without: A self-determination theory perspective. In A. Linley & S. Joseph (Eds.), *Positive psychology in practice.* Hoboken, NJ: Wiley.

Crocker, J., Luhtanen, R. K., Cooper, M. L., & Bouvrette, A. (2003). Contingencies of self-worth in college students: Theory and measurement. *Journal of Personality and Social Psychology, 85,* 894–908.

Deci, E. L., & Ryan, R. M. (1985). *Intrinsic motivation and self-determination in human behavior.* New York: Plenum.

Deci, E. L., & Ryan, R. M. (1995). Human autonomy: The basis for true self-esteem. In M. Kernis (Ed.), *Agency, efficacy, and self-esteem* (pp. 31–49). New York: Plenum.

Deci, E. L., & Ryan, R. M. (2000). The "what" and the "why" of goal pursuits: Human needs and the self-determination of behavior. *Psychological Inquiry, 11,* 227–268.

Epstein, M. (1995). *Thoughts without a thinker.* New York: Basic Books.

Gagné, M., Ryan, R. M., & Bargmann, K. (2003). Autonomy support and need satisfaction in the motivation, and well-being of gymnasts. *Journal of Applied Sport Psychology, 15,* 372–390.

Grolnick, W. S. (2003). *The psychology of parental control: How well-meant parenting backfires.* Mahwah, NJ: Lawrence Erlbaum Associates, Inc.

Kasser, T., Ryan, R. M., Couchman, C., & Sheldon, K. M. (2003). Materialistic values: Their causes and consequences. In T. Kasser & A. D. Kanner (Eds.), *Psychology and the consumer culture: The struggle for a good life in a materialistic world* (pp. 11–28). Washington, DC: American Psychological Association.

Kasser, T., Ryan, R. M., Zax, M., & Sameroff, A. J. (1995). The relations of maternal and social environments to late adolescents' materialistic and prosocial values. *Developmental Psychology, 31,* 907–914.

Kernis, M. H. (2003). Optimal self-esteem and authenticity: Separating fantasy from reality. *Psychological Inquiry, 14,* 83–89.

Paulhus, D. L., & Williams, K. M. (2002). The dark triad of personality: Narcissism, Machiavellianism, and psychopathy. *Journal of Research in Personality, 36,* 556–563.

Rogers, C. (1963). The actualizing tendency in relation to "motives" and to consciousness. In M. R. Jones (Ed.), *Nebraska symposium on motivation* (Vol. 11, pp. 1–24). Lincoln, NE: University of Nebraska Press.

Ryan, R. M. (1982). Control and information in the intrapersonal sphere: An extension of cognitive evaluation theory. *Journal of Personality and Social Psychology, 43,* 450–461.

Ryan, R. M., & Brown, K. W. (2003). Why we don't need self-esteem: Basic needs, mindfulness, and the authentic self. *Psychological Inquiry, 14,* 71–76.

Ryan, R. M., & Deci, E. L. (2000). Self-determination theory and the facilitation of intrinsic motivation, social development and well-being. *American Psychologist, 55,* 68–78.

Ryan, R. M., & Deci, E. L. (2004). Avoiding death and engaging life as accounts of meaning and culture: A comment on Pyszczynski, Greenberg, Solomon, Arndt, and Schimel (2004). *Psychological Bulletin, 130*, 473–477.

Ryan, R. M., & Kuczkowski, R. (1994). The imaginary audience, self-consciousness, and public individuation in adolescence. *Journal of Personality, 62*, 219–238.

Ryan, R. M., LaGuardia, J. G., Solky-Butzel, J., Chirkov, V. & Kim, Y. (2005). On the interpersonal regulation of emotions: Emotional reliance across gender, relationships and cultures. *Personal Relationships, 12*, 145–163.

Ryan, R. M., Sheldon, K. M., Kasser, T., & Deci, E. L. (1996). All goals are not created equal: An organismic perspective on the nature of goals and their regulation. In P. M. Gollwitzer & J. A. Bargh (Eds.), *The psychology of action: Linking cognition and motivation to behavior* (pp. 7–26). New York: Guilford.

17

Making Diamonds Out of Coal: The Role of Authenticity in Healthy (Optimal) Self-Esteem and Psychological Functioning

BRIAN M. GOLDMAN

*P*ublic opinion often proclaims that self-esteem confers many healthy benefits for people. However, an in-depth understanding of its influence on healthy functioning is still emerging. Most research on self-esteem phenomena has studied its *level*: the degree to which one's feelings of self-worth or acceptance are generally positive or negative. These studies have found that high self-esteem is often linked with a myriad of positive outcomes including greater subjective well-being (Myers & Diener, 1995), and self-confidence (O'Brien & Epstein, 1988).

An alternative perspective proposes that there is a downside to high self-esteem (e.g., Kernis & Goldman, 1999). From this perspective, high self-esteem can undermine the emergence of substantial healthy adjustment in part by stifling the creation of an authentic self-view (i.e., a comprehensive recognition of one's positive and negative qualities). For instance, people with high self-esteem tend to engage in self-serving biases (Tennen & Herzberger, 1987). That is, they typically attribute their successes to internal causes (e.g., "I'm brilliant!") but explain undesired outcomes in terms of external reasons (e.g., "That test was stupid and unfair!"). High self-esteem has also been linked with extremely inflated feelings of self-worth, or narcissism (e.g., Goldman, Kernis, Foster, Piasecki, & Hermann, 2004). Taken as a whole, this alternative perspective depicts people with high self-esteem to have a highly restrictive self-view that chronicles their positive qualities when not lauding their achievements. Although a chorus of compliments may ring like a melody, it may also impede personal growth and healthy adjustment. After all, openness to feedback (both positive and negative) may initiate important changes that result in self-enrichment.

These contrasting views of high self-esteem raise concerns about the overall role of self-esteem in substantially contributing to healthy psychological functioning. For instance, is high self-esteem more indicative of healthy adjustment or of an overly restrained and distorted (e.g., glorified) self-view? Is there an "optimal" self-esteem, and if so, how best to characterize it?

IS HIGH SELF-ESTEEM "OPTIMAL"?

Attempts to reconcile the conflicting views of high self-esteem have resulted in some researchers' suggesting that self-esteem level is a multifaceted construct (Baumeister, Campbell, Kreuger, & Vohs, 2003; Kernis, 2003). Thus, whether one's self-esteem optimizes or even remotely confers healthy benefits to psychological functioning depends on a consideration of characteristics in addition to its level (e.g., Crocker & Wolfe, 2001; Kernis & Paradise, 2002). Kernis and Goldman (1999) described self-esteem in terms of *fragile* or *secure* forms that vary along four theoretical components of self-esteem: *stability, contingency, congruence, and defensiveness*. Below, I briefly discuss these components in differentiating among fragile and secure forms of high self-esteem. Extensive discussion of and evidence supporting the distinction between *fragile high self-esteem* and *secure high self-esteem* can be found elsewhere (e.g., Kernis, 2003; Kernis & Goldman, 2005a; Kernis & Paradise, 2002).

Optimal Self-esteem: Decomposing Fragile and Secure Forms of High Self-Esteem

Fragile high self-esteem refers to positive feelings of self-worth that (1) exhibit substantial short-term fluctuations in contextually based feelings of self-worth (i.e., *unstable*); (2) depend upon achieving specific outcomes (i.e., *contingent*); (3) are discrepant with implicit feelings of self-worth, (i.e., *incongruent*); and (4) reflect an unwillingness to admit to possessing negative feelings of self-worth (i.e., *defensive*). In contrast, *secure high self-esteem* reflects positive feelings of self-worth that: (1) exhibit minimal short-term variability from day-to-day experiences (i.e., *stable*); (2) arise from satisfying core psychological needs, not from attaining specific outcomes (i.e., *true*); (3) are concordant with positive implicit feelings of self-worth (i.e., *congruent*); and (4) are open to recognizing negative self-aspects (i.e., *genuine*).

In addition, *fragile high self-esteem* reflects feelings of positive self-regard that are highly susceptible to either real or imagined threats to one's self-worth. People with fragile high self-esteem presumably navigate through their life experiences with feelings of *positive self-regard* as their prime directive (Kernis, 2003). Thus, their feelings of self-worth require continual validation that is fueled by chronic use of *self-esteem maintenance strategies* (e.g., *self-enhancement* and *self-protection*) to sustain and promote their positive self-regard and to buffer and defend against perceived self-esteem threats (Kernis & Goldman, 2003). *Secure high self-esteem* people also have positive feelings of self-worth; however they "like, value, and accept themselves, imperfections and all" (Kernis, 2003, p. 3). As such, their feelings of positive self-regard are thought to arise naturally from successfully meeting life's challenges, rather than resulting from the successful use of self-esteem maintenance strategies (Kernis, 2003).

In contrast to fragile high self-esteem, secure high self-esteem is theorized to reflect a *"strong sense of self"* such that positive feelings of self-worth are well-anchored within one's self (Kernis, Paradise, Whitaker, Wheatman, & Goldman, 2000). When compared to those with secure high self-esteem (and sometimes even low self-esteem), people with fragile high self-esteem tend to exhibit greater maladjustment (see Kernis & Goldman, 2003 for review). Thus, high self-esteem that also reflects greater amounts of secure forms of self-esteem should reflect more healthy or optimal psychological functioning. Kernis (2003) therefore proposed that *"optimal self-esteem"* reflects the sum total of all the secure components of self-esteem (i.e., "stable," "true," "congruent," and "genuine"). Optimal self-esteem may be intimately linked with the construct of *psychological authenticity* in substantially contributing to healthy functioning (Kernis, 2003; Kernis & Goldman, 2005a, 2005b). Below I describe authenticity in general and its role in healthy functioning.

LINKING PSYCHOLOGICAL AUTHENTICITY, HEALTHY FUNCTIONING, AND OPTIMAL SELF-ESTEEM

Psychological authenticity can be conceptualized as a dynamic set of processes whereby one's full inherent nature is discovered and explored, accepted, imbued with meaning, and actualized (Maslow, 1968; Rogers, 1959). Rogers (1961) emphasized that authenticity emerges as people actualize their inherent nature and potentialities by achieving congruence between their self-concept and their immediate experiences. Thus, being authentic (i.e., being one's *true-self*) involves compatibility between one's self-knowledge and one's accompanying experiences. When individuals are in contact with their core self they are said to become more *"fully functioning"* (Rogers, 1961) and therefore exhibit healthy adjustment. Consistent with this view, Goldman, Kernis, Piasecki, Hermann, and Foster (2004, Study 1) found that individuals' *psychological well-being* (Ryff, 1989) was greater, and it subsequently increased over a four week period, to the extent that their goals "reflected who they really are as a person." Such findings suggest that *authentic goal pursuits* (i.e., those that resonate with one's true sense of self) are linked with healthy functioning.

The prior discussion suggests that psychological authenticity along with secure and high forms of self-esteem (optimal) appear to converge in their promoting of healthy functioning. In addition, they may reflect complementary processes that support the operation of one another. For example, Kernis and Goldman (2004b) suggest that having optimal self-esteem may increase individuals' likelihood to try new and challenging endeavors that, in turn, foster their becoming more fully functioning.

Likewise, self-determination theory (SDT; Deci & Ryan, 1985; Deci & Ryan, 1995; Deci & Ryan, 2000) holds that authentic functioning is reflected by actions that directly satisfy people's core psychological needs for autonomy, competence, and relatedness. As such, Kernis, Paradise, Whitaker, Wheatman, & Goldman (2000) proposed that people with more secure, as opposed to fragile high self-esteem would *regulate* their goal-oriented behaviors with greater *self-determination*. In support of their hypothesis, Kernis et al. (2000) found that the more stable (i.e., secure) or higher individuals' self-esteem, the more their goals were pursued for highly self-determined *intrinsic* (e.g., fun or pleasure) or *identified* reasons (e.g., personally expressive, important to their growth and development) and the less they were pursued for non self-determined reasons. That is, the higher and more stable individuals' self-esteem, the less their goals were regulated by *introjects* (i.e., attempts to reduce feelings of guilt or anxiety) or by attempts to satisfy *external* contingencies (i.e., attaining rewards and avoiding punishments). In addition, Kernis et al. (2000) also found that the higher and more stable individuals' self-esteem, the greater their *self-concept clarity* (Campbell, Trapnell, Heine, Katz, Lavallee, & Lehman, 1996). Taken as a whole, the prior findings suggest that when aspects of optimal self-esteem are operative people tend to be in contact with themselves and to act in ways that express and satisfy their core psychological needs. In contrast, fragile or low self-esteem may function as a barrier to healthy and authentic functioning by perhaps fostering *false-self behaviors* (Harter, 1997) or even *alienation* from one's self (Horney, 1950). To further examine the interrelationship between self-esteem and authenticity processes, I now turn to a recently proposed multicomponent conceptualization of *dispositional authenticity* (Goldman & Kernis, 2002; Kernis, 2003).

Dispositional Authenticity, Optimal Self-Esteem and Healthy Functioning

Dispositional authenticity can be defined as the unobstructed operation of one's core or true self in one's daily enterprise (Goldman & Kernis, 2002; Kernis, 2003). Specifically, it is theorized to reflect the following four separable but related components: (1) *awareness* (i.e., self-understanding); (2) *unbiased processing* (i.e., objectivity in self-evaluation); (3) *behavior* (i.e., congruence between one's values, needs, and actions); and (4) *relational orientation* (i.e., being open, honest, and genuine in one's close relationships). Highly operative authenticity is presumed to be reflected in high self-understanding, objectivity in self-evaluations, acting in ways that resonate with core self aspects (e.g., self-determined), and sincerity in close relationships (Kernis & Goldman, 2005a, 2005b). As such, dispositional authenticity may provide a broad reservoir of inner resources to aid in healthy functioning.

Empirically, higher composite scores on a measure of dispositional authenticity (Authenticity Inventory; AI Version 1; Goldman & Kernis, 2001) have been linked with greater *life-satisfaction* and *positive affectivity* (Goldman & Kernis, 2002). Similarly, using a revised version of the same measure (AI Version 2), Goldman et al. (2004, Study 2) found that greater authenticity composite scores inversely correlated with *depression* and *negative affectivity*, but positively correlated with each of Ryff's (1989) multicomponent measure of *psychological well-being* (i.e., self-acceptance, positive relationships with others, autonomy, environmental mastery, purpose in life, and personal growth). Individual differences in dispositional authenticity have also been linked with various markers of optimal self-esteem. Specifically, higher authenticity composite scores positively correlated with self-esteem level but negatively correlated with *contingent self-esteem* (Goldman & Kernis, 2002; Goldman et al., 2004, Study 2). In addition, higher authenticity scores correlated with greater *self-esteem stability* (Hermann & Kernis, 2004). Thus, greater dispositional authenticity more strongly relates to high self-esteem that is secure rather than fragile.

Developing a Strong Sense of Self: Tying Optimal Self-Esteem and Authenticity Processes

The extent that people function authentically has considerable implications for their self-esteem and vice versa. For instance, authenticity may provide both the foundation for achieving secure (and ultimately optimal) high self-esteem and the processes through which secure (and optimal) high self-esteem relates to healthy psychological adjustment (Kernis & Goldman, 2005a). As such, the extent to which authenticity is operative is likely to affect the degree to which individuals may avoid some of the trappings of fragile high self-esteem. Below I discuss how breakdowns in the components of authenticity may be implicated in undermining healthy (i.e., secure and optimal) self-esteem development and psychological adjustment.

Breakdowns in Dispositional Authenticity

The awareness component of authenticity (i.e., self-understanding) may influence optimal self-esteem development by its contribution to self-knowledge construction. For instance, when self-knowledge is largely unclear, inaccurate, or incomplete corresponding feelings of self-worth may be more directly tied to external sources of information (e.g., how one performs relative to others). As such, individuals may habitually seek out opportunities for self-evaluation in order to "fill in the gap". In support of this contention, Goldman et al. (2004, Study 2) found that higher awareness and composite scores involved *social comparisons* that were less frequent for ability dimensions (Gibbons & Buunk, 1998) and were less motivated by self-enhancement (Gibbons, Benhow, & Gerrard, 1994). Thus, over time lower authenticity levels may result in more fragile self-esteem (e.g., contingent) by promoting the acquisition of self-knowledge that is largely informed by, and attuned to, external as opposed to internal referents.

Biased processing of self-relevant information may also promote fragile self-esteem by influencing people's subsequent behavioral choices. For instance, positive bias in processing may increase self-esteem fragility when people mistakenly enact tasks well beyond their range of competence (e.g., enrolling in calculus when struggling with mathematics). In addition, behavioral authenticity breakdowns, such as enacting a false self (e.g., not "voicing" one's true feelings or opinions), have been linked to lower self-esteem levels (Harter, 1997). Finally, relational authenticity breakdowns are likely to reflect important changes in self-esteem. The extent that people feel valued or accepted by others may largely determine their overall level of self-esteem (e.g., Harter, 1990, 1993; Leary & Downs, 1995). Thus, by being inauthentic with their intimates (e.g., not being open and honest) people may erode relationship qualities (e.g., feelings of trust or intimacy) that, in turn, affect the extent that they feel valued by their partners.

Healthy Alternatives for Reducing Fragile High Self-esteem

Taken as a whole, the prior sections suggest that when authenticity processes are largely inoperative fragile self-esteem may be created or sustained. Substantial reductions to fragile self-esteem are not likely to occur from deliberate pursuits for enhancing positive feelings of self-regard. Rather, collaboration between authenticity and self-esteem processes is important for reducing self-esteem fragility and for fostering healthy self-esteem development. By developing one's capacity and ability to be aware of and understanding of one's self, processing self-relevant information objectively, behaving in accord with one's core values and needs, and by functioning genuinely in one's close relationships, one may further develop secure (and ultimately optimal) self-esteem. Thus, by engaging in endeavors that maximize the components of authenticity (e.g., heightening one's awareness through *mindfulness* training; see Brown & Ryan, 2003) people may confer healthy benefits to their self-esteem development and psychological functioning.

Despite the benefits that presumably result from authentic functioning, its development may not always "feel good." Authenticity development may initially be cost prohibitive for some (e.g., realizing one's weaknesses), but should confer long-term substantial benefits to healthy functioning. The distinction of well-being in terms of hedonic pleasures or happiness (i.e., "subjective") and eudaemonic forms (i.e., psychological self-realization and meaning) (see Ryan & Deci, 2002) may be pertinent in understanding the unique and shared contributions of authenticity and self-esteem to healthy functioning. Specifically, relative to self-esteem level, authenticity may exert a less direct influence on *subjective well-being* (e.g., *positive affectivity, life-satisfaction*) but not necessarily psychological well-being (e.g., *autonomy, purpose in life*). For example, people's levels of subjective well-being, such as feelings of happiness, are perhaps more directly tied to the extent to which they also have positive feelings of self-worth than to whether they possess high (perhaps even low) amounts of self-understanding or objectivity in their self-evaluations. Consistent with the prior line of reasoning, Goldman (2004) found that higher ratings of individuals' *self-esteem* and *dispositional authenticity* levels significantly predicted higher subsequent ratings (approximately one month later) of *life-satisfaction* (Diener, Emmons, Larson, & Griffin, 1985) and *psychological well-being* (Ryff, 1989). Furthermore, when controlling for the influence of one another, *self-esteem* ratings uniquely predicted *life-satisfaction* scores, however both *self-esteem* and *authenticity* independently predicted *psychological well-being* scores. The findings from Goldman (2004) suggest that substantial psychological adjustment is realized through the collaboration of self-esteem with authenticity.

In conclusion, substantive healthy adjustment should be considered with respect to the extent to which people's feelings of self-worth are rooted in the unobstructed operation of their true selves (e.g., self-understanding, objectivity in self-evaluation, etc.). By developing their authenticity people may become empowered to act in ways that more directly satisfy their core psychological needs. In doing so, they may also minimize self-esteem fragility and maximize secure (and ultimately optimal) self-esteem development. In my view, when optimal self-esteem and authenticity processes are both highly operative, people further develop and actualize their core or true self in becoming more fully functioning and substantially healthy.

REFERENCES

Baumeister, R. F., Campbell, J. D., Kreuger, J. I., & Vohs, K. D. (2003) Does high self-esteem cause better performance, interpersonal success, happiness, or healthier lifestyles? *Psychological Science in the Public Interest, 4*(1), 1–44.

Brown, K. W., & Ryan, R. M. (2003). The benefits of being present: Mindfulness and its role in psychological well-being. *Journal of Personality and Social Psychology, 84*, 822–848.

Campbell, J. D., Trapnell, P. D., Heine, S. J., Katz, I. M., Lavallee, L. F., & Lehman, D. R. (1996). Self-concept clarity: Measurement, personality correlates, and cultural boundaries. *Journal of Personality and Social Psychology, 70*, 141–156.

Crocker, J., & Wolfe, C. T. (2001). Contingencies of self-worth. *Psychological Review, 108*, 593–623.

Deci, E. L., & Ryan, R. M. (1985). The general causality orientation scale: Self-determination in personality. *Journal of Personality and Social Psychology, 19*, 109–134.

Deci, E. L., & Ryan, R. M. (1995). Human agency: The basis for true self-esteem. In M. H. Kernis (Ed.), *Efficacy, agency, and self-esteem* (pp. 31–50). New York: Plenum.

Deci, E. L., & Ryan, R. M. (2000). The "what" and "why" of goal pursuits: Human needs and the self-determination of behavior. *Psychology Inquiry, 11*, 227–269.

Diener, E., Emmons, R., Larsen, R., & Griffin, S. (1985). The satisfaction with life scale. *Journal of Personality and Social Psychology, 49*, 71–75.

Gibbons, F. X., Benhow, C. P., & Gerrard, M. (1994) From top dog to bottom half: Social comparison strategies in response to poor performance. *Journal of Personality and Social Psychology, 67*, 638–652.

Gibbons, F. X., & Buunk, B. P. (1998). Individual differences in social comparison: Development and validation of a measure of social comparison orientation. *Journal of Personality and Social Psychology, 76*, 129–142.

Goldman, B. M. (2004). *The interrelated roles of dispositional authenticity, self-processes, and global role-functioning in affecting psychological adjustment.* Unpublished doctoral dissertation, University of Georgia, Athens.

Goldman, B. M., & Kernis, M. H. (2001). *Development of the Authenticity Inventory.* Unpublished data, University of Georgia, Athens.

Goldman, B. M., & Kernis, M. H. (2002). The role of authenticity in healthy psychological functioning and subjective well-being. *Annals of the American Psychotherapy Association, 5*(6), 18–20.

Goldman, B. M., Kernis, M. H., Foster, J. D., Piasecki, R., & Hermann, A. (2004). *Exercising one's daimon: Dispositional authenticity and self-expressive goal pursuits as predictors of well-being.* Manuscript in preparation.

Harter, S. (1990). Causes, correlates and the functional role of global self-worth: A life-span perspective. In R. Sternberg & J. Kolligian, Jr (Eds.), *Competence considered* (pp. 67–98). New Haven, CT: Yale University Press.

Harter, S. (1993). Causes and consequences of low self-esteem in children and adolescents. In R. F. Baumeister (Ed.), *Self-Esteem: The puzzle of low self-regard* (pp. 87–116). New York: Plenum Press.

Harter, S. (1997). The personal self in social context: Barriers to authenticity. In R. D. Ashmore & L. Jussim (Eds.), *Self and identity: Fundamental issues* (pp. 81–105). New York: Oxford University Press.

Hermann, A., & Kernis, M. H. (2004). *Growth and defensive motivations in healthy self-esteem functioning.* Unpublished Master's thesis, University of Georgia, Athens.

Kernis, M. H. (2003). Toward a conceptualization of optimal self-esteem. *Psychological Inquiry*, 1–26.

Kernis, M. H., & Goldman, B. M. (1999). Self-esteem. In D. Levinson, J. Ponzetti, P. Jorgenson (Eds.), *Encyclopedia of human emotions* (pp. 593–600). New York: Macmillan Library Reference.

Kernis, M. H., & Goldman, B. M. (2003). Stability and variability in the self-concept and self-esteem. In M. Leary & J. Tangney (Eds.), *Handbook of self and identity* (pp. 106–127). New York: Guilford Press.

Kernis, M. H., & Goldman, B. M. (2005a). From thought and experience to behavior and interpersonal relationships: A multicomponent conceptualization of authenticity. In A. Tesser, J. V. Wood, & D. A. Stapel (Eds.), *On building, defending, and regulating the self: A psychological perspective* (pp. 31–52). New York: Psychology Press.

Kernis, M. H., & Goldman, B. M. (2005b). Authenticity, social motivation, and psychological adjustment. In J. P. Forgas, K. D. Williams, & S. M. Laham (Eds.) *Social motivation: Conscious and unconscious processes* (pp. 210–227). Cambridge, UK: Cambridge University Press.

Kernis, M. H., & Paradise, A. W. (2002). Distinguishing between secure and fragile forms of high self-esteem. In E. L. Deci & R. M. Ryan (Eds.), *Handbook of self-determination research* (pp. 330–360). Rochester, NY: University of Rochester Press.

Kernis, M. H., Paradise, A. W., Whitaker, D., Wheatman, S., & Goldman, B. (2000). Master of one's psychological domain? Not likely if one's self-esteem is unstable. *Personality and Social Psychology Bulletin*, 26, 1297–1305.

Leary, M. R., & Downs, D. L. (1995). Interpersonal functions of the self-esteem motive: The self-esteem system as a sociometer. In M. H. Kernis (Ed.), *Efficacy, agency, and self-esteem* (pp. 31–50). New York: Plenum.

Maslow, A. H. (1968). *Toward a psychology of being.* (2nd ed.) Princeton, NJ: Van Nostrand.

Myers, D. G., & Diener, E. (1995). Who is happy? *Psychological Science*, 6, 10–19.

O'Brien, E. J., & Epstein, S. (1988) The Multidimensional Self-Esteem Inventory: Professional manual. Odessa, FL: Psychological Assessments Resources.

Rogers, C. (1959). A theory of therapy, personality, and interpersonal relationships, as developed in the client-centered framework. In S. Koch (Ed.), *Psychology: A study of science* (Vol. 3., pp. 184–256). New York: McGraw-Hill.

Rogers, C. (1961). *On becoming a person: A therapist's view of psychotherapy.* Boston: Houghton Mifflin.

Ryan, R. M., & Deci, E. L. (2002). On assimilating identities to the self: A self-determination theory perspective on internalization and integrity within cultures. In M. Leary & J. Tangney (Eds.), *Handbook of self and identity*. New York: Guilford Press.

Ryff, C. (1989). Happiness is everything, or is it? Explorations on the meaning of psychological well-being. *Journal of Personality and Social Psychology*, 57, 1069–1081.

Tennen, H., & Herzberger, S. (1987). Depression, self-esteem, and the absence of self-protective attributional biases. *Journal of Personality and Social Psychology*, 52, 72–80.

Section II

Development and Determinants of Self-Esteem

Question 6

What developmental processes are associated with the emergence of self-esteem? At what age can children rightfully be said to possess self-esteem? To what extent is self-esteem genetically transmitted? What roles do family, peer groups, and other childhood experiences play in the development of self-esteem?

*T*his set of essays focuses on developmental processes associated with the emergence of self-esteem.

Harter describes the developmental trajectories, first of domain-specific self-evaluations, then of global feelings of self-worth (the latter emerging on average around age 8). She then describes two broad classes of self-esteem determinants anchored in the perspectives of James (i.e., ratio of successes to aspirations) and Cooley (i.e., internalized opinions of others toward self). Harter discusses the implications of each perspective for self-esteem change and concludes by considering the role of genetic influences on self-esteem.

Kaplan focuses on the development of the self-esteem motive (to maximize positive self-feelings), which he views "...as the normal outcome of the infant's initial dependency upon human beings for satisfaction of basic biological needs...." Kaplan describes a series of processes through which "...the child acquires the need to behave in ways that will evoke positive self-attitudes and avoid negative self-attitudes—a need expressed as self-esteem motive." Kaplan concludes by speculating on processes associated with individual differences in the self-esteem motive.

Hart, Atkins, and Tursi focus on recent research that suggests that the roles of self-understanding and parental behaviors in children's self-esteem may be more nuanced than previously thought. For example, recent behavioral genetics studies suggest that individual differences in children's self-esteem are attributable to genetic and non-shared environmental influences, but not to shared environmental influences. In addition, Hart and his colleagues review other recent research that they suggest corroborates the partial independence of self-esteem from self-understanding. They discuss the implications of such findings for future research.

18

The Development of Self-Esteem

SUSAN HARTER

*I*n considering the issue of the emergence of self-esteem, an important developmental question concerns the age at which an appreciation for one's worth as a person, as a self, first emerges. Two broad classes of constructs drive these processes, cognitive-developmental level and socialization. At the outset, it becomes critical to discriminate between the age at which children are able to *verbalize* a sense of their self-esteem versus when they appear to manifest it behaviorally in their actions and demeanor. Young children (ages 2–3) begin to use self-relevant pronouns such as "I" and "Me" and may be able to make domain-specific self-evaluations such as "I can run fast", "I know my letters and numbers". These represent rudimentary signs that they can begin to evaluate concrete behavioral attributes about the self in terms of their valence, namely positive versus negative attributes. However, due to normative cognitive-developmental limitations, they cannot yet conceptualize the fact that they are a *person*, much less that personhood carries with it a sense of self-worth or self-esteem. Thus, young children do not possess a conscious, verbalizable concept of their self-esteem.

Does this mean that they do not manifest a sense of positivity or negativity about their behavior, about their seeming value? No. In fact, children clearly exude such a sense of their worth through their actions, what we have labeled "behaviorally-manifest self-esteem" (Haltiwanger, 1989; Harter, 1990, 1999). Asking teachers of children aged 4 through 7, what behaviors discriminated between high and low self-esteem through a Q-sort procedure, we discovered a reliable cluster of behaviors that differentiated the two groups. The behaviors that defined high self-esteem children included displays of confidence, exploration, curiosity, purposefulness, as well as such behaviors as smiling and pride in wanting to share the products of their activities (e.g., pictures, crafts) with others. In contrast, low self-esteem young children were judged to be reticent and withdrawn, primarily onlookers who showed lack of confidence, exploration, curiosity, pride, purposefulness, and who rarely smiled. Thus, in the minds of adult observers, there are clear conceptions of what distinguishes high vs. low self-esteem young children with regard to the behaviors they display.

Why might the behaviors that discriminate between these two groups become important? To the extent that low self-esteem children show lack of exploration, confidence, and purposefulness, they will be less motivated to develop competence, to master skills appropriate for their developmental level, and to engage in social interactions and skills that will be needed at subsequent stages. Thus, there are critical outcomes that behaviorally manifest self-esteem will predict.

THE EMERGENCE OF VERBALIZABLE GLOBAL SELF-ESTEEM

From a developmental perspective, when do children develop a verbalizable concept of their global self-esteem, their overall worth as a person? Moreover, what determines whether such an evaluation is positive or negative? Findings (see Harter, 1990, 1999) reveal that it is not until about the age of 8 that children can comprehend that they are a person who can reflect on the fact that they are happy with themselves, overall, or conversely unhappy with whom they are as a person. Prior to this age, they can evaluate domain-specific aspects of competence (cognitive, physical) or adequacy (appearance, conduct, social acceptance), but they do not yet have the cognitive skills necessary to realize that these discrete evaluations can somehow be combined to form a more global sense of their overall worth as a person. In addition, the judgments in these discrete, differentiated domains are, for the vast majority of young children, extremely positive. From a cognitive-developmental perspective, young children cannot yet make the discrimination between their *actual* competence or adequacy and their *ideal* competence or adequacy. Rather they tend to respond to instruments in terms of their ideals. They also lack the cognitive ability to engage in social comparison *for the purposes of self-evaluation* (Ruble & Frey, 1991). Finally, their perspective-taking skills are in the process of development and they cannot yet completely or accurately evaluate the perceptions of what significant others (e.g., parents, peers) think about the self (Selman, 1980).

Theories of the Causes of Self-Esteem that Become Applicable from Middle Childhood and Beyond

Many investigators of the self have turned to two historical scholars of the self who identified causes of self-esteem in adult populations. Both James (1892) and Cooley (1902) advanced theories of such causes, albeit different antecedents. For James, one's level of self-esteem and one's global evaluation of worth as a person was a reflection of perceptions of competence or adequacy in domains of *importance*, in life arenas where one had aspirations for success. Thus, if one were performing well in domains that were valued, high self-esteem would result. If, in contrast, one were performing poorly in domains of importance, then low self-esteem would be the outcome. Critical to James' theory is the fact that one does not have to be a superstar in all domains. Rather, one can *discount* the importance of domains in which one is not performing well, one can attempt to avoid that domain, which, in turn, should protect one's high self-esteem. Low self-esteem individuals continue to tout the importance of domains in which they are not performing well, thus, leading to a discrepancy between high importance and low perceived competence or adequacy. It is this discrepancy that takes its psychological toll, leading to devaluation of the self (Harter, 1999).

From a neo-Piagetian developmental perspective (e.g., Fischer, 1980), young children do not have the cognitive ability to engage in these Jamesian processes. They do not have a concept of global self-esteem, nor can they make a distinction between their perceived adequacy and the importance of success (analogous to a real versus ideal self-evaluation), each of which is a necessary component of James' model. However, by age 8, on average, and older, these processes are in place.

Cooley (1902) put forth a very different model of the antecedents of self-esteem (for adults) that focused on social-psychological determinants. Cooley advanced the concept of the "looking glass self", as a metaphor for these processes. The essence of Cooley's formulation was that others' opinions of self were critical to the development of a concept of one's self-esteem. That is, significant others are the mirror into which we gaze for information about what they think of us. These perceptions are then incorporated into self-judgments about one's worth as a person. If one thinks that others value them highly as a person, then high self-esteem will result. If one perceives that others view them negatively, then one will develop low self-esteem.

From a developmental perspective, young children do not yet have the cognitive and social processes necessary to construct a sense of their self-esteem based on the principles Cooley put forth. As noted earlier, they do not yet possess a concept of their global self-esteem. Moreover, they have not yet mastered the social perspective-taking skills to infer how others might evaluate them globally as a person. However, by about the age of 8, these skills are sufficiently developed such that Cooley's determinants of global self-esteem are in place.

The cognitive and social advances that emerge in middle childhood make both James' and Cooley's theory of the causes of self-esteem powerful determinants of one's level of self-esteem (see Harter, 1999). They also translate into the *individual differences* that begin to emerge in middle childhood with regard to level of self-esteem. There is much more variability in the level of self-esteem beginning in middle childhood and beyond, precisely because of the cognitive limitations of the young child that protect them from thinking negatively about themselves. Thus, self-esteem is very high. However, the cognitive "advances" to emerge developmentally can represent liabilities (see Harter, 1999), leading to more negative self-esteem. What do we mean by this?

From a Jamesian perspective, the ability to differentiate the *importance of success* from one's *actual abilities* sets the stage for the realization that one may not be performing up to expectations. This will erode one's overall sense of one's worth as a person, one's self-esteem. A child's new-found capacity to utilize social comparison, for the purpose of self-evaluation, will mean that the vast majority who cannot be at the top of the ladder of success will experience lower self-esteem. From the position of Cooley, the ability to assess the opinions of others toward the self, a new perspective-taking ability, may represent a liability to the extent that in middle childhood and beyond, one may perceive that significant others do not value them. Thus, if they internalize these opinions, Cooley's contention, they will then develop low self-esteem.

The empirical evidence (see Harter, 1990, 1993, 1999) provides clear support that beginning in middle childhood, both James' and Cooley's formulations are alive and well in predicting the level of self-esteem from middle childhood and beyond, to late adulthood. Moreover, these are not competing theories. Each contributes to the prediction of global self-esteem. The findings reveal a clear additive model. That is, each of these formulations contributes to our prediction of level of self-esteem (see Figure 18.1). Thus, those with the lowest self-esteem are those who both report low approval from others and feel most inadequate in domains of importance. Those with the highest self-esteem report high approval from others in conjunction with self-perceptions of success in arenas they deem important.

Elsewhere, our findings revealing that the opinions of certain significant others are more important than others and that particular domains are more important to self-esteem have been presented in detail (Harter, 1999). Noteworthy is the very robust finding that across the life span, perceptions of one's physical appearance and global self-esteem are inextricably linked, with correlations ranging from .65 to .82. Moreover, those basing their self-esteem on perceived attractiveness are far more likely to devalue their appearance, their self-esteem, and report depression. Adopting this meta-theory is particularly pernicious for females in our society.

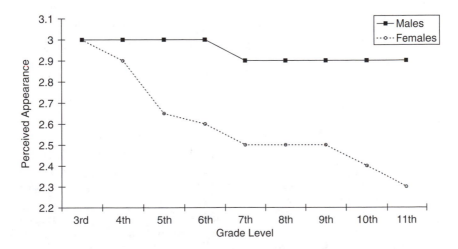

FIGURE 18.1 Perceived physical appearance for males and females as a function of grade level (reproduced from Harter (1999) with permission from Guilford Press).

Can Self-Esteem Change?

Given these formulations, and their developmental origins, can self-esteem become altered or does one's early experience cement one's level of self-esteem forever? Clearly, early experience is an important determinant but if there are major changes in the causes of self-esteem change, then self-esteem will change in tandem. Thus, children with low self-esteem can move to higher levels of self-worth if they can adjust the ratio of their competence/adequacy and importance of success. How might one do this? James suggested a formula: one either increases one's competence/adequacy or one decreases the importance of success in areas where one feels inadequate. These may not be easy goals to achieve, however they represent two hypothetical avenues. That is, one can strive to increase the importance of those domains where one does feel adequate and/or discount the importance of domains in which one feels inadequate. With regard to Cooley's formulation, one can try to occupy social niches where one's talents are acknowledged. This, again, is difficult for children, particularly if parents are disapproving. Other solutions include finding a special adult; for example, a grandparent, a teacher, a coach, the parent of a friend, or a peer group who are approving and can therefore be a boon to self-esteem (see Harter, 1999).

The issue of change is more complex than this, however. The question of whether self-esteem *as a construct* is an unchangeable *trait* or whether it is changeable or more state-like is bogus, as recent research is documenting (see Harter, 2004). The construct of self-esteem, itself, is neither a trait nor a state, by definition. Rather, findings now reveal that for *some* individuals the construct is stable over time or trait-like whereas for others it varies over either time or situation. Our research provides three strands of evidence to support this claim (as does work by DuBois, 2002).

First, we have examined change over time during the transition from high school to college, over an eight-month period. Here, we discovered three groups of students. One group reported no change in self-esteem. One group reported gains in self-esteem. A third group reported losses in self-esteem. Thus, the first group reported stability over time, whereas the other two groups both reported change (see Harter, 1999).

In a second strand of research, we have introduced the construct of "relational" self-esteem or self-worth (see Harter, 1999, 2004). We documented the fact that many individuals report different levels of self-esteem depending upon the relational context (i.e., with parents, teachers, male classmates, and female classmates), thus showing variability across contexts. However, a minority showed consistency, that is no differences in self-esteem, across these contexts. Thus, for some individuals there is variability, for others there is not.

Finally, we have assessed self-reported *fluctuations* in self-esteem asking adolescents to indicate whether their self-esteem does not typically change from day to day or whether it changes several times a day, a week, or a month. Here, again, we found that for some individuals, there are virtually no fluctuations in self-esteem whereas for others, there are minor to major fluctuations.

Other Possible Causes: Genetic Influences?

The discussion above has focused on psychological mechanisms that account for a child's level of self-esteem. For many years, these have been the prevailing theories. Recently, neurological and genetic models have come to the fore, the 1990s were declared the decade of the brain, and it became obvious that our splintered fields needed to be integrated if we are truly to understand development and human behavior. Thus, how might such a genetic perspective be applied to differences in levels of self-esteem in children? I am not a geneticist, nor have I done such work. Some findings suggest (statistical) heritability of self-esteem. The empirical findings cannot be disputed (see McGuire, Manke, Kimberly, Saudino, Reiss, Hetherington, & Plomin, 1999; Neiss, Sedikides, & Stevenson, 2002).

However, does this mean that there is a "self-esteem" gene? I think not. Might there be heritability, yes. What might be a thoughtful explanation? We know a great deal about heritability from many strong studies of intelligence, temperament, athleticism, and creativity. There are also considerable data demonstrating the heritability of conditions such as various learning disabilities, autism, and ADHD (see Pennington, 2002). These studies can be linked to the formulations above. That is, if the genetic throw of the dice causes a child to be intellectually competent, athletically competent, attractive by current societal standards, and if parents reward those characteristics and reinforce their importance, then according to James and our own findings, this child is on the path to high self-esteem. If children are genetically blessed with a sociable temperament, and are rewarded for their sociability by parents, teachers, and peers, then, from a Cooley perspective, they will receive positive feedback that will enhance their self-esteem. Thus, I would see the constructs that I have identified as mediators of self-esteem, impacted by genetics, but not that there is a direct connection between genes and self-esteem.

REFERENCES

Cooley, C. H. (1902). *Human nature and the social order.* New York: Charles Scribner's Sons.

DuBois, D. (Chair). (2002, April). *Change and stability in self-esteem during adolescence: The long and the short of it.* Symposium conducted at the Biennial Meeting of the Society for Research in Child Development, New Orleans.

Fischer, K. W. (1980). A theory of cognitive development: The control and construction of hierarchies of skills. *Psychological Review, 87,* 477–531.

Haltiwanger, J. (1989). *Behavioral referents of presented self-esteem in young children.* Paper presented at the meeting of the Society for Research in Child Development, Kansas City, MO.

Harter, S. (1990). Causes, correlates, and the functional role of global self-worth: A lifespan perspective. In R. Sternberg & J. Kolligian (Eds.), *Competence considered* (pp. 67–98). New Haven, CT: Yale University Press.

Harter, S. (1993). Causes and correlates of low self-esteem in children and adolescents. In R. F. Baumeister (Ed.), *Self-esteem: The puzzle of low self-regard* (pp. 87–116). New York: Plenum.

Harter, S. (1999). *The construction of the self*. New York: The Guilford Press.

Harter, S. (2004). The developmental emergence of self-esteem: Individual differences in change and stability. In D. Mroczek & T. Little (Eds.), *The handbook of personality development*. Hillsdale, NJ: Lawrence Erlbaum Associates, Inc.

James, W. (1892). *Psychology: The briefer course*. New York: Henry Holt.

McGuire, S., Manke, B., Saudino, K. J., Reiss, D., Hetherington, E. M., & Plomin, R. (1999). Perceived competence and self-worth during adolescence: A longitudinal behavioral genetic study. *Child Development, 70*, 1283–1296.

Neiss, M. B., Sedikides, C., & Stevenson, J. (2002). Self-esteem: A behavioural genetic perspective. *European Journal of Personality, 16*, 351–367.

Pennington, B. F. (2002). *The development of psychopathology*. New York: The Guilford Press.

Ruble, D. N., & Frey, K. S. (1991). Changing patterns of comparative behavior as skills are acquired: A functional model of self-evaluation. In J. Suls & T. A. Wills (Eds.), *Social comparison: Comtemporary theory and research* (pp. 70–112). Hillsdale, NJ: Lawrence Erlbaum Associates, Inc.

Selman, R. L. (1980). *The growth of personal understanding*. New York: Academic Press.

19

Development of the Self-Esteem Motive

HOWARD B. KAPLAN

*T*he self-esteem motive is viewed as the normal outcome of the infant's initial dependency upon adult human beings for satisfaction of basic biological needs, among which perhaps the most apparent (to the infant) is hunger. From the base of biological dependency the person is said to pass through the stages of learning to need other people, to need the expression of positive attitudes toward oneself from others, and finally to need the expression of positive self-attitudes.

THE NEED FOR OTHER PEOPLE

Since the infant is in fact dependent upon the parent surrogate for the satisfaction of basic needs, in time and with the development of increasing discriminative ability the infant may be expected to subjectively associate need satisfaction with the presence of specific adult figures. For example, the infant will come to perceive a relationship between the instances in which his hunger is assuaged on the one hand and the presence of the mother on the other hand: The probability is far greater that the infant's hunger will be assuaged if the mother or mother surrogate is present than if she is not present. As the presence of an adult figure increasingly becomes associated with need satisfaction, the former phenomenon comes to evoke the same kind of responses as the initial need satisfaction. Just as the total need satisfaction experience (feeding) or intrinsic aspects of it (the nipple, the taste of milk, the stomach filling up) evoke feelings of pleasure, tension reduction, and so on, so does the associated phenomenon, the presence of the adult figure, come to evoke pleasurable experiences. Just as the presentation of a stimulus associated with the feeding experience (the sight of the bottle or a breast) evokes positive excitatory emotional responses in anticipation of need satisfaction (feeding) so does the presentation of the parent come to evoke similar emotional responses. In short, the perception of the mother's presence evokes pleasurable emotional

responses in the infant. Thus, the mother's presence becomes an intrinsically gratifying experience for the infant where formerly it was only gratifying for the infant
in conjunction with the satisfaction of the infant's biological needs. The mother's
presence is now said to be an acquired need (independent of its association with
satisfaction of the infant's biological needs), to have positive motivational significance just as the satisfaction of biological needs is said to have positive motivational significance. Just as the infant cries for relief of his hunger so will he (given
his newly acquired needs) cry for the presence of his mother whether or not he is
aware of current biological needs.

THE NEED FOR POSITIVE ATTITUDES FROM OTHERS

Insofar as the mother and/or other adults have been motivationally significant features of his environment the infant is likely to become extremely sensitive to their
presence and to the phenomena associated with their presence—i.e., the range of
behaviors manifested by the adult figures. In her continuing role of ministering to
the physical needs of the infant, the mother or mother surrogate will produce a
variety of behaviors, including facial expressions, that sometimes take a form an
observer might describe as a smile and at other times assume a form that might
be described as a frown; at times her body posture might be described as relaxed
and at other times rigid; on occasion her gestures and acts might be described as
expressing approval or love and on other occasions as expressing annoyance or disapproval; on some occasions her vocalizations might be harsh, loud, and frequent
while on other occasions her vocalizations might be soothing, quiet, and infrequent. The mother will tend to display some rather than other of these culturally
patterned behaviors depending upon concrete circumstances; and which of these
behaviors are performed might well be associated with the degree to which the
infant experiences need satisfaction. Thus, during the acts of feeding or washing
the infant the mother might characteristically be relaxed, smile, and speak softly,
while during periods in which the harassed mother must delay feeding the hungry infant she might characteristically speak in loud and harsh tones and handle
the infant roughly.

The mother's behavioral responses toward the child that accompany (or result
in) the child's experience of need satisfaction (pleasure) or need dissatisfaction
(pain) might be responses that are unrelated to the child's behavior, as when she
expresses annoyance toward the child because she had an argument with a friend
or behaves kindly toward the infant because her husband complimented her. Or,
perhaps more probably, the mother's behaviors toward the child that are associated
with the infant's experience of pleasure or pain might be responses to the infant's
behavior, as when the mother claps, smiles, and hugs the infant who has displayed
a new ability, or when the mother yells at or slaps the infant for overturning a vase.
In either case, to the extent that certain behaviors by the mother do in fact consistently appear in conjunction with, or result in, the infant's experience of need
gratification the infant will likely come to subjectively associate these behaviors
with these experiences of need gratification (or need frustration).

These behaviors by the mother, which in fact are displayed in conjunction with the acts of satisfying (or frustrating) the infant's need (such as hunger or the otherwise avoidance of physical pain) and which are subjectively associated by the infant with the experience of satisfaction or frustration, might be described briefly as expressions of parental attitudes. That is, if an observer or the mothers themselves were asked to interpret the meaning of these maternal behaviors they would likely interpret them in terms of expressions of positive or negative emotional responses.

As these maternal attitudes become increasingly associated in the infant's awareness with experiences of satisfaction or frustration of his physical needs the expressions of attitudes themselves come to evoke the same kinds of emotional responses that the experiences of physical need satisfaction or frustration evoked. Just as the experience of hunger evoked subjective feelings of distress, so would the expressions of negative attitudes toward the child (harsh tones, loud voice, rough handling, turning away, saying "naughty") by the mother now evoke subjective feelings of distress *even in circumstances in which the infant was not aware of current frustration of physical needs*. Just as the experience of alleviation of hunger evoked feelings of pleasure, satisfaction, or tension release so are such feelings now evoked by expressions of positive attitudes (a soft vocal tone, a caress, drawing near, saying "good boy") by the mother toward the child, again, independently of any current experience by the infant of satisfaction of physical needs. Thus, as a result of the infant's sensitivity to the range of behaviors associated with the mother's presence (an acquired need) and of the infant's discrimination between maternal behaviors that are consistently associated with the circumstances of satisfying, or frustrating the infant's physical needs, the expression of positive (negative) maternal attitudes has become an intrinsically gratifying (distressing) experience where formerly its gratificational relevance was in conjunction with the experience of physical need satisfaction (frustration). The infant may be said to have acquired a need to evoke positive attitudinal responses (and to avoid negative attitudinal responses) by the mother. The attitudinal responses of the mother have achieved motivational significance in that the subject will so behave as to evoke the expression of positive attitudes and to avoid the expression of negative attitudes by the mother toward himself (just as the satisfaction of physical needs present at birth and the presence of the mother, a need acquired since birth, were said to have motivational significance in that the subject behaves so as to achieve satisfaction of these needs).

THE NEED FOR POSITIVE SELF-ATTITUDES

It has been asserted that the child who has acquired the need to evoke positive (and to avoid negative) attitudinal responses from others in his environment would attempt to behave so far as possible in ways that would satisfy this need. However, if this goal is to be achieved certain conditions must be fulfilled. Although, as has been stated above, the attitudinal responses to the child by adult figures may occasionally be the consequence of factors unrelated to the child's attributes, it is more often the case that expressions of positive or negative attitudes toward the child by others are consequences of the behaviors and characteristics manifested by the child. The adults' attitudinal responses represent in large measure culturally patterned expressions of their perceptions and evaluations of the degree to which the child's behaviors and attributes conform to the (again, in large measure) culturally patterned normative expectations that the adults apply to the child. To the extent that the child manifests "approved" behaviors and attributes, others will respond with expressions of positive attitudes, and to the extent that the child manifests "disapproved" behaviors and attributes, others will respond with expressions of negative attitudes.

Insofar as certain of his behaviors and attributes are consistently associated with the actual occurrence of motivationally significant experiences (i.e., being the object of positive or negative attitudinal responses) the subject will learn to *subjectively associate* the attitudinal responses of others with his own attributes and behaviors. For example, he is able to perceive that people consistently express "positive" attitudes (laugh, pay attention, say "good boy") when he behaves in certain ways (smiles, walks, plays with a ball, eats his food) and consistently express "negative" attitudes (frown, yell at him, say "don't") when he behaves in other ways (cries, sits passively, plays with a doll, throws his food).

Because of the perceived association between the child's attributes and behaviors on the one hand and the attitudinal responses of the other people on the other hand, the child becomes emotionally invested in being able to anticipate what sorts of attitudinal responses will be expressed by others toward particular subject traits and behaviors. The ability of the subject to successfully predict the attitudinal responses of others to particular subject attributes or behaviors would permit (within limits) the individual to behave in ways that would satisfy the acquired need to maximize the expression of positive (and minimize the expression of negative) attitudes by others toward the subject. That is, the subject could purposively behave in ways that would predictably evoke the desired attitudinal responses to the subject by others.

Such an ability would involve the subject in adopting the perspective of the other person and vicariously responding to himself *as if* he were the other person. That is, the subject in his own imagination would perceive, evaluate, and attitudinally respond to himself, as the other person would be presumed to respond. The subject could then vary his own behavior in a way that was consistent with the expectation that the other would respond with positive rather than negative attitudes.

In the course of imagining how the other person responds (or would respond) to the subject attitudinally, the subject expresses an attitude toward himself that is the symbolic representation of the imagined attitudinal response of the other person and then responds to his own attitudinal expression as if the other person had actually expressed the attitude. In view of the symbolic association between the subject's own attitudinal expression and the imagined attitudinal responses of others, and in view of the subject's previously discussed acquired need to be the object of positive attitudinal responses (and to avoid being the object of negative attitudinal responses) by others, the subject would be expected to respond to his own expressions of positive attitudinal responses toward himself with feelings of satisfaction, gratification, tension release, and so on, and would be expected to respond to his own negative attitudinal responses to himself with feelings of tension, subjective distress, depression, and so on. The subject's own attitudinal responses to himself thus become motivationally significant. Through their original association with the imagined attitudes of others, the subject's attitudinal expressions toward himself tend to consistently evoke relatively gratifying/distressing emotional experiences. The subject at this point may be said to have acquired the need to respond to himself in terms of positive attitudes and thereby to evoke further gratifying emotional experiences and to avoid responding to himself in terms of negative attitudes that would evoke continued experiences of subjective distress. In short, the subject is now said to have acquired the need to maximize the experience of positive self-attitudes and to minimize the experience of negative self-attitudes. Stated in another way, the subject has acquired the self-esteem motive.

In summary, the self-esteem motive is seen as the normal outcome of processes that may be traced back to the infant's initial dependence upon adult figures for satisfaction of physical needs. Through the association between experiences of satisfaction of physical needs and the presence of adult figures the infant acquires a need for the physical presence of adult figures and becomes particularly sensitive to the phenomena associated with the presence of adults (i.e., the range of adult behaviors). The infant's perception of the actually existing association between satisfaction/frustration of its physical needs and particular adult behaviors (which an observer or the adult in question might describe as expressions of positive or negative attitudes) leads to the infant's acquisition of a need to be the object of positive attitudes (and to avoid being the object of negative attitudes) expressed by significant other adults. In order to maximize the satisfaction of this acquired need, the child adopts the role of the other adults and perceives, evaluates, and expresses attitudes toward himself from their point of view in order to permit himself to behave in ways that he imagines will evoke positive attitudes from others, and the child then responds to his own expressions of attitudes toward himself as if they were in fact the expressed attitudes of others with positive or negative affect. In this way, through the symbolic association between the imagined attitudinal responses of others and his own attitudinal responses toward himself, the child acquires the need to behave in ways that will evoke positive self-attitudes and avoid negative self-attitudes—a need expressed as self-esteem motive.

INDIVIDUAL DIFFERENCES IN THE SELF-ESTEEM MOTIVE

In the normal course of events, then, the child will develop the self-esteem motive; that is, the child will experience distressful self-feelings in response to negative self-evaluations. Accordingly, he will experience the need to respond in ways that will assuage these feelings and forestall occasions for such negative self-feelings. The near universal process through which the self-esteem motive develops will be forestalled only by the relatively rare circumstances in which the child is the object of uniformly punitive, uniformly rewarding, or totally random responses by the child's significant others, regardless of the child's attributes or behaviors.

However, while the processes for developing a self-esteem motive are near universal, the frequency and continuity of experiencing a need to attain or restore self-esteem (or, more to the point, to assuage or forestall feelings of self-derogation) is highly variable. Individual differences in the activation of the self-esteem motive are a function of the child's self-perception of having highly (dis)valued attributes, performing highly (dis)valued behaviors, and otherwise having salient (dis)valued experiences (failures or successes, acceptance or rejection by significant others). Variability in these self-judgments is a function of the child's actual experiences of failure or success in achieving valued goals, and of evoking positive or negative attitudes from significant others. From the beginning children will vary in their experiences depending upon the level of expectations imposed on the child and the biogenetic, psychosocial, and sociocultural resources provided to the child at birth and onward. Not the least significant of these resources is the nature and effectiveness of adaptive, coping, or defense mechanisms that may permit the individual in varying degrees to forestall, redefine, or assuage the distress associated with self-devaluing circumstances.

Although variation in the experiences that directly or indirectly affect self-esteem begin at birth (and even earlier), variation in the experience of perception of self-devaluing circumstances presumes the capacity to become an object to oneself, i.e., the capacity for self-referent responses. Since self-cognition, in general, and self-evaluation, in particular, presumes the development of language (that allows the symbolic representation of oneself to oneself) it is to be expected that individual differences in self-esteem (that is, the need for self-esteem) will become apparent around the time that the child develops language. At that time the child's variable self-awareness of self-devaluing experiences, and correlated negative self-feelings evoked by the self-awareness, to that degree will stimulate the self-esteem motive, i.e., the need to attain or restore higher levels of positive self-evaluations and correlated positive self-feelings.

FURTHER READING

Kaplan, H. B. (1975). *Self-attitudes and deviant behavior*. Pacific Palisades, CA: Goodyear.

Kaplan, H. B. (1980). *Deviant behavior in defense of self*. New York: Academic Press.

Kaplan, H. B. (1986). Psychosocial stress from the perspective of self theory. In H. B. Kaplan (Ed.), *Psychosocial stress: Perspectives on structure, theory, life course, and methods* (pp. 175–244). San Diego, CA: Academic Press.

Kaplan, H. B. (1986). *Social psychology of self-referent behavior*. New York: Plenum Press.

Kaplan, H. B. & R. J. Johnson. (2001). *Social deviance: Testing a general theory*. New York: Kluwer Academic/Plenum.

20

Origins and Developmental Influences on Self-Esteem

DANIEL HART, ROBERT ATKINS, and NATASHA TURSI

THE SELF-ESTEEM THEORETICAL TRADITION

*T*he origins of and developmental influences on self-esteem have fascinated generations of psychologists. A century of theorizing and research has resulted in a broad consensus that self-esteem is the joint product of (1) *reflective self-evaluations*, and (2) the *appraisals of others*. The first of these notions can be traced to William James, who wrote that:

> our self-feeling in this world depends entirely on what we *back* ourselves to be and do. It is determined by the ratio of our actualities to our supposed potentialities; a fraction of which our pretensions are the denominator and the numerator our success: thus, Self-esteem = Success / Pretensions. Such a fraction may be increased as well by diminishing the denominator as by increasing the numerator. (James, 1890, pp. 310–311)

This definition suggests that self-esteem is the byproduct of an individual's reflective weighing of successes and aspirations and seemingly specifies a developmental sequence in which knowledge of the self precedes self-esteem.

Cooley (1922) proposed that pride or shame in oneself is determined in large part by one's inferences concerning *others' appraisals* of the self. If others are believed to judge the self favorably, then self-esteem is high; if one's family and friends are perceived as judging the self negatively, then low self-esteem should result. Cooley's ideas concerning social influences on self-esteem were the foundation for thousands of studies examining the relation of self-esteem to the perceived perceptions of significant others—particularly parents—a line of work that continues through today. Developmentally, Cooley's theory requires as a prerequisite to self-esteem the awareness that others have perspectives on the self, a capability that is probably present in toddlers.

PROBLEMS WITH THE TRADITIONAL ACCOUNT

The traditional account of self-esteem development is undoubtedly correct in large measure. A voluminous research literature abundant with findings supportive of both James' and Cooley's tenets has accumulated over the past 50 years. For example, in her review of the literature in the *Handbook of Child Psychology*, Harter concluded that there "is a growing body of empirical evidence revealing that parental approval is particularly critical in determining the self-esteem of children, supporting the [Cooley's] looking-glass-self formulation" (1998, p. 583), and in the same chapter reported that there is considerable evidence consistent with James' theory of self-esteem.

In our view, however, there are exciting new findings in a variety of areas which demonstrate that the traditional account must be supplemented by new paradigms, if self-esteem is to be understood fully. In the sections that follow, we highlight these findings.

Self-Esteem has Both State and Trait Qualities

Within an individual, self-esteem varies from moment to moment and from context to context. A child may judge the self to be a success with peers—and experience high self-esteem during play—but judge that the self is ineffective at school. Research with adults (discussed elsewhere in this volume) suggests that the study of variability in self-esteem over the course of a day or a week provides extremely important insights into personality functioning. Unfortunately, there is exceedingly little developmental research on this topic (and consequently we do not discuss it in this chapter; for one example of this kind of work, see Kernis, Brown, & Brody, 2000). Most of the developmental research on self-esteem has focused on the stable, trait-like facets of self-esteem, presuming, correctly as it turns out, that some individuals are typically very positive in their self-evaluations while others are chronically negative in their self-appraisals. Because this assumption is dominant in the field, our discussion in the following sections focuses on self-esteem as a trait.

Individual Differences in Self-Esteem are Heritable

As we noted earlier, most theorists have assumed that children's self-esteem is influenced by parental appraisals. From this theoretical perspective, parents who think negatively of their children are inculcating negative self-esteem in them, while parents who view their children positively foster positive self-regard. This belief has become a foundation in American folk psychology regarding child rearing (Damon, 1995). Moreover, there is abundant research suggesting that parents who behave coldly have children with low self-esteem (e.g., Killeen & Forehand, 1998). Unfortunately, however, much of the research which reports correlations of parental and family characteristics with children's self-esteem and concludes that parental behavior or communication influences self-esteem in children fails to consider the possibility that it is parental *genes*, not *parental behavior*, which accounts for the similarity of parents to their children. Only through sophisticated research designs—either correlational studies which permit the separate estimation of parents' genetic and behavioral influences on their children or experimental studies in which parental appraisals are changed—is it possible to determine whether parental appraisals influence children's self-esteem. These kinds of sophisticated studies are exceedingly rare.

However, there are a few behavioral genetic studies, which demonstrate that individual differences in self-esteem are *not* accounted for by differences in family environments. Based on patterns of correlations among twins, non-twin siblings, and siblings who share the genes of only one parent, McGuire and colleagues (McGuire, Manke, Saudino, Reiss, Hetherington, & Plomin, 1999) inferred that variability in adolescents' general self-esteem and other facets of self-evaluation was attributable to genetic sources and to environmental influences unique to each child in a family. Other behavioral genetic studies (e.g., Kendler, Gardner, & Prescott, 1998) converge on the same conclusions. These findings suggest that the shared environment, in this case the family/household, is uncorrelated with children's levels of self-esteem.

One example that demonstrates this important point is the nontraditional family setting, consisting of parents and adopted, unrelated children. The behavioral genetics evidence suggests that the fact that these children share a common home environment would not influence their global levels of self-esteem; in other words, sharing a common home environment does not lead children in such families to develop similar feelings of self-worth. Adoptive parents with low levels of self-esteem who create a cold home environment apparently are no more likely to have adoptive children with low self-esteem than are high self-esteem adoptive parents whose home is warm and positive. Such findings undermine common assumptions about the role of the family in shaping self-esteem in children.

While the shared environment of the family does not influence self-esteem in children, this does not mean that self-esteem level is fully determined by genes. As mentioned above, behavioral geneticists have concluded that non-shared environments—unique environmental influences—predict children's levels of self-esteem as well. For example, even children raised in the same family experience different external environmental influences, and these unique influences appear to influence levels of self-esteem. These unique environmental influences include schools, peers, and social circles, and different patterns of parental treatment. Children's interactions with these and other influences affect their self-esteem. To some extent, these unique environments may be a result of children's qualities; for example, parental behavior is shaped by children's unique personalities. Siblings may have significantly dissimilar personalities, which trigger different parental responses.

In our view, the behavioral genetic research on self-esteem leads to the rejection of claims that family environment and parenting style (at least to the extent that the latter refers to parental behavior that is similar across siblings) accounts for individual differences in self-esteem.

A few behavioral genetic studies have attempted to estimate the relative importance of genetic and shared environmental influences on self-esteem *change over time.* The findings from this work suggest that change in self-esteem is attributable to genetic and non-shared environmental influences, but not to shared environmental influences (see Neiss, Sedikides, & Stevenson, 2002 for a review). Again, the inference is that family environments are not influential in change in self-esteem.

Self-Esteem is Increasingly Stable with Age

Individual differences in self-esteem emerge in childhood and become increasingly stable with age (the test–retest correlation for a 1 year interval is estimated to be .4 for 8-year-olds and rises to .5 for teenagers (Trzesniewski, Donnellan, & Robins, 2003), a pattern nearly identical to that observed in personality traits. The substantial stability of individual differences suggests that self-esteem must be partially independent of the *understanding* of self, that is, the collection of traits, features, and beliefs, which individuals ascribe to themselves. Damon and Hart (1988) demonstrated that self-understanding changes across childhood and adolescence, with both the specific attributes attributed to the self and the organization among them evidencing regular developmental transformation. In other words, the research suggests that self-esteem can remain stable while self-understanding changes, just as the stability of personality traits indicates that they are independent of any age-specific attitudes or beliefs. This is not to suggest that James' claim that self-esteem is associated with the assessment of successes and aspirations is totally wrong—even young children's self-assessments correspond to their abilities and qualities (e.g., Marsh, Ellis, & Craven, 2002)—but it is to claim that self-esteem is not wholly a product of this kind of evaluation.

Self-Appraisals are a Subset of Evaluations of the World

Recent research demonstrates that individuals differ in the propensity to make negative evaluations about the world (Robinson, Vargas, Tamir, & Solberg, 2004). Moreover, individual differences in this propensity are correlated with measures of negative mood and somatic complaints, a pattern that is similar to that observed among measures of self-esteem and assessments of psychopathology. This suggests that measures of self-esteem index the broad, stable, trait-like tendency to make negative evaluations about the world—all objects of appraisal are judged more or less the same—rather than specific judgments concerning the self's qualities. In other words, self-esteem may be a domain-specific reflection of a general appraisal of the world. This turns around the Jamesian presumption that self-esteem is a derivative of the reflective appraisal of self (Harter, 1998); it is to postulate instead that the propensity to make negative evaluations about the world determines the identification of the self's successes and aspirations.

Self-Esteem is Open to Social Influence and Can be Changed

Our discussion to this point has emphasized the importance of factors that contribute to stable individual differences in self-esteem. However, self-esteem is not an encapsulated human quality, impervious to environmental influence. Indeed, self-evaluation is influenced by social context across cultures (Marsh & Hau, 2003). For example, the transition from elementary school to middle school depresses self-esteem in young teenagers (e.g., Seidman, Allen, Aber, Mitchell, & Feinman, 1994), which suggests that change in social context affects the evaluative appraisal of oneself. Moreover, childhood self-esteem can be changed, at least for short periods of time, through targeted interventions (Haney & Durlak, 1998). While relatively little is known about the durability of change in self-esteem produced by either transition from one social context to another or as a result of intentional interventions, the existence of these sorts of effects demonstrates that self-esteem is influenced by social context.

SELF-ESTEEM AS A DEVELOPMENTAL CONSTRUCT

A century of theorizing and research leads to the conclusion that childhood self-esteem has its conceptual base in the understanding of self and that it is influenced by social context. The evidence for accepting this conclusion cannot be reviewed here, as there are thousands of relevant studies.

However, we believe that the new research, which we outlined above, leads to a more nuanced understanding of self-esteem than was possible for theorists of 50 years ago. The behavioral genetic findings of the last two decades demonstrate that family environments and parenting styles have little systematic influence on children's self-esteem, an insight not available to the field in the 1950s. Similarly, the evidence of the high stability of self-esteem and the fact that individuals may be broadly biased in the tendency to evaluate the world negatively or positively is both relatively new and rich with potential insights for our understanding of self-esteem.

The new research adds vitality to the study of childhood self-esteem. We have learned a great deal over the past century of work, but we have learned as well that all we believed about the origins and development of self-esteem is unlikely to be true. The future holds great promise for the study of the extent to which childhood self-esteem is independent of the individual's reflective appraisal of self, the degree to which self-esteem reflects unique information about the self as opposed to broad construals of the world, the malleability of self-esteem in social context and in intentional interventions, and the paths of influence from family to childhood self-appraisals. These are all areas in which traditional wisdom must be augmented by new findings from the next century of research.

REFERENCES

Cooley, C. H. (1922). *Human nature and the social order*. New York: Charles Scribner's Sons.

Damon, W. (1995). *Greater expectations: Overcoming the culture of indulgence in America's homes and schools*. New York: The Free Press.

Damon, W., & Hart, D. (1988). *Self-understanding development in childhood and adolescence*. New York: Cambridge University Press.

Haney, P., & Durlak, J. A. (1998). Changing self-esteem in children and adolescents: A meta-analytic review. *Journal of Clinical Child Psychology, 27*, 423–433.

Harter, S. (1998). The development of self-representations. In N. Eisenberg (Ed.), *Handbook of child psychology: Vol. 3, Social, emotional, and personality development* (pp. 553–617). New York: Wiley.

James, W. (1890). *The principles of psychology: Volume 1.* New York: Holt.

Kendler, K. S., Gardner, C. O., & Prescott, C. A. (1998). A population-based twin study of self-esteem and gender. *Psychological Medicine, 28*, 1403–1409.

Kernis, M., Brown, A., & Brody, G. (2000). Fragile self-esteem in children and its associations with perceived patterns of parent–child communication. *Journal of Personality, 68*(2), 225–253.

Killeen, M. R., & Forehand, R. (1998). A transactional model of adolescent self-esteem. *Journal of Family Psychology, 12*, 132–148.

Marsh, H. W., Ellis, L. A., & Craven, R. G. (2002). How do preschool children feel about themselves? Unraveling measurement and multidimensional self-concept structure. *Developmental Psychology, 38*, 376–393.

Marsh, H. W., & Hau, K. (2003). Big-fish-little-pond effect on academic self-concept. *American Psychologist, 58*, 364–376.

McGuire, S., Manke, B., Saudino, K. J., Reiss, D., Hetherington, E. M., & Plomin, R. (1999). Perceived competence and self-worth during adolescence: A longitudinal behavioral genetic study. *Child Development, 70*, 1283–1296.

Neiss, M. B., Sedikides, C., & Stevenson, J. (2002). Self-esteem: A behavioral genetic perspective. *European Journal of Personality, 16*, 351–367.

Robinson, M. D., Vargas, P. T., Tamir, M., & Solberg, E. C. (2004). Using and being used by categories: The case of negative evaluations and daily well-being. *Psychological Science, 15*, 521–526.

Seidman, E., Allen, L., Aber, J. L., Mitchell, C., & Feinman, J. (1994). The impact of school transitions in early adolescence on the self-system and perceived social context of poor urban youth. *Child Development, 65*, 507–522.

Trzesniewski, K. H., Donnellan, M. B., & Robins, R. W. (2003). Stability of self-esteem across the life span. *Journal of Personality and Social Psychology, 84*, 205–220.

Question 7

Does self-esteem ever truly change? What aspects of self-esteem are more resistant to change than are others? How can a person modify his or her self-esteem? What are the central ingredients of a personal program to change one's self-esteem?

*T*his set of essays focuses on self-esteem change, both by individuals themselves and through structured intervention programs. As a group, these essays offer many important and nonmutually exclusive suggestions for enhancing self-esteem.

Mruk's favored approach to changing self-esteem is anchored in qualitative research in which self-esteem is considered a joint function of competence and worthiness, i.e., feelings of self-worth emerge from competently exhibiting certain kinds of behaviors. Mruk reviews clinical techniques used to change self-esteem and describes his own intervention program consisting of five weekly group sessions. He concludes by noting difficulties associated with modifying only the worthiness dimension of self-esteem and on the difficulties associated with modifying defensive high self-esteem.

Tevendale and Dubois first review evidence that although self-esteem exhibits considerable stability, it can and does change in many individuals. Like Mruk, these authors advocate that personal and formal intervention programs be theoretically based and include a thorough understanding of fundamental self-esteem concepts. Moreover, understanding both objective and subjective factors involved in self-esteem change processes is essential. As they note, interventions that increase individuals' actual day-to-day mastery experiences and social connectedness have proven to be most successful.

In the final essay in this section, Vonk distinguishes processes that enhance fragile vs. secure forms of self-esteem. After reviewing the implications of self-determination theory and sociometer theory for enhancing self-esteem, Vonk reports findings from her internet-based study in which participants completed diaries and researchers heightened either self-contact/autonomy or social approval. Findings indicated that, relative to a control group, only the self-esteem of individuals in the social approval group improved over time. Vonk suggests, "…that positive regard by others, even if it only temporary, is the 'entrance' to true self-esteem changes…"

21

Changing Self-Esteem: Research and Practice

CHRISTOPHER J. MRUK

There are at least three major ways of defining self-esteem that are active in the field today. Self-esteem can be seen primarily in terms of *competence* as James (1890/1983) suggested over a century ago when he talked about the ratio of one's pretensions to successes. Self-esteem can also be viewed largely as a form of *worthiness*, a definition that appears to be the most frequently used in the literature today (Baumeister, Smart, & Boden, 1996). However, self-esteem can be understood as the product of a relationship between the variables of *competence and worthiness* (Branden, 1969), where feelings of worth are generated by competently exhibiting certain types of behavior. Although there is evidence that self-esteem can change when defined in any of these ways, there are two reasons that the strongest case may be made when using the third approach.

First, research methods capable of accessing self-esteem as it is lived by real people in real life seem to favor understanding the phenomenon in terms of competence and worthiness. For example, one of the earliest investigations of self-esteem at the lived level is found in Epstein's (1979) ecological work. In one particularly revealing design, he asked subjects to keep a record of their experiences over a period of several consecutive weeks and to monitor them for fluctuations in self-esteem. The volunteers were also instructed to describe in some detail one experience per week that enhanced their self-esteem and one that lessened it. These data, in turn, were examined in terms of the types of situations that generated changes in self-esteem, the kinds of emotions that were experienced at the time, as well as the behaviors that accompanied them. He found that two types of experiences affected self-esteem most directly: those that involved success or failure and those that involved acceptance or rejection. Of course, success and failure often depend on competence, or the lack of it, and it is clear that being accepted or rejected by meaningful others can readily affect one's sense of worthiness.

Other such research examines how self-esteem affects, and is affected by, making certain types of decisions. These situations, called "central conflicts" (Jackson, 1984), often arise for people when one set of deeply held positive values they hold are challenged by an opposing set of deeply held negative beliefs about themselves or their abilities. An example can be found in a situation where an individual believes he or she should act one way, such as independently, but then behaves in the opposite way, such as by being dependent in an unhealthy relationship. Another might involve knowing what one should do in a difficult situation, but then failing to do so because of lack of courage. What makes the conflict central is that in such moments, a person finds his or her self-esteem "at-stake." To paraphrase Branden (1969), such times question an individual's "competence at living and worthiness to do so" because they can only be resolved in one of two ways. A person may face the dilemma competently, which affirms their worth as an individual and increases self-esteem. Or an individual may fail to handle the situation competently, which leads to an acute sense of unworthiness and results in a loss of self-esteem (Mruk, 1983). In other words, work that focuses on how self-esteem is actually lived indicates quite clearly that it can and does change—for better *and* for worse!

Although some might be tempted to dismiss such research because it is based on qualitative work, doing so would be a mistake because of the fact that there are serious limits to researching self-esteem with quantitative methods alone. For example, Epstein noted that having access to people's experience over time is very important because

> Self-report estimates are usually based on impressions gained over repeated observations, whereas laboratory studies usually investigate responses in a single setting on a single occasion. On this basis alone there is reason to suspect that laboratory findings, as customarily obtained, are often low in replicability and generality, and cannot therefore establish strong relationships with findings obtained on other occasions by other means (1979, p. 52).

Perhaps even more important is the fact that qualitative methods are the only ones we have for researching certain dimensions of human experience, namely, those that involve meaning. Jackson (1984), for example, pointed out that

> Experimental investigation is based on the criteria of prediction and replication... But this is only one *kind* of criterion, and it establishes only one kind of knowledge. There are other kinds of knowledge that elude the criteria of prediction and replication; and a specific example is knowledge about self-esteem as a meaningful experience in a person's life. This kind of knowledge resides in a system of relations that is unique and irreducible in each separate instance. Such knowledge cannot be captured by a method that breaks it down into standard components. The experiment, however, is designed to perform exactly this kind of reduction. *It is aimed at washing out the very information which we seek—namely, information about unique and specific constellations of personal meaning* (pp. 216–217).

In short, qualitative research shows that self-esteem can change and that such methods have a legitimate place in the field because they can access certain aspects of human phenomena, which others cannot.

At the same time, it is important to remember that although meaning cannot be measured, other aspects of self-esteem can and must be measured. Such quantitative research provides the second reason that we can say it is possible to change self-esteem and more. This kind of work usually involves measuring self-esteem, introducing a variable that may affect it, and then assessing self-esteem again to see whether any change occurs. One design focuses on measuring self-esteem as a function of treating a mental health disorder, such as depression, addiction, and so forth (O'Brien & Epstein, 1983, 1988). Another makes changing self-esteem the central issue by having people participate in programs designed for this purpose (Bartoletti & O'Brien, 2003; Hakim-Larson & Mruk, 1997). Not only does this type of correlational work show that self-esteem can change, but it also shows that it is possible to generate change by programmatic intervention.

Of course, it is well known that even though correlational research is more quantitative, there are methodological issues to consider here as well (Smelser, 1989; Wells & Marwell, 1976). Many of them concern attempting to measure self-esteem and include such problems as the limits of self-report methods and the ceiling effect. However, there are instruments that attempt to address such problems, such as the Multidimensional Self-Esteem Inventory or MSEI (O'Brien & Epstein, 1983, 1988). One strength of this measure is that its key scales can be grouped into those that assess competence and those that measure worthiness, which makes it very comprehensive. Another is that unlike most self-esteem tests, the MSEI includes a defensiveness scale that helps deal with the above mentioned problems. For example, the index aims to identify "false positives," such as those made by people who may have an inflated sense of worthiness or one that is not based on corresponding realities of competent behavior. The measure acts as a validity scale for assessing self-esteem by reducing the likelihood of confusing positive responses that reflect genuine self-esteem with those that are given to cover up self-esteem problems, such as insecurity, certain forms of defensiveness, or even narcissism.

Now that there is reason to believe that self-esteem can change and that we can design programs to help that happen, it is possible to consider what components are necessary to create an effective approach. I investigated this question (Mruk, 2006) by examining two things: clinical techniques or practices that are said to increase self-esteem and the common features of major self-esteem programs of the 1990s. This work resulted in two types of findings. One is that there are at least nine clinical techniques often used when attempting to change self-esteem. They are: providing acceptance, offering positive feedback, modeling, increasing problem-solving ability, cognitive restructuring, assertiveness training, natural self-esteem moments, two types of therapeutic formats (individual and group work, but especially the latter), and practice. The other concerns the underlying features that standard self-esteem enhancement programs (Bednar & Peterson, 1995; Burns, 1993; Frey & Carlock, 1989; Pope, McHale, & Craighead, 1988) seem to have in common. They are: setting up a systematic or step-by-step approach, including assessment as a part of the process, emphasizing the role of the facilitator, and employing some of the nine techniques identified above.

The results indicate that there are two different types of "crucial ingredients" necessary for changing self-esteem programmatically: using particular types of clinical techniques and organizing them systematically in a way that includes assessment, a series of structured activities, and personal guidance. A logical way to build an effective self-esteem enhancement program, then, is to base it on both sets of factors and to do so in a way that is consistent with one's definition of self-esteem. I developed a program to test this hypothesis (Mruk, 1999, 2006). It is a step-by-step approach that consists of moving through five progressively sequenced, two-hour group sessions at the rate of one per week. Each session focuses on a particular aspect of self-esteem and includes specific steps placed in sequential order. The first week begins by helping people understand self-esteem in terms of competence and worthiness. The second involves assessing the participant's current level of self-esteem using the MSEI and discussing results. The third focuses on enhancing worthiness by employing techniques that facilitate its growth, such as cognitive restructuring. In the fourth, the focus shifts to increasing competence by developing better problem-solving skills. The program concludes with a fifth week that includes designing an individualized self-esteem action plan for the future. Pre and post testing using the MSEI indicates that the program is effective (Bartoletti & O'Brien, 2003; Hakim-Larson & Mruk, 1997). While much more work is needed to generalize any further, it can be said that there are specific techniques that address the major components of self-esteem and that they can be organized so as to produce change systematically.

Given that self-esteem can change either naturally or programmatically and that each path involves certain types of key processes, it is now possible to address the last issue: What aspects of changing self-esteem seem to be more difficult than others? I have encountered two types of particularly difficult problems in this regard. The first one concerns how important it is for researchers and practitioners in this field to define self-esteem as carefully as they can. Although it seems clear to me that defining this phenomenon in terms of competence and worthiness is a most comprehensive and useful approach, this position is in the minority. Yet, it is undeniable that programs aimed primarily at enhancing worthiness, which is by far the most popular approach, have been heavily criticized over the past decade, and rightly so. The main problem seems to be that programs that simply help make people feel good about themselves regardless of actual performance produce no lasting positive results and may even have negative long-term consequences. The latter includes such possibilities as fostering unrealistic expectations, inadvertently helping people to develop narcissism, and facilitating certain forms of antisocial behavior (Baumeister et al., 1996; Damon, 1995; Leo, 1990). Building a program based on competence and worthiness is not as vulnerable to such failings because one balances the other. In other words, competence in appropriate behaviors generates a sense of worthiness that is earned, and a sense of worthiness that is earned makes engaging in behavior that diminishes worthiness less attractive and less likely.

The second difficulty is a practical one. In general, self-esteem has been divided into three types (Coopersmith, 1967). One of them is high, positive, or healthy self-esteem. According to the definition being used here, this type of self-esteem comes from a sense of worthiness that results from demonstrating appropriate forms of competence, a goal toward which we all should strive. Low self-esteem, by contrast, stems from some sort of deficiency in both areas. However, since such a state is painful by nature, most people who suffer it know they do and usually wish to alter the condition. The dynamics of discomfort and awareness often generate motivation to change, which makes it relatively easy to offer help to those who suffer the condition. Unfortunately, the third type, often called defensive self-esteem, is more problematic because it involves a lack of balance that is difficult to perceive and, therefore, resistant to change. People who live a condition characterized by competence but low worthiness, for instance, tend to focus on their abilities rather than facing their weakness. Those with worthiness but little competence are caught in a similar bind because their view of themselves is not supported by reality. In either case, a lack of awareness associated with defensive self-esteem creates a vulnerability to certain kinds of threats, namely things that may lessen a fragile sense of worthiness or an inadequate sense of competence, respectively. Typically, such defensiveness takes the form of simple denial or avoidance, which is hard enough to work through, as any clinician will confirm. Sometimes, however, the dynamics of defensive self-esteem can involve anger, aggressiveness, or even more problematic forms of acting out. Such possibilities make self-esteem work of this type more difficult, but also more important—for society as well as for the person.

REFERENCES

Bartoletti, M., & O'Brien, E. J. (2003). *Self-esteem, coping and immunocompetence: A correlational study*. Poster session presented at the annual meeting of the American Psychological Association, Toronto, Canada.

Baumeister, R., Smart, L., & Boden, J. (1996). Relation of threatened egotism to violence and aggression: The dark side of self-esteem. *Psychological Review, 103,* 5–33.

Bednar, R., & Peterson, S. (1995). *Self-esteem: Paradoxes and innovations in clinical theory and practice* (2nd ed.). Washington, DC: American Psychological Association.

Branden, N. (1969). *The psychology of self-esteem.* New York: Bantam.

Burns, D. (1993). *Ten days to self-esteem: The leader's manual.* New York: Quill.

Coopersmith, S. (1967). *The antecedents of self-esteem.* San Francisco: Freeman.

Damon, W. (1995). *Great expectations: Overcoming the culture of indulgence in our homes and schools.* New York: Free Press.

Epstein, S. (1979). The ecological study of emotions in humans. In K. Blankstein (Ed.), *Advances in the study of communications and affect* (pp. 47–83). New York: Plenum.

Frey, D., & Carlock, C. J. (1989). *Enhancing self-esteem* (2nd ed.). Muncie, IN: Accelerated Development.

Hakim-Larson, J., & Mruk, C. (1997). Enhancing self-esteem in a community mental health setting. *American Journal of Orthopsychiatry, 67,* 655–659.

Jackson, M. (1984). *Self-esteem and meaning: A life historical investigation.* Albany: State University of New York.

James, W. (1983). *The principles of psychology*. Cambridge, MA: Harvard University Press. (Original work published 1890)

Leo, J. (1990, May 18). Damn, I'm good! *U.S. News and World Report*, p. 21.

Mruk, C. (2006). *Self-esteem research, theory, and practice: Toward a positive psychology of self-esteem* (3rd ed.). New York: Springer.

Mruk, C. (1999). *Self-esteem: Research, theory, and practice* (2nd ed.). New York: Springer.

Mruk, C. (1983). Toward a phenomenology of self-esteem. In A. Giorgi, A. Barton, & C. Maes (Eds.), *Duquesne studies in phenomenological psychology* (Vol. 4, pp. 137–148). Pittsburgh: Duquesne University Press.

O'Brien, E., & Epstein, S. (1983, 1988). *MSEI: The multidimensional self-esteem inventory*. Odessa, FL: Psychological Assessment Resources.

Pope, A., McHale, S., & Craighead, E. (1988). *Self-esteem enhancement with children and adolescents*. New York: Pergamon Press.

Smelser, N. J. (1989). Self-esteem and social problems: An introduction. In A. M. Mecca, N. J. Smelser, & J. Vasconcellos (Eds.), *The social importance of self-esteem* (pp. 294–326). Berkeley, CA: University of California Press.

Wells, E. L., & Marwell, G. (1976). *Self-esteem: Its conceptualization and measurement*. Beverly Hills, CA: Sage.

22

Self-Esteem Change: Addressing the Possibility of Enduring Improvements in Feelings of Self-Worth

HEATHER D. TEVENDALE and DAVID L. DUBOIS

*M*ost definitions of self-esteem suggest that it is a stable and enduring characteristic. Rosenberg (1965), for example, described self-esteem as "the evaluation which an individual makes and *customarily maintains* with regard to himself [or herself]; it expresses an attitude of approval or disapproval" (p. 5, emphasis added). Whether or not self-esteem is indeed stable, however, is an important question that has received considerable attention in the research literature (Harter & Whitesell, 2003). The occurrence of short-term fluctuations in self-esteem for many individuals has been convincingly demonstrated (Kernis, Cornell, Sun, & Berry, 1993). This essay, however, examines whether self-esteem can change in a more enduring manner. Additionally, a consideration of those aspects of self-esteem that may be more or less resistant to long-term change is undertaken. We conclude with a discussion of strategies that individuals may be able to use in a personal change program to modify their self-esteem.

DOES SELF-ESTEEM CHANGE?

Developmental research provides evidence that self-esteem does change over the life course. Overall, findings of this research suggest that the average level of self-esteem is notably high during early childhood before becoming established at a somewhat lower level during middle and late childhood and then declines during the transition to adolescence (Eccles, Wigfield, Flanagan, Miller, Reuman, & Yee, 1989; Marsh, 1989; Marsh, Barnes, Cairns, & Tidman, 1984; Robins, Trzesniewski, Tracy, Gosling, & Potter, 2002; Savin-Williams & Demo, 1984; Twenge & Campbell, 2001). A recent large-scale ($n = 326{,}641$), cross-sectional, internet-based study also found evidence of change in levels of self-esteem during adulthood (Robins et al., 2002).

These findings suggest that the self-esteem of adults tends to increase during their mid- to late 20s as well as in their 50s and 60s, but decrease significantly among adults of age 70 and older (Robins et al., 2002).

The preceding trends reflect only average self-esteem scores across all study participants and thus provide data only about mean group change over time. It is possible, however, that even when the average level of self-esteem changes with age, the self-esteem of different individuals relative to others in their age group may remain largely the same if everyone tends to shift to a similar degree. Conversely, even when there is little or no change in the group mean level of self-esteem, there may be considerable flux in self-esteem levels of different individuals with the increases of some offsetting the decreases of others. For these reasons, studies restricted to analyses of group averages provide limited information regarding whether the self-esteem of individuals changes and, if so, to what extent and with what degree of permanency.

One approach to gauging the extent of change in self-esteem at the individual level is to compute correlations between scores on a measure of self-esteem for a given set of individuals across different time points. These correlations indicate the degree to which the relative ordering of individuals according to their reported levels of self-esteem is maintained over time (this is also referred to as rank-order stability). Thus, lower test–retest correlations will occur to the extent that individuals are changing in self-esteem over time and reported levels of self-esteem are increasing over time for some individuals and decreasing for others. A meta-analysis of these types of correlations found evidence of moderate stability in self-esteem levels (correlations ranged from .40 to .65; correlations corrected for measurement error ranged from .53 to .71) over an average time interval of 3.2 years (SD = 4.4; Trzesniewski, Donnellan, & Robins, 2003). Stability was lowest in childhood, increasing from adolescence to adulthood, and then decreasing from adulthood to old age. This pattern of findings is similar to that found in a meta-analysis of personality trait stability (Roberts & DelVecchio, 2000).

To examine change and stability in self-esteem over time at the individual level more directly, several studies have employed cluster analysis. This statistical procedure has been used to group individuals by their pattern of responses on a measure of self-esteem administered repeatedly over time. In a two-year, longitudinal study of 128 early adolescents experiencing the transition from elementary school to junior high (Hirsch & DuBois, 1991), cluster analysis revealed four groups of youth who were distinguished by their trajectories of self-esteem over four waves of assessment: consistently high (35%), chronically low (13%), steeply declining (21%), and small increase (31%). Similar trajectories of change were identified in a larger study of youth (n = 1160) assessed four times from 6th through 10th grade (Zimmerman, Copeland, Shope, & Dielman, 1997). Nearly half of the sample in this study comprised a consistently high self-esteem group and 13% a consistently low self-esteem group, whereas approximately 20% were in moderate and rising self-esteem and steadily decreasing self-esteem groups, respectively. Taken together these studies suggest that slightly more than half of adolescents experience little or no change in their levels of self-esteem even over periods as long as 4 years, whereas 20% experience decreases in self-esteem and another 20–30% experience increases in self-esteem.

The answer to whether self-esteem ever truly changes appears to be yes. In addition to evidence that the typical level of self-esteem changes in somewhat predictable ways over the course of development, it appears that there is only moderate stability of relative levels of self-esteem within any age group and that, at least during adolescence, individual trajectories of increasing or decreasing self-esteem are not uncommon. At the same time, it seems that self-esteem over the life course may be fairly stable such that even during periods of expected change (i.e., adolescence), stability is at least as common as patterns of growth or decline.

WHAT ASPECTS OF SELF-ESTEEM ARE DIFFICULT TO CHANGE?

Given evidence that self-esteem is stable over time for many people, consideration must be given to what may make self-esteem resistant to change. Self-verification theory posits that individuals are invested in maintaining consistent views of themselves (Swann, Rentfrow, & Guinn, 2002). Stable self-perceptions are believed to provide a feeling of security, as well as guidance regarding social interactions. Findings from experimental research, for example, indicate that people will make significant efforts to verify existing self-concepts by seeking self-confirmatory feedback and choosing interaction partners more likely to confirm self-views, even negative ones (see Swann, 1990, for a review). Attempts to maintain existing self-concepts are more likely for important rather than unimportant self-views (Swann & Pelham, 2002). Thus, aspects of self-evaluation that are central to an individual's overall sense of self-worth may be the most difficult to change.

It also may be difficult to change aspects of self-esteem that are based on personal characteristics that are themselves difficult to alter. For example, aspects of self-esteem related to social interactions may be challenging to modify because the personality traits that contribute to social success (e.g., extraversion) have been indicated to be quite stable (Roberts & DelVecchio, 2000). Additionally, individuals who are not successful socially in one environment, such as youth who are rejected by their peers, may have negative social experiences in other environments (Hardy, Bukowski, & Sippola, 2002). For such individuals, efforts to obtain increased social support or validation in new environments may have the effect of reinforcing, rather than ameliorating, feelings of low self-esteem that stem from a sense of social inadequacy.

Similar considerations apply to aspects of self-esteem that are influenced by factors in the person's environment that are difficult to change or avoid. Illustratively, thinness is a pervasive standard for what constitutes physical attractiveness in Western culture (Thompson & Stice, 2001). Individuals with higher body weight, furthermore, are less likely to date and more likely to experience other types of social rejection (Halpern, Udry, Campbell, & Suchindran, 1999; Neumark-Sztainer,

Falkner, Story, Perry, Hannan, & Mulert, 2002). For an individual who is overweight, avoiding exposure to negative appearance related feedback or the message that thinness is the standard for attractiveness is likely to be difficult.

Children and adolescents, in particular, have limited control over the environments within which they must function. Youth have restricted personal autonomy (Harter & Whitesell, 2003) and, thus, limited influence over the schools they attend, the peer groups to which they are exposed, and their home life. Adults typically have more freedom to select the environments in which they function. There are, however, many circumstances that can make leaving a given environment difficult. For example, although troubled marriages and problematic work environments have been indicated to negatively influence self-esteem (Saks & Ashforth, 1997; Shackelford, 2001; Voss, Markiewicz, & Doyle, 1999; Wiener, Muczyk, & Martin, 1992), one can imagine many reasons (e.g., children's needs, financial constraints) why individuals might be unable to easily remove themselves from these types of situations.

HOW CAN SELF-ESTEEM BE CHANGED?

These considerations highlight the potential for both psychological and environmental challenges to any efforts that an individual might make to deliberately enhance his or her self-esteem. Nonetheless, as noted, there is considerable evidence that changes in self-esteem do occur throughout the life span. This, of course, is not equivalent to demonstrating that self-esteem can be purposefully modified in a positive direction. However, findings from evaluations of programs designed to enhance self-esteem provide persuasive evidence that this type of change is possible as well (Haney & Durlak, 1998; Hattie, 1992). In a meta-analysis of esteem-enhancement programs for children, adolescents, and adults, Hattie (1992) reported an average effect size of .37 across 89 studies. This finding indicates that positive change on self-concept or self-esteem was evident for 65% of participants in the typical intervention. The size of the effect reported is indicative of moderate gains in self-esteem. Whether such gains are lasting and thus sustained over time has not been sufficiently investigated.

Hattie (1992) found that interventions intended to increase self-esteem directly or indirectly were similarly effective. The majority of the direct programs were didactic and individually focused. These programs typically are geared toward helping participants identify and appreciate positive sources of self-esteem in their lives and toward teaching cognitive-behavioral techniques that can be used in combating psychological threats to self-esteem (e.g., listing evidence disputing negative self-evaluations). Programs termed indirect were more likely to address skills and behaviors that may form the basis for making self-evaluations (e.g., enhancing academic achievement). A comprehensive psychosocial approach in which attention is given to the "inner" and "outer" forces affecting self-esteem may produce the best results (Hamachek, 1994).

Components from self-esteem enhancement interventions may be adapted for the purposes of a personal change program. However, just as group-based self-esteem programs with a basis in theory are more effective (Haney & Durlak, 1998), attempts by an individual to change his or her self-esteem are likely to be more successful if the individual has a sound understanding of the factors that are most likely to influence feelings of self-worth. As a first step, an individual seeking to change his or her self-esteem thus should become familiar with fundamental concepts about how self-esteem is developed and maintained.

James (1890) theorized that self-esteem is formed by comparing perceptions of one's accomplishments to expectations of competence. From a multidimensional view of the self-system, these types of comparisons occur in multiple areas (e.g., work, relationships with family, physical appearance). Resulting appraisals for each domain then contribute to an overall sense of self-worth (Byrne, 1996; Harter, 1999). The specific domains that contribute most to self-esteem vary across individuals. Research, however, consistently indicates that both experiences of mastery or success and a sense of being valued by significant others are fundamentally important sources of self-esteem (Harter, 1999; Twenge & Campbell, 2001). Individuals seeking to raise their self-esteem thus should examine how positive or negative their self-evaluations are across a range of domains including performance at work, school, and other activities of personal importance (e.g., athletics or hobbies), as well as in regard to the quality of their relationships with friends, family, and romantic partners. Self-evaluations of appearance also merit consideration given that body image is one of the strongest predictors of overall feelings of self-worth (Harter, 1999).

Once those domains that seem likely to be the biggest culprits in lowering self-esteem are identified, the next step would be to assess the likely sources of one's negative self-evaluations within different domains. It may be useful to distinguish aspects of low self-esteem that stem primarily from objective personal or environmental factors (e.g., a lack of skills needed to perform well at one's job or an adverse work environment) and those that are attributable to more subjective, psychological factors. Two classes of psychological factors that should be considered are unrealistic beliefs about personal deficits (e.g., a conviction that one is unsuccessful at one's job despite receiving positive evaluations) and the adoption of unreasonably high expectations or standards that cannot be met (e.g., a feeling that one must do better than any other employee at all aspects of work; Shirk, Burwell, & Harter, 2003).

Cognitive processes leading to low self-esteem such as overly critical self-perceptions or perfectionistic tendencies can be addressed by standard cognitive therapy techniques (Beck, 1995; Freeman, Pretzer, Fleming, & Simon, 1990; Young, 1999). General cognitive therapy methods have been adapted for individual use via self-help workbooks such as *Mind Over Mood* (Greenberger & Padesky, 1995). Workbook exercises can be utilized to challenge automatic thoughts, beliefs, and assumptions that are fueling negative self-evaluations. For example, systematically examining evidence that does not support negative beliefs about oneself may enable more favorable self-evaluations to take root in those areas (e.g., I've received positive evaluations from my supervisor which suggests that I am doing well at work). These modified beliefs, in turn, can provide the foundation for enhanced overall feelings of self-worth.

It also is important to recognize that the preceding types of techniques, if practiced in the extreme, paradoxically carry the risk of proving harmful to self-esteem (not to mention one's overall health and well-being). Consider, for example, a pervasive tendency to discount or "filter out" evidence of one's shortcomings. Although this type of denial might bolster (or at least protect) a person's self-esteem in the short term, departures from reality like this are more likely in the long run to jeopardize one's chances for sustaining a favorable sense of self-worth (DuBois, 2003). Taking action to address personal limitations is apt to be a more fruitful approach because this has the potential to lead to actual improvements in skills and functioning and thus provide a more sustained source of positive self-evaluation.

In accordance with these considerations, several of the interventions that have proved most successful at enhancing levels of self-esteem are oriented toward increasing participants' actual day-to-day experiences of mastery and social connectedness (DuBois, 2003). These include interventions that focus primarily on skill development, as well as those that seek to modify aspects of the environment. For a personal self-esteem change program, efforts could be geared toward strengthening one's skills or performance within areas where objective skill or performance limitations are identified as contributing to negative self-evaluations. For example, with respect to the areas of work and personal relationships, a person might pursue additional education to facilitate career advancement and endeavor to strengthen social skills through work with a therapist. As noted, programs that change environmental factors (e.g., restructuring schools) also have been found to be an effective means of improving feelings of self-worth (DuBois, 2003). Individuals, of course, may have difficulty personally modifying such aspects of their environments. Nonetheless, a person may be able to make some headway in this regard by seeking out new environments that are more affirming and by avoiding or taking steps to modify those aspects of a current environment that are damaging to self-esteem. For example, continuing with the previous example, in the area of work the person might attempt to find a new job that is a better match for his or her skills and in the area of personal relationships the person could seek marital therapy to help decrease critical feedback from a spouse.

CONCLUSION

Self-esteem appears to be fairly stable for most people most of the time. It is equally apparent, however, that levels of self-esteem do change over the life course and, furthermore, that self-esteem can be increased deliberately through planned interventions. Striving to alter personal beliefs and expectations that detract from feelings of self-worth and concerted efforts to engineer more frequent experiences of success and social connectedness in one's day-to-day life are both viable avenues for improving self-esteem. Given the inherent challenges, the involvement of significant others who can provide support for positive change is a recommended component of any plan to improve self-esteem.

REFERENCES

Beck, J. S. (1995). *Cognitive therapy: Basics and beyond.* New York: Guilford.

Byrne, B. M. (1996). *Measuring self-concept across the life span.* Washington, DC: American Psychological Association.

DuBois, D. L. (2003). Self-esteem, adolescence. In T. P. Gullotta & M. Bloom (Eds.) and T. P. Gullotta & G. Adams (Section Eds.), *Encyclopedia of primary prevention and health promotion* (pp. 953–961). New York: Kluwer Academic/Plenum.

Eccles, J. S., Wigfield, A., Flanagan, C. A., Miller, C., Reuman, D., & Yee, D. (1989). Self-concept, domain values, and self-esteem: Relations and changes at early adolescence. *Journal of Personality, 57,* 283–310.

Freeman, A., Pretzer, J., Fleming, B., & Simon, K. M. (1990). *Clinical applications of cognitive therapy.* New York: Plenum.

Greenberger, D., & Padesky, C. A. (1995). *Mind over mood.* New York: Guilford Press.

Halpern, C. T., Udry, J. R., Campbell, B., & Suchindran, C. (1999). Effects of body fat on weight concerns, dating, and sexual activity: A longitudinal analysis of Black and White adolescent girls. *Developmental Psychology, 35,* 721–736.

Hamachek, D. (1994). Changes in the self from a developmental/psychosocial perspective. In T. M. Brinthaupt & R. P. Lipka (Eds.), *Changing the self: Philosophies, techniques, and experiences* (pp. 21–68). Albany: State University of New York Press.

Haney, P., & Durlak, J. (1998). Changing self-esteem in children and adolescents: A meta-analytic review. *Journal of Clinical Child Psychology, 27,* 423–433.

Hardy, C. L., Bukowski, W. M., & Sippola, L. K. (2002). Stability and change in peer relationships during the transition to middle-level school. *Journal of Early Adolescence, 22,* 117–142.

Harter, S. (1999). *The construction of the self: A developmental perspective.* New York: Guilford Press.

Harter, S., & Whitesell, N. R. (2003). Beyond the debate: Why some adolescents report stable self-worth over time and situation, whereas others report changes in self-worth. *Journal of Personality, 71,* 1027–1058.

Hattie, J. (1992). *Self-concept.* Hillsdale, NJ: Lawrence Erlbaum Associates, Inc.

Hirsch, B. J., & DuBois, D. L. (1991). Self-esteem in early adolescence: The identification and prediction of contrasting longitudinal trajectories. *Journal of Youth and Adolescence, 20,* 53–72.

James, W. (1890). *The principles of psychology* (Vol. 1). New York: Holt.

Kernis, M. H., Cornell, D. P., Sun, C., & Berry, A. (1993). There's more to self-esteem than whether it is high or low: The importance of stability of self-esteem. *Journal of Personality and Social Psychology, 65,* 1190–1204.

Marsh, H.W. (1989). Age and sex effects in multiple domains of self-concept: Preadolescence to adulthood. *Journal of Educational Psychology, 81,* 417–430.

Marsh, H. W., Barnes, J., Cairns, L., & Tidman, M. (1984). Self-Descriptive Questionnaire: Age and sex effects in the structure and level of self-concept for preadolescent children. *Journal of Educational Psychology, 76,* 940–956.

Neumark-Sztainer, D., Falkner, N., Story, M., Perry, C., Hannan, P. J., & Mulert, S. (2002). Weight-teasing among adolescents: Correlations with weight status and disordered eating behaviors. *International Journal of Obesity & Related Metabolic Disorders, 26,* 123–131.

Roberts, B. W., & DelVecchio, W. F. (2000). The rank-order consistency of personality traits from childhood to old age: A quantitative review of longitudinal studies. *Psychological Bulletin, 126,* 3–25.

Robins, R. W., Trzesniewski, K. H., Tracy, J. L., Gosling, S. D., & Potter, J. (2002). Global self-esteem across the life span. *Psychology and Aging, 17,* 423–434.

Rosenberg, M. (1965). *Society and the adolescent self-image.* Princeton, NJ: Princeton University Press.

Saks, A. M., & Ashforth, B. E. (1997). A longitudinal investigation of the relationships between job information sources, applicant perception of fit, and work outcomes. *Personnel Psychology, 50,* 395–426.

Savin-Williams, R. C., & Demo, D. H. (1984). Developmental change and stability in adolescent self-concept. *Developmental Psychology, 20,* 1100–1110.

Shackelford, T. K. (2001). Self-esteem in marriage. *Personality & Individual Differences, 30,* 371–390.

Shirk, S., Burwell, R., & Harter, S. (2003). Strategies to modify low self-esteem in adolescents. In M. Reinecke, F. Dattilio, & A. Freeman (Eds.), *Cognitive therapy with children and adolescents: A casebook for clinical practice* (pp. 189–213). New York: Guilford Press.

Swann, W. B. (1990). To be adored or to be known: The interplay of self-enhancement and self-verification. In R. M. Sorrentino & E. T. Higgins (Eds.), *Handbook of motivation and cognition* (Vol. 2, pp. 408–480). New York: Guilford Press.

Swann, W. B., & Pelham, B. W. (2002). Who wants out when the going gets good? Psychological investment and preference for self-verifying college roommates. *Journal of Self and Identity, 1,* 219–233.

Swann, W. B., Rentfrow, P. J., & Guinn, J. (2002). Self-verification: The search for coherence. In M. Leary & J. Tangney (Eds.), *Handbook of self and identity.* New York: Guilford Press.

Thompson, J. K., & Stice, E. (2001). Thin-ideal internalization: Mounting evidence for a new risk factor for body-image disturbance and eating pathology. *Current Directions in Psychological Science, 10,* 181–183.

Trzesniewski, K. H., Donnellan, M. B., & Robins, R. W. (2003). Stability of self-esteem across the life span. *Journal of Personality and Social Psychology, 84,* 205–220.

Twenge, J. M., & Campbell, W. K. (2001). Age and birth cohort differences in self-esteem: A cross-temporal meta-analysis. *Personality and Social Psychology Review, 5,* 321–344.

Voss, K., Markiewicz, D., & Doyle, A. B. (1999). Friendship, marriage and self-esteem. *Journal of Social & Personal Relationships, 16,* 103–122.

Wiener, Y., Muczyk, J. P., & Martin, H. J. (1992). Self-esteem and job involvement as moderators of the relationship between work satisfaction and well-being. *Journal of Social Behavior & Personality, 7,* 539–554.

Young, J. E. (1999). *Cognitive therapy for personality disorders: A schema-focused approach* (3rd ed.). Sarasota, FL: Professional Resource Press/Professional Resource Exchange.

Zimmerman, M. A., Copeland, L. A., Shope, J. T., & Dielman, T. E. (1997). A longitudinal study of self-esteem: Implications for adolescent development. *Journal of Youth and Adolescence, 26,* 117–141.

23

Improving Self-Esteem

ROOS VONK

I describe three ways in which self-esteem can be raised. The first way, using self-deception and self-enhancement, is deemed ineffective because it produces defensive, fragile self-esteem. The second way is from within, through self-contact and autonomy. However, there is no experimental evidence that this is sufficient to produce changes in self-esteem. The third way is to boost people's self-esteem by being accepting and approving of them, thus elevating their sociometer and their sense of relatedness. Research suggests that this is effective and that it can engender long-term changes in self-esteem, because outward reaffirmation produces the conditions that promote self-growth and self-determination.

IMPROVING SELF-ESTEEM

In raising the question "Can self-esteem change?", we implicitly mean, "Can self-esteem be enhanced?" Although many theorists have argued that higher self-esteem is not the panacea that many in our society believe it to be (Baumeister, Campbell, Krueger, & Vohs, 2003; Damon, 1995a, 1995b; Dawes, 1994; Hewitt, 1998; London, 1997), it is generally assumed that higher self-esteem is better: It is, among other things, associated with higher mental and physical health (Taylor & Brown, 1988; Taylor, Lerner, Sherman, Sage, & McDowell, 2003) and stability in relationships (Murray, Holmes, Griffin, Bellavia, & Rose, 2001).

Because we know all the strategies and defenses that people use to maintain their self-esteem (see, e.g., Baumeister, 1998; Blaine & Crocker, 1993; Crocker & Park, 2003), the most obvious answer to the question how to raise self-esteem, is to use these strategies. To name but a few, self-esteem may be raised if people learn to:

- attribute their failures and moral transgressions to external or unstable causes, and their successes to their own qualities;
- selectively remember successes by giving more attention to them, and focus on their positive qualities by spending more time thinking about them;
- compare themselves with others who are less well off when things are bad.

Although some of these strategies are actually recommended by positive psychologists (e.g., Seligman, 1998), I do not believe that they produce desirable outcomes at all. Granted, they might work in raising self-esteem, but this produces the kind of self-esteem that is associated with self-deception and with maladaptive responses when the self is threatened, such as aggression (Baumeister, Smart & Boden, 1996; Kernis et al., 1993), excessive self-enhancement (cf. Heatherton & Vohs, 2000; Vohs & Heatherton, 2001), and derogation of others (e.g., Aberson, Healy, & Romero, 2000; Fein & Spencer, 1997).

The reason is simple: This type of self-esteem is not genuine, because it is based on distortion and does not concord with the facts of life. One of these facts is that people have flaws, make failures, and are rejected. A sense of self-esteem that denies these facts will always twist with reality. As a consequence, the self-concept continuously needs to be safeguarded; the individual can never truly relax and be at ease with the self.

DEFENSIVE VS. SECURE SELF-ESTEEM

The above problem is inherent to fragile, defensive high self-esteem. This kind of self-esteem typically is based on reaffirmation by external sources. These sources may vary from person to person (Crocker & Wolfe, 2001; cf. James, 1890): For some, self-esteem depends on being the best in school or work, for others on the love of their family, and for still others on how they look. In part because of these contingencies, self-esteem is unstable (Kernis & Waschull, 1995): Across multiple assessments, it shows more fluctuations than secure self-esteem.

Fragile self-esteem is not rooted in a fundamental sense of self-worth. This is also evidenced by results from implicit measures of self-esteem, such as the name-letter effect (Nuttin, 1985, 1987): People with high self-esteem tend to have a higher preference for the letters of their own name (Koole & Pelham, 2002). Because letter preferences can be assessed without participants' awareness of what is being assessed, this effect is assumed to reflect an unconscious, implicit evaluation of the self. A recent study by Bosson, Brown, Zeigler-Hill, and Swann (2003) confirms that participants with high explicit and low implicit self-esteem (a weak name-letter effect) are particularly likely to engage in defensive, ego-repairing processes.

Secure self-esteem, on the other hand, is not contingent because it is derived from within. According to self-determination theory (Deci & Ryan, 1995, 2002), this type of self-esteem is associated with high self-determination, that is (1) knowing one's inner self; and (2) behaving autonomously, in accordance with one's true needs—as opposed to external forces (e.g., the need to please others or achieve success). Secure self-esteem is grounded in unconditional positive regard for oneself (cf. Rogers, 1959, 1961). Depending on how their caregivers have responded to them, and the resultant attachment style they have developed (cf. Ainsworth, Blehar, Waters, & Wall, 1978; Bowlby, 1980), people differ in whether they have a firm sense of self-worth that is stable and noncontingent, and does not need to be deserved or protected.

The question, then, becomes: Can self-esteem be enhanced from within, independent from others' approval? Can it be enhanced without the "cheap tricks" discussed earlier, by increasing self-determination instead? This would imply breaking the cycle of wanting to please others, being successful, or whatever it takes to maintain fragile self-esteem, because these efforts only make the individual more focused toward the outside world—hence making it increasingly less likely that self-contact and autonomy develop. In effect, I think that breaking this cycle and restoring self-determination is exactly what is attempted in many psychotherapeutic interventions.

Unfortunately, there is not much experimental evidence that promoting self-determination has the effect of raising self-esteem. In the extant literature, self-determination and "true" self-esteem are examined as individual differences variables. As a consequence of early childhood experiences, people have acquired a particular position on the "true" self-esteem continuum, and they have to do with that. Indeed, the self-determination literature (Deci & Ryan, 2002) is based largely on correlational research. These correlations do show that self-determination is negatively related to self-esteem instability, contingency, and positively to self-esteem, self-acceptance, and self-concept clarity (in our own data, Vonk, Jolij, Stoeller, & Boog, 2006, these correlations are all in the .20–.25 range). However, as we have argued elsewhere (Brandt & Vonk, Chapter 29, this volume), in self-report data all of these correlations may be explained by one common underlying factor, which is the self-theory "I'm doing fine."

Thus, empirically the exact causal paths in these relations are unknown, and theoretically, self-determination is seen to be rooted in early childhood. Consequently, little is known about interventions that could enhance self-determination and genuine self-esteem among adults.

SELF-ESTEEM AS A SOCIOMETER: THE ROLE OF OTHERS

In self-determination theory, self-esteem can be gained by increasing self-contact and autonomy in choices, rather than depending on reaffirmation by others. This view stands in sharp contrast with sociometer theory (Leary & Baumeister, 2000; Leary, Tambor, Terdal, & Downs, 1995). Based on people's fundamental need to belong (Baumeister & Leary, 1995), sociometer theory poses that self-esteem is an evolutionarily adaptive instrument that tells people how they are doing as a member of their group, and whether others are accepting them. This view implies that "true" self-esteem, which does not depend on any social contingencies, such as described by Deci and Ryan (1995) and Kernis (2003), is an illusion. Imagine for one moment a person who does not accomplish anything, is not liked by others, contributes nothing to the group or to society in general, yet retains a solid sense of self-esteem. From this perspective, it may be argued that being entirely non-responsive to others' appraisals is a reflection of maladjustment (Leary, 1999). People's self-worth is sensitive to their social environment, and very functionally so.

Thus, being accepted by others is a major contingency for everyone. In line with this view, Leary and his colleagues have demonstrated that social rejection or disapproval produces sharp declines in participants' self-esteem; these effects occurred regardless of their initial self-esteem level (Leary, Haupt, Strausser, & Chokel, 1998) and regardless of whether they themselves acknowledged that their self-esteem depended on others (Leary et al., 2003). Similarly, social approval and acceptance enhanced self-esteem (Leary et al., 2003). These results suggest that self-esteem can indeed be raised, simply by being accepting and giving positive regard. However, we do not know whether others' appraisals can have long-term effects. It is conceivable that the beneficial effects of praise and acceptance subside as soon as the positive feedback ends (e.g., a day after the experiment or, in everyday life, when a Rogerian psycho-therapy ends, or when a friendship or relationship changes).

Note that self-determination theory acknowledges the important role of others as well; self-esteem is not seen as emerging in a social vacuum. Acceptance and positive regard by others are important because they fulfil people's need for relatedness. As long as the acceptance is unconditional, people will not be bothered with the issue of how to please others in order to be liked, and they can maintain their self-contact and autonomy. According to sociometer theory, however, self-esteem may drop when, for whatever reason, the positive feedback declines. This may happen when the feedback is conditional, but also when the provider of the feedback disappears off the stage. Note that, eventually, all external, social sources of self-esteem are contingent to some extent, because even a parent or spouse who provides unconditional positive regard may disappear from one's life at some point. The development of a sense of self-esteem that is sustained in such circumstances requires at least some inner, autonomous basis.

CHANGING SELF-ESTEEM: THE INWARD VS. OUTWARD ROUTE

In a recent experiment (Vonk et al., 2006), we attempted to enhance self-esteem by means of two distinct interventions; one "inward," based on autonomy and self-contact, and the other "outward," based on social reaffirmation. We also examined the long-term effects of these interventions. Participants (N = 3408 completed) filled out questionnaires at home via Internet on 12 occasions (T1–T12), throughout a period of 8 months. (At present, the study is still continuing and we are up to T16.)

In the second month of the study (after T3), three experimental groups were created. All of the three groups kept filling out questionnaires (e.g., on self-esteem, coping, authenticity, self-growth, happiness) every 2 weeks. The control group did nothing in addition to this. Participants in the "inward" experimental group were asked to start keeping a diary at least twice a week during 6 weeks (i.e., up to T6). They were given specific directions that were designed to enhance their self-contact and autonomy. For instance, they were encouraged to regard the writing as "talking to yourself" about anything that was on their minds, and not to show their writings to anyone at all. They were also told that they were doing the writing for themselves; that it was part of the study, but that it was OK to skip it if for whatever reason it was inconvenient or they did not feel like it, in which case they could do it later. (Self-report measures indicate that the large majority of participants was highly motivated and did write at least twice a week.)

In the "outward" experimental group, participants were also invited to start keeping a diary, but these participants were instructed to send in their diary by e-mail twice a week. Within 1 or 2 days after sending it, these participants always received a personal comment on their diary from a trained psychologist. So, within the 6-weeks period, they sent in their diary and received a comment twelve times. To avoid that a personal relationship with the psychologist would develop, there was a team of five psychologists who wrote their comments anonymously and alternated across participants. Participants were told that the comments were not intended to help them solve problems, but simply to show them that we were reading their diaries and to encourage them to keep writing. The comments were between 100 and 250 words. They were entirely personalized, but they were always supportive and approving of what the participant was doing or the way in which she/he reflected upon it. We assumed that, in this condition, participants' attention would be directed outwardly; during writing they would not be talking to themselves, but to their image of the psychologist who liked and appreciated them.

Results showed that after 2 weeks of diary writing (i.e., at T4), self-esteem of these participants had already increased. This increase progressed further at T5 and T6. For participants in the "inward" condition, on the other hand, increases in self-esteem and self-determination were similar to those in the control group. Thus, writing a private diary and, thereby, turning attention inward, did not have any effects over and above the small effects of the self-reflection that were induced merely by responding to the questionnaires every 2 weeks.

Contrary to what we expected, the effects of the positive feedback lasted some time beyond the week in which the feedback was terminated. At T7 (2 weeks after termination), there was no decrease in self-esteem whatsoever. Remarkably, in a follow-up study conducted more than 4 months after the diary intervention, participants in the "outward" group were still significantly higher on implicit self-esteem (i.e., the name-letter effect) than the other two groups.

Although it is possible that our "inward" manipulation by means of the diary method was not effective, these results do suggest that changes in self-esteem can quite effectively be induced by means of approval and acceptance by others. Interestingly, another effect of the positive feedback was that contingent self-esteem (assessed at T10) decreased and that self-determination (assessed at T6) increased (especially choice/autonomy), as compared with the other two groups. Thus, whereas these participants in fact demonstrated the crucial influence of others on self-esteem, they were utterly unaware of this influence and started to see themselves as more autonomous and less dependent upon others' approval.

This result corroborates Cooley's comment that we live "in the minds of others without knowing it, just as we walk the solid ground without thinking how it bears us up" (1902, p. 208). In effect, what we did for the participants in the "outward" group is to create a more solid ground for them. Paradoxically, it appears that, the more solid the ground—i.e., the more others are accepting and approving—the more people become unaware of what they are walking on, and the higher is their sense of autonomy. When the road gets bumpy, on the other hand—when people cannot rely on others' reaffirmation—they become aware of it. This is when self-esteem becomes contingent and "shaky," and when people may enter the cycle of looking to receive reaffirmation from others, thereby losing self-contact and autonomy.

OUTWARD TURNING INWARD

The results from our study converge with those of longitudinal studies that refute the idea that self-esteem is developed in childhood and remains stable across the life span. Dramatic changes in self-esteem do occur in adulthood, but they are typically associated with major life transitions, such as marriage, parenthood, job loss or promotion, or entering junior high school, high school, or college (Basic Behavioral Science Task Force of the NAMHC, 1996). Presumably, these changes are connected to changes in support and acceptance by one's peer group or spouse, or changes in how one's performance is evaluated. Eventually, this may produce changes in self-esteem that persist until the individual's life changes again.

It is noteworthy, however, that in our study some of the changes were maintained until long after the intervention, and occurred on implicit measures (although stability of self-esteem was not affected by the intervention). This suggests that the change was far more than "skin deep," and that the reaffirmation from others induced an increase in genuine self-esteem. In my view, that is exactly what happened: When people feel accepted and appreciated—in sociometer theory, when their sociometer is lifted; in self-determination theory, when their need for relatedness is satisfied—they start to feel safe and relaxed. The positive embedding by others is like a comfortable cushion that protects them, so they feel at ease and can drop their defenses. These are precisely the conditions that promote openness, self-growth, self-contact, and other "sixtiesh" variables, thus producing changes from within [cf. Greenberg, Pyszczynski, & Goldenberg (2003), who note that people first need to feel safe in order for growth and self-expansion motives to arise]. Indeed, our results also show that participants who received positive feedback rated higher on self-growth and authenticity (at T5, i.e., during the intervention period).

In sum, I suggest that positive regard by others, even if it is only temporary, is the "entrance" to true self-esteem changes: When people are accepted and reaffirmed by others, they feel that they are on solid ground. Because they are utterly unaware of how shaky the ground is, and how dependent their self-boost is upon others, they start to feel relaxed and autonomous. They become more open and less defensive, and their self-determination, self-growth, and other intrinsic drives are enhanced. As a consequence, their self-esteem is reinforced from within. Because of this, the change may last until long after the social approval, and it may even be permanent if there are no major changes in the individual's life. But, unfortunately, as the social environment can instigate increases in true self-esteem, it can instigate decreases just as well.

REFERENCES

Aberson, C. L., Healy, M., & Romero, V. (2000). Ingroup bias and self-esteem: A meta analysis. *Personality & Social Psychology Review, 4*(2), 157–173.

Ainsworth, M. D. S., Blehar, M. C., Waters, E., & Wall, S. (1978). *Patterns of attachment: A psychological study of the strange situation.* Hillsdale, NJ: Lawrence Erlbaum Associates.

Basic Behavioral Science Task Force of the National Advisory Mental Health Council (1996). Basic behavioral science research for mental health: Vulnerability and resilience. *American Psychologist, 51,* 22–38.

Baumeister, R. F. (1998). The self. In D. Gilbert, S. T. Fiske, & G. Lindzey (Eds.), *Handbook of social psychology* (4th ed., Vol. 1, pp. 680–740). New York: McGraw-Hill.

Baumeister, R. F., Campbell, J. D., Krueger, J. I., & Vohs, K. D. (2003). Does high self-esteem cause better performance, interpersonal success, happiness, or healthier lifestyles? *Psychological Science in the Public Interest, 4,* 1–44.

Baumeister, R. F., & Leary, M. R. (1995). The need to belong: Desire for interpersonal attachments as a fundamental human motivation. *Psychological Bulletin, 117*(3), 497–529.

Baumeister, R. F., Smart, L., & Boden, J. M. (1996). Relation of threatened egotism to violence and aggression: The dark side of high self-esteem. *Psychological Review, 103*(1), 5–33.

Blaine, B., & Crocker, J. (1993). Self-esteem and self-serving biases in reactions to positive and negative events: An integrative review. In R. F. Baumeister (Ed.), *Self-esteem: The puzzle of low self-regard* (pp. 55–85). New York: Plenum Press.

Bosson, J. K., Brown, R. P., Zeigler-Hill, V., & Swann, W. B. Jr. (2003). Self-enhancement tendencies among people with high explicit self-esteem: The moderating role of implicit self-esteem. *Self and Identity, 2,* 169–187.

Bowlby, J. (1980). *Attachment and loss, vol. III: Loss: Sadness and depression.* New York: Basic Books.

Brandt, A. C., & Vonk, R. (2006). Who do you think you are? On the link between self-knowledge and self-esteem. In M. H. Kernis (Ed.), *Self-esteem issues and answers.* New York: Psychology Press.

Cooley, C. H. (1902). *Human nature and the social order.* New York: Scribners.

Crocker, J., & Park, L. E. (2003). Seeking self-esteem: Construction, maintenance, and protection of self-worth. In M. Leary & J. Tangney (Eds.), *Handbook of self and identity* (pp. 291–313). New York: Guilford.

Crocker, J., & Wolfe, C. T. (2001). Contingencies of self-worth. *Psychological Review, 108*(3), 593–623.

Damon, W. (1995a, February 15). 'I'm terrific'—and demoralized. *Education Week, 33.*

Damon, W. (1995b). *Greater expectations: Overcoming the culture of indulgence in our homes and schools.* New York: Free Press.

Dawes, R. M. (1994). *House of cards: Psychology and psychotherapy built on myth.* New York: Free Press.

Deci, E. L., & Ryan, R. M. (1995). Human autonomy: The basis for true self-esteem. In M. Kernis (Ed.), *Efficacy, agency and self-esteem* (pp. 31–49). New York: Plenum.

Deci, E. L., & Ryan, R. M. (Eds.). (2002). *Handbook of self-determination research.* Rochester, NY: University of Rochester Press.

Fein, S., & Spencer, S. J. (1997). Prejudice as self-image maintenance: Affirming the self through derogating others. *Journal of Personality and Social Psychology*, *73*(1), 31–44.

Greenberg, J., Pyszczynski, T., & Goldenberg, J. L. (2003). Freedom vs. fear: On the defense, growth, and expansion of the self. In J. Greenberg, S. L. Koole, & T. Pyszczynski (Eds.), *Handbook of experimental existential psychology*. New York: Guilford.

Heatherton, T. F., & Vohs, K. D. (2000). Interpersonal evaluations following threats to self: Role of self-esteem. *Journal of Personality and Social Psychology*, *78*, 725–736.

Hewitt, J. P. (1998). *The myth of self-esteem: Finding happiness and solving problems in America*. New York: St. Martin's Press.

James, W. (1890). *The principles of psychology*. Cambridge, MA: Harvard University Press.

Kernis, M. H. (2003). Toward a conceptualization of optimal self-esteem. *Psychological Inquiry*, *14*, 1–26.

Kernis, M. H., Cornell, D. P., Sun, C.-r., Berry, A., & Harlow, T. (1993). There's more to self-esteem than whether it is high or low: The importance of stability of self-esteem. *Journal of Personality and Social Psychology*, *65*(6), 1190–1204.

Kernis, M. H., & Waschull, S. B. (1995). The interactive roles of stability and level of self-esteem: Research and theory. In M. P. Zanna (Ed.), *Advances in experimental social psychology* (Vol. 27, pp. 93–141). San Diego, CA: Academic Press.

Koole, S. L., & Pelham, B. W. (2002). On the nature of implicit self-esteem: The case of the name letter effect. In S. Spencer & M. P. Zanna (Eds.), *Motivated social perception: The ninth Ontario symposium*. Hillsdale, NJ: Lawrence Erlbaum Associates.

Leary, M. R. (1999). The social and psychological importance of self-esteem. In R. M. Kowalski & M. R. Leary (Eds.), *The social psychology of emotional and behavioral problems*. Washington, DC: American Psychological Association.

Leary, M. R., & Baumeister, R. F. (2000). The nature and function of self-esteem: sociometer theory. *Advances in experimental social psychology*, *32*, 1–62.

Leary, M. R., Gallagher, B., Fors, E., Buttermore, N., Baldwin, E., Kennedy, K., & Mills, A. (2003). The invalidity of disclaimers about the effects of social feedback on self-esteem. *Personality and Social Psychology Bulletin*, *29*, 623–636.

Leary, M. R., Haupt, A. L., Strausser, K. S., & Chokel, J. T. (1998). Calibrating the sociometer: The relationship between interpersonal appraisals and the state self-esteem. *Journal of Personality & Social Psychology*, *74*(5), 1290–1299.

Leary, M. R., Tambor, E. S., Terdal, S. K., & Downs, D. L. (1995). Self-esteem as an interpersonal monitor: The sociometer hypothesis. *Journal of Personality & Social Psychology*, *68*(3), 518–530.

London, T. (1997). The case against self-esteem: Alternative philosophies toward self that would raise the probability of pleasurable and productive living. *Journal of Rational Emotive & Cognitive-Behavior Therapy*, *15*, 19–29.

Murray, S. L., Holmes, J. G., Griffin, D. W., Bellavia, G., & Rose, P. (2001). The mismeasure of love: How self-doubt contaminates relationship beliefs. *Personality & Social Psychology Bulletin*, *27*(4), 423–436.

Nuttin, J. M. J. (1985). Narcissism beyond Gestalt and awareness: The name letter effect. *European Journal of Social Psychology*, *15*, 353–361.

Nuttin, J. M. J. (1987). Affective consequences of mere ownership: The name letter effect in twelve European languages. *European Journal of Social Psychology*, *17*, 381–402.

Rogers, C. R. (1959). The essence of psychotherapy: A client-centered view. *Annals of Psychotherapy, 1*, 51–57.

Rogers, C. R. (1961). The process equation of psychotherapy. *American Journal of Psychotherapy, 15*, 27–45.

Seligman, M. E. P. (1998). *Learned optimism* (2nd ed.). New York: Pocket Books (Simon & Schuster).

Taylor, S. E., & Brown, J. D. (1988). Illusion and well-being: A social psychological perspective on mental health. *Psychological Bulletin, 103*(2), 193–210.

Taylor, S. E., Lerner, J. S., Sherman, D. K., Sage, R. M., & McDowell, N. K. (2003). Portrait of the self-enhancer: Well adjusted and well liked or maladjusted and friendless? *Journal of Personality & Social Psychology, 84*, 165–176.

Vohs, K. D., & Heatherton, T. F. (2001). Self-esteem and threats to self: Implications for self-construals and interpersonal perceptions. *Journal of Personality and Social Psychology, 81*, 1103–1118.

Vonk, R., Jolij, J., Stoeller, T., & Boog, I. (2006): *Effects of unconditional positive regard and self-reflection on self-esteem*. Manuscript in preparation.

Question 8

How much do interpersonal as compared with intrapersonal processes influence self-esteem? What are these processes?

*T*his set of essays focuses on the extent to which intrapersonal as compared with interpersonal processes influence self-esteem. This issue resides at the heart of many core self-esteem processes that remain points of contention among current self-esteem researchers and theorists. Not surprisingly, then, each contributor argues passionately for a point of view that is at times at odds with each of the others.

Moller, Friedman, and Deci argue that to assess the relative influence on self-esteem of interpersonal and intrapersonal processes, one must first distinguish true from contingent self-esteem and developmental from proximal influences. The authors suggest that the extent to which self-esteem is true depends on the interplay of internal growth-oriented needs and the social environment. True self-esteem develops when these needs are satisfied, whereas contingent self-esteem develops when these needs are not satisfied. The authors argue that interpersonal processes play a more central role in determining people's level of contingent as opposed to true self-esteem.

Leary begins his essay by describing three general approaches to self-esteem processes, which he labels *private self-evaluation, passive appraisal, and active appraisal*. Next, he argues that active appraisal approaches (which include sociometer and terror management theories) account best for the functional significance of self-esteem. Finally, consistent with the interpersonal nature of sociometer theory, Leary argues that "...virtually all influences on self-esteem fundamentally involve factors that have real, potential, or imagined implications for the person's acceptability to other people."

Swann and Seyle argue that it is difficult, if not impossible, to distinguish intrapersonal from interpersonal processes. Instead, they prefer to think of these processes as two sides of the same coin. Consequently, they believe that it will be especially fruitful to identify principles that govern their interplay. One such principle is the role of self-verification processes in the maintenance of self-concept and self-esteem. Swann and Seyle briefly review these processes, paying special attention to recent research that focuses on self-esteem per se.

24

A Self-Determination Theory Perspective on the Interpersonal and Intrapersonal Aspects of Self-Esteem

ARLEN C. MOLLER, RON FRIEDMAN, and EDWARD L. DECI

*U*nderstanding the relative influence of interpersonal and intrapersonal processes on self-esteem requires making two important distinctions. The first is the type of self-esteem, namely whether true self-esteem or contingent self-esteem is being considered (Deci & Ryan, 1995; Ryan & Deci, 2004). The second is whether developmental antecedents of self-esteem or current social-contextual influences are being considered. The two types of self-esteem have different developmental, as well as different proximal, antecedents, and they are associated with different outcomes.

True self-esteem represents a form of intrinsic satisfaction with oneself that is relatively stable and, by its nature, is not particularly salient to the person. In other words, people high in true (i.e., noncontingent) self-esteem are less concerned with self-esteem and with evaluating the self as an object (Ryan & Brown, 2003). True self-esteem constitutes a deep sense of feeling worthy, such that one's self is not continually being put to the test. It tends naturally to accompany a high level of autonomous motivation. Contingent self-esteem, in contrast, is more superficial and is dependent on matching criteria such as performing up to an achievement standard, controlling one's emotions, amassing wealth, or becoming famous, depending on what criteria have been internalized (i.e., introjected) and are thus salient to the person. It is characterized by objective self-awareness—that is, seeing oneself "through others' eyes" (Duval & Wicklund, 1972; Plant & Ryan, 1985).

DEVELOPMENTAL INFLUENCES

According to self-determination theory (SDT), the degree to which people's self-esteem is true versus contingent is based in the dialectic between (1) their innate growth-oriented strivings to fulfill universal psychological needs for autonomy, competence, and relatedness and (2) the social environment that either supports or thwarts those strivings. If, developmentally, people experience ongoing satisfaction of the basic needs, they tend to become secure within themselves and to experience a sense of true self-worth that is relatively stable and is not a source of focus or concern. True self-esteem is thus generated by an inherently active, growth-oriented tendency that flourishes under conditions of basic need satisfaction.

If, in contrast, people experience deficiencies in satisfaction of the basic needs beginning at early ages, their sense of self will be less secure, and it is likely that they will be forever striving for extrinsic goals or standards that would connote significance or worth. Thus, contingent self-esteem is based on deficits in need satisfaction and is accordingly more defensive in nature. It is associated with more controlled forms of self-regulation—specifically, with introjected regulation, which involves the motives to prove one's worth, to feel prideful, and to avoid guilt and shame.

The relatively widespread socialization practice of conditional regard (or withdrawal of love) involves parents providing attention and affection to their children when the children behave as the parents desire. This practice tends to thwart children's needs for autonomy because the children have to relinquish autonomy in order to get love. Interestingly, however, research shows that it also tends to thwart their need for relatedness because the children do not feel accepted for who they are (Assor, Roth, & Deci, 2004). This socializing approach involves contingencies upon which parents' esteem for their children is based, and Assor et al. also found that the children tended to introject the contingencies, subsequently feeling an inner compulsion to do as their parents required. Thus, the children tended to esteem themselves only when they had lived up to the introjected standards, so their self-worth was unstable, their feelings of satisfaction after successes were fleeting, and their shame and guilt after failure were very strong.

Developmentally, then, the SDT analysis maintains that interpersonal processes (namely the amount of need satisfaction provided by significant others through, for example, noncontingent love) play an important role in determining the degree to which true versus contingent self-esteem will be central. To the extent that, during their childhood years, people's basic psychological needs are on-goingly satisfied within their social environment, they will experience stable high levels of true self-esteem and they will function in ways that are authentic and psychologically healthy. To the extent that the needs are not satisfied, the people's self-esteem will be contingent.

Our statement that social environments play an important role in the degree to which people experience true (as opposed to contingent) self-esteem is not equivalent to saying that the interpersonal environment determines or programs people's type or level of self-esteem. People are proactive organisms, and do not simply accept self-esteem contingencies that the environment presses upon them, nor do they simply accept the level of regard the social environment expresses toward them. Rather, the type and level of people's self-esteem represent the best accommodation they are able to make within their social environment. When faced with antagonistic, non-nurturing, need-thwarting social contexts, the best that people can typically do is develop contingent self-esteem, which will vary in level depending on their effectiveness at meeting the standards. Accordingly, intrapersonal processes are also central in the development of true versus contingent self-esteem, namely, (1) people's growth-oriented tendencies which are oriented toward healthy development and are reflected in a high level of true self-esteem and (2) their basic psychological needs for autonomy, competence, and relatedness which energize the tendency toward growth. These intrapersonal processes, in interaction with the interpersonal context that either supports or thwarts need satisfaction and growth, are the bases for the developmental outcome of true versus contingent self-esteem.

TWO ALTERNATIVE VIEWS

Our view stands in sharp contrast to two other contemporary views of self-esteem: sociometer theory (Leary & Baumeister, 2000) and terror management theory (Greenberg, Solomon, & Pyszczynski, 1997). Sociometer theory suggests that people's selves and their levels of self-esteem are entirely a function of their social environment. This theory, which does not differentiate true from contingent self-esteem, views the level of self-esteem to be a function of whether the social environment is accepting. The theory deals only with what we call contingent self-esteem. Further, the theory views self-esteem almost exclusively as an interpersonal process of trying to avoid rejection. As such, the theory considers only the need for relatedness to be important for self-esteem, whereas SDT research has shown that all three basic needs—the needs for competence, autonomy, and relatedness—are essential for high self-esteem (Reis, Sheldon, Gable, Roscoe, & Ryan, 2000).

Terror management theory (Greenberg et al., 1997) proposes that people have a need for self-esteem that shields them from the terror of their inevitable death. Self-esteem accrues from satisfying external or introjected cultural standards. Terror management theory focuses on contingent self-esteem and describes the process of acquiring self-esteem as an interpersonal process. Thus, they have given little attention to true self-esteem, which we maintain is a growth or expansion process rather than a defensive or security-based one.

PROXIMAL SOCIAL-CONTEXTUAL INFLUENCES

Developmentally, within SDT, the dialectic of the proactive organism and the social environment affects the degree to which people develop a high level of true self-esteem, or alternatively become oriented toward having their feelings of worth be contingent upon whether they meet specified standards. If people have experienced substantial need satisfaction, they are likely to have a relatively stable high sense of true self-esteem, which does not require ongoing affirmation in the proximal social context.

However, if their development has been characterized by non-need-satisfying experiences, they will become increasingly dependent upon feedback from the immediate situation to signify their worthiness. In other words, if people's basic psychological needs have been thwarted to the point that they do not feel good about themselves intrinsically, they will focus attention on establishing self-worth based upon controlling standards and relevant feedback. Thus, central proximal factors in people's level of (contingent) self-esteem will be how others relate to them and what messages others convey, whether explicitly or implicitly, about their performance, their likability, and their worth.

When the processes of contingent self-esteem are central for people, the standards against which their worth is assessed will to some extent be external, but they will, to a substantial degree, have been introjected. Holding rigidly internalized standards, people will then evaluate themselves against those standards and will be looking to others for affirmation that the standards have been met and thus that they are worthy individuals.

To summarize, true self-esteem, in the ongoing sense, is primarily an intrapersonal process in which people feel a relatively deep and stable sense of worth and are not dependent on ongoing affirmation to maintain their own sense of value. In contrast, contingent self-esteem has a much more prominent interpersonal component. Specifically, contingent self-esteem involves introjected standards, which, although intrapersonal, were taken in from the interpersonal world and require continual buttressing from that world. As such, the proximal social context plays an important part in contingent self-esteem because it provides much of the feedback that signifies whether or not people have met the conditions that are required for feeling good about themselves.

CONTINGENT SELF-ESTEEM ELABORATED

In a developmental sense, it is people's experiences of need thwarting, resulting from socialization practices such as conditional regard, that result in their introjecting contingencies of worth and thus having a strong orientation toward contingent self-esteem. Then, at any given time, their level of self-esteem (i.e., of contingent self-esteem) will depend on how well they have done in meeting the standards and getting the interpersonal reassurance that is necessary for someone with contingent self-esteem to feel lovable and worthy. For contingent self-esteem, the level can thus fluctuate substantially from low to high, and much of the fluctuation will depend on interpersonal occurrences (see Kernis, 2003). Further, the instability inherent in contingent self-esteem leaves people reactive to transient events in the environment, which tend to prompt acts of hostility and aggression when the people's self-evaluations of worth are threatened (Kernis, Grannemann, & Barclay, 1989). Individuals for whom self-esteem is unstable will also tend to react strongly to negative events and overestimate the duration of those negative events (Kernis & Waschull, 1995).

CONTINGENCIES OF SELF-WORTH

Crocker and Wolfe (2001) proposed that people's self-esteem is contingent upon their performance in various life domains to the degree that those domains are personally meaningful to them. From this perspective, then, all self-esteem is considered contingent. As in sociometer theory and terror management theory, the Crocker and Wolfe view focuses on the level of contingent self-esteem, which in all three theories is said to result from being successful in meeting some type of interpersonal standard.

With regard to the SDT concept of true (i.e., noncontingent) self-esteem, Crocker and Wolfe (2001) said that true self-esteem might exist but is quite rare. Our view, in contrast, is that people do, to some extent, have true self-esteem, so the interesting issues relate to the degree to which individuals' self-esteem is true vs. contingent. We predict, of course, that the degree to which self-esteem is true as opposed to contingent is a reliable predictor of well-being.

Crocker and colleagues also suggested that the types of contingencies that are central to people's self-esteem differ in various ways; for example, some are more internal, others more external. More internal sources such as being virtuous are said to be more controllable by the person than are external sources such as an attractive appearance or others' approval. Accordingly, the internal sources have been found to be more positively related to self-esteem (Crocker, Luhtanen, Cooper, & Bouvrette, 2003).

SDT similarly predicts that these externally mediated criteria are likely to be associated with lower self-esteem, as research has shown that aspiring for and achieving extrinsic goals such as wealth, fame, and attractive appearance are associated with poorer well-being than aspiring for and attaining intrinsic goals such as personal growth, affiliation, and generativity (Kasser & Ryan, 1996, 2001). Indeed, we would argue that identifying with these "internal" or intrinsic goals and values is likely to support or bolster true self-esteem because these goals and values are more directly need satisfying than are the extrinsic or externally focused goals and values.

CONCLUSION

From the perspective of self-determination theory the relative influence on self-esteem of interpersonal and intrapersonal process depends on the type of self-esteem. The degree to which a person's self-esteem is true is a function of internal growth-oriented processes interacting with the social environment, which either satisfies or thwarts the basic psychological needs for competence, autonomy, and relatedness. Satisfaction of these needs is essential for nourishing the growth-oriented processes and for establishing true self-esteem. True self-esteem is considered relatively stable and is not very salient to the person, so he or she is not engaged in continual self-evaluation. In contrast, to the degree that the basic needs are not well met during development, the deficits will result in self-esteem being contingent, so people will be faced with the ongoing task of proving their worth by meeting standards of excellence. In this case, interpersonal processes will play a much more central role in determining people's level of self-esteem.

To whatever degree true self-esteem is rare, our view is that psychological theories ought not simply treat that paucity as an immutable status quo but instead would do well to work toward advocating the developmental and social contextual conditions that will make it more prevalent.

REFERENCES

Assor, A., Roth, G., & Deci, E. L. (2004). The emotional costs of parents' conditional regard: A self-determination theory analysis. *Journal of Personality*, 72, 47–89.

Crocker, J., Luhtanen, R. K., Cooper, M. L., & Bouvrette, A. (2003). Contingencies of self-worth in college students: Theory and measurement. *Journal of Personality and Social Psychology*, 85, 894–908.

Crocker, J., & Wolfe, C. T. (2001). Contingencies of self-worth. *Psychological Review*, 108, 593–623.

Deci, E. L., & Ryan, R. M. (1995). Human autonomy: The basis for true self-esteem. In M. Kernis (Ed.), *Efficacy, agency, and self-esteem* (pp. 31–49). New York: Plenum.

Duval, S., & Wicklund, R. A. (1972). *A theory of objective self awareness*. New York: Academic Press.

Greenberg, J., Solomon, S., and Pyszczynski, T. (1997). Terror management theory of self-esteem and cultural worldviews: Empirical assessments and conceptual refinements. In M. P. Zanna (Ed.), *Advances in experimental social psychology* (Vol. 29, pp. 61–139). San Diego, CA: Academic Press.

Kasser, T., & Ryan, R. M. (1996). Further examining the American dream: Differential correlates of intrinsic and extrinsic goals. *Personality and Social Psychology Bulletin*, 22, 280–287.

Kasser, T., & Ryan, R. M. (2001). Be careful what you wish for: Optimal functioning and the relative attainment of intrinsic and extrinsic goals. In P. Schmuck & K. M. Sheldon (Eds.), *Life goals and well-being: Towards a positive psychology of human striving* (pp. 115–129). Goettingen: Hogrefe & Huber Publishers.

Kernis, M. H. (2003). Toward a conceptualization of optimal self-esteem. *Psychological Inquiry*, 14, 1–26.

Kernis, M. H., Grannemann, B. D., & Barclay, L. C. (1989). Stability and level of self-esteem as predictors of anger arousal and hostility. *Journal of Personality and Social Psychology*, 56, 1013–1022.

Kernis, M. H., & Waschull, S. B. (1995). The interactive roles of stability and level of self-esteem: Research and theory. In M. P. Zanna (Ed.), *Advances in experimental social psychology* (Vol. 27, pp. 93–141). San Diego, CA: Academic Press.

Leary, M. R., & Baumeister, R. F. (2000). The nature and function of self-esteem: Sociometer theory. In M. P. Zanna (Ed.), *Advances in experimental social psychology* (Vol. 32, pp. 1–62). San Diego, CA: Academic Press.

Plant, R. W., & Ryan, R. M. (1985). Intrinsic motivation and the effects of self-consciousness, self-awareness, and ego-involvement: An investigation of internally controlling styles. *Journal of Personality*, 53, 435–449.

Reis, H. T., Sheldon, K. M., Gable, S. L., Roscoe, J., & Ryan, R. M. (2000). Daily well-being: The role of autonomy, competence, and relatedness. *Personality and Social Psychology Bulletin*, 26, 419–435.

Ryan, R. M., & Brown, K. W. (2003). Why we don't need self-esteem: On fundamental needs, contingent love, and mindfulness. *Psychological Inquiry, 14*, 71–76.

Ryan, R. M., & Deci, E. L. (2004). Avoiding death and engaging life as accounts of meaning and culture: A comment on Pyszczynski, Greenberg, Solomon, Arndt, and Schimel. *Psychological Bulletin, 130*, 473–477.

25

To What Extent is Self-Esteem Influenced by Interpersonal as Compared with Intrapersonal Processes? What are These Processes?

MARK R. LEARY

aking a wide view of the theories that have emerged since James' (1890) groundbreaking discussion of self-esteem, one can distinguish three broad categories of perspectives that differ in the degree to which they assume that self-esteem is (or, at least, ought to be) influenced by interpersonal factors. I begin by reviewing these three approaches, and then critically examine the role of interpersonal and intrapersonal factors in self-esteem.

The first perspective maintains that healthy self-esteem should not be affected by interpersonal evaluations. Although differing in specifics, these theories, which I will collectively call the *private self-evaluation perspective*, share the assumption that mature, well-adjusted people should evaluate themselves according to their own internal standards—and, thus, feel good or bad about themselves to the degree that those standards are or are not met—but their personal self-evaluations should not be affected by the appraisals of other people. To the extent that a person's self-esteem is based on other people's evaluations, the individual is regarded as inauthentic, maladjusted, or overly concerned with approbation. This assumption can be found, among other places, in humanistic psychology (Rogers, 1959) and in the writings of May (1983).

In contrast to the private self-evaluation perspective, the *passive appraisal perspective* asserts that self-esteem is naturally affected by other people's evaluations, as well as other events that have self-relevant implications. The passive appraisal perspective conceptualizes self-esteem as a summary self-judgment based on an amalgam of interpersonal and intrapersonal information, along with direct experience with the environment. The modifier "passive" refers to the fact that these approaches see self-esteem as merely a reflection of various sources of self-relevant information and do not assume that self-esteem *does* anything in particular with this information (although it may have incidental effects on social perception, affect, and motivation). This approach can be traced to Cooley, Mead, and other symbolic interactionists, who asserted that people's perceptions of themselves depend heavily upon their beliefs about how they are perceived by other people (e.g., reflected appraisals). Contemporary incarnations of the passive appraisal perspective acknowledge that reflected appraisals are only one source of information, among many, upon which people base their self-esteem. The passive appraisal perspective seems to have been the implicit view of most social and personality psychologists for the past three decades.

The *active appraisal perspective* builds upon the passive appraisal perspective by suggesting that self-esteem is affected by interpersonal factors because, in one way or another, self-esteem is inherently involved in processing certain kinds of social information. Active appraisal theories view self-esteem as part of a process by which people actively seek to assess their interpersonal, social, or cultural standing. For example, Barkow (1980) proposed that self-esteem is a subjective reflection of the individual's dominance and social status. Barkow suggested that human self-esteem is a psychological remnant of nonhuman dominance hierarchies and that people seek to have high self-esteem because behaving in ways that enhance self-esteem increases their prestige, status, and access to resources. Similarly, terror management theory (Solomon, Greenberg, & Pyszczynski, 1991) offers an active, functional perspective on self-esteem. According to terror management theory, self-esteem reflects the degree to which people believe they are valued participants in a meaningful world. Further, people seek self-esteem because high self-esteem buffers them against the paralyzing terror that arises from their awareness of their fragility and mortality in an uncertain world. A third active appraisal perspective, sociometer theory (Leary & Baumeister, 2000; Leary & Downs, 1995), views self-esteem as part of a psychological system that monitors the person's relational value (or, more colloquially, interpersonal acceptance and rejection). Put simply, self-esteem is a subjective gauge of the person's relational value. These theories differ in important ways but each conceptualizes self-esteem as inherently responsive to interpersonal events and suggests that it is impossible to understand the nature of self-esteem without considering its functional connection to the interpersonal or cultural world.

In my view, logical, evolutionary, and empirical considerations provide the greatest support for the active appraisal perspective. Even if my own preferred explanation (i.e., sociometer theory) should ultimately be found to be fatally flawed, I would find it hard to accept theories that divorce self-esteem from interpersonal events, particularly from the real and imagined judgments of other people. Although many considerations point to the fact that self-esteem serves some important function linked to the person's place in his or her social world, I will discuss only two of the most important.

THE FUNCTIONAL QUESTION

Self-esteem appears to be a human universal. Although the specific factors that affect self-esteem may differ by culture, no one has yet found a group of people who do not experience changes in how they feel about themselves as a result of their own actions and others' evaluations of them, who are indifferent to these self-relevant feelings, or who do not generally prefer to feel good rather than bad about themselves. The universality of the experience strongly suggests that self-esteem is probably an evolutionary adaptation that, like other affectively based experiences, likely served some important function in helping our prehistoric ancestors deal with the challenges and opportunities of their everyday lives. Even if one dismisses evolution in favor of a social constructionist account of self-esteem, it is nonetheless reasonable to assume that a universally adopted social construction must serve some important function.

The private self-evaluation and the passive appraisal perspectives do not easily account for the function of self-esteem. Advocates of the private self-evaluation perspective sometimes suggest that self-esteem signals that people are behaving authentically—i.e., consistently with who they really are (Deci & Ryan, 1995; Rogers, 1959)—but no one has identified the tangible, evolutionarily significant benefits of being authentic. (Indeed, occasional inauthenticity might be expected to be more adaptive if it enhances survival and reproductive success.) And, unless authenticity has adaptive benefits, why would self-esteem be a universal and integral part of the human psyche?

The passive appraisal perspective fares only slightly better in explaining the function of self-esteem. Having an accurate self-concept is undoubtedly beneficial, and reflected appraisals are an important source of information about oneself. Thus, a symbolic interactionist account can explain why people seek feedback from their interpersonal environments and why self-esteem is strongly affected by interpersonal factors. Yet, the passive appraisal perspectives do not articulate the benefits that derive from *feeling* good or bad about oneself (i.e., experiencing low vs. high self-esteem) as a consequence of social feedback. Data show not only that self-esteem is not as strongly related to emotion and behavior as is often imagined but that, when it is, low and high self-esteem may be concomitants rather than causes of positive and negative outcomes (Baumeister, Campbell, Krueger, & Vohs, 2003; Colvin & Block, 1994; Leary et al., 1997; Mecca, Smelser, & Vasconcellos, 1989).

In contrast, theories that adopt an active appraisal perspective make the function of self-esteem explicit, albeit in different ways. Dominance theory suggests that self-esteem is involved in maintaining relative dominance (Barkow, 1980), terror management theory proposes that self-esteem buffers people against paralyzing anxiety that would compromise their well-being (Solomon et al., 1991), and sociometer theory asserts that self-esteem is involved in monitoring and responding to events that have implications for interpersonal acceptance and rejection (Leary & Baumeister, 2000). I find it more plausible that self-esteem evolved to serve adaptive functions such as these than either to manage aspects of people's intrapsychic lives or to serve as a mere scorecard of reflected appraisals.

THE INTERPERSONAL BASIS OF SELF-ESTEEM

Of course, one could potentially propose an active, functional theory of self-esteem that did not involve interpersonal processes whatsoever. For example, Bednar, Wells, and Peterson (1989) suggested that the function of self-esteem is to provide people with feedback regarding their own adequacy in dealing with threats, and Harber (2003) suggested that self-esteem tells people whether they can trust their own emotions. Yet, a viable theory of self-esteem must account for the fact that interpersonal factors exert a uniquely strong influence on self-esteem, even among people who adamantly claim that their self-esteem is impervious to such influences (Leary, Gallagher, Fors, Buttermore, Baldwin, Lane, & Mills, 2003). Furthermore, evidence does not support the idea that interpersonal influences on self-esteem necessarily reflect maladjustment. Self-esteem seems to be fundamentally connected to the real and imagined evaluations of other people, even among well-functioning individuals.

Research suggests that self-esteem is affected primarily by events that have implications for people's acceptability in the eyes of other people (i.e., "relational value;" Leary & Baumeister, 2000). For example, the primary dimensions on which people evaluate themselves—physical appearance, competence, positive social qualities (i.e., likeability), and adherence to social norms—are central determinants of both the degree to which people are accepted or shunned and the degree to which they have high or low self-esteem (e.g., Fleming & Courtney, 1984). Similarly, research on contingencies of self-worth show that people base their feelings of self-worth on seven primary attributes—academics, appearance, approval from others, competition, family support, God's love, and virtue (Crocker, Luhtanen, Cooper, & Bouvrette, 2003)—each of which has important interpersonal implications. (Even "God's love" has a clear social element, albeit an "intertheopersonal" one.) The fact that the primary bases of self-esteem are so strongly social creates problems for the notion that people whose self-esteem is affected by others' evaluations are psychologically disturbed, except perhaps for sociopaths (who may be the only individuals whose self-esteem is unaffected by interpersonal feedback). All three of the active appraisal theories described above can explain these findings, but in my view, sociometer theory offers the most parsimonious explanation of why self-esteem is so strongly influenced by interpersonal events (for comparisons of these approaches, see Leary, 2002, 2004; Leary, Cottrell, & Phillips, 2001).

Occasionally, one will observe instances in which an event that does not appear to have any important interpersonal implications affects a person's self-esteem. So, for example, being dismissed as a fool by a complete stranger in a foreign city can make people feel bad about themselves, and people may also lose self-esteem after failing at a task that other people do not care about (or may even disparage). In my view, such anomalies reflect one of three processes. First, if, as sociometer theory suggests, the self-esteem system evolved to monitor social acceptance, it emerged over millions of years in which hominids spent their lives in the same clan and rarely encountered other people. Thus, the system may not automatically distinguish people whose judgments we should care about from those whose judgments are irrelevant. People may deliberately override the sociometers by deciding to dismiss a particular negative evaluation (Leary, 2004), but their first reaction to almost any relational devaluation is to feel bad. Second, once people learn that certain attributes—such as appearance, likeability, or competence—are important for social acceptance, they may automatically react to threats on those dimensions even when nothing is currently at stake. Essentially, such reactions have become functionally autonomous (Allport, 1937). Finally, because the sociometer must not only respond to actual threats to social acceptance but anticipate them as well, an inconsequential evaluation in one context may nonetheless warn the individual about similarly negative evaluations in future situations that do matter.

Importantly, the active appraisal theories do not deny that self-esteem is affected by intrapersonal processes, including people's private self-evaluations. After all, interpretations of interpersonal events are invariably filtered through people's existing beliefs, including their beliefs about themselves. Thus, how people perceive themselves does affect how they think they are regarded by others and, thus, their self-esteem. Furthermore, "trait" self-esteem—a person's typical or average level of self-esteem—can be construed as the resting position of the person's sociometer in the absence of explicit interpersonal feedback, essentially an intrapersonal "set point" that influences a person's state self-esteem in any particular situation (Leary & MacDonald, 2003). People's chronic beliefs about their relational value are one source of input into their self-esteem.

CONCLUSION

Although self-esteem is affected by both interpersonal and intrapersonal factors, virtually all influences on self-esteem fundamentally involve factors that have real, potential, or imagined implications for the person's acceptability to other people. Thus, the antecedents of self-esteem, whether proximally interpersonal or intrapersonal, are ultimately rooted in people's concerns with other people's perceptions and evaluations of them.

REFERENCES

Allport, G. W. (1937). *Personality: A psychological interpretation*. New York: Holt.

Baumeister, R. F., Campbell, J. D., Krueger, J. I., & Vohs, K. D. (2003). Does high self-esteem cause better performance, interpersonal success, happiness, or healthier lifestyles? *Psychological Science in the Public Interest, 4*, 1–44.

Barkow, J. (1980). Prestige and self-esteem: A biosocial interpretation. In D. R. Omark, F. F. Strayer, & D. G. Freedman (Eds.), *Dominance relations: An ethological view of human conflict and social interaction* (pp. 319–332). New York: Garland STPM.

Bednar, R. L., Wells, M. G., & Peterson, S. R. (1989). *Self-esteem: Paradoxes and innovations in clinical theory and practice*. Washington, DC: American Psychological Association.

Colvin, C. R., & Block, J. (1994). Do positive illusions foster mental health? An examination of the Taylor and Brown formulation. *Psychological Bulletin, 116*, 3–20.

Crocker, J., Luhtanen, R. K., Cooper, M. L., & Bouvrette, A. (2003). Contingencies of self-worth in college students: Theory and measurement. *Journal of Personality and Social Psychology, 85*, 894–908.

Deci, E. L., & Ryan, R. M. (1995). Human agency: The basis for true self-esteem. In M. H. Kernis (Ed.), *Efficacy, agency, and self-esteem* (pp. 31–50). New York: Plenum.

Fleming, J. S., & Courtney, B. E. (1984). The dimensionality of self-esteem II: Hierarchical facet model for revised measurement scales. *Journal of Personality and Social Psychology, 46*, 404–421.

Harber, K. D. (2003, October). *Self esteem and the use of emotions as information.* Paper presented at the meeting of the Society of Southeastern Social Psychologists, Greensboro, NC.

James, W. (1890). *The principles of psychology.* New York: Dover.

Leary, M. R. (2002). The interpersonal basis of self-esteem: Death, devaluation, or deference? In J. Forgas & K. D. Williams (Eds.), *The social self: Cognitive, interpersonal, and intergroup perspectives.* New York: Psychology Press.

Leary, M. R. (2004). The function of self-esteem in terror management theory and sociometer theory: A comment on Pyszczynski, Greenberg, Solomon, Arndt, and Schimel. *Psychological Bulletin, 130*, 478–482.

Leary, M. R. (2004). The sociometer, self-esteem, and the regulation of interpersonal behavior. In R. F. Baumeister & K. D. Vohs (Eds.), *Handbook of self-regulation: Research, theory, and applications.* New York: Guilford.

Leary, M. R., & Baumeister, R. F. (2000). The nature and function of self-esteem: Sociometer theory. In M. P. Zanna (Ed.), *Advances in experimental social psychology* (Vol. 32, pp. 1–62). San Diego, CA: Academic Press.

Leary, M. R., Cottrell, C. A., & Phillips, M. (2001). Deconfounding the effects of dominance and social acceptance on self-esteem. *Journal of Personality and Social Psychology, 81*, 898–909.

Leary, M. R., & Downs, D. L. (1995). Interpersonal functions of the self-esteem motive: The self-esteem system as a sociometer. In M. Kernis (Ed.), *Efficacy, agency, and self-esteem.* New York: Plenum.

Leary, M. R., Gallagher, B., Fors, E. H., Buttermore, N., Baldwin, E., Lane, K. K., & Mills, A. (2003). The invalidity of personal claims about self-esteem. *Personality and Social Psychology Bulletin, 29*, 623–636.

Leary, M. R., & MacDonald, G. (2003). Individual differences in self-esteem: A review and theoretical integration. In M. R. Leary & J. P. Tangney (Eds.), *Handbook of self and identity* (pp. 401–418). New York: Guilford Press.

Leary, M. R., Tambor, E., Terdal, S., & Downs, D. L. (1995). Self-esteem as an interpersonal monitor: The sociometer hypothesis. *Journal of Personality and Social Psychology, 68*, 518–530.

May, R. (1983). *The discovery of being.* New York: Norton.

Mecca, A. M., Smelser, N. J., & Vasconcellos, J. (1989). *The social importance of self-esteem.* Berkeley, CA: University of California Press.

Rogers, C. (1959). A theory of therapy, personality, and interpersonal relationships, as developed in the client-centered framework. In S. Koch (Ed.), *Psychology: A study of a science* (Vol. 3, pp. 184–256). New York: McGraw-Hill.

Solomon, S., Greenberg, J., & Pyszczynski, T. (1991). A terror management theory of social behavior: The psychological functions of self-esteem and cultural worldviews. In M. Zanna (Ed.), *Advances in experimental social psychology* (Vol. 24, pp. 91–159). Orlando, FL: Academic Press.

26

The Antecedents of Self-Esteem

WILLIAM SWANN, JR. and D. CONOR SEYLE

*D*oes self-esteem grow out of intrapsychic or interpersonal processes? This seemingly straightforward question is actually trickier than it appears to be. The complexity stems from the fact that intrapsychic and interpersonal processes are mutually influential. As such, determining which of the two sets of processes are dominant is a little like asking whether the process of respiration is influenced more by the quality of one's lungs or the quality of the air in the surrounding environment. Obviously, both sets of variables affect the outcome. The question, then, is how intrapersonal and interpersonal processes interact to produce self-esteem.

Among the first to ask where self-esteem comes from were the early symbolic interactionists. Cooley (1902), for example, argued persuasively that we don't just "know" who we are; rather, we infer our self-views from our experiences with others, especially those who are important to us and whose opinions we trust (e.g., Mead, 1934; Rosenberg, 1973). Research inspired by attachment theory (Bowlby, 1969) supports the idea that we use the manner in which others treat us as a source of self-knowledge (Ainsworth, Blehar, Waters, & Wall, 1978). For example, children of caregivers who are warm and responsive conclude that their caregivers value and respect them and consequently develop relatively positive self-views (e.g., Arend, Gove, & Sroufe, 1979; Cassidy, 1988). Such children subsequently thrive. Even as late as adolescence, they are perceived as more socially skilled and self-confident than children of cold or insensitive mothers (Schulman, Elicker, & Sroufe, 1994; Sroufe, Carlson, & Shulman 1993).

Once derived from social interaction, self-views tend to persist over time, whether they are positive or negative (e.g., Shrauger & Shoeneman, 1979; Trzesniewski, Donnellan, & Robins, 2003). Indeed, some researchers have shown that self-conceptions and related psychological structures remain stable over periods as long as 35 years (e.g., Block, 1981; Costa & McCrae, 1980). Such continuity is at least partially due to unintended interpersonal considerations: Stability in the reactions people elicit due to constancy in their social class, physical appearance, and so on. In addition, however, people's motivation to maintain their self-views

(Lecky, 1945; Swann, 1983) appears to play a role. Both interpersonal and intrapsychic factors may underlie this motivation. From an interpersonal perspective, unwavering self-views stabilize people's behavior, which, in turn, makes them more predictable to their relationship partners (e.g., Athay & Darley, 1981; Goffman, 1959). From an intrapsychic perspective, stable self-views serve as the lenses through which we perceive reality, lenses that imbue our worlds with meaning. Hence, if people's self-views shift, their ability to make sense of social reality will be compromised.

For both interpersonal and intraspychic reasons, then, people may make active efforts to ensure that their environments provide them with a steady supply of *self-verifying* feedback. One strategy they may employ involves the display of "identity cues"—appearances, physical environments, and possessions that tell others who they are (Goffman, 1959). For example, Gosling, Ko, Mannarelli, and Morris (2002) recently reported that people structure their bedrooms and offices in ways that communicated their identities to others. In their study, just as some brought observers to recognize their self-perceived "messiness," others brought them to see them as relatively "tidy." As a result, even before people open their mouths, their interaction partners may already be primed to regard them as they regard themselves.

People may also attain self-verification by gravitating toward some relationship partners and avoiding others (e.g., Swann, Rentfrow, & Guinn, 2002). Thus, for example, research has shown that people choose to interact with evaluators who see them as they see themselves (e.g., Hixon & Swann, 1993; Robinson & Smith-Lovin, 1992; Swann, Wenzlaff, Krull, & Pelham, 1992). This pattern emerges even when people have negative self-views. That is, when people with negative self-views (i.e., associated with low self-esteem or depression) are given a choice to interact with people who have positive or negative impressions of them, they choose to interact with those who have correspondingly negative perceptions of them (Swann, Pelham, & Krull, 1989; Swann, Stein-Seroussi, & Giesler, 1992). And it is not merely that people with negative self-views choose negative evaluators to avoid positive ones (whom they might fear will come to reject them)—when such individuals have a choice of interacting with a negative evaluator versus being in a different experiment, they display a preference for the negative evaluator (Swann, Wenzlaff, & Tafarodi, 1992).

And what if people somehow wind up interacting with partners whose appraisals challenge their self-views? Initially, people may attempt to bring such partners to see them congruently (e.g., Swann & Hill, 1982, Swann & Read, 1981, study 2). Failing this, they may withdraw from the relationship, either psychologically or through divorce (e.g., Cast & Burke, 2002; De La Ronde & Swann, 1998; Ritts & Stein, 1995; Swann, Hixon, & De La Ronde, 1992). This tendency is also symmetric with respect to self-esteem: just as people who valued themselves were apt to withdraw from negative spouses, people who *de*valued themselves withdrew from positive partners (Swann et al., 1992). A parallel process unfolds in the work place. That is, people who devalued themselves were more apt to quit their jobs when they received raises as compared to pay cuts (Schroeder, Josephs & Swann, 2004).

Even if all of the foregoing efforts to create self-confirming social environments fail, people's self-views may bias their information-processing activities in ways that make their experiences seem more self-verifying than they are in reality. For example, Swann and Read (1981, Study 1) showed that participants with positive self-views spent longer scrutinizing evaluations when they anticipated that the evaluations would be positive and people with negative self-views spent longer scrutinizing evaluations when they anticipated that the evaluations would be negative. Memory processes may be similarly biased. In a follow-up study, Swann and Read (1981, Study 3) discovered that participants who perceived themselves positively remembered more positive than negative statements, and those who perceived themselves negatively remembered more negative than positive statements. Finally, numerous investigators have shown that people tend to interpret information in ways that reinforce their self-views. For example, Markus (1977) found that people endorse the validity of feedback only insofar as it fits with their self-views. Similarly, Story (1998) reported that just as people with high self-esteem recalled evaluations as being more favorable than was warranted, people with low self-esteem recalled them as being overly negative.

Together, such attentional, encoding, retrieval, and interpretational processes may systematically skew people's perceptions of social reality. For this reason, even when people happen to wind up with relationship partners who perceive them in a manner that challenges their self-views, they may fail to appreciate the discrepancy fully.

The foregoing research suggests that interpersonal and intrapersonal processes are intricately interwoven with one another. Which brings us back to the question that this essay is designed to address: "To what extent is self-esteem influenced by interpersonal as compared with intrapersonal processes?" The foregoing analysis suggests that this question is based on two tenuous assumptions. The first is that self-esteem is an autonomous structure that resides inside people like their livers, spleens, or hearts. The problem with this notion is that it tempts people to mistake an abstraction (what self-esteem really is) for a thing (what the word "structure" connotes to many people). In reality, self-esteem is a fiction we construct to make sense of who we are, what others think of us, and how we should behave. This fiction is at the same time an interpretation of the experiences we have and a guide to the type of experiences we seek: less a fixed structure than a constantly updated filter, which colors our perceptions of social reality.

The second tenuous assumption underlying the question we were asked to answer is that intrapersonal and interpersonal processes can be readily distinguished. In reality, we believe that the interpersonal and intrapersonal processes that give rise to feelings of self-esteem are like two sides of the same coin. As Mead noted, "No hard and fast line can be drawn between our own selves and the selves of others, since our own selves exist and enter as such into our experience only insofar as the selves of others exist and enter as such into our experience also." Mead's comments thus highlight the difficulty of separating the interpersonal and intrapersonal processes involved in self-esteem, for the intrapersonal concepts can exist only insofar as they receive nourishment from the interpersonal arena which is in turn guided by intrapersonal processes.

Our discomfort with attempting to divide the influences on self-esteem into interpersonal versus personal influences may well create a sense of déjà vu for those familiar with recent analyses of the relative influence of traits versus situations (e.g., Higgins, 1990; Swann & Seyle, 2005) or genes versus environment (e.g. Turkheimer, 1991). Inevitably, these approaches resolve through the development of a theory that does not treat the two sides as independent, but instead as mutually supportive interacting elements (e.g., Gilbert, 1998; Ridley, 2003; Swann & Seyle, 2005; Turkheimer, 1991).

A similar approach must be taken when examining the question of interpersonal versus intrapersonal determinants of self-esteem. Although these processes are obviously conceptually distinct, in practice they may be deeply interwoven and mutually influential. We should thus work to identify the principles that govern their interplay rather than contemplate whether one dominates the other.

REFERENCES

Ainsworth, M. D. S., Blehar, M. C., Waters, E., & Wall, S. (1978). *Patterns of attachment: A psychological study of the strange situation*. Hillsdale, NJ: Lawrence Erlbaum Associates, Inc.

Arend, R., Gove, F., & Sroufe, L. A. (1979). Continuity of individual adaptation from infancy to kindergarten: A predictive study of ego-resiliency and curiosity in preschoolers. *Child Development, 50*, 950–959.

Athay, M., & Darley, J. M. (1981). Toward an interaction centered theory of personality. In N. Cantor & J. F. Kihlstrom (Eds.), *Personality, cognition, and social interaction* (pp. 281–308). Hillsdale, NJ: Lawrence Erlbaum Associates, Inc.

Block, J. (1981). Some enduring and consequential structures of personality. In A. I. Rabin, J. Arnoff, A. M. Barclay, & R. A. Zucker (Eds.), *Further explorations in personality*. New York: Wiley.

Bowlby, J. (1969). *Attachment and loss, Vol. 1, Attachment*. New York: Basic Books.

Cassidy, J. (1988). Child–mother attachment and the self in six year-olds. *Child Development, 59*, 121–134.

Cast, A. D., & Burke, P. D. (2002). A theory of self-esteem. *Social Forces, 80*, 1041–1068.

Cooley, C. H. (1902). *Human nature and the social order*. New York: Charles Scribner's Sons.

Costa, B. T. Jr., & McCrae, R. R. (1980). Still stable after all these years: Personality as a key to some issues in adulthood and old age. In P. B. Baltes & O. G. Brim (Eds.), *Life span development and behavior* (Vol. 3). New York: Academic.

De La Ronde, C., & Swann, W. B. Jr. (1998). Partner verification: Restoring shattered images of our intimates. *Journal of Personality and Social Psychology, 75*, 374–382.

Gilbert, D. T. (1998). Ordinary personology. In D. T. Gilbert, S. Fiske, & G. Lindzey (Eds.), *The handbook of social psychology* (4th ed., Vol. 2, pp. 89–150). New York: Random House.

Goffman, E. (1959). *The presentation of self in everyday life*. New York: Anchor Books.

Gosling, S. D., Ko, S. J., Mannarelli, T., & Morris, M. E. (2002). A room with a cue: Judgments of personality based on offices and bedrooms. *Journal of Personality and Social Psychology, 82*, 379–398.

Higgins, E. T. (1990). Personality, social psychology, and cross-situation relations: Standards and knowledge activation as a common language. In L. A. Pervin (Ed.), *Handbook of personality: Theory and research* (pp. 301–338). New York: Guilford Press.

Hixon, J. G., & Swann, W. B. Jr. (1993). When does introspection bear fruit? Self-reflection, self-insight, and interpersonal choices. *Journal of Personality and Social Psychology, 64*, 35–43.

Lecky, P. (1945). *Self-consistency: A theory of personality.* New York: Island Press.

Markus, H. (1977). Self-schema and processing information about the self. *Journal of Personality and Social Psychology, 35*, 63–78.

Mead, G. H. (1934). *Mind, self and society.* Chicago: University of Chicago Press.

Ridley, M. (2003). *Nature via nurture: Genes, experience, and what makes us human.* New York: Harper Collins.

Ritts, V., & Stein, J. R. (1995). Verification and commitment in marital relationships: An exploration of self-verification theory in community college students. *Psychological Reports, 76*, 383–386.

Robinson, D. T., & Smith-Lovin, L. (1992). Selective interaction as a strategy for identity maintenance: An affect-control model. *Social Psychology Quarterly, 55*, 12–28.

Rosenberg, M. (1973). Which significant others? *American Behavioral Scientist, 16*, 829–860.

Schroeder, D. Josephs, R., & Swann, W. B. (2004). *Foregoing lucrative employment to preserve low self-esteem.* Unpublished manuscript, University of Texas, Austin.

Schulman, S., Elicker, J., & Sroufe, A. (1994). Stages of friendship growth in preadolescents as related to attachment history. *Journal of Social and Personal Relationships, 11*, 341–361.

Shrauger, J. S., & Schoeneman, T. J. (1979). Symbolic interactionist view of self-concept: Through the looking glass darkly. *Psychological Bulletin, 86*, 549–573.

Sroufe, L. A., Carlson, E., & Shulman, S. (1993). Individuals in relationships: Development from infancy through adolescence. In Funder, D. C., Parke, R. D., Tomlinson-Keasey, C., & Widamen, K. (Eds.), *Studying lives through time: Personality and development.* Washington, DC: American Psychological Association.

Story, A. L. (1998). Self-esteem and memory for favorable and unfavorable personality feedback. *Personality and Social Psychology Bulletin, 24*, 51–64.

Swann, W. B. Jr. (1983). Self-verification: Bringing social reality into harmony with the self. In J. Suls & A. G. Greenwald (Eds.), *Social psychological perspectives on the self* (Vol. 2, pp. 33–66). Hillsdale, NJ: Lawrence Erlbaum Associates, Inc.

Swann, W. B. Jr., & Hill, C. A. (1982). When our identities are mistaken: Reaffirming self-conceptions through social interaction. *Journal of Personality and Social Psychology, 43*, 59–66.

Swann, W. B., Hixon, J. G., & De La Ronde, C. (1992). Embracing the bitter 'truth': Negative self-concepts and marital commitment. *Psychological Science, 3*, 118–121.

Swann, W. B. Jr., Pelham, B. W., & Krull, D. S. (1989). Agreeable fancy or disagreeable truth? How people reconcile their self-enhancement and self-verification needs. *Journal of Personality and Social Psychology, 57*, 782–791.

Swann, W. B. Jr., & Read, S. J. (1981). Self-verification processes: How we sustain our self-conceptions. *Journal of Experimental Social Psychology, 17*, 351–372.

Swann, W. B. Jr., Rentfrow, P. J., & Guinn, J. (2002). Self-verification: The search for coherence. In M. Leary & J. Tangney (Eds.), *Handbook of self and identity.* New York: Guilford.

Swann, W. B. Jr. & Seyle, C. (2005). Personality psychology's comeback and its emerging symbiosis with social psychology. *Personality and Social Psychology Bulletin, 31,* 155–165.

Swann, W. B. Jr., Stein-Seroussi, A., & Giesler, B. (1992). Why people self-verify. *Journal of Personality and Social Psychology, 62,* 392–401.

Swann, W. B., Wenzlaff, R. M., Krull, D. S., & Pelham, B. W. (1992). Allure of negative feedback: Self-verification strivings among depressed persons. *Journal of Abnormal Psychology, 101,* 293–306.

Swann, W. B. Jr., Wenzlaff, R. M., & Tafarodi, R. W. (1992). Depression and the search for negative evaluations: More evidence of the role of self-verification strivings. *Journal of Abnormal Psychology, 101,* 314–317.

Trzesniewski, K. H., Donnellan, M. B., & Robins, R. W. (2003). Stability of self-esteem across the life span. *Journal of Personality and Social Psychology, 84,* 205–220.

Turkheimer, E. (1991). Individual and group differences in adoption studies of IQ. *Psychological Bulletin, 110*(3), 392–405.

Question 9

How are self-esteem and self-knowledge linked? Are these links direct or indirect?

*T*his set of essays focuses on associations between self-knowledge and self-esteem. Hoyle reviews empirical literature that focuses on these links. As he notes, the clearest findings involve valence of self-knowledge, particularly negative self-knowledge and self-esteem level. More specifically, the proportion and complexity of negative self-knowledge relate inversely to self-esteem. Interestingly, these same features of self-knowledge relate to stability of self-esteem, independent of its level.

Showers and Zeigler-Hill discuss the interplay between the content and structure of self-knowledge and self-esteem. Their essay is mostly conceptual in nature, in that they discuss the potential role of such structural factors as self-complexity, compartmentalization, and self-discrepancies. The authors suggest that the power of these structural features generally lies in their capacity to cushion the adverse impact of negative self-beliefs.

Brandt and Vonk argue that while having a well-defined and confident idea of who you are relates to high and healthy self-esteem, so does having positive illusions about the self. They suggest that this apparent paradox can be resolved by first noting that having a clear sense of self does not necessarily mean that this self-knowledge is accurate. It follows, the authors argue, that positive illusions, explicit self-esteem, and self-concept clarity stem from the same basic theory— "I'm doing fine."

27

Self-Knowledge and Self-Esteem

RICK H. HOYLE

*T*he self is an organized, dynamic, and reflexive system of self-referent thoughts, feelings, and motives that shape people's experience of themselves, others, situations, and social relations (Hoyle, Kernis, Leary, & Baldwin, 1999; Mischel & Morf, 2003). The raw material of the self-system is the self-referent information that accumulates in memory with experience and with the passage of time (Greenwald & Banaji, 1989; Kihlstrom & Cantor, 1984). Mental representations of the self draw on this accumulated store of information, providing an organized and efficient context for processing information and planning behavior (Markus, 1977; Mischel & Morf, 2003). The content, structure, and accessibility of these mental representations vary across individuals, and within individuals across situations, giving rise to questions about the implications of variability in the characteristics of self-knowledge for personal and social experience. Of particular interest is the link between characteristics of self-knowledge and self-esteem.

RELEVANT CHARACTERISTICS OF SELF-KNOWLEDGE

Self-knowledge varies along three dimensions of potential relevance to self-esteem: valence, organizational structure, and lucidness. Of these three, the most obviously relevant to self-esteem is valence. Virtually all self-knowledge, whether manifestly evaluative or not, has evaluative connotations that, broadly speaking, can be classified as positive or negative (Greenwald, Bellezza, & Banaji, 1988). To the extent that individual bits of self-knowledge can be classified as positive or negative, the body of self-knowledge can be characterized in *valence* terms. If these bits of self-knowledge are rated in terms of importance, then self-knowledge can further be described in terms of the *relative importance of positive and negative self-knowledge* (e.g., Pelham & Swann, 1989).

The volume of self-referent information in memory is sufficiently large that it must be arrayed in an organized manner in order to meet the information processing needs of the individual (Showers & Zeigler-Hill, 2003). The organizational structure of self-knowledge varies along three related dimensions of potential relevance to self-esteem. Building on the valence distinction, *evaluative organization* concerns the degree to which positive and negative self-knowledge across mental representations of the self is compartmentalized or integrated (Showers, 1992a). Two additional dimensions ignore the valence distinction, focusing instead on the associations among mental representations of the self. *Self-concept differentiation* concerns the mental representation of oneself in prominent roles (Donahue, Robins, Roberts, & John, 1993). Greater differentiation is reflected in less overlap among self-representations across roles. *Self-complexity* focuses on mental representations of the self more broadly, emphasizing the number and interrelatedness of self-representations (Linville, 1985, 1987). Greater complexity is defined as more distinct representations of the self in memory (cf. Rafaeli-Mor, Gotlib, & Revelle, 1999). Returning to the valence distinction, it has proven profitable to distinguish between the complexity of positive and negative self-knowledge (Morgan & Janoff-Bulman, 1994; Woolfolk, Novalany, Gara, Allen, & Polino, 1995).

Self-knowledge also varies in lucidness. That is, some people seem to know themselves better than others (Wilson & Dunn, 2004). This variability in the lucidness of self-knowledge is reflected in two characteristics: clarity and certainty. *Self-concept clarity* concerns the articulation of self-knowledge and manifests as more extreme, temporally stable, and internally consistent knowledge of the self (Campbell, 1990). A related characteristic of self-knowledge is *self-certainty*, reflected in the precision of self-descriptions (Baumgardner, 1990). As with self-complexity, self-certainty can refer to all self-knowledge or positive and negative self-knowledge separately.

An important feature of these characteristics is their focus on self-referent information of which the individual is aware. It seems likely that implicit self-knowledge—information about the self of which the individual is not conscious at a particular point in time—is relevant for self-esteem as well (Devos & Banaji, 2003). Yet, although researchers have made significant strides in the measurement of implicit processes (including self-evaluation), strategies for measuring the characteristics just described for implicit self-knowledge have not yet been developed. For that reason, my review of the empirical literature on self-knowledge and self-esteem is limited to explicit self-knowledge—the working self-concept (Markus & Kunda, 1986)—and explicit self-esteem.

ARE SELF-KNOWLEDGE AND SELF-ESTEEM RELATED?

Relatively few published studies have focused specifically on the association between characteristics of self-knowledge and self-esteem. Fortunately, a number of published studies focused on self-knowledge more generally have included a measure of global self-esteem. Along with relevant findings from these studies, I present findings from two previously unpublished data sets (Ns = 193 and 237) that include a measure of self-esteem as well as measures of many of the characteristics of self-knowledge just reviewed.

One might expect the strongest link between self-esteem and self-knowledge to be in terms of valence—the more positive people's self-knowledge, particularly when positive bits of self-knowledge are important, the higher their global feelings of self-worth. Although this association has not been examined explicitly, the proportion of negative self-knowledge is routinely included as a covariate in investigations of evaluative organization. The coefficients of association (either zero-order correlation coefficients or semi-partial correlation coefficients controlling for other covariates entered in the model at the same time) across these studies range from $-.31$ (Showers, 1992a) to $-.48$ (Showers, 1992b). Because the proportion of negative self-knowledge is often entered with other covariates, these studies may underestimate the simple association between negative self-knowledge and self-esteem. Indeed, in the new data sets the zero-order r values between the proportion of negative self-knowledge and global self-esteem are $-.38$ and $-.50$. One might also consider the relative importance of positive vs. negative self-knowledge. When included in a regression equation with measures of positive and negative content, this variable is modestly associated with global self-esteem ($r = .15$; Showers, 1992a). The relative importance of positive self-knowledge is available only in one of the previously unpublished data sets; the zero-order r with self-esteem is .07. These findings indicate a substantial association between the valence of self-knowledge and global self-esteem and a possible small association between the relative importance of positive vs. negative self-knowledge self-esteem.

Significantly more findings have been published that index the association between organizational structure of self-knowledge and self-esteem. The preponderance of this work focuses on self-complexity. The zero-order correlation between self-complexity, without distinguishing between positive and negative self-knowledge, is modest and negative ($r = -.11$ and $-.22$ in the new data sets), suggesting that a larger number of distinct self-representations in memory is a liability in terms of self-appraisal (cf. Campbell, Chew, & Scratchley, 1991; Lutz & Ross, 2003). This curious result is clarified when self-complexity is considered separately for positive and negative self-knowledge. The correlation between positive self-complexity and self-esteem varies around zero (e.g., Rhodewalt, Madrian, & Cheney, 1998), ranging from $-.05$ (Woolfolk et al., 1995) to .15 (Morgan & Janoff-Bulman, 1994); in the new data sets, the rs are $-.08$ and $-.12$. None of these coefficients is statistically significant, suggesting that the complexity of positive self-knowledge is, by and large, unrelated to global self-esteem. In contrast, the association between negative self-complexity and global self-esteem is robustly negative, ranging from $-.22$ and $-.28$ in the previously unpublished data sets, to r of $-.36$ and $-.42$ in published findings [Morgan & Janoff-Bulman (1994) and Wookfolk et al. (1995), respectively]. The correlation between positive and negative self-complexity averages about .40, ranging from .18 in one of the new data sets to .59 in one of the studies reported by Woolfolk et al. (1995). To summarize, the overall complexity of self-knowledge is modestly negatively associated with self-esteem; however, when self-complexity is indexed separately for positive and negative self-knowledge, the association is fully attributable to the complexity of negative self-knowledge.

A somewhat different view of the self-complexity–self-esteem relation focuses on the sensitivity of self-esteem to evaluative feedback as a function of self-complexity. According to the affective extremity hypothesis, greater complexity of self-knowledge should be associated with less sensitivity of state self-esteem to evaluative feedback. This prediction has been supported in multiple studies, yielding an effect size of about $r = .24$ (Linville, 1985; Renaud & McConnell, 2002; cf. Rhodewalt et al., 1998). To a modest degree, the more complex people's self-knowledge is, the less their state self-esteem increases following positive feedback or decreases following negative feedback.

Self-concept differentiation does not distinguish between positive and negative self-knowledge and focuses specifically on mental representations of oneself in roles. Zero-order correlations with global self-esteem range from $-.30$ (Bigler, Neimeyer, & Brown, 2001) to $-.39$ (Donahue et al., 1993; see also Lutz & Ross, 2003). Research on a similar conceptualization of organizational structure with a focus on goals found an r of $.19$ between coherence (i.e., low differentiation) of self-referent goals and self-esteem (Sheldon & Kasser, 1995).

The association between evaluative organization and self-esteem typically is evaluated controlling for proportion of negative self-knowledge. Moreover, the association between evaluative organization and self-esteem is expected to vary depending on whether, on balance, positive or negative self-knowledge is more important (Showers, 1992a). In random samples from the normal population, the expectation is for a positive association between evaluative integration and self-esteem. Although published findings correspond with this expectation (Showers, 1992a, 1992b), the association is modest and negative in the two new data sets $(r = -.14$ and $-.21)$, controlling for proportion of negative self-knowledge. The association between evaluative organization and self-esteem varies from moderately positive to moderately negative and is contingent on other (frequently unmeasured) characteristics of self-knowledge.

The lucidness of self-knowledge—i.e., how well it is articulated in memory—should be associated with self-esteem as well. Specifically, high self-esteem should co-occur with greater clarity and certainty of self-knowledge (Baumgardner, 1990; Campbell, 1990). Published findings indicate that this is indeed the case. High self-esteem is associated with greater extremity, temporal stability, and internal consistency of self-knowledge (Campbell, 1990) as well as with self-reports of self-concept clarity (Bigler et al., 2001; Campbell, Trapnell, Heine, Katz, Lavallee, & Lehmann, 1996); correlations with self-reports typically exceed $.60$. The association between self-esteem and self-certainty is more modest, with high self-esteem people evincing more certainty across a range of descriptive terms (Baumgardner, 1990). When those terms are grouped according to valence—mirroring the treatment of self-complexity—I find that self-esteem is essentially unrelated to the certainty of positive self-knowledge $(r = -.09)$ but modestly associated with the certainty of negative self-knowledge $(r = -.15)$.

The two previously unpublished data sets allow for further, more detailed exploration of these associations. For instance, in light of the fact that it is now widely accepted that self-esteem varies along multiple dimensions (e.g., Kernis, Cornell, Sun, Berry, & Harlow, 1993), it would be informative to know whether characteristics of self-knowledge correlate with other aspects of self-esteem. One data set includes a measure of instability of self-esteem along with measures of self-complexity, evaluative organization, and proportion of negative self-knowledge for 177 university students. Zero-order rs indicate that instability of self-esteem is associated with self-knowledge that is more negative ($r = .25$), higher in negative self-complexity ($r = .16$), and more evaluatively compartmentalized ($r = .29$). These correlations persist after controlling for level of self-esteem (partial $r = .18$, .17, and .25, respectively), suggesting that self-knowledge is associated with stability of self-esteem above and beyond the association with either level of self-esteem.

Because there is conceptual overlap among the various characteristics of self-knowledge, it would also be informative to determine the unique contribution of each to the prediction of global feelings of self-worth. A simultaneous regression equation ($N = 237$), including proportion of negative self-knowledge, evaluative organization, and positive and negative self-complexity produced a multiple R of .51, with proportion of negative self-knowledge ($sr = .48$) and negative self-complexity ($sr = .18$) accounting for virtually all of the association. A parallel analysis where instability of self-esteem was used as the outcome produced a multiple R of .34. Significant predictors were proportion of negative self-knowledge ($sr = .12$) and evaluative organization ($sr = .21$). These findings underscore the robust association between valence of self-knowledge and global self-esteem and suggest that the association of other characteristics of self-knowledge and self-esteem varies depending on whether the focus is level or stability of self-esteem.

A final set of analyses focuses specifically on characteristics relevant to negative self-knowledge. Specifically, I tested two moderator hypotheses. The first examined whether evaluative organization and negative self-complexity interact to influence self-esteem. The logic of this hypothesis is that highly complex self-knowledge that is compartmentalized from positive self-knowledge should have negative implications for feelings of self-worth beyond the unqualified effect of each variable. The effect was nonsignificant. A second moderator hypothesis examined the interaction of the proportion of negative self-knowledge and negative self-complexity based on the logic that a relatively large proportion of complex self-knowledge should adversely influence global self-esteem beyond the main effects of each variable (Malle & Horowitz, 1995). This effect was nonsignificant as well. These analyses indicate that proportion of negative self-knowledge, evaluative organization, and negative self-complexity are additively associated with global self-esteem.

CONCLUSIONS

Although the potential link between self-knowledge and self-esteem has received little direct attention from self researchers, I was able to glean a sufficient number of relevant empirical findings from the broader literature on self-knowledge to draw tentative conclusions about the association. The clearest finding is that characteristics reflecting the valence of self-knowledge are most strongly associated with the level of global self-esteem. The most relevant self-knowledge in this regard is negative self-knowledge: Individuals who report more negative self-knowledge that is complex and integrated with positive self-knowledge and about which they are certain also report relatively lower self-esteem. The two principal contributors to this pattern are proportion and complexity of negative self-knowledge, which are additively associated with self-esteem.

A novel finding is the association between stability of self-esteem and these same features of valenced self-knowledge. Importantly, these associations are independent of associations of both stability of self-esteem and characteristics of self-knowledge with level of self-esteem. These findings underscore the view that stability is a relevant feature of self-esteem that functions relatively independent of the level of self-esteem (Kernis et al., 1993) and suggest a potentially fruitful new direction for research on the sources of instability.

A number of key questions remain to be addressed regarding the association between self-knowledge and self-esteem. For instance, it is not clear from studies completed to date whether the association is causal and, if so, in which direction the causal influence runs. Relatedly, with rare exception, the work to date has focused on "off-line" assessment; that is, assessment of self-knowledge when the self is not actively engaged in meaningful information processing. On-line assessment would provide valuable information regarding the processes that underlie the association between self-knowledge and self-esteem, and a more accurate index of the association between them. Finally, although the literature on implicit self-esteem has grown rapidly (for a review, see Farnham, Greenwald, & Banaji, 1999), the form and functioning of implicit self-knowledge has received little attention (relevant work is reviewed by Devos & Banaji, 2003). Findings from new research in these areas would fill in important details in the emerging picture of the self-system.

REFERENCES

Baumgardner, A. H. (1990). To know oneself is to like oneself: Self-certainty and self-affect. *Journal of Personality and Social Psychology*, 58, 1062–1072.

Bigler, M., Neimeyer, G. J., & Brown, E. (2001). The divided self revisited: Effects of self-concept clarity and self-concept differentiation on psychological adjustment. *Journal of Social and Clinical Psychology*, 20, 396–415.

Campbell, J. D. (1990). Self-esteem and clarity of the self-concept. *Journal of Personality and Social Psychology*, 59, 538–549.

Campbell, J. D., Chew, B., & Scratchley, L. S. (1991). Cognitive and emotional reactions to daily events: The effects of self-esteem and self-complexity. *Journal of Personality*, 59, 473–505.

Campbell, J. D., Trapnell, P. D., Heine, S. J., Katz, I. M., Lavallee, L. F., & Lehmann, D. R. (1996). Self-concept clarity: Measurement, personality, correlates, and cultural boundaries. *Journal of Personality and Social Psychology*, 70, 141–156.

Devos, T., & Banaji, M. R. (2003). Implicit self and identity. In M. R. Leary & J. P. Tangney (Eds.), *Handbook of self and identity* (pp. 153–175). New York: Guilford Press.

Donahue, E. M., Robins, R. W., Roberts, B. W., & John, O. P. (1993). The divided self: Concurrent and longitudinal effects of psychological adjustment and social roles on self-concept differentiation. *Journal of Personality and Social Psychology*, 64, 834–846.

Farnham, S. D., Greenwald, A. G., & Banaji, M. R. (1999). Implicit self-esteem. In D. Abrams & M. Hogg (Eds.), *Social identity and social cognition* (pp. 230–248). Oxford, UK: Blackwell.

Greenwald, A. G., & Banaji, M. R. (1989). The self as a memory system: Powerful, but ordinary. *Journal of Personality and Social Psychology, 57*, 41–54.

Greenwald, A. G., Bellezza, F. S., & Banaji, M. R. (1988). Is self-esteem a central ingredient of the self-concept? *Personality and Social Psychology Bulletin, 14*, 34–45.

Hoyle, R. H., Kernis, M. H., Leary, M. R., & Baldwin, M. W. (1999). *Selfhood: Identity, esteem, regulation.* Boulder, CO: Westview Press.

Kernis, M. H., Cornell, D. P., Sun, C., Berry, A., & Harlow, T. (1993). There's more to self-esteem than whether it's high or low: The importance of stability of self-esteem. *Journal of Personality and Social Psychology, 65*, 1190–1204.

Kihlstrom, J. F., & Cantor, N. (1984). Mental representations of the self. In L. Berkowitz (Ed.), *Advances in experimental social psychology* (Vol. 17, pp. 1–47). New York: Academic Press.

Linville, P. W. (1985). Self-complexity and affective extremity: Don't put all your eggs in one cognitive basket. *Social Cognition, 3*, 94–120.

Linville, P. W. (1987). Self-complexity as a cognitive buffer against stress-related illness and depression. *Journal of Personality and Social Psychology, 52*, 663–676.

Lutz, C. J., & Ross, S. R. (2003). Elaboration versus fragmentation: Distinguishing between self-complexity and self-concept differentiation. *Journal of Social and Clinical Psychology, 22*, 537–559.

Malle, B. F., & Horowitz, L. M. (1995). The puzzle of negative self-views: An explanation using the schema concept. *Journal of Personality and Social Psychology, 68*, 470–484.

Markus, H. (1977). Self-schemata and processing information about the self. *Journal of Personality and Social Psychology, 35*, 63–78.

Markus, H., & Kunda, Z. (1986). Stability and malleability of the self-concept. *Journal of Personality and Social Psychology, 51*, 858–866.

Mischel, W., & Morf, C. C. (2003). The self as a psycho-social dynamic processing system: A meta-perspective on a century of the self in psychology. In M. R. Leary & J. P. Tangney (Eds.), *Handbook of self and identity* (pp. 15–43). New York: Guilford Press.

Morgan, H. J., & Janoff-Bulman, R. (1994). Positive and negative self-complexity: Patterns of adjustment following traumatic versus non-traumatic life experiences. *Journal of Social and Clinical Psychology, 13*, 63–85.

Pelham, B. W., & Swann, W. B. (1989). From self-conceptions to self-worth: On the sources and structure of global self-esteem. *Journal of Personality and Social Psychology, 57*, 672–680.

Rafaeli-Mor, E., Gotlib, I. H., & Revelle, W. (1999). The meaning and measurement of self-complexity. *Personality and Individual Differences, 27*, 341–356.

Renaud, J. M., & McConnell, A. R. (2002). Organization of the self-concept and the suppression of self-relevant thoughts. *Journal of Experimental Social Psychology, 38*, 79–86.

Rhodewalt, F., Madrian, J. C., & Cheney, S. (1998). Narcissism, self-knowledge organization, and emotional reactivity: The effect of daily experiences on self-esteem and affect. *Personality and Social Psychology Bulletin, 24*, 75–87.

Sheldon, K. M., & Kasser, T. (1995). Coherence and congruence: Two aspects of personality integration. *Journal of Personality and Social Psychology, 68*, 531–543.

Showers, C. J. (1992a). Compartmentalization of positive and negative self-knowledge: Keeping bad apples out of the bunch. *Journal of Personality and Social Psychology*, *62*, 1036–1049.

Showers, C. J. (1992b). Evaluatively integrative thinking about characteristics of the self. *Personality and Social Psychology Bulletin*, *18*, 719–729.

Showers, C. J., & Zeigler-Hill, V. (2003). Organization of self-knowledge: Features, functions, and flexibility. In M. R. Leary & J. P. Tangney (Eds.), *Handbook of self and identity* (pp. 47–67). New York: Guilford Press.

Wilson, T. D., & Dunn, E. W. (2004). Self-knowledge: Its limits, value, and potential for improvement. *Annual Review of Psychology*, *55*, 493–518.

Woolfolk, R. L., Novalany, J., Gara, M. A., Allen, L. A., & Polino, M. (1995). Self-complexity, self-evaluation, and depression: An examination of form and content within the self-schema. *Journal of Personality and Social Psychology*, *68*, 1108–1120.

28

Pathways Among Self-Knowledge and Self-Esteem: They Are Direct or Indirect?

CAROLIN J. SHOWERS and VIRGIL ZEIGLER-HILL

Research on the structure and organization of self-knowledge suggests that the links between self-knowledge and self-esteem are often indirect. The general theme of this work is that specific self-beliefs can have more or less impact depending on how they are organized in relation to other self-knowledge (Showers & Zeigler-Hill, 2003). In other words, structural features of the self may serve as important moderators of the impact of self-knowledge on self-esteem. These structural features include self-schemas, category structures (including self-complexity, differential importance, and compartmentalization), and features of self-definition (including self-concept clarity and contingencies of self-worth).

In contrast to abstract discussions of self from philosophical and psychodynamic perspectives, the cognitive perspective provided a concrete model for the empirical study of self. Early cognitive models suggested essentially a one-to-one correspondence between the content of self-beliefs and self-esteem (cf. Rosenberg, 1965). In this view, the more positive one's beliefs about the self, the higher one's self-esteem; conversely, people with low self-esteem should have a greater proportion of negative self-beliefs. In other words, the links between self-esteem and self-knowledge were direct. However, ideas about self-structure were lurking even though they were not the focus of early cognitive research. For example, Combs and Snygg (1959) diagrammed the self as a series of concentric circles corresponding to the perceived centrality of a set of self-beliefs. This structural feature suggests that a belief is processed differently depending on its centrality, with more central beliefs having greater impact on overall thoughts and feelings about the self. Today, we also know that central self-beliefs are less vulnerable to external influences such as transient mood (Sedikides, 1995).

Not surprisingly, even William James (1890/1963) ventured into the structural realm and articulated some possible pathways that might link self-knowledge and self-esteem. First, he introduced the notion of multiple selves ["...a man has as many social selves as there are individuals who recognize him and carry an image of him in their mind" (p. 294)], thereby laying the ground work for the view that self-knowledge may be tied to specific contexts. Hence, context could potentially moderate the impact of a given self-belief on self-esteem. Modern cognitive perspectives on the self take the notion of multiple selves as a basic assumption (Banaji & Prentice, 1994; Cantor, Markus, Niedenthal, & Nurius, 1986; Markus & Wurf, 1987), for instance describing the current self as a transaction of person, situation, and audience (Schlenker & Weigold, 1989).

James (1890/1963) also linked self-knowledge to self-esteem by an indirect pathway when he defined self-esteem as the ratio of one's beliefs to one's pretensions. In other words, the impact of self-beliefs is moderated by one's standards or expectations. Today, self-discrepancy theory elaborates on the motivational and emotional consequences of perceiving a gap between the current actual self and one's expectations for what one ideally would or should be (Higgins, Bond, Klein, & Strauman, 1986).

ACCESSIBILITY AS A MODERATOR OF SELF-KNOWLEDGE

As interest in a cognitive perspective on the self moved from the more traditional focus on stable cognitive beliefs to a focus on dynamic cognitive processes, the accessibility of specific self-beliefs was viewed as an index of underlying structure (Markus, 1977; Segal, 1988). Studies of self-schemata demonstrated the preferential accessibility of attributes that an individual identified as extreme and important. For example, depressed persons may be characterized by negative self-schemas, and demonstrate this by responding *ME* more quickly to the negative attributes that describe them than do nondepressed persons (e.g., Bargh & Tota, 1988). Thus, negative self-beliefs are not only more prevalent in depressed than nondepressed persons, they are more accessible. More generally, however, response latency techniques allow self-researchers to distinguish self-beliefs that are merely available from those that are both available and highly accessible. Accessibility then is a factor that should moderate the impact of a valenced item of self-knowledge on self-esteem. The self-schema research made it clear that self-knowledge could be available without being accessible (e.g., those negative words to which nondepressed persons said *ME*). However, the literature did not go so far as to identify meaningful subgroups of individuals who benefited from this moderating effect (e.g., who had high availability, but low accessibility of negative beliefs).

CATEGORY STRUCTURE AS A MODERATOR OF SELF-KNOWLEDGE

Theoretically speaking, the underlying structure of the self-concept can be modeled as an associative or even a connectionist network (Bower, 1981; Smith, Coats, & Walling, 1999). However, most empirical studies focus only on category structures assessed at a basic level (cf. Rosch, 1978). In this view, self-knowledge is organized into a set of self-aspect categories. The categories allow individuals to manage the enormous repertoire of self-beliefs from which they draw in constructing responses to specific contexts. One basic individual difference is the sheer number of self-categories ("differentiation") and the content of the dimensions along which they are formed (e.g., me as a professor; me in a bad mood). This differentiation of the self-concept into distinct categories of self-knowledge, typically corresponding to multiple selves, is a fundamental structural feature that potentially mitigates the impact of specific items of self-knowledge on overall thoughts and feelings about the self.

In any given situation, only the most relevant categories of self-knowledge are activated to form the working self-concept (Markus & Wurf, 1987). Social psychologists have identified several features of self-structure that may affect the activation of specific categories of self-knowledge in specific contexts and, hence, their impact on self-esteem. These structural features include self-complexity, differential importance, compartmentalization, self-discrepancies, and possible selves.

Self-Complexity

Individuals with high self-complexity (Linville, 1985, 1987) have many distinct self-aspect categories. That is, they have many multiple selves with non-overlapping attributes. According to Linville's model, high self-complexity can moderate the impact of positive and negative self-beliefs on the self-concept, because a given belief that appears in only one of many multiple selves should affect only a small proportion of the total self-concept. In contrast, individuals with low self-complexity should show affective extremity because the activation of a single positive or negative attribute or self-category will implicate a much greater proportion of the total self. For individuals with low self-complexity, the path from self-knowledge to self-esteem is much more direct than it is for more complex individuals.

Differential Importance

When multiple domains or aspects of the self are differentiated with respect to importance (Pelham & Swann, 1989), the impact of self-knowledge on self-esteem may vary. Positive or negative beliefs about the self in an unimportant domain may have little impact on self-esteem, whereas valenced beliefs in important domains will prevail. Of course, even in the latter case, alternative strategies may be used to protect, maintain, or enhance self-esteem despite important negative beliefs (Tesser, 2000). Nonetheless, adjusting the perceived importance of domains in which one has strong positive or negative experiences may be a very useful coping strategy that mitigates the impact of valenced self-knowledge on self-esteem.

Compartmentalization and Integration

Compartmentalization and integration (Showers, 2002) should also have moderating effects on the links between valenced self-knowledge and self-esteem. In compartmentalized self-structures, positive and negative self-beliefs are segregated into distinct self-aspect categories (e.g., me as a creative scholar; me during final exams). In contrast, the self-aspect categories of integrative self-structures contain a mixture of positive and negative beliefs (e.g., me as a student: hardworking, disorganized, intelligent, anxious). Compartmentalized structures may accommodate many negative self-beliefs with little impact on self-esteem if the categories that contain those beliefs are perceived to be of low importance. That is, when positive compartments are most important, compartmentalized individuals should have very high self-esteem. In general, individuals with integrative self-structures should have moderate self-esteem. Compartmentalized individuals with important negative categories should have very low self-esteem, whereas integrative individuals will be able to ameliorate important negative characteristics by linking them to more positive attributes. Thus, the impact of valenced self-knowledge on self-esteem is altered by links to other positive and negative self-beliefs in compartmentalized or integrative structures.

Over the long term, compartmentalized and integrative structures may alter the links between self-knowledge and self-esteem in other ways. For example, successful compartmentalization may ultimately lead to the exclusion from self of compartmentalized attributes as their self-aspect categories become less and less important. In this way, compartmentalization may contribute to self-change. Some findings suggest that the effort involved in successful integration may be difficult to maintain over time, and that integration is best used as a temporary strategy to handle salient negative attributes (Showers & Kling, 1996; Showers & Zeigler-Hill, 2004). Finally, because integration keeps both positive and negative self-beliefs in mind, it may be a relatively realistic representation of self, with specific advantages for adjustment (e.g., resilience), even though self-esteem may be moderate (Showers, Limke, & Zeigler-Hill, 2004).

Self-Discrepancies and Possible Selves

The feature of self-structure highlighted by self-discrepancy theory is the gap between one's perceived actual attributes and those that one ideally should or would possess (Higgins, 1987). Thus, the impact of any specific self-belief on self-esteem depends on whether that attribute (or its opposite) is a part of the self that one should or ideally would be. Thus, the ought self and the ideal self are the standards that determine the impact of current self-beliefs. Interestingly, possible selves which similarly represent selves that one might become in the future, are thought to provide motivation, i.e., goals that one strives for or to avoid (Cross & Markus, 1991). Thus, a positive possible self (e.g., successful doctor) may mitigate the impact of current negative self-knowledge (e.g., overworked student).

SELF-DEFINITION AS A MODERATOR OF SELF-KNOWLEDGE

Self-concept clarity refers to the confidence with which an individual can endorse self-attributes (Baumgardner, 1990; Campbell, Trapnell, Heine, Katz, Lavallee, & Lehman, 1996). This definitional property of one's self-attributes may also moderate the association between specific attributes and self-esteem. High self-clarity is correlated with both high self-esteem and stability of self-esteem (Kernis, Paradise, Whitaker, Wheatman, & Goldman, 2000). Individuals with high self-clarity may make decisions with confidence because they can easily match themselves to situations that fit them well (Setterlund & Niedenthal, 1993). This ability to choose environments and tasks for which they are well-suited may be both self-enhancing and stabilizing. In contrast, individuals with lower self-concept clarity tend to have lower self-esteem. Although self-clarity should be adaptive for those with predominantly positive self-concepts, it remains unclear whether certainty about the self-concept would be beneficial for individuals with negative self-concepts. For these individuals, uncertainty about their negative attributes could potentially minimize the impact of these negative self-beliefs and may allow for an increased possibility of self-change in comparison to very certain negative self-beliefs. The possible long-term benefits of low self-concept clarity for individuals with negative self-beliefs have yet to be fully explored.

DIRECTIONS OF CAUSALITY

Although a traditional cognitive view would imply that items of self-knowledge are the building blocks of self-esteem, it is possible that this process is bi-directional or even reversed. For example, if self-esteem is acquired as a global entity (e.g., from interactions with approving or securely attached others that communicate an overall sense of self-worth), specific positive self-beliefs may derive from this global positive self-view that guides the encoding of experience. Global self-esteem may drive the development of structural features that facilitate processes associated with that level of self-esteem. So, for example, low self-esteem may create low self-complexity or low self-concept clarity. It is hard to imagine a truly direct path from self-esteem to self-knowledge, because self-esteem would serve as a guide for the process of interpreting and encoding experience. At the very least, experience would serve as an important moderator of these processes.

INDIRECT PATHWAYS AFFORD FLEXIBILITY

In virtually all of the literature on features of self-structure, it appears that direct paths from self-knowledge to self-esteem remain. In analyses of self-esteem, the sheer positivity or negativity of a person's self-beliefs predicts the lion's share of the variance, whereas structural features tend to explain the noise in the data (e.g., Marsh, 1986). As more reliable and diagnostic measures of self-structure are developed it may be possible to account for more variance. Of course, when the self-concept is basically positive, a direct path from self-knowledge to self-esteem should be advantageous. The power of the structural features typically lies in their ability to cushion the impact of negative self-beliefs. Nonetheless, several theories suggest that the flexibility afforded by these structural mechanisms will ultimately serve an important function for most individuals, because most people acknowledge at least some important negative self-attributes or confront significant negative experiences at various times in their lives. For example, when the links between self-knowledge and self-esteem are direct and immediate, self-esteem may tend to be unstable, as the individual reacts strongly to the short-term activation of specific positive or negative attributes (cf. Kernis & Goldman, 2003). The existence of direct pathways also suggests that self-esteem may be constructed in a contingent fashion, i.e., that an individual feels that possession of certain self-attributes—e.g., attractive, loved by family, respected by others, moral/ethical—determines overall self-worth (cf. Crocker & Park, 2003). Finally, direct pathways between self-knowledge and self-esteem would seem to preclude many kinds of discrepancies between implicit and explicit self-esteem, some of which may be important for effective functioning (cf. Devos & Banaji, 2003). Thus, even though the direct pathways between self-knowledge and self-esteem often appear quite strong, indirect paths are especially interesting because of their critical role in psychological functioning when they do come into play.

REFERENCES

Banaji, M. R., & Prentice, D. A. (1994). The self in social contexts. *Annual Review of Psychology, 45*, 297–332.

Bargh, J. A., & Tota, M. E. (1988). Context-dependent automatic processing in depression: Accessibility of negative constructs with regard to self but not others. *Journal of Personality and Social Psychology, 54*, 925–939.

Baumgardner, A. H. (1990). To know oneself is to like oneself: Self-certainty and self-affect. *Journal of Personality and Social Psychology, 58*, 1062–1072.

Bower, G. H. (1981). Mood and memory. *American Psychologist, 36*, 129–148.

Campbell, J. D., Trapnell, P. D., Heine, S. J., Katz, I. M., Lavallee, L. F., & Lehman, D. R. (1996). Self-concept clarity: Measurement, personality correlates, and cultural boundaries. *Journal of Personality and Social Psychology, 70*, 141–156.

Cantor, N., Markus, H., Niedenthal, P., & Nurius, P. (1986). On motivation and the self-concept. In R. M. Sorrentino & E. T. Higgins (Eds.), *Handbook of motivation and cognition: Foundations of social behavior* (pp. 96–121). New York: Guilford Press.

Combs, A. W., & Snygg, D. (1959). *Individual behavior: A perceptual approach to behavior* (Rev. ed.). Oxford, England: Harpers.

Crocker, J., & Park, L. E. (2003). Seeking self-esteem: Construction, maintenance, and protection of self-worth. In M. R. Leary & J. P. Tangney (Eds.), *Handbook of self and identity* (pp. 291–313). New York: Guilford Press.

Cross, S., & Markus, H. (1991). Possible selves across the life span. *Human Development, 34*, 230–255.

Devos, T., & Banaji, M. R. (2003). Implicit self and identity. In M. R. Leary & J. P. Tangney (Eds.), *Handbook of self and identity* (pp. 153–175). New York: Guilford Press.

Higgins, E. T. (1987). Self-discrepancy: A theory relating self and affect. *Psychological Review, 94*, 319–340.

Higgins, E. T., Bond, R. N., Klein, R., & Strauman, T. (1986). Self-discrepancies and emotional vulnerability: How magnitude, accessibility, and type of discrepancy influence affect. *Journal of Personality and Social Psychology, 51*, 5–15.

James, W. (1963). *The principles of psychology*. New York: Holt. (Original work published 1890)

Kernis, M. H., & Goldman, B. M. (2003). Stability and variability in self-concept and self-esteem. In M. R. Leary & J. P. Tangney (Eds.), *Handbook of self and identity* (pp. 106–127). New York: Guilford Press.

Kernis, M. H., Paradise, A. W., Whitaker, D. J., Wheatman, S. R., & Goldman, B. N. (2000). Master of one's psychological domain? Not likely if one's self-esteem is unstable. *Personality and Social Psychology Bulletin, 26*, 1297–1305.

Linville, P. W. (1985). Self-complexity and affective extremity: Don't put all of your eggs in one cognitive basket. *Social Cognition, 3*, 94–120.

Linville, P. W. (1987). Self-complexity as a cognitive buffer against stress-related illness and depression. *Journal of Personality and Social Psychology, 52*, 663–676.

Markus, H. (1977). Self-schemata and processing information about the self. *Journal of Personality and Social Psychology, 35*, 63–78.

Markus, H., & Wurf, E. (1987). The dynamic self-concept: A social psychological perspective. *Annual Review of Psychology, 38*, 299–337.

Marsh, H. W. (1986). Global self-esteem: Its relation to specific facets of self-concept and their importance. *Journal of Personality and Social Psychology, 51*, 1224–1236.

Pelham, B. W., & Swann, W. B. (1989). From self-conceptions to self-worth: On the sources and structure of global self-esteem. *Journal of Personality and Social Psychology, 57*, 672–680.

Rosch, E. (1978). Principles of categorization. In E. Rosch & B. B. Loyd (Eds.), *Cognition and categorization* (pp. 27–48). Hillsdale, NJ: Lawrence Erlbaum Associates, Inc.

Rosenberg, M. (1965). *Society and the adolescent self-image*. Princeton, NJ: Princeton University Press.

Schlenker, B. R., & Weigold, M. F. (1989). Goals and the self-identification process: Constructing desired identities. In L. Pervin (Ed.), *Goal concepts in personality and social psychology* (pp. 243–290). Hillsdale, NJ: Lawrence Erlbaum Associates Inc.

Sedikides, C. (1995). Central and peripheral self-conceptions are differentially influenced by mood: Tests of the differential sensitivity hypothesis. *Journal of Personality and Social Psychology, 69*, 759–777.

Segal, Z. V. (1988). Appraisal of the self-schema construct in cognitive models of depression. *Psychological Bulletin, 103*, 147–162.

Setterlund, M. B., & Niedenthal, P. M. (1993). "Who am I? Why am I here?": Self-esteem, self-clarity, and prototype matching. *Journal of Personality and Social Psychology, 65*, 769–780.

Showers, C. J. (2002). Integration and compartmentalization: A model of self-structure and self-change. In D. Cervone & W. Mischel (Eds.), *Advances in personality science* (pp. 271–291). New York: Guilford Press.

Showers, C. J., & Kling, K. C. (1996). Organization of self-knowledge: Implications for recovery from sad mood. *Journal of Personality and Social Psychology, 70,* 578–590.

Showers, C. J., Limke, A., & Zeigler-Hill, V. (2004). Self-structure and self-change: Applications to psychological treatment. *Behavior Therapy, 35,* 167–184.

Showers, C. J., & Zeigler-Hill, V. (2003). Organization of self-knowledge: Features, functions, and flexibility. In M. R. Leary & J. P. Tangney (Eds.), *Handbook of self and identity* (pp. 47–67). New York: Guilford Press.

Showers, C. J., & Zeigler-Hill, V. (2004). Organization of partner knowledge: Relationship outcomes and longitudinal change. *Personality and Social Psychology Bulletin, 30,* 1198–1210.

Smith, E. R., Coats, S., & Walling, D. (1999). Overlapping mental representations of self, in-group, and partner: Further response time evidence and a connectionist model. *Personality and Social Psychology Bulletin, 25,* 873–882.

Tesser, A. (2000). On the confluence of self-esteem maintenance mechanisms. *Personality and Social Psychology Review, 4,* 290–299.

29

Who Do You Think You Are? On the Link Between Self-Knowledge and Self-Esteem

AAFJE C. BRANDT and ROOS VONK

W ho am I? Being able to answer this question is widely assumed to be essential for healthy psychological functioning. A well-defined self-concept facilitates the processing of self-relevant information (Bargh, 1982), predicts life satisfaction (Jones, 2001) and psychological adjustment (Bigler, Neimeyer, & Brown, 2001; Campbell, Assenand, & Di Paula, 2003), leads to a sense of self-continuity (Gergen & Gergen, 1988), and is related to stability in evaluations of the self (Kernis & Waschull, 1995) and to high levels of self-esteem (e.g., Baumgardner, 1990; Campbell, 1990; Campbell, Trapnell, Heine, Katz, Lavallee, & Lehman, 1996).

The degree to which the self-concept is stable, consistent, clear, and confidently defined is referred to as self-concept clarity (Campbell, 1990; Campbell et al., 1996). It pertains to the knowledge components of the self: What traits do I possess? What are my physical characteristics? What are my roles and goals in life? The construct makes no assertion about the valence of the characteristics; the typical measure of self-concept clarity merely asks people about the extent to which self-conceptions are clear and confident.

Considerable amounts of research have particularly contributed to the notion that a clear self-concept is strongly related to positive evaluations of the self (e.g., Baumgardner, 1990; Campbell, 1990; Campbell et al., 1996). People who are high in self-esteem tend to describe themselves in a confident and well-articulated manner that is stable over time, whereas people with more negative self-evaluations typically use more uncertain self-descriptions that have a tendency to fluctuate (Campbell, 1990). Also, when their self-evaluations are stable over time, people generally show high levels of self-concept clarity (Kernis & Waschull, 1995).

Apparently, there is a strong connection between having a clear sense of who you are and liking yourself. This is not a new idea: For long the belief predominated that the mentally healthy person has a clear view on reality (for a review, see Jourard & Landsman, 1980). However, during the past two decades more and more evidence has come to light that well-adjusted and happy people do not have clear views on themselves at all (Taylor and Brown, 1988). On the contrary, those with normal, functional levels of self-regard typically engage in a wide range of behaviors that distort the processing of self-relevant information. For example, people judge positive traits to be far more characteristic of themselves than negative traits (Brown, 1986), overestimate the control they have over chance-determined events (see Crocker, 1982, for a review), more easily forget information related to their failures than their successes (Silverman, 1964), and see abilities that they are not good at as common, but abilities that they master as rare and distinctive (Marks, 1984). Most of these and other distortions do not seem to occur in the way moderately depressed or people low in self-esteem view themselves (e.g., Brown, 1986; Kuiper & MacDonald, 1982).

These findings suggest that distorted rather than clear self-perceptions are related to having positive feelings toward the self. This is a remarkable diagnosis considering that positive self-regard is also strongly correlated with self-concept clarity (e.g., Baumgardner, 1990; Campbell, 1990; Campbell et al., 1996). So on the one hand, research suggests that knowing who you are contributes to self-esteem, but on the other hand it seems that self-esteem is promoted by illusions about the self, i.e., by not knowing who you are. How can these two findings be reconciled?

To understand this, we must take a closer look at the construct of self-concept clarity. The building stones of self-concept clarity are the beliefs people have about themselves, about their traits, their appearances, their virtues and their flaws. The more confident, stable, and consistent these beliefs are, the clearer the self-concept is. Clarity of the self-concept, however, does not in any way imply *accuracy* of the self-concept (Campbell et al., 1996). A self-concept is clear to the extent that people have a clear idea of who they *think* they are. Theoretically, people who have a very confident and well-articulated theory about who they are and what defines them, could be totally inaccurate on the basis of other criteria, such as their behaviors or observations by others.

The notion that having a clear self-concept does not mean that one is aware of one's actual assets and characteristics, suggests that a clear sense of self can be obtained without having to seek accurate self-knowledge. We can erroneously think we are unique in our qualities, focus on our successes, forget about our mistakes and still have a sound feeling that we know who we are. What is important is that we *believe* that we know who we are.

Knowing that self-concept clarity does not reflect accuracy of self-knowledge but, rather, a set of subjective self-beliefs, the paradox of self-esteem being linked to both distorted self-views and a clear self-concept becomes less paradoxical. Since truthfulness is not a necessity for a clear self-concept, the belief that we know who we are can develop through routes that are to some extent biased and self-serving. As noted above, people often process self-relevant information in an overly favorable way (e.g., Brown, 1986; Marks, 1984; Silverman, 1964), but even when this leads to self-knowledge and self-beliefs that are not in agreement with reality, this is not necessarily a threat to the clarity of the self-concept. As long as these biases foster beliefs about the self, they promote self-concept clarity, independent of their accuracy. Support for this notion lies in the finding that self-concept clarity is moderately correlated to self-deception: The higher people are in self-concept clarity, the more likely they are to engage in self-deceptive behaviors in general (Brandt & Vonk, 2004). So, ironically, those who are inclined to be somewhat dishonest toward themselves, tend to have clearer self-concepts.

This suggests that *believing* that we know ourselves might in some respects be similar to positive illusions such as believing that we have control over chance-determined situations and viewing positive traits as more characteristic of our personalities than negative ones. One thing that positive illusions and thinking that we know who we are have in common is that their relationship with reality is disputable. Another resemblance is that, despite that, all of these beliefs are also positively correlated with self-esteem, suggesting that they might be advantageous for mental health.

In trying to understand the relationship between having a clear sense of self and high self-esteem, various explanations have been offered. For example, Campbell (1990) suggests that individuals who have uncertain self-concepts are more dependent on self-relevant information and are more susceptible to and influenced by this information than are people with more articulated self-views. Baumgardner (1990) proposes that knowing who we are gives us the opportunity to take control over future outcomes because it enables us to seek circumstances that allow us to maximize our successes and minimize our failures. If either of these explanations would be fully true, there should not only be a relation between self-concept clarity and explicit self-esteem, but also between self-concept clarity and *implicit* self-esteem. Yet, when correlating self-concept clarity to implicit feelings of self-worth measured by name-letter preference (see Kitayama & Karasawa, 1997; Koole & Pelham, 2003; Nuttin, 1985) while controlling for explicit self-esteem, Brandt and Vonk (2004) found no relation between the two, whereas they did find a substantial correlation between self-concept clarity and explicit self-esteem. So having a clear sense of self is related to self-reported levels of self-esteem, suggesting that believing that we know who we are, is connected to believing that we like ourselves. But apparently, this belief does not predict to what extent we like ourselves on a more unaware, intuitive level, which unsettles existing explanations about the relation between self-esteem and having a clear sense of self.

If being confident about who you are is not connected to more automatic and consciously unaccessible feelings of self-worth, what accounts for the relation between knowing who you are and positive explicit levels of self-esteem? We suggest that both confidence about who you are and explicit self-esteem originate from the same underlying self-theory, which is: "I'm doing fine". This basic theory produces several beliefs, including "I know who I am" and "I like myself".[1] Believing that we are doing well leads us to state that we feel worthy, and convinces us that we have clear views on ourselves. It also leads to biases in the processing of self-relevant information, reflected in positive illusions about the self. This in turn might result in distorted self-views such as unrealistic optimism and self-deception. In support of this notion, Brandt and Vonk (2004) found a modest but significant correlation between explicit self-esteem and self-deception, but no relation between implicit feelings of self-worth and self-deception.

In sum, substantial amounts of research have shown that having a well-defined and confident idea of who you are is related to healthy, positive feelings of self-worth. Paradoxically, having illusions about ourselves is also connected to high self-esteem. This paradox can be understood once we realize that having a clear sense of self does not mean that our self-knowledge is accurate, and that this relationship mainly exists on an explicit level of self-esteem. We therefore argue that positive illusions, as well as explicit self-esteem, and self-concept clarity, stem from the same basic self-theory, "I'm doing fine".

NOTES

1. The belief "I know who I am" is in our view most strongly reflected in the Self-Concept Clarity Scale (Campbell et al., 1996), which is a self-report scale that asks people directly to what extent they feel their self-concept is clear and stable. However, several other measures are used to tap self-concept clarity, such as extremity, reaction times, and confidence intervals related to self-descriptions (e.g., Baumgardner, 1990; Campbell, 1990). We argue that these measures also reflect the belief "I know who I am", since people who think they know themselves, actually have well-defined ideas about where they stand at a multitude of personality characteristics. This conviction can result in extreme, fast, and confident self-descriptions, reflecting a clear, yet not necessarily accurate, self-concept.

REFERENCES

Bargh, J. A. (1982). Attention and automaticity in the processing of self-relevant information. *Journal of Personality and Social Psychology, 43,* 425–436.

Baumgardner, A. H. (1990). To know oneself is to like oneself: Self-certainty and self-affect. *Journal of Personality and Social Psychology, 58,* 1062–1072.

Bigler, M., Neimeyer, G. J., & Brown, E. (2001). The divided self revisited: Effects of self-concept clarity and self-concept differentiation on psychological adjustment. *Journal of Social and Clinical Psychology, 20,* 396–415.

Brandt, A. C., & Vonk, R. (2004). *Self-esteem, self-deception, and perceptions of self-knowledge.* Unpublished data.

Brown, J. D. (1986). Evaluations of self and others: Self-enhancement biases in social judgments. *Social Cognition, 4,* 353–376.

Campbell, J. D. (1990). Self-esteem and clarity of the self-concept. *Journal of Personality and Social Psychology, 59,* 538–549.

Campbell, J. D., Assenand, S., & Di Paula, A. (2003). The structure of the self-concept and its relation to psychological adjustment. *Journal of Personality, 71,* 115–140.

Campbell, J. D., Trapnell, P. D., Heine, S. J., Katz, I. M., Lavallee, L. F., & Lehman, D. R. (1996). Self-concept clarity: Measurement, personality correlates, and cultural boundaries. *Journal of Personality and Social Psychology, 70,* 141–156.

Crocker, J. (1982). Biased questions in judgment of covariations studies. *Personality and Social Psychology Bulletin, 8,* 214–220.

Gergen, K. J., & Gergen, M. M. (1988). Narrative and the self as relationship. In L. Berkowitz (ed.), *Advances in experimental social psychology* (Vol. 21, pp. 17–56). San Diego, CA: Academic Press.

Jones, R. S. (2001). *A correlational examination of the effects of personality, self-concept, and social role salience on the life satisfaction of adult women students.* Dissertation. The George Washington University, Washington, DC.

Jourard, S. M., & Landsman, T. (1980). *Healthy psychology: An approach from the viewpoint of humanistic psychology* (4th ed.). New York: Macmillan.

Kernis, M. H., & Waschull, S. B. (1995). The interactive roles of stability and level of self-esteem: Research and theory. In M. P. Zanna (Ed.), *Advances in experimental social psychology* (Vol. 27, pp. 93–141). San Diego, CA: Academic Press.

Kitayama, S., & Karasawa, M. (1997). Implicit self-esteem in Japan: Name letters and birthday numbers. *Personality and Social Psychology Bulletin, 23*, 736–742.

Koole, S. L., & Pelham, B. W. (2003). On the nature of implicit self-esteem: The case of the name letter effect. In S. Spencer, S. Fein, & M. P. Zanna (Eds.), *Motivated social perception: The Ontario Symposium* (pp. 93–116). Hillsdale, NJ: Lawrence Erlbaum Associates.

Kuiper, N. A., & MacDonald, M. R. (1982). Self and other perception in mild depressives. *Social Cognition, 1*, 233–239.

Marks, G. (1984). Thinking one's abilities are unique and one's opinions are common. *Personality and Social Psychology Bulletin, 10*, 203–208.

Nuttin, J. M. (1985). Narcissism beyond gestalt and awareness: The name letter effect. *European Journal of Social Psychology, 15*, 353–361.

Silverman, I. (1964). Self-esteem and differential responsiveness to success and failure. *Journal of Abnormal and Social Psychology, 69*, 115–119.

Taylor, S. E., & Brown, J. D. (1988). Illusion and well-being: A social psychological perspective on mental health. *Psychological Bulletin, 103*, 193–210.

Question 10

How can parents and teachers facilitate optimal self-esteem in children and adolescents?

*T*he essays in this section focus on what parents and teachers can do to facilitate optimal self-esteem in children and adolescents.

Grolnick and Beiswenger review the literature on parent and teacher influences on children's self-esteem, as viewed through the lens of self-determination theory. From this perspective, "...caretaker qualities of involvement, autonomy support and structure, aspects of the environment that facilitate the fulfillment of psychological needs, are associated with self-esteem." As the authors describe, the literature amply supports the contention "...that when these needs are fulfilled, children construct a healthy sense of self that allows them to approach the world with confidence."

Branden presents his "six pillars of self-esteem": living consciously, self-acceptance, self-responsibility, self-assertiveness, living purposefully, and self-integrity. He then points out the numerous ways that parents and teachers can facilitate these pillars. In Branden's view, the roots of self-esteem lie not in our accomplishments per se, "...but in those internally generated practices that, among other things, make it possible for us to achieve—all the self-virtues listed above."

Covington argues "...that most issues regarding self-esteem and its promotion as they regard parents and teachers revolve around matters of achievement and "well-doing," and around the child's self-perceived sense of ability. After reviewing the controversy surrounding the "self-esteem movement," Covington offers five recommendations for caretakers that include fostering learning for learning's sake, minimizing academic competition with others, and focusing on improvement in the face of failure.

30

Facilitating Children's Self-Esteem: The Role of Parents and Teachers

WENDY S. GROLNICK and KRISTA L. BEISWENGER

S elf-esteem, the evaluative aspect of the self-concept, has been linked to important outcomes in children, such as enhanced well-being (Rosenberg, 1965; Wilson, 1991), lower symptomatology (i.e., depression and anxiety; Harter, 1999), and more positive peer relations (Coopersmith, 1967). Thus, it is not surprising that a great deal of research has focused on the socialization of children's self-esteem. In this paper, we focus on the contributions of parents and teachers to children's self-esteem.

Before delving into parental and teacher factors that may facilitate self-esteem in children, it is important to address what self-esteem means in children. According to Harter (1985), very young (preschool) children make global judgments about their competence in an all-or-none fashion (i.e., *I am either all good or all bad*). Most children of this age judge themselves as all good. As children move into middle childhood, they begin to differentiate their competence in different areas. For example, they may see themselves as good in school but not strong in athletics. At the same time, they develop a general sense of their worthiness as a person, which may be only partly related to their domain-specific evaluations. It is this overall sense of self or self-worth that we address in this paper.

Coopersmith (1967, p. 4) states, "By self-esteem we refer to the evaluation which the individual makes and customarily maintains with regard to himself; it expresses an attitude of approval or disapproval, and indicates the extent to which the individual believes himself to be capable, successful, significant and worthy." Similarly, Rosenberg (1965, p. 31) suggests, "When we speak of high self-esteem we shall simply mean that the individual considers himself worthy... Low self-esteem, on the other hand, implies self-rejection, self-dissatisfaction, and self-contempt." We use these definitions as a starting point for our discussion of socialization of self-esteem.

In order to address the factors that facilitate self-esteem, one needs a theoretical framework. Most previous research on the role parents and teachers play in children's self-esteem adopts a symbolic interactionist perspective. This theory expands upon Cooley's (1902) notion of the "looking-glass self" and William James' (1890) conception of the social self. According to this perspective, one constructs a self-view through significant others' appraisals of the self. These "reflected appraisals" become the basis for self-esteem. Thus, from this viewpoint, children's self-esteem is enhanced when others view the child positively. Many studies support this notion by showing that children who perceive positive relations with significant others tend to show high self-esteem (Barber, Chadwick, & Oerter, 1992; Demo, Small, & Savin-Williams, 1987; Felson & Zielinski, 1989; Gecas & Schwalbe, 1986; Hoelter & Harper, 1987; Mead, 1934).

Although we do not doubt that children pick up on others' appraisals of them, this theory represents a passive notion of how children construct an experience of self. Consistent with recent concepts of socialization (Grolnick, Ryan, & Deci, 1997; Kuczynski, Harach, & Bernardini, 1999), children play an active role in their development. Development is an active process in which children differentiate and integrate aspects of their internal and external environments (Deci & Ryan, 1985). This process occurs through an interplay between the needs that children bring and the environments they encounter.

Self-determination theorists propose that a healthy sense of self involves fulfilling three psychological needs (Deci & Ryan, 1985, 1987). These needs include: (1) the need for competence, or the feeling that one is capable and effective in one's environment (White, 1959); (2) the need for autonomy, or the sense that one is the owner of his/her actions and has a sense of choice (deCharms, 1968; Heider, 1958); and (3) the need for relatedness, or the feeling that one is connected to and supported by significant others (Ainsworth, Blehar, Waters, & Wall, 1978; Bowlby, 1969; Harlow, 1958). Fulfillment of these needs facilitates the growth process, and an integrated sense of self develops. Research indicates that feelings of autonomy, competence, and relatedness are associated with psychological well-being (Reis, Sheldon, Gable, Roscoe, & Ryan, 2000) and feelings of vitality (Ryan & Frederick, 1997).

From a self-determination perspective, parents and teachers can facilitate children's self-esteem by providing environments that foster feelings of autonomy, competence, and relatedness. We argue that contexts characterized by involvement, autonomy support, and structure are particularly important for helping children fulfill these psychological needs.

First, children's self-esteem can be facilitated by an environment characterized by positive *involvement*. Involved caretakers provide resources (e.g., time, support, availability) that help children experience success and feel competent in their environments (Grolnick & Slowiaczek, 1994). Involvement not only fosters children's feelings of competence but also builds a sense of relatedness to these caretakers.

A second aspect of interpersonal environments conducive to self-esteem is *autonomy support* (Deci & Ryan, 1985). Caretaker autonomy support involves providing children with a sense of choice about their actions and supporting their intentions by encouraging children to initiate action and solve problems on their own (Grolnick & Ryan, 1989). When children experience autonomy support, they feel that their actions emanate from within and are not pressured or controlled by others. It is only when one feels ownership of one's actions that successes build a healthy sense of competence.

Third, parents and teachers can help children fulfill these three needs by providing *structure*. Structure involves providing information and establishing helpful guidelines that communicate reasonable expectations (Grolnick & Ryan, 1989). When children are provided with clear, consistent guidelines at home, they tend to feel more in control of their successes in school (Grolnick & Ryan, 1989). Knowing what adults expect of them helps children develop more realistic goals that they can achieve within the boundaries established, thus enhancing the feeling that they can master their world (i.e., a sense of competence). Together, involvement, autonomy support, and structure are vehicles through which parents and teachers can facilitate feelings of autonomy, competence, and relatedness, thereby fostering children's self-esteem.

Based on self-determination theory, we organize our review of research on parental facilitators of self-esteem into three areas—involvement, autonomy support, and structure. Although many studies use different terms to describe these relevant dimensions, the constructs discussed within each section share basic similarities.

INVOLVEMENT

Under the construct of involvement we include studies that assess factors such as parent support, participation, and communication with children and adolescents. Most studies on the socialization of self-esteem have focused on the effects of "family support." Thomas, Gecas, Weigert, and Rooney (1974, p. 11) describe two important components of support: (1) "communicating to the child something of his inherent worth," and (2) "approving of the child's efforts to have an effect on the environment and simultaneously letting the child know that they are there if he or she needs them." Thus, support is a general rubric for a variety of positive, accepting, and involved behaviors. Hoelter and Harper (1987), using adolescents' perceptions of their families as supportive (e.g., *My family listens to me*; *My family supports the things I do*), and Barber et al. (1992), using adolescents' retrospective reports of their mothers' and fathers' supportive behavior (e.g., *She/he made me feel she/he was there if I needed him/her*), each found that supportive behavior was associated with adolescent self-worth, as assessed by the Rosenberg (1965) scale.

Involved behavior, defined as time spent together, participation in activities, and interest in the child, has also been linked to self-esteem. Adolescents who report that their parents participate in educational and recreational activities with them report higher self-esteem (Demo et al., 1987). Coopersmith (1967) showed that children with high self-esteem rated their mothers as more likely to know their friends and be concerned and interested in them than children with low self-esteem. Rosenberg (1979) also found that parents of children with high self-esteem were more interested in their child and his/her activities.

Affection has also been a target of several studies. Children of mothers who were rated by interviewers as more affectionate with their children were higher in self-esteem, whereas mothers of children with lower self-esteem were perceived as having more distant relationships with their children (Bachman, 1970; Coopersmith, 1967).

Links between parent support and self-esteem may be bi-directional (Felson & Zielinski, 1989), i.e., there may be child-to-parent as well as parent-to-child effects. With regard to child-to-parent effects, children with higher self-esteem, for example, may *evoke* more support from their parents. Further, children's self-esteem may color their perceptions of their parents, as children with higher self-esteem may screen negative events and perceptions while those with low self-esteem may screen out the positive.

In order to address the direction-of-effects, several studies have utilized longitudinal designs. For example, Felson and Zielinski (1989) used a cross-lagged design and assessed children's perceptions of parental support and self-esteem over a 1-year period. These authors provided support for both directions of effect; controlling for earlier self-esteem, girls who perceived greater communication, affection, and praise from their parents were higher in self-esteem 1 year later than those perceiving less support. Only parental praise predicted self-esteem for boys. In addition, controlling for earlier parental support, self-esteem predicted the amount of praise children reported, supporting a child-to-parent effect. A longitudinal study by Roberts and Bengtson (1996) investigating only parent-to-child effects, showed that children who reported experiencing more affectual closeness with their parents were higher in self-esteem at baseline and 20 years later (controlling for earlier self-esteem) than those with low self-esteem. These findings suggest that parental affection may facilitate children's self-esteem in adulthood.

In sum, there is strong support for positive associations between parent involvement, affection, and support and children's self-esteem. The research literature supports the notion that when children's needs for relatedness are met (i.e., when children feel loved, accepted, and valued by those around them) they develop a positive self-feeling that enables them to approach the world with confidence.

AUTONOMY SUPPORT

Less self-esteem research has focused on parenting factors relevant to autonomy supportive versus controlling styles. Coopersmith (1967) examined a number of variables related to controlling styles. Mothers of children with high self-esteem were less likely to use corporal punishment and love withdrawal, two more controlling discipline methods, than those with low self-esteem. Further, mothers of children with high self-esteem were more likely to endorse children's right to an independent opinion and feel that their child should have a voice in planning and decision-making than mothers of children with low self-esteem.

Findings by Kernis, Brown, and Brody (2000) also support this theory. Parents' use of what we would call autonomy supportive problem-solving methods with their children (e.g., seeking child input, working together, recognizing children's feelings) was positively associated with self-esteem in children. On the other hand, controlling problem solving strategies (e.g., ignoring child input, insisting on the parent's solution) and parental use of psychological control (e.g., guilt induction, love contingency) were related to low self-esteem in children.

In a longitudinal study, Grolnick, Kurowski, and Dunlap (2000) assessed children's perceptions of their parents' autonomy support and self-esteem in sixth grade and then after the transition to junior high in seventh grade. Controlling for sixth grade self-worth, children whose parents increased or remained steady in autonomy support evidenced greater gains in self-esteem than children whose parents became more controlling over the transition.

Possible gender differences in how parental control relates to children's self-esteem are evident in several studies. For example, in a study by Demo et al. (1987), parental control (i.e., adolescents' perceptions of their parents as restrictive and controlling) was negatively associated with daughters' but not sons' self-esteem. Similarly, Barber et al. (1992) found that negative control was positively associated with self-derogation for both boys and girls while use of induction was positively associated with self-esteem for girls only. While Graybill (1978) reported similar negative relations between children's perceptions of parent control and self-esteem for both boys and girls, Gecas and Schwalbe (1986) found that these relations were stronger for boys than girls and for fathers rather than mothers.

While less research has addressed the relation of autonomy support to self-esteem and some studies have found gender differences, overall the literature supports the notion that parents who help children develop feelings of autonomy by encouraging their initiations and involving them in decision making and planning, foster children's self-esteem.

STRUCTURE

We could find only a few studies that examined parental structure and children's self-esteem. Contrary to the zeitgeist of the time, which suggested that permissive styles would facilitate self-esteem, Coopersmith (1967) found that mothers of boys with high self-esteem were less permissive, had higher standards, and were more firm in their enforcement of rules. Kernis et al. (2000) also related parental consistency in discipline to children's self-esteem. Though not examining self-esteem per se, Grolnick and Ryan (1989) found that parental provision of structure was associated with children's understanding of the sources of control in their environments. Such a sense of control would likely contribute to positive self-feelings. Clearly, further work on this question is warranted.

TEACHERS

There is less research on teachers' contributions to children's self-esteem than parents', but the few studies that have been done support the importance of involvement, autonomy support, and structure. For example, in a longitudinal study in which adolescents were followed across the transition to junior high, adolescents who perceived higher levels of teacher support and involvement at Time 1 reported greater self-esteem and lower levels of depression than those perceiving less nurturance (Reddy, Rhodes, & Mulhall, 2003). Further, adolescents who perceived increases in teacher support over the transition tended to evidence greater gains in self-esteem over time. Ryan and Grolnick (1986) found that perceived teacher autonomy support was related to greater self-esteem, perceived cognitive competence, and academic motivation in elementary school children. Further, relevant to structure, Nelson (1984) found that the degree to which teachers stressed order and organization (along with amount of teacher involvement and support) was associated with overall student self-esteem. Finally, fostering feelings of relatedness in the classroom is also important. Adolescents who report greater feelings of relatedness and more positive representations of teachers also report higher general self-worth (Ryan, Stiller, & Lynch, 1994). Thus teacher involvement, autonomy support, and structure in the classroom seem to be associated with optimal self-esteem in children and adolescents.

Our review of the literature on the socialization of self-esteem supports a self-determination framework in which caretaker qualities of involvement, autonomy support and structure, aspects of the environment that facilitate the fulfillment of psychological needs, are associated with self-esteem. This literature suggests that when these needs are fulfilled, children construct a healthy sense of self that allows them to approach the world with confidence.

REFERENCES

Ainsworth, M. D. S., Blehar, M. C., Waters, E., & Wall, S. (1978). *Patterns of Attachment*. Hillsdale, NJ: Lawrence Erlbaum Associates, Inc.

Bachman, J. G. (1970). *Youth in transition* (Vol. 2). Ann Arbor, MI: Institute for Social Research, University of Michigan.

Barber, B. K., Chadwick, B. A., & Oerter, R. (1992). Parental behaviors and adolescent self-esteem in the United States and Germany. *Journal of Marriage and the Family*, 54(1), 128–141.

Bowlby, J. (1969). *Attachment and loss, Vol. 1*. New York: Basic Books.

Cooley, C. H. (1902). *Human nature and the social order*. New York: Charles Scribner's Sons.

Coopersmith, S. (1967). *The antecedents of self-esteem*. San Francisco: WH Freeman.

deCharms, R. (1968). *Personal causation: The internal affective determinants of behavior*. New York: Academic.

Deci, E. L., & Ryan, R. M. (1985). *Intrinsic motivation and self-regulation in human behavior*. New York: Plenum.

Deci, E. L., & Ryan, R. M. (1987). The support of autonomy and control of behavior. *Journal of Personality and Social Psychology*, 53, 1024–1037.

Demo, D. H., Small, S. A., & Savin-Williams, R. C. (1987). Family relations and the self-esteem of adolescents and their parents. *Journal of Marriage and the Family*, 49, 705–715.

Felson, R. B., & Zielinski, M. A. (1989). Children's self-esteem and parental support. *Journal of Marriage and the Family*, 51(3), 727–735.

Gecas, V., & Schwalbe, M. L. (1986). Parental behavior and adolescent self-esteem. *Journal of Marriage and the Family*, 48(1), 37–46.

Graybill, D. (1978). Relationship of maternal child-rearing behaviors to children's self-esteem. *The Journal of Psychology*, 100, 45–47.

Grolnick, W. S., Kurowski, C. O., & Dunlap, K. G. (2000). Parental resources and the transition to junior high. *Journal of Research on Adolescence, 10*(4), 465–488.

Grolnick, W. S., & Ryan, R. M. (1989). Parent styles associated with children's self-regulation and competence in school. *Journal of Educational Psychology, 81*, 143–154.

Grolnick, W. S., Ryan, R. M., & Deci, E. L. (1997). Internalization within the family: The self-determination theory perspective. In J. E. Grusec & L. Kuczynski (Eds.), *Parenting and children's internalization of values: A handbook of contemporary theory* (pp. 135–161). New York: Wiley.

Grolnick, W. S., & Slowiaczek, M. L. (1994). Parents' involvement in children's schooling: A multidimensional conceptualization and motivational model. *Child Development, 65*(1), 237–252.

Harlow, H.F. (1958). The nature of love. *American Psychologist, 13*, 673–685.

Harter, S. (1985). Competence as a dimension of self-evaluation: Toward a comprehensive model of self-worth. In R. Leahy (Ed.), *The development of the self* (pp. 55–122). New York: Academic.

Harter, S. (1999). *The construction of the self*. New York: Guilford Press.

Heider, F. (1958). *The psychology of interpersonal relations*. New York: Wiley.

Hoelter, J., & Harper, L. (1987). Structural and interpersonal family influences on adolescent self-conception. *Journal of Marriage and the Family, 49*(1), 129–139.

James, W. (1890). *The principles of psychology*. New York: Dover (reprinted 1950).

Kernis, M. H., Brown, A. C., & Brody, G. H. (2000). Fragile self-esteem in children and its associations with perceived patterns of parent–child communication. *Journal of Personality, 68*(2), 225–252.

Kuczynski, L., Harach, L., & Bernardini, C. (1999). Psychology's child meets sociology's child: Agency, influence, and power in parent–child relationships. *Contemporary Perspectives on Family Research, 1*, 21–52.

Mead, G. H. (1934). *Mind, self, and society*. Chicago: Chicago University Press.

Nelson, G. (1984). The relationships between dimensions of classroom and family environments on the self-concept, satisfaction, and achievement of grade 7 and 8 students. *Journal of Community Psychology, 12*(3), 276–287.

Reddy, R., Rhodes, J. E., & Mulhall, P. (2003). The influence of teacher support on student adjustment in the middle school years: A latent growth curve study. *Development and Psychopathology, 15*, 119–138.

Reis, H. T., Sheldon, K. M., Gable, S. L., Roscoe, J., & Ryan, R. M. (2000). Daily well-being: The role of autonomy, competence, and relatedness. *Personality and Social Psychology Bulletin, 26*(4), 419–435.

Roberts, E. L., & Bengston, V. L. (1996). Affective ties to parents in early adulthood and self-esteem across 20 years. *Social Psychology Quarterly, 59*(1), 96–106.

Rosenberg, M. (1965). *Society and the adolescent self-image*. Princeton, NJ: Princeton University Press.

Rosenberg, M. (1979). *Conceiving the self*. New York: Basic Books.

Ryan, R. M., & Frederick, C. (1997). On energy, personality, and health: Subjective vitality as a dynamic reflection of well-being. *Journal of Personality, 65*(3), 529–565.

Ryan, R. M., & Grolnick, W. S. (1986). Origins and pawns in the classroom: Self-report and projective assessments of individual differences in children's perceptions. *Journal of Personality and Social Psychology, 50*(3), 550–558.

Ryan, R. M., Stiller, J., & Lynch, J. H. (1994). Representations of relationships to teachers, parents, and friends as predictors of academic motivation and self-esteem. *Journal of Early Adolescence, 14*(2), 226–249.

Thomas, D. L., Gecas, V., Weigert, A., & Rooney, E. (1974). *Family socialization and the adolescent*. Lexington, MA: DC Heath.

White, R. (1959). Motivation reconsidered: The concept of competence. *Psychological Review, 66*, 297–333.

Wilson, W. J. (1991). The truly disadvantaged: The inner city, the underclass, and public policy. Chicago: University of Chicago Press.

31

Nurturing Self-Esteem in Young People

NATHANIEL BRANDEN

*I*f we are to consider how self-esteem is best nurtured in young people, we must first be clear on what we mean by "self-esteem." So I shall begin with a definition.

Self-esteem is the disposition to experience oneself as being competent to cope with the basic challenges of life, and as being worthy of happiness. Thus, it consists of two components: (1) *self-efficacy*—confidence in one's ability to think, learn, choose, and make appropriate decisions; and (2) *self-respect*—confidence that love, friendship, achievement, success—in a word, happiness—are natural and appropriate (Branden, 1994).

If a person felt inadequate to face the normal challenges of life, if he or she lacked fundamental self-trust or confidence in his or her mind, we would recognize the presence of a self-esteem deficiency, no matter what other assets the person possessed. The same would be true if a person lacked a basic sense of self-respect, felt unworthy of the love or respect of others, felt undeserving of happiness, or was fearful of asserting thoughts, wants, or needs.

Self-esteem is not the euphoria or buoyancy that may be temporarily induced by a drug, a compliment, or a love affair. If it is not grounded in reality, if it is only a delusion in someone's consciousness—if it is not built over time through such practices as living consciously, self-responsibly, and with integrity, discussed below—it is not self-esteem (Branden, 1997a).

We cannot "give" a child self-esteem; but we can support the practices that will lead a child to self-esteem, and abstain from the actions that tend to undermine a child's self-esteem.

Over more than four decades of practicing psychotherapy, I have been preoccupied with the question of what people are doing right when they are strengthening their self-esteem and what they are doing wrong when they are undermining it. In *The six pillars of self-esteem* (Branden, 1994), I examine the six practices that I have found to be essential for nurturing self-esteem, and that have been indispensable to my work as a therapist. Here, I can only suggest the briefest essence of "the six pillars."

The practice of living consciously: respect for facts; being present to what we are doing while we are doing it; seeking and being eagerly open to any information, knowledge, or feedback that bears on our interests, values, goals, and projects; seeking to understand not only the world external to self but also our inner world, so that we do not act out of self-made blindness (Branden, 1997b).

The practice of self-acceptance: the willingness to own, experience, and take responsibility for our thoughts, feelings, and actions, without evasion, denial, or disowning—and also without self-repudiation; the virtue of realism applied to the self.

The practice of self-responsibility: realizing that we are the author of our choices and actions; that each one of us is responsible for our life and well-being, and for the attainment of our goals; and that if we need the cooperation of other people to achieve our goals, we must offer values in exchange, since no one exists merely to serve us (Branden, 1997a).

The practice of self-assertiveness: being authentic in dealings with others; treating our values and person with decent respect in our social interactions; willingness to stand up for our ideas and ourselves in appropriate ways in appropriate contexts.

The practice of living purposefully: identifying our short-term and long-term goals or purposes and the actions needed to attain them (formulating an action-plan); organizing behavior in the service of those goals; monitoring action to be sure we stay on track; and paying attention to outcome to recognize if we need to go back to the drawing board.

The practice of personal integrity: living with congruence between what we know, what we profess, and what we do; manifesting our professed values in action. One of the simplest applications of living consciously and being self-responsible is being conscious of—and taking responsibility for—the words coming out of one's mouth. If adults did so, they would not be so prone to make the kind of statements that can devastate a young person's self-esteem. "What's the matter with you? Can't you do anything right?" When I hear adults talking to a child abusively, I inquire, "What is your purpose? Have you found that insulting a child's intelligence raises the level of performance?" I ask teachers: "Have you found ridicule to be an effective tool for facilitating learning?" *Pay attention to outcome!*

Or, a lesson in self-acceptance: 5-year-old Jennie bursts into the room and screams, "I hate my brother!" Mother number one says, "What a terrible thing to say! You don't mean it! You *can't* hate him! He's your *brother!*" What is she teaching? Self-alienation and self-doubt. Mother number two says, "Wow! You're really feeling mad at your brother *right now!* Want to tell me about it, sweetheart?" What is she teaching? Self-acceptance and the non-catastrophizing of negative emotions (Branden, 1987).

Clearly, parents and teachers can make it easier or harder for a young person to develop self-esteem. They can make it easier or harder for a young person to learn the six practices and make them an integral part of his or her life. However, they cannot inspire these practices in young people if they do not manifest them in their own behavior. In this area, modeling is essential to effective teaching. According to Stanley Coopersmith's landmark study of the family origins of self-esteem, the parents of children with high self-esteem tend to have high self-esteem themselves (Coopersmith, 1967).

The six practices provide a standard for assessing parental and teaching policies. Do these policies encourage or discourage consciousness, self-acceptance, self-responsibility, self-assertiveness, purposefulness, and integrity? Do they raise or lower the probability that a young person will learn self-esteem-supporting behaviors?

The issue of what supports—or subverts—self-esteem is present virtually from the beginning of life. A child has no more basic requirement, as far as parental behavior is concerned, than that of safety and security. This entails the satisfaction of physiological needs, protection from the elements, and basic care-taking in all its obvious respects. It entails the creation of an environment in which the child can feel nurtured and safe.

In this context, the process of separation and individuation can unfold (Mahler, Pine, & Bergman, 1975). A mind that can later learn to trust itself can begin to emerge. A person with a confident sense of boundaries can develop.

Today we know that touch is essential for a child's healthy development. Through touch we send sensory stimulation that helps the infant's brain to develop. Through touch we convey love, caring, comfort, support, and nurturing.

As the process of growth continues, a child who is treated with love tends to internalize the feeling and to experience him or herself as lovable. Love is conveyed by verbal expression, nurturing actions, and the pleasure and joy parents show in the sheer fact of the child's being.

An effective parent can convey anger or disappointment without signaling withdrawal of love—and can teach without resorting to rejection, humiliating behavior, or physical or emotional abuse, all of which can damage a child's fragile sense of self.

A child whose thoughts and feelings are treated with acceptance tends to internalize the response and to learn self-acceptance. Acceptance is conveyed, not necessarily by agreement, which is not always possible, but by listening to and acknowledging the child's thoughts and feelings, and by not chastising, arguing, lecturing, psychologizing, or insulting.

A child who is treated with respect tends to learn self-respect. Stated simply, respect is conveyed by addressing the child with the same good-mannered courtesy one normally extends to adults. A home—or a classroom—in which people talk to one another with benevolent respect is an environment that supports self-esteem.

When praise is in order, convey appreciation *of behavior*, and do so realistically. *Do not make extravagant, global statements about the child's intelligence or ability*—because they make the child feel anxious and unseen. When criticism of behavior is necessary, do so respectfully, with regard for the dignity of the recipient. *Do not indulge in character assassination* (Ginott, 1972).

When parents express their pleasure in and appreciation of a child's questions or observations or thoughtfulness, they are encouraging the exercise of consciousness or mindfulness. When they respond positively and respectfully to a child's efforts at self-expression, or invite such self-expression, they encourage self-assertiveness. When they acknowledge and show appreciation for a child's truthfulness, they encourage integrity. In short, catch a child doing something right and convey pleasure and appreciation at the sight of it.

How parents respond when children make mistakes can be fateful for self-esteem. If a child is ridiculed or chastised or punished for making a mistake—or if a parent steps in impatiently, saying "Here, let me do it!"—the child cannot feel free to struggle and learn. A natural process of growth is sabotaged. A child who does not feel accepted by parents if he or she makes a mistake may learn to practice *self*-rejection in response to mistakes. Consciousness is muted, self-acceptance is undermined, self-assertiveness and self-responsibility are suppressed. It is more useful to ask, "What have you learned? What might you do differently next time?"

An effective way to stimulate expanded consciousness in young people is to avoid asking questions that can be answered with a yes or no and to ask instead questions that require *thought*. For instance, instead of asking, "Did you have a good time at the circus?"—ask, "What was the most interesting (or exciting) thing you saw at the circus?" Or "What's your favorite book (or class) and what do you like about it?"

There is no end to the possible ways one might encourage the six practices in young people; here, it has been possible to indicate only a few. I turn now to some of the ways in which teachers can contribute to the development of self-esteem in their students.

To many students, school represents a "second chance"—an opportunity to acquire a better sense of self and a better vision of life than was offered in their home. A teacher who projects confidence in a child's competence and goodness can be a powerful antidote to a family in which such confidence is lacking and perhaps the opposite perspective is being conveyed. A teacher who treats boys and girls with respect can provide enlightenment for a child struggling to understand human relationships and who comes from a home where such respect does not exist. A teacher who refuses to accept a child's negative self-concept and relentlessly holds to a better view of the child's potential has the power—sometimes—to save a life. A client once said to me, "It was my fourth grade teacher who made me aware that a different kind of humanity existed than my family—she gave me a vision to inspire me."

"Feel good" notions of self-esteem are harmful rather than helpful. Yet, if one examines the proposals offered to teachers on how to raise students' self-esteem, many are the kind of trivial nonsense that gives self-esteem a bad name, such as praising and applauding a child for virtually everything he or she does, dismissing the importance of objective accomplishments, handing out gold stars on every possible occasion, and propounding an "entitlement" idea of self-esteem that leaves it divorced from both behavior and character. One of the consequences of this approach is to expose to ridicule the whole self-esteem movement in the schools.

A few words, as an aside, on the relationship of self-esteem to external achievements in school or beyond. To observe that the practice of living purposefully is essential to well-realized self-esteem should not be understood to mean that the measure of a person's worth is his or her external achievements. We admire achievements—in ourselves and in others—and it is natural and appropriate to do so. But this is not the same thing as saying that our achievements are the measure or ground of our self-esteem. The root of our self-esteem, as I have discussed at length elsewhere (Branden, 1994) is not our achievements but those internally generated practices that, among other things, *make it possible for us to achieve*—all the self-virtues mentioned above.

If the proper goal of education is to provide students with a foundation in the basics needed to function effectively in the modern world, then nothing is more important than building courses on the art of critical thinking into every school curriculum. And if self-esteem means confidence in our ability to cope with the challenges of life, is anything more important than learning how to use one's mind? This means learning, not *what* to think, but *how* to think.

In an information-age economy, where everyone's chief capital asset is what they carry between their ears, the ability to think independently is valued far above mere obedience. Individual teachers and designers of curricula need to ask themselves: How does my work contribute to the process of young people becoming thinking, innovative, creative human beings?

To give a child the experience of being accepted and respected does not mean to signal that "I expect nothing of you." Teachers who want children to give their best must convey that *that is what they expect.* Children often interpret the absence of such expectations as evidence of contempt.

We know that a teacher's expectations tend to turn into self-fulfilling prophecies. If a teacher expects a student to get an A—or a D—either way, expectations tend to become realities. If a teacher knows how to convey, "I am absolutely convinced you can master this subject and I expect you to, and I will give you all the help you need," the child feels nurtured, supported, and inspired.

If a proper education has to include an understanding of thinking, it also has to include an understanding of feelings. A teacher is in a position to teach children a rational respect for feelings coupled with an awareness that one can accept a feeling without having to be ruled by it. For self-esteem, this is an issue of the highest importance.

Students can learn to own when they are afraid, and accept it, and (for instance) still go to the dentist when it is necessary to do so. They can learn to admit when they are angry, and talk about it, and not resort to fists. They can learn to recognize when they are hurt, and own the feeling, and not put on a phony act of indifference. They can learn to witness their feelings of impatience and excitement, and breathe into them, and yet not go out to play until they have finished their homework. They can learn to recognize their sexual feelings, and accept them, and not be controlled by them in self-destructive ways. They can learn to recognize and accept their emotions *without losing their minds.*

The last issue I will mention, equally applicable to parents and teachers, is the need to ask, "What do I want from this child? Obedience or cooperativeness?" If I want obedience, fear may be an appropriate feeling to encourage. If I want cooperativeness, then I must speak not to a child's fear, but to a child's *mind.*

If, in dealing with a young person, we remember that we are addressing a *mind,* the simplest conversation can be a vehicle for supporting and strengthening self-esteem. Such are a few of the ways in which parents and teachers can contribute to the self-esteem of young people.

REFERENCES

Branden, N. (1987). *How to raise your self-esteem*. New York: Bantam Books.

Branden, N. (1994). *The six pillars of self-esteem*. New York: Bantam Books.

Branden, N. (1997a). *Taking responsibility*. New York: Simon & Schuster.

Branden, N. (1997b). *The art of living consciously*. New York: Simon & Schuster.

Coopersmith, S. (1967). *The antecedents of self-esteem*. San Francisco: WH Freeman & Company.

Ginott, H. (1972). *Teacher and child*. New York: Macmillan.

Mahler, M.S., Pine, F., & Bergman, A. (1975). *The psychological birth of the human infant*. New York: Basic Books.

32

How Can Optimal
Self-Esteem Be Facilitated
in Children and
Adolescents by Parents
and Teachers?

MARTIN V. COVINGTON

T his question is not as straightforward as might seem at first glance. As with all complicated questions, answers for this one also depend on how the terms of the debate are set out and on one's assumptions about the nature of the phenomenon at hand. And, a debate it has been! The notion of self-esteem is not only one of the most important concepts of our time, but also one of the most controversial, especially when applied to matters of child-rearing, schooling, and social policy. Thus, it is important that I begin with a clear definition of self-esteem, followed by an analysis of the nature of the controversy, and conclude with a theoretical and empirically based perspective that hopefully paves the way for some constructive answers.

A DEFINITION

Any consideration of the issues involved here must acknowledge that the research literature on self-esteem is truly massive, and this does not count that huge volume of writings found in the popular press. Fortunately, my task is made somewhat easier by the fact that the wording of the question provides some boundaries for our deliberations which I take to mean a consideration of the kinds of factors or conditions that adult care-givers, teachers, and parents alike, can mobilize to foster a sense of self-esteem in their wards. Nathaniel Branden's broad definition of self-concept (1987) seems most appropriate in this context: "who and what we think we are...our physical and psychological traits, our assets and liabilities, and, above all, our self-esteem. Self-esteem is the evaluative component of self-concept." (p. 6)

I will use the term self-worth interchangeably with self-esteem to represent this evaluative component, which refers to a person's self-assessments as to whether he or she is valued by others or not, able or unable, loveable or reprehensible. These personal judgments about one's worth, as Branden correctly argues, depend in turn on judgments about one's personal assets, which in the case of schooling translates largely into assessments as to whether or not one's mental abilities are sufficient to master the academic curriculum. When one adds an evaluative component to this particular measure of one's self-esteem, stated in the starkest terms, it implies that individuals are only as worthy or valued as their achievements. Because this test of one's worth is widely endorsed across our society, it is not surprising to find that often it not only represents the underlying ethos of many classrooms at all educational levels, but is also endorsed by many parents as well. Some parents hold their children to exacting standards of excellence, which in itself is admirable enough. However, when these expectations are accompanied by an implied threat of being ostracized if one does not succeed, then both self-esteem and achievement are victimized. But we are getting slightly ahead of our story. Based on this particular definition, I will argue that most issues regarding self-esteem and its promotion as they regard parents and teachers revolve around matters of achievement and "well-doing," and around the child's self-perceived sense of ability.

THE CONTROVERSY

Now what is so controversial about the concept of enhancing self-esteem? Basically, there are two distinct positions on the matter of taking deliberate steps to enhance feelings of self-regard in young people. The first position—that of pro-esteem advocates, is that enhancing feelings of self-acceptance is the ultimate goal of all social interactions, the education enterprise included. In effect, it is thought that positive feelings of self-regard are a worthwhile goal in its own right, and that when these feelings exist in abundance good things happen to people including, importantly in the school context, increased scholastic achievement. This position holds that positive self-esteem is the natural birthright of all humans—a gift, in short, and one bestowed whether it is deserved or not. From this perspective, then, self-esteem is best enhanced by treating others with respect and support, and with direct reminders of their value and uniqueness, irrespective of any actual achievements.

While no one would discount the humanizing value of respect, trust, and nurturance, the critics of this view dispute the nature of self-esteem just described, question the effectiveness of the methods proposed for its initiation, and offer up empirical evidence which casts doubt on the implied casual relationship between self-esteem and academic performance. First and foremost, although numerous research studies have demonstrated a positive relationship between self-esteem variables and academic achievement, the magnitude of these correlations is extremely small; indeed, typically so minuscule that in one study, for instance, variations in self-esteem measures accounted for less than three percent of the variations in achievement records (for review, see Covington, 1992). Moreover, such correlations, even had they been more substantial, lend no particular plausibility to the theory they self-esteem causes achievement gains: the alternative hypothesis, that is, increased achievement causes positive feelings of self-regard, remains equally plausible.

Second, quite apart from these empirical findings, critics maintain that self-esteem is best conceptualized not as a gift to which all persons are entitled as human beings, but rather as a reward for doing something well (e.g., Krauthammer, 1990). They maintain that the gravest injustice that schools could inflict would be to encourage children to be happy without their having earned it. Moreover, one wonders if by fostering good feelings alone, many of the traditional reasons for learning and striving to improve would disappear, including dissatisfaction with one's life circumstances.

Despite this assault, many pro-esteem advocates have attempted to maintain the moral high-ground, disbelieving that anyone would doubt the importance—indeed, the urgency, of trying to improve children's perceptions of their own worth. As these contesting positions have crystallized over time, we are often left with the unhelpful statement of the issues in the form of a mutually exclusive dichotomy of goals: whether students should become good learners or feel good about themselves.

Fortunately, we are better informed about the nature of the relationship between self-esteem and academic performance than either advocates or critics acknowledge. Recent research from our laboratory and the findings of other colleagues have verified the underlying dynamics that firmly place self-esteem dynamics in the midst of the achievement process. Rather than relying on simple one-to-one correlations between feelings of self-regard and achievement of the kinds described above, we have explored the complex networking of many factors as they interact among themselves over time and eventually influence the academic performance of the learner. These data were subject to statistical techniques that allow for the presumption of causality. Several findings are critical to our story:

First, when self-esteem is defined around Branden's evaluative emphasis on one's self-judgments about personal strengths and limitations (e.g., "how able are you to do well on this task?"), the evidence convincingly demonstrates that positive self-evaluations play a substantial role in causing increases in academic performance. Pro-esteem advocates have it right in this instance: self-esteem factors are clearly implicated in the achievement process.

Second, a subtle, nuanced qualification is needed here. The influence of self-esteem on performance is largely indirect, that is, it operates through various mediators, the most important of which are the reasons (or motives) for learning in the first place! For those learners whose reasons for learning involve positive goals—for instance, becoming the best one can be, to learn to care for others, or merely to satisfy one's curiosity, then the entire network of influential factors work in harmony and unison toward enhanced achievement. These reasons for learning are associated with the belief that one has the ability to meet the challenge of the tasks at hand. If, however, one's reasons for learning are more self-promotional or defensive in nature—for instance, striving to succeed in order to avoid failure and its implication that one is incompetent, or to prove one's superiority over others, then academic performance flags largely because of the interfering effects of the fear that one may not succeed. In this case, these reasons for learning tend to be associated with self-doubts about one's ability.

Third, critics are also correct, at least on one point. Positive self-regard seems to depend on achieving worthwhile goals, not merely deserving respect, but actually earning it. Every thing in our data underscores the critical role played by feelings of pride at having achieved something of value as a trigger for continued striving (Covington, 2002). Yet, these critics have overlooked another reality. High grades and other noteworthy accomplishments alone are no guarantee for personal fulfillment. As we have noted, feelings of worthiness also depend on the right reasons for learning, and when these reasons are wrong, that is, driven by fear or self-doubt, the foundation on which one's worth is built remains tenuous.

Incidentally, this is one reason why the simple one-to-one correlations between self-regard measures and achievement are so low. This simple linkage does not take into account the reasons for learning. For example, the prediction of pro-esteem advocates that high self-regard causes noteworthy achievements can be turned upside down when someone with low self-esteem actually performs well. In this case, the individual may do well because he is driven to avoid failure and feelings of worthlessness. It is not that self-worth considerations are not important—obviously, they are, even in this counterintuitive example. The problem with past thinking is that the key role of motives for learning has never been properly acknowledged by either critics or advocates.

RECOMMENDATIONS

Based on this fuller and more balanced understanding of the role of self-esteem factors in the achievement process, what recommendations can be made to the care-givers of young learners regarding the enhancement of self-esteem? I propose a series of five interlocking observations:

1. For parents and teachers alike, it is best to assume that self-acceptance is a by-product of achieving something meaningful to the learner. Attempts to encourage self-worth in the learner simply by reinforcing their status as being "special" will fail if feelings of "well-being" are not justified by "well-doing."

2. Having emphasized the importance of creating meaningful achievements, the ways youngsters achieve is also critical for the facilitation of self-esteem. Caregivers need to recognize that self-confidence is best strengthened when learners are challenged incrementally, with the prospects for success maximized when children are allowed to set achievement goals themselves and to modify them as needed so that when failures to meet them occur, disappointments serve to renew the child's resolve to continue, not demoralize them. Helping children think

of learning in terms of a series of goals, and encouraging in them the capacity to set moderate subgoals along the way is as important a skill as any subject-matter content. In this connection, children should be encouraged to take responsibility for planning and carrying out plans for learning as soon as developmentally appropriate. A significant aspect of a sense of "well-being," as we have seen, is a conviction of self-confidence to succeed and the independence of judgment to rearrange circumstances as the need arises.

3. Of vital importance, yet a reality often overlooked, as already noted, is that one's successes will strengthen a sense of self-regard only when the reasons for learning are positive. But how do care-takers encourage those positive, intrinsically-satisfying reasons associated with the growth of feelings of self-worth—such as satisfaction of one's curiosity or learning in order to benefit others? The challenge is especially difficult when we realize that many classrooms (as well as some homes) are structured around an implicitly competitive norm. Because of these competitive rules of the "learning game," children often must compete with their peers for a limited number of rewards, a condition which forces them into a position of trying to avoid failure, not necessarily to succeed. Such fear-driven reasons diminish self-respect, even should they succeed.

4. Caregivers can help youngsters be resilient in such failure-prone circumstances by encouraging positive definitions of their worth, mainly encouraging students to do the "best they can" and to focus on improvement rather than "doing better than others." This mind set is powerfully important not only from a self-esteem perspective, but also because the evidence suggests that students who see schools as an opportunity to better themselves are likely to stay in school longer, whereas those who see school as a contest in which students must try to outscore others are more likely to drop out sooner, probably to avoid the fear and anxiety that often results from such confrontations (Covington, 1998).

5. Given the importance of the motivational factors in the decision to continue in school, parents often fear the wrong thing. Far from being worried if their children do not enter the frenzied "rat-race" for grades in competitive contests, they should start worrying when their children do. All too often the result is not excellence, but self-doubt, anger, and a decline in caring about learning. What matters ultimately regarding the facilitation of self-acceptance is not performance per se, but learning; and not for short-term learning gains but learning for the right reasons.

REFERENCES

Branden, N. (1987). *How to raise your self-esteem.* New York: Bantam Books.

Covington, M. V. (1992). *Making the grade: A self-worth perspective on motivation and school reform.* New York: Cambridge University Press.

Covington, M. V. (1998). *The will to learn: A guide for motivating young people*. New York: Cambridge University Press.

Covington, M. V. (2002). Rewards and intrinsic motivation: A needs-based developmental perspective. In T. Urdan & F. Pajares (Eds.), *Motivation of adolescents*. New York: Academic Press.

Krauthammer, C. (1990). Education: Doing bad and feeling good. *Time Magazine, 135* (6), 78.

Section III

Self-Esteem and Psychological Functioning

Question 11

How central is self-esteem to psychological functioning and well-being? If central, why and through what processes? If not central, how can we explain the current preoccupation with it in US society?

*T*he essays in this section address the degree of self-esteem's centrality to psychological functioning and well-being. The contributors to this question present a wide range of views that reflect the complexities of the issues involved. The first two essays focus on self-esteem as an individual difference variable and the third focuses on self-esteem processes per se.

Solomon argues in his essay that self-esteem is an essential component of psychological functioning because it allows humans to function without crippling anxiety. Solomon presents the terror management theory (TMT) perspective that self-esteem reflects the belief that one is a person of value in a world of meaning. "All human beings thus require self-esteem, although the manner in which they obtain and maintain it varies a great deal depending upon the standards of value espoused in specific social roles by specific cultures, which often differ quite dramatically." Solomon offers several reasons for Americans' current preoccupation with self-esteem, one of which he believes is their increasing difficulty acquiring and maintaining self-esteem.

In her essay, Koch reviews data that link high self-esteem to positive outcomes such as happiness and life satisfaction and low self-esteem to negative outcomes such as suicide and criminal behavior. She then turns to a recent literature review that calls into question the importance of self-esteem to psychological functioning. Koch suggests that "Despite the lack of evidence suggesting that self-esteem plays a central role in functioning and well-being, a popular obsession with self-esteem remains." She offers several explanations for this obsession, which she concludes is a largely western phenomenon.

In their essay, Tesser and Martin present a process view of self-esteem and argue that the pursuit of self-relevant goals is central to psychological functioning. They suggest that these goals typically involve personal values or self-characteristics, instigate changes in feelings of self-worth, involve certain emotions, and are mutually substitutable. Tesser and Martin argue that failure to obtain self-relevant goals, especially when substitution is not available, will undermine well-being and heighten negative states such as depression and rumination. They present evidence to bolster these assertions.

33

Self-Esteem is Central to Human Well-Being

SHELDON SOLOMON

Life...is arduous, difficult, a perpetual struggle. It calls for gigantic courage and strength. More than anything, perhaps, creatures of illusion as we are, it calls for confidence in oneself. Without self-confidence, we are as babes in the cradle.

Virginia Woolf, *A Room of One's Own*

S elf-esteem was recognized as an utterly essential and uniquely human affectation by the earliest psychologists. William James, in *Principles of Psychology* (1890) argued that self-esteem is a basic and fundamental human need: "The emotions themselves of self-satisfaction and abasement are of a unique sort, each as worthy to be classed as a primitive emotional species as are, for example, rage and pain." However, it took almost a century for experimental social psychologists to become interested in understanding what self-esteem consists of, how it is acquired and maintained, what functions it serves, and how it does so.

SELF-ESTEEM: WHAT, WHY AND HOW

The first empirically substantiated theoretical approach to delineating the nature and function of self-esteem was terror management theory (TMT; Greenberg, Pyszczynski, & Solomon, 1986, 1997); TMT was in turn derived from cultural anthropologist Ernest Becker's (1971, 1973, 1975) interdisciplinary pursuit of the motivational underpinnings of human behavior. According to Becker, and following Darwin, human beings share with all forms of life a biological propensity for survival, but are unique by virtue of their sophisticated cognitive capacities in their awareness of the ultimate futility of this most basic biological imperative. In other words, only human beings (small children and idiots excepted) are aware of the inevitability of death, that death can occur at any time for reasons that often cannot be anticipated or controlled, and that they are fragile and vulnerable corporeal entities: respiring pieces of defecating, fornicating, flatulent, post-nasal dripping meat who are no more significant or enduring than ferns, fleas, and ferrets.

Human beings would be potentially incapacitated with abject terror if they were perpetually preoccupied with these frightening existential realities. Accordingly, Becker and TMT hypothesize that cultural worldviews emerged—humanly constructed beliefs about reality shared by individuals in a group that (1) imbue the world with meaning and stability and offer some hope of symbolic (e.g., by noteworthy accomplishments or amassing great fortunes) or literal (e.g., the afterlives promised by most religions) immortality; and (2) supply opportunities for individuals to perceive themselves as uniquely valuable and significant participants in the cosmic drama to which they subscribe through the provision of social roles with associated standards of appropriate conduct. Meeting or exceeding these standards yields *self-esteem*: the belief that one is a person of value in a world of meaning. Self-esteem is thus the primary psychological mechanism by which cultural worldviews mitigate the debilitating dread that might otherwise render humans unable to function with a modicum of equanimity in their daily affairs.

TMT posits that self-esteem acquires its anxiety buffering qualities in the context of the socialization process. At birth, human infants are utterly vulnerable and dependent, and especially prone to intense anxiety when their basic needs are unsatisfied. Bowlby (1969) argued that this raw undifferentiated terror is the psychological impetus for the formation of infants' attachment to their primary caretakers. Parental provision of protection and sustenance provides positive feelings of safety and satiety, and is at first provided unconditionally. During socialization, however, parental approval becomes contingent on engaging in certain culturally prescribed activities (e.g., eating with a fork) and refraining from others (e.g., picking your nose and wiping your finger on the seat of the Lexus). Now feeling safe and secure becomes associated with being "good," and anxiety and insecurity with being "bad." This is how self-esteem initially becomes an effective anxiety-buffer. And then later in childhood, youngsters begin to realize that their parents are human and mortal and thus ultimately incapable of protecting them from life's dangerous vicissitudes, so they begin to (quite unconsciously) transfer their psychological allegiance to the cultural worldview and garner self-esteem by adhering to standards of value associated with their social roles as fledgling members of their culture.

In sum, self-esteem, from a TMT perspective, consists of the belief that one is a person of value in a world of meaning; and the primary function of self-esteem is to buffer anxiety in a creature utterly devoted to life, but painfully aware of the inevitability and always looming prospect of death. All human beings thus require self-esteem, although the manner in which they obtain and maintain it varies a great deal depending upon the standards of value espoused in specific social roles by specific cultures, which often differ quite dramatically. Highly valued behaviors in one culture are often utterly despised in another; e.g., the ancient Greeks were very tolerant, and indeed fond of homosexuality, while these activities are currently vilified by fundamentalist Christians and Muslims (who agree on little else these days). Self-esteem is thus never directly obtained by any individual in a cultural vacuum; it is always at least in part a reflection of prevailing cultural constructs and social norms.

SELF-ESTEEM AS CULTURALLY CONSTRUCTED ANXIETY BUFFER: EMPIRICAL EVIDENCE

A large body of evidence is in accord with the proposition that the self-esteem is negatively correlated with state and trait anxiety, and positively correlated with a host of desirable psychological, physiological, and behavioral outcomes (for a review, see Solomon, Greenberg, & Pyszczynski, 1991). Additionally, momentarily elevated or dispositionally high self-esteem (1) reduces anxiety and physiological arousal in response to threatening stimuli (Greenberg et al., 1992); (2) reduces vulnerability denying defensive distortions (Greenberg, Pyszczynski, Solomon, Pinel, Simon, & Jordan, 1993); and (3) reduces or eliminates cultural worldview defense in response to mortality salience (specifically, after thinking about one's own death, the tendency to have more positive reactions to similar others or those who uphold cherished cultural values and the concurrent tendency to derogate and aggress against dissimilar others or those who violate cherished cultural precepts; Harmon-Jones, Simon, Greenberg, Pyszczynski, Solomon, & McGregor, 1997.) More recent work has also demonstrated that reminders of death instigate efforts to procure self-esteem. For example, Taubman Ben-Ari, Florian, and Mikulincer (1999) showed that mortality salience increased risky driving behavior (both self-reports and on a driving simulator) among Israeli soldiers who valued their driving ability as a source of self-esteem. There is thus a large body of empirical evidence that provides convergent support for the TMT conception of self-esteem as an anxiety buffer with particular potency in matters pertaining to death (for an extensive review of this literature see Pyszczynski et al., 2004).

WHY ARE AMERICANS CURRENTLY SO PREOCCUPIED WITH SELF-ESTEEM?

Although psychologists are not in unanimous agreement that self-esteem is of central importance to human beings' psychological well-being (see, e.g., Baumeister, Campbell, Krueger, & Vohs, 2003), there is little dispute that Americans are presently, for better or worse, excessively preoccupied with obtaining and maintaining adequate levels of self-regard (e.g., using self-esteem as a search term on Google.com on 18 December 2003 produced 2,270,000 results). Why might this be the case?

First, people may be increasingly concerned with self-esteem as part of a broad evolutionary trend toward escalating self-awareness. Nietzsche (1887/1974, p. 299) speculated that:

> ...the development of language and the development of consciousness...go hand in hand....The human being inventing signs is at the same time the human being who becomes ever more keenly conscious of himself. It was only as a social animal that man acquired self-consciousness—which he is still in the process of doing, more and more.

Perhaps then as human beings become more and more aware of themselves as objects of their own subjective experience, there is a commensurate increase in concerns about self-worth. And to the extent this is true preoccupation with self-esteem should be rising independent of specific cultural milieus.

Second, American culture is most assuredly on the high end of the individual side of the individualism–collectivism continuum proposed by cross-cultural psychologists (e.g., Markus & Kitayama, 1991; Triandis, 1994) to account for different thoughts, feelings, and behaviors of people in different cultures. Thus, people in individualistic cultures may, of necessity, be more likely to focus attention on themselves rather than their group and be more concerned about their self-esteem as a result. If so, then preoccupation with self-esteem should be more pronounced in individualistic cultures.

Finally, and I suspect most importantly, Americans are currently preoccupied with self-esteem because they are having an increasingly difficult time acquiring and maintaining it (just like you really never think about needing air as long as there's lots to breath but oxygen becomes a very salient desire when it is in short supply). At the start of the third millennium, too many Americans are clinically depressed, chemically dependent, chronically bored, or just plain unhappy. According to the National Institute of Mental Health, 19 million Americans are depressed each year, 10 times the rate of depression following World War II; adolescent suicide among males is up 300% since the 1960s; 25% of the children in America are adversely affected by alcoholism in their families; Valium and Prozac are daily fare for millions. Eating disorders and obsessive compulsive behaviors abound. Too many Americans are overweight, out of shape, and spend most of their time snacking, shopping, or watching television to see who can drink the most yak urine on *Fear Factor* while anxiously awaiting the next round of humiliating rejections on *American Idol* or staged pummeling from the World Wrestling Federation. Why? Have people always been this miserable and disoriented, or is there something about our specific time and place that makes for a toxic psychological atmosphere?

From a TMT perspective, all of these problems are (at least in part) the result of pervasive low self-esteem that occurs when people subscribe to cultural worldviews with standards of value that are generally unattainable for the average individual. For example, Christianity at its best stresses that all people are equal in the eyes of God and therefore a person working as a dipstick for a cesspool is no less eligible for a heavenly afterlife than the President or the Pope as long as each of them behave with integrity while on Earth; all people are consequently potentially able to meet or exceed the standards of value provided by a Christian worldview and obtain self-esteem in doing so. Conversely, contemporary American culture places almost exclusive emphasis on physical beauty and material wealth and power as the primary standards by which self-esteem is procured. But physical beauty, defined in our culture as being perpetually young and thinner than a piece of linguini, cannot be easily, if ever, attained by most of us. Similarly, material wealth is equally difficult for the average individual to acquire, because in a capital-based economic order there can be no millionaires without hordes of relative paupers who generate those riches by providing cheap labor and mindless consumption of revenue-generating products. However, Americans are told from the moment they're born that this is the Land of Opportunity and anyone with sufficient desire and effort can be successful, implying implicitly or explicitly that those who are not fantastically wealthy are therefore personally responsible for their meager accomplishments. Consequently, the average American, neither rich nor beautiful, tends to perceive him or her self negatively, and suffer deficits in self-worth accordingly.

Hungarian anthropologist Geza Roheim (1934) anticipated this rather unhappy state of affairs 70 years ago when he observed:

> We have evolved a state of things in which everybody must be a hero, must do something, achieve something, in order to become an ordinary…member of society. The architect must always build new houses and outdo his rivals, the author must invent new plots for books, the business man must develop his business, the employee tries to get a better employment: everybody is rushing about in a state of feverish haste, emphatically doing something….Civilized adults, like children, depend on an ever-increasing number of other adults for the gratification of their wishes. The process of growing up, once a biological process, has now become an achievement.

SUMMARY AND CONCLUSION

Self-esteem is an absolutely essential attribute in a sentient life form aware of, and disinclined to accept, the inevitability of death. By embedding ourselves in culturally constructed conceptions of reality and adhering to the demands of the social roles we inhabit in the context of our cultural worldviews, human beings can obtain self-esteem—the belief that we are persons of value in worlds of meaning. Self-esteem makes anxiety-free action possible; without it, we would be as Virginia Woolf put it: "as babes in the cradle." All human beings thus require self-esteem, but the manner by which it is obtained and maintained depends on the specific demands of cultural dictates that are wildly discrepant across cultures. People will tend to be exceptionally concerned with matters pertaining to self-worth when standards for attaining self-esteem are difficult or impossible to meet. One way therefore to judge the quality and viability of a culture is to ask to what extent there are sufficient social roles with attainable standards to ensure that as many people as possible are capable of securing this very necessary psychological asset—self-esteem.

REFERENCES

Baumeister, R. F., Campbell, J. D., Krueger, J. I., & Vohs, K. D. (2003). Does high self-esteem cause better performance, interpersonal success, happiness, or healthier lifestyles? *Psychological Science in the Public Interest, 4*, 1–44.

Becker, E. (1971). *The birth and death of meaning.* New York: Free Press.

Becker, E. (1973). *The denial of death.* New York: Free Press.

Becker, E. (1975). *Escape from evil*. New York: Free Press.

Bowlby, J. (1969). *Attachment and loss: Vol. 1. Attachment*. New York: Basic Books.

Greenberg, J., Pyszczynski, T., & Solomon, S. (1986). The causes and consequences of a need for self-esteem: A terror management theory. In R. F. Baumeister (Ed.), *Public self and private self* (pp. 189–212). New York: Springer.

Greenberg, J., Pyszczynski, T., Solomon, S., Pinel, E., Simon, L., & Jordan, K. (1993). Effects of self-esteem on vulnerability-denying defensive distortions: Further evidence of an anxiety-buffering function of self-esteem. *Journal of Experimental Social Psychology, 29*, 229–251.

Greenberg, J., Solomon, S., & Pyszczynski, T. (1997). Terror management theory of self-esteem and cultural worldviews: Empirical assessments and conceptual refinements. In Mark Zanna (Ed.), *Advances in experimental social psychology* (Vol. 29, pp. 61–139). Orlando, FL: Academic Press.

Greenberg, J., Solomon, S., Pyszczynski, T., Rosenblatt, A., Burling, J., Lyon, D., & Simon, L. (1992). Assessing the terror management analysis of self-esteem: Converging evidence of an anxiety-buffering function. *Journal of Personality and Social Psychology, 63*, 913–922.

Harmon-Jones, E., Simon, L., Greenberg, J., Pyszczynski, T., Solomon, S., & McGregor, H. (1997). Terror management theory and self-esteem: Evidence that increased self-esteem reduces mortality salience effects. *Journal of Personality and Social Psychology, 72*, 24–36.

James, W. (1890). *Principles of psychology*. New York: Henry Holt.

Markus, H., & Kitayama, S. (1991). Culture and the self: Implications for cognition, emotion, and motivation. *Psychological Review, 98*, 224–253.

Nietzsche, F. (1974). *The gay science*. New York: Vintage Books. (Original work published 1887)

Pyszczynski, T., Greenberg, J., Solomon, S., Arndt, J., & Schimel, J. (2004). Why do people need self-esteem? A theoretical and empirical review. *Psychological Bulletin, 130*, 435–468.

Roheim, G. (1934). The evolution of culture. *International Journal of Psycho-Analysis, XV*, 387–418.

Solomon, S., Greenberg, J., & Pyszczynski, T. (1991). A terror management theory of social behavior: The psychological functions of self-esteem and cultural worldviews. In M. Zanna (Ed.), *Advances in experimental social psychology* (Vol. 24, pp. 91–159). Orlando, FL: Academic Press.

Taubman Ben-Ari, O., Florian, V., & Mikulincer, M. (1999). The impact of mortality salience on reckless driving: A test of terror management mechanisms. *Journal of Personality and Social Psychology, 76*, 35–45.

Triandis, H. (1994). *Culture and social behavior*. New York: McGraw-Hill.

34

Examining the Role of Self-Esteem in Psychological Functioning and Well-Being

ERIKA J. KOCH

*I*s self-esteem central to functioning? An initial examination of the self-esteem literature suggests that it is. Research has linked low self-esteem with a wealth of negative emotions and behaviors, including anxiety, loneliness, jealousy, unsafe sex, teenage pregnancy, criminal behavior, eating disorders, substance abuse, depression, and membership in deviant groups (Leary, Schreindorfer, & Haupt, 1995). People with low self-esteem seem to be less resilient than people with high self-esteem, as they have fewer domains from which to self-affirm when threatened (Spencer, Josephs, & Steele, 1993). Low self-esteem may even carry negative consequences in relationships: people with low self-esteem may mistakenly perceive rejection where it does not exist and may overly scrutinize problems with their romantic partners (Murray, Rose, Bellavia, Holmes, & Kusche, 2002). Similarly, rejection apparently affects people with low self-esteem more strongly than it affects people with high self-esteem (Sommer & Baumeister, 2002), and even ambiguous cues about social situations may prime rejection for people with low (but not high) self-esteem (Koch, 2002).

Given the wealth of negative emotions and behaviors linked to low self-esteem, it is not surprising that many efforts to raise self-esteem today focus on children, presumably in the hopes of preventing later negative outcomes. Contemporary esteem-boosting efforts may be rooted in earlier work such as Coopersmith's (1967), which suggested that children's low self-esteem was associated with neuroses, psychoses, and a general inability to cope with life. Coopersmith thus served as an early advocate for interventions to raise children's self-esteem. More recently, researchers such as Harter (1993) have suggested that low self-esteem is a risk factor for suicide and depression. Thus, in both children and adults, low self-esteem is associated with various negative outcomes.

Conversely, numerous findings link high self-esteem with various positive outcomes, including initiative, happiness, socioeconomic status, and general life satisfaction (e.g., Baumeister, Campbell, Krueger, & Vohs, 2003; Kwan, Bond, & Singelis, 1997; Twenge & Campbell, 2002). Recent promising findings suggesting self-esteem's benefits also include an apparent prevention of bulimia (Baumeister et al., 2003), and a historical decrease in negative social indicators (e.g., violent crime, suicide) coinciding with a rise in self-esteem (Twenge & Campbell, 2001). At a broader level, recent theorizing suggests that self-esteem may provide a buffer against anxiety about death (Greenberg, Pysczynski, & Solomon, 1986). In sum, to quote a top-selling introductory psychology text, "High self-esteem—a feeling of self-worth—pays dividends" (Myers, 2001, p. 514).

A CLOSER LOOK AT THE SELF-ESTEEM RESEARCH

If high self-esteem indeed yields such dividends, then self-esteem would certainly be central to functioning. Are such dividends, though, actually the result of high self-esteem? A closer examination of the literature suggests that self-esteem is, in actuality, not central to functioning. A recent, comprehensive review of the self-esteem literature revealed scant evidence that self-esteem actually *causes* positive outcomes, with the possible exception of happiness (which, unlike other outcomes examined, can be assessed only through self-report; Baumeister et al., 2003). Although school systems and educators have widely promoted self-esteem, the evidence that boosting self-esteem actually bolsters academic performance is weak, with effects ranging from nonsignificant to negligible (Baumeister et al., 2003). Even the architects of one of the most ambitious self-esteem promotion efforts—the California Task Force to Promote Self-Esteem and Personal and Social Responsibility—ultimately admitted that the relationships between self-esteem and desired behaviors were disappointingly low (Baumeister et al., 2003; Swann, 1996).

If high self-esteem does not promote positive behaviors, might low self-esteem nevertheless promote negative behaviors? Research suggests that it does not. For example, contrary to early speculation, a recent review of the literature concluded that no evidence currently exists to suggest that low self-esteem causes aggression (Baumeister, Smart, & Bowden, 1996). In fact, threatened egoism (or narcissism) apparently creates aggression (Bushman & Baumeister, 1998). Furthermore, given the correlational nature of much of the research suggesting negative consequences of low self-esteem, the wealth of negative behaviors associated with low self-esteem may be *causes* of low self-esteem, rather than *consequences* of low self-esteem (Leary et al., 1995).

The findings that high self-esteem does not necessarily promote positive outcomes, and that low self-esteem does not necessarily promote negative outcomes, call into question the efforts to raise self-esteem. As early as 1890, William James suggested that one method to raise self-esteem simply involved lowering one's "pretensions," or what one strives to achieve. In other words, raising one's self-esteem may simply require lowering one's standards. Attempts to raise self-esteem may ultimately prove counterproductive, as children may fail to learn the difference between acceptable and unacceptable work. They may not experience the unique positive feeling of earning a good grade when esteem-boosting praise is given regardless of the quality of work (Baumeister et al., 2003). Similarly, a recent meta-analytic review reveals that high school and college students' self-esteem scores do not show significant relationships with social indicators, and as self-esteem scores have increased historically, objective indicators of competency (e.g., Scholastic Aptitude Test scores) have decreased (Twenge & Campbell, 2001). Experimental evidence also indicates that when people feel socially accepted, they may experience high self-esteem even in the face of failure, suggesting that efforts to shield self-esteem from negative performance feedback may be misguided (Koch & Shepperd, 2003).

Furthermore, research revealing the "darker" side of high self-esteem suggests that having high self-esteem will not necessarily lead to healthy psychological functioning (Baumeister et al., 1996). For example, high yet unstable self-esteem is associated with heightened levels of aggression under conditions of threat (Kernis & Waschull, 1995). High self-esteem may foster experimentation in risky behaviors (Baumeister et al., 2003), and people with high self-esteem may resist threatening information relevant to their risk behaviors, ultimately resulting in unrealistically low perceptions of risk (Boney-McCoy, Gibbons, & Gerrard, 1999; Smith, Gerrard, & Gibbons, 1997). Thus, high self-esteem may not be the psychological cure that once seemed so promising.

THE PREOCCUPATION WITH SELF-ESTEEM

Despite the lack of evidence suggesting that self-esteem plays a central role in functioning and well-being, a popular obsession with self-esteem remains. Since the self-esteem movement blossomed in the late 1970s, self-esteem has pervaded American culture. Recent researchers have documented an increase in self-esteem research, as well as the mainstream prevalence of self-esteem on the World Wide Web (Baumeister et al., 2003; Twenge & Campbell, 2001). Although the self-esteem movement initially focused on adults (Twenge & Campbell, 2001), the movement soon extended to children and persists today. A recent web search for "self-esteem program" yielded 2,430 hits (November 2003), revealing a multitude of story books, workshops, and lesson plans—many with their own corresponding testimonials. Self-esteem even has its own web site—self-esteem.com—that purports to teach its viewers how to raise their self-esteem and handle various psychological difficulties.

Given the lack of evidence suggesting self-esteem's benefits, what might explain the United States' persistent preoccupation with self-esteem? Several possibilities come to mind. First, the popular definition of self-esteem may not match the psychological definition of self-esteem. Perhaps confusion arises because people use "self-esteem" as an umbrella term, encompassing not only positive self-feelings but also general feelings of happiness. Second, the notion that self-esteem yields positive outcomes is intuitive. Because high self-esteem feels good, people may naturally conclude that it results in positive consequences. A common-sense interpretation of the correlations between self-esteem and positive outcomes suggests that self-esteem actually *leads to* those outcomes. Thus, even those familiar with some psychological research might conclude that self-esteem causes various positive outcomes.

The continued interest in self-esteem may also stem from the desire for a "quick fix" to solve complex social problems (Swann, 1996). As a prime example, the California Task Force to Promote Self-Esteem and Personal and Social Responsibility apparently resulted partly from concern over California's state budget: "people with self-esteem produce income and pay taxes...[people without self-esteem] tend to be users of taxes" (as cited in Baumeister et al., 2003). The belief that increasing self-esteem will both bolster the economy and cure social ills may be quite tempting. If successful, implementing a single program to boost self-esteem might be considerably less difficult and costly than implementing multiple programs designed to curtail drug use, teenage pregnancy, or dropout rates.

Similar temptation may appear in the classroom. Policies such as social promotion—passing children on to the next grade level regardless of academic performance—may reflect the belief that bolstering and preserving children's self-esteem ultimately reaps academic benefits. Furthermore, grade inflation may in part stem from concern over protecting students' self-esteem by refraining from assigning low grades. In support of this possibility, cross-cultural evidence suggests that North American teachers are more reluctant to give challenging assignments that potentially threaten self-esteem, whereas Japanese teachers are more likely to believe that children thrive when challenged (Heine, Lehman, Markus, & Kitayama, 2003).

IS THE PREOCCUPATION WITH SELF-ESTEEM IN THE UNITED STATES A CULTURAL ARTIFACT?

Such cross-cultural differences suggest that the current fascination with self-esteem may be unique to particular cultures. Perhaps as a logical extension of the United States' historically increasing individualism (e.g., Twenge & Campbell, 2001), Americans have become progressively more concerned with acquiring self-esteem. While self-esteem research has proliferated in the United States (Twenge & Campbell, 2001), self-esteem research has not flourished in Japan (Heine et al., 2003).

Such differences in research emphases may reflect cross-cultural differences in the conceptualization of the self. A fundamental difference across cultures involves the construal of the self: *independent* selves (presumably the products of individualistic cultures) are autonomous, self-contained, and focused on personal goals, whereas *interdependent* selves (presumably the products of collectivist cultures) are intimately connected to others in a social network, situationally bound, and focused on social harmony (Markus & Kitayama, 1991; Triandis, 1989). Western societies such as the United States tend to promote an independent view of the self, whereas Eastern societies such as Japan tend to promote an interdependent self.

As compared to Western cultures, non-Western cultures display a lack of esteem-boosting pursuits. This cross-cultural difference may reflect differences in the sources of self-esteem. In societies such as the United States, self-esteem may derive primarily from feelings of social acceptance and personal competence (e.g., Koch & Shepperd, 2003; Twenge & Campbell, 2001). In contrast, maintenance of social harmony forms the basis of self-esteem in interdependent cultures, and self-esteem is best understood within the social context (Markus & Kitayama, 1991). Self-esteem as the United States knows it may be a Western phenomenon, and self-satisfaction or culturally appropriate fulfillment of social roles may be the closest non-Western equivalent (Markus & Kitayama, 1991). The term "self-esteem" may not even be appropriate for interdependent cultures, as pride in accomplishments is not necessarily valued in non-Western cultures (Markus & Kitayama, 1991). In fact, the Japanese have had to import a term equivalent to "self-esteem," as indigenous words apparently carried more negative connotations (Heine et al., 2003).

Perhaps as a reflection of cross-cultural differences in the importance placed on self-esteem, the distribution of self-esteem scores appears quite different in the United States versus Japan. In the US, the distribution of a group of people completing a self-esteem instrument typically reveals that people classified as having "low" self-esteem by a median split procedure actually have scores that fall around the theoretical midpoint—not the low end—of the instrument (Tice, 1993). Thus, distributions of self-esteem scores in the US tend to be skewed, rather than normal. In contrast, distributions of self-esteem scores in Japan tend to be normal rather than skewed (Heine et al., 2003).

Americans' persistent pursuit of self-esteem may seem strange in countries such as Japan. As part of the interdependent self, the Japanese orientation is more self-critical than self-promoting, with a constant goal of improving rather than merely feeling good. Apparently, the Japanese do not pursue happiness as readily as Americans do, and they view self-assertion as immature and self-promotion as alienating (Heine et al., 2003; Markus & Kitayama, 1991). Differences in the pursuit of self-esteem also appear in differences in what comprises life satisfaction. Relationship harmony is a greater predictor of life satisfaction in Hong Kong than in the US, and conversely, self-esteem is a greater predictor of life satisfaction in the US than in Hong Kong (Kwan et al., 1997).

CONCLUSION

Although intuitive, the prediction that psychological functioning requires self-esteem has received surprisingly little empirical support. Despite the appeal of considering self-esteem a cure for social and psychological ills, research does not suggest that raising self-esteem will in turn promote positive behavior, reduce negative behavior, or foster academic or professional competence. In fact, self-esteem may be more a function of perceived acceptance than actual (or perceived) competence. For example, recent correlational research suggests that self-esteem is more strongly related to feelings of acceptance than feelings of competence, and similar experimental evidence suggests that rejection feedback lowers self-esteem, although failure feedback by itself does not (Koch & Shepperd, 2003). Optimal functioning may require a sense of self-efficacy (e.g., Bandura, 1997) without requiring a sense of high self-esteem. Similarly, satisfying a "need to belong" (Baumeister & Leary, 1995) may require feeling accepted by others, rather than feeling high self-esteem per se. Finally, although the United States may continue indefinitely with its self-esteem obsession, cultures that do not share an independent conceptualization of the self seem to find this obsession strange. The lack of universality of the quest for self-esteem also calls into question the necessity of it in everyday functioning.

ACKNOWLEDGMENT

I wish to thank James Shepperd and Lahnna Catalino for their comments.

REFERENCES

Bandura, A. (1997). *Self-efficacy: The exercise of control*. New York, NY: WH Freeman.

Baumeister, R. F., Campbell, J. D., Krueger, J. I., & Vohs, K. D. (2003). Does high self-esteem cause better performance, interpersonal success, happiness, or healthier lifestyles? *Psychological Science in the Public Interest, 4*, 1–44.

Baumeister, R. F., & Leary, M. R. (1995). The need to belong: Desire for interpersonal attachment as a fundamental human motivation. *Psychological Bulletin, 117*, 497–529.

Baumeister, R. F., Smart, L., & Boden, J. M. (1996). Relation of threatened egotism to violence and aggression: The dark side of high self-esteem. *Psychological Review, 103*, 5–33.

Boney-McCoy, S., Gibbons, F. X., & Gerrard, M. (1999). Self-esteem, compensatory self-enhancement, and the consideration of health risk. *Personality and Social Psychology Bulletin, 25*, 954–965.

Bushman, B. J., & Baumeister, R. F. (1998). Threatened egotism, narcissism, self-esteem, and direct and displaced aggression: Does self-love or self-hate lead to violence? *Journal of Personality and Social Psychology, 75*, 219–229.

Coopersmith, S. (1967). *The antecedents of self-esteem*. San Francisco, CA: WH Freeman.

Greenberg, J., Pysczynski, T., & Solomon, S. (1986). The causes and consequences of a need for self-esteem: A terror management theory. In R. F. Baumeister (Ed.), *Public self and private self* (pp. 189–212). New York: Springer.

Harter, S. (1993). Causes and consequences of low self-esteem in children and adolescents. In R. F. Baumeister (Ed.), *Low self-esteem: The puzzle of low self-regard* (pp. 87–116). New York, NY: Plenum Press.

Heine, S. J., Lehman, D. R., Markus, H. R., & Kitayama, S. (2003). Is there a universal need for positive self-regard? *Psychological Review, 106*, 766–794.

Kernis, M. H., & Waschull, S. B. (1995). The interactive roles of stability and level of self-esteem: Research and theory. *Advances in Experimental Social Psychology, 27*, 93–141.

Koch, E. J. (2002). Relational schemas, self-esteem, and the processing of social stimuli. *Self and Identity, 1*, 271–279.

Koch, E. J., & Shepperd, J. A. (2003). Is self-esteem more than a sociometer? Testing competence and acceptance explanations of self-esteem. Manuscript submitted for publication.

Kwan, V. S. Y., Bond, M. H., & Singelis, T. M. (1997). Pancultural explanations for life satisfaction: Adding relationship harmony to self-esteem. *Journal of Personality and Social Psychology, 73*, 1038–1051.

Leary, M. R., Schreindorfer, L. S., & Haupt, A. L. (1995). The role of low self-esteem in emotional and behavioral problems: Why is low self-esteem dysfunctional? *Journal of Social and Clinical Psychology, 14*, 297–314.

Markus, H. R., & Kitayama, S. (1991). Culture and the self: Implications for cognition, emotion, and motivation. *Psychological Review, 98*, 224–253.

Murray, S. L., Rose, P., Bellavia, G. M., Holmes, J. G., & Kusche, A. G. (2002). When rejection stings: How self-esteem constrains relationship-enhancement processes. *Journal of Personality and Social Psychology, 83*, 556–573.

Myers, D. G. (2001). *Psychology* (6th ed.). New York: Worth Publishers.

Smith, G. E., Gerrard, M., & Gibbons, F. X. (1997). Self-esteem and the relation between risk behavior and perceptions of vulnerability to unplanned pregnancy in college women. *Health Psychology, 16*, 137–146.

Sommer, K. L., & Baumeister, R. F. (2002). Self-evaluation, persistence, and performance following implicit rejection: The role of trait self-esteem. *Personality and Social Psychology Bulletin, 28*, 926–938.

Spencer, S. J., Josephs, R. A., & Steele, C. M. (1993). Low self-esteem: The uphill struggle for self-integrity. In R. F. Baumeister (Ed.), *Low self-esteem: The puzzle of low self-regard* (pp. 21–36). New York, NY: Plenum Press.

Swann, W. B. (1996). *Self-traps: The elusive quest for higher self-esteem.* New York, NY: WH Freeman.

Tice, D. M. (1993). The social motivations of people with low self-esteem. In R. F. Baumeister (Ed.), *Low self-esteem: The puzzle of low self-regard* (pp. 37–53). New York, NY: Plenum Press.

Triandis, H. C. (1989). The self and social behavior in differing cultural contexts. *Psychological Review, 96*, 506–520.

Twenge, J. M., & Campbell, W. K. (2001). Age and birth cohort differences in self-esteem: A cross-temporal meta-analysis. *Personality and Social Psychology Review, 5*, 321–344.

Twenge, J. M., & Campbell, W. K. (2002). Self-esteem and socioeconomic status: A meta-analytic review. *Personality and Social Psychology Review, 6*, 59–71.

35

Self-Esteem Processes are Central to Psychological Functioning and Well-Being

ABRAHAM TESSER and LEONARD L. MARTIN

S elf-esteem does not have a universally agreed upon meaning. For some, self-esteem is an entity associated with individuals. Some people have more of it; some have less of it. Some people are variable with respect to it; some are stable. It is an individual difference that psychologists think makes a difference. An alternative perspective, one that we find more congenial, is to address self-esteem as a process involving goal pursuit. We believe that this process is important to psychological functioning and to personal well-being.

SELF-ESTEEM PROCESSES ARE CENTRAL

From our perspective, self-esteem involves *goal states* some of which are common to most individuals; others of which are idiosyncratic. What these goals states have in common is that they are *a significant part of the self-definition*. They are the personally relevant end states toward which we strive. They may pertain to moral dictums (e.g., be honest), they may pertain to competencies (e.g., build strong furniture), or they may pertain to social recognitions (e.g., be a good son; don't be excluded from the group.) Not all goals are self-definitional nor are they all related to self-esteem. A person may be hungry, for example, but whether the person has a hamburger is not necessarily part of the person's self-definition. On the other hand, whether the person adheres to the Atkins diet may very well be self-defining. What we are referring to as self-esteem ties these self-relevant goals together.

Self-related goals function as do other goals. As such they have the properties of docility (individuals settle upon the shortest/easiest path to the goal), persistence (individuals cease pursuing the goal only after the goal has been attained or abandoned), and equifinality (there are many paths to the same goal). So, how does one distinguish self-relevant goals from other goals? We describe four ways.

First, different kinds of goals often can be distinguished from one another via self-report. People tend to describe their pursuit of self-relevant goals in terms as of their personal values, the kind of person they are, or simply because it is the right thing to do, i.e., a moral imperative. The pursuit of non-self-relevant goals is often explained in terms of instrumentalities that have no implications for self-worth, e.g., I am pursuing this goal because a person has to eat, because it is the law, in order to get a good salary/raise. Stated this way, the term *self-relevant goal* has a clear resonance with the concept of intrinsic interest. We avoid using the latter term, however, because that term often carries with it a set of theoretical assumptions that are orthogonal to our present purposes. For example, theorists concerned with intrinsic interest often omit the elaboration of the accoutrement of goal completion. For these theorists, engaging in the activity, regardless of outcome seems to be enough. We suggest that outcomes of self-relevant goal pursuit are consequential to a larger and connected self-system. This distinction may become clearer as we discuss other unique aspects of self-relevant goals.

More central to present concerns is the observation that progress toward self-goals is associated with changes in feelings of self-worth or self-esteem. In an interesting study, Quinn and Crocker (1999) measured the extent to which participants endorsed the Protestant Ethic. They also measured each participant's weight and feelings of self-worth. Not surprisingly, normal weight individuals generally reported higher self-worth than obese individuals. Importantly, this relationship held only for those who strongly endorsed the Protestant Ethic. There was no association for those who did not endorse it.

These findings make sense in the context of a goal view of self-worth. Self-control is an important part of the Protestant ethic, so for those who endorse this ethic controlling one's weight is self-relevant. For these people, failure to control their weight is a sign that they are morally weak, whereas being in good shape is a sign they are morally strong. Individuals who do not endorse the Protestant ethic do not make these inferences. Thus, failure to control one's weight lowers self-worth only where controlling one's weight is significant to the self. Note also that although weight control is self-relevant for endorsers, one would hardly call controlling one's weight an intrinsic interest or activity.

Self-relevant goals also differ from other goals in the kinds of emotions with which they are associated. All goals lead to positive emotions, e.g., joy, happiness, as we approach those goals and negative emotions such as frustration, anger as progress is slowed or stopped. Self-relevant goals, however, are also associated with "self emotions" such as pride, shame, guilt, and embarrassment. Important self-standards are central to triggering each of these emotions and these emotions are associated with behaviors that lead to self-relevant behaviors. For example, the experience of shame is associated with the desire to hide the self and guilt with attempts to make personal reparation (Tangney, 2002). These emotions play a crucial role in self-regulation and social functioning (Keltner & Beer, in press).

A fourth characteristic of self-relevant goals is that they are substitutable for one another. According to Lewin, when one behavior substitutes for another we can infer that the two behaviors serve the same goal. There are some quite compelling demonstrations that self-relevant behaviors can substitute for one another. The classic demonstration by Steele and Liu (1983) showed that allowing people to affirm themselves in one domain decreased dissonance reduction in a different domain. It is worth noting that all participants in the study engaged in the self-affirming activity. However, it was only among those for whom that activity was self important that the dissonance was reduced. It is also worth noting that there is nothing special about self-affirmation in this regard. Additional work suggests that dissonant behaviors can affect the propensity to self-affirm and a variety of other self-relevant behaviors, e.g., those resulting in social comparison can affect and be affected by both of these (Tesser, 2000, 2001; Tesser, Crepaz, Collins, Cornell, & Beach, 2000). This mutual substitutability can be easily explained by assuming that each type of behavior serves a common goal, i.e., maintenance of self-worth (Tesser, Martin, & Cornell, 1996).

We have suggested that self-esteem is central to psychological functioning. The preceding paragraphs suggest that individual concerns with self-esteem are frequent; that the processes associated with maintaining or experiencing positive or negative self-feelings are broad and encompass almost every area of human functioning. Are goal-related self-esteem processes also associated with happiness and well-being? Again, we would argue in the affirmative.

SELF-ESTEEM-RELATED PROCESSES ARE IMPORTANT TO WELL-BEING

If our analysis is correct, then failure to obtain self-relevant goals, particularly if substitution is not available, should lead to negative states of well-being. Such states should manifest themselves as negative affect, depression, rumination, and lowered self-esteem (Martin & Tesser, 1996; Martin, Tesser, & McIntosh, 1993). Indeed, there is evidence consistent with this logic.

Koole, Smeets, van Knippenberg, and Dijksterhuis (1999) reported a series of three studies that directly addressed these issues. In these experiments, participants were randomly assigned to either a success or a failure condition on a self-relevant task. Some participants were given a chance to affirm themselves. From our perspective, affirmation is an alternative route to the goal of maintaining positive self-evaluation. Results over the three studies showed that failure resulted in increased rumination, increased negative affect, and lowered self-esteem compared to success. However, the opportunity to affirm the self eliminated the negative consequences of failure. Participants who failed but self-affirmed showed no rumination, no decrease in self-esteem, and no increase in negative affect. In sum, self-related goals play a consequential role in affecting indicators of well-being. Moreover, the functioning of these goals highlights the kind of systemic effects i.e., substitution, inherent in our process view of self-esteem.

We have suggested that problems can arise when the opportunity to substitute goals is unavailable. A substitute may be unavailable for at least two reasons. The situation may not permit substitution or the person may fail to adopt the substitution that a situation affords. A series of studies by McIntosh, Harlow, and Martin [1995; see also McIntosh, Martin, & Jones (1997)] addressed this second possibility. They measured individual differences in the extent to which an individual is able to shift goals. That is some individuals, i.e., "linkers," report that their happiness is contingent on satisfying specific goals; whereas others indicate that they could be happy even if their present goals were unmet. By implication, linkers cannot see the possibility of other (substitute) goals satisfying them. As a result, we would expect linkers to be more likely to ruminate about unattained goals and experience negative affect. This is the case. More specifically, for linkers compared to non-linkers the correlation between negative life events and depression was stronger. Similarly, for linkers compared to non-linkers the correlations between number of hassles and both depression and rumination were stronger.

In conclusion, we take a process view of self-esteem. We argue that self-esteem is involved in the playing out of self-relevant goals. It is central in that many goals are self-relevant and they are systemic, i.e., being mutually substitutable for one another. At the same time, the playing out of the self-relevant goal process appears to have nontrivial effects on well-being. The failure to satisfy self-relevant goals, either directly or via substitution, leaves the individual susceptible to rumination, negative affect, depression, or lowered self-esteem.

REFERENCES

Keltner, D., & Beer, J. S. (in press.). Self conscious emotion and self-regulation. In A. Tesser, J. W. Wood, & D. W. Stapel (Eds.), *On building, defending and regulating the self: A psychological perspective*. New York: Psychology Press.

Koole, S. L., Smeets, K., van Knippenberg, A., & Dijksterhuis, A. (1999). The cessation of rumination through self-affirmation. *Journal of Personality & Social Psychology*, 77(1), 111–125.

Martin, L., & Tesser, A. (1996). Some ruminative thoughts. In R. S. Wyer (Ed.), *Advances in social cognition* (Vol. 9, pp. 1–48). Hillsdale, NJ: Lawrence Erlbaum Associates, Inc.

Martin, L. L., Tesser, A., & McIntosh, W. D. (1993). Wanting but not having: The effects of unattained goals on thoughts and feelings. In D. M. Wegner & J. W. Pennebaker (Eds.), *The handbook of mental control* (pp. 552–572). New York: Prentice-Hall.

McIntosh, W. D., Harlow, T. F., & Martin, L. L. (1995). Linkers and nonlinkers: Goal beliefs as a moderator of the effects of everyday hassles on rumination, depression, and physical complaints. *Journal of Applied Social Psychology*, 25(14), 1231–1244.

McIntosh, W. D., Martin, L. L., & Jones, J. B. III (1997). Goal beliefs, life events, and the malleability of people's judgments of their happiness. *Journal of Social Behavior & Personality*, 12(2), 567–575.

Quinn, D. M., & Crocker, J. (1999). When ideology hurts: Effects of belief in the Protestant ethic and feeling overweight on the psychological well-being of women. *Journal of Personality & Social Psychology*, 77(2), 402–414.

Steele, C. M., & Liu, T. J. (1983). Dissonance processes as self-affirmation. Journal of *Personality and Social Psychology*, 45, 5–19.

Tangney, J. P. (2002). Self-conscious emotions: The self as a moral guide. In A. Tesser, D. A. Stapel, & J. W. Wood (Eds.), *Self and motivation: Emerging psychological perspectives* (pp. 97–118). Washington, DC: APA.

Tesser, A. (2000). On the confluence of self-esteem maintenance mechanisms. *Personality and Social Psychology Review*, 4, 290–299.

Tesser, A. (2001). On the plasticity of self defense. *Current Directions in Psychological Science, 10*, 66–69.

Tesser, A., Crepaz, N., Collins, J. C., Cornell, D., & Beach, S. R. H. (2000). Confluence of self defense mechanisms: On integrating the self zoo. *Personality and Social Psychology Bulletin, 26*, 1476–1489.

Tesser, A., Martin, L., & Cornell, D. (1996). On the substitutability of self-protective mechanisms. In P. M. Gollwitzer & J. A. Bargh (Eds.), *The psychology of action: Linking motivation and cognition to behavior* (pp. 48–68). New York: Guilford.

Question 12

Are striving for and possessing high self-esteem always positive or healthy? What are the costs and benefits of directly orienting one's daily behaviors toward seeking high self-esteem?

The essays in this section address the costs and benefits of possessing and striving for high self-esteem.

Crocker begins her essay by describing some costs and benefits of possessing high trait self-esteem. As she notes, the clearest benefits of high trait self-esteem are experiencing positive emotions and possessing positive and certain self-concepts. Costs to possessing high trait self-esteem are most apparent following ego-threat. She then turns to her own work that focuses on the costs and benefits of pursuing self-esteem. This work demonstrates that although pursing self-esteem may have some short-term emotional and motivational benefits, they are overshadowed by costs to individuals' autonomy, learning, interpersonal relationships, and mental and physical health.

Rhodewalt also elaborates some of the costs of pursuing high self-esteem. He first distinguishes secure (true, authentic, and stable) from insecure (contingent, inauthentic, and unstable) high self-esteem and asserts that the latter is unhealthy and problematic precisely because it involves constant self-esteem striving. Rhodewalt provides a self-regulatory framework to characterize fragile high self-esteem individuals' attempts to validate positive self-evaluations about which they are insecure. He suggests that, ironically, these strivings may only serve to perpetuate individuals' insecurity and uncertainty.

Wood, Anthony, and Foddis take a different tack and focus on the specific question of whether individuals with low trait self-esteem benefit from striving for high self-esteem. They distinguish between "self-evaluative" and "non-self-evaluative" methods and describe mechanisms by which self-evaluative methods may be ineffective or detrimental. Self-evaluative methods include positive self-statements and success experiences. The authors propose that whereas these methods may backfire for a variety of reasons, non-self-evaluative methods may sometimes be helpful precisely because they avoid these detrimental self-evaluative processes.

36

Having and Pursuing Self-Esteem: Costs and Benefits

JENNIFER CROCKER

W ith a few notable exceptions, most research on self-esteem has focused exclusively on level of trait self-esteem—whether people typically or characteristically have high or low self-regard. Independent of whether people have high or low trait self-esteem, however, they may pursue self-esteem. That is, they may organize their behavior around the goal of maintaining, protecting, or enhancing self-esteem by demonstrating that they have certain abilities or qualities (Crocker & Park, 2004a). People with either high or low trait self-esteem may pursue self-esteem.

BENEFITS AND COSTS OF HAVING HIGH SELF-ESTEEM

Hundreds of studies have demonstrated the benefits of having high trait self-esteem. The clearest benefits are the positive emotions, and the positive and certain self-concepts that accompany high self-esteem.

Emotional Benefits

Self-esteem is strongly related to the affective tone of daily life, with high self-esteem people reporting more positive affect, more life satisfaction, less anxiety, less hopelessness, and fewer depressive symptoms than people who are low in self-esteem. Self-esteem is the strongest predictor of life satisfaction in the United States, outstripping other predictors such as age, income, education, physical health, and marital status, and all other psychological variables. These effects are typically large, with correlations around .60. Although high self-esteem is strongly correlated with positive emotions, evidence that it causes them is less clear (Baumeister, Campbell, Krueger, & Vohs, 2003).

Self-Concept Benefits

Self-esteem is also related to the beliefs people hold about themselves. High self-esteem people believe they are intelligent, attractive, and popular (Baumeister et al., 2003). Although high self-esteem people acknowledge that they had flaws or made mistakes in the distant past, they see their present or recent past selves in a particularly positive light, believing they have changed for the better even when concurrent evaluations suggest they have not (Ross, 2002; Wilson & Ross, 2001). High self-esteem people believe they are superior to others in many domains, and they expect their futures to be rosy relative to others (Taylor & Brown, 1988). Consequently, high self-esteem people have more self-confidence than low self-esteem people, especially following an initial failure (Baumeister et al., 2003).

Objective Benefits

In light of the positive emotions and favorable beliefs about the self associated with high self-esteem, it seems reasonable to think that people who have high self-esteem fare better in terms of the objective outcomes they experience in life—that they would not only be happier but also richer, more successful, better loved, and perhaps even more attractive than low self-esteem people. Although researchers have long speculated that high self-esteem also has objective benefits, these hypothesized benefits are typically small or nonexistent. For example, a recent and extensive review concluded that high self-esteem produces pleasant feelings and enhanced initiative, but does not cause high academic achievement, good job performance, or leadership, nor does low self-esteem cause violence, smoking, drinking, taking drugs, or becoming sexually active at an early age (Baumeister et al., 2003).

Costs

Some recent evidence suggests that high self-esteem has costs, especially under conditions of ego threat. For example, high self-esteem people are more likely to persist in the face of failure, but this creates problems when failure is unavoidable and persistence does not pay (Baumeister et al., 2003). High self-esteem people under ego threat become overconfident and take risks, sometimes losing money as a result (Baumeister, Heatherton, & Tice, 1993).

Although having high self-esteem has strong emotional benefits for the self, it may have costs for other people. For example, the positive and certain self-concepts of high self-esteem people often lead them to become hostile, defensive, and blaming when things go badly (Blaine & Crocker, 1993). High self-esteem people become less likable, whereas low self-esteem people become more likable under ego threat (Heatherton & Vohs, 2000; Vohs & Heatherton, 2001).

Conclusions

In general, it seems likely that both low and high self-esteem are helpful or adaptive in some situations, and not adaptive in others. Because low self-esteem people doubt their abilities and worry about whether others will accept them, they tend to integrate feedback from others (Brockner, 1984), yet lack the self-confidence to act on their goals, or drive others away through their need for reassurance (Joiner, Alfano, & Metalsky, 1992). Because high self-esteem people tend to think well of themselves, and overestimate their intelligence, attractiveness, and likability, they may be less realistic about their strengths and weaknesses than people who score lower on measures of self-esteem (Taylor & Brown, 1988). These positive illusions can be helpful or unhelpful, depending on the circumstances. For example, the positive self-views associated with high self-esteem may be helpful for asking the boss for a raise, but interfere with understanding her feedback about areas in which one needs to improve before a raise is forthcoming. Although focusing on one's strengths and minimizing one's weaknesses often foster positive mood, optimism, and perseverance, when one's weaknesses interfere with accomplishing important goals and can be addressed, the exaggeratedly positive and highly certain self-views of high self-esteem may be an obstacle to recognizing and addressing their weaknesses and accomplishing their goals.

BENEFITS AND COSTS OF PURSUING SELF-ESTEEM

In contrast to most research on the costs and benefits of *having* high or low trait self-esteem, my own research is focused on the costs and benefits of *pursuing* self-esteem. This research focuses on what people believe they need to be or do to have worth and value as a person, and how they regulate their behavior around the goal of demonstrating that they *are* those things. Generally, people want to prove that they have the abilities or qualities that they believe give them value or worth as a person (Crocker & Park, 2004a). Although pursuing self-esteem and having self-esteem might seem logically connected (Pyszczynski & Cox, 2004; Sheldon, 2004), they are both theoretically and empirically distinct; people with both high and low trait self-esteem can pursue self-esteem, and pursuing self-esteem is not a guarantee that one will be successful, and achieve high self-esteem (Crocker & Park, 2004b). Successful pursuit of self-esteem raises state self-esteem, but the magnitude of the boost to self-esteem is smaller than the drop in self-esteem when one fails at this pursuit (Crocker, Karpinski, Quinn, & Chase, 2003; Crocker, Sommers, & Luhtanen, 2002). In other words, the pursuit of self-esteem may paradoxically lower self-esteem more than it raises it, and lead to a relentless quest for self-esteem.

The pursuit of self-esteem, when it is successful, has emotional and motivational benefits, but both short- and long-term costs, diverting people from fulfilling their fundamental human needs for competence, relatedness, and autonomy, and leading to poor self-regulation and mental and physical health (Crocker & Park, 2004a). When they pursue self-esteem, people often create the opposite of what they need to thrive, and inflict costs on others as well. People pursue self-esteem through different avenues, and some of these have higher costs than others, but even "healthier" ways of pursuing self-esteem have costs (Crocker & Park, 2004a).

Emotional and Motivational Benefits and Costs

When people pursue self-esteem, they become ego-involved in events. Success means not only, "I succeeded," but also, "I am worthy." Failure means not only "I failed," but also "I am worthless." Consequently, when people succeed in a domain in which their self-worth is invested, they experience intense positive emotions, and when they fail they experience intense negative emotion (Crocker & Park, 2004a). These emotions shape motivation; people seek the "high" they get from succeeding at the pursuit of self-esteem, but want to avoid the "low" associated with failure (Wolfe & Crocker, 2003).

Costs for Autonomy
When people pursue self-esteem, they are susceptible to stress, pressure, and anxiety because failure suggests they are worthless. As Deci and his colleagues suggest, "The type of ego involvement in which one's "worth" is on the line—in which one's self-esteem is contingent upon an outcome—is an example of internally controlling regulation that results from introjection. One is behaving because one feels one has to and not because one wants to, and this regulation is accompanied by the experience of pressure and tension" (Deci, Eghrari, Patrick, & Leone, 1994, p. 121). Students whose self-esteem is contingent on academic performance experience pressure to succeed and lose intrinsic motivation. College students who base their self-esteem on academic performance report experiencing more time pressure, academic struggles, conflicts with professors and teaching assistants, and pressure to make academic decisions than less contingent students (Crocker & Luhtanen, 2003).

Costs for Learning
The pursuit of self-esteem interferes with learning and mastery (Covington, 1984). When people have self-validation goals, mistakes, failures, criticism, and negative feedback are self-threats rather than opportunities to learn and improve. Because negative self-relevant information in domains of contingent self-worth implies that one is lacking the quality on which self-esteem is staked, people resist and challenge such information (Baumeister, 1998). If failure or negative feedback cannot be explained away, people search for other ways to restore their self-esteem, for example compensatory self-enhancement or downward comparison. When self-worth is at stake, people want to avoid failure, even if doing so undermines learning (Covington, 1984). For example, students with contingent self-worth in the academic domain report that they would be willing to cheat if they were unable to succeed at a task (Covington, 1984). All of these reactions to self-threat are focused on maintaining, protecting, or restoring self-esteem following negative self-relevant information, rather than learning from the experience.

Costs to Relationships
When people pursue self-esteem, relatedness is hindered because they become focused on themselves at the expense of others' needs and feelings. People pursuing self-esteem want to be superior to others. Consequently, other people become competitors and enemies rather than supports and resources. Whether the response is distancing, avoidance, and withdrawal, or blaming, anger, and aggression, connections with others are sacrificed. These

defensive reactions may result in isolation and disconnection from others and hinder the formation of meaningful, authentic, supportive relationships (Crocker & Park, 2004a).

Costs for Self-Regulation

The pursuit of self-esteem interferes with self-regulation. Because self-esteem has powerful consequences for emotion, when self-esteem is threatened, people often indulge in immediate impulses to make themselves feel better, giving short-term affect regulation priority over other self-regulatory goals (Tice et al., 2001). Procrastination and self-handicapping, for example, protect self-esteem by creating excuses for failure, but decrease the chances of success. The failures of self-regulation that result from the emotional distress associated with self-esteem threat can result in self-destructive behavior (Baumeister, 1997).

Costs for Mental Health

People who tend to approach situations and events with self-esteem goals are high in symptoms of depression (Dykman, 1998). The tendency to overgeneralize negative events to the worth of the entire self, characteristic of people with self-esteem goals, is related to depression and prospectively predicts the development of depressive symptoms (Carver, 1998). Instability of self-esteem caused by success and failure in domains of contingency can contribute to depressive symptoms (Kernis et al., 1998). For example, temporal variability in self-esteem, together with life stress, prospectively predicted the onset of depressive symptoms in a sample of college students (Roberts & Kassel, 1997).

Costs for Physical Health

Although research has not directly examined the links, the pursuit of self-esteem likely has long-term costs to physical health. Self-esteem goals may lead to physical health problems through anxiety and stress. People with self-esteem goals tend to be highly anxious (Dykman, 1998), and anxiety has negative effects on health (Suinn, 2001). Stress and anxiety are associated with activation of the pituitary–adrenal–cortical system, which releases corticosteroids from the adrenal cortex (Hellhammer & Wade, 1993), compromising immune system functioning, and resulting in greater susceptibility to illnesses such as upper respiratory infections (Kiecolt-Glaser, Cacioppo, Malarkey, & Glaser, 1992). People who pursue self-esteem also tend to be hostile, especially when they experience threats to self-worth (Kernis, Brown, & Brody, 2000). Hostility is a risk factor for coronary heart disease, and also diminishes immune system functioning (Kiecolt-Glaser et al., 1992). Pursuing self-esteem may lead to physical health problems through unhealthy coping behavior, such as abuse of alcohol, and other health-risk behaviors such as smoking, tanning, excessive dieting, and use of steroids (Leary, Tchividjian, & Kraxberger, 1994).

Conclusion

The pursuit of self-esteem has short-term emotional benefits, and some motivational benefits, but it has both immediate and long-term costs for autonomy, learning, relationships, and mental and physical health. People typically are more aware of the emotional benefits of pursuing self-esteem, and surprisingly unaware of the wide range of costs that pursuing self-esteem has in their lives, and the lives of those around them. The emotional benefits of successful pursuit of self-esteem are intense and immediate, obscuring the longer-term costs, especially the costs to others. Recognizing the costs of pursuing self-esteem can threaten self-esteem, so people may avoid the self-reflection required to fully appreciate those costs. When people are unaware of the costs of their pursuit of self-esteem, they may be caught in a misery of their own making.

REFERENCES

Baumeister, R. F. (1997). Esteem threat, self-regulatory breakdown, and emotional distress as factors in self-defeating behavior. *Review of General Psychology, 1*, 145–174.

Baumeister, R. F. (1998). The self. In D. T. Gilbert, S. T. Fiske, & G. Lindzey (Eds.), *The handbook of social psychology* (4th ed., Vol. 2, pp. 680–740). New York: McGraw-Hill.

Baumeister, R. F., Campbell, J. D., Krueger, J. I., & Vohs, K. D. (2003). Does high self-esteem cause better performance, interpersonal success, happiness, or healthier lifestyles? *Psychological Science in the Public Interest, 4*, 1–44.

Baumeister, R. F., Heatherton, T. F., & Tice, D. M. (1993). When ego threats lead to self-regulation failure: Negative consequences of high self-esteem. *Journal of Personality and Social Psychology, 64*, 141–156.

Blaine, B., & Crocker, J. (1993). Self-esteem and self-serving biases in reactions to positive and negative events: An integrative review. In R. F. Baumeister (Ed.), *Self-esteem: The puzzle of low self-regard* (pp. 55–85). Hillsdale, NJ: Lawrence Erlbaum Associates, Inc.

Brockner, J. (1984). Low self-esteem and behavioral plasticity: Some implications of per-sonality and social psychology. In L. Wheeler (Ed.), *Review of personality and social psychology* (Vol. 4, pp. 237–271). Beverly Hills, CA: Sage.

Carver, C. S. (1998). Generalization, adverse events, and development of depressive symptoms. *Journal of Personality, 66*, 607–619.

Covington, M. V. (1984). The self-worth theory of achievement motivation: Findings and implications. *Elementary School Journal, 85*, 5–20.

Crocker, J., Karpinski, A., Quinn, D. M., & Chase, S. (2003). When grades determine self-worth: Consequences of contingent self-worth for male and female engineering and psychology majors. *Journal of Personality and Social Psychology, 85*, 507–516.

Crocker, J., & Luhtanen, R. K. (2003). Level of self-esteem and contingencies of self-worth: Unique effects on academic, social, and financial problems in college stu-dents. *Personality and Social Psychology Bulletin, 29*, 701–712.

Crocker, J., & Park, L. E. (2004a). The costly pursuit of self-esteem. *Psychological Bulletin, 130*, 392–414.

Crocker, J., & Park, L. E. (2004b). Reaping the benefits of pursuing self-esteem without the costs? Response to comments on Crocker and Park (2004). *Psychological Bulletin, 130*, 430–434.

Crocker, J., Sommers, S. R., & Luhtanen, R. K. (2002). Hopes dashed and dreams fulfilled: Contingencies of self-worth and admissions to graduate school. *Personality and Social Psychology Bulletin, 28*, 1275–1286.

Deci, E. L., Eghrari, H., Patrick, B. C., & Leone, D. R. (1994). Facilitating internalization: The self-determination theory perspective. *Journal of Personality*, *62*, 119–141.

Dykman, B. M. (1998). Integrating cognitive and motivational factors in depression: Initial tests of a goal-orientation approach. *Journal of Personality and Social Psychology*, *74*, 139–158.

Heatherton, T. F., & Vohs, K. D. (2000). Interpersonal evaluations following threat to self. *Journal of Personality and Social Psychology*, *78*, 725–736.

Hellhammer, D. H., & Wade, S. (1993). Endocrine correlates of stress vulnerability. *Psychotherapy and Psychosomatics*, *60*, 8–17.

Joiner, T. E., Alfano, M. S., & Metalsky, G. I. (1992). When depression breeds contempt: Reassurance seeking, self-esteem, and rejection of depressed college students by their roommates. *Journal of Abnormal Psychology*, *101*, 165–173.

Kernis, M. H., Brown, A. C., & Brody, G. H. (2000). Fragile self-esteem in children and its associations with perceived patterns of parent–child communication. *Journal of Personality*, *68*, 225–252.

Kernis, M. H., Whisenhunt, C. R., Waschull, S. B., Greenier, K. D., Berry, A. J., Herlocker, C. E., & Anderson, C. A. (1998). Multiple facets of self-esteem and their relations to depressive symptoms. *Personality and Social Psychology Bulletin*, *24*, 657–668.

Kiecolt-Glaser, J., Cacioppo, J., Malarkey, W., & Glaser, R. (1992). Acute psychological stressors and short-term immune changes: What, why, for whom and to what extent? *Psychosomatic Medicine*, *53*, 345–362.

Leary, M. R., Tchividjian, L. R., & Kraxberger, B. E. (1994). Self-presentation can be hazardous to your health: Impression management and health risk. *Health Psychology*, *13*, 461–470.

Pyszczynski, T., & Cox, C. (2004). Can we really do without self-esteem? A comment on Crocker and Park (2004). *Psychological Bulletin*, *130*, 425–429.

Roberts, J. E., & Kassel, J. D. (1997). Labile self-esteem, life stress, and depressive symptoms: Prospective data testing a model of vulnerability. *Cognitive Therapy and Research*, *21*, 569–589.

Ross, M. (2002). *It feels like yesterday: The social psychology of subjective time judgments.* Paper presented at the annual meeting of the Society for Personality and Social Psychology, Savannah, GA.

Sheldon, K. M. (2004). The benefits of a "sidelong" approach to self-esteem need satisfaction: A comment on Crocker and Park (2004). *Psychological Bulletin*, *130*, 421–424.

Suinn, R. M. (2001). The terrible twos—anger and anxiety. *American Psychologist*, *56*, 27–36.

Taylor, S. E., & Brown, J. D. (1988). Illusion and well-being: A social-psychological perspective on mental health. *Psychological Bulletin*, *103*, 193–210.

Vohs, K. D., & Heatherton, T. F. (2001). Self-esteem and threats to self: Implications for self-construals and interpersonal perceptions. *Journal of Personality and Social Psychology*, *81*, 1103–1118.

Wilson, A. E., & Ross, M. (2001). From chump to champ: People's appraisals of their earlier and present selves. *Journal of Personality and Social Psychology*, *80*, 572–584.

Wolfe, C. T., & Crocker, J. (2003). What does the self want? Contingencies of self-worth and goals. In S. Spencer, S. Fein, M. P. Zanna, & J. M. Olson (Eds.), *The Ontario symposium: Motivated social perception* (Vol. 9, pp. 147–170). Hillsdale, NJ: Lawrence Erlbaum Associates, Inc.

37

Possessing and Striving for High Self-Esteem

FREDERICK RHODEWALT

*I*n a classic comedy routine, Professor Irwin Corey was asked why did he wear sneakers. The self-proclaimed world's foremost authority on everything said that it was really two questions. He then launched into a lengthy monologue about "Why?" being the essential question that has occupied philosophers for centuries. In response to the second question, Professor Corey replied, "Do I wear sneakers? Yes!" In my view, in order to attempt an answer to the focal question of this essay, "Are striving for and possessing high self-esteem always healthy?," one must answer at least two questions. The first asks, is all high self-esteem the same? This is a very complex question, however, I am not alone in arguing that the answer is no. That being the case, the answer to the question of the healthiness of possessing and striving for high self-esteem is easy; it depends on the type of high self-esteem one possesses.

POSSESSING HIGH SELF-ESTEEM: HEALTHY OR UNHEALTHY?

What constitutes high self-esteem is an essential question that has occupied personality and social psychologists for decades. Global self-esteem is comprised of feelings of self-worth, self-liking, and acceptance (Brown, 1986; Kernis, 2003; Rosenberg, 1965). Low self-esteem then, reflects negative, neutral, or mildly positive global feelings about the self and high self-esteem indicates positive feelings of self-worth, self-liking, and acceptance. However, the current consensus is that self-esteem falls along a continuum from true or optimal to unauthentic or contingent (Crocker & Wolfe, 2001; Deci & Ryan, 1995; Kernis, 2003). Kernis (2003) suggests the broad categories of secure and fragile self-esteem to describe this dichotomy. With regard to the question of possessing and striving for high self-esteem, it is evident that possessing secure self-esteem is preferable to fragile self-esteem. In fact, one might argue that possessing secure self-esteem by its very nature does not require striving for it. In contrast, possessing fragile self-esteem requires constant striving for the purposes of maintaining and protecting these positive but fragile self-feelings.

But what does it mean to have fragile self-esteem? One answer is that fragile self-esteem is self-esteem that is based upon meeting standards or contingencies of worth (Crocker & Wolfe, 2001). Possessing self-esteem becomes the goal and striving to meet imposed contingencies the mechanism (Crocker & Nuer, 2003). The contingencies can be those imposed by others, for example, the child's belief that she will not be loved unless she excels in school or introjected, as in the child's belief that he is worthwhile only if he excels in school. Possessing high self-esteem that is contingent in this way is as unhealthy because failing to meet these standards leads to self-esteem devaluation (Crocker & Wolfe, 2001), instability (Kernis, 2003), and defensive and often hostile attempts to protect and repair positive but fragile self-esteem (Baumeister, Smart, & Boden, 1996).

There is a second way to construe self-esteem that, I believe, lends itself to examining the costs of possessing and striving for high self-esteem. Self-esteem is also a central element in self-regulation (Rhodewalt & Tragakis, 2003). In this view, self-esteem is both an input and an outcome of goal-directed, *self-involved* activity. However, it is a more salient input and output for those with fragile self-esteem than it is for those with secure self-esteem. Our self-regulatory model of self-esteem broaches the issue of contingency from a different angle than that taken by other researchers in the field. If self-regulation involves a continuous assessment of how we are doing compared to some standard, then all self-esteem is contingent because it involves feelings of worth that come from effectively meeting standards, demonstrating competence, and achieving social acceptance. It is the on-line affective and self-evaluative reactions to these comparisons that is the basis of the experience of self-esteem.

A second element of our self-regulatory model of self-esteem is that it emphasizes the linkages between global self-esteem and the specific self-evaluations that undergird it. The model embraces William James' (1890) position that self-esteem arises in large part from a tally of our standings on specific self-evaluations weighted for how important the specific dimensions are to self-definition (Campbell, 1990; Pehlam, 1995; Pelham & Swann, 1989). Consistent with this view, Pelham (1995) has shown that a measure of differential importance of an individual's self-evaluations significantly predicts his or her global self-esteem. The linkage between global self-esteem and self-evaluations is further illustrated in Tafarodi and Swann's (1995) finding that global self-esteem is composed of the somewhat independent dimensions of self-liking and self-competency. I contend that self-evaluations of competency and acceptance are the pathways by which global self-esteem is linked to the social context in which the individual is functioning. Global self-esteem is seldom directly on the line while self-evaluations of competency and acceptance often are, especially for those with fragile self-esteem.

From our self-regulatory perspective, people who possess high but fragile self-esteem have the goal of clarifying and validating important self-evaluations. This general goal is intensified by specific situational demands. That is, if people are unsure about their competencies or insecure about their acceptance by others, then situations that require displays of competency or tests of the strength of their acceptance pose threats to their self-evaluations and, consequently, to their self-esteem. It is in such circumstances that self-esteem regulation is fully engaged and the costs of the pursuit of self-esteem may be assessed. I will illustrate this point with the example of competency but mention that the same analysis applies to self-evaluations of acceptance (Rhodewalt & Vohs, 2005).

Because competency presumes the capacity to produce desired outcomes, success and failure performance feedback implies something about the degree to which one possesses the competency in question. Therefore, performance outcomes become linked to one's self-worth via the diagnostic information such outcomes provide about competency. Herein lies a potential critical difference between secure and fragile self-esteem. Secure self-esteem is supported by outcome contingent, self-evaluations of competency, and acceptance. That is, a secure individual's pride in her athletic ability is based on a performance history in which successes were clearly and unambiguously linked to the individual's actions. Fragile high self-esteem we contend is associated with self-appraisals of competency and related feelings of self-esteem that are based on personal histories which include ambiguous and inconsistent experiences (Rhodewalt & Tragakis, 2003; see also Jones & Berglas, 1978 for a similar argument). Although they may believe that they possess desired competencies, they are not confident in these assessments.

To summarize, possessing high but fragile self-esteem is not "healthy" because fragile self-esteem is "high maintenance" self-esteem. One of the costs of possessing fragile self-esteem is that it requires its chronic pursuit, a topic addressed in the following section.

PURSUING HIGH SELF-ESTEEM: HEALTHY OR UNHEALTHY?

What are the consequences of having high self-esteem built upon positive but uncertain self-evaluations of competency and acceptance? Two lines of research from my laboratory speak to this question and illustrate the utility of the self-regulation approach to the study of fragile self-esteem. Research on self-handicapping behavior (Rhodewalt & Tragakis, 2002) and our self-regulatory processing model of narcissism (Morf & Rhodewalt, 2001; Rhodewalt, 2001; Rhodewalt & Sorrow, 2003) illustrate the relations among self-esteem, self-regulation, and social interactions. The generic model is that individuals who possess positive but uncertain self-evaluations rely on their social interactions for validation and maintenance of these positive self-images. They are proactive in that they employ a collection of intra- and interpersonal strategies that distort the meaning of self-relevant feedback. Self-esteem regulation is intra-personally based to the extent that it arises and proceeds primarily within the head of the person and involves interpretations and distortions of meaning. The purpose of these tactics is to allow interpretations of self and situation that preserve desired self-evaluations. Self-esteem regulation is interpersonally based to the extent that the person uses other people to bolster feelings and thoughts about the self. These strategies allow people to modify their thoughts or feelings about others, alter perceived relationship closeness, or constrain and channel others' responses so that the desired self-image is confirmed.

Intra-Personal Self-Esteem Regulation

People in general are quite adroit at interpreting social feedback in a self-enhancing way. For example, people persistently offer internal attributions for success and external attributions for failure (Miller & Ross, 1975; Weary, 1978). However, individuals with fragile, uncertain self-esteem—narcissists (Rhodewalt, Madrian, & Cheney, 1998, see also Kernis, 2001) and self-handicappers (Harris & Snyder, 1986; Kernis, Grannemann, & Barclay, 1992)—appear to be more excessive in the self-aggrandizing attributions they offer for their outcomes. We observe this most clearly in studies that provide participants with response noncontingent success feedback. Narcissists persistently attribute such feedback to superior ability or competency. Our studies reveal that narcissists make self-aggrandizing attributional claims that they cannot meet (Rhodewalt & Morf, 1998; Rhodewalt, Tragakis, & Finnerty, 2003). Thus, one cost of this strategy is that uncertainty is perpetuated and failure or the threat of failure is more frequent and threatening.

In sum, evidence suggests that fragile, high self-esteem individuals engage in intra-personal esteem regulation in order to protect or enhance self-esteem. However, they do so at a cost because the biased interpretations of social feedback sustain the underlying uncertainty and thus necessitate future defensive regulation.

Interpersonal Self-Esteem Regulation

Self-esteem regulation is also achieved through interpersonal means. High, fragile self-esteem is tied closely to public behaviors, social interactions, or interpersonal relationships. Rhodewalt (2005; Rhodewalt et al., 1998) reports a series of daily diary studies in which narcissists display high but unstable self-esteem that is more closely entrained to the quality of their social interactions than is the self-esteem of less narcissistic individuals. Given that their self-esteem is so closely derived from their interactions with others, it is not surprising that they attempt to manipulate their relationships strategically in order to protect the self.

Not only do narcissists use others for self-esteem bolstering and protection, they often do so in way that harms the very relationships upon which they are dependent for self-esteem support. This point is illustrated in a study by Morf and Rhodewalt (1993), which examined narcissistic interpersonal relations in the context of self-evaluation maintenance process (SEM; Tesser, 1988). SEM behaviors involve thinking about and relating to close others in ways that enhance or protect one's self-esteem. For example, when a person is outperformed by a friend in a domain that is important to the person's self-evaluation, one response is to derogate the friend on other dimensions. Morf and Rhodewalt (1993) demonstrated that compared to less narcissistic individuals, narcissists experiencing comparison threat were more likely to derogate the threatening partner in a face to face interaction. Narcissists engage in interpersonal self-esteem maintenance in ways that potentially disrupt or harm the relationship.

CONCLUSION

Is possessing and striving for self-esteem always healthy? In this essay, I have attempted to argue that possessing secure self-esteem is healthy because under normal circumstances possessing it does not require striving for it. Rather, it is fragile, high self-esteem that is problematic because it is based on positive self-evaluations about which the individual is uncertain and insecure. Thus, these individuals are chronically self-involved in their activities and chronically striving for evidence that validates their positive self-evaluations. They do so via intra- and interpersonal strategies that may be effective in the short term but accrue intra- and interpersonal costs as well.

I point to lack of clarity regarding competence and acceptance as the toxic element in unhealthy high self-esteem because uncertainty shapes interaction goals (see Campbell, 1990; Kernis, 1993; and Swann & Schroeder, 1995 for similar propositions). For example, Swann (1983, 1985) has emphasized the importance of self-concept confidence or clarity in self-verification processes. According to Swann, people orchestrate their social worlds in an attempt to verify confidently held self-views because consensus about the self bolsters the predictability and controllability of the social environment. What about important, but uncertain self-views? Swann, Griffin, Predmore, and Gaines (1987) found that for less confidently held self-conceptions people sought self-enhancement. Thus, for individuals who are unsure of themselves, their self-presentational behavior involves "wishful thinking" in that they hope to acquire evidence that they are who they would like to be.

Rhodewalt and Tragakis (2002) have coined the term *self-solicitation* to refer to the interaction goal and strategic behaviors involved in seeking social feedback that enables one to maintain or protect desired or "hoped for" self-image. Self-solicitation then encompasses a set of interaction strategies that constrain others so that they provide feedback which supports the precarious self-view. As evidenced by research reviewed earlier, such strategies do accomplish this goal. However, this attributional manipulation can cause other interpretive ambiguities for the self-solicitor. Foremost is the possible awareness that the feedback was not unsolicited. At some level, self-solicitors have to be concerned about the hand their strategic interpersonal behaviors played in eliciting and shaping the feedback they receive. It is ironic that the strategies employed by uncertain individuals to maintain and protect and desired self-conceptions are often the implements that sustain their uncertainty. Self-solicitors become caught in an unending cycle of interpersonal self-evaluation and self-esteem regulation (cf. Morf & Rhodewalt, 2001). Perhaps then, striving for self-esteem among these individuals is unhealthy because their strivings impede the goal they seek, secure self-esteem.

ACKNOWLEDGMENTS

I would like to thank Michael Kernis for asking important questions and providing provocative answers.

REFERENCES

Baumeister, R. F., Smart, L., & Boden, J. M. (1996). Relation of threatened egotism to violence and aggression: The dark side of high self-esteem. *Psychological Review, 103,* 5–33.

Brown, J. D. (1986). Evaluations of self and others: Self-enhancement biases in social judgment. *Social Cognition, 4,* 353–376.

Campbell, J. (1990). Self-esteem and clarity of the self-concept. *Journal of Personality and Social Psychology, 59,* 538–549.

Crocker, J., & Nuer, N. (2003). The insatiable quest for self-worth. *Psychological Inquiry, 14,* 31–34.

Crocker, J., & Wolfe, C. T. (2001). Contingencies of self-worth. *Psychological Review, 108,* 593–623.

Harris, R. N., & Snyder, C. R. (1986). The role of uncertain self-esteem in self-handicapping. *Journal of Personality and Social Psychology, 51,* 451–458.

James, W. (1890). *The principles of psychology, Vol. 1.* New York: Holt.

Jones, E. E., & Berglas, S. (1978). Control of attributions about the self through self-handicapping strategies: The appeal of alcohol and the role of underachievement. *Personality and Social Psychology Bulletin, 4,* 200–206.

Kernis, M. H. (1993). The roles of stability and level of self-esteem in psychological functioning. In R. Baumeister (Ed.), *Self-esteem: The puzzle of low self-regard* (pp. 167–182). New York: Plenum Press.

Kernis, M. H. (2001). Following the trail from narcissism to fragile self-esteem. *Psychological Inquiry, 12,* 223–225.

Kernis, M. (2003). Toward a conceptualization of optimal self-esteem. *Psychological Inquiry, 14,* 1–26.

Kernis, M. H., Grannemann, B. D., & Barclay, L. C. (1992). Stability of self-esteem: Assessment, correlates, and excuse making. *Journal of Personality, 60,* 621–644.

Miller, D. T., & Ross, M. (1975). Self-serving biases in the attribution of causality: Fact or fiction? *Psychological Bulletin, 82,* 213–225.

Morf, C. C., & Rhodewalt, F. (1993). Narcissism and self-evaluation maintenance: Explorations in object relations. *Personality and Social Psychology Bulletin, 19,* 668–676.

Morf, C. C., & Rhodewalt, F. (2001). Unraveling the paradoxes of narcissism: A dynamic self-regulatory processing model. *Psychological Inquiry, 12,* 177–196.

Pelham, B. W. (1995). Self-investment and self-esteem: Evidence for a Jamesian model of self-worth. *Journal of Personality and Social Psychology, 69,* 1141–1150.

Pelham, B. W., & Swann, W. B. Jr. (1989). From self-conceptions to self-worth: On the sources and structure of global self-esteem. *Journal of Personality and Social Psychology, 57,* 672–680.

Rhodewalt, F. (2005). Social motivation and object relations: Narcissism and interpersonal self-esteem regulation. In J. Forgas, K. Williams, & W. Von Hippel (Eds.), *Social motivation.* New York: Cambridge University Press.

Rhodewalt, F. (2001). The social mind of the narcissist: Cognitive and motivational aspects of interpersonal self-construction. In J. P. Forgas, K. Williams, & L. Wheeler (Eds.), *The social mind: Cognitive and motivational aspects of interpersonal behavior* (pp. 177–198). New York: Cambridge University Press.

Rhodewalt, F., Madrian, J., & Cheney, S. (1998). Narcissism and self-esteem instability: The effects of self-knowledge organization and daily social interaction on self-esteem and affect. *Personality and Social Psychology Bulletin, 24,* 75–87.

Rhodewalt, F., & Morf, C. C. (1998). On self-aggrandizement and anger: A temporal analysis of narcissism and affective reactions to success and failure. *Journal of Personality and Social Psychology, 74*, 672–685.

Rhodewalt, F., & Sorrow, D. (2003). Interpersonal self-regulation: Lessons from the study of narcissism. In M. Leary & J. P. Tangney (Eds.), *Handbook of self and identity*. New York: Guilford Press.

Rhodewalt, F., & Tragakis, M. (2002). Self-handicapping and the social self: The costs and rewards of interpersonal self-construction. In J. Forgas & K. Williams (Eds.), *The social self: Cognitive, interpersonal, and intergroup perspectives* (pp. 121–143). Philadelphia, PA: Psychology Press.

Rhodewalt, F., & Tragakis, M. (2003). Self-esteem and self-regulation: Toward optimal studies of self-esteem. *Psychological Inquiry, 14*, 66–70.

Rhodewalt, F., Tragakis, M., & Finnerty, J. (2003). *Narcissism and self-handicapping: Linking self-aggrandizement to behavior*. University of Utah. Manuscript submitted for publication.

Rhodewalt, F., & Vohs, K. D. (2005). Defensive strategies, motivation, and the self: A self-regulatory process view. In A. Elliot & C. Dweck (Eds.), *Handbook of competence and motivation*. New York: Guilford Press.

Rosenberg, M. (1965). *Conceiving the self*. New York: Basic Books.

Swann, W. B. (1983). Self-verification: Bringing social reality into harmony with the self. In J. Suls & A. Greenwald (Eds.), *Psychological perspectives on the self* (Vol. 2, pp. 33–66). Hillsdale, NJ: Lawrence Erlbaum Associates, Inc.

Swann, W. B. (1985). The self as architect of social reality. In B. Schlenker (Ed.), *The self and social life* (pp. 100–125). New York: McGraw-Hill.

Swann, W. B., Griffin, J. J., Predmore, S. C., & Gaines, B. (1987). The cognitive-affective crossfire: When self-consistency confronts self-enhancement. *Journal of Personality and Social Psychology, 52*, 881–889.

Swann, W. B., & Schroeder, D. G. (1995). The search for beauty and truth: A framework for understanding reactions to evaluations. *Personality and Social Psychology Bulletin, 21*, 1307–1318.

Tafarodi, R. W., & Swann, W. B. Jr. (1995). Self-liking and self-competence as dimensions of global self-esteem: Initial validation of a measure. *Journal of Personality Assessment, 65*, 322–342.

Tesser, A. (1988). Toward a self-evaluation maintenance model of social behavior. In L. Berkowitz (Ed.), *Advances in experimental social psychology* (Vol. 21, pp. 181–227). New York: Academic Press.

Weary, G. B. (1978). Self-serving biases in the attribution process: A re-examination of the fact or fiction question. *Journal of Personality and Social Psychology, 36*, 56–71.

38

Should People with Low Self-Esteem Strive for High Self-Esteem?

JOANNE V. WOOD, DANU B. ANTHONY, and
WALTER F. FODDIS

*P*eople who have high self-esteem (HSEs) are happier and psychologically healthier than people who have low self-esteem (LSEs; Baumeister, Campbell, Krueger, & Vohs, 2003), and are more likely to have satisfying and stable relationships (e.g., Leary & MacDonald, 2003). Does this mean that LSEs should strive to have high self-esteem? We suspect that they should not, at least not directly. We propose that certain methods for elevating state self-esteem—those that readily engage self-evaluative processes—can be ineffective or even backfire for LSEs.

Similarly, Kernis (2003) and Crocker and Park (2004) have proposed that striving for high self-esteem is detrimental. They argued that the goal to enhance self-esteem leads to excessive defensiveness and interferes with fundamental needs, ultimately resulting not in "true" high self-esteem, but in contingent or unstable self-esteem. Although these views may well be correct, our focus in this essay is different. We distinguish between "self-evaluative" and "non-self-evaluative" methods, and focus on specific mechanisms by which self-evaluative methods may be ineffective or worse. We also propose that relatively non-self-evaluative methods may benefit state self-esteem.

We warn at the outset that our thinking about this self-evaluative/non-self-evaluative distinction is in a nascent stage. Considerable empirical work is needed to verify the distinction and to examine underlying mechanisms. What we are most confident of at this point is that self-evaluative methods can, under some circumstances, be harmful to state self-esteem. In our lab, surprising results have emerged for two experiences that are widely believed to boost self-esteem: positive self-statements and success events.

POSITIVE SELF-STATEMENTS CAN BACKFIRE

The belief that people benefit from positive self-statements is widely held in North America. It is promoted by the mass media, including television shows (e.g., *Oprah*) and magazines. Bookstore shelves groan under self-help books concerning self-esteem, many of which advocate the daily use of such self-statements as, "I am loving, lovable, and loved" (Sheehan, 1998, p. 40) and "Every day I like myself more" (McQuaig, 1986, p. 55).

Despite the widespread belief that positive self-statements are beneficial, we have found that they can be useless or worse (Wood, Lee, & Perunovic, 2004). For example, in one experiment, we cued participants to repeat the phrase, "I am a lovable person" four times a minute for 4 minutes (Wood et al., 2004). Disguised measures of mood suggested that HSE participants felt happier, but LSEs felt worse, relative to participants who did not repeat the phrase. In another experiment, we examined the use of positive self-statements to prepare for stressful situations. We led participants to believe that they would meet with a stranger of the opposite sex, during which time they would be evaluated for their social skills (Lee & Wood, 2004). Results revealed that for people who were insecure in their social skills—and therefore most likely LSE—repeating the phrase, "I feel very confident. People like me and I have good social skills," triggered negative thoughts about themselves.

In sum, we have evidence that sometimes, when LSEs repeat highly positive self-statements, their moods get worse, not better; their feelings about themselves worsen, rather than improve; and their self-related thoughts become more negative, not positive. Thus, positive self-statements can be harmful for the people who seem to "need" them the most. In contrast, for HSEs, positive self-statements can boost thoughts and feelings about themselves.

SUCCESSES BENEFIT HSEs MUCH MORE THAN LSEs

Perhaps a more effective route to boosting state self-esteem would involve not self-*persuasion* (as from positive self-statements), but an *experience* that would convince LSEs of their self-worth, such as achieving a success. Indeed, it has become well-accepted that LSEs and HSEs both benefit from success (e.g., Brown & Dutton, 1995). Contrary to this view, we have found that success is experienced differently by LSEs and HSEs (Wood, Heimpel, Newby-Clark, & Ross, 2005). Although success brings pleasure to both groups, it raises LSEs' anxiety, and, paradoxically, triggers negative self-relevant thoughts. In two experiments, we manipulated success by leading some participants to think they had performed superbly on several tests of "cognitive abilities." LSEs in the success condition reported more tension and more physical symptoms of anxiety (e.g., trembling) than HSEs, as well as more than LSEs in the no-feedback condition. Our studies also uncovered similar self-esteem differences in anxiety and in self-relevant thoughts for successes in everyday life.

UNDERLYING MOTIVATIONS AND MECHANISMS

Why do positive self-statements and successes fail or backfire? We propose that self-evaluative methods arouse inhibiting motivations, heighten self-focused attention, and exacerbate the salience of self-discrepancies from one's standards.

Arousing Inhibiting Motivations

Positive self-statements and success experiences may arouse motivations in LSEs to self-verify and self-protect. Swann's self-verification theory proposes that people try to maintain their self-views, because stable self-views afford clarity and predictability (Swann & Schroeder, 1995). Success and positive self-statements may trigger LSEs' self-verification motives because they contradict LSEs' doubts about their competence and self-worth (Brown & McGill, 1989; Pinel & Swann, 1996). The second motive, self-protectiveness, was proposed by Baumeister, Tice, and Hutton (1989). Baumeister et al. argued that whereas HSEs aim for self-enhancement, LSEs aim for self-protection; HSEs strive to feel good about themselves and to be seen favorably by others, whereas LSEs strive instead to avoid revealing their deficiencies. Several empirical studies have supported this portrait of LSEs as self-protective (e.g., Wood, Giordano-Beech, Taylor, Michela, & Gaus, 1994). In the eyes of a self-protective person, a success may provide new opportunities to reveal one's deficiencies. LSEs may fear that their success is fragile and will reverse, or that it will bring higher standards that they cannot achieve (cf. Blaine & Crocker, 1993). After the success of being hired for a new job, for example, LSEs may worry that they cannot meet other people's expectations (Wood et al., 2005).

These two motives—self-verification and self-protection—are likely to fuel the mechanisms we discuss next.

Heightening Self-Focused Attention

Direct, self-evaluative methods of improving self-esteem necessarily involve focusing attention on the self (cf. Crocker & Park, 2004; Leary, 2004). Self-focused attention has at least three untoward effects to which LSEs should be especially vulnerable. First, self-focus intensifies one's emotional state (Wood & Dodgson, 1996). Because LSEs are generally more anxious and depressed than HSEs (Leary & Downs, 1995), self-focus should exacerbate these feelings. Second, self-focus may disrupt social functioning (e.g., Reis, Sheldon, Gable, Roscoe, & Ryan, 2000) by decreasing one's ability to empathize with others or to embrace others' support and love.

A third effect of self-focus is that it intensifies attention to one's standards (Carver & Scheier, 1998). Such attention can facilitate adaptive self-regulation, but it also can be painful and counterproductive for LSEs (Wood & Dodgson, 1996; Wood, Saltzberg, Neale, Stone, & Rachmiel, 1990). In particular, we propose that positive self-statements and successes often remind LSEs that they do not measure up to their standards. Because of the centrality of such processes, we discuss them in detail next.

Intensifying Salience of Self-Discrepant Standards

Previous theory and evidence concerning feedback receipt and attitude change lead us to suspect that when LSEs achieve a success or repeat a positive self-statement, they fairly automatically compare this information to their self-conceptions to judge its fit (Eisenstadt & Leippe, 1994; Jussim, Yen, & Aiello, 1995). This process can yield memories and thoughts that confirm or disconfirm the information. For example, after succeeding on a test of "cognitive abilities," LSEs may recall a math test on which they failed. Information about the self also leads people to compare their self-conceptions to their ideal standards (e.g., Aronson, Blanton, & Cooper, 1995). LSEs in particular may readily think of ways in which they fall short of their ideals. Hence, even positive information about the self may serve as a painful reminder of one's "self-discrepancies" (Higgins, 1987).

When LSEs repeat the statement, "I am a lovable person," then, they may say to themselves, "But I know I'm not as lovable as I could be, or as lovable as X..." When a violinist with LSE hears applause for a beautiful solo, she may enjoy it, but soon think of flaws in her performance, recall occasions when she did not play well, think of true virtuosos who play far better, or worry that she cannot repeat her fine performance next time.

WHAT SELF-EVALUATIVE METHODS FAIL TO DO

Consider also what self-evaluative methods do not do. First, to the extent that people have feelings about themselves that are beyond their awareness (e.g., Jordan, Spencer, & Zanna, 2002), self-evaluative methods such as self-statements are incomplete, because they address only conscious thoughts and feelings. Second, theorists have argued that secure high self-esteem requires meeting the needs of competence, autonomy, and relatedness (Ryan & Deci, 2000), as well as "authenticity"—thinking, feeling, and acting in ways that reflect one's true self (Kernis, 2003; Kernis & Goldman, 2005). If so,[1] self-evaluative methods seem to offer little. Following advice to repeat something self-discrepant may undermine one's autonomy, and is unlikely to make one feel competent. Although successes should serve one's competence needs, they may not benefit self-esteem when they are pursued to serve "extrinsic" goals, such as monetary reward or fame (Ryan & Deci, 2000), or when they occur in an "external" domain, such as physical appearance, rather than in an "internal" domain, such as moral virtue (e.g., Crocker & Luhtanen, 2003; Foddis, Wood, & Moore, 2004). Moreover, as we have already suggested, the self-focus engendered by self-evaluative methods may interfere with relatedness needs.

WHAT *DOES* BOOST SELF-ESTEEM?

If we are correct about the dangers of self-evaluative methods, three strategies may be effective in boosting LSEs' state self-esteem: (1) teaching LSEs to engage in less self-destructive self-evaluation; (2) encouraging LSEs to direct their self-focus to their positive features; and (3) reminding LSEs of valued qualities while bypassing the self-evaluative process.

Training LSEs to engage in more adaptive self-evaluation is the basic goal of cognitive-behavioral therapies for self-esteem (e.g., Warren, McLellarn, & Ponzoha, 1988). Therapists encourage LSEs to replace irrational and harsh self-related thoughts with more realistic, beneficent alternatives. This approach is promising, but more studies are needed that include control groups that rule out such confounds as therapist attention and placebo effects.

The second strategy involves focusing LSEs' self-evaluation on their desirable qualities rather than on their weaknesses. LSEs do have attributes that they value (Anthony, Wood, Holmes, & Cameron, 2004; Pelham, 1991). Listing one's favorable attributes appears to raise state self-esteem (McGuire & McGuire, 1996). One function of friends and partners may be to remind one of one's qualities. Arndt and his colleagues showed that participants' defensiveness can be reduced when they are reminded of people who accept them unconditionally and when others validate their expression of their "true" selves (Arndt, Schimel, Greenberg, & Pyszczynski, 2002; Schimel, Arndt, Pyszczynski, & Greenberg, 2001). Remarkably, Murray, Holmes, and Griffin (1996, 2000) showed that when LSEs are loved by a spouse who sees more virtue in them than they themselves do, their self-esteem increases over a year.

When LSEs focus on their good points, however, danger awaits. As described earlier, even positive feedback can remind LSEs of standards that they are not meeting. The hazards of self-evaluation for LSEs are illustrated in studies that have examined the seemingly benign activity of listing one's desirable attributes. Although doing so can raise self-esteem (McGuire & McGuire, 1996), it does not under conditions that undermine one's confidence (Briñol & Petty, 2003). For example, when people high in self-doubt recalled examples of their self-confidence, their state self-esteem dropped if they were required to list 12 examples (Hermann, Leonardelli, & Arkin, 2002). Participants apparently inferred from their difficulty in retrieving 12 examples that they did not meet the standard of self-confidence after all.

Similarly, although others' admiration can make one feel good, it may not help to be admired for the wrong reasons. Arndt and his colleagues showed that participants' defensiveness was *not* reduced when they received social approval for their accomplishments, rather than for qualities that reflected their "true" inner selves (Arndt et al., 2002; Schimel et al., 2001). We suspect that for LSEs in particular, admiration for one's accomplishments may suggest that others' love is conditional on their meeting certain standards.

We are suggesting, then, that for LSEs, any self-evaluation—even if focused initially on positive attributes—is hazardous. But how can LSEs ever feel better about themselves without evaluating themselves? It seems that what is required is the third strategy—to subtly remind LSEs of features they like about themselves, without triggering a thorough self-evaluation in that domain, and especially not of their entire selves. Positive moods may fill this bill; they enhance positive thoughts and feelings about the self (e.g., Brown & Mankowski, 1993), yet they inhibit self-focused attention (Green, Sedikides, Saltzberg, Wood, & Forzano, 2003), and can encourage a style of thinking that is not careful or analytical (Isen, 1987).

Steele's "self-affirmation" tasks may operate similarly. When participants simply complete a scale highlighting a value they cherish (e.g., politics, aesthetics), they do not engage in the strategies they normally use to reduce dissonance (e.g., Spencer, Josephs, & Steele, 1993).[2] Completing such a values scale also diminishes LSEs' defensiveness as they await an evaluative task (Spencer, Fein, & Lomore, 2001). Self-affirmation tasks of this type may heighten self-focus mildly, but they should not lead to self-focus in domains in which people typically self-evaluate, such as achievements or social attractiveness. Rather, completing a scale that concerns one's value may subtly allow people to express an authentic, favorable aspect of themselves (à la Kernis, 2003) without triggering a full-blown self-evaluation.

CONCLUSION

What distinguishes the methods that elevate state self-esteem from those that are ineffective? Speculation is hazardous, because (1) methods empirically demonstrated to raise self-esteem are scarce, (2) methods may be effective for different reasons, and (3) the effective methods probably differ from the ineffective methods on many dimensions. It is also unclear whether methods effective for raising state self-esteem, even if used frequently, will have a lasting impact on trait self-esteem. However, one feature that the methods that are effective in raising state self-esteem seem to have in common—and a way in which they differ from positive self-statements and success experiences—is that they do not seem likely to automatically instigate self-evaluation processes. Being in a positive mood, engaging in a self-affirmation task (à la Steele), thinking of a person who has accepted oneself unconditionally, and being loved are less likely to trigger self-focused attention or comparisons with one's ideal standards. Hence, these methods may "fly under the radar," and thereby avoid stimulating deleterious self-evaluative processes. Research is needed to test these possibilities.

NOTES

1. We say "if" because although evidence supports these ideas, clear causal connections between either authentic functioning or meeting the three needs and high self-esteem have not been demonstrated. The most convincing evidence comes from within-person studies that show that specific experiences in which people feel competent, autonomous, and connected to others are also experiences in which their self-esteem is heightened (e.g., Reis et al., 2000). These studies are correlational, however, so it is not clear that meeting these needs *causes* self-esteem to increase. Perhaps when people feel good about themselves, they can more readily do what is required to satisfy their needs.

2. A reduction in defensiveness (such as in the Arndt et al. studies and in many self-affirmation studies) seems to imply a boost in state self-esteem, yet the same

manipulations that reduce defensiveness often do not yield changes on dependent measures of self-esteem. However, obtaining such changes on self-report measures may require complicated circumstances (Pyszczynski, Greenberg, Solomon, Arndt, & Schimel, 2004), so we see these methods as promising in their impact on state self-esteem.

REFERENCES

Anthony, D. B., Wood, J. V., Holmes, J. G., & Cameron, J. J. (2004). *It's what's inside that counts... Or is it?: Interpersonal self-concept and global self-esteem.* Poster presentation at the 2004 International Association for Relationship Research conference, Madison, WI.

Arndt, J., Schimel, J., Greenberg, J., & Pyszczynski, T. (2002). The intrinsic self and defensiveness: Evidence that activating the intrinsic self reduces self-handicapping and conformity. *Personality and Social Psychology Bulletin, 28,* 671–683.

Aronson, J., Blanton, H., & Cooper, J. (1995). From dissonance to disidentification: Selectivity in the self-affirmation process. *Journal of Personality and Social Psychology, 68,* 986–996.

Baumeister, R. F., Campbell, J. D., Krueger, J. I., & Vohs, K. D. (2003). Does high self-esteem cause better performance, interpersonal success, happiness, or healthier lifestyles? *Psychological Science in the Public Interest, 4,* 1–44.

Baumeister, R. F., Tice, D. M., & Hutton, D. G. (1989). Self-presentational motivations and personality differences in self-esteem. *Journal of Personality, 57,* 547–579.

Blaine, B., & Crocker, J. (1993). Self-esteem and self serving biases in reactions to positive and negative events: An integrative review. In R. F. Baumeister (Ed.), *Self-esteem: The puzzle of low self-regard* (pp. 55–85). New York: Plenum Press.

Briñol, P., & Petty, R. E. (2003). Overt head movements and persuasion: A self-validation analysis. *Journal of Personality & Social Psychology, I,* 1123–1139.

Brown, J. D., & Dutton, K. A. (1995). The thrill of victory, the complexity of defeat: Self-esteem and people's emotional reactions to success and failure. *Journal of Personality and Social Psychology, 68,* 712–722.

Brown, J. D., & Mankowski, T. A. (1993). Self-esteem, mood, and self-evaluation: Changes in mood and the way you see you. *Journal of Personality and Social Psychology, 64,* 421–430.

Brown, J. D., & McGill, K. L. (1989). The cost of good fortune: When positive life events produce negative health consequences. *Journal of Personality and Social Psychology, 57,* 1103–1110.

Carver, C. F., & Scheier, M. F. (Eds.). (1998). *On the self-regulation of behavior.* New York: Cambridge University Press.

Crocker, J., & Luhtanen, R. K. (2003). Level of self-esteem and contingencies of self-worth: Unique effects on academic, social and financial problems in college students. *Personality and Social Psychology Bulletin, 29,* 701–712.

Crocker, J., & Park, L. E. (2004). The costly pursuit of self-esteem. *Psychological Bulletin, 130,* 392–414.

Eisenstadt, D., & Leippe, M. R. (1994). The self-comparison process and self-discrepant feedback: Consequences of learning you are what you thought you were not. *Journal of Personality and Social Psychology, 67,* 611–626.

Foddis, W. F., Wood, J. V., & Moore, K. (2004, May). *How self-esteem and narcissism differ in sources of self-esteem.* Poster presentation at the American Psychological Society 16th Annual Convention, Chicago, IL.

Green, J. D., Sedikides, C., Saltzberg, J. A., Wood, J., & Forzano, L. B. (2003). Happy mood decreases self-focused attention. *British Journal of Social Psychology, 42,* 147–157.

Hermann, A. D., Leonardelli, G.J., & Arkin, R.M. (2002). Self-doubt and self-esteem: A threat from within. *Personality and Social Psychology Bulletin, 28,* 395–408.

Higgins, E. T. (1987). Self-discrepancy: A theory relating self and affect. *Psychological Review, 94,* 319–340.

Isen, A. M. (1987). Positive affect, cognitive processes, and social behavior. In L. Berkowitz (Ed.), *Advances in experimental social psychology* (Vol. 20, pp. 203–253). New York: Academic Press.

Jordan, C. H., Spencer, S. J., & Zanna, M. P. (2002). "I love me… I love me not": Implicit self-esteem, explicit self-esteem, and defensiveness. In S. J. Spencer, S. Fein, M. P. Zanna, & J. M. Olson (Eds.), *Motivated social perception: The Ontario symposium* (Vol. 9, pp. 117–145). Mahwah, NJ: Lawrence Erlbaum Associates, Inc.

Jussim, L., Yen, H., & Aiello, J. R. (1995). Self-consistency, self-enhancement, and accuracy in reactions to feedback. *Journal of Experimental Social Psychology, 31,* 322–356.

Kernis, M. H. (2003). Toward a conceptualization of optimal self-esteem. *Psychological Inquiry, 14,* 1–26.

Kernis, M. H., & Goldman, B. M. (2005). From thought and experience to behavior and interpersonal relationships: A multicomponent conceptualization of authenticity. In Tesser, A., Wood, J. V., & Stapel, D. (Eds.). *The psychology of self: On the edge of understanding* (pp. 31–52). New York: Psychology Press.

Leary, M. R. (2004). *The curse of the self: Self-awareness, egoism, and the quality of human life.* New York: Oxford University Press.

Leary, M. R., & Downs, D. L. (1995). Interpersonal functions of the self-esteem motive: The self-esteem system as a sociometer. In M. H. Kerins (Ed.), *Efficacy, agency, and self-esteem. Plenum series in social/clinical psychology* (pp. 123–144). New York: Plenum Press.

Leary, M. R., & MacDonald, G. (2003). Individual differences in self-esteem: A review and theoretical integration. In M. R. Leary & J. P. Tangney (Eds.), *Handbook of self and identity* (pp. 401–418). New York: Guilford Press.

Lee, J., & Wood, J. V. (2004). *Positive self-statements in evaluative situations.* Unpublished raw data.

McGuire, W. J., & McGuire, C. V. (1996). Enhancing self-esteem by directed-thinking tasks: Cognitive and affective positivity asymmetries. *Journal of Personality and Social Psychology, 70,* 1117–1125.

McQuaig, J. H. (1986). *Like yourself and live.* Toronto: Rexdale, Hunter Carlyle Publishing.

Murray, S. L., Holmes, J. G., & Griffin, D. W. (1996). The self-fulfilling nature of positive illusions in romantic relationships: Love is not blind, but prescient. *Journal of Personality and Social Psychology, 71,* 1155–1180.

Murray, S. L., Holmes, J. G., & Griffin, D. W. (2000). Self-esteem and the quest for felt security: How perceived regard regulates attachment processes. *Journal of Personality and Social Psychology, 78,* 478–498.

Pelham, B. W. (1991). On the benefits of misery: Self-serving biases in the depressive self-concept. *Journal of Personality and Social Psychology, 61,* 670–681.

Pinel, E. C., & Swann, W. B. (1996). *The cognitive-affective crossfire revisited: Affective reactions to self-discrepant evaluations.* Unpublished manuscript, University of Texas, Austin.

Pyszczynski, T., Greenberg, J., Solomon, S., Arndt, J., & Schimel, J. (2004). Why do people need self-esteem? A theoretical and empirical review. *Psychological Bulletin, 130,* 435–468.

Reis, H. T., Sheldon, K. M, Gable, S. L., Roscoe, J., & Ryan, R. M. (2000). Daily well-being: The role of autonomy, competence, and relatedness. *Personality and Social Psychology Bulletin, 26,* 419–435.

Ryan, R. M., & Deci, E. L. (2000). Self-determination theory and the facilitation of intrinsic motivation, social development, and well-being. *American Psychologist, 55,* 68–78.

Schimel, J., Arndt, J., Pyszczynski, T., & Greenberg, J. (2001). Being accepted for who we are: Evidence that social validation of the intrinsic self reduces general defensiveness. *Journal of Personality and Social Psychology, 80,* 35–52.

Sheehan, E. (1998). *Low self-esteem: Your questions answered.* Shaftesbury: Element Books Ltd.

Spencer, S. J., Fein, S., & Lomore, C. D. (2001). Maintaining one's self-image vis-à-vis others: The role of self-affirmation in the social evaluation of the self. *Motivation and Emotion, 25,* 41–65.

Spencer, S. J., Josephs, R. A., & Steele, C. M. (1993). Low self-esteem: The uphill struggle for self-integrity. In R. F. Baumeister (Ed.), *Self-esteem: The puzzle of low self-regard* (pp. 21–36). New York: Plenum Press.

Swann, W. B., & Schroeder, D. G. (1995). The search for beauty and truth: A framework for understanding reactions to evaluations. *Personality and Social Psychology Bulletin, 21,* 1307–1318.

Warren, R., McLellarn, R.W., & Ponzoha, C. (1988). Rational-emotive therapy vs. general cognitive-behavior therapy in the treatment of low self-esteem and related emotional disturbances. *Cognitive Therapy and Research, 12,* 21–37.

Wood, J. V., & Dodgson, P.G. (1996). When is self-focused attention an adaptive coping response?: Rumination and overgeneralization versus compensation. In I. G. Sarason, G. R. Pierce, & B. R. Sarason (Eds.), *Cognitive interference: Theories, methods, and findings* (pp. 231–259). Hillsdale, NJ: Lawrence Erlbaum Associates, Inc.

Wood, J. V., Giordano-Beech, M., Taylor, K. L., Michela, J. L., & Gaus, V. (1994). Strategies of social comparison among people with low self-esteem: Self-protection and self-enhancement. *Journal of Personality and Social Psychology, 67,* 713–731.

Wood, J. V., Heimpel, S. A., Newby-Clark, I., & Ross, M. (2005). Snatching defeat from the jaws of victory: Self-esteem differences in the experience and anticipation of success. *Journal of Personality and Social Psychology, 89,* 764–780.

Wood, J. V., Lee, J., & Perunovic, W. Q. E. (2004). *Positive thinking: Power for some, peril for others.* Unpublished manuscript, University of Waterloo.

Wood, J. V., Saltzberg, J. A., Neale, J. M, Stone, A. A, & Rachmiel, T. B. (1990). Self-focused attention, coping responses, and distressed mood in everyday life. *Journal of Personality and Social Psychology, 58,* 1027–1036.

Question 13

What is the place of self-esteem in therapeutic settings? To which disorders is it most relevant?

The essays in this section focus on the role of self-esteem in psychological disorders and therapeutic settings. Each essay provides compelling evidence in support of the clinical relevance of self-esteem processes.

Roberts focuses his essay on the notion that self-esteem processes can illuminate both the etiology and effective treatment of a number of clinical conditions. First, he discusses established findings pertaining to the role of unstable self-esteem as a risk factor in promoting depressive symptoms following stressful events. Next, he reviews evidence pertaining to self-esteem level as a potential moderator of the relation between attributional styles and depression, and to self-esteem contingencies in eating disorders. Roberts concludes his essay with a discussion of self-esteem as a treatment outcome.

O'Brien, Bartoletti, Leitzel, and O'Brien examine extensive connections among self-esteem, psychopathology, and psychotherapy. First, they discuss the role of self-esteem in diagnosing various forms of psychopathology, including mood, personality, and eating disorders. In addition, they consider self-esteem as an outcome measure, as an independent variable in psychotherapy interventions, and as a factor associated with therapist effectiveness. O'Brien and colleagues illustrate the extensive involvement of self-esteem processes in many aspects of psychopathology and psychotherapy.

DeHart and Tennen describe what they view as primary functions of self-esteem (promote positive affect, goal attainment, and interpersonal relationships) and relate these functions to the therapeutic enterprise. They also focus on self-esteem dynamics as manifest in depression and narcissistic personality disorder. Specifically, the authors discuss the relevance of stability of self-esteem and implicit self-esteem in understanding and treating emotional disorders. In addition, Dehart and Tennen advocate for a daily process approach to understanding self-esteem processes in emotional disorders and psychotherapy.

39

Self-Esteem from a Clinical Perspective

JOHN E. ROBERTS

From a clinical perspective, self-esteem (SE) has the potential to shed light on both the etiology and the effective treatment of a number of clinical conditions. In this chapter, I highlight some of the established findings, as well as what I see as the important questions and conceptual issues. Unorthodox ideas concerning the pathways by which SE could be associated with clinical conditions are raised, including reverse causation, SE deficits as part of a clinical condition's prodrome (i.e., early subclinical symptomatology), and indirect causal pathways involving behavior and the environment. Different conceptualizations of the nature of vulnerable SE are also highlighted.

SELF-ESTEEM IN DEPRESSION

SE has been most extensively investigated in depression, and this work can serve as a framework for anticipating issues that are likely to emerge as research develops on other clinical conditions. Given that feelings of worthlessness are part of the diagnostic criteria for depression (as well as a number of other clinical conditions), research designs need to guard against the possibility that SE deficits are simply a symptom of the disorder itself, a prodrome to the disorder (i.e., an early symptom), or a scar of past episodes (Roberts & Gamble, 2001). Given that we cannot experimentally manipulate SE (at least not in a meaningful manner in this clinical context), we need to be sensitive to the possibility that associations between SE and depression result from third variables. Consequently, plausible common causes of SE and depression, such as the personality dimension neuroticism (Schmitz, Kugler, & Rollnik, 2003), are sometimes used as covariates in data analyses (e.g., Roberts & Gotlib, 1997; S. Roberts & Kendler, 1999).

A number of prospective studies have now demonstrated that individuals with temporally unstable or labile SE are at risk for developing depressive symptoms subsequent to stressful life events (e.g., Butler et al., 1994; Roberts & Monroe, 1992; Kernis et al., 1998). Individuals whose SE is more unstable over time are prone to developing greater depressive symptoms following life stressors compared to those with more stable SE. However, this effect seems to be largely limited to individuals who are initially low in depressive symptoms (Roberts & Gotlib, 1997; Roberts & Kassel, 1997; Roberts & Monroe, 1992; though also see Crocker, Karpinski, Quinn, & Chase, 2003), and particularly among those who are initially low in symptoms but who have a past history of more serious depression (Roberts & Gotlib, 1997; Roberts & Kassel, 1997; see also Gable & Nezlek, 1998). These findings suggest that unstable SE might be involved in the onset of depressive symptoms, but not the maintenance of already present depressive symptomatology. Interestingly, preliminary research suggests that the exact opposite phenomenon occurs in the maintenance of already existing depression. Specifically, clinically depressed individuals with greater perceived stability of their SE at the start of treatment tend to have a poor treatment response, particularly when coupled with feelings of worthlessness (Roberts, Shapiro, & Gamble, 1999). It may be that temporal variability in SE contributes to the onset of depression, but once clinical depression sets in stability reflects an ingrained negative self-image that is resistant to change. Different processes may be involved in the onset versus maintenance of symptoms, and research samples that indiscriminately include all levels of symptomatology potentially yield misleading findings.

Although these findings appear both reliable and distinct from level of SE (i.e., high versus low SE), which does not consistently predict the development of depression (see Roberts & Monroe, 1999 for a review), the underlying mechanisms by which unstable SE contributes to depression are not established. At least three as yet untested mechanisms appear plausible. First, given their tenuous and unstable self-representations, it may be that individuals with unstable SE have difficulty recruiting concrete mental representations of coping responses, leading to less effective problem solving. Consequently, stressors that would otherwise be brief and minor become prolonged and threatening. Second, individuals with unstable SE may respond to threats with anger (Kernis, Grannemann, & Barclay, 1989) or excessive reassurance seeking from others, leading to interpersonal stressors that in turn amplify depression (Joiner & Metalsky, 2001). These first two models suggest that the effects of unstable SE on depression are indirect and are mediated by "stress generation" (Roberts & Ciesla, 2000). The final model suggests a more direct effect; there may be greater spreading activation of negative representations of self following stressors among those with unstable SE, which leads to pervasive negative thinking about the self, world, and future (the so-called "negative cognitive triad") and the development of depressive symptoms.

Another growing body of research suggests that SE works together with negative attributional style in creating vulnerability to depressive symptomatology. According to the hopelessness theory of depression (Abramson, Alloy, & Metalsky, 1989), individuals with negative attributional styles (e.g., the tendency to attribute negative events to stable, general and internal causes) are prone to hopelessness when confronted with stressors, and hopelessness in turn leads to depression. Although a number of studies have shown that negative attributional style increases the impact of stress on the development of depressive symptoms, this effect appears to be stronger among those with low compared to high SE (Abela & Payne,

2003; Metalsky, Joiner, Hardin, & Abramson, 1993; Robinson, Garber, & Hilsman, 1995; Southall & Roberts, 2002). Metalsky et al. (1993) assert that high SE breaks the connection between negative attributional style, hopelessness and depression, but exactly how this happens is left unexplained.

Regardless of level of SE, we would expect that negative attributional styles will impact one's outlook on the future when confronted with stressful life events—as a result of stability attributions, adversity would be expected to continue into the future; as a result of generality attributions, adversity would be expected to be pervasive across life domains; and as a result of internality attributions, adversity would be viewed as resulting from something internal to the person. Though the future would not look bright, those with higher SE appear resistant to developing generalized hopelessness and depression. Why? Somehow, high SE buffers against the toxic effects of these attributions and allows these individuals to remain engaged and active in life. Perhaps a different form of hopelessness arises—hopelessness about the external situation but not about the value and worth of the self.

From the depression literature, several themes emerge. First, the effects of various facets of SE play different roles in the onset versus maintenance of the condition. Second, SE interacts with other risk factors, such as life stress and attributional style, in the prediction of depression. Third, more complex models of SE that include facets beyond level contribute to our understanding. Finally, it should be noted that SE may mediate the effects of adverse parenting and insecure attachment on the development of depressive symptoms emerging later in life (Gamble & Roberts, 2005; Garber, Robinson, & Valentiner, 1997; Roberts, Gotlib, & Kassel, 1996). Each of these issues is likely to be important in research exploring SE in other mental disorders.

SELF-ESTEEM IN OTHER CLINICAL CONDITIONS

From both diagnostic and theoretical standpoints, SE plays a pivotal role in a number of clinical conditions beyond depression. For example, one of the cardinal symptoms of eating disorders involves the overvaluing of body shape on SE. This view suggests that individuals with SE contingencies based on body shape will be at risk for eating disorders. Consistent with this perspective there is evidence that females who base their SE on body shape are at risk for developing eating disorder symptoms (Crocker, 2002; Geller, Johnston, Madsen, Goldner, Remic, & Birmingham, 1998), as are females who base their SE on intimate relationships (Geller, Zaitsoff, & Srikameswaran, 2002). Furthermore, a series of studies has demonstrated that low SE prospectively predicts symptoms of bulimia in interaction with perfectionism and the perception of being overweight. Specifically, perfectionistic women who perceive themselves as being overweight are at risk for developing symptoms of bulimia if they have low SE, but not if they have high SE (Vohs et al., 2001; Vohs, Bardone, Joiner, & Abramson, 1999).

Although both clinical theory (e.g., Heimberg & Becker, 2002) and diagnostic criteria emphasize the importance of SE issues in the social anxiety disorders (social phobia and avoidant personality disorder), there is a paucity of empirical work examining the role of SE in these conditions. Cross-sectional studies have demonstrated that social anxiety is correlated with low SE on explicit measures of self-worth (Kocovski & Endler, 2000; de Jong, 2002), but not on implicit measures (de Jong, 2002). Likewise, according to both diagnostic criteria and clinical theory, several personality disorders including narcissistic, avoidant, dependent and borderline personality disorders are rooted in SE deficits, but again there is little well-designed empirical research. One exception is a recent study demonstrating that borderline features are associated with both lower levels of SE and less stability of SE from one day to the next (Tolpin, Gunthert, Cohen, & O'Neill, 2004). Interestingly, two disorders raise issues concerning the global versus domain-specific nature of SE—body dysmorphic disorder and gender identity disorder. The former involves strong negative evaluation of a specific body part (e.g., one's nose), whereas the latter involves negative evaluation of one's assigned sex. To what extent is extreme dissatisfaction with a body part or negative evaluation of one's gender conceptually similar to the SE construct?

SELF-ESTEEM IN TREATMENT

To what extent are improvements in SE per se important in treatment? In other words, should interventions directly target SE as an end in itself? Consistent with this idea, some clinicians have developed programs that are specifically designed to raise SE (e.g., McKay & Fanning, 1992; Mruk, 1995; Newns, Bell, & Thomas, 2003). Likewise, cognitive therapists emphasize work on modifying beliefs about the self (e.g., Beck, 1995), including schema—deeply ingrained beliefs such as "I am fundamentally unlovable," "I am unable to function on my own" and "I am morally bad" (Young, 1994). This work involves teaching clients to treat their thoughts (including their beliefs related to self-worth) as hypotheses rather than as hard truths. Clients would learn to examine the evidence for and against their negative beliefs, develop methods of testing these beliefs, and consider alternative beliefs that are more consistent with the facts. They would also learn to systematically monitor and challenge logical errors in their thinking—so-called "cognitive distortions"—such as black and white thinking and overgeneralization.

A second perspective suggests that improvements in SE are primarily important as a means to other ends, for example, helping the client feel good enough and competent enough to try making a behavioral change. Within this perspective, SE is relevant in terms of facilitating adaptive behavior. For example, the standard treatment for specific phobias involves exposure to the feared stimulus and the standard treatment for obsessive–compulsive disorder involves exposure to the feared stimulus (typically a frightening thought or image, or a "contaminated" object) with response prevention (i.e., preventing the ritualistic behavior that typically follows contact with the feared stimulus). Both cases are enormously challenging for the client, and consequently one of the most challenging tasks for the clinician is to help the client muster the psychological resources necessary to engage in treatment. SE would be a necessary ingredient for change, but would not be directly related to the actual mechanism of change—in this case habituation to feared stimuli.

A final perspective suggests that treatment should work toward decreasing self-focus and preoccupation with self-worth. In other words, the therapist should help the client decrease the struggle against negative self-evaluative thoughts. Paradoxically, the struggle for SE itself may be problematic for many individuals (Crocker & Park, 2004). Consistent with this possibility, low SE among depressed patients who are highly self-focused and ruminative is predictive of poor response to behavioral treatment (Ciesla & Roberts, 2002). Given their elevated self-focus and rumination, these patients are likely to be highly preoccupied with their negative thoughts about themselves. Perhaps this idea is best exemplified among individuals with narcissistic (Morf & Rhodewalt, 2001) and borderline personality disorders. Such individuals find any feelings of inadequacy intolerable and wreak interpersonal havoc in their frantic efforts to avoid such feelings. In fact, recent developments in clinical practice emphasize the importance of acceptance in which the client learns to tolerate previously rejected aspects of themselves rather than struggling to change them (Hayes, Strosahl, & Wilson, 1999; Linehan, 1993; Segal, Williams, & Teasdale, 2002). This process may involve habituation to negative internal experience, including feelings of inadequacy and guilt, and learning to ease the struggle for positive self-worth.

If SE becomes a focus in treatment, it is important that the clinician assess the nature and functional impact of the client's SE issues. Rather than being a monolithic construct, SE appears to have a multifaceted nature, and this perspective needs to be incorporated in clinical work. For example, Greenier, Kernis, and Waschull (1995) raise the possibility that unstable SE can arise from different causal pathways. Unstable SE that results from high ego involvement in which the client is continuously involved in self-evaluative processes would have different treatment implications than unstable SE that results from an impoverished self-concept. One of the key aspects in case conceptualization involves a functional assessment of how SE issues and related behaviors impact the client's life. For example, does the client verbalize negative self-statements? What situations do these behaviors tend to occur in? What are the consequences of this behavior? As an example, in some cases of depression feelings of worthlessness lead to social withdrawal, isolation, and inactivity. The resulting loss of reinforcement and reward in turn directly contributes to depression (see Lewinsohn, Hoberman, & Hautzinger, 1985). In such cases, it may be more productive to concentrate efforts at improving social activity rather than directly trying to increase SE.

CONCLUSIONS

Various facets of SE appear to be associated with risk for depression, and perhaps other clinical disorders as well. Likewise, they appear to be involved in the process of recovery. However, the causal pathways by which SE is associated with clinical disorders and their treatment are unclear—it may be that the causal effects of SE are largely indirect and are mediated by behavior and the environment. Paradoxically, it may be that preoccupation with one's view of self is most problematic for some individuals as it interferes with the pursuit of goals and engagement with life and the experience of reinforcement and reward from the environment. Greater attention to the mechanisms by which SE is associated with mental disorders would be productive in both clinical practice and research. Such a functional analytic approach would examine the actual consequences of SE deficits in the person's life, including interpersonal, behavioral, and environmental consequences, and how those consequences contribute to clinical conditions. Finally, given the close association between aspects of SE and various mental disorders, it would be wise for social and personality researchers to consider the possibility that some of their findings are the result of elevated levels of clinical symptoms, such as depression, rather than SE deficits per se.

REFERENCES

Abela, J. R. Z., & Payne, A. V. L. (2003). A test of the integration of the hopelessness and self-esteem theories of depression in school children. *Cognitive Therapy and Research, 27,* 519–535.

Abramson, L. Y., Alloy, L. B., & Metalsky, G. I. (1989). Hopelessness depression: A theory-based subtype of depression. *Psychological Review, 96,* 358–372.

Beck, J. S. (1995). *Cognitive therapy: Basics and beyond.* New York: Guilford Press.

Butler, A. C., Hokanson, J. E., & Flynn, H. A. (1994). A comparison of self-esteem liability and low trait self-esteem as vulnerability factors for depression. *Journal of Personality and Social Psychology, 66,* 166–177.

Ciesla, J. A., & Roberts, J. E. (2002). Self-directed thought and response to treatment for depression: A preliminary investigation. *Journal of Cognitive Psychotherapy: An International Quarterly, 16,* 435–453.

Crocker, J. (2002). The costs of seeking self-esteem. *Journal of Social Issues, 58,* 597–615.

Crocker, J., Karpinski, A., Quinn, D. M., & Chase, S. K. (2003). When grades determine self-worth: Consequences of contingent self-worth for male and female engineering and psychology majors. *Journal of Personality and Social Psychology, 85,* 507–516.

Crocker, J., & Park, L. E. (2004). The costly pursuit of self-esteem. *Psychological Bulletin, 130,* 392–414.

de Jong, P. J. (2002). Implicit self-esteem and social anxiety: Differential self-favouring effects in high and low anxious individuals. *Behaviour Research & Therapy, 40,* 501–508.

Gable, S. L., & Nezlek, J. B. (1998). Level and instability of day-to-day psychological well-being and risk for depression. *Journal of Personality and Social Psychology, 74,* 129–138.

Gamble, S. A., & Roberts, J. E. (2005). Adolescents' perceptions of primary caregivers and depressive symptomatology: The mediating roles of attachment security and self-esteem. *Cognitive Therapy and Research, 25,* 123–141.

Garber, J., Robinson, N. S., & Valentiner, D. (1997). The relation between parenting and adolescent depression: Self-worth as a mediator. *Journal of Adolescent Research, 12,* 12–33.

Geller, J., Johnston, C., Madsen, K., Goldner, E. M., Remic, R. A., & Birmingham, C. L. (1998). Shape- and weight-based self-esteem and the eating disorders. *International Journal of Eating Disorders, 24,* 285–298.

Geller, J., Zaitsoff, S. L., & Srikameswaran, S. (2002). Beyond shape and weight: Exploring the relationship between nonbody determinants of self-esteem and eating disorder symptoms in adolescent females. *International Journal of Eating Disorders, 32,* 344–351.

Greenier, K. D., Kernis, M. H., & Waschull, S. B. (1995). Not all high (or low) self-esteem people are the same: Theory and research on stability of self-esteem. In M. H. Kernis (Ed.), *Efficacy, agency, and self-esteem* (pp. 51–68). New York: Plenum Press.

Hayes, S. C., Strosahl, K. D., & Wilson, K. G. (1999). *Acceptance and commitment therapy: An experiential approach to behavior change.* New York: Guilford Press.

Heimberg, R. G., & Becker, R. R. (2002). *Cognitive-behavioral group therapy for social phobia.* New York: Guilford Press.

Joiner, T. E., & Metalsky, G. I. (2001). Excessive reassurance seeking: Delineating a risk factor involved in the development of depressive symptoms. *Psychological Science, 12,* 371–378.

Kernis, M. H., Grannemann, B. D., & Barclay, L. C. (1989). Stability and level of self-esteem as predictors of anger arousal and hostility. *Journal of Personality and Social Psychology, 56,* 1013–1022.

Kernis, M. H., Whisenhunt, C. R., Waschull, S. B., Greenier, K. D., Berry, A. J., Herlocker, C. E., & Anderson, C. A. (1998). Multiple facets of self-esteem and their relations to depressive symptoms. *Personality and Social Psychology Bulletin, 24,* 657–668.

Kocovski, N. L., & Endler, N. S. (2000). Social anxiety, self-regulation, and fear of negative evaluation. *European Journal of Personality, 14,* 347–358.

Lewinsohn, P. M., Hoberman, H., Teri, L., & Hautzinger, M. (1985). An integrative theory of depression. In S. Reiss & R. Bootzin (Eds.), *Theoretical issues in behavior therapy* (pp. 331–359). New York: Academic Press.

Linehan, M. M. (1993). *Cognitive-behavioral treatment of borderline personality disorder.* New York: Guilford Press.

McKay, M., & Fanning, P. (1992). *Self-esteem.* Oakland, CA: New Harbinger Publications.

Metalsky, G. I., Joiner, T. E., Hardin, T. S., & Abramson, L. Y. (1993). Depressive reactions to failure in a naturalistic setting: A test of the hopelessness and self-esteem theories of depression. *Journal of Abnormal Psychology, 102,* 101–109.

Morf, C. C., & Rhodewalt, F. (2001). Unraveling the paradoxes of narcissism: A dynamic self-regulatory processing model. *Psychological Inquiry, 12,* 177–196.

Mruk, C. (1995). *Self-esteem: Research, theory, and practice.* New York: Springer.

Newns, K., Bell, L., & Thomas, S. (2003). The impact of a self-esteem group for people with eating disorders: An uncontrolled study. *Clinical Psychology and Psychotherapy, 10,* 64–68.

Roberts, J. E., & Ciesla, J. A. (2000). Stress generation in the context of depressive disorders. In G. Fink (Ed.), *Encyclopedia of stress* (pp. 512–518). San Diego, CA: Academic Press.

Roberts, J. E., & Gamble, S. A. (2001). Cognitive characteristics of previously depressed adolescents. *Personality and Individual Differences, 30,* 1023–1037.

Roberts, J. E., & Gotlib, I. H. (1997). Temporal variability in global self-esteem and specific self-evaluation as prospective predictors of emotional distress: Specificity in predictors and outcome. *Journal of Abnormal Psychology, 106,* 521–529.

Roberts, J. E., Gotlib, I. H., & Kassel, J. D. (1996). Adult attachment security and symptoms of depression: The mediating roles of dysfunctional attitudes and low self-esteem. *Journal of Personality and Social Psychology, 70,* 310–320.

Roberts, J. E., & Kassel, J. D. (1997). Labile self-esteem, stressful life events, and depressive symptoms: Prospective data testing a model of vulnerability. *Cognitive Therapy and Research, 21,* 569–589.

Roberts, J. E., & Monroe, S. M. (1992). Vulnerable self-esteem and depressive symptoms: Prospective findings comparing three alternative conceptualizations. *Journal of Personality and Social Psychology*, 62, 804–812.

Roberts, J. E., & Monroe, S. M. (1999). Vulnerable self-esteem and social processes in depression: Toward an interpersonal model of self-esteem regulation. In T. Joiner & J. Coyne (Eds.), *The interactional nature of depression: Advances in interpersonal approaches* (pp. 149–187). Washington, DC: American Psychological Association.

Roberts, J. E., Shapiro, A. M., & Gamble, S. (1999). Level and perceived stability of self-esteem prospectively predict depressive symptoms during psychoeducational group treatment. *British Journal of Clinical Psychology*, 38, 425–429.

Roberts, S. B., & Kendler, K. S. (1999). Neuroticism and self-esteem as indices of the vulnerability to major depression in women. *Psychological Medicine*, 29, 1101–1109.

Robinson, N. S., Garber, J., & Hilsman, R. (1995). Cognitions and stress: Direct and moderating effects on depressive versus externalizing symptoms during the junior high school transition. *Journal of Abnormal Psychology*, 104, 453–463.

Schmitz, N., Kugler, J., & Rollnik, J. (2003). On the relation between neuroticism, self-esteem, and depression: Results from the National Comorbidity Survey. *Comprehensive Psychiatry*, 44, 169–176.

Segal, Z. V., Williams, J. M. G., & Teasdale, J. D. (2002). *Mindfulness-based cognitive therapy for depression*. New York: Guilford Press.

Southall, D., & Roberts, J. E. (2002). Attributional style and self-esteem in vulnerability to adolescent depressive symptoms following life stress: A 14-week prospective study. *Cognitive Therapy and Research*, 26, 563–579.

Tolpin, L. H., Gunthert, C. K., Cohen, L. H., & O'Neill, S. C. (2004). Borderline personality features and instability of daily negative affect and self-esteem. *Journal of Personality*, 72, 111–138.

Vohs, K. D., Bardone, A. M., Joiner, T. E., & Abramson, L. Y. (1999). Perfectionism, perceived weight status, and self-esteem interact to predict bulimic symptoms: A model of bulimic symptom development. *Journal of Abnormal Psychology*, 108, 695–700.

Vohs, K. D., Voelz, Z. R., Pettit, J. W., Bardone, A. M., Katz, J., Abramson, L. Y., Heatherton, T. F., & Joiner, T. E. (2001). Perfectionism, body dissatisfaction, and self-esteem: An interactive model of bulimic symptom development. *Journal of Social and Clinical Psychology*, 20, 476–497.

Young, J. E. (1994). *Cognitive therapy for personality disorders: A schema-focused approach*. Sarasota, FL: Professional Resource Press.

40

Self-Esteem, Psychopathology, and Psychotherapy

EDWARD J. O'BRIEN, MIA BARTOLETTI, and JEFFREY D. LEITZEL

*T*his essay considers two issues. First, we examine self-esteem issues in diagnosing psychopathology in the DSM-IV-TR (American Psychiatric Association, 2000). We then consider how self-esteem research can help develop an empirical basis for the DSM (Beutler & Malik, 2002), and how psychiatric observations may increase understanding of biological effects on self-esteem. Second, we consider self-esteem as an outcome measure, as an independent variable in psychotherapy interventions, and as a factor influencing therapist effectiveness.

SELF-ESTEEM AND PSYCHOPATHOLOGY[1]

Self-esteem has been linked to a wide variety of psychopathologies (Silverstone, 1991). A search of the DSM-IV-TR shows that the term "self-esteem" appears in 24 different diagnostic contexts, as a criterion for disorders (e.g., dysthymia), as a criterion for disorders being considered for inclusion in future DSM editions (e.g., depressive personality disorder), and as an associated feature of disorders (e.g., social phobia). Complicating the linkages between self-esteem and the DSM is the fact that there are over 70 different "self" terms in the DSM-IV-TR[2] with many having meanings that overlap with self-esteem, including, for example: arrogant self-appraisal, grandiose sense of self, inflated self-appraisal, low self-worth (dirtiness, worthlessness), self-assured (cocky), self-blame, self-confidence, self-critical, self-deprecation, self-doubts, self-evaluation, and self-reproach. Such casual language usage complicates the task of understanding linkages between self-esteem and psychopathology in the DSM.

Self-Esteem and Mood Disorders

The largest number of associations between self-esteem and psychopathology involve mood disorders where self-esteem is a diagnostic criterion for each disorder.

Chronic and pervasive low self-esteem is a diagnostic criterion for dysthymic disorder. Low self-esteem (described as "feelings of worthlessness or excessive or inappropriate guilt") is a defining criterion of a depressive episode that is required to diagnose major depression. Grandiose high self-esteem is a criterion used to define hypomanic and manic episodes, which are diagnostic when linked to instability of mood in cyclothymic and bipolar disorders. Cyclothymia involves chronic instability in mood and self-esteem whereas bipolar disorder is defined in more acute terms with self-esteem varying from extreme worthlessness to grandiosity.

Several new diagnoses are being considered for inclusion in the DSM (Appendix B, DSM-IV-TR) that involve self-esteem dysfunction. All of these disorders are linked to depressive symptoms and include low self-esteem as a diagnostic criterion: postpsychotic depressive disorder of schizophrenia, minor depressive disorder, recurrent brief depressive disorder, mixed anxiety–depressive disorder, and depressive personality disorder.

Negative self-evaluation is one element of Beck's cognitive triad in depression (e.g., DeRubeis, Tang, & Beck, 2001). Self-esteem has been shown to be related in a linear manner to a spectrum of levels of depression, ranging from nondepressed to major depression, with several subclinical depression levels in between that are associated with serious psychosocial problems (Gotlib, Lewinsohn, & Seeley, 1995; Lewinsohn, Solomon, Seeley, & Zeiss, 2000). While there is strong empirical evidence for a link between self-esteem and depression, etiological issues remain ambiguous. That is, we are uncertain about whether self-esteem disturbance is a risk factor for mood disorders, an empirical marker for mood disorders, or a consequence of mood disorders ("scar" hypothesis) (Abela, 2002; Butler, Hokanson, & Flynn, 1994; Roberts & Monroe, 1999; Shahar & Davidson, 2003). Harter (1999) argues that self-esteem may be both a risk factor and a consequence of depression (in different individuals and/or at different times for the same individual).

Personality Disorders

Self-esteem dysfunction is a diagnostic criterion and/or an associated feature for dependent, avoidant, narcissistic, antisocial, and borderline personality disorders. Low self-esteem is a criterion for dependent and avoidant personality disorders while grandiose high self-esteem is a criterion for narcissistic personality disorder and an associated feature for antisocial personality disorder. Instability of self-image is a defining feature of borderline personality disorder. Comorbidity of personality disorders with mood disorders usually suggests a poor prognosis, but research on this point is inconsistent (e.g., Kuyken, Kurzer, DeRubeis, Beck, & Brown, 2001; Morrison, Bradley, & Westen, 2003).

Anxiety Disorders

Self-esteem level is not a criterion for any anxiety disorder. However, self-esteem is considered to be an associated issue that may be relevant in several anxiety disorders. For example, individuals suffering from social phobia are said to be hypersensitive to criticism, to evaluate themselves negatively, and to have low self-esteem. Someone suffering from posttraumatic stress disorder (PTSD) may be self-blaming after a physical attack, or have feelings of being "damaged" by sexual abuse. Most anxiety disorders, including generalized anxiety and obsessive-compulsive disorder, have high comorbidities with mood disorders (Brown & Barlow, 2002; Morrison et al., 2003; Rasmussin & Eisen, 1988) and symptoms of low self-esteem. Finally, adjustment disorders[3] often involve low self-esteem symptoms.

Schizophrenia-Spectrum Disorders

Low self-esteem is a diagnostic criterion for schizoaffective disorder. While self-esteem is not involved in the diagnosis of schizophrenia, research with schizophrenia patients shows that they report low self-esteem. Barrowclough, Tarrier, Humphreys, Ward, Gregg, & Andrews (2003) found that criticism patients experience over their positive symptoms of schizophrenia was associated with low self-esteem and with the exacerbation of symptoms.

Eating Disorders

Self-esteem issues are associated features in the disorders of anorexia and bulimia nervosa. In these disorders, body appearance is thought to play too central a role in self-esteem and/or the client shows body image distortion related to self-esteem. Interestingly, evaluation of body appearance is highly correlated with global self-esteem (.65 and .64) in normal populations (Harter, 1999; and O'Brien & Epstein, 1988, respectively) as well as in these patient groups.

Other Disorders

Self-esteem is an associated feature of a number of other disorders including: learning disorders, stuttering, attention deficit-hyperactivity disorder, conduct disorder, oppositional defiant disorder, substance abuse disorders, gender identity disorder, encopresis, and enuresis. The link to self-esteem often involves stigma effects on patients with these disorders (e.g., teasing by peers because of a learning disorder). Stigma effects on self-esteem may play a role in most DSM diagnoses. In the case of conduct disorder and oppositional defiant disorder, the link to self-esteem involves unstable, grandiose, and defensive self-esteem in an outward bravado that may, in some individuals, mask underlying feelings of low self-esteem.[4]

Bridges between Self-Esteem and the DSM

Self-esteem theory and research have considerable potential for establishing a more empirical foundation for the DSM. Studies of self-esteem show two somewhat independent dimensions, level of self-esteem and variability or instability of self-esteem (e.g., Kernis, 2003) that correspond to the two dimensions used for the diagnosis of all mood disorders, level, and lability of mood. Work is needed to directly test theories of disease entity versus continuum models in these two dimensions of self-esteem and mood (Meehl, 1995; Joiner & Schmidt, 2002).

Disease entity models underlie the DSM medical model and are premised on the notion that psychological disorders correspond to categories or types that can be defined by rules of inclusion based on symptom presence or absence (e.g., Houts, 2002). For example, a patient must show five of nine presence–absence symptoms (e.g., depressed mood, feelings of worthlessness) to meet the diagnostic criterion for having a major depressive episode. In the disease entity approach, an individual either has the disease (meets the diagnostic criteria for inclusion) or does not have the disease.

In contrast, continuum models are premised on the notion that symptoms associated with adjustment and psychopathology vary along continua from normal functioning to various levels of pathological functioning. Most personality and clinical research in psychology is based on the continuum model (Joiner & Schmidt, 2002). For example, the continuum model would argue that mood can vary from "normal" depression in everyday life to moderately severe and extreme depressions. Based on the continuum model, determining what constitutes a clinical level of depression involves setting a somewhat arbitrary cut point based on severity and duration of depressive moods. Individuals who do not meet such an arbitrary cut point criterion may still be suffering from significant problems that impact on their ability to function (e.g., Lewinsohn et al., 2000). Rather than a presence–absence decision, the continuum model would locate an individual's standing on depression somewhere on a more-or-less normal curve with a corresponding T-score or percentile score to indicate where that individual stands along a continuum in comparison to a normative comparison group.

Empirical studies of normal and pathological mood level and lability are needed to further evaluate disease entity versus continuum models. Future studies of self-esteem should further examine the correlates of different levels of self-esteem and instability with mood level and lability (e.g., Kernis, 2003; Gotlib et al., 1995; Lewinsohn et al., 2000). For example, at what level does low self-esteem show implications for depression? At what level does high self-esteem become associated with narcissism? What are "normal" levels of self-esteem and mood instability and at what point does such instability begin to interfere with psychological adjustment and well being? At an instrumentation level there is a need to develop self-report and/or judge rating methods to support a more empirical basis for judgments of level of pathology rather than the "presence–absence" tests in the current DSM. Empirical studies are needed to identify symptoms that covary and should therefore be clustered together, cut points for establishing level of dysfunction, and level of individual symptom (versus presence–absence) needed for the determination of clinical significance of a symptom.

Analyses of self-esteem instability (e.g., Kernis, 2003) show particular promise in increasing our understanding of levels of cyclothymic and bipolar disorders. The many categorical classifications in this area of the DSM (Bipolar I, Bipolar II, mixed episodes, single and recurrent major depressive episodes, acute versus chronic mood lability in bipolar versus cyclothymic) would benefit greatly from empirical studies utilizing self-monitoring methods employed by Kernis and others to directly observe variability in self-esteem and mood (which will almost certainly turn out to be a continuum varying from minimal to dramatic instability).

It may be worth moving toward including ratings of self-esteem level and variability in future versions of the DSM or other diagnostic manuals (e.g., the ICD). This would be similar to the experimental inclusion in the DSM-IV-TR of dimensional ratings (absent, mild, moderate, severe) of psychotic, disorganized, and negative symptoms in schizophrenia. Inclusion of similar ratings for self-esteem level and instability would allow accumulation of more empirical findings about the actual topography of self-esteem symptoms as they relate to the many disorders in the DSM. For example, a rating system of self-esteem level and stability as normal or problematic (at mild, moderate, or serious levels) could add significantly to our empirical understanding of patterns of self-esteem dysfunction in various psychopathologies.

Self-esteem research may also benefit from medical model research. For example, psychiatric studies may suggest important biological issues to be incorporated into self-esteem models that at times seem rather "cerebral" in their psychosocial focus. For example, self-esteem instability is likely affected by genetic and biochemical factors that may at times take away joy in life (and self) and at other times turn joy into seemingly uncontrollable passion (Newman, Leahy, Beck, Reilly-Harrington, & Gyuli, 2002).

SELF-ESTEEM AND TREATMENT INTERVENTIONS

Self-Esteem as an Outcome Measure

The Smith, Glass, and Miller (1980) metaanalysis found self-esteem to be a common psychotherapy outcome measure. Self-esteem continues to be a widely used outcome measure in humanistic therapies (Elliot, 2002) and is often an implicit (e.g., as a component part of the CES-D depression measure) and/or explicit outcome measure in cognitive-behavioral and other treatments (e.g., Alden, 1989; Kubany et al., 2004; Rossello & Bernal, 1999; Watson, Gordon, Stermac, Kalogerakos, & Steckley, 2003). Self-esteem has been used as an outcome measure and positive changes in self-esteem have been demonstrated with well thought out and targeted interventions for virtually all clinical presenting problems from career indecision to depression, personality disorders, and schizophrenia (e.g., Elliot, Greenberg, & Lietaer, 2004). Self-esteem measures have also detected treatment failures where ill-considered interventions have been applied to nontargeted populations and have achieved poor outcomes (e.g., Lynam et al., 1999; Scheier & Kraut, 1979).

Unresolved self-esteem issues are often present in clients once they complete time-limited and manualized therapies (e.g., Gutierres & Todd, 1997; Kubany et al., 2004). While there are encouraging outcomes in the treatment of depression and anxiety disorders, many (sometimes most) clients with these disorders fail to respond, only partially respond, drop out, or only temporarily improve in response to therapy (Westen & Morrison, 2001). Clinical trials outcome studies typically treat "pure" cases and exclude clients who have comorbid or subclinical personality problems such as self-esteem, inhibition, and attachment problems (Morrison et al., 2003). The presence of such problems adds considerably to the difficulties and time required for effective treatment. Morrison et al. pointed out that multi-symptomatic cases are the norm in clinical practice. A key aspect of what is often left undone in clinical trials studies may involve addressing core aspects of self-esteem issues. McMullin (1999) suggested that clinicians should consider the ratio between the dozens of clinical interventions used to change a client's negative self-esteem versus the thousands of negative life experiences, over decades of life, involving many individuals with whom the client was quite intimately involved. Consideration of this ratio may help therapists appreciate the time and effort required to bring about lasting change in core self-evaluation.

Self-Esteem Change as an Independent Variable

Our discussion of self-esteem change processes comes from humanistic and cognitive behavioral therapies. Changing self-esteem has been a key goal in client-centered therapy (Rogers, 1959). However, self-esteem enhancement is but one of several goals in this therapy. As one strives to bring the client's actual self into alignment with her or his ideal self (Rogers' definition of self-esteem), it is important for the client to also address organismic levels of experience. Consider the example of a student who feels negatively about parental disapproval over his poor school performance. A Rogerian therapist would view this problem in terms of the student's striving for external rewards. It may be that the student is majoring in the wrong discipline so as to please his parents and may need to find a major that better fits his experiential world. The therapist's job is not to support the student in achieving self-esteem but to help him find sources of self-esteem that are congruent with his inner experience. The therapist in this case would convey unconditional positive regard for the client while empathically helping the student develop his sense of inner direction.

Research shows that therapists achieve more positive outcomes when they have genuine positive regard for the client and show empathy for the client's experience (Beutler et al., 2004; Elliot et al., 2004; Sachse & Elliot, 2002). The magnitude of these effects on outcome is not large (similar to the modest but consistently positive effects of a collaborative therapist-client relationship). Beck's cognitive behavioral therapy (CBT) explicitly includes the "Rogerian triad" as a key element (Hollon & Beck, 2004). Self-esteem change, then, can come from the positive reflected appraisals from the therapist who is empathically helping the client find internal sources of genuine or authentic self-esteem.

In addition to the Rogerian triad, CBT for depression involves correcting low self-esteem as one part of the cognitive triad of depression (Hollon & Beck, 2004). CBT includes psychoeducation to help clients become aware of negative "self-talk" and the depressing impact of such talk and the beliefs on which it is based. Client self-monitoring of cognitive and emotional processes related to depression helps identify areas where automatic thoughts are maintaining depressed mood. Identification of "cognitive errors" in self-appraisal follows from client self-monitoring and therapy interviews. Correcting such errors as all-or-none thinking, overgeneralization, and selective attention to negative life experiences may enhance the client's self-esteem (e.g., Young, Weinberger & Beck, 2001; Clarke, Hawkins, Murphy, Sheeber, Lewinsohn, & Seeley, 1995).

Mruk (1999) created a self-esteem change program based on empirically validated strategies taken from humanistic and CBT approaches and ideas derived from other therapies. In addition to the phenomenological and CBT intervention efforts described above, Mruk's program involves psychoeducation regarding the nature and effects of self-esteem and defensiveness. It also includes goal setting and implementation of a self-esteem change project in a structured 5-week group therapy program. Initial outcomes with Mruk's program have been positive (Hakim-Larson & Mruk, 1997). Bartoletti (2004) recently initiated a clinical trials (wait list control) outcome study of Mruk's approach with a college counseling population. Bartoletti will examine whether Mruk's program can achieve positive changes in self-esteem, constructive thinking, explanatory style, and immunocompetence (Immunoglobulin A levels) while not bringing about increases in narcissism.

Self-Esteem of the Therapist

This essay will end by considering the self-esteem of the therapist. The therapist's own well-being may play an important role in her or his ability to help others. Jennings & Skovholt (1999) identified "master therapists" based on peer nominations. These master therapists were found to be mentally healthy and mature people who attended to their own well-being and who had a healthy, authentic sense of self-importance that was neither grandiose nor overly humble. On the other end of the continuum, a significant number of therapists develop personal problems that interfere with their ability to function effectively (Norcross, Geller, & Kurzawa, 2000). Beutler et al. (2004) found a modest but consistently positive link between the therapist's personal adjustment and her/his therapeutic effectiveness. Therapists who successfully care for their own optimal self-esteem and emotional well-being are thus more likely to be effective in their work with clients.

This essay examined connections among self-esteem, psychopathology, and psychotherapy. Self-esteem issues are extensively involved in many aspects of psychopathology. The conceptual and methodological sophistication of self-esteem research has much to offer in creating a stronger empirical basis for future editions of the DSM (Kupfer, First, & Regier, 2002). Consideration of self-esteem issues also has the potential for focusing psychotherapy efforts on achieving deeper and more lasting changes in the lives of clients.

NOTES

1. For simplicity of reference, most of our statements about links between self-esteem and the diagnosis of mental disorders come from the DSM-IV-TR. We will note when we use sources other than the DSM.

2. Approximately 20 of these terms involve the use of "self" as a proxy for "the person". For example, self-masturbation refers to a physical, not a cognitive process. Over 50 of the "self" terms refer to concepts relevant to the self-esteem and self-concept literatures.

3.   Note that while adjustment disorders are considered separate from anxiety disorders in the DSM, we are considering them here due to their association with difficulty in coping with stress.

4.   Our review of linkages between self-esteem and the DSM is certainly not exhaustive (e.g., we have not considered conditions such as relationship, occupational, abuse & neglect, or identity problems). Hopefully, we have given a sense of the many interconnections to be explored between self-esteem and psychopathology in the DSM.

REFERENCES

Abela, J. R. Z. (2002). Depressive mood reactions to failure in the achievement domain: A test of the integration of the hopelessness and self-esteem theories of depression. *Cognitive Therapy & Research, 26*(4), 531–552.

Alden, L. (1989). Short-term structured treatment for avoidant personality disorder. *Journal of Consulting and Clinical Psychology, 57*(6), 756–764.

American Psychiatric Association. (2000). *Diagnostic and statistical manual of mental disorders* (4th ed., Text Revision). Washington, DC: American Psychiatric Association.

Barrowclough, C., Tarrier, N., Humphreys, L., Ward, J., Gregg, L., & Andrews, B. (2003). Self-esteem in schizophrenia: Relationships between self-evaluation, family attitudes, and symptomatology. *Journal of Abnormal Psychology, 112*(1), 92–99.

Bartoletti, M. (2004). *Effects of self-esteem change on psychological and physiological measures of well-being.* Unpublished doctoral dissertation proposal, Marywood University, Scranton, PA.

Beutler, L. E., & Malik, M. L. (Eds.). (2002). *Rethinking the DSM: A psychological perspective.* Washington, DC: American Psychological Association.

Beutler, L. E., Malik, M. L., Alimohamed, S., Harwood, T. M., Talebi, H., Noble, S., & Wong, E. (2004). Therapist variables. In M. J. Lambert (Ed.), *Bergen and Garfield's handbook of psychotherapy and behavior change* (5th ed., pp. 227–306). New York: Wiley.

Brown, T. A., & Barlow, D. H. (2002). Classification of anxiety and mood disorders. In D. H. Barlow (Ed.), *Anxiety and its disorders: The nature and treatment of anxiety and panic* (pp. 292–327). New York: The Guilford Press.

Butler, A. C., Hokanson, J. E., & Flynn, H. A. (1994). A comparison of self-esteem lability and low trait self-esteem as vulnerability factors for depression. *Journal of Personality and Social Psychology, 66*(1), 166–177.

Clarke, G. N., Hawkins, W., Murphy, M., Sheeber, L., Lewinsohn, P. M., & Seeley, J. R. (1995). Targeted prevention of unipolar depressive disorder in an at-risk sample of high school adolescents: A randomized trial of a group cognitive intervention. *Journal of the American Academy of Child and Adolescent Psychiatry, 34,* 312–321.

DeRubeis, R. J., Tang, T. Z., & Beck, A. T. (2001). Cognitive therapy. In K. S. Dobson (Ed.), *Handbook of cognitive-behavioral therapies* (2nd ed., pp. 349–392). New York: Guilford Press.

Elliot, R. (2002). The effectiveness of humanistic therapies: A meta-analysis. In D. J. Cain & J. Seeman (Eds.), *Humanistic psychotherapies: Handbook of research and practice* (pp. 57–81). Washington, DC: American Psychological Association.

Elliot, R., Greenberg, L. S., & Lietaer, G. (2004). Research on experiential psychothera-pies. In M. J. Lambert (Ed.), *Bergen and Garfield's handbook of psychotherapy and behavior change* (5th ed., pp. 493–539). New York: Wiley.

Gotlib, I. H., Lewinsohn, P. M., & Seeley, J. R. (1995). Symptoms versus a diagnosis of depression: Differences in psychosocial functioning. *Journal of Consulting and Clinical Psychology, 63*, 90–100.

Gutierres, S. E., & Todd, M. (1997). The impact of childhood abuse on treatment out-comes of substance users. *Professional Psychology: Research & Practice, 28*(4), 348–354.

Hakim-Larson, J., & Mruk, C. (1997). Enhancing self-esteem in a community mental health setting. *American Journal of Orthopsychiatry, 67*(4), 655–659.

Harter, S. (1999). *The construction of the self: A developmental perspective.* New York: Guilford Press.

Hollon, S. D., & Beck, A. T. (2004). Cognitive and cognitive behavioral therapies. In M.J. Lambert (Ed.), *Garfield and Bergin's handbook of psychotherapy and behavior change: An empirical analysis* (5th ed., pp. 447–492). New York: Wiley.

Houts, A. C. (2002). Discovery, invention, and the expansion of the modern diagnostic and statistical manuals of mental disorders. In L. E. Beutler & M. L. Malik (Eds.), *Rethinking the DSM: A psychological perspective* (pp. 17–65). Washington, DC: American Psychological Association.

Jennings, L., & Skovholt, T. (1999). The cognitive, emotional and relational characteristics of master therapists. *Journal of Counseling Psychology, 46*(1), 3–11.

Joiner, T. E. J., & Schmidt, N. B. (2002). Taxometrics can "do diagnostics right" (and it isn't quite as hard as you think). In L. E. Beutler & M. L. Malik (Eds.), *Rethinking the DSM: A psychological perspective* (pp. 107–120). Washington, DC: American Psychological Association.

Kernis, M. H. (2003). Toward a conceptualization of optimal self-esteem. *Psychological Inquiry, 14*(1), 1–26.

Kubany, E. S., Hill, E. E., Owens, J. A., Iannce-Spencer, C., McCaig, M. A., Tremayne, K. J., & Williams, P. L. (2004). Cognitive trauma therapy for battered women with PTSD (CTT-BW). *Journal of Consulting and Clinical Psychology, 72*, 3–18.

Kupfer, D. J., First, M. B., & Regier, D. A. (Eds.). (2002). *A research agenda for DSM-V.* Washington, DC: American Psychiatric Association.

Kuyken, W., Kurzer, N., DeRubeis, R. J., Beck, A. T., & Brown, G. K. (2001). Response to cognitive therapy in depression: The role of maladaptive beliefs and personality disorders. *Journal of Consulting & Clinical Psychology, 69*(3), 560–566.

Lewinsohn, P. M., Solomon, A., Seeley, J. R., & Zeiss, A. (2000). Clinical implications of "subthreshold" depressive symptoms. *Journal of Abnormal Psychology, 109* (2), 345–351.

Lynam, D. R., Milich, R., Zimmerman, R., Novak, S. P., Logan, T. K., Martin, C., Leukfeld, C., & Clayton, R. (1999). Project DARE: No effects at 10-year follow-up. *Journal of Consulting and Clinical Psychology, 67*(4), 590–593.

McMullin, R. E. (1999). *The new handbook of cognitive therapy techniques* (2nd ed.). New York: W.W. Norton & Co.

Meehl, P. E. (1995). Bootstraps taxometrics: Solving the classification problem in psy-chopathology. *American Psychologist, 50*(4), 266–275.

Morrison, K. H., Bradley, R., & Westen, D. (2003). The external validity of controlled clin-ical trials of psychotherapy for depression and anxiety: A naturalistic study. *Psychology & Psychotherapy: Theory, Research & Practice, 76*(2), 109–132.

Mruk, C. J. (1999). *Self-esteem: Research, theory, and practice* (2nd ed.). New York: Springer.

Newman, C. F., Leahy, R. L., Beck, A. T., Reilly-Harrington, N. A., & Gyulai, L. (2002). *Bipolar disorder: A cognitive therapy approach*. Washington, DC: American Psychological Association.

Norcross, J. C., Geller, J. D., & Kurzawa, E. K. (2000). Conducting psychotherapy with psychotherapists: I. Prevalence, patients, and problems. *Psychotherapy: Theory, Research, Practice, Training, 37*(3), 199–205.

O'Brien, E. J., & Epstein, S. (1988). *MSEI the multidimensional self-esteem inventory: Professional manual*. Odessa, FL: Psychological Assessment Resources.

Rasmussen, S. A., & Eisen, J. L. (1988). Clinical and epidemiologic findings of significance to neuropharmacologic trials in OCD. *Psychopharmacology Bulletin, 24*(3), 466–470.

Roberts, J. E., & Monroe, S. M. (1999). Vulnerable self-esteem and social processes in depression: Toward an interpersonal model of self-esteem regulation. In T. Joiner & J. C. Coyne (Eds.), *The interactional nature of depression: Advances in interpersonal approaches* (pp. 149–187). Washington, DC: American Psychological Association.

Rogers, C. R. (1959). A theory of therapy, personality and interpersonal relationships as developed in the client-centered framework. In S. Koch (Ed.), *Psychology: A study of science* (Vol. 3, pp. 184–256). New York: McGraw-Hill.

Rossello, J., & Bernal, G. (1999). The efficacy of cognitive-behavioral and interpersonal treatments for depression in Puerto Rican adolescents. *Journal of Consulting & Clinical Psychology, 67*(5), 734–745.

Sachse, R., & Elliott, R. (2002). Process-outcome research on humanistic therapy variables. In D. J. Cain (Ed.), *Humanistic psychotherapies: Handbook of research and practice* (pp. 83–115). Washington, DC: American Psychological Association.

Scheirer, M. A., & Kraut, R. E. (1979). Increasing educational achievement via self concept change. *Review of Educational Research, 49*(1), 131–150.

Shahar, G., & Davidson, L. (2003). Depressive symptoms erode self-esteem in severe mental illness: A three-wave, cross-lagged study. *Journal of Consulting & Clinical Psychology, 71*(5), 890–900.

Silverstone, P. H. (1991). Low self-esteem in different psychiatric conditions. *British Journal of Clinical Psychology, 30*(2), 185–188.

Smith, M. L., Glass, G. V., & Miller, T. I. (1980). *The benefits of psychotherapy*. Baltimore, MD: Johns Hopkins University Press.

Watson, J. C., Gordon, L. B., Stermac, L., Kalogerakos, F., & Steckley, P. (2003). Comparing the effectiveness of process-experiential with cognitive-behavioral psychotherapy in the treatment of depression. *Journal of Consulting & Clinical Psychology, 71*(4), 773–781.

Westen, D., & Morrison, K. (2001). A multidimensional meta-analysis of treatments for depression, panic, and generalized anxiety disorder: An empirical examination of the status of empirically supported therapies. *Journal of Consulting & Clinical Psychology, 69*(6), 875–899.

Young, J. E., Weinberger, A. D., & Beck, A. T. (2001). Cognitive therapy for depression. In D. H. Barlow (Ed.), *Clinical handbook of psychological disorders: A step-by-step treatment manual* (3rd ed., pp. 264–308). New York: Guilford Press.

41

Self-Esteem in Therapeutic Settings and Emotional Disorders

TRACY DEHART and HOWARD TENNEN

S elf-esteem plays a key role in most formulations of psychopathological processes (Cooper, 1986) and in many models of therapeutic technique (Bednar, Wells, & Peterson, 1989). For several highly prevalent emotional disorders, such as depression and borderline personality, vulnerable self-esteem is a defining characteristic. For other disorders, such as narcissistic personality and eating disorders, fluctuations in self-esteem triggered by stressful interpersonal encounters prompt self-destructive behavior and maladaptive responses to others. We begin this brief chapter with an overview of the primary functions of self-esteem and the relevance of these functions to therapeutic efforts. We then illustrate how the dynamics of self-esteem are manifested in psychopathology through the lens of two emotional disorders, depression and narcissistic personality disorder. Next, we discuss how unconscious aspects of self-esteem pose a significant challenge to therapists. Finally, we offer daily process methodology as a promising way to examine self-esteem disturbances in emotional disorders and the therapeutic processes designed for their alleviation.

SELF-ESTEEM IN THE THERAPEUTIC SETTING

Previous theorizing on the self posits that high self-esteem promotes positive affect, goal achievement, and interpersonal relationships (Leary, Tambor, Terdal, & Downs, 1995). We believe that each of these self-esteem functions plays an important role in the therapeutic process.

Promotes Positive Affect

Most people seek psychotherapy because they are experiencing distressing negative emotions. A good deal of evidence demonstrates that people with low self-esteem experience more negative emotions than their high self-esteem counterparts because of the way they respond to threatening information and how they regulate their moods. Whereas people with high self-esteem typically respond to threatening information by protecting or maintaining their positive beliefs about the self, people with low explicit self-esteem respond to such information by experiencing a diminished sense of self (Greenberg & Pyszczynski, 1985; Steele, 1988; Swann, 1987; Taylor & Brown, 1988; Tesser, 1988). Individuals with low self-esteem also recall fewer positive thoughts and memories in response to negative moods, and they dampen their positive moods compared with individuals with high self-esteem (Dodgson & Wood, 1998; Smith & Petty, 1995; Wood, Heimpel, & Michela, 2003).

Goal Attainment

Self-esteem is also linked to the therapeutic process in that individuals with higher self-esteem maintain higher goal expectancies and persist in the face of initial setbacks (Bandura, 1997; Maddux, 1995). Positive outcome expectancies are key to successful psychotherapy outcomes because clients' assessments of the effectiveness of therapy are based mainly on their therapy expectations, rather than on therapist factors (Horvath & Luborsky, 1993). Because negative expectations about therapeutic outcomes presumably influence actual outcomes (Affleck, Tennen, & Rowe, 1991), these negative therapeutic expectancies are likely to become a self-fulfilling prophecy. In fact, psychotherapy clients with low self-esteem may be doubly challenged in psychotherapy: Their low expectations that therapy will be successful contribute to less effective therapeutic outcomes, and their lack of persistence in therapy when things are not going well make them likely candidates for premature treatment termination. Indeed, to the extent that their low expectations in therapy contribute to slow progress, low self-esteem individuals actually *create* a pessimistic therapeutic climate in which they are inclined to respond by disengaging from treatment.

Interpersonal Relationships

Clients' and therapists' self-esteem contribute to a positive therapeutic alliance, which in turn influences treatment outcomes (Bowlby, 1982; Horvath & Luborsky, 1993; Zetzel, 1970). Because people with low self-esteem have a history of feeling rejected, they are especially sensitive to signs of potential rejection (Leary et al., 1995; Murray, Holmes, & Griffin, 2000). For example, according to the dependency regulation model, relationship-specific expectancies of acceptance play a central role in regulating people's perceptions of their relationship partners (Murray et al., 2000). In fact, the contingency between perceived acceptance and people's regard for their relationship partners becomes overlearned and is elicited automatically (DeHart, Pelham, & Murray, in press). Therefore, individuals with low self-esteem may only be satisfied with their therapists when they believe that their therapists view them positively. Moreover, their perception of not being positively regarded may result in low self-esteem people derogating or challenging their therapists. These self-regulatory dynamics sow the seeds for negative therapeutic reactions and treatment failures, and thus represent another significant challenge for therapists.

In short, self-esteem influences the therapeutic process from beginning to end. Dysfunctional regulation of self-esteem and affect often brings the individual into therapy, may have a negative influence on the client–therapist relationship, and fosters a pessimistic therapeutic climate. Unfortunately, this is not the recipe for successful psychotherapy and may result in the client disengaging and eventually terminating treatment.

SELF-ESTEEM AND PSYCHOLOGICAL DISORDERS

As mentioned above, people's overall feelings of worth and acceptance play an important role in their psychological functioning. However, the dynamics of self-esteem vary among emotional disorders. We have selected one disorder from DSM IV's (APA, 1999) Axis I, major depressive disorder, and one from Axis II, narcissistic personality disorder, in which self-esteem plays an especially important role. We discuss how implicit (i.e., unconscious, relatively uncontrolled, and overlearned) and explicit (i.e., consciously considered and relatively controlled) self-esteem motives are related to each disorder, and we highlight potential difficulties that certain manifestations of implicit self-esteem pose for the therapeutic process.

Major Depressive Disorder

Major depressive disorder is characterized by a depressed mood, loss of interest or pleasure in activities, and disturbances in thought processes (APA, 1999, p. 327). Both psychoanalytic and cognitive formulations underscore the role of early relationships with significant others in the development of the disorder (Basch, 1975; Brown & Harris, 1989; Jacobson, 1975; Rado, 1968). For example, early psychodynamic perspectives asserted that depression is the result of unconscious anger felt toward the loss of an ambivalent attachment relationship, which is directed toward the self (Arieti & Bemporad, 1978; Basch, 1975). In addition, aggression is viewed as a defensive effort to ward off feelings of depression and to regulate self-esteem (Jacobson, 1975). On the other hand, cognitive formulations contend that early experiences create beliefs about the self that serve as vulnerability factors, which in turn interact with subsequent negative experiences to initiate and maintain depression (Bandura, 1997; Beck, Rush, Shaw, & Emery, 1979; Brown & Harris, 1978, 1989; Maddux, 1995; Pyszczynski, Holt, & Greenberg, 1987). In short, psychoanalytic and cognitive theories suggest that loss of self-esteem and poor self-esteem regulation in the face of adverse events are key features of depression.

Despite their many differences, psychodynamic and cognitive perspectives agree that self-esteem is a vulnerability factor for depression, and there is empirical support for the causal link between low self-esteem and depression (Brown & Harris, 1978, 1989). Recently, clinical and social psychologists have argued that it is not low self-esteem per se, but rather labile self-esteem, that is related to depression (Butler, Hokanson, & Flynn, 1994; Kernis, Grannemann, & Mathis, 1991; Roberts & Monroe, 1992, 1994). Presumably, negative events activate negative self-evaluations among individuals with labile self-esteem, which in turn compromises their ability to regulate depressed moods. However, most of this research has measured unstable self-esteem (the standard deviation of people's self-esteem over time) rather than labile self-esteem per se (see Butler et al., 1994 for an exception).

Self-esteem may also be related to the belief that one can exercise control over dysfunctional thought processes, negative affect associated with depression, and behaviors that impair interactions with others (Bandura, 1997; Maddux & Meier, 1995). This line of reasoning, derived from self-efficacy theory, proposes that when individuals believe that they lack the ability to control their world and to repair the emotional damage elicited by negative events, feelings of hopelessness may develop (Abramson, Metalsky, & Alloy, 1989; Brown & Harris, 1978). In fact, many cognitive therapies enhance clients' coping skills by fostering self-efficacy (Bandura, 1997; Maddux & Meier, 1995). Specifically, cognitive therapies increase people's beliefs that they can control the outcomes of negative events, control and change negative thought patterns, and obtain desired goals. These therapies assume that clients have conscious control over and can easily change their dysfunctional thought patterns. However, beliefs that are overlearned and elicited automatically may not be amenable to conscious control.

Depressed individuals also experience relationship difficulties (Brown & Harris, 1978; Davila, Bradbury, Cohan, & Tochluk, 1997; Fincham, Beach, Harold, & Osborne, 1997). For example, wives who are depressed act in ways that elicit rejection from their partners, which results in them feeling more distressed (Davila et al., 1997). A client's depression can also influence the therapeutic relationship. Because people's beliefs about the self can influence the imagined appraisals of others (Kenny, 1994; Shrauger & Schoeneman, 1979), the negative self-appraisals of depressed individuals make them inclined to anticipate, and perhaps even evoke signs of rejection from the therapist that interfere with the therapeutic alliance.

Narcissistic Personality Disorder

Narcissistic personality disorder is characterized by a grandiose sense of self-importance, constant need for admiration from others, lack of empathy, and interpersonal exploitativeness (APA, 1999, p. 661). Most psychodynamic perspectives on narcissism point to the important role of early object relations in the development of the disorder (Cooper, 1986; Kernberg, 1975; cf. Lasch, 1979, Nemiah, 1973). That is, early relationships with parents who are rejecting, neglectful, disapproving and do not meet the child's needs are internalized into negative feelings about others as well as feelings of inferiority and insecurity (Nemiah, 1973). Therefore, a vulnerable self-structure develops, and narcissistic individuals try constantly to compensate for their insecurities by exaggerating their accomplishments, preoccupying themselves with thoughts of success, and seeking excessive admiration from others.

Clinical conceptions depict narcissistic individuals as demonstrating emotional instability, despite their grandiose sense of self (Kernberg, 1975; Kohut, 1986; Nemiah, 1973). Narcissists' excessively positive self-views are believed to be defensive and mask underlying insecurities (Kernberg, 1975), which is consistent with research and theory on subclinical levels of narcissism among young adults who have high explicit and low implicit self-esteem (Brown & Bosson, 2001; Jordan, Spencer, Zanna, Hoshino-Browne, & Correll, 2003; Kernis, 2003). In addition, people with high explicit and low implicit self-esteem respond defensively to self-concept threats (Bosson, Brown, Ziegler-Hill, & Swann, 2003; Jordan et al., 2003). This inconsistency between explicit and implicit self-views may contribute to the narcissist's emotional instability (Emmons, 1987; Reich, 1986) and aggression in response to self-threat (Bushman & Baumeister, 1998).

Another reason why narcissistic clients experience emotional instability is because they set excessively high goals for themselves that they fail to meet (Kernberg, 1975; Kohut, 1986; Lasch, 1979; Nemiah, 1973). In fact, it has been argued that narcissistic individuals may be especially well suited for bureaucratic institutions because of the ambition and confidence they exude (Lasch, 1979). However, their vulnerable self-esteem makes them particularly sensitive to criticism or setbacks, and their awareness of this sensitivity makes it difficult for narcissists to take risks. Excessively high personal goals, an impoverished sense of self, and extreme sensitivity to criticism converge in individuals with pathological narcissism to engender unstable self-esteem (Rhodewalt, Madrian, & Cheney, 1998), which in turn generates affective instability.

Narcissistic individuals also have impaired interpersonal relationships. They are caught in an approach–avoidance dilemma. On the one hand, they must rely on the admiration of others to combat the negative appraisals they maintain about themselves—appraisals that they are unable to regulate (Stolorow, 1986). At the same time, however, they are terrified of becoming emotionally dependent on others because others are viewed "as without exception undependable" (Lasch, 1979, p. 84). Problems relying on others make it difficult for the narcissist to form a productive client–therapist relationship (Bromberg, 1986; Cooper, 1986; Lasch, 1979). A major goal in the psychodynamic treatment of narcissistic individuals is to make their unconscious insecurities more consciously available (Kernberg, 1975; Kohut & Wolf, 1986; White, 1986). Then, their insecurities may be more fully integrated into conscious beliefs.

THE ROLE OF IMPLICIT SELF-ESTEEM IN THE TREATMENT OF EMOTIONAL DISORDERS

Many people are unable to articulate self-concept vulnerabilities as a part of their conscious belief systems (Pelham, DeHardt, & DeHart, 2003; Wenzlaff & Bates, 1998). This, we believe, poses a thorny problem for cognitive therapists. Specifically, how does one go about consciously restructuring a set of overlearned beliefs that are elicited automatically? The integration of the psychoanalytic concept of the unconscious with advances within cognitive psychology in measuring implicit beliefs (Epstein, 1994) holds considerable promise for our understanding of how unconscious self-concept vulnerabilities might contribute to emotional disorders. For example, investigators have recently begun to use indirect methods to determine whether people at risk for depression engage in biased information processing (Alloy, Abramson, & Francis, 1999; Hedlund & Rude, 1995; Wenzlaff & Bates, 1998). These findings indicate that the accessibility of negative self-relevant thoughts may provide a way to assess vulnerability to depression. That they were derived from experimental investigations guided by cognitive psychological theory should make such findings palatable to cognitive therapists.

Psychoanalytic approaches to psychotherapy have long acknowledged the importance of unconscious working models. In fact, one of the cornerstones of psychoanalytic therapy is its attempt to change people's unconscious beliefs about self and others by having the client project these beliefs onto the analyst. Then, the analyst helps recondition these implicit beliefs by repeatedly responding to the client in ways that do not replicate childhood interactions with significant others. However, people's implicit self-evaluations appear to be most informative when assessed under conditions of threat or cognitive load (Bowlby, 1982; Jones, Pelham, Mirenberg, & Hetts, 2002; Koole, Dijksterhuis, & van Knippenberg, 2001; Pelham, Koole, Hardin, Hetts, Seah, & DeHart, 2005). For example, self-concept threat seems to activate beliefs that are typically not available to conscious reflection (Jones et al., 2002; Pelham et al., 2005). Therefore, we encourage therapists to begin using additional techniques that evoke self-concept threat or induce cognitive load, to help uncover and change self-concept vulnerabilities that lie outside of conscious awareness.

A DAILY PROCESS APPROACH TO SELF-ESTEEM IN EMOTIONAL DISORDERS AND IN PSYCHOTHERAPY

A growing literature now demonstrates the unique potential of daily process designs—commonly referred to as daily diary recording (Stone, Lennox, & Neale, 1985), ecological momentary assessment (EMA; Stone & Shiffman, 1994), or experience sampling methodology (ESM; Csikszentmihalyi & Larson, 1984)—to capture hypothesized psychological processes in situ. Indeed, several investigations described in this chapter used daily process methods (Butler et al., 1994; Kernis et al., 1991; Rhodewalt et al., 1998; Roberts & Monroe, 1992). Yet, only rarely have investigators addressed temporal associations depicted in the clinical literature and in theories describing self-esteem's role in emotional disorders (Tennen & Affleck, 1996; Tennen, Affleck, Armeli, & Carney, 2000; Tolpin, Gunthert, Cohen, & O'Neill, 2004).

Invariably, clinical and social psychological theories of disturbances in self-esteem posit if–then contingencies in daily life, and how a particular disorder alters these contingencies. As described in this chapter, these theories depict responses to self-threatening information, thoughts and memories evoked by negative moods, behavioral responses to setbacks, and self-regulation efforts in response to negative emotions. We believe that the inherently idiographic nature of these if–then contingencies is exceptionally well suited to study through daily process designs. Fortunately, the behavioral, cognitive, and emotional contingencies described throughout this chapter fit well with the ways people portray their everyday lives in recounting experiences in psychotherapy sessions and in daily social exchanges. This natural tendency should serve as a resource to therapists.

Finally, daily process methods can provide unique implicit and explicit self-esteem related outcome indicators in studies of the psychotherapy's effectiveness. Rather than comparing pretreatment and posttreatment levels of self-esteem as indicators of effective treatment, daily process methods would allow clinical researchers to examine changes in how low self-esteem clients respond to self-threatening information, whether after treatment they are better able to evoke positive memories when they experience negative moods, and if treatment made them more resilient to setbacks in their daily lives. These are the very processes described by traditional clinical theory and current social psychological models of self-esteem.

REFERENCES

Abramson, L. Y., Metalsky, G. I., & Alloy, L. B. (1989). Hopelessness depression: A theory-based subtype of depression. *Psychological Review, 96*, 358–372.

Affleck, G., Tennen, H., & Rowe, J. (1991). *Infants in crisis: How parents cope with new-born intensive care and its aftermath.* New York: Springer.

Alloy, L. B., Abramson, L. Y., & Francis, E. L. (1999). Do negative cognitive styles confer vulnerability to depression? *Current Direction in Psychological Science, 8*, 128–132.

American Psychiatric Association. (1999). *Diagnostic and statistical manual of mental disorders* (4th ed.). Washington, DC: American Psychiatric Association.

Arieti, S., & Bemporad, J. (1978). *Severe and mild depression: The psychotherapeutic approach.* New York: Basic Books.

Bandura, A. (1997). Self-efficacy: The exercise of control. New York: W. H. Freeman.

Basch, M. F. (1975). Toward a theory that encompasses depression: A revision of existing causal hypotheses in psychoanalysis. In E. J. Anthony & T. Benedek (Eds.), *Depression and human existence* (pp. 485–515). Boston: Little, Brown and Company.

Beck, A. T., Rush, A. J., Shaw, B. F., & Emery, G. (1979). *Cognitive therapy of depression.* New York: Guilford Press.

Bednar, R. L., Wells, M. G., & Peterson, S. R. (1989). *Self-esteem: Paradoxes and innovations in clinical theory and practice.* Washington, DC: American Psychological Association.

Bosson, J. K., Brown, R. P., Zeigler-Hill, V., & Swann, W. B. (2003). Self-enhancement tendencies among people with high explicit self-esteem: The moderating role of implicit self-esteem. *Self and Identity, 2*, 169–187.

Bowlby, J. (1982). *Attachment and loss* (Volume 1: Attachment). London: Hogarth Press.

Bromberg, P. M. (1986). The mirror and the mask: On narcissism and psychoanalytic growth. In A. P. Morrison (Ed.), *Essential papers on narcissism* (pp. 420–463). New York: New York University Press.

Brown, R. P., & Bosson, J. K. (2001). Narcissus meets Sisyphus: Self-love, self-loathing, and the never-ending pursuit of self-worth. *Psychological Inquiry, 12*, 210–213.

Brown, G. W., & Harris, T. (1978). *Social origins of depression: A study of psychiatric disorder in women.* New York: The Free Press.

Brown, G. W., & Harris, T. (1989). Depression. In G. W. Brown & T. O Harris (Eds.), *Life events and illness* (pp. 49–89). New York: Guilford Press.

Bushman, B. J., & Baumeister, R. F. (1998). Threatened egotism, narcissism, self-esteem, and direct and displaced aggression: Does self-love or self-hate lead to violence? *Journal of Personality & Social Psychology, 75*, 219–229.

Butler, A. C., Hokanson, J. E., & Flynn, H. A. (1994). A comparison of self-esteem lability and low trait self-esteem as vulnerability factors for depression. *Journal of Personality and Social Psychology, 66*, 166–177.

Cooper, A. M. (1986). Narcissism. In A. P. Morrison (Ed.), *Essential papers on narcissism* (pp. 111–141). New York: New York University Press.

Csikszentmihalyi, M., & Larson, R. (1984). *Being adolescent: Conflict and growth in the teenage years.* New York: Basic Books.

Davila, J., Bradbury, T. N., Cohan, C. L., & Tochluk, S. (1997). Marital functioning and depressive symptoms: Evidence for a stress generation model. *Journal of Personality and Social Psychology, 73*, 849–861.

DeHart, T., Pelham, B. W., & Murray, S. L. (in press). Implicit dependency regulation: Self-esteem, relationship closeness, and implicit evaluation of close others. *Social Cognition.*

Dodgson, P. G., & Wood, J. V. (1998). Self-esteem and the cognitive accessibility of strengths and weaknesses after failure. *Journal of Personality and Social Psychology, 75*, 178–197.

Emmons, R. A. (1987). Narcissism: Theory and measurement. *Journal of Personality and Social Psychology, 52*, 11–17.

Epstein, S. (1994). Integration of the cognitive and the psychodynamic unconscious. *American Psychologist, 49*, 709–724.

Fincham, F. D., Beach, S. R., Harold, G. T., & Osborne, L. N. (1997). Marital satisfaction and depression: Different causal relationships for men and women? *Psychological Science, 8*, 351–357.

Greenberg, J., & Pyszczynski, T. (1985). Compensatory self-inflation: A response to the threat to self-regard of public failure. *Journal of Personality and Social Psychology, 49*, 273–280.

Hedlund, S., & Rude, S. S. (1995). Evidence of latent depressive schemas in formerly depressed individuals. *Journal of Abnormal Psychology, 104*, 517–525.

Horvath, A. O., & Luborsky, L. (1993). The role of the therapeutic alliance in psychotherapy. *Journal of Consulting and Clinical Psychology, 61*, 561–573.

Jacobson, E. (1975). The regulation of self-esteem. In E. J. Anthony & T. Benedek (Eds.), *Depression and human existence* (pp. 169–180). Boston: Little, Brown and Company.

Jones, J. T., Pelham, B. W., Mirenberg, M. C., & Hetts, J. J. (2002). Name letter preferences are not merely mere exposure: Implicit egotism as self-regulation. *Journal of Experimental Social Psychology, 38*, 170–177.

Jordan, C. H., Spencer, S. J., Zanna, M. P., Hoshino-Browne, E., & Correll, J. (2003). Secure and defensive high self-esteem. *Journal of Personality and Social Psychology, 85*, 969–978.

Kenny, D. A. (1994). *Interpersonal perception: A social relations analysis.* New York: Guilford Press.

Kernberg, O. F. (1975). *Borderline conditions and pathological narcissism.* New York: Jason Aronson, Inc.

Kernis, M. H. (2003). Toward a conceptualization of optimal self-esteem. *Psychological Inquiry, 14*, 1–26.

Kernis, M. H., Grannemann, B. D., & Mathis, L. C. (1991). Stability of self-esteem as a moderator of the relation between level of self-esteem and depression. *Journal of Personality and Social Psychology, 61*, 80–84.

Kohut, H. (1986). Forms and transformations of narcissism. In A. P. Morrison (Ed.), *Essential papers on narcissism* (pp. 60–68). New York: New York University Press.

Kohut, H., & Wolf, E. S. (1986). The disorders of the self and their treatment: An outline. In A. P. Morrison (Ed.), *Essential papers on narcissism* (pp. 175–197). New York: New York University Press.

Koole, S. L., Dijksterhuis, A., & van Knippenberg, A. (2001). What's in a name: Implicit self-esteem and the automatic self. *Journal of Personality and Social Psychology, 80*, 669–685.

Lasch, C. (1979). *The culture of narcissism: American life in an age of diminishing expectations.* New York: W. W. Norton & Company, Inc.

Leary, M. R., Tambor, E. S., Terdal, S. K., & Downs, D. L. (1995). Self-esteem as an interpersonal monitor: The sociometer hypothesis. *Journal of Personality and Social Psychology, 68*, 518–530.

Maddux, J. E. (1995). Self-efficacy theory: An introduction. In J. E. Maddux (Ed.), *Self-efficacy, adaptation, and adjustment* (pp. 3–27). New York: Plenum Press.

Maddux, J. E., & Meier, L. J. (1995). Self-efficacy and depression. In J. E. Maddux (Ed.), *Self-efficacy, adaptation, and adjustment* (pp. 143–172). New York: Plenum Press.

Murray, S. L., Holmes, J. G., & Griffin, D. (2000). Self-esteem and the quest for felt security: How perceived regard regulates attachment processes. *Journal of Personality and Social Psychology, 78*, 478–498.

Nemiah, J. C. (1973). *Foundations of psychopathology.* New York: Jason Aronson, Inc.

Pelham, B. W., DeHardt, T. K., & DeHart, T. (2003). *Implicit vulnerability to depression: Evidence for a latent depressive self-schema.* Unpublished manuscript, State University of New York, Buffalo.

Pelham, B. W., Koole, S. L., Hardin, C. D., Hetts, J. J., Seah, E., & DeHart, T. (2005). Gender moderates the relation between implicit and explicit self-esteem. *Journal of Experimental Social Psychology, 41*, 84–89.

Pyszczynski, T., Holt, K., & Greenberg, J. (1987). Depression, self-focused attention, and expectancies for positive and negative future life events for self and others. *Journal of Personality and Social Psychology, 52*, 994–1001.

Rado, S. (1968). The problem of melancholia. In W. Gaylin (Ed.), *The meaning of despair: Psychoanalytic contributions to the understanding of depression* (pp. 70–95). New York: Science House.

Reich, A. (1986). Pathologic forms of self-esteem regulation. In A. P. Morrison (Ed.), *Essential papers on narcissism* (pp. 44–59). New York: New York University Press.

Rhodewalt, F., Madrian, J. C., & Cheney, S. (1998). Narcissism, self-knowledge, organization, and emotional reactivity: The effect of daily experience on self-esteem and affect. *Journal of Personality & Social Psychology, 24*, 75–87.

Roberts, J. E., & Monroe, S. M. (1992). Vulnerable self-esteem and depressive symptoms: Prospective findings comparing three alternative conceptualizations. *Journal of Personality and Social Psychology, 62*, 804–812.

Roberts, J. E., & Monroe, S. M. (1994). A multidimensional model of self-esteem in depression. *Clinical Psychology Review, 14*, 161–181.

Shrauger, S. J., & Schoeneman, T. J. (1979). Symbolic interactionist view of self-concept: Through the looking glass darkly. *Psychological Bulletin, 86*, 549–573.

Smith, S. M., & Petty, R. E. (1995). Personality moderators of mood congruency effects on cognition: The role of self-esteem and negative mood regulation. *Journal of Personality and Social Psychology, 68*, 1092–1107.

Steele, C. M. (1988). The psychology of self-affirmation: Sustaining the integrity of the self. In L. Berkowitz (Ed.), *Advances in experimental social psychology* (Vol. 21, pp. 261–302). New York: Academic Press.

Stolorow, R. D. (1986). Toward a functional definition of narcissism. In A. P. Morrison (Ed.), *Essential papers on narcissism* (pp. 198–208). New York: New York University Press.

Stone, A. A., Lennox, S., & Neale, J. M. (1985). Daily coping and alcohol use in a sample of community adults. In S. Shiffman & T. A. Wills (Eds.), *Coping and substance abuse* (pp. 199–220). New York: Academic Press.

Stone, A. A., & Shiffman, S. (1994). Ecological momentary assessment (EMA) in behavioral medicine. *Annals of Behavioral Medicine, 16*, 199–202.

Swann, W. B. Jr. (1987). Identity negotiation: Where two roads meet. *Journal of Personality & Social Psychology, 53*, 1038–1051.

Taylor, S. E., & Brown, J. D. (1988). Illusion and well-being: A social-psychological perspective on mental health. *Psychological Bulletin, 103*, 193–210.

Tennen, H., & Affleck, G. (1996). Daily processes in coping with chronic pain. Methods and analytic strategies. In M. Zeidner & N. S. Endler (Eds.), *Handbook of coping: Theory, research, and applications* (pp. 151–180). New York: Wiley.

Tennen, H., Affleck, G., Armeli, S., & Carney, M. A. (2000). A daily process approach to coping: Linking theory, research, and practice. *American Psychologist, 55*, 626–636.

Tesser, A. (1988). Toward a self-evaluation maintenance model of social behavior. In L. Berkowitz (Ed.), *Advances in experimental social psychology* (Vol. 21, pp. 181–227). San Diego, CA: Academic Press.

Tolpin, L. H., Gunthert, K. C., Cohen, L. H., & O'Neill, S. C. (2004). Borderline personality features and instability of daily negative affect and self-esteem. *Journal of Personality, 72*, 111–137.

Wenzlaff, R. M., & Bates, D. E. (1998). Unmasking a cognitive vulnerability to depression: How lapses in mental control reveal depressive thinking. *Journal of Personality and Social Psychology, 75*, 1559–1571.

White, M. T. (1986). Self relations, object relations, and pathological narcissism. In A. P. Morrison (Ed.), *Essential papers on narcissism* (pp. 143–174). New York: New York University Press.

Wood, J. V., Heimpel, S. A., & Michela, J. L. (2003). Savoring versus dampening: Self-esteem differences in regulating positive affect. *Journal of Personality and Social Psychology, 85*, 566–580.

Zetzel, E. R. (1970). *The capacity for emotional growth.* New York: International Universities Press, Inc.

Question 14

What is the evolutionary significance of self-esteem?

T he last question in this section focuses on the evolutionary significance of self-esteem.

Hill and Buss suggest that a comprehensive evolutionary psychological model of self-esteem would need to incorporate six distinct psychological mechanisms. Specifically, they "...propose that self-esteem is not a unitary construct, but rather a collection of internal representations, monitoring mechanisms, updating mechanisms, evaluative mechanisms, motivational mechanisms, and mechanisms designed to generate behavioral output." In addition, they offer suggestions for how to clarify which components of self-esteem are domain-specific and which operate more broadly across a range of contexts.

Kirkpatrick and Ellis assert that self-esteem "...reflects the operation of numerous evolved psychological mechanisms designed by natural selection to monitor specific aspects of the self in relation to other." The authors propose a number of domain-specific models of self-esteem based on functional rather than descriptive criteria and they review evidence supporting several functional domains and their differential relations to other types of criterion variables.

Campbell and Foster argue that support exists for the evolutionary basis of a relatively unelaborated form of self-esteem. In other words, they suggest that our ancestors likely possessed positive self-feelings that were linked to important adaptive tasks, such as social exclusion. The authors then argue that much of what scholars currently refer to as self-esteem is a culture-specific elaboration of this "proto" self-esteem. They provide evidence to support these assertions and offer some speculations pertaining to the cultural history of the self.

42

The Evolution of Self-Esteem

SARAH E. HILL and DAVID M. BUSS

*E*volutionary psychology seeks to synthesize fundamental principles of evolutionary biology with modern psychological theories, leading to testable hypotheses about the design of the human mind. This synthesis has proved useful in guiding the discovery of previously unknown phenomena, generating new predictions not produced by prior psychological models, and providing cogent theories about entire domains of functioning such as mating, parenting, kinship, cooperation, and aggression (Buss, 2004; Pinker, 2002). Self-esteem—a domain of exceptional importance—has recently come under the theoretical lens of evolutionary psychology (Barkow, 1989; Kirkpatrick & Ellis, 2001, this volume; Kirkpatrick, Waugh, Valencia, & Webster, 2002; Leary & Downs, 1995).

One early evolutionary theorist hypothesized that the self-concept is a composite of internal representations of individual characteristics that affect reproductive fitness (Barkow, 1989). Attributes expected to influence individuals' self-concepts are many, such as health, physical prowess, prestige, status, attractiveness, alliances, and resources, all of which have been integral to solving adaptive problems throughout human evolutionary history. Evolutionarily informed work on the self continued when Leary and Downs (1995) proposed a *sociometer* theory of self-esteem. The sociometer theory describes self-esteem as an internal gauge designed to monitor individuals' successes in interpersonal relationships, particularly the degree to which they are being included or excluded from social groups, and to motivate corrective actions when one's level of social inclusion gets dangerously low. Kirkpatrick and Ellis (2001), in an important conceptual elaboration, extend the sociometer theory by proposing that what is currently referred to as "self-esteem" is actually a collection of sociometers or self-esteems, each designed to monitor inclusion and motivate behavior in functionally distinct social domains such as mating, coalitional relationships, and prestige hierarchies (Kirkpatrick & Ellis, 2001, this volume; Kirkpatrick et al., 2002).

Each of the multiple self-esteem mechanisms is hypothesized to have been designed by natural selection to monitor information about the self that corresponds to solving a specific and recurrent adaptive problem faced by our evolutionary ancestors. The information so gained is hypothesized to activate psychological and behavioral processes designed to calibrate the information acquired through such monitoring and use it to solve specific adaptive problems (Kirkpatrick et al., 2002). These proposed functions of self-esteem are similar to resource holding potential (RHP) assessment, the hypothesized mechanism by which non-human animals gauge their competitive ability relative to their peers in order to facilitate optimal competitive behavior (for comparisons of self-esteem and RHP see Barkow, 1989; Gilbert, 1989; Wenegrat, 1984).

This essay, building on the work of these previous authors, offers two proposals for the eventual goal of developing a comprehensive evolutionary psychological model of self-esteem. The first involves clearly separating the distinct psychological mechanisms hypothesized to be involved in self-esteem experiences based on their function. That is, we propose that self-esteem is not a unitary construct, but rather a collection of internal representations, monitoring mechanisms, updating mechanisms, evaluative mechanisms, motivational mechanisms, and mechanisms designed to generate behavioral output. The second suggestion centers on one way to clarify which components of self-esteem are domain-specific and which operate across a range of domains—a potentially contentious issue in the field of evolutionary psychology.

SIX PSYCHOLOGICAL COMPONENTS OF SELF-ESTEEM

Throughout human evolutionary history, individuals have competed against one another for access to resources that others were simultaneously seeking to acquire. Choosing the range of behaviors that will lead to an adaptive problem's successful solution has depended simultaneously on the predicted abilities of oneself and the anticipated behaviors of relevant others. Striving for a particular socially-mediated outcome without gauging both one's own abilities *and* the comparative abilities of relevant competitors could lead to futile attempts, wasted effort, banishment, or death. The problem of keeping track of one's own abilities has thus been an important selection pressure that has shaped human psychology. One hypothesized cognitive solution to this reliably occurring selection pressure is the ability to *maintain internal representations* of one's own talents and abilities. Keeping track of these values allows one to make prudent behavioral decisions in light of this information. Furthermore, it provides a referent by which to compare oneself to relevant others in social and socially-competitive situations.

For instance, an individual would refer to the internal representation of their desirability to members of the opposite sex to make an informed decision about whether it would be best to compete with his or her peers for access to a potential love interest or whether to look for love elsewhere. Although we concur with Barkow, Leary, and Kirkpatrick and Ellis that the *social* aspects of these internal representations will be most important, we note that some important internal representations will be either nonsocial or not necessarily social (e.g., ability to start a fire to cook meat; finding one's way home after being lost in the woods).

Thus, the first psychological component of self-esteem is the ability to maintain cognitive representations of one's traits and abilities to solve specific adaptive problems.

Second, as Leary and Downs (1995) and Kirkpatrick and Ellis (2001) have likewise proposed, mechanisms designed to *monitor* one's performance, and especially one's standing with respect to relevant others, are also components of self-esteem. The ability to receive input from the environment about how one's own performance in a specific adaptive domain compares to one's peers provides a means by which to become informed of changes in the self or changes in one's relevant competition. For instance, individuals looking for a romantic partner can monitor how their own desirability and the desirability of their same-sexed competition change over time or based on cues they receive from the social environment. Like Kirkpatrick and Ellis (2001), we expect these *monitoring mechanisms* to be functionally domain-specific. That is, we expect that performance will be monitored in as many domains as there are adaptive problems to solve.

One's abilities to solve specific adaptive problems can change dramatically from year to year, month to month, day to day, or even moment to moment. An individual's abilities may change due to success or failure in a hunt, the birth or death of a child, an increase in age, acquisition of experience, health, sickness, alliance formation, coalitional weakening, kinship ascension, and other factors. In women, these abilities may change with phase of the ovulatory cycle (Kimura, 2000). The problem of incorporating this important contextual information into the self-concept to influence behavioral decisions has been an important selection pressure that has shaped human psychology. Humans are proposed to have evolved psychological mechanisms designed to update the self-concept based on new information about the self. These *updating mechanisms*, of course, rely on information provided by the monitoring mechanisms. But they are distinct, in that informational output from the monitoring can result in: (1) no change in internal representations, (2) an increase in perception of one's abilities or attributes relative to others, or (3) a decrease in perception of one's abilities or attributes. Thus, the output of monitoring mechanisms provides input into updating mechanisms, which in turn result in changes in internal representations. For instance, if a woman looking for a romantic partner receives information via her monitoring mechanisms that she is becoming increasingly attractive relative to her peers, we expect the updating mechanisms will update her internal representation of her desirability to potential mates.

We hypothesize that it is ultimately such changes in self-perceived abilities to solve specific adaptive problems that cause the affective shifts that demarcate self-esteem experiences. Therefore, we propose that the fourth component of self-esteem is composed of cognitive adaptations designed to evaluate the internal representations. When this *affective evaluation* is applied to stable internal representations, we can refer to it as *trait self-esteem*. When it is applied to the updates, changes, or fluctuations in internal representations, we can refer to it as *state self-esteem*. We note that some theorists reserve the concept of "self-esteem" to refer to this affective evaluation, relegating the non-affective components to the concept of "self-concept."

None of these four proposed psychological mechanisms could have evolved, however, unless they produced behavior that affected the reproductive fitness of the bearers of these mechanisms over the period during which they evolved and are maintained. Therefore, a fifth component of this system must serve a *motivational function*. We propose that the affective component of self-esteem has been designed to motivate individuals to choose behavioral options that are most appropriate, given the newly updated state of their internal representation. The loss of self-esteem that accompanies the rejection of a mating overture, for example, could motivate social derogation of the rejecter to preserve reputation, increase one's own efforts to improve one's mate value, or change the quality of the mates toward which one makes future overtures (Buss, 2003). Just as the emotion of jealousy can motivate behaviors ranging from vigilance to violence (Buss & Shackelford, 1997), we expect that the behavioral output motivated by changes in self-esteem will be highly varied as well, ranging perhaps from altruism to suicide.

A complete description of the cognitive architecture of self-esteem requires a sixth component—*the specific behavioral output*. Since we hypothesize that self-esteem sends a signal to the self that there has been a change in one's ability to solve a specific adaptive problem, the best behavioral solution to that adaptive problem is expected to change. Just as a professional athlete changes his game in the face of an injury, individuals suffering from a loss of self-esteem are similarly expected to adjust their behaviors to make the most of the situation they are in and prevent their competition from exploiting their weakness. Although extraordinarily challenging for theorists, we suggest that a comprehensive evolutionary theory of self-esteem will eventually include each of these six components.

ON THE GENERALITY OF SELF-ESTEEM ACROSS DOMAINS AND SEXES

From an evolutionary perspective, the single-function sociometer theory of self-esteem advanced by Leary and Downs (1995), although superior to its predecessors, is too narrow in scope to capture the varied adaptive problems self-esteem mechanisms were designed to solve. Furthermore, it lacks details about the requisite cognitive architecture needed to solve those problems. Different adaptive problems require different adaptive solutions. What leads to value as a mate differs, to some extent, from what leads to value as a coalition member. For instance, although cues to fertility may be critical for mate value, they are largely irrelevant to one's value in a warfare coalition. Conversely, willingness to risk one's life in battle may contribute to value in a warfare coalition, but detract from one's value as a parent. Our ideas for a more comprehensive theory of self-esteem maintain that individuals' psychologies have been designed to monitor success within each of a number of specific adaptive domains, not merely the domain of social inclusion or exclusion.

Furthermore, we expect that many design features of the six components of self-esteem will be *sharply sex-differentiated*—a critical theoretical position lacking in prior theories of self-esteem. Since we have hypothesized that self-esteem has been designed to track and update adaptive problem-solving ability, we expect that self-esteem experiences will reflect the type and salience of the adaptive problems that the sexes have faced differently over evolutionary time. For instance, since resource acquisition potential is a more important part of men's than women's mate value (Buss, 1989), resources acquisition is a more salient adaptive problem for men than it is for women. We therefore expect that any changes on dimensions relating to resource acquisition and defense will affect men's self-esteem more than women's self-esteem. Physical attractiveness is a more important component of women's than men's mate value, so achieving and maintaining a certain level of physical attractiveness is a more salient adaptive problem for women than it is for men. We expect that changes on this dimension will affect women's more than men's self-esteem (Buss, 1989). Indeed, it has been demonstrated that body image plays a significant role in an individual's self-esteem, but more so for females than males (Hamida, Mineka, & Bailey, 1998).

Sex differences in the qualities that lead to value as a mate, ally, kin member, and coalition member should lead to corresponding sex differences in self-esteem. Thus, the argument for domain-specificity articulated by Kirkpatrick and Ellis (2001) can be extended fully to sex-linked functional specificity.

Nonetheless, we believe that the arguments for specificity can be carried too far, and may overlook a critical fact—that some attributes contribute to the successful solution of problems *across* adaptive domains. One example is health. Good health enhances one's value as a mate, as an ally, as a coalition member, and as a kin member, as well as making oneself a more formidable status competitor. Therefore, becoming ill should cause a decrease in self-esteem across these domains, and a return to robust health should cause an increase in self-esteem across these domains. Social status, to take another example, is an attribute that is important in the mating domain as well as in the domains of same-sex dyadic alliances, coalitions, and kinships. Where self-assessed traits will be relevant to multiple adaptive domains, invoking entirely separate self-assessment mechanisms for each domain of self-esteem both lacks parsimony and entails postulating the existence of costly redundant cognitive and neural architecture.

These conceptual clarifications offer a principled means to generate predictions about the causes and consequences of self-esteem, and the causes and consequences of changes in self-esteem. They also offer one solution to the positive manifold found in correlations of self-esteem across different facets and domains. To the extent that the same attributes contribute to one's value to social others across domains, rises in self-esteem in one domain (e.g., one's evaluation of oneself as a desirable mate) should correlate positively with elevations in self-esteem in other domains (e.g., one's evaluation of oneself as a desirable coalition member). To the extent that the attributes that contribute to social value differ across domains, we predict that self-esteem will show specificity. Thus, the "global" self-esteem often found as a result of modest positive correlations across facets may reflect the fact that some of the same attributes contribute to esteem on multiple facets. This formulation provides a principled way to predict where generality will be found and where specificity will be found.

The same meta-theoretical reasoning can be applied to predictions about sex difference and sex similarities in self-esteem effects. To the degree that the same attributes contribute to social value for men and women (e.g., health), then increments or decrements on those attributes should show the same effects on self-esteem for men and women equally. To the degree that different attributes contribute to social value for men and women, increments and decrements on those attributes should show sex-linked effects on self-esteem. This formulation provides a principled framework for predicting where sex differences will be found and where they will be absent, ultimately contributing to a more comprehensive and evolutionarily grounded theory of self-esteem.

ACKNOWLEDGMENT

We thank Bruce Ellis and Michael Kernis for helpful suggestions on an earlier draft of this chapter

REFERENCES

Barkow, J. (1989). *Darwin, sex, and status*. Toronto: University of Toronto Press.

Buss, D. M. (1989). Sex differences in human mate preferences: Evolutionary hypotheses testing in 37 cultures. *Behavioral and Brain Sciences, 12*, 1–49.

Buss, D. M. (2003). *The evolution of desire: Strategies of human mating* (Rev. ed.). New York: Basic Books.

Buss, D. M. (2004). *Evolutionary psychology: The new science of the mind* (2nd ed.). Boston: Allyn & Bacon.

Buss, D. M., & Shackelford, T. K. (1997). From vigilance to violence: Mate retention tactics in married couples. *Journal of Personality and Social Psychology, 72*, 346–361.

Gilbert, P. (1989). *Human nature and suffering*. Hillsdale, NJ: Erlbaum.

Hamida, S. B., Mineka, S., & Bailey, J. M. (1998). Sex differences in controllability of mate value: An evolutionary perspective. *Journal of Personality and Social Psychology, 75*, 953–966.

Kimura, D. (2000). *Sex and cognition*. New York: Bradford Books.

Kirkpatrick, L. A., & Ellis, B. J. (2001). An evolutionary-psychological approach to self-esteem: Multiple domains and multiple functions. In M. Clark & G. Fletcher (Eds.), *The Blackwell handbook of social psychology, Vol. 2: Interpersonal processes* (pp. 411–436). Oxford: Blackwell Publishers.

Kirkpatrick, L. A., Waugh, C. E., Valencia, A., & Webster, G. D. (2002). The functional domain specificity of self-esteem and the differential prediction of aggression. *Journal of Personality and Social Psychology, 82*, 756–767.

Leary, M. R., & Downs, D. L. (1995). Interpersonal functions of the self-esteem motive: The self-esteem system as a sociometer. In M. H. Kernis (Ed.), *Efficacy, agency, and self-esteem* (pp. 123–144). New York: Plenum.

Pinker, S. (2002). *The blank slate*. New York: Viking.

Wenegrat, B. (1984). *Sociobiology and mental disorder: A new view*. Menlo Park, CA: Addison Wesley.

43

The Adaptive Functions of Self-Evaluative Psychological Mechanisms

LEE A. KIRKPATRICK and BRUCE J. ELLIS

A ccording to contemporary evolutionary psychology, the brain/mind comprises a host of domain-specific mechanisms and systems designed by natural selection to solve adaptive problems faced recurrently by our ancestors (e.g., Buss, 1995; Tooby & Cosmides, 1992). Over evolutionary time, the genetic recipes for mechanisms and systems that proved (on average) to be more adaptive than alternative designs—where adaptive refers specifically to inclusive fitness or reproductive success—were retained as species-typical traits. These mechanisms organize behavior by selectively attending to particular kinds of input information (environmental cues, internal states, etc.), processing this information via various forms of inferential rules, and generating behavioral output.

Because humans have evolved to be a highly social species, many of the most important adaptive problems we face involve negotiating our social world. Such adaptive problems include, for example, problems related to mating (selection, attraction, and retention of mates), problems related to competition for resources (negotiation of status hierarchies, formation and maintenance of alliances), problems related to acquiring assistance and support from others (selection and maintenance of friendships), and problems related to intergroup conflict. Our evolved psychological architecture therefore should include specialized systems designed by natural selection as solutions to these adaptive problems. The functional organization of these diverse systems must differ qualitatively from one another because the adaptive problems and their solutions vary greatly across domains.

Virtually all such systems include, as part of their adaptive design, input mechanisms designed to assess domain-relevant features of the environment (e.g., availability of valuable resources), domain-relevant features of other individuals (e.g., size and strength of competitors for these resources), and domain-relevant features of the self (e.g., one's own size and strength). Because the particular features of environments, other individuals, and the self that are relevant to a particular adaptive domain vary greatly—e.g., mechanisms for evaluating potential mates must differ qualitatively from mechanisms for evaluating competitors for resources—such evaluative mechanisms must themselves be differentiated and contain domain-specific circuitry.

We submit that what psychologists have traditionally referred to as *self-esteem* reflects the operation of one such class of mechanisms, namely those designed for evaluating the self in relation to others in the context of these diverse social-cognitive psychological systems. In this way our view has much in common with sociometer theory (e.g., Leary & Downs, 1995) in rejecting the conceptualization of self-esteem as a goal or motive in itself, in favor of a model in which self-esteem represents a gauge or index designed to provide input into systems designed to serve other (adaptive) goals or motives. Our model departs from Leary's, however, in suggesting that (1) there are multiple such "sociometers" associated with functionally distinct social-psychological systems, and (2) these sociometers have many functions which also vary across relationship domains. In this brief essay, we illustrate our view with only a few specific examples; see Kirkpatrick and Ellis (2001) for a more complete discussion.

RANK AND STATUS

Many if not most social species are characterized by (usually intrasexual) hierarchies of what has been variously termed rank, status, or dominance. High rank confers the benefit of access to desirable resources such as food, nesting sites, and mates, but also introduces adaptive problems related to defending and maintaining one's rank; low rank necessitates alternative strategies for obtaining resources and appeasing dominant competitors. Social animals therefore must possess some kind of self-evaluative mechanism to keep track of their place in the hierarchy in order to choose adaptively among behavioral strategies whose differential adaptiveness is contingent on rank. Many theorists have suggested that human self-esteem is related to relative position in dominance hierarchies (e.g., Barkow, 1989; Gilbert, Price, & Allan, 1995).

In many species, rank is determined primarily by physical size and strength and maintained by force. However, violent fights between individuals in such species tend to be rare, because both parties are able to quickly size up the relative strength of the potential opponent versus oneself; the weaker individual, facing almost certain defeat, will either steer clear of the encounter or explicitly concede the battle by displaying species-specific signals of submission. Thus, self-perceived rank or dominance is crucial in guiding adaptive behavioral choices between attacking and conceding in potentially conflictual encounters, and for displaying rank-appropriate behaviors to others.

Human status hierarchies are undoubtedly more complex than those of other species. For example, human dominance, like that of chimpanzees (de Waal, 1982) is largely a function of strength of political alliances rather than individual size and strength. Moreover, Henrich and Gil-White (2001) suggest that humans have evolved a unique system of status competition that is functionally distinct from *dominance*. Whereas dominance, as in other species, is a means of attaining and maintaining status by force or threat of force, *prestige* is a form of status that is freely conferred by others in recognition of valuable skills or knowledge from which they hope to benefit (e.g., via social learning). Perceiving oneself as high in prestige should activate behavioral strategies designed to attract and maintain a *clientele* who will offer resources in exchange for sharing skills and knowledge; perceiving oneself as low in prestige should activate systems designed to identify prestigious individuals and join their clienteles. According to Henrich and Gil-White, dominance and prestige hierarchies differ greatly in the behavioral strategies adopted by high- and low-status individuals within them. For example, low-status individuals in a prestige hierarchy seek proximity and eye contact with the high-status individual, whereas submissive individuals in dominance hierarchies avoid encounters and eye contact with dominants.

We therefore believe that humans possess at least two self-evaluative mechanisms related to self-perceived dominance and self-perceived prestige, respectively. It is also possible that a third mechanism related to self-perceived status—that is, the social rank resulting from whichever process was used to attain it—may function separately (but receive input from) dominance- and prestige-assessment mechanisms. Much previous research on human *dominance* and self-esteem might be clarified by differentiating and separately measuring these functionally distinct processes.

MATING

As a consequence of countless genetic, developmental, and environmental factors, people vary greatly in terms of their value as potential mates. Over the course of human evolution, preferences for certain characteristics of mates have evolved because mating with some kinds of individuals was on average more adaptive—again, in a strict inclusive-fitness sense—than with others. Although such preferences are assumed to be species-universal (at least within sexes), people do not always get what they desire. Assortative mating is a dynamic process that depends not only on people's ideal preferences, but also the preferences of potential partners. If individuals adopted a mate-seeking strategy that followed the rule, *mate with the highest-value partner with which you are able*, they would eventually find themselves mated with an equal-valued partner after a potentially long process of trial and error (Ellis & Kelley, 1999).

However, effort invested into seeking and attracting mates is costly in terms of time, energy, and resources. A more adaptive strategy, then, would be to use knowledge of one's own *mate value* (MV) to guide and focus the search for a mate. Such a system would prevent low-MV individuals from wasting hopeless effort in trying to attract potential mates who are certain to reject them, and also prevent high-MV individuals from squandering the opportunity to obtain high-quality mates by choosing poorly. For these and other reasons, numerous theorists have suggested that self-esteem tracks self-evaluations of mate value (e.g., Dawkins, 1982; Kenrick, Groth, Trost, & Sadalla, 1993; Wright, 1994) and functions to calibrate aspiration levels when choosing mates (Kirkpatrick & Ellis, 2001).

A mechanism for assessing one's own MV confers other adaptive benefits as well. Even if a low-MV individual were able to attract an unusually high-MV mate, it would subsequently be costly to retain that mate. In a mismatched mated pair, the higher-value mate will be continually tempted by attractive alternatives; having little to gain by staying in the relationship and much potentially to gain by abandoning it, such individuals would be expected to invest less heavily in the relationship. The low-value mate, in contrast, will be saddled with ongoing expenditures of time and resources to retain the mate. Similar arguments apply to relative investments in offspring. Indeed, male zebra finches manipulated experimentally to enhance their mate value (Burley, 1986) and Pygmy men of high rank (Hewlett, 1991) have been shown to spend disproportionately less time and effort caring for their offspring, with mates picking up the slack.

COALITIONS AND ALLIANCES

In humans, as in many other primates, social structure involves not only competition between individuals, but between groups of individuals. In chimpanzees, for example, troops compete with other neighboring troops, and within-troop alliances compete with other within-troop alliances, for territory and other resources (de Waal, 1982). Inclusion in social groups at various levels of organization is therefore crucial, and humans should possess psychological mechanisms designed to monitor the current state of one's coalitions and alliances and one's inclusion within them.

At the macro level, humans organize themselves into groups ranging from bands (a few dozen individuals), to tribes (hundreds), chiefdoms (thousands) and states (Diamond, 1997). Whatever the organization of a given society, local groups compete with other local groups, sometimes violently. Humans should therefore possess psychological mechanisms designed to index the degree to which one is integrated within such a community, and (perhaps separately) the relative value and strength of this group. Such social self-esteem (or *collective* self-esteem; Luhtanen & Crocker, 1992) plays a central role in social identify theory (Tajfel, 1982; Tajfel & Turner, 1986).

At a more micro level, people form smaller alliances of various sizes that compete with one another within tribes and nations. Friendship groups are valuable social units in which resources are shared to mutual benefit of included individuals, and friendships provide allies in conflicts with individuals in other groups. A psychological mechanism designed to monitor one's inclusion in such relationships is reflected in the previous theories of self-esteem that focus on perceptions of social acceptance or belongingness (e.g., Baumeister & Leary, 1995; Leary & Downs, 1995).

SUMMARY AND CONCLUSIONS

We maintain that what psychologists refer to as "self-esteem" reflects the operation of numerous evolved psychological mechanisms designed by natural selection to monitor specific aspects of the self in relation to others. These self-evaluative mechanisms perform a wide variety of adaptive functions in the context of psychological systems designed to guide behavior adaptively with respect to mate selection, status competition, coalition formation, and other social domains.

This view has a number of important implications for answering other fundamental questions about self-esteem examined in this book. Regarding the function of self-esteem, for example, our view converges with that of Leary and colleagues (e.g., Leary & Downs, 1995) in rejecting the notion that maintaining high self-esteem is a fundamental human motive or goal; rather, self-esteem functions in the service of psychological systems that are organized around other motives or goals. However, it is certainly possible for the positive affect associated with high self-perceived "self-esteem"—i.e., high mate value, prestige, dominance, or social inclusion—to function as a psychological reward and thus lead people to behave in ways designed to produce those feelings, in much the same way as drugs or alcohol (Leary & Baumeister, 2000).

Regarding the structure of self-esteem, our view diverges from other extant models of self-esteem "domain-specificity" by differentiating domains in functional rather than merely descriptive terms. Moreover, it raises important questions about the nature of "global" self-esteem vis-à-vis domain-specific mechanisms. There is no such thing as a generically "good person" because, for example, the (adaptive) criteria defining a good mate differ from those defining a dominant competitor; consequently, it is not clear what (adaptive) function would be served by judgments about one's own generic "goodness." Because some specific traits are valued by others across multiple domains—e.g., physical strength renders a male both a valuable mate and a valuable coalition partner—domain-specific self-evaluations are moderately correlated across domains. While it therefore is possible to construct internally consistent measures of global self-esteem, an important question for future research is whether global self-esteem is merely epiphenomenal or proves functionally important in its own right.

Research in our own labs is beginning to demonstrate that functionally distinct domains of self-esteem, as we have conceptualized them, are differentially related to other kinds of variables. For example, we have shown self-perceived superiority and perceived social inclusion to significantly predict aggression in opposite directions, with global self-esteem unrelated to aggression (Kirkpatrick, Waugh, Valencia, & Webster, 2002). We believe that the conceptualization and measurement of self-esteem in this way will similarly prove useful in clarifying many other empirical questions in the self-esteem literature. (See Kirkpatrick & Ellis, 2001 for a discussion of potential applications of our view to several well-known topics in the self-esteem literature.)

REFERENCES

Barkow, J. J. (1989). *Darwin, sex, and status: Biological approaches to mind and culture.* Toronto: University of Toronto Press.

Baumeister, R. F., & Leary, M. R. (1995). The need to belong: Desire for interpersonal attachments as a fundamental human motivation. *Psychological Bulletin, 117,* 497–529.

Burley, N. (1986). Sexual selection for aesthetic traits in species with biparental care. *American Naturalist, 127,* 415–445.

Buss, D. M. (1995). Evolutionary psychology: A new paradigm for psychological science. *Psychological Inquiry, 6,* 130.

Dawkins, R. (1982). *The extended phenotype.* San Francisco: WH Freeman.

de Waal, F. (1982). *Chimpanzee politics: Power and sex among apes.* Baltimore: Johns Hopkins University Press.

Diamond, J. (1997). *Guns, germs, and steel: The fates of human societies.* New York: Norton.

Ellis, B. J., & Kelley, H. H. (1999). The pairing game: A classroom demonstration of the matching phenomenon. *Teaching of Psychology, 26,* 118–121.

Gilbert, P., Price, J., & Allan, S. (1995). Social comparison, social attractiveness, and evolution: How might they be related? *New Ideas in Psychology, 13,* 149–165.

Henrich, J., & Gil-White, F. J. (2001). The evolution of prestige: Freely conferred deference as a mechanism for enhancing the benefits of cultural transmission. *Evolution and Human Behavior, 22,* 165–196.

Hewlett, B. S. (1991). *Intimate fathers: The nature and context of Aka pygmy paternal infant care.* Ann Arbor: University of Michigan Press.

Kenrick, D. T., Groth, G. E., Trost, M. R., & Sadalla, E. K. (1993). Integrating evolutionary and social exchange perspectives on relationships: Effects of gender, self-appraisal, and involvement level on mate selection criteria. *Journal of Personality and Social Psychology, 64,* 951–969.

Kirkpatrick, L. A., & Ellis, B. J. (2001). An evolutionary-psychological approach to self-esteem: Multiple domains and multiple functions. In G. Fletcher & M. Clark (Eds.), *The Blackwell handbook of social psychology: Vol. 2: Interpersonal processes* (pp. 411–436). Oxford, England: Blackwell.

Kirkpatrick, L. A., Waugh, C. E., Valencia, A., & Webster, G. D. (2002). The functional domain specificity of self-esteem and the differential prediction of aggression. *Journal of Personality and Social Psychology, 82,* 756–767.

Leary, M. R., & Baumeister, R. F. (2000). The nature and function of self-esteem: Sociometer theory. In M. Zanna (Ed.), *Advances in experimental social psychology* (pp. 1–62). San Diego, CA: Academic.

Leary, M. R., & Downs, D. L. (1995). Interpersonal functions of the self-esteem motive: The self-esteem system as a sociometer. In M. H. Kernis (Ed.), *Efficacy, agency, and self-esteem* (pp. 123–144). New York: Plenum.

Luhtanen, R., & Crocker, J. (1992). A collective self-esteem scale: Self-evaluation of one's social identity. *Personality and Social Psychology Bulletin, 18,* 302–318.

Tajfel, H. (1982). Social psychology of intergroup relations. *Annual Review of Psychology, 33,* 1–39.

Tajfel, H., & Turner, J. C. (1986). The social identity theory of intergroup behavior. In S. Worchel & W. Austin (Eds.), *Psychology of intergroup relations* (2nd ed., pp. 7–24). Chicago: Nelson-Hall.

Tooby, J., & Cosmides, L. (1992). The psychological foundations of culture. In J. H. Barkow, L. Cosmides, & J. Tooby (Eds.), *The adapted mind* (pp. 19–136). New York: Oxford University Press.

Wright, R. (1994). *The moral animal: The new science of evolutionary psychology.* New York: Pantheon.

44

Self-Esteem: Evolutionary Roots and Historical Cultivation

W. KEITH CAMPBELL and JOSHUA D. FOSTER

S hould self-esteem be thought of as an adaptive, evolutionary trait, or is it a more recent, perhaps Western, social creation? In this chapter, we argue that there is support for an evolutionary basis of self-esteem in a relatively unelaborated form. By this, we mean that our ancestors had positive feelings surrounding the self and that these were linked to positive outcomes on important tasks, such as social inclusion. However, these positive feelings were not conceptualized or expressed as "self-esteem" or any psychological or linguistic variant. We then argue that much of what we currently describe as self-esteem is a cultural, specifically recent and Western, elaboration and amplification of this "proto" self-esteem. Put another way, a social psychologist traveling back in time 50,000 years would not have received meaningful responses other than confusion to the question "Do you have high self-esteem?" With probing, however, this same psychologist would have found that the self was seen as positive and that the level of positivity was associated with success in various endeavors.

EVOLUTIONARY ROOTS OF SELF-ESTEEM

Contemplation of an evolutionary basis for self-esteem results in several predictions. First, self-esteem should show variance. Second, it should be heritable. Third, it should in all likelihood confer some adaptive advantage on the possessor. The first two predictions have been supported empirically—there is clearly variance in self-esteem (e.g., Twenge & Crocker, 2002) and self-esteem is heritable (e.g., Neiss, Sedikides, & Stevenson, 2002). The third prediction is a little more problematic. In order to test it, one needs to establish how self-esteem *could* be advantageous. One possibility is that self-esteem could serve as a simple reward for adaptive behaviors. For example, success at a hunting task might be followed by a temporary boost of self-esteem. This would reinforce the hunting behavior thus making it more probable in the future. This *simple reinforcement model* is unlikely, however, because self-esteem does not share the immediate impact and short duration of classic reinforcers (e.g., sugar pellets). Likewise, the outcome of the hunting task (i.e., attainment of food) would serve as a primary reinforcer in and of itself.

Self-esteem could also directly facilitate adaptive behaviors. It is possible that individuals with high self-esteem were more successful at important life tasks than those with low self-esteem, and that this differential success was caused by self-esteem. This *fitness model* of self-esteem is reasonable, but the data from modern samples generally do not bear it out. Men with high self-esteem report having more sexual partners, for example, but this likely reflects contingencies of self-worth rather than self-esteem facilitating mating (for a review, see Baumeister & Tice, 2000). Likewise, the association between socioeconomic status and self-esteem is small and the causal chain likely extends from success to self-esteem (Twenge & Campbell, 2002). Finally, in a large review of the self-esteem literature, there was minimal evidence found that self-esteem caused much beyond positive affect and activity initiation (Baumeister, Campbell, Krueger, & Vohs, 2003). Of course, a core level of self-enhancement (i.e., positive affect associated with the self, optimism, confidence) may be related to success, both now and in our adaptive environment (Sedikides & Skowronski, 2000, 2003). This self-enhancement, however, is not the same as an elaborated sense of self-esteem.

Finally, self-esteem could serve to convey information to the organism. There are several examples of such *informational models* in contemporary social psychology, several of which are explicitly grounded in evolutionary theory. The sociometer model (Leary & Baumeister, 2000), for example, suggests that self-esteem is a marker of belongingness (a recent revision of the sociometer model links self-esteem directly to mate value; Brase & Guy, 2004). Likewise, the self-evaluation maintenance model (Tesser, 1988) and recent extensions of social comparison models (e.g., the evolutionary approach of Gilbert, Price, & Allan, 1995), as well as the contingencies of self-worth model (Crocker, Luhtanen, Cooper, & Bouvrette, 2003), argue that self-esteem can be viewed as an outcome of success, social standing, physical appearance, etc.—all of which are predictors of reproductive fitness. Finally, Kirkpatrick's (Kirkpatrick & Ellis, 2001) evolutionary model of self-esteem is a complex example of an informational model, with different forms of self-esteem indicating performance at and activating responses to important tasks such as maintaining social inclusion, mating, and competition. Taken together, these information models make theoretical sense, have good empirical support in contemporary samples, and suggest a highly plausible evolutionary function of self-esteem—specifically, that self-esteem serves to inform us about our social standing and our general movement toward or away from desirable or undesirable evolutionary outcomes.

In sum, the evolutionary function of self-esteem was most likely to be informational. Nevertheless, we propose that self-esteem did not exist in our ancestral past in the elaborated form that it does in the contemporary US. The social environment in which we evolved was not highly supportive of self-esteem in the form of public displays of success or superiority. Instead, it took a brief (in evolutionary time) cultural chain of events to shape proto self-esteem into what we think of today as self-esteem.

THE CULTIVATION OF SELF-ESTEEM

If self-esteem has deep and strong evolutionary roots, then there should be evidence that it was possessed by our hunter–gatherer (HG) forbearers. Unfortunately, we do not have direct evolutionary data on self-esteem, nor even self-esteem data from modern HG groups (who may serve as a proxy for our historical forbearers). Therefore, much of the argument made below will be by necessity speculative.

Prehistoric Society and Self-Esteem

It is likely that early human HG groups had the ingredients for self-esteem. They likely had a self-concept, a concept of social standing (e.g., esteem), and an attitudinal system with likes and dislikes (Sedikides & Skowronski, 2000, 2003). However, the nature of early HG groups, based on archeological data and studies of modern, immediate return HG groups such as the Hadza of Tanzania, suggests that the importance of a linguistically and conceptually elaborate sense of self-esteem was minimal. We make this statement based on the several pieces of evidence derived from the analyses of Boehm (1999) and Martin (1999): (1) Early HG groups were egalitarian in nature. There was little in the way of social hierarchy and there was broad sharing of resources (e.g., meat). (2) The basic self-concept in HG groups was not elaborated. One was either a male/hunter or a female/gatherer. One could also be younger or older. There was not the proliferation of identities that was observed with the dawning of culture. Certainly, one could be better or worse at these limited social roles, but because of the egalitarian system, one would be taunted, ridiculed, pressured or even killed if he or she bragged excessively or became dominant, aggressive, or possessive. (3) These HG groups generally had a fission–fusion social model. Basically, if one group did not like me, I could leave (i.e., fission). I could then survive on my own, or join another group without difficultly (i.e., fusion). Thus, group belongingness would be less important than in later societies. (4) Inflated self-enhancement emerges in the context of ambiguity (e.g., Dunning, Meyerowitz, & Holzberg, 1989) and in non-close relationships (e.g., Sedikides, Campbell, Reeder, & Elliot, 1998). There was little room for either in HG groups. The success of a hunter or gatherer was objectively apparent to all in the group. There was little illusion or strategic self-definition (e.g., I am a "people person"). Likewise, small HG groups were close knit with most members being related by blood and history. This minimizes self-enhancement publicly as well as privately.

Historic Culture and Self-Esteem

If self-esteem has been strongly and differentially cultivated by modern societies, levels of self-esteem should vary cross-culturally and cross-temporally. The data are consistent with this position. We start with a quick detour into a speculative cultural history of the self.

In the earliest civilizations of Sumeria and later in the more advanced civilizations of Egypt, social roles were highly structured. There was a social hierarchy with slaves on the bottom, and warriors, priests and kings on the top. This structure was seen as invariant and cosmically ordained—specifically, social positions were associated with astrological bodies and patterns (e.g., Pharaoh associated with the sun) (Campbell, 1972). There was little room for individualism and self-esteem. Such as it was, self-esteem would be more evident in royal or priestly castes.

The evolution of civilization brought us Eastern (India and the Far East) and Western (Europe and the Levant) cultural centers. Eastern cultures placed less emphasis on individuality, with strong caste systems in India and the Confucian system in the Far East. Western cultures placed more emphasis on the individual, notably in Ancient Greece and, more prominently, in enlightenment Europe (i.e., mid-17th to mid-18th centuries) (Campbell, 1972). It is precisely the emergence of this enlightened individualism that would be predicted to spawn self-esteem as a conceptually elaborate trait. Of course, it is difficult to report hard empirical data for the historical difference between East and West. However, there is a wealth of data suggesting that self-esteem and self-enhancement are currently more pronounced in the West, so much so that some researchers have questioned whether individuals in the East are at all motivated to enhance self-esteem (Heine, Lehman, Markus, & Kitayama, 1999). We do not take this extreme stance; nevertheless, there is reliable cross-sectional meta-analytic evidence that white samples have roughly one third of a standard deviation higher self-esteem than do Asian samples (Twenge & Crocker, 2002), consistent with a stronger Western tendency toward self-enhancement and individualism. This same cross-cultural pattern is also observed with narcissism (Foster, Campbell, & Twenge, 2003). Likewise, a striking ethnographic study of child rearing in the US and Taiwan reports evidence that this difference is not a matter of degree, but rather a qualitative difference in the meaning of and importance placed on self-esteem (Miller, Wang, Sandel, & Cho, 2002). Indeed, these authors argued that for many in rural China, self-esteem has no real meaning.

Although tales of hubris and of men standing up to the gods are prevalent in Greek mythology, from Odysseus and Icarus to Prometheus and Narcissus, it is difficult to make a clear case for Ancient Greek self-esteem (cf. Baumeister, 1987). There is, however, clear etymological evidence that self-esteem was a concept that emerged during the European enlightenment. Specifically, a search of the Oxford English Dictionary (OED) reveals that the word "self-esteem" first occured in writing at the beginning of the enlightenment (1657, in Baker's *Sancta Sophia*). This was part of a larger linguistic trend of using "self" as a prefix. According to the OED, this trend started in the mid-16th and flourished in the mid-17th centuries. The emergence of self-esteem can be compared to related words. For example, "esteem" was first used in the 1450s—200 years before "self-esteem." Likewise, "pride" first appeared in English ca. 1000, "power" in 1297, "satisfaction" in 1400, and "happiness" in 1591. This etymological evidence corresponds to a wealth of evidence from literary and other historical accounts that portray the emergence of the self during this period (Baumeister, 1987). Of course, one could argue that self-esteem has always existed but was called by another name, such as pride or honor. We would argue that pride and honor likely correlate with self-esteem, but that they reflect different cultural systems. Honor, for example, emerges in a distinct cultural system that is heavily influenced by martial values (for an excellent discussion, see Nisbett & Cohen, 1999). A culture of honor is different from a culture of self-esteem, and likely has different and more ancient cultural roots.

After the emergence of self-esteem as a concept in the mid-17th century, the concept of self-esteem took a small place in the psychological lexicon, thanks to the writings of William James (1890). James, however, like many of those who wrote before him, had an ambivalent view of self-esteem. Equating self-esteem with success/pretensions, James noted (p. 311):

> Everything added to the Self is a burden as well as a pride. A certain man who lost every penny during our civil war went and actually rolled in the dust, saying he had not felt so free and happy since he was born.

Certainly, this was not a terrific sales pitch for self-esteem as a universal need. The pushing of self-esteem on American culture did not occur until the 1960s and 1970s (for a review, see Twenge & Campbell, 2001). During this time, self-esteem changed from a largely technical term that was hedonically ambiguous, to a common self-description that was seen as positive, desirable, and often necessary. This push was derived largely from the work of Maslow (e.g., 1970) and others, but was taken in a direction not necessarily intended by these originators. In particular, the *California Task Force to Promote Self-Esteem and Personal and Social Responsibility* argued that self-esteem could play an important role in mitigating a range of societal ills such as poverty, drug use, and premarital sex (Mecca, Smelser, & Vasconcellos, 1989). This "self-esteem movement" led to an explosion of public interest in self-esteem and a perception that self-esteem is a necessary component to basic human functioning. Indeed, the concept of self-esteem has now become so prevalent that to measure self-esteem effectively, all one needs to do is have participants rate the statement: "I have high self-esteem" (Robins, Hendin, & Trzesniewski, 2001). Whereas the enlightenment period introduced the world to the concept of self-esteem, the self-esteem movement made it a part of our everyday lexicon. It also made the possession of high self-esteem not just desirable but an apparent cure-all to many of the problems of society.

What success has the self-esteem movement had in increasing the self-esteem of Americans? There is cross-temporal meta-analytic data beginning in the mid-1960s. From 1968 to 1994, self-esteem has increased over one half of a standard deviation in mixed-gender samples, and over a full standard deviation in male samples (Twenge & Campbell, 2001). These data clearly demonstrate a cultural underpinning of self-esteem. What is especially powerful is that these cultural effects emerged over a relatively short period of time, roughly one generation. In evolutionary time, this represents the blink of eye.

SUMMARY

We argue that self-esteem is an evolved trait that conveyed some advantage to early humans. In particular, self-esteem likely provided information about social standing and performance in other areas of life. We also argue that self-esteem, as we know it in the contemporary West, is largely a cultural amplification of this "proto" self-esteem. Self-esteem emerged in the early enlightenment as an hedonically ambiguous trait, and became a central element of identity starting in the 1960s in the US. Cultural shifts, such as the self-esteem movement in the US, served to shape modern Westernized conceptualizations of self-esteem into what they are today—far removed from our evolutionary past.

REFERENCES

Baumeister, R. F. (1987). How the self became a problem: A psychological review of historical research. *Journal of Personality and Social Psychology, 52*, 163–176.

Baumeister, R. F., Campbell, J. D., Krueger, J. I., & Vohs, K. D. (2003). Does high self-esteem cause better performance, interpersonal success, happiness, or healthier lifestyles? *Psychological Science in the Public Interest, 4*, 1–44.

Baumeister, R. F., & Tice, D. M. (2000). *The social dimension of sex*. New York: Allyn & Bacon.

Boehm, C. (1999). *Hierarchy in the forest*. Cambridge, MA: Harvard University Press.

Brase, G. L., & Guy, E. C. (2004). The demographics of mate value and self-esteem. *Personality and Individual Differences, 36*, 471–484.

Campbell, J. (1972). *Myths to live by*. New York: Viking Press.

Crocker, J., Luhtanen, R. K., Cooper, M. L., & Bouvrette, A. (2003). Contingencies of self-worth in college students: Theory and measurement. *Journal of Personality and Social Psychology, 85*, 894–908.

Dunning, D., Meyerowitz, J. A., & Holzberg, A. D. (1989). Ambiguity and self-evaluation: The role of idiosyncratic trait definitions in self-serving assessments of ability. *Journal of Personality and Social Psychology, 57*, 1082–1090.

Foster, J. D., Campbell, W. K., & Twenge, J. M. (2003). Individual differences in narcissism: Inflated self-views across the lifespan and around the world. *Journal of Research in Personality, 37*, 469–486.

Gilbert, P., Price, J. S., & Allan S. (1995). Social comparison, social attractiveness and evolution: How might they be related? *New Ideas in Psychology, 13*, 149–165.

Heine, S. J., Lehman, D. R., Markus, H. R., & Kitayama, S. (1999). Is there a universal need for positive self-regard? *Psychological Review, 106*, 766–794.

James, W. (1890). *The principles of psychology*. New York: Henry Holt.

Kirkpatrick, L. A., & Ellis, B. J. (2001). An evolutionary-psychological approach to self-esteem: Multiple domains and multiple functions. In M. Clark & G. Fletcher (Eds.), *The Blackwell handbook of social psychology, Vol. 2: Interpersonal processes* (pp. 411–436). Oxford, UK: Blackwell.

Leary, M. R., & Baumeister, R. F. (2000). The nature and function of self-esteem: Sociometer theory. In M. P. Zanna (Ed.), *Advances in experimental social psychology* (Vol. 32, pp. 1–62). San Diego, CA: Academic Press.

Martin, L. L. (1999). I-D compensation theory: Some implications of trying to satisfy immediate-return needs in a delayed-return culture. *Psychological Inquiry, 10*, 195–209.

Maslow, A. H. (1970). *Motivation and personality* (2nd ed.). New York: Harper & Row.

Mecca, A. M., Smelser, N. J., & Vasconcellos, J. (Eds.). (1989). *The social importance of self-esteem.* Berkeley, CA: University of California Press.

Miller, P. J., Wang, S., Sandel, T., & Cho, G. E. (2002). Self-esteem as folk theory: A comparison of European American and Taiwanese mothers' beliefs. *Parenting: Science & Practice, 2,* 209–239.

Neiss, M. B., Sedikides, C., & Stevenson, J. (2002). Self-esteem: A behavioural genetic perspective. *European Journal of Personality, 16,* 351–367.

Nisbett, R. E., & Cohen, D. (1999). *The culture of honor: The psychology of violence in the South.* Boulder, CO: Westview Press.

Robins, R. W., Hendin, H. M., & Trzesniewski, K. H. (2001). Measuring global self-esteem: Construct validation of a single item measure and the Rosenberg Self-Esteem scale. *Personality and Social Psychology Bulletin, 27,* 151–161.

Sedikides, C., Campbell, W. K., Reeder, G. D., & Elliot, A. J. (1998). The self-serving bias in relational context. *Journal of Personality and Social Psychology, 74,* 378–386.

Sedikides, C., & Skowronski, J. J. (2000). On the evolutionary functions of the symbolic self: The emergence of self-evaluation motives. In A. Tesser, R. Felson, & J. Suls (Eds.), *Psychological perspectives on self and identity* (pp. 91–117). Washington, DC: APA Books.

Sedikides, C., & Skowronski, J. J. (2003). Evolution of the self: Issues and prospects. In M. R. Leary & J. P. Tangney (Eds.), *Handbook of self and identity* (pp. 594–609). New York: Guilford.

Tesser, A. (1988). Toward a self-evaluation maintenance model of social behavior. In L. Berkowitz (Ed.), *Advances in experimental social psychology* (Vol. 21, pp. 181–227). New York: Academic Press.

Twenge, J. M., & Campbell, W. K. (2001). Age and birth cohort differences in self-esteem: A cross-temporal meta-analysis. *Personality and Social Psychology Review, 5,* 321–344.

Twenge, J., & Campbell, W. K. (2002). Self-esteem and socioeconomic status: A meta-analytic review. *Personality and Social Psychology Review, 6,* 59–71.

Twenge, J. M., & Crocker, J. (2002). Race and self-esteem: Meta-analyses comparing Whites, Blacks, Hispanics, Asians, and American Indians. *Psychological Bulletin, 128,* 371–408.

Section IV

Self-Esteem in Social Context

Question 15

How does self-esteem relate to close relationship dynamics?

This set of essays examines self-esteem dynamics within close relationships. As a group, they leave little doubt about the importance of self-esteem in close relationships.

Murray writes about the nature of relationship contingencies and their consequences. She first describes situations that highlight various risks that occur in close relationships. Next, she describes how being secure in one's partner's positive regard allows people to put their relationship ahead of self-protection. Unfortunately, as revealed in Murray's research, the doubts of low self-esteem individuals have some adverse consequences. She concludes her essay by suggesting conditions that may make it easier for individuals with low self-esteem to be more optimistic.

Baldwin suggests that self-esteem dynamics inextricably intertwine with relationship dynamics, even though the connections may not be apparent or conscious. As he notes, "Self-esteem feelings arise from a host of evaluative procedures and expectations, and these are for the most part learned and then maintained in the context of close relationships." Baldwin describes these dynamics within parent-child relationships and in relationships more broadly. In addition, Baldwin discusses his research on the operation of relational schemas and their implications for self-esteem processes.

Berenson and Downey discuss the overlap between low self-esteem and high rejection sensitivity. For example, both are associated with increased readiness to perceive and react to cues of potential rejection by others. However, Berenson and Downey suggest that the nature of their insecurities and motivations may be different. For individuals with low self-esteem, the concern over rejection lies in the message it communicates about their worth or competence. In contrast, for individuals high in rejection sensitivity, rejection raises concerns about the availability of others' care in time of need.

45

Self-Esteem: Its Relational Contingencies and Consequences

SANDRA L. MURRAY

"Of all the forms of caution, caution in love is perhaps the most fatal to true happiness."

B. Russell, *The Conquest of Happiness*

W hy are people with low self-esteem less likely to find happiness in both dating and marital relationships than people with high self-esteem (e.g., Fincham & Bradbury, 1993; Hendrick, Hendrick, & Adler, 1988; Karney & Bradbury, 1997; Kelly & Conley, 1987; Murray, Holmes, & Griffin, 1996a, 1996b)? I argue that people with low self-esteem are less satisfied largely because they are too hesitant in reaching optimistic conclusions about their partner's care and attachment, and as a consequence, they too readily react to the risks of interdependence by putting cautious, self-protective thoughts and behaviors at a greater psychological premium than more relationship-enhancing thoughts and behaviors.

In developing these arguments, I first describe the many common situations in relationship life that highlight the risks of dependence, and thus, necessitate the kinds of motivated cognitive processes that put relationship-enhancement and self-protection motives in conflict. Next, I outline how a relationship-specific sense of felt security in a partner's positive regard and acceptance allows people to take the necessary risk of putting relationship-enhancement ahead of self-protection. I then explain why low self-esteem people are less likely to find this sense of felt security than high self-esteem people, and describe the detrimental and self-fulfilling consequences of such doubts for both relationship- and self-evaluations. I conclude on a more optimistic note by pointing to the conditions that can result in low self-esteem people risking more optimistic and more accurate conclusions about their partner's regard and acceptance.

POSITIVE ILLUSIONS AND THE PRESSURE FOR CONVICTION

Just as romantic life is replete with situations, such as an affectionate hug or a comforting remark, that can affirm and bolster self-esteem, it is also filled with situations that highlight the risks of rejection and the potential practical and self-esteem costs of depending on another person's fallible good will (Braiker & Kelley, 1979; Holmes, 2002; Kelley, 1979). For instance, if Harry has transgressed and broken a promise, Sally must decide whether to risk letting her outcomes depend on Harry's actions again in the future. In such situations, the cautious or self-protective choice is most often the choice that minimizes dependence on the other person's goodwill. In this scenario, deciding not to trust Harry's promises and reducing her reliance on Harry for the satisfaction of her own goals, likely protects Sally from feeling let down and rejected in the future. However, such a self-protective choice also compromises Sally's trust in Harry, and limits Harry's future opportunities to demonstrate his trustworthiness, putting the well-being of the relationship at greater risk.

In the face of such dilemmas, people in satisfying dating and marital relationships seem to throw inferential caution to the wind—and think and behave in ways that put protecting the welfare of the relationship ahead of self-protection (see Murray, 1999, for a review). For instance, people in satisfying marriages generously attribute their partner's transgressions to transient features of the situation (Bradbury & Fincham, 1990). They also inhibit self-protective inclinations to respond in kind to a partner's misdeeds, and instead, respond constructively (Rusbult, Verette, Whitney, Slovik, & Lipkus, 1991). Perhaps a consequence of such situated generosity is that people in satisfying dating and marital relationships see strengths in their imperfect partner, which they do not see in others (Rusbult, Van Lange, Wildschut, Yovetich, & Verette, 2000), and these strengths are also not apparent to their friends (Murray, Holmes, Dolderman, & Griffin, 2000a) or even to their partner (Murray, Holmes, & Griffin, 1996a; Neff & Karney, 2002).

REGULATING RISK: THE NATURE OF DEPENDENCE REGULATION

Casting doubt aside in these ways seems to require a kind of psychological insurance policy. For instance, people only allow themselves to risk giving their partner the cognitive and behavioral benefit of the doubt, and putting a positive spin on the available evidence, when they believe their partner's positive regard, acceptance, and love is secure (Murray, Holmes, & Griffin, 2000b; Murray, Holmes, Griffin, Bellavia, & Rose, 2001). After all, Sally is not likely to feel as vulnerable in forgiving Harry's transgressions if she expects Harry to be equally forgiving of her own foibles. In other words, people actively regulate closeness (and thus dependence) with a sense of felt security, and they do not let themselves risk vulnerability unless they are confident that the potential for rejection is minimal. This process of dependence regulation means that dating and married intimates find more to value in their partner the more loved they feel (Murray et al., 2001) and the more positively they feel about their partner's regard for them (Murray et al., 2000b). Conversely, distancing oneself from the relationship is a self-protective defense for people who acutely perceive that their partners are not all that committed to the relationship.

To find this sense of felt security in a partner's acceptance, people likely need to believe that each partner brings comparable personal strengths (and liabilities) to the relationship (Murray, Rose, Holmes, Derrick, Podchaski, Bellavia, & Griffin, 2005). To feel secure people may need to feel that they are just as good a person as their partner (and that their partner also shares this perception). In lay psychophysical terms, the perceived worth of one's own qualities need to be roughly equivalent to the perceived worth of one's partner's qualities. After all, to the extent that Harry feels inferior to Sally on most dimensions, and assumes that Sally sees these imbalances, how could he construct a justification for her positive regard and love that he would find logically satisfying?

How Self-Esteem Affects Felt Security

Unfortunately, people with low self-esteem have greater difficulty finding sufficient reason to trust in their own worthiness of love, and by extension, their partner's positive regard and acceptance (Murray et al., 2000b, 2001). Low self-esteem people typically possess less positive, more uncertain, and more conflicted beliefs about themselves than high self-esteem people (e.g., Baumeister, 1993; Baumgardner, 1990; Campbell, 1990). In terms of their own relational appeal, low self-esteem people describe themselves as possessing far fewer desirable interpersonal traits than their partner (Murray et al., 2003), qualities they believe are necessary for securing another's positive regard and acceptance (Baldwin & Sinclair, 1996; Roberts, Gotlib, & Kassel, 1996). Moreover, in both dating and marital relationships, low self-esteem people naively and incorrectly assume that their partner sees them in the same negative light as they see themselves (Murray et al., 2000b). Accordingly, lows may often find themselves having trouble explaining why a partner who sees so many faults in them, and who seems so superior to them would really care for them, or remain committed. In contrast, the confidently held, positive self-views of high self-esteem people may provide a readily accessible, compelling accounting for a partner's care and commitment (no matter how desirable that partner's qualities may appear).

Thus, low self-esteem people generally lack the level of confidence in their partner's positive regard, acceptance, and care they need to satisfy felt security goals. In fact, even low self-esteem people whose marriages have already lasted as long as 10 years underestimate their partner's love for them (Murray et al., 2001). Accordingly, the chronic activation of this goal (whether conscious or not) should sensitize lows to information relevant to the satisfaction of this goal (e.g., Bargh & Ferguson, 2000; Gardner, Pickett, & Brewer, 2000; Holmes & Rempel, 1989; Vorauer & Ross, 1996)—specifically, the perceived "if–then" contingencies warranting interpersonal acceptance (Baldwin, 1992).

Imagine, for instance, that Sally gets criticized at work for failing to complete a project on time. To the extent that she feels unsure of Harry's regard, Sally may be reluctant to disclose this personal failure for fear that he might be angry or disappointed with her. Consistent with this logic, low self-esteem people react to experimentally induced doubts about their intelligence or considerateness with greater concerns about their dating partner's likely rejection (Murray et al., 1998). In fact, lows even react to experimental boosts to their intelligence by expressing greater agitation about the prospect of their partner's rejection (Murray, Holmes, MacDonald, & Ellsworth, 1998). Now imagine that Sally comes home to find Harry in a generally irritable mood, grumbling about the lack of food in the fridge. Rather than brushing this off, Sally may worry that such grumbling signifies broader displeasure with her or the relationship. In fact, people with lower self-esteem over-interpret their dating partner's (hypothetical) negative moods, and see them as symptomatic of their partner's ill feelings toward them (Bellavia & Murray, 2003). They also react to experimentally induced signs of a partner's irritation by anticipating rejection (Murray, Rose, Bellavia, Holmes, & Kusche, 2002).

As these examples illustrate, lows are not likely to be all that even-handed in their search for evidence of care. Instead, they seem to process information in risk-averse ways, too ready to generalize from signs of rejection and too hesitant to trust signs of acceptance. Even though detecting signs of rejection might hurt in the short term, such a bias toward rejection cues may better protect intimates who feel less positively regarded by their partner against the greater hurt of inferring acceptance, risking attachment, and then later reaching the all the more hurtful conclusion that they were never really accepted at all.

On the other side of the coin, confident expectations that a partner sees positive qualities in oneself may inoculate people with high self-esteem against all but the most threatening situations. For highs, felt security goals are likely to be largely satiated (and thus quiescent). Rather than looking for signs of the partner's approval, they may instead approach their relationships with an eye toward confirming and maintaining benevolent expectations about the partner's care. Consistent with this hypothesis, high self-esteem people do not read rejection in the minor signs of their partner's annoyance (Murray et al., 2002), and, they actually compensate for experimentally induced doubts about their own intelligence or considerateness by exaggerating how much their partner accepts and loves them (Murray et al., 1998).

How Self-Esteem Affects Conviction

How does their greater sensitivity to perceiving rejection then affect low self-esteem people's capacity to put the needed positive mental and behavioral spin on difficult situations? In specific situations, the tendency to read rejection and hurt in day-to-day events may make it difficult for low self-esteem people to respond constructively to difficulties. Instead, they might react to the self-esteem sting of rejections with anger and with the self-protective step of actively distancing from the source of the hurt—the partner or relationship. Devaluing the partner, lashing out behaviorally, or reducing feelings of closeness—all are likely to function to lessen the acute threat to self-esteem posed by the feeling of being rejected (Murray et al., 1998). After all, one need not believe the message if the messenger can be discredited.

Consistent with this logic, people typically react to acute rejection experiences by strangers by aggressing against those who ostracized them, suggesting that people's most immediate impulse is to return hurts in a tit-for-tat fashion (Twenge, Baumeister, Tice, & Stucke, 2001). In romantic relationships, people who are dispositionally prone to questioning another's acceptance also seem to react in this self-protective (perhaps self-vindicating) way. Low self-esteem people respond to induced anxieties about rejection by derogating their partner's traits (Murray et al., 1998; Murray et al., 2002). More anxiously attached (and thus lower self-esteem) women also display greater anger toward their partner in situations in which their partner may not have been as responsive as they hoped (Rholes, Simpson, & Orina, 1999). Women chronically high on rejection sensitivity (and lower on self-esteem) also respond to a potential dating partner's disinterest by evaluating that partner more negatively (Ayduk, Downey, Testa, Yen, & Shoda, 1999). They are also more likely to initiate conflicts on days after they felt more rejected by their partner, and simply priming rejection-related words activates hostility-related thoughts for these women (Ayduk et al., 1999).

In contrast, for people with high self-esteem, resilient expectations of acceptance seem to lessen the self-esteem sting of rejection in ways that might allow them to put protecting the relationship ahead of defending against a perceived blow to the self. As a result, people who feel more positively regarded may inhibit the tit-for-tat impulse to hurt the partner in return, and instead, more readily compensate for signs of difficulty by drawing closer to their partner, enhancing the value of their partner and relationship. Supporting this point, high self-esteem people responded to the prospect that their dating partner was annoyed by some unknown aspect of their personality by reporting greater feelings of closeness to their partner (Murray et al., 2002, Study 2).

IMPLICATIONS FOR RELATIONSHIP WELL-BEING

The existing research thus suggests that low self-esteem people are less happy in both dating and marital relationships because they harbor unwarranted and unwanted doubts about their partner's positive regard and love (Murray et al., 2000b). In trying to assuage these concerns, lows turn to the behavioral evidence where they (incorrectly) see evidence for their concerns. They then respond to their feeling of being acutely rejected by derogating their partner, and thereby distancing themselves from the source of the hurt (Murray et al., 1998, 2002). Unfortunately, such cycles are likely to have detrimental self-fulfilling effects as relationships progress. The results of a longitudinal study of dating couples revealed that the partners of lows became more disaffected and disillusioned with them as time passed, suggesting that the self-protective behavior of lows eventually elicits the rejection they initially feared (Murray et al., 2000b).

Apart from eroding the self-esteem resource of a loving, admiring partner, the relationship insecurities of lows may eventually further undermine their own sense of self-worth. Interpersonal theorists on self-esteem argue that feelings of self-worth reflect a sense of connection to others, and that low self-esteem (acute and chronic) reflects a need for approval and interpersonal connections (Kernis, Cornell, Sun, Berry, & Harlow, 1993; Leary, Tambor, Terdal, & Downs, 1995; Nezlek, Kowalski, Leary, Blevins, & Holgate, 1997; Rudich & Vallacher, 1999). In romantic relationships, people with low self-esteem should be particularly likely to rely on their perceptions of their partner's regard and love as a gauge of their own self-worth. Specifically, our longitudinal study of dating couples revealed that people who felt less positively regarded internalized their (incorrect) perceptions of their dating partner's regard, and came to see themselves more negatively over the course of a year (Murray et al., 2000b).

ROOM FOR OPTIMISM

In light of these pernicious, self-fulfilling effects, is there any room for optimism in considering the relationship futures of low self-esteem people? Earlier I reasoned that low self-esteem people doubt their partner's regard in part because they see their partner as bringing more interpersonal strengths and fewer weaknesses to the relationship than they do (Murray et al., 2005). If that is the case, putting the partner more within the "league" or psychological grasp of lows, should alleviate their rejection anxieties. In a recent series of experiments, we found that humanizing the partner by pointing to their failures in being considerate, or their culpability for a past conflict, boosted the state self-esteem of lows and heightened their confidence in their partner's acceptance (Murray et al., 2005). Upgrading people's sense of their own relational appeal by pointing to the ways in which their traits provided an easy fit to other, potential partners' personalities had a similar, ameliorative effect for lows.

Rather than being directly dispositional in nature, the relationship problems of lows likely stem from the indirect consequences of relationship-specific, and modifiable, representations that put the partner on a pedestal relative to the self. The popular media has often speculated that at some level (whether conscious or not), low self-esteem people really want to feel unloved, and want to sabotage their relationship. From a related, self-verification perspective (Swann, Hixon, & De La Ronde, 1992), such insecurities may arise because epistemic needs for certainty result in lows simply assuming that their partner sees them in the same relatively negative light as they see themselves (Murray et al., 2000b, 2001). Our most recent findings suggest that felt security in a partner's acceptance is more a statement about one's own worth in relation to the partner's—a much more dyadic, and dynamic construct (Kelley, 1983).

From this perspective, lows and highs may both be motivated to see themselves and their close partners in ways that make them feel more secure in a specific relationship. For instance, low self-esteem people who feel relatively shy and unsociable seek information that might disconfirm such self-perceptions from a novel interaction partner (Bernichon, Cook, & Brown, 2003). In dating relationships, both lows and highs want their partner to see them as more physically attractive than they see themselves (Swann, Bosson, & Pelham, 2002). Similarly, lows and highs in both dating and marital relationships also want their partner to see them more positively on relationally oriented qualities, such as warmth, responsiveness, and tolerance (Murray et al., 2000b). Lows and highs both also prefer romantic partners that validate and enhance or affirm the self (Katz & Beach, 2000), presumably because such partners would be more likely to remain attached and committed.

To conclude, our most recent experimental research complements existing research that suggests that the self-evaluation motives of low self-esteem people may not seem all that different from highs—if the situation is structured appropriately (see Mischel & Shoda, 1995). In fact, in situations that put the partner on less of a pedestal relative to the self, and thus, afford reason to trust in the partner's acceptance, lows are not any more cautious than highs. In these safe contexts, lows are just as psychologically equipped to defend their relationship against threat as highs—risking the kinds of motivated and benevolent transformations of the evidence that typically characterize high self-esteem people (Murray et al., 2003).

REFERENCES

Ayduk, O., Downey, G., Testa, A., Yen, Y., & Shoda, Y. (1999). Does rejection elicit hostility in rejection sensitive women? *Social Cognition, 17,* 245–271.

Baldwin, M. W. (1992). Relational schemas and the processing of social information. *Psychological Bulletin, 112,* 461–484.

Baldwin, M. W., & Sinclair, L. (1996). Self-esteem and "if...then" contingencies of interpersonal acceptance. *Journal of Personality and Social Psychology, 71,* 1130–1141.

Bargh, J. A., & Ferguson, M. J. (2000). Beyond behaviorism: On the automaticity of higher mental processes. *Psychological Bulletin, 126,* 925–945.

Baumeister, R. F. (1993). *Self-esteem: The puzzle of low self-regard.* New York: Plenum Press.

Baumgardner, A. H. (1990). To know oneself is to like oneself: Self-certainty and self-affect. *Journal of Personality and Social Psychology, 58,* 1062–1072.

Bellavia, G., & Murray, S. L. (2003). Did I do that? Self-esteem related differences in reactions to romantic partners' moods. *Personal Relationships, 10,* 77–96.

Bernichon, T., Cook, K. E., & Brown, J. D. (2003). Seeking self-evaluative feedback: The interactive role of global self-esteem and specific self-views. *Journal of Personality and Social Psychology, 84,* 194–204.

Bradbury, T. N., & Fincham, F. D. (1990). Attributions in marriage: Review and critique. *Psychological Bulletin, 107,* 3–23.

Braiker, H. B., & Kelley, H. H. (1979). Conflict in the development of close relationships. In R. L Burgess & T. L. Huston (Eds.), *Social exchange in developing relationships* (pp. 135–168). New York: Academic Press.

Campbell, J. D. (1990). Self-esteem and clarity of the self-concept. *Journal of Personality and Social Psychology, 59,* 538–549.

Fincham, F. D., & Bradbury, T. N. (1993). Marital satisfaction, depression and attributions: A longitudinal analysis. *Journal of Personality and Social Psychology, 64,* 442–452.

Gardner, W., Pickett, C. L., & Brewer, M. B. (2000). Social exclusion and selective memory: How the need to belong influences memory for social events. *Personality and Social Psychology Bulletin*, 26, 486–496.

Hendrick, S. S., Hendrick, C., & Adler, N. L. (1988). Romantic relationships: Love, satisfaction, and staying together. *Journal of Personality and Social Psychology*, 54, 980–988.

Holmes, J. G. (2002). Interpersonal expectations as the building blocks of social cognition: An interdependence theory perspective. *Personal Relationship*, 9, 1–26.

Holmes, J. G., & Rempel, J. K. (1989). Trust in close relationships. In C. Hendrick (Ed.), *Review of personality and social psychology: Close relationships* (Vol. 10, pp. 187–219). Newbury Park, CA: Sage.

Karney, B. R., & Bradbury, T. N. (1997). Neuroticism, marital interaction, and the trajectory of marital satisfaction. *Journal of Personality and Social Psychology*, 72, 1075–1092.

Katz, J., & Beach, S. R. H. (2000). Looking for love? Self-verification and self-enhancement effects on initial romantic attraction. *Personality and Social Psychology Bulletin*, 26, 1526–1539.

Kelley, H. H. (1979). *Personal relationships: Their structures and processes*. Hillsdale, NJ: Lawrence Erlbaum Associates.

Kelley, H. H. (1983). Love and commitment. In H. H. Kelley, E. Berscheid, A. Christensen, J. H. Harvey, T. L. Huston, G. Levinger, E. McClintock, L. A. Peplau, & D. R. Peterson (Eds.), *Close relationships* (pp. 265–314). New York: W. H. Freeman.

Kelly, E. L., & Conley, J. J. (1987). Personality and compatibility: A prospective analysis of marital stability and marital satisfaction. *Journal of Personality and Social Psychology*, 52, 27–40.

Kernis, M. H., Cornell, D. P., Sun, C. R., Berry, A., & Harlow, T. (1993). There's more to self-esteem than whether it is high or low: The importance of stability of self-esteem. *Journal of Personality and Social Psychology*, 65, 1190–1204.

Leary, M. R., Tambor, E. S., Terdal, S. K., & Downs, D. L. (1995). Self-esteem as an interpersonal monitor: The sociometer hypothesis. *Journal of Personality and Social Psychology*, 68, 518–530.

Mischel, W., & Shoda, Y. (1995). A cognitive-affective system theory of personality: Reconceptualizing situations, dispositions, dynamics, and invariance in personality structure. *Psychological Review*, 102, 246–268.

Murray, S. L. (1999). The quest for conviction: Motivated cognition in romantic relationships. *Psychological Inquiry*, 10, 23–34.

Murray, S. L., Holmes, J. G., Dolderman, D., & Griffin, D. W. (2000a). What the motivated mind sees: Comparing friends' perspectives to married partners' views of each other. *Journal of Experimental Social Psychology*, 36, 600–620.

Murray, S. L., Holmes, J. G., & Griffin, D. (1996a). The benefits of positive illusions: Idealization and the construction of satisfaction in close relationships. *Journal of Personality and Social Psychology*, 70, 79–98.

Murray, S. L., Holmes, J. G., & Griffin, D. W. (1996b). The self-fulfilling nature of positive illusions in romantic relationships: Love is not blind, but prescient. *Journal of Personality and Social Psychology*, 71, 1155–1180.

Murray, S. L., Holmes, J. G., & Griffin, D. W. (2000b). Self-esteem and the quest for felt security: How perceived regard regulates attachment processes. *Journal of Personality and Social Psychology*, 78, 478–498.

Murray, S. L., Holmes, J. G., Griffin, D. W., Bellavia, G., & Rose, P. (2001). The mismeasure of love: How self-doubt contaminates relationship beliefs. *Personality and Social Psychology Bulletin, 27*, 423–436.

Murray, S. L., Holmes, J. G., MacDonald, G., & Ellsworth, P. (1998). Through the looking glass darkly? When self-doubts turn into relationship insecurities. *Journal of Personality and Social Psychology, 75*, 1459–1480.

Murray, S. L., Rose, P., Bellavia, G., Holmes, J., & Kusche, A. (2002). When rejection stings: How self-esteem constrains relationship-enhancement processes. *Journal of Personality and Social Psychology, 83*, 556–573.

Murray, S. L., Rose, P., Holmes, J. G., Derrick, J., Podchaski, E., Bellavia, G., & Griffin, D. W. (2005). Putting the partner within reach: A dyadic perspective on felt security in close relationships. *Journal of Personality and Social Psychology, 88*, 327–347.

Neff, L. A., & Karney, B. R. (2002). Judgments of a relationship partner: Specific accuracy but global enhancement. *Journal of Personality, 70*, 1079–1112.

Nezlek, J. B., Kowalski, R. M., Leary, M. R., Blevins, T., & Holgate, S. (1997). Personality moderators of reactions to interpersonal rejection: Depression and trait self-esteem. *Personality and Social Psychology Bulletin, 23*, 1235–1244.

Rholes, S. W., Simpson, J. A., & Orina, M. M. (1999). Attachment and anger in an anxiety-provoking situation. *Journal of Personality and Social Psychology, 76*, 940–957.

Roberts, J. E., Gotlib, I. H., & Kassel, J. D. (1996). Adult attachment security and symptoms of depression: The mediating roles of dysfunctional attitudes and low self-esteem. *Journal of Personality and Social Psychology, 70*, 310–320.

Rudich, E. A., & Vallacher, R. R. (1999). To belong or to self-enhance? Motivational bases for choosing interaction partners. *Personality and Social Psychology Bulletin, 25*, 1387–1404.

Rusbult, C., E., Van Lange, P. A. M., Wildschut, T., Yovetich, N. A., & Verette, J. (2000). Perceived superiority in close relationships: Why it exists and persists. *Journal of Personality and Social Psychology, 79*, 521–545.

Rusbult, C. E., Verette, J., Whitney, G. A., Slovik, L. F., & Lipkus, I. (1991). Accommodation processes in close relationships: Theory and preliminary research evidence. *Journal of Personality and Social Psychology, 60*, 53–78.

Swann, W. B., Bosson, J. K., & Pelham, B. W. (2002). Different partners, different selves: Strategic verification of circumscribed identities. *Personality and Social Psychology Bulletin, 28*, 1215–1228.

Swann, W. B., Hixon, J. G., & De La Ronde, C. (1992). Embracing the bitter "truth": Negative self-concepts and marital commitment. *Psychological Science, 3*, 118–121.

Twenge, J. M., Baumeister, R. F., Tice, D. M., & Stucke, T. S. (2001). If you can't join them, beat them: Effects of social exclusion on aggressive behavior. *Journal of Personality and Social Psychology, 81*, 1058–1069.

Vorauer, J. D., & Ross, M. (1996). The pursuit of knowledge in close relationships: An informational goals analysis. In G .J. O. Fletcher & J. Fitness (Eds.), *Knowledge structures in close relationships: A social psychological approach* (pp. 369–396). Mahwah, NJ: Lawrence Erlbaum Associates.

46

Self-Esteem and Close Relationship Dynamics

MARK W. BALDWIN

*I*t can be easy to lose sight of the relevance of close relationships to self-esteem. After all, thinking about oneself seems one of the most private, self-contained things one can do. The key to appreciating the influence of close relationships on self-esteem, and vice versa, is to recognize that self-esteem dynamics are virtually always, at some deep level, tied in with relationship dynamics—even when the connection may not be conscious or apparent. I will start with a brief overview of some of the ways in which relationships influence self-esteem, both developmentally and in the here-and-now, and then examine the reverse influence, of self-esteem on relationships. I will conclude by noting that because interpersonal dynamics may become "internalized," they may no longer be immediately apparent to casual inspection or theorizing. Fortunately, social cognitive methods can be applied to reveal the ongoing links between self-esteem and significant relationships.

THE INFLUENCE OF RELATIONSHIPS ON SELF-ESTEEM

Let us begin by considering a broad definition of close relationships, as "ongoing patterns of interactions that involve affectively strong bonds between individuals and considerable interdependence, such as romantic and marital relationships, friendships, and parent-child relationships" (Aron, 2003, p. 442). In short, these are the important relationships in our lives in which we typically have abundant exposure to the other person, often involving the expression of many of our most personal characteristics, thoughts, emotions, and so on. It is not too much of an exaggeration to say that our confident sense of who we are is predicated on the "shared reality" (Hardin & Higgins, 1996; Mead, 1934) that emerges from interactions with others, particularly with these people who know us the most deeply, and with whom we negotiate our sense of identity in the give and take of day-to-day interaction. As a result, most of the factors that can be identified as playing a role in self-esteem are at their most intense in the context of close relationships, whether one speaks of assessments of one's social acceptability, comparison to others, or satisfaction of basic social needs. Research supports this observation, generally finding a significant moderate correlation between people's self-esteem and the quality, nature, and stability of their relationships, whether with family and friends (e.g., Voss, Markiewicz, & Doyle, 1999), with parents (e.g., Harter, 1999) or with romantic partners (e.g., Hendrick, Hendrick, & Adler, 1988).

Self-esteem feelings arise from a host of evaluative procedures and expectations, and these are for the most part learned and then maintained in the context of close relationships. This principle is perhaps easiest to see in the parent–child context, where the initial outline of the self-attitude is etched by the dynamics of the primary relationship (see, e.g., Moretti & Higgins, 1999, for a detailed discussion). If the child learns that when seeking support and warmth from the parent, he or she tends to find a valuable self reflected in the parent's eyes, the result is likely to be genuine high self-esteem and self-acceptance rooted in a secure sense of attachment (e.g., Brown, 1993; Mikulincer, 1995). Parental affection is seldom 100% unconditional, of course, and children are well-attuned to the dynamics of social feedback. Children learn to evaluate themselves by internalizing evaluative communications from parents and, to a lesser extent, siblings. Young children can often be heard talking to themselves, for example, imitating the kinds of things their parents might say, such as, "Bad girl!" or "You can do it!" They mimic the attributional patterns, standard-setting, and evaluative tone to which they are exposed. Gradually this self-referential speech becomes internalized, as these patterns of interaction become habits of thought (Baldwin, 1997). In ideal circumstances, the internalized voices are relatively benign and encouraging, but if the parent sets extremely high and demanding standards for performance, the child may become self-critical and perfectionistic (Koestner, Zuroff, & Powers, 1991; Moretti & Higgins, 1999). To the extent that the parent rewards positive behavior or successes with affection but uses withdrawal of love to try to discourage misbehavior, the child may develop highly contingent or conditional self-esteem, in which positive feelings of self-worth are only accessible in the context of certain kinds of successes or positive behaviors (Rogers, 1959).

Although the relationship between child and parent is in some ways the easiest to analyze, in terms of the link between self-esteem and the interpersonal dynamics of social evaluation and acceptance, the same factors continue to apply as the social world extends beyond the family and home context. Throughout life, whether with peers, authority figures, or intimate relationship partners, people continue to experience new forms of relatedness and can internalize these as frames for self-experience. We know, for example, that people often experience significantly different levels of self-esteem depending on whom they are with: They might feel very confident and generally good about themselves with a supportive friend, but anxious and insecure with a judgmental religious leader or pathetically unacceptable with a rejecting ex-spouse (e.g., Harter, Waters, & Whitesell, 1998). Similarly, they might feel a secure sense of self in the context of relationships where they feel that their basic needs of relatedness, competency, and autonomy are being met, but feel worse about themselves if these needs are blocked in some way (LaGuardia, Ryan, Couchman, & Deci, 2000). The general rule seems to be that positive self-esteem arises from the sense that one is loved and valued by one's significant others, and that one can anticipate positive regard from others (e.g., Baldwin & Baccus, 2003; Baldwin & Keelan, 1999). People who are securely attached to a loved one, who believe that their partner cares about them, values them, and will support them in times of need, tend to report high self-esteem (Mikulincer, 1995). The benefit of a supportive relationship goes beyond just good feelings: Over time, people with a romantic partner who views them very positively gradually start to act in a manner that approaches their own self-ideal (e.g., Drigotis, Rusbult, Wieslquist, & Whitton, 1999). Conversely, the costs of a relationship suffused with criticism can be significant, as demonstrated by a study in which the strongest predictor of relapse after treatment for depression was found to be the perceived criticalness of the subject's spouse (Hooley & Teasdale, 1989).

THE INFLUENCE OF SELF-ESTEEM ON RELATIONSHIPS

I would not wish to imply that everyone's self-esteem is forever at the mercy of whatever kind of image is reflected back by the people around them. For one thing, once people have formed an idea of how they are perceived, this preconception tends to shape the way they *think* others view them (see Tice and Wallace (2003) for a review). Beyond that, people's self-esteem level, dynamics, and needs also play a role in the kinds of relationship dynamics they attempt to create—and ultimately end up creating (which may not be the same!). Indeed, the link between self-esteem and conduct in close relationships works both ways.

One obvious mechanism whereby self-esteem influences relationships is through partner choice. Not all relationships are open to this source of influence—it is notoriously difficult to choose one's biological parents, for example—but often there is enough flexibility in the selection of friends or romantic partners that self-esteem can play a significant role. For example, people often seek to associate with others who will help satisfy their specific needs relating to self-esteem. Several studies have shown that whereas individuals with low self-esteem tend to seek others who accept them for being "nice," individuals with high self-esteem often seek those who will respect them and reinforce their positive self-views (e.g., Rudich & Vallacher, 1999). Narcissists, in particular, have been found to pursue social admiration even to the point of choosing a partner who worships them unreservedly or brings to the table socially desirable characteristics such as good looks (thereby bringing admiration from others), rather than choosing a partner who might be a source of secure attachment and true intimacy (Campbell, 1999). Sometimes sub-optimal partner choices may appear baffling to observers, who wonder why (other) people seem compelled to make the same mistakes over and over. There are several possible explanations for this (e.g., Freud's analysis of the repetition compulsion), but one leading candidate is that people have a powerful need for a sense of coherence and regularity in their interpersonal life. Therefore, once they become accustomed to being seen and treated in a particular way, they may seek relationships that re-establish this familiar pattern. In Swann and colleagues' research, for example, individuals with low self-esteem surprisingly chose to interact with others who saw them negatively, even if more positive evaluators were available. In one study of married couples, people who did not feel accurately perceived by their partner (even on dimensions where their own self-view was negative) tended to react negatively to the partner and withdraw from intimacy (see Swann, Rentfrow, and Guinn (2003) for a review).

Once in a relationship, partners become interdependent in their pursuit of their self-esteem related motives, and their efforts to coordinate self-views can resemble a complex dance. People love to bask in the reflected glory of their partner's success and talents, for example, and often seem to consider their partner's personal assets and resources their own (Aron, Aron, Tudor, & Nelson, 1991). As Self-Evaluation Maintenance theory (Tesser, Millar, & Moore, 1988) points out, though, all is not so sweet if the two partners' strengths are in the same general domain of activity. Then comparison and competition rear their ugly heads, often causing discomfort until a delicate balance or compartmentalization can be worked out (e.g., "I tend to cook meat dishes, which I am better at, whereas she tends to cook vegetarian dishes"). People who feel their self-esteem threatened by a friend's successes may even act to undermine those successes (Tesser & Smith, 1980). As these examples demonstrate, when people are able to satisfy their self-esteem needs together, relationship dynamics can be harmonious and fulfilling, but if the partners' esteem-regulation tendencies do not mesh well, this can be a source of conflict (e.g., MacDonald, Zanna, & Holmes, 2000).

A final dynamic whereby self-esteem shapes relationship quality is through behavioral confirmation. In this form of self-fulfilling prophecy an individual with low self-esteem, who anticipates that others will be critical and rejecting, somehow manages to produce exactly this kind of response from interaction partners. There is ample evidence for this pattern (e.g., Curtis & Miller, 1986; Downey, Freitas, Michaelis, & Khouri, 1998; Riggs & Cantor, 1984), although there is still more work to be done on illuminating the exact mechanism. Presumably, insecure individuals act in an uncertain, pessimistic, socially dependent manner and may either defensively withdraw or else give off impressions of dissatisfaction, anxiety and hostility that interaction partners find objectionable (see, e.g., Schütz, 1998). In any case, low self-esteem individuals often end up re-creating the kinds of unsatisfying relationships that produced their insecurity in the first place.

INTERNALIZATION MAY OBSCURE THE LINKS BETWEEN SELF-ESTEEM AND RELATIONSHIP DYNAMICS

Given all of the evidence demonstrating that self-esteem is intertwined with relationship dynamics it is, perhaps, difficult to understand why this connection is often under-appreciated. It seems that laypersons and researchers alike, particularly in the context of Western individualism, often do not perceive or acknowledge the ongoing influence of social factors in self-esteem. When social psychologists write about self-esteem, for example, we usually acknowledge the social roots of self-experience by mentioning James's *social self* or Cooley's *looking-glass self*. Often overlooked, though, is the degree to which adult self-esteem remains connected to social existence. We need to keep in mind that self-esteem dynamics, and related affects such as pride, self-admiration, shame, and self-loathing, are firmly based in our nature as social animals (Baldwin & Baccus, 2004).

I believe the reason relational factors tend to be overlooked is that, as I have indicated, they are often "internalized." It seems obvious that people can and do think about significant others who are not in the room—even those who are long deceased, like a critical parent or a supportive grandparent—and this can profoundly influence their self-evaluations. Making matters a bit more complex, however, is that these influences can occur implicitly, outside of conscious awareness. To fully understand the reciprocal influence of self-esteem and relationship dynamics, then, researchers are increasingly using modern social cognitive approaches to look "inside the head" of the self-evaluator. From a social cognitive point of view, interpersonal knowledge is represented in what are often called *working models* (Bowlby, 1973) or *relational schemas* (Baldwin, 1992). These structures represent an interpersonal configuration consisting of an image of self (e.g., a self-schema as "worthy") along with an associated image of other (e.g., an other-schema as "responsive and caring"). These representations of self and other are embedded in an interpersonal script, characterizing typical if–then patterns of relatedness in that relationship (e.g., "if I need something, then she will take care of me"). Troublesome self-esteem dynamics, then, can arise from relational configurations such as those where a "loser self" and "critical other" are associated with a script such as "If I fail, then he will reject me" (cf. Rogers, 1959). Conversely, specific thoughts about and evaluations of the self can activate relevant interpersonal structures and influence the perception of ongoing interactions.

From this point of view, the experience of self-evaluation—even when a person is alone looking in a mirror—is shaped by accessible relational schemas that define evaluative dynamics and serve as a kind of "private audience" for self-reflection. Research has shown, for example, that just thinking about a significant other for a few minutes can activate the relational schema associated with that relationship, which can then shape self-evaluations. In some studies, research participants who visualized someone they knew who was very critical or judgmental were later highly critical of themselves after a failure (Baldwin, 1994; Baldwin & Holmes, 1987). In another study of the cognitive mechanisms involved, participants primed this way showed an information-processing pattern typically exhibited by chronically low self-esteem individuals: Being shown words related to "failure" made them significantly faster, a second later, to recognize words related to "rejection" (Baldwin & Sinclair, 1996). Thus, as several self-theorists have argued, self-criticalness and low self-esteem typically involve the cognitive activation of a relationship dynamic in which failures or personal shortcomings are associated with rejection or contempt from significant others (cf. Rogers, 1959).

An important aspect of the phenomenon of internalization is that often—perhaps usually—the underlying relational cognition takes place implicitly, outside of awareness. When a person with a failure–rejection relational schema fails in some important domain, activation can spread automatically (within

250 ms; Baldwin, Baccus, & Fitzsimons, 2004) to the representation of being rejected. An image of people frowning or jeering may never enter awareness, therefore: The feeling of being a contemptible, rejected loser simply arises in consciousness as if from nowhere. Additional evidence that much of this can take place outside of awareness comes from subliminal priming studies in which, for example, graduate students who were subliminally exposed to the scowling face of their judgmental department chair evaluated their own work more harshly than normal (giving it a C+ as opposed to A− in control conditions; Baldwin, Carrell, & Lopez, 1990). These students, and other participants in similar social cognitive studies, were seated alone while they engaged in self-evaluation, and were not aware of any influence the primes might have had on their personal self-esteem reactions. Nonetheless, the results demonstrate the powerful impact of implicit relational factors in shaping self-evaluation.

Although much of the research on relational factors in self-esteem tends to focus on the causes and consequences of self-critical reactions, it is important to note that implicit relational cognition can produce positive, as well as negative, self-esteem responses. Several studies have now demonstrated that when people are primed with relational schemas representing secure, noncontingent acceptance, they tend to exhibit self-accepting, nondefensive high self-esteem, and they do not show the if–then, failure–rejection contingency pattern associated with low self-esteem dynamics (Baldwin & Sinclair, 1996; Baldwin & Holmes, 1987; Mikulincer & Shaver, 2005). Moreover, research participants who play a computer game that repeatedly pairs their own name with images of warm acceptance from others later show increases on measures of implicit self-esteem (Baccus, Baldwin, & Packer, 2004). These social cognitive findings are very consistent with research showing that people in healthy close relationships often become more secure over time.

Self-esteem is inextricably enmeshed with close relationship dynamics, then, whether these dynamics are being played out with a relationship partner "in the real world" or even just entirely "inside the head." This principle is supported in research using correlational techniques, longitudinal designs, diary methods, experimental manipulations, and social cognitive approaches. My hope is that as implicit cognitive processes become better understood, and methods for assessing internalized interpersonal dynamics become better developed, the links between self-esteem and close relationship factors will become even better recognized than they are now.

REFERENCES

Aron, A. (2003). Self and close relationships. In M. R. Leary & J. P. Tangney (Eds.), *Handbook of self and identity* (pp. 442–461). New York: Guilford.

Aron, A., Aron, E. N., Tudor, M., & Nelson, G. (1991). Close relationships as including other in the self. *Journal of Personality and Social Psychology, 60*, 241–253.

Baccus, J. R., Baldwin, M. W., & Packer, D. (2004). Increasing implicit self-esteem through classical conditioning. *Psychological Science, 15*, 498–502.

Baldwin, M. W. (1992). Relational schemas and the processing of social information. *Psychological Bulletin, 112*, 461–484.

Baldwin, M. W. (1994). Primed relational schemas as a source of self-evaluative reactions. *Journal of Social and Clinical Psychology, 13*, 380–403.

Baldwin, M. W. (1997). Relational schemas as a source of if–then self-inference procedures. *Review of General Psychology, 1*, 326–335.

Baldwin, M. W., & Baccus, J. R. (2003). Relational knowledge and an expectancy-value approach to self-esteem. In S. J. Spencer, S. Fein, M. P. Zanna, & J. M. Olson (Eds.), *Motivated social perception: The Ontario Symposium* (Vol. 9, pp. 171–194). Mahwah, NJ: Lawrence Erlbaum Associates.

Baldwin, M. W., & Baccus, J. R. (2004). Maintaining a focus on the social goals underlying self-conscious emotions. *Psychological Inquiry, 15*, 139–144.

Baldwin, M. W., Baccus, J. R., & Fitzsimons, G. M. (2004). Self-esteem and the dual processing of interpersonal contingencies. *Self and Identity, 3*, 81–93.

Baldwin, M. W., Carrell, S. E., & Lopez, D. F. (1990). Priming relationship schemas: My advisor and the Pope are watching me from the back of my mind. *Journal of Experimental Social Psychology, 26*, 435–454.

Baldwin, M. W., & Holmes, J. G. (1987). Salient private audiences and awareness of the self. *Journal of Personality and Social Psychology, 53*, 1087–1098.

Baldwin M. W., & Keelan, J. P. R. (1999). Interpersonal expectations as a function of self-esteem and sex. *Journal of Social and Personal Relationships, 16*, 822–833.

Baldwin, M. W., & Sinclair, L. (1996). Self-esteem and "if...then" contingencies of interpersonal acceptance. *Journal of Personality and Social Psychology, 71*, 1130–1141.

Bowlby, J. (1973). *Attachment and loss: Separation, anxiety and anger.* New York: Basic Books.

Brown, J. (1993). Self-esteem and self-evaluation: Feeling is believing. In J. Suls (Ed.), *Psychological perspectives on the self* (pp. 27–58). Hillsdale, NJ: Lawrence Erlbaum Associates.

Campbell, W. K. (1999). Narcissism and romantic attraction. *Journal of Personality and Social Psychology, 77*, 1254–1270.

Curtis, R. C., & Miller, K. (1986). Believing another likes or dislikes you: Behaviors making the beliefs come true. *Journal of Personality & Social Psychology, 51*, 284–290.

Downey, G., Freitas, A. L., Michaelis, B., & Khouri, H. (1998). The self-fulfilling prophecy in close relationships: Rejection sensitivity and rejection by close partners. *Journal of Personality and Social Psychology, 75*, 545–560.

Drigotis, S. M., Rusbult, C. E., Wieselquist, J., & Whitton, S. W. (1999). Close partner as sculptor of the ideal self: Behavioral affirmation and the Michelangelo phenomenon. *Journal of Personality and Social Psychology, 77*, 293–323.

Hardin, C. D., & Higgins, E. T. (1996). Shared reality: How social verification makes the subjective objective. In R. M. Sorrentino & E. T. Higgins (Eds.), *Handbook of motivation and cognition, Vol. 3: The interpersonal context* (pp. 28–84). New York: Guilford Press.

Harter, S. (1999). *The construction of the self: A developmental perspective.* New York: Guilford Press.

Harter, S., Waters, P., & Whitesell, N. R. (1998). Relational self worth: Differences in perceived worth as a person across interpersonal contexts among adolescents. *Child Development, 69*, 756–766.

Hendrick, S. S., Hendrick, C., & Adler, N. L. (1988). Romantic relationships: Love, satisfaction, and staying together. *Journal of Personality and Social Psychology, 54*, 980–988.

Hooley, J. M., & Teasdale, J. D. (1989). Predictors of relapse in unipolar depressives: Expressed emotion, marital distress, and perceived criticism. *Journal of Abnormal Psychology, 98*, 229–235.

Koestner, R., Zuroff, D. C., & Powers, T. A. (1991). Family origins of adolescent self-criticism and its continuity into adulthood. *Journal of Abnormal Psychology, 100*, 191–197.

LaGuardia, J. G., Ryan, R. M., Couchman, C. E., & Deci, E. (2000). Within-person variation in security of attachment: A self-determination theory perspective on attachment, need fulfillment, and well-being. *Journal of Personality and Social Psychology, 79*, 367–384.

MacDonald, G., Zanna, M. P., & Holmes, J. G. (2000). An experimental test of the role of alcohol in relationship conflict. *Journal of Experimental Social Psychology, 36*, 182–193.

Mead, G. H. (1934). *Mind, self, and society.* Chicago: University of Chicago Press.

Mikulincer, M. (1995). Attachment style and the mental representation of the self. *Journal of Personality and Social Psychology, 69*, 1203–1215.

Mikulincer, M., & Shaver, P. R. (2005). Mental representations of attachment security: Theoretical foundations for a positive psychology. In M. Baldwin (Ed.), *Interpersonal cognition* (pp. 233–266). New York: Guilford.

Moretti, M. M., & Higgins, E. T. (1999). Own versus other standpoints in self-regulation: Developmental antecedents and functional consequences. *Review of General Psychology, 3*, 188–223.

Riggs, J. M., & Cantor, N. (1984). Getting acquainted: The role of the self-concept and preconceptions. *Personality and Social Psychology Bulletin, 10*, 432–445.

Rogers, C. R. (1959). Therapy, personality and interpersonal relationships. In S. Koch (Ed.), *Psychology: A study of a science* (Vol. 3). Toronto: McGraw-Hill.

Rudich, E. A., & Vallacher, R. R. (1999). To belong or to self-enhance? Motivational bases for choosing interaction partners. *Personality and Social Psychology Bulletin, 25*, 1387–1404.

Schütz, A. (1998). Coping with threats to self-esteem: The differing patterns of subjects with high versus low self-esteem in first-person accounts. *European Journal of Personality, 12*, 169–186.

Swann, W. B. Jr., Rentfrow, P. J., & Guinn, J. S. (2003). Self-verification: The search for coherence. In M. R. Leary & J. P. Tangney (Eds.), *Handbook of self and identity* (pp. 367–383). New York: Guilford.

Tesser, A., Millar, M., & Moore, J. (1988). Some affective consequences of social comparison and reflection processes: The pain and pleasure of being close. *Journal of Personality and Social Psychology, 54*, 49–61.

Tesser, A., & Smith, J. (1980). Some effects of friendship and task relevance on helping: You don't always help the one you like. *Journal of Experimental Social Psychology, 16*, 582–590.

Tice, D. M., & Wallace, H. M. (2003). The reflected self: Creating yourself as (you think) others see you. In M. R. Leary & J. P. Tangney (Eds.), *Handbook of self and identity* (pp. 91–105). New York: Guilford.

Voss, K., Markiewicz, D., & Doyle, A. B. (1999). Friendship, marriage and self-esteem. *Journal of Social and Personal Relationships, 16*, 103–122.

47

Self-Esteem and Rejection Sensitivity in Close Relationships

KATHY BERENSON and GERALDINE DOWNEY

Both trait self-esteem and fluctuations in self-esteem are associated with aspects of relationship dynamics: for example, the extent to which members of a couple feel satisfied with the relationship, give one another the "benefit of the doubt" in ambiguous situations, or show various affective reactions, such as depression and anger (e.g., Kernis, Cornell, Sun, Berry, & Harlow, 1993; Murray, Holmes, & Griffin, 2000). Yet, despite its volume, the literature on self-esteem has many fundamental inconsistencies, and there remains little consensus about just *how* self-esteem relates to various psychological and interpersonal phenomena (Tangney & Leary, 2003). In this paper we aim to elucidate the processes linking self-esteem with relationship dynamics, drawing upon research on the processes predicted by rejection sensitivity as a point of comparison.

The construct of self-esteem (SE) involves individual differences in global valuation of the self, studied both as a stable characteristic and as a temporary state. People differ substantially in what they believe is important to their SE. Whereas some may largely base SE on being accepted by a particular person, by a group of people, or by people in general, others may base SE on more "autonomous" qualities, such as personal values, abilities, or faith. An interpersonal experience can only have an impact on SE to the extent that the person believes that it means something about their worth, therefore, people with interpersonal self-worth contingency beliefs are at heightened risk for fluctuations in their mood and SE on the basis of others' feedback (Crocker, Luhtanen, Cooper, & Bouvrette, 2003). People whose self esteem is characteristically low or frequently plunges in relationship contexts, therefore learn to prepare themselves for such interpersonal threats, through readily activated cognitive/affective processes. In this sense, their interpersonal patterns appear similar to those individuals who are high in rejection sensitivity (RS), a construct rooted in attachment theory and interpersonal psychodynamic theories, defined by the tendency to anxiously expect rejection (see Levy, Ayduk, & Downey, 2001).

Both low SE and high RS are associated with increased readiness to perceive and react to cues for potential rejection in others' behavior; furthermore, both dispositions are maintained, in part, by self-fulfilling prophecies, in that they promote negative interpersonal behaviors that undermine relationships. Studies have consistently shown a moderately strong inverse correlation between the Rosenberg Self-Esteem Scale and the Rejection Sensitivity Questionnaire (e.g., $r = -.33$, Downey & Feldman, 1996). Nevertheless, research has typically found that outcomes of theoretical interest are predicted by RS even after SE has been controlled (Downey & Feldman, 1996; Mendoza-Denton, Downey, Davis, & Pietrzak, 2002). We propose that beyond their similarities, SE and RS involve distinct insecurities and motivations that would predict distinct processing dynamics when evoked by the potential for rejection in a close relationship.

INSECURITY AND ATTENTION TO EXPECTED INTERPERSONAL THREAT

Our conceptualization of the links between SE, RS, and relationship dynamics begins with motivated monitoring of interpersonal situations on dimensions of acceptance/rejection, as do other theoretical models of SE (e.g., Baldwin & Keelan, 1999; Leary, Haupt, Strausser, & Chokel, 1998; Leary, Tambor, Terdal, & Downs, 1995). The process of attending to, interpreting, and responding to interpersonal cues is influenced by expectations developed over the course of one's cognitive-social learning history, and triggered by relevant features of new relationship situations. When the evoked expectations are negative, concern with the potential for threat increases attention to threat-relevant cues, and in turn, increases the likelihood that threat will be perceived. As predicted by this model, a history of painful rejection experiences has been associated with both low SE (Harter, 1999) and with high RS (Feldman & Downey, 1994). Moreover, consistent with their negative expectations, people with low SE are more likely than others to perceive their romantic partners in a negative, critical light (Murray, Rose, Bellavia, Holmes, & Kusche, 2002), and similar patterns are shown among people with high RS (Downey & Feldman, 1996).

The tendency to vigorously monitor dimensions of acceptance/rejection can be understood as having developed to minimize risks for harm. Yet, potential rejection may be threatening to people in different ways, and for different reasons. SE that is generally low or frequently plunges promotes concern about rejection because of the message it communicates about self-worth, competence, or social status. When evoked in a close relationship, potential threats to SE primarily motivate people to protect the self—avoiding rejection becomes important so as to not be found lacking by someone whose evaluation matters. On the other hand, RS promotes concern about rejection because of the message that it conveys about the availability of others' care in times of need. Although some high RS people may try to avoid activating their concerns about rejection by avoiding relationships, when involved in a close relationship they are motivated not to be abandoned or neglected by the person they have trusted with their vulnerability, and thus readily prioritize the prevention of potential rejections at a cost to the self. Therefore, even though the basic process of monitoring threat predicted by low SE and high RS is the same, the nature of the threats and primary motivations for monitoring them are distinct. Furthermore, these two dispositions should have distinct implications for relationship dynamics when the potential for rejection by an important other arises.

Strategies for facing the prospect of an expected rejection in an interpersonal situation are likely to depend on how much control a person believes he or she can have over the ultimate outcome—e.g., appraisal of the likelihood that efforts to prevent the rejection could be successful, and the certainty with which social cues are perceived as conveying definitive rejection. Low SE is associated with low self-efficacy, and cognitive biases that would make rejection seem inevitable ("depressive certainty"). When faced with rejection cues, people with low SE are less likely than high SE individuals to actively engage in rejection-prevention strategies (Sommer & Baumeister, 2002). Helplessness, defeatism, bitterness, and decreases in interpersonal investment are therefore expected to centrally characterize the reactions to rejection cues associated with low SE. It is as though low SE reduces the threshold for interpreting interpersonal cues as definitive rejections about which nothing can be done but to assign blame, and to give up on the relationship as a potential context for acceptance. By contrast, the relationship processing promoted by RS should centrally involve defensively motivated proactive strategies for maintaining connection to the significant other, involving vigilant attention to early signals for potential rejection and effort to prevent its realization.

REJECTION SENSITIVITY AND DEFENSIVELY MOTIVATED PROACTIVE STRATEGIES

Drawing on research on the neurobiology of emotion (Cacioppo & Gardner, 1999; Lang, Bradley, & Cuthbert, 1990; LeDoux, 1996; Ohman, 2000), RS is proposed to operate as part of a Defensive Motivational System that when activated, mobilizes arousal, attention, and behavior in the service of self-protection (Downey & Ayduk, 2004). Because remaining close to the significant other who is the source of the potential threat is typically a central motivation of high RS individuals, the fight-or-flight responses usually associated with activation of a Defensive Motivational System would not be initially preferred. Instead, automatic responses to the earliest warning signs for potential rejection involve attempts to prevent realization of the threat by anticipating and accommodating the partner's wishes, even at the expense of other personal goals. In this defensively motivated state, high levels of affective arousal and a threat-oriented attentional focus are thus accompanied by inhibitory tactics such as freezing, trying to be inconspicuous, or trying to please (see also Gray, 1987, 2000). Experimental evidence demonstrates that under conditions involving likely, but not yet definite, rejection, high RS predicts increased efforts to gain acceptance (e.g., self-silencing or ingratiating behavior) relative to conditions involving acceptance cues or more definitive rejection cues, whereas low SE does not. In fact, under conditions of likely rejection, low SE predicts decreased ingratiating behavior (Romero-Canyas, Downey, Cavanaugh, & Pelayo, 2006). Of course, when used too often or indiscriminately, rejection-preventive efforts can contribute to interpersonal dysfunction. For example, RS predicts young women's self-reported willingness to do things they believe to be wrong or that make them uncomfortable to maintain a relationship (Downey & Ayduk, 2004; Purdie & Downey, 2000).

Expecting and attending to rejection cues increases readiness to perceive them, and once a rejection is perceived to have occurred, RS predicts hostile reactions (Ayduk, Downey, Testa, Yen, & Shoda, 1999; Downey, Feldman, & Ayduk, 2000), depressive symptoms (Ayduk, Downey, & Kim, 2001), and negative reactions from others (Downey, Freitas, Michaelis, & Khouri, 1998). These aspects of the relationship dynamics associated with RS people bear similarity to those associated with low SE (e.g., Murray et al., 2002), yet further distinctions between them can also be expected. Relative to low SE, high RS should predict more intense affective and behavioral reactions to perceived rejection as a result of the prolonged physiological arousal involved in Defensive Motivational System activation. The reactions to rejection associated with RS are also likely to appear more erratic because they would often follow a period of rejection-prevention efforts in which negative responses to the partner are suppressed. For example, sudden shifts from solicitousness to hostility, or from anxious hopefulness about a relationship to despair, that are characteristic of high RS individuals with Borderline Personality Disorder are an extreme illustration of this dynamic. By contrast, low SE predicts skipping straight past the phase of anxious rejection-prevention efforts (Romero-Canyas & Downey, 2005). Because interpreting a cue as a definitive rejection short-circuits activation of the Defensive Motivational System, co-occurring low SE may often have a dampening effect on the rejection-preventive efforts and intense, erratic reactions to rejection predicted by high RS alone.

EVALUATING THE MEANING OF REJECTION EXPERIENCES

Even when an interpersonal cue is interpreted as a definitive indicator of rejection, the relationship dynamics that ensue and subsequent implications for social learning about the self and others depend in part on whether the rejection is blamed on the self or on the other. Blaming others can protect SE from rejections perpetrated by people who are not deeply significant to the self. For example, work on sensitivity to race-based rejection (Mendoza-Denton, Downey, Purdie, Davis, & Pietrzak, 2002), suggests that African-American students who are sensitive to rejection based on their race do not experience low SE because they tend to attribute rejection to the racism of the perpetrating group (see also Crocker & Major, 1989). To the extent that a relationship is particularly close, intimate, or otherwise an important basis for self-definition, however, cognitive interpretations that undermine positive regard for the partner or the stability of the relationship are less likely to be effective for protecting the self. In fact, there is some evidence that the tendency to derogate a romantic partner is more typical of people with low, rather than high SE (Murray et al., 2002). Derogating others is also a central component of the faulty interpersonal self-regulation that narcissists employ to maintain their unrealistically inflated and readily threatened self-views, at a cost to their relationships and well-being (Morf & Rhodewalt, 2002). Over time, the interpersonal consequences of blaming important others for perceived rejection can be expected to perpetuate concerns about rejection and also to increase associated negative outcomes. For example, the tendency of high RS processing dynamics to undermine relationships increases exposure to negative social feedback and in turn, takes a toll on SE (Ayduk, Mendoza-Denton, Mischel, Downey, Peake, & Rodriguez, 2000).

The extent to which a person believes that their self-worth and interpersonal acceptance are contingent upon one another adds a further dimension to the interpretation of threat cues, and further elucidates the association between SE and RS concerns. That is, when self-worth is defined as interpersonally contingent, attending to signs that others may not provide needed nurturance can be predicted to evoke concerns about the adequacy of the self. Likewise, when others' acceptance is believed to be contingent upon unstable personal qualities (e.g., high achievement, physical beauty, or selfless behavior), and when the potential loss of this acceptance would be of great concern, attending to indicators of the self's inadequacy can be predicted to prime anxious expectations for rejection. Thus, the tendency for concerns about self-worth and interpersonal acceptance to be evoked in tandem is addressed in our model, yet because we define SE and RS concerns as distinct, we do not predict that they will necessarily occur together in the absence of relevant contingency beliefs. Of course, negative feedback about the self or an important relationship typically evokes negative mood, and may do so even when the feedback is not believed to have broader negative implications for self worth (Crocker et al., 2003). Accounting for shared negative mood effects seems particularly important if future research is to untangle the relationship processing dynamics associated with SE and RS.

CONCLUDING COMMENTS

We have attempted to elucidate the processes that we believe link SE with relationship dynamics by comparing and contrasting them with the processes predicted by RS, an associated disposition. As indicated, both SE and RS concerns promote increased attention to rejection cues, and a readiness to perceive and respond to them that has negative consequences for relationships. Moreover, believing that self-worth and interpersonal acceptance are contingent upon one another may lead the activation of concerns about SE and RS to readily co-occur. Beyond such links between low SE and high RS, however, we have proposed that these dispositions involve distinct sets of insecurities and motivations, and predict distinct processing dynamics when evoked by the threat of rejection in a close relationship. Specifically, RS predicts vigorous, often exaggerated efforts to prevent potential rejection threats from being realized, patterns that we expect would add an intense and erratic quality to depressed and angry reactions when rejection is ultimately perceived to have occurred. Low SE, by contrast, predicts the prioritization of self-protection over interpersonal bonds in interpreting and reacting to rejections that are assumed to be inevitable. In other words, we propose that whereas RS operates as part of a Defensive Motivational System functioning to prevent the loss of nurturing relationships, SE primarily influences relationship processing of an evaluative nature.

REFERENCES

Ayduk, O., Downey, G., & Kim, M. (2001). Rejection sensitivity and depressive symptoms in women. *Personality & Social Psychology Bulletin, 27*, 868–877.

Ayduk, O., Downey, G., Testa, A., Yen, Y., & Shoda, Y. (1999). Does rejection elicit hostility in rejection sensitive women? *Social Cognition, 17*, 245–271.

Ayduk, O., Mendoza-Denton, R., Mischel, W., Downey, G., Peake, P. K., & Rodriguez, M. (2000). Regulating the interpersonal self: Strategic self-regulation for coping with rejection sensitivity. *Journal of Personality and Social Psychology, 79*, 776–792.

Baldwin, M. W., & Keelan, J. P. R. (1999). Interpersonal expectations as a function of self esteem and sex. *Journal of Personality and Social Psychology, 60*, 241–253.

Cacioppo, J. T., & Gardner, W. L. (1999). Emotions. *Annual Review of Psychology, 50*, 191–214.

Crocker, J., Luhtanen, R. K., Cooper, M. L., & Bouvrette, A. (2003). Contingencies of self-worth in college students: Theory and measurement. *Journal of Personality and Social Psychology, 85*, 894–908.

Crocker, J., & Major, B. (1989). Social stigma and self-esteem: The self-protective properties of stigma. *Psychological Review, 96*, 608–630.

Downey, G., & Ayduk, O. (2004). *Correlates of rejection sensitivity in college students.* Unpublished Data. Columbia University.

Downey, G., & Feldman, S. (1996). Implications of rejection sensitivity for intimate relationships. *Journal of Personality & Social Psychology, 70*, 1327–1343.

Downey, G., Feldman, S., & Ayduk, O. (2000). Rejection sensitivity and male violence in romantic relationships. *Personal Relationships, 7*, 45–61.

Downey, G., Freitas, A., Michaelis, B., & Khouri, H. (1998). The self-fulfilling prophecy in close relationships: Rejection sensitivity and rejection by romantic partners. *Journal of Personality & Social Psychology, 75*, 545–560.

Feldman, S., & Downey, G. (1994). Rejection sensitivity as a mediator of the impact of childhood exposure to family violence on adult attachment behavior. *Development and Psychopathology, 6*, 231–247.

Gray, J. A. (1987). *The psychology of fear and stress* (2nd ed.). New York: Mc Graw-Hill.

Gray, J. A. (2000). Three fundamental emotional systems. In P. E. R. J. Davidson (Ed.), *The nature of emotion* (pp. 243–247). New York: Oxford University Press.

Harter, S. (1999). *The construction of the self: A developmental perspective.* New York: Guilford.

Kernis, M. H., Cornell, D. P., Sun, C., Berry, A., & Harlow, T. (1993). There's more to self-esteem than whether it's high or low: The importance of stability of self-esteem. *Journal of Personality and Social Psychology, 65*, 1190–1204.

Kernis, M. H., & Goldman, B. M. (2003). Stability and variability in self-concept and self esteem. In Leary, M. R. & Tangney, J. P. (eds.), *Handbook of self and identity* (pp. 106–127). New York: Guilford.

Lang, P., Bradley, M., & Cuthbert, B. (1990). Emotion, attention, and the startle reflex. *Psychological Review*, 97(3), 377–395.

Leary, M. R., Haupt, A. L., Strausser, K. S., & Chokel, J. T. (1998). Calibrating the sociometer: The relationship between interpersonal appraisals and the state self-esteem. *Journal of Personality & Social Psychology*, 74, 1290–1299.

Leary, M. R., Tambor, E. S., Terdal, S. K., & Downs, D. L. (1995). Self-esteem as an interpersonal monitor: The sociometer hypothesis. *Journal of Personality and Social Psychology*, 68, 518–530.

LeDoux, J. (1996). *The emotional brain*. New York: Touchstone.

Levy, S., Ayduk, O., & Downey, G. (2001). The role of rejection sensitivity in people's relationships with significant others and valued social groups. In M. Leary (Ed.), *Interpersonal rejection* (pp. 251–289). New York: Oxford University Press.

Mendoza-Denton, R., Downey, G., Purdie, V., Davis, A., & Pietrzak, J. (2002). Sensitivity to status-based rejection: Implications for African American students' college experience. *Journal of Personality & Social Psychology*, 83, 896–918.

Morf, C., & Rhodewalt, F. (2001). Unraveling the paradoxes of narcissism: A dynamic self-regulatory processing model. *Psychological Inquiry*, 12, 177–196.

Murray, S. L., Holmes, J. G., & Griffin, D. W. (2000). Self-esteem and the quest for felt security: How perceived regard regulates attachment processes. *Journal of Personality and Social Psychology*, 78, 478–498.

Murray, S. L., Rose, P., Bellavia, G. M., Holmes, J. G., & Kusche, A. G. (2002). When rejection stings: How self-esteem constrains relationship-enhancement processes. *Journal of Personality and Social Psychology*, 83, 556–573.

Ohman, A. (2000). Evolutionary, cognitive, and clinical perspectives. In M. L. J. M. Haviland-Jones (Ed.), *Handbook of emotions* (pp. 573–593). New York: Guilford.

Purdie, V., & Downey, G. (2000). Rejection sensitivity and adolescent girls' vulnerability to relationship-centered difficulties. *Child Maltreatment*, 5, 338–349.

Romero-Canyas, R., & Downey, G. (2005). Rejection sensitivity as a predictor of affective and behavioral responses to interpersonal stress: A defensive motivational system. In K. D. Williams, J. P. Forgas, & W. von Hippel (Eds.), *The social outcast: Ostracism, social exclusion, rejection, and bullying*. New York: Psychology Press.

Romero-Canyas, R., Downey, G., Cavanaugh, T., & Pelayo, R. (2006). Paying to belong: Who tries excessively to gain acceptance following rejection? The link between rejection sensitivity and ingratiation after rejection. Manuscript under review, Columbia University.

Sommer, K. L., & Baumeister, R. F. (2002). Self-evaluation, persistence, and performance following implicit rejection: The role of trait self-esteem. *Personality & Social Psychology Bulletin*, 28, 926–938.

Tangney, J. P., & Leary, M. R. (2003). The next generation of self research. In Leary, M. R. & Tangney, J. P. (eds.), *Handbook of self and identity* (pp. 667–675). New York: Guilford.

Question 16

What is the interface between culture and self-esteem? Is self-esteem a uniquely Western concept? How do the groups to which we belong, and our own and others' feelings about those groups (collective self-esteem), influence our personal self-esteem, and vice versa?

*T*he essays in this section focus on the interface between self-esteem and culture. The first two essays represent the ongoing debate in the literature about the universal need for positive self-regard.

Kitayama asserts that the assumed centrality of self-esteem may not generalize to Asian cultures. He presents evidence indicating that while self-enhancement is common among Americans, it is elusive among Japanese, whereas the reverse is true for self-effacement. Kitayama suggests that this self-effacement reflects spontaneous self-appraisals and not merely self-presentation. In addition, he suggests that cultural differences in self-appraisals may be a function of the kinds of social situations experienced.

Sedikides and Gaertner present research indicating the primacy of the personal self over the collective self. In addition, the authors argue against the cultural relativism of self-esteem, instead of arguing (and presenting evidence) for the universalism of self-esteem and associated self-enhancement processes. The authors present findings indicating that while self-enhancement is a universal process, it is expressed differently in eastern and western culture.

Twenge presents evidence that the amount of individualism present in a culture at a given point of time relates to culture members' level of self-esteem. Specifically, as American culture became more individualistic from the late 1960s to the mid-1990s, young people reported higher levels of self-esteem. Twenge concludes that self-esteem is not a uniquely Western concept, although some non-Western cultures emphasize self-criticism rather than preservation of individual self-esteem.

48

Does Self-Esteem Matter Equally Across Cultures?

SHINOBU KITAYAMA

O ne assumption that is central in the current social psychological literature concerns the significance of self-esteem. Conceptualized as positive appraisal of the self (Rosenberg, 1965), self-esteem is assumed to mediate many psychological processes including self-perception and self-regulation. Thus, evidence suggests that individuals are motivated to maintain high self-esteem and, moreover, that this motivation influences friend choice (Tesser, 1988), self-perception and evaluation (Taylor & Brown, 1988), and causal attribution of success and failure (Miller & Ross, 1975). Indeed, this motivation is so strong that positive views of the self that are attained are often described as illusory (Taylor & Brown, 1988). Moreover, self-esteem and its close correlates such as autonomy, control, and efficacy are strongly implicated in subjective well-being and social adjustment (Diener & Diener, 1995). Yet, one major limitation of this impressive array of evidence used to support the assumed centrality of self-esteem is that almost all of it comes from European-American middleclass cultures. In fact, as I shall discuss below, the validity of this assumption may be severely compromised in many other cultures. In making this argument, I will rely especially on our own cross-cultural studies involving North Americans and Japanese.

CULTURE AND SELF

We have argued that European-American middleclass cultures strongly foster models of the self as independent (Kitayama & Uchida, 2004; Markus & Kitayama, 1991, 2004). The self is defined primarily in terms of its internal attributes such as abilities, competence, and personality traits. This cultural assumption is grounded in a number of practices (for example, merit pay system in social institutions) and discourses (for example, the view of competence and intellectual ability as fixed and innate) that are congruous with it. As a consequence, the centrality of self-esteem in defining the self is often taken for granted and perceived to be natural. Moreover, in these independent cultural contexts, self-enhancing perceptions are positively sanctioned, reinforced, and therefore internalized as a highly automatized response tendency (Paulhus & Levitt, 1987). It may then be expected that individuals engaging in these cultures are strongly motivated to confirm the positivity of their internal attributes of the self.

In contrast, Asian cultures strongly sanction very different models of the self as interdependent. The self is defined primarily in terms of its relationships with others and, therefore, its connectedness and embeddedness in meaningful relationships is quite central in the self. This cultural assumption is bolstered by myriad practices (for example, seniority system in social institutions) and associated discourses (for example, the view of competence and abilities malleably cultivated and developed through immersion in the pertinent social world). In these cultural contexts, it is one's connectedness and engagement with others in a relationship that is central (Kitayama, Mesquita, & Karasawa, in press). In particular, self-esteem, as positive appraisal of the self, is often antithetical to this ever-important task of interdependence. For example, an expression of ability and accomplishment may easily invite envy of others. Or going one's own way in a group setting is often perceived as disrupting of group harmony. Not surprisingly, in Asian interdependent cultural contexts, an expression of high self-esteem is often perceived as a sign of insecurity, incompetence (Yoshida, Kojo, & Kaku, 1982), and psychological vulnerabilities (Miller, Wang, Sandel, & Cho, 2002). In these cultural contexts, then, self-critical or self-effacing self-perceptions may be encouraged, reinforced, and eventually internalized to form a habitual response tendency.

SELF-ENHANCEMENT AND SELF-CRITICISM

Empirical evidence for the centrality of self-esteem in North America stems largely from the literature on self-enhancement. Although individuals occasionally refrain from being overly self-serving, they usually recruit a variety of different tactics to maintain and enhance their self-esteem (Taylor & Brown, 1988). This phenomenon of self-enhancement probably qualifies as one of the most replicable effects in social psychology.

However, self-enhancement is quite elusive if not totally absent in many Asian cultural contexts. For example, Kitayama, Takagi, and Matsumoto (1994) reviewed 22 studies that were then available in Japan on causal attribution of success and failure. In none of these studies, any obviously self-serving tendencies could be identified. This is indeed in sharp contrast with quite robust self-serving effects that are typical among European-Americans. Likewise, a false-uniqueness effect (wherein individuals report themselves to be positively unique in their own group) is very weak among Japanese. For example, for each of more than 50 different personality traits, Matsumoto (2000, described in Kitayama & Markus, 2000) asked both Americans and Japanese to estimate the proportion of others in their universities who were better than themselves. For virtually *all* the traits, Americans underestimated this proportion, thereby demonstrating a robust psychological bias to over-estimate their positive uniqueness. In contrast, Japanese showed this effect only for approximately half of the traits tested. For the remaining traits, they showed an opposite bias of effacing themselves. Thus, while Japanese do sometimes show a self-enhancing effect (Brown & Kobayashi, 2002; Sedikides, Gaertner, & Toguchi, 2003), in view of all available evidence, such an effect appears to be an exception that needs to be accounted for (Heine, 2005).

It is important to note that self-effacement or criticism observed in Asian cultures is likely to reflect, at least in part, spontaneous appraisals of the self rather than tactical self-presentations. There are three reasons for this conclusion. First, self-effacement, criticism, or non-enhancement of self have been often demonstrated under conditions of complete anonymity. Quite informative are a small number of studies that explicitly compare private versus public conditions. Interestingly, although effacement or criticism might be expected to be more pronounced in the public condition than in the private condition, this in fact is often not the case (Heine, Lehman, Markus, & Kitayama, 1999; Kitayama et al., 1994).

Second, self-effacement or criticism has been repeatedly observed in Japan with unobtrusive behavioral measures. For example, Heine, Takata, and Lehman (2000) provided both American and Japanese respondents with a series of feedbacks on their performance in a standard intellectual task. The feedbacks were manipulated in such a way that half of the respondents were informed that their performance was poorer than average (failure condition) while the remaining half were informed that their performance was better than average (success condition). The dependent variable was the number of feedbacks the respondents requested before convincing themselves of their own ability in the task. Americans requested significantly fewer feedbacks in the success condition than in the failure condition, thereby demonstrating a strong self-enhancing effect. In contrast, Japanese requested significantly fewer feedbacks in the failure condition than in the success condition. Thus, they demonstrated an equally reliable effect in the opposite, self-effacing or critical direction.

Third, there is evidence that self-enhancing perceptions in North America and self-effacing perceptions in Asia are promoted by culturally scripted ways in which daily situations are construed and made meaningful. For example, imagine Sally—an American girl—has received 80 points in an exam. It is likely that her mother praises her by drawing each other's attention to the accomplishment, namely, 80 points. In contrast, Vincent—a Chinese boy, who has received just the same score, might be reminded by his mother of the 20 points that are still missing! In order to examine the potential variability of situational construals in more systematic fashion, Kitayama, Markus, Matsumoto, and Norasakkunkit (1997) asked both Americans and Japanese to describe as many situations as possible where their own self-esteem was increased (called the success situations) or decreased (called the failure situations). Out of the pool of the situations thus collected, 400 were randomly sampled so that there were equal numbers of both American-made versus Japanese-made situations and success versus failure situations. These situations were then presented to new groups of American and Japanese respondents, who were asked to imagine that they were in each of the situations and then to indicate whether and to what extent their own self-esteem would increase or decrease.

The results were quite revealing. To begin with, Americans reported that their self-esteem would increase more in the success situations than it would decrease in the failure situations—another manifestation of a self-enhancing effect. In contrast, Japanese reported that their self-esteem would decrease more in the failure situations than it would increase in the success situations, thus, demonstrating an equally reliable bias toward self-effacement or criticism. More importantly for the purpose of the present discussion, however, American-made success situations were more effective than their Japanese-made counterparts in increasing self-esteem. Moreover, this was the case for both American and Japanese respondents. In contrast, Japanese-made failure situations were more effective than their American-made counterparts in depressing self-esteem and, moreover, this was true for both Japanese and American respondents. This last set of findings suggests that the collective environment (constituted by a set of situational construals) has a capacity to foster and reinforce the culturally authenticated forms of self-perception, namely, self-enhancement in North America and self-effacement or criticism in Japan.

It is important to note that self-critical or self-effacing perceptions of the self in Asia may not be totally negative. These perceptions are socially and culturally sanctioned. First, Asian cultures strongly sanction and emphasize incremental theories of abilities and competence (rather than entity theories) and, as a consequence, relatively negative self-perceptions may not necessarily imply that the self is permanently deficient. Instead, these perceptions are taken as an initial starting point for future improvement (Heine et al., 2001). Moreover, self-critical perceptions may also signal a willingness to fit-in and be a member of a cohesive, interdependent relationship. They therefore are likely to solicit positive responses from others in a relationship. Predominant interpersonal positive affect that is exchanged in these cultural contexts is likely to be that of sympathy, compassion, and empathy (Kitayama & Markus, 2000).

Here is a paradox, however: Asians receive positive responses from others only insofar as they maintain negative self-appraisals. If they should use these positive social feedbacks to change their self-appraisals in a positive direction ("Oh, I think I am actually quite smart because people are saying that!"), their friends would stop sending the positive feedbacks. Nevertheless, the positive affect communicated from the others is likely to be associated with the mental representation of the self even though these associations are not recognized as such at an explicit, conscious level. On the basis of this line of reasoning, we have suggested that in closely knit interdependent social relationships, negative self-appraisals at an explicit level are likely to coexist with positive self-evaluations at an implicit level. Consistent with this analysis, we have demonstrated that implicit self-evaluations as measured by an Implicit Association Test (Kitayama & Uchida, 2003) and name letter effect (Kitayama & Karasawa, 1997) are as positive among Japanese as among Americans.

INTERDEPENDENCE IN INDEPENDENT CULTURES

Having emphasized the cultural variation in self-evaluation, I should hasten to add that it is an overstatement if one argues that the combination of implicit self-regard and explicit self-criticism or effacement is fixed or limited solely to Asia or other non-Western regions of the world. On the contrary, our analysis suggests that this pattern of self-evaluations is fostered by interdependent social relations. Kitayama and Uchida (2003) therefore argued that "the psychological capacities for both self-enhancement and self-criticism are both available for all individuals, but they are differentially activated and integrated into the cross-culturally variable patterns of social life" (p. 481). We thus predicted and found that this pattern of self-evaluations was quite common even among Americans when they were tested in a context of close, interdependent social relationship. Our first study applied a modified version of Implicit Association Test to both Japanese and Americans and showed that the above pattern occurs in both cultures if the self is evaluated vis-à-vis one's actual friend. Moreover, in our second study, we showed that when placed in a context that has neither actual nor presumed emotional interdependence, both Japanese and Americans manifest positive self-evaluations at both explicit and implicit levels.

The Kitayama and Uchida (2003) data suggests that one major source of cross-cultural difference in the self lies in the cross-culturally divergent distribution of different kinds of social situations and attendant social relations therein. Specifically, as compared to North American cultures, Asian cultures may be composed of a greater number and variety of situations that are typically construed to involve close, emotionally interdependent social relations. Likewise, as compared to Asian cultures, American cultures may be composed of a greater number and variety of situations that are typically construed to involve social relations where each participant interacts with others as an independent, rational actor who pursues his or her self-interests.

CONCLUDING REMARKS

Self-esteem, defined as positive appraisal of the internal or personal self, is commonly available in all known cultures. Yet, the extent to which self-esteem is elaborated and integrated into broader systems of regulating cognition, emotion, and motivation depends crucially on culture. In some cultures such as middleclass North American cultures, self-esteem is a central anchor of social behavior and self-perception. Individuals are therefore motivated to maintain, enhance, and defend it, resulting in a variety of self-enhancing psychological biases. Moreover, this motivation often yields a variety of negative consequences that are usually masked and backgrounded in cultural discourses (Crocker & Park, 2004). However, the last decade of cultural psychological research has established that this impressive array of findings does not travel well across its cultural boundaries. In particular, in Asian cultures self is construed to be a relational entity. Social connectedness and embeddedness assume primacy over self-esteem. Moreover, negative side effects of high self-esteem are clearly recognized and highlighted in cultural discourses (Miller et al., 2002).

The cultural variability I pointed out in this commentary might be somewhat unnerving to many social psychologists because this emerging evidence might seem to spoil the ever-important goal of finding universal principles of psychological processes. However, universality may best be established empirically rather than posited as a matter of faith. Indeed, the human is an animal that has evolved to adjust itself to an environment of its own creation, namely culture. This cultural environment can highlight self-esteem or background it. It can also make self-esteem quite important for one's mental health, but it might alternatively make it quite dysfunctional in adjusting to the society. The fundamental biological unity of the human species does not imply uniformity in psychological processes (Shweder, 2003). On the contrary, the human becomes functionally complete only when it is immersed into a cultural environment (Tomasello, 1999). Human psychological processes are therefore likely to be flexibly adjusted to the needs and demands posed by the specific cultural environment (Kitayama, Ishii, Imada, Takemura, & Ramaswamy, in press). And the evidence available so far suggests that much of what we know about self-esteem in social psychology today may be contingent on the North American, mostly middleclass cultures. I therefore concur with Crocker and Park (2004) in their assessment that "the pursuit of self-esteem is a particularly American phenomenon, born of the nation's founding ideologies" (p. 405). The time, however, is ripe now for the discipline to pursue a goal of becoming a truly universal human science by taking culture seriously and conceptualizing the human mind as fully embedded in and fundamentally afforded and enabled by the cultural matrix of social life.

REFERENCES

Brown, J. D., & Kobayashi, C. (2002). Self-enhancement in Japan and America. *Asian Journal of Social Psychology*, 5, 145–168.

Crocker, J., & Park, L. E. (2004). The costly pursuit of self-esteem. *Psychological Bulletin*, 130, 392–414.

Diener, E., & Diener, M. (1995). Cross cultural correlates of life satisfaction and self-esteem. *Journal of Personality and Social Psychology*, 68, 653–663.

Heine, S. J. (2005). Where is the evidence for pancultural self-enhancement? A reply to Sedikides, Gaertner, & Toguchi. *Journal of Personality and Social Psychology*, 89, 531–538.

Heine, S. J., Kitayama, S., Lehman, D. R., Takata, T., Ide, E., Lueng, C., & Matsumoto, H. (2001). Divergent consequences of success and failure in Japan and North America: An investigation of self-improving motivations and malleable selves. *Journal of Personality and Social Psychology*, 81, 599–615.

Heine, S. J., Lehman, D. R., Markus, H. R., & Kitayama, S. (1999). Is there a universal need for positive self-regard? *Psychological Review*, 106, 766–794.

Heine, S. J., Takata, T., & Lehman, D. R. (2000). Beyond self-presentation: Evidence for self-criticism among Japanese. *Personality and Social Psychology Bulletin*, 26, 71–78.

Kitayama, S., & Karasawa, M. (1997). Implicit self-esteem in Japan: Name letters and birthday numbers. *Personality and Social Psychology Bulletin*, 23, 736–742.

Kitayama, S., & Markus, H. R. (2000). The pursuit of happiness and the realization of sympathy: Cultural patterns of self, social relations, and well-being. In E. Diener & E. Suh (Eds.), *Subjective well-being across cultures*. Cambridge, MA: MIT Press.

Kitayama, S., Ishii, K., Imada, T., Takemura, K., & Ramaswamy, J. (in press). Voluntary settlement and the spirit of independence: Evidence from Japan's "Northern Frontier". *Journal of Personality and Social Psychology*.

Kitayama, S., Markus, H. R., Matsumoto, H., & Norasakkunkit, V. (1997). Individual and collective processes in the construction of the self: Self-enhancement in the United States and self-criticism in Japan. *Journal of Personality and Social Psychology, 72,* 1245–1267.

Kitayama, S., Mesquita, B., & Karasawa, M. (in press). Cultural affordances and emotional experience: Socially engaging and disengaging emotions in Japan and the United States. *Journal of Personality and Social Psychology.*

Kitayama, S., Takagi, H., & Matsumoto, H. (1994). Cultural psychology of Japanese self: I. causal attribution of success and failure. *Japanese Psychological Review, 38,* 247–280.

Kitayama, S., & Uchida, Y. (2003). Explicit self-criticism and implicit self-regard: Evaluating self and friend in two cultures. *Journal of Experimental Social Psychology, 39,* 476–482.

Kitayama, S., & Uchida, Y. (2004). Interdependent agency: An alternative system for action. In R. Sorrentino, D. Cohen, J. M. Olson, & M. P. Zanna (Eds.), *Culture and social behaviour: The Ontario symposium* (Vol. 10, pp. 165–198). Mahwah, NJ: Lawrence Erlbaum Associates, Inc.

Markus, H. R., & Kitayama, S. (1991). Culture and the self: Implications for cognition, emotion, and motivation. *Psychological Review, 98,* 224–253.

Markus, H. R., & Kitayama, S. (2004). Models of agency: Sociocultural diversity in the construction of action. In V. Murphy-Berman & J. J. Berman (Eds.), *Cross-cultural differences in perspectives on the self: Nebraska symposium on motivation* (Vol. 49, pp. 1–57). Lincoln: University of Nebraska Press.

Matsumoto, H. (2000). *False uniqueness effect in Japan and the US.* Unpublished manuscript, Kyoto University.

Miller, D., & Ross, M. (1975). Self-serving biases in the attribution of causality: Fact or fiction? *Psychological Bulletin, 82,* 213–225.

Miller, P. J., Wang, S.-H., Sandel, T., & Cho, G. E. (2002). Self-esteem as folk theory: A comparison of European American and Taiwanese mothers' beliefs. *Parenting, 2,* 209–239.

Paulhus, D. L., & Levitt, K. (1987). Desirable responding triggered by affect: Automatic egotism? *Journal of Personality and Social Psychology, 52,* 245–259.

Rosenberg, M. (1965). *Society and the adolescent self-image.* Princeton, NJ: Princeton University Press.

Sedikides, C., Gaertner, L., & Toguchi, Y. (2003). Pancultural self-enhancement. *Journal of Personality and Social Psychology, 84,* 60–79.

Shweder, R. A. (2003). *Why do men barbecue?: Recipes for cultural psychology.* Cambridge, MA: Harvard University Press.

Taylor, S. E., & Brown, J. D. (1988). Illusion and well-being: A social psychological perspective on mental health. *Psychological Bulletin, 103,* 193–210.

Tesser, A. (1988). Toward a self-evaluation maintenance model of social behavior. In L. Berkowitz (Ed.), *Advances in experimental social psychology* (Vol. 21, pp. 181–227). San Diego, CA: Academic Press.

Tomasello, M. (1999). *The cultural origins of human cognition.* Cambridge, MA: Harvard University Press.

Yoshida, T., Kojo, K., & Kaku, H. (1982). A study on the development of self-presentation in children. *Japanese Journal of Educational Psychology, 30,* 30–37.

49

Primacy of Personal over Collective Self and Cultural Considerations

CONSTANTINE SEDIKIDES and LOWELL GAERTNER

The proposition that group membership (collective self or self-esteem) influences personal self (or self-esteem) has acquired truism status in social and personality psychology. This broad proposition was supported initially by data suggesting that enhancement of the collective self (i.e., ingroup bias in the form of intergroup discrimination) provided a boost to personal self-esteem (e.g., Oakes & Turner, 1980). A flurry of research, however, criticized the initial findings both on methodological (e.g., Berkowitz, 1994) and episte-mological (e.g., Schiffmann & Wicklund, 1992) grounds. Indeed, subsequent evidence has not been consistent with the hypothesis (for reviews, see Aberson, Healy, & Romero, 2000; Brown, 2000; Rubin & Hewstone, 1998). Alternative support for the proposition comes from a more refined need-deficit hypothesis, according to which low personal self-esteem motivates intergroup discrimination as a means of replenishing the personal self-esteem deficit (e.g., Hogg & Abrams, 1990). Findings, however, are inconsistent with such a hypothesis and indicate that individuals low in personal self-esteem are *less* likely to engage in ingroup bias than those high in personal self-esteem (Aberson et al., 2000; Crocker & Luhtanen, 1990). In summary, the collective self does not seem to decisively shape the personal self.

How about the alternative direction of causation, though? Does the personal self shape the collective self? We believe that this effect is stronger, and recent evidence backs our claim.

Rationale for this claim is derived from our primary research (Gaertner, Sedikides, & Graetz, 1999) as well as a meta-analysis (Gaertner, Sedikides, Vevea, & Iuzzini, 2002). In the basic experimental paradigm, either the personal or collective self is threatened (e.g., via unfavorable feedback) or praised (e.g., via favorable feedback). Participants whose personal (relative to collective) self is threatened consider the threat more severe, report a more negative mood, feel angrier, and derogate to a greater extent the source of threat. In a similar vein, participants react more strongly to praise of the personal than collective self. Finally, when the personal self is threatened, participants shift identification from the personal to the collective self (i.e., ingroup), whereas they do not shift identification toward the personal self when the collective self is threatened. This research establishes the motivational and emotional primacy of the personal over the collective self. (For additional supportive evidence, see Eidelman & Biernat, 2003.)

More importantly, the personal self serves as a cognitive basis for the formation of the collective self (i.e., novel ingroups). The basic experimental paradigm is as follows (Gramzow, Gaertner, & Sedikides, 2001). In the first session, participants judge whether each of several positive and negative behaviors is congruent or discrepant with the personal self. In the second session, participants are classified into a novel ingroup or outgroup, learn that the previously seen behaviors allegedly were performed by either ingroup or outgroup members, and recall the behaviors. Based on previous research (e.g., Sedikides, 1993; Sedikides & Green, 2000), we assumed that negative and self-discrepant behaviors are most threatening: Participants would expect *not* to perform such behaviors. If participants relied on the personal self for the formation of the collective self, they would expect for ingroup members *not* to perform such behaviors either. Thus, when confronted with the unexpected—ingroup members enacting negative and self-discrepant behaviors— they would engage in relatively deep processing trying to reconcile the new information with their positive expectancies. The result would be elevated recall for negative, self-discrepant, ingroup attributes only. Indeed, this is what we found. The personal self serves as a springboard for the collective self.

This view also accounts for evaluative favoritism in the minimal group paradigm (Gramzow & Gaertner, 2003). The favorable evaluation of the ingroup over the outgroup is more strongly associated with personal rather than collective self-esteem. Collective self-esteem does not predict evaluative favoritism when personal self-esteem is controlled. The personal self serves as an evaluative basis for novel ingroups, a statement consistent with Aberson et al.'s (2000) meta-analytic conclusion.

Is the primacy of the personal over the collective self a Western phenomenon? In an influential article, Heine, Lehman, Markus, and Kitayama (1999) highlighted a seemingly striking difference between mean self-esteem scores of Westerners (e.g., Americans, Canadians) and Easterners (e.g., Japanese) on a standard self-esteem inventory (e.g., Rosenberg self-esteem scale). Specifically, Westerners' self-esteem scores were skewed, with the majority of respondents reporting moderately high to very high self-esteem. In contrast, Easterners' self-esteem scores were normally distributed. Additionally, Heine et al. pointed out that Japanese self-enhance substantially less than Americans, and, on occasion, they self-efface. Heine et al. concluded that "the need for self-regard … is not a universal, but rather is rooted in significant aspects of North American culture" (p. 766).

We believe that there are reasons to doubt the cultural relativism of self-esteem. In support of their argument, Heine et al. (1999) stated that the constructs self-esteem and self-regard are not widespread in Japanese culture. Neither were they widespread in American culture before the 1960s (Twenge & Campbell, 2001). The lack of lay terms to define psychological states or processes does not necessarily imply their absence, as would be the case with such phenomena as cognitive dissonance, pluralistic ignorance, and false consensus effect. Interestingly, terms equivalent to self-esteem do exist abundantly in Japanese culture: need for face, need for *gambaru* (doing one's best), need for relational esteem, and need to be a good cultural member (Heine et al., 1999, pp. 786–788). Thus, cultural universalism of self-esteem is a more plausible alternative. Our claim is bolstered by several lines of empirical and theoretical inquiry, such as the evolutionary adaptiveness of self-esteem (Barkow, 1980; Kirkpatrick & Ellis, 2001), the developmental (Harter, 1998) and social (Leary & Baumeister, 2000) relevance of self-esteem, the trait-like characteristics of self-esteem (Robins, Trzesniewski, Tracy, Gosling, & Potter, 2002; Trzesniewski, Donnellan, & Robins, 2003), and the existential functions (e.g., buffering against death-anxiety; Pyszczynski, Greenberg, Solomon, Arndt, & Schimel, 2004) of self-esteem.

Additionally, there are good reasons to doubt the cultural relativism of self-enhancement, of which self-esteem is a valid signature. A distinction needs to be drawn between implicit and explicit self-enhancement. The evidence is over-whelmingly in favor of the proposition that implicit self-enhancement is universal. Implicit measures, such as name-letter preferences, birth date preferences, or semantic priming paradigms, reveal that Easterners have a highly favorable self-image (Hoorens, Nuttin, Erdelyi-Herman, & Pavakanun, 1990; Kitayama & Karasawa, 1997). Moreover, both Japanese and Americans regard the self more positively and less negatively than they regard others, as manifested in response time latencies (Kitayama & Uchida, 2003; Kobayashi & Greenwald, 2003).

Still, why is it that Japanese self-enhance less than Americans on explicit measures? Sedikides, Gaertner, and Toguchi (2003) provided an explanation. People are sensitive to and strive to fulfil culturally sanctioned norms, internalize the dimensions that imply successful role fulfilment, and evaluate themselves favorably on these dimensions. Japanese value collectivistic dimensions (traits or behaviors), whereas Americans value individualistic dimensions. Hence, Japanese will self-enhance on collectivistic, and Americans on individualistic, dimensions. These hypotheses received strong empirical backing. In one experiment, Japanese considered themselves superior to other group members on collectivistic, but not individualistic, dimensions. Americans, however, considered themselves superior to other group members on individualistic, but not collectivistic, dimensions. In a conceptual replication, Americans with an interdependent self-construal self-enhanced on collectivistic dimensions, whereas Americans with an independent self-construal self-enhanced on individualistic dimensions. As hypothesized, personal importance of the judgmental dimension mediated these findings, for both types of participants. Finally, a comprehensive meta-analysis (Gaertner, Sedikides, & Vevea, 2003) corroborated the above patterns.

Our research (Sedikides et al., 2003) demonstrates that self-enhancement, albeit universal, is expressed differently in Eastern and Western culture. Recent investigations have documented additional ways in which culture shapes the expression of self-enhancement motivation. One is self-presentation: It is less acceptable in Eastern than in Western culture to present the self favorably. Controlling for self-presentational concerns, however, Easterners are as self-enhancing as Westerners (Kobayashi & Greenwald, 2003; Kudo & Numazaki, 2003; Kurman, 2003). Another, conceptually similar, way is indirectness: Japanese strategically refrain from self-enhancement, but expect a close other (e.g., parent, sibling, friend) to enhance on their behalf (Muramoto, 2003). Thus, Japanese self-enhance through the eyes of close relationships. Still another way is competition: Japanese are as self-enhancing as Americans when they compete against an opponent, but are self-effacing in a competition-free relationship (Takata, 2003).

A final critical piece of evidence for the universality of self-enhancement is the relation between self-enhancement and psychological health. A positive relation between the two constructs is well-established in Western culture (Taylor, Lerner, Sherman, Sage, & McDowell, 2003; Updegraff & Taylor, 2000). Importantly, this relation also holds in Eastern culture. Self-serving attributions, self-favoring social comparisons, self-efficacy, and optimism are negatively associated with depression and positively associated with self-esteem and life satisfaction in China (Anderson, 1999), Hong Kong (Stewart et al., 2003), Korea, (Chang, Sanna, & Yang, 2003), Bosnia (Bonanno, Field, Kovacevic, & Kaltman, 2002), and Singapore (Kurman, 2003; Kurman & Siram, 1997). Furthermore, in both Japan and the United States, high self-esteem individuals self-enhance more than low self-esteem individuals (Kobayashi & Brown, 2003; Kurman, 2003).

In summary, although culture influences the expression of self-enhancement motivation, in both the East and the West individuals want to feel good about themselves. Self-enhancement and the need for self-esteem are universal.

REFERENCES

Aberson, C. L., Healy, M. R., & Romero, V. L. (2000). Ingroup bias and self-esteem: A meta-analysis. *Personality and Social Psychology Review, 4*, 157–173.

Anderson, C. A. (1999). Attributional style, depression, and loneliness: A cross-cultural comparison of American and Chinese students. *Personality and Social Psychology Bulletin, 5*, 482–499.

Barkow, J. (1980). Prestige and self-esteem: A biosocial interpretation. In D. R. Omark, F. F. Strayer, & D. G. Freedman (Eds.), *Dominance relations* (pp. 319–332). New York: Garland.

Berkowitz, N. H. (1994). Evidence that subjects' expectancies confound intergroup bias in the Tajfel minimal group paradigm. *Personality and Social Psychology Bulletin, 20*, 184–195.

Bonanno, G. A., Field, N. P., Kovacevic, A., & Kaltman, S. (2002). Self-enhancement as a buffer against extreme adversity: Civil war in Bosnia and traumatic loss in the United States. *Personality and Social Psychology Bulletin, 28*, 184–196.

Brown, R. (2000). Social identity theory: Past achievements, current problems and future challenges. *European Journal of Social Psychology Review, 30*, 745–778.

Chang, E. C., Sanna, L. J., & Yang, K. (2003). Optimism, pessimism, affectivity, and psychological adjustments in US and Korea: A test of a mediation model. *Personality and Individual Differences, 34*, 1195–1208.

Crocker, J., & Luhtanen, R. (1990). Collective self-esteem and ingroup bias. *Journal of Personality and Social Psychology, 58*, 60–67.

Eidelman, S., & Biernat, M. (2003). Derogating black sheep: Individual or group protection? *Journal of Experimental Social Psychology, 39*, 602–609.

Gaertner, L., Sedikides, C., & Vevea, J. L. (2003). *East meets West with tactical self-enhancement: Cultural manifestations of a universal motive*. Unpublished manuscript, University of Tennessee.

Gaertner, L., Sedikides, C., & Graetz, K. (1999). In search of self-definition: Motivational primacy of the individual self, motivational primacy of the collective self, or contextual primacy? *Journal of Personality and Social Psychology, 76,* 5–18.

Gaertner, L., Sedikides, C., Vevea, J., & Iuzzini, J. (2002). The "I," the "We," and the "When:" A meta-analysis of motivational primacy in self-definition. *Journal of Personality and Social Psychology, 83,* 574–591.

Gramzow, R. H., & Gaertner, L. (2003). *Self-esteem and favoritism toward novel in-groups: The Self as an evaluative base*. Manuscript in preparation, Northeastern University.

Gramzow, R. H., Gaertner, L., & Sedikides, C. (2001). Memory for ingroup and outgroup information in a minimal group context: The self as an informational base. *Journal of Personality and Social Psychology, 80,* 188–205.

Harter, S. (1998). The development of self-representations. In W. Damon & N. Eisenberg (Eds.), *Handbook of child psychology* (5th ed., Vol. 3, pp. 553–617). New York: Wiley.

Heine, S. H., Lehman, D. R., Markus, H. R., & Kitayama, S. (1999). Is there a universal need for positive self-regard? *Psychological Review, 106,* 766–794.

Hogg, M. A., & Abrams, D. (1990). Social motivation, self-esteem, and social identity. In D. Abrams & M. A. Hogg (Eds.), *Social identity theory: Constructive and critical advances* (pp. 28–47). New York: Springer-Verlag.

Hoorens, V., Nuttin, J. M., Erdelyi-Herman, I., & Pavakanun, U. (1990). Mastery pleasure versus mere ownership: A quasi-experimental cross-cultural and cross-alphabetical test for the name letter effect. *European Journal of Social Psychology, 20,* 181–205.

Kirkpatrick, L. A., & Ellis, B. J. (2001). An evolutionary-psychological approach to self-esteem: Multiple domains and multiple functions. In G. J. O. Fletcher & M. S. Clark (Eds.), *The Blackwell handbook of social psychology, Vol. 2: Interpersonal processes* (pp. 411–436). Oxford, UK: Blackwell.

Kitayama, S., & Karasawa, M. (1997). Implicit self-esteem in Japan: Name letters and birthday numbers. *Personality and Social Psychology Bulletin, 23,* 736–742.

Kitayama, S., & Uchida, Y. (2003). Explicit self-criticism and implicit self-regard: Evaluating self and friend in two cultures. *Journal of Experimental Social Psychology, 39,* 476–482.

Kobayashi, C., & Brown, J. D. (2003). Self-esteem and self-enhancement in Japan and America. *Journal of Cross-Cultural Psychology, 34,* 567–580.

Kobayashi, C., & Greenwald, A. G. (2003). Implicit-Explicit differences in self-enhancement for Americans and Japanese. *Journal of Cross-Cultural Psychology, 34,* 522–541.

Kudo, E., & Numazaki, M. (2003). Explicit and direct self-serving bias in Japan: Reexamination of self-serving bias for success and failure. *Journal of Cross-Cultural Psychology, 34,* 511–521.

Kurman, J. (2003). Why is self-enhancement low in certain collectivistic cultures?: An investigation of two competing explanations. *Journal of Cross-Cultural Psychology, 34,* 496–510.

Kurman, J., & Siram, N. (1997). Self-enhancement, generality of self-evaluation, and affectivity in Israel and Singapore. *Journal of Cross-Cultural Psychology, 28,* 421–441.

Leary, M. R., & Baumeister, R. F. (2000). The nature and function of self-esteem: Sociometer theory. In M. Zanna (Ed.), *Advances in experimental social psychology* (Vol. 32, pp. 1–62). San Diego: Academic Press.

Muramoto, Y. (2003). An indirect self-enhancement in relationship among Japanese. *Journal of Cross-Cultural Psychology*, *34*, 552–566.

Oakes, P. J., & Turner, J. C. (1980). Social categorization and intergroup behaviour: Does minimal intergroup discrimination make social identity more positive? *European Journal of Social Psychology*, *10*, 295–302.

Pyszczynski, T., Greenberg, J., Solomon, S., Arndt, J., & Schimel, J. (2004). Why do people need self-esteem? A theoretical and empirical review. *Psychological Bulletin*, *130*, 435–468.

Robins, R. W., Trzesniewski, K. H., Tracy, J. L., Gosling, S. D., & Potter, J. (2002). Global self-esteem across the lifespan. *Psychology and Aging*, *17*, 423–434.

Rubin, M., & Hewstone, M. (1998). Social identity theory's self-esteem hypothesis: A review and some suggestions for clarification. *Personality and Social Psychology Review*, *4*, 157–173.

Schiffmann, R., & Wicklund, R. A. (1992). The minimal group paradigm and its minimal psychology: On equating social identity with arbitrary group membership. *Theory and Psychology*, *2*, 29–50.

Sedikides, C. (1993). Assessment, enhancement, and verification determinants of the self-evaluation process. *Journal of Personality and Social Psychology*, *65*, 317–338.

Sedikides, C., Gaertner, L., & Toguchi, Y. (2003). Pancultural self-enhancement. *Journal of Personality and Social Psychology*, *84*, 60–70.

Sedikides, C., & Green, J. D. (2000). On the self-protective nature of inconsistency/negativity management: Using the person memory paradigm to examine self-referent memory. *Journal of Personality and Social Psychology*, *79*, 906–922.

Stewart, S. M., Byrne, B. M., Lee, P. W. H., Ho, L. M., Kennard, B. D., Hughes, C., & Emslie, G. (2003). Personal versus interpersonal contributions to depressive symptoms among Hong Kong adolescents. *International Journal of Psychology*, *38*, 160–169.

Takata, T. (2003). Self-enhancement and self-criticism in Japanese culture: An experimental analysis. *Journal of Cross-Cultural Psychology*, *34*, 542–551.

Taylor, S. E., Lerner, J. S., Sherman, D. K., Sage, R. M., & McDowell, N. K. (2003). Portrait of the self-enhancer: Well adjusted and well liked or maladjusted and friendless? *Journal of Personality and Social Psychology*, *84*, 165–176.

Trzesniewski, K. H., Donnellan, M. B., & Robins, R. W. (2003). Stability of self-esteem across the life span. *Journal of Personality and Social Psychology*, *84*, 205–220.

Twenge, J. M., & Campbell, W. K. (2001). Age and birth cohort differences in self-esteem: A cross-temporal meta-analysis. *Personality and Social Psychology Review*, *5*, 321–344.

Updegraff, J. A., & Taylor, S. E. (2000). From vulnerability to growth: The positive and negative effects of stressful life events. In J. Harvey & E. Miller (Eds.), *Loss and trauma: General and close relationship perspectives* (pp. 3–28). Philadelphia, PA: Brunner-Routledge.

50

What is the Interface between Culture and Self-Esteem?

JEAN M. TWENGE

S elf-esteem is traditionally defined as a person's evaluation of him/herself. Despite the internal nature of the concept, however, there are many external determinants of self-esteem. One of the most important is the level of individualism in a culture at a given time. I will begin my answer by describing the influence of historical period on individualism and self-esteem.

TIME PERIODS AS CULTURES AND THEIR INFLUENCES ON SELF-ESTEEM

Just as regions differ in culture, the larger sociocultural environment changes over time even within nations. A child growing up in the United States in the 1950s experienced a very different culture than a child growing up in the 1980s. The considerable changes in social trends during this time led to a number of changes in individuals, including increases in anxiety and depression (Lewinsohn, Rohde, Seeley, & Fischer, 1993; Twenge, 2000) and greater externality in locus of control (Twenge, Zhang, & Im, 2004). Thus birth cohort changes, as a proxy for shifts in the larger social environment, are an example of the influence of culture on individuals.

Several social trends suggest that responses to self-esteem questionnaires may have changed during the last 40 years. First, American culture has become more individualistic. As Baumeister (1987) documented, the general trend in Western society has been toward a more self-focused conception of the individual. This trend accelerated during the late 1960s and early 1970s. While duty to country and social norms once ruled American life, rampant individualism soon became the rule. "Doing your own thing" was increasingly fashionable (Frum, 2000; Fukuyama, 1999), and pollsters noted that "the rage for self-fulfillment" had spread everywhere (Yankelovich, 1981, p. 3). Empirical evidence from psychology also suggests that the individualistic philosophy was growing in popularity. While

American parents in the postwar era valued obedience in their children, by the 1970s and 1980s they placed more importance on independence and good judgment (Remley, 1988). In addition, scores on an individualism measure derived from the California Psychological Inventory increased markedly between the 1950s and the 1980s (Gough, 1991, cited in Roberts & Helson, 1997).

Not only did the general societal ethos promote the self, but a "self-esteem movement" (an offshoot of the "human potential" and "self-growth" movements) gained prevalence. Increasingly, proclaiming that you loved, cherished, and valued yourself was no longer an immodest proposition (Jones, 1980; Rosen, 1998; Swann, 1996). Americans were told to "be your own best friend" and seek self-fulfillment (Ehrenreich & English, 1978; Frum, 2000). While considering changes in self-esteem, we labeled this new attitude the "culture of self-worth" (Twenge & Campbell, 2001).

The concept of self-esteem was also increasingly publicized and discussed among laypeople as well as psychologists, a trend that may have had a direct effect on participants' responses to self-esteem measures (Gergen, 1973). Magazine articles, books, and television talk shows discussed self-esteem and its importance. Popular music reflected this trend, sometimes in amusing ways. In 1986, Whitney Houston's song "The Greatest Love of All" was a number one single. On first listening to the song, many people thought Houston was singing about an all-consuming romance, or perhaps about love for children. However, the song is about loving yourself: "I never found anyone to fulfill my needs," Houston sings. "So I learned to depend on me ... I found the greatest love of all inside of me ... learning to love yourself is the greatest love of all." In 1994, an alternative rock band called Offspring recorded a song called "Self-Esteem" about a young man who allows people to treat him badly. By the late 1990s, then, laypeople not only knew what self-esteem was, but they also knew how to diagnose themselves when they came up lacking.

In addition, school programs set out to increase children's self-esteem (e.g., Ammerman & Fryrear, 1975; Blume, 1989; Outwater, 1990; Swann, 1996; for a review, see Haney & Durlak, 1998). The programs emphasized self-worth in a very general way, encouraging students to feel "special" and "applaud themselves" (Seligman, 1995). Students also recited "affirmations" of their own self-worth and wore t-shirts emblazoned with such slogans as "I'm lovable and capable" (Swann, 1996, p. 4). School assignments also encouraged this self-focus; Sykes (1995) notes that a common student project across the country was a collection of self-descriptions, likes, and dislikes called "All About Me." A meta-analysis (Haney & Durlak, 1998) found that self-esteem interventions such as these increased children's self-esteem, on average, more than half a standard deviation.

I thought that these influences might work to raise young people's self-esteem, or at the very least might raise their scores on measures of self-esteem. Working with my colleague Keith Campbell, I performed a meta-analysis on college students' scores on the Rosenberg Self-Esteem Scale (RSE) between 1968 and 1994. Across more than a hundred studies, we found that college students' self-esteem scores increased about two-thirds of a standard deviation over this 26-year period (Twenge & Campbell, 2001). Thus, 1990s college undergraduates scored considerably higher in self-esteem compared to their late 1960s counterparts. It is possible that today's undergraduates actually do feel better about themselves compared to the college students of the 1960s. It could also be that college students now speak the language of self-esteem and understand that one is supposed to possess copious amounts of this supposedly precious substance. Given the strong and documented shift toward individualism in the culture, however, it is likely that at least some of the change results from this increasing focus on the self. After all, if one is a functioning, happy human being, focusing on the self is more likely to lead to self-love than self-hate (e.g., Taylor & Brown, 1988). This study shows the influence of culture on self-esteem: As American culture became more individualistic, focused on the needs of the self, and popularized the concept of self-esteem, young people reported higher levels of self-esteem.

This also helps answer the question about self-esteem perhaps being a uniquely Western concept. Although the concept is probably not unique to the West or to any specific time period, it is clear that the society-wide focus on self-esteem and its consequences may be unique to the West in the decades since 1970. If a researcher walked up to someone on the street in 1965 and asked "Do you have high self-esteem?" the person probably would have replied, "Do I have high *what?*" In 1965, the *Reader's Guide to Periodical Literature* did not have a single listing for articles on self-esteem (nor did it list any articles under self-respect or self-love: Twenge & Campbell, 2001). Now, of course, magazines cover the topic extensively, and the average layperson can discuss self-esteem at length, especially the importance of children's self-esteem.

HOW REGIONAL CULTURE AND ETHNICITY INFLUENCE SELF-ESTEEM

Self-esteem is also influenced by culture in its more traditional incarnation: a system of behavior promoted in a certain region or ethnic group. Many studies have found that Asians and Asian-Americans report lower self-esteem compared to White Americans (Crocker, Luhtanen, Blaine, & Broadnax, 1994; for a review, see Twenge & Crocker, 2002). Steve Heine and his colleagues have recently published an extensive line of research showing that Asian cultures place a higher value on self-criticism, in contrast to the American emphasis on self-esteem (Heine, Takata, & Lehman, 2000). After failing at one task, Asian students were more likely to choose to do that task again (in order to improve their performance), whereas American students were more likely to choose a new task, presumably to protect their self-concept (Heine, Kitayama, Lehman, Takata, Ide, Leung, & Matsumoto, 2001). Japanese students do not self-enhance even when responses are completely anonymous (Heine & Lehman, 1995). This tendency toward self-criticism may exist because it promotes harmony in relationships (Heine, Lehman, Markus, & Kitayama, 1999).

As noted above regarding change over time, levels of individualism may be particularly important for predicting levels of self-esteem within a certain culture. Individualism and an independent self-construal promote maintaining and enhancing self-esteem, particularly through efforts to stand out or be superior to others. This tendency is weaker or even absent in some cultures that emphasize the interdependent self-construal, where harmony in social relations is a more important goal (Heine et al., 1999; Markus & Kitayama, 1991). When individualism and collectivism are measured separately, it is individualism that correlates highly with self-esteem (Oyserman, Coon, & Kemmelmeier, 2002).

The results of Oyserman et al.'s (2002) meta-analysis also help explain the self-esteem differences between Americans of different ethnic backgrounds. Earlier in the century, psychologists assumed that Blacks would have low self-esteem given the prejudice and discrimination they faced. Since the late 1970s, however, Blacks have reported higher self-esteem than Whites (Gray-Little & Hafdahl, 2000; Twenge & Crocker, 2002). Some research and theory has argued that stigma could be used as self-protection, which could bolster Black self-esteem (e.g., Crocker & Major, 1989; Rowley, Sellers, Chavous, & Smith, 1998). However, stigma as self-protection cannot explain the lower self-esteem of Asian-Americans, who also faced prejudice and discrimination in the United States (although— arguably—not as much as Blacks). Oyserman et al.'s results, however, show that Blacks are higher in individualism than Whites, who do not differ significantly from Hispanics, who in turn are higher than Asian-Americans. This exactly mirrors the relationship between ethnicity and self-esteem in the United States, where Blacks score higher than Whites, Whites score marginally higher than Hispanics, and Hispanics score higher than Asian-Americans (Twenge & Crocker, 2002). This suggests, once again, that individualism is a crucial component for high self-esteem.

THE IMPORTANCE OF COLLECTIVE SELF-ESTEEM

Some researchers have wondered if the lower levels of individual self-esteem in some cultures are replaced by higher levels of collective self-esteem (Crocker, Luhtanen, Blaine, & Broadnax, 1994; Phinney, 1990). Collective self-esteem refers to valuing the groups and collectives one belongs to. Although Asians and Blacks agreed that their racial groups are often viewed negatively by Whites, both groups had high levels of collective self-esteem (Crocker et al., 1994). Asian students' collective self-esteem for their group was equal to White students' collective self-esteem, and Blacks' collective self-esteem was significantly higher. However, notice that these results are very similar to those for individual self-esteem, with Blacks scoring higher than Whites. There is a small discrepancy for Asians; compared to Whites, Asians have lower individual self-esteem and equal collective self-esteem. Thus, collective self-esteem can only partially, and not fully, account for the White-Asian difference in individual self-esteem.

The emphasis on self-criticism and self-improvement in Asian cultures also carries over to groups. When Heine and Lehman (1997) asked students to compare their own university with a rival university, Canadian students displayed an in-group enhancement bias, whereas Japanese students did not. Similarly, Americans claimed that their neighborhood's emergency preparedness was better than their city's as a whole; in contrast, Japanese citizens said the opposite (that their neighborhood was not as prepared as the rest of the city: Kitayama, Karasawa, Markus, & Lehman, 1998). This suggests that collective self-esteem does not take the place of individual self-esteem in Asian cultures, as Asians are critical of their ingroups as well as of their individual selves.

A recent meta-analysis found that collective self-esteem does not predict ingroup bias, but group identification does (Aberson, Healy, & Romero, 2000). Thus, group identity may predict behavior more strongly than collective self-esteem. In addition, the authors point out that individual self-esteem may predict the enhancement of one's group; this suggests that individual and collective self-esteem may be two sides of the same coin.

CONCLUSION

Self-esteem is influenced by culture in many different ways: through time period, regional norms, and the subcultures of ethnic groups. Self-esteem is not a uniquely Western concept, but the emphasis on self-esteem in modern Western culture is at an all-time high. Many non-Western cultures emphasize self-criticism rather than the preservation of individual self-esteem. Overall, it is very important to consider the cultural origins of self-esteem. Although self-esteem is the most internal of concepts, its sources outside the self are many and varied.

REFERENCES

Aberson, C. L., Healy, M., & Romero, V. (2000). Ingroup bias and self-esteem: A meta-analysis. *Personality and Social Psychology Review, 4*, 157–173.

Ammerman, M. S., & Fryrear, J. L. (1975). Photographic enhancement of children's self-esteem. *Psychology in the Schools, 12*, 319–325.

Baumeister, R. F. (1987). How the self became a problem: A psychological review of historical research. *Journal of Personality and Social Psychology, 52*, 163–176.

Blume, J. A. (1989). The effects of implementing a self-esteem curriculum guide on self-esteem and performance of elementary school children. (Doctoral dissertation, California School of Professional Psychology at Los Angeles, 1989). *Dissertation Abstracts International, 50*, 1935A.

Crocker, J., Luhtanen, R., Blaine, B., & Broadnax, S. (1994). Collective self-esteem and psychological well-being among white, black, and Asian college students. *Personality and Social Psychology Bulletin, 20*, 503–513.

Crocker, J., & Major, B. (1989). Social stigma and self-esteem: The self-protective properties of stigma. *Psychological Review, 96*, 608–630.

Ehrenreich, B., & English, E. (1978). *For her own good: 150 years of the experts' advice to women.* New York: Doubleday.

Frum, D. (2000). *How we got here: The 70s, the decade that brought you modern life (for better or worse).* New York: Basic Books.

Fukuyama, F. (1999). *The great disruption: Human nature and the reconstitution of social order.* New York: Free Press.

Gergen, K. J. (1973). Social psychology as history. *Journal of Personality and Social Psychology, 26*, 309–320.

Gough, H. (1991). *Scales and combinations of scales: What do they tell us, what do they mean?* Paper presented at the 99th annual convention of the American Psychological Association, San Francisco, August 1991.

Gray-Little, B., & Hafdahl, A. R. (2000). Factors influencing racial comparisons of self-esteem: A quantitative review. *Psychological Bulletin, 126,* 26–54.

Haney, P., & Durlak, J. A. (1998). Changing self-esteem in children and adolescents: A meta-analytic review. *Journal of Clinical Child Psychology, 27,* 423–433.

Heine, S. J., Kitayama, S., Lehman, D. R, Takata, T., Ide, E., Leung, C., & Matsumoto, H. (2001). Divergent consequences of success and failure in Japan and North America: An investigation of self-improving motivations and malleable selves. *Journal of Personality and Social Psychology, 81,* 599–615.

Heine, S. J., & Lehman, D. R. (1995). Cultural variation in unrealistic optimism: Does the West feel more vulnerable than the East? *Journal of Personality and Social Psychology, 68,* 595–607.

Heine, S. J., & Lehman, D. R. (1997). The cultural construction of self-enhancement: An examination of group-serving biases. *Journal of Personality and Social Psychology, 72,* 1268–1283.

Heine, S. J., Lehman, D. R., Markus, H. R., & Kitayama, S. (1999). Is there a universal need for positive self-regard? *Psychological Review, 106,* 766–795.

Heine, S. J., Takata, T., & Lehman, D. R. (2000). Beyond self-presentation: Evidence for self-criticism among Japanese. *Personality and Social Psychology Bulletin, 26,* 71–78.

Jones, L. Y. (1980). *Great expectations: America and the Baby Boom generation.* New York: Coward, McCann, & Geoghegan.

Kitayama, S., Karasawa, M., Markus, H. R., & Lehman, D. (1998). Construction of self-esteem in everyday conversation: A Japanese/U.S. comparison. Unpublished manuscript.

Lewinsohn, P., Rohde, P., Seeley, J., & Fischer, S. (1993). Age-cohort changes in the lifetime occurrence of depression and other mental disorders. *Journal of Abnormal Psychology, 102,* 110–120.

Markus, H. R., & Kitayama, S. (1991). Culture and the self: Implications for cognition, emotion, and motivation. *Psychological Review, 98,* 224–253.

Outwater, A. D. (1990). An intervention project to improve body image and self-esteem in sixth-grade boys and girls as a potential prevention against eating disorders (Doctoral dissertation, the Union Institute, 1990). *Dissertation Abstracts International, 51,* 4029A.

Oyserman, D., Coon, H. M., & Kemmelmeier, M. (2002). Rethinking individualism and collectivism: Evaluation of theoretical assumptions and meta-analyses. *Psychological Bulletin, 128,* 3–72.

Phinney, J. S. (1990). Ethnic identity in adolescents and adults: Review of research. *Psychological Bulletin, 108,* 499–514.

Remley, A. (1988, October). From obedience to independence. *Psychology Today, 22,* 56–59.

Roberts, B. W., & Helson, R. (1997). Changes in culture, changes in personality: The influence of individualism in a longitudinal study of women. *Journal of Personality and Social Psychology, 72,* 641–651.

Rosen, B. C. (1998). *Winners and losers of the information revolution: Psychosocial change and its discontents.* Westport, CT: Praeger.

Rowley, S. J., Sellers, R. M., Chavous, T. M., & Smith, M. A. (1998). The relationship between racial identity and self-esteem in African American college and high school students. *Journal of Personality and Social Psychology, 74,* 715–724.

Seligman, M. (1995). *The optimistic child*. New York: Houghton Mifflin.

Swann, W. B. (1996). *Self-traps: The elusive quest for higher self-esteem*. New York: W. H. Freeman.

Sykes, C. J. (1995). *Dumbing down our kids: Why American children feel good about themselves but can't read, write, or add*. New York: St. Martin's Griffin.

Taylor, S. E., & Brown, J. D. (1988). Illusion and well-being: A social psychological perspective on mental health. *Psychological Bulletin, 103*, 193–210.

Twenge, J. M. (2000). The age of anxiety? Birth cohort change in anxiety and neuroticism, 1952–1993. *Journal of Personality and Social Psychology, 79*, 1007–1021.

Twenge, J. M., & Campbell, W. K. (2001). Age and birth cohort differences in self-esteem: A cross-temporal meta-analysis. *Personality and Social Psychology Review, 5*, 321–344.

Twenge, J. M., & Crocker, J. (2002). Race and self-esteem: Meta-analyses comparing Whites, Blacks, Hispanics, Asians, and American Indians and comment on Gray-Little and Hafdahl (2000). *Psychological Bulletin, 128*, 371–408.

Twenge, J. M., Zhang, L., & Im, C. (2004). It's beyond my control: A cross-temporal meta-analysis of increasing externality in locus of control, 1960–2002. *Personality and Social Psychology Review, 8*, 308–319.

Yankelovich, D. (1981). *New rules*. New York: Bantam.

Question 17

What role does self-esteem play in society's ills such as suicide, delinquency, drugs, violence? What about in society's triumphs, such as great art, music, and scientific achievements?

The essays in this section focus on the role that self-esteem plays in society's ills and triumphs. The authors vary widely in the stances they take on this issue.

Owens and McDavitt take the position that although self-esteem has very real effects within the context of the broader society, these effects are not always definitive. They review evidence that low self-esteem may be associated with negative outcomes such as social isolation, depression, suicide, and delinquency, while high self-esteem may be associated with positive outcomes such as creativity and a proactive stance toward life in general. The authors suggest that findings such as these point to the importance of the self-esteem motive for both individuals and society.

Pyszczynski offers a largely conceptual piece. He addresses the relevance of self-esteem to society through the lens of Terror Management Theory, which emphasizes the ties that bind self-esteem to social values. The author suggests that the motive to achieve self-esteem generally is a civilizing force that provides the motivational impetus to live up to cultural standards of value, energizing the pursuit of important personal goals and behaviors that are of value to society. However, a potential drawback is that self-esteem sometimes is contingent on being superb in whatever domain one is pursuing.

Tice and Gailliot take the controversial position that self-esteem plays little, if any, role in society's ills and triumphs. In their view, self-esteem often plays a complex role in many phenomena and empirical research often does not support its presumed causal significance. Rather, the authors assert that self-esteem often is an outcome of such phenomena as academic and work performances and social interactions. On the other hand, they do acknowledge that stability of self-esteem can clarify the role of self-esteem in various phenomena.

51

The Self-Esteem Motive: Positive and Negative Consequences for Self and Society

TIMOTHY J. OWENS and ALYSON R. MCDAVITT

There are many ways to address the question: What role does self-esteem play in society's ills and triumphs? In this essay, we confine our thoughts to the essence of this question: self-esteem as a social force; or, the influence that self-concept, and thus self-esteem, has on broader society. This effect can manifest itself in two ways—first, through social trends such as rates of teenage drinking, suicide, and delinquency; and second, through more macro phenomena such as social movements and war. The direction we take means confining our thoughts to the singular and cumulative effects of individual self-esteem (the generally positive or negative attitude an individual takes toward him- or herself) rather than to collective or social self-esteem as a social force.

Since the editor has asked us to consider such broad topics as self-esteem's putative role in societal triumphs such as great art, music, and scientific achievement, we must necessarily veer partially into the realm of speculation. This causes us some anxiety since the first author has been openly critical of many self-esteem entrepreneurs' over inflated and sometimes baseless claims of the concept's power to solve all manner of individual and social problems (Owens & Stryker, 2001).[1] We thus tread lightly into the arena of speculation and do so only when it makes theoretical sense. But why speculate at all? Quite simply, there is a dearth of empirically supported research on self-esteem's role in "societal triumphs." Our aim, therefore, is hopefully to stimulate future research while avoiding wholly baseless claims about self-esteem that may simply add grist to the self-esteem entrepreneurs' mills, add to the public's misperceptions of the concept, and bring it into further disrepute in some quarters of the academy and the media.[2]

We wish to focus the reader's attention on the importance of the self-esteem motive, or the fundamental desire humans have to think well of themselves (Kaplan, 1975; Allport, 1961; Rosenberg, 1979). Indeed, many self-theorists regard this motive as universally dominant in the human motivational system (James, 1890; Kaplan, 1975; Rosenberg, 1979).[3]

However, focusing on the protection and enhancement of one's self-esteem necessarily paints an incomplete picture. Other mechanisms certainly come into play as well. To that end, we also draw on four basic principles of self-concept—and thus self-esteem—formation (Rosenberg, 1979). They are: *reflected appraisals* (seeing oneself through others' eyes), *social comparisons* (comparing oneself to others), *self-attributions* (drawing conclusions about one's worth and efficacy by observing and then judging one's own successes and failures), and *psychological centrality* (the weight or importance individuals assign to their various personal attributes, identities, and abilities).

We turn now to a general comparison of high self-esteem people and low self-esteem people. This is followed by more pointed discussions of self-esteem's role in social problems and in societal triumphs.

HIGH SELF-ESTEEM PEOPLE VERSUS LOW SELF-ESTEEM PEOPLE

What exactly are the consequences of high and low self-esteem for individuals? First, several researchers have found that persons with high self-esteem and low self-esteem differ in their cognitive orientations and in their general attitudes toward life. While high self-esteem (hereafter HSE) individuals tend to be more proactive and optimistic, low self-esteem (hereafter LSE) individuals tend to be more reactive and pessimistic (Rosenberg & Owens, 2001). Having LSE has been found to be associated with a tendency to withdraw and isolate one's self from others (Gibson, 1981; Peck & Kaplan, 1995; Rosenberg & Owens, 2001; Sniderman & Citrin, 1971) and has also been correlated with depression and anxiety (Rosenberg & Owens, 2001; Owens, 1994).

Because of their tendency to withdraw, LSE people are less likely to participate in political activities such as voting (Gibson, 1981; Sniderman & Citrin, 1971). In addition, LSE people, in contrast to HSE people, not only tend to have differing levels of political participation, but also differing political beliefs. People with HSE are more likely to vote and participate in nonvoting political activities (Peck & Kaplan, 1995) while also showing a greater tendency toward liberal, democratic views as well as possessing higher tolerance for "unpopular" political groups (Sullivan, Marcus, Feldman, & Pierson, 1981). This tends to be untrue for LSE people because of their general avoidance of risk and criticism (Rosenberg & Owens, 2001).

While LSE has not generally been associated with political participation, it has been argued that LSE could lead individuals to seek social movement activism in order to better their self-regard (à la the self-esteem motive) (Kaplan & Liu, 2000). Owens and Aronson (2000) make the opposite argument while also making a distinction between individual self-esteem (ISE) and social self-esteem (SSE). ISE is equivalent to personal self-esteem and SSE is the esteem generally conferred upon a particular social group or category of people by the wider society. Owens and Aronson argue that when there is a discrepancy between ISE and SSE, particularly when ISE is relatively high compared with a low level of perceived SSE, some individuals will likely take action in order to correct this imbalance, as the self-esteem motive would suggest. Moreover, social movement activism can be an emotionally grueling experience owing to the internal and external politics surrounding movement activism (see Goodwin, Jasper, & Polletta, 2001; Jasper, 1997). This is not an atmosphere generally conducive to attracting and keeping LSE people. They tend to socially isolate themselves from others, but when with others, avoid confrontation, fear criticism, and presume a personal affront or *faux pas* just around the corner (Rosenberg & Owens, 2001).

One's level of self-esteem may also affect decision-making. Persons with LSE tend to be more indecisive than HSE people (Rosenberg & Owens, 2001) while also being more susceptible to persuasion (Gibson, 1981). Looking at a group of California judges, Gibson (1981, p. 117) found that judges with HSE were less likely than those with LSE to feel restricted by "traditional socialization forces" and were able "independently to evaluate role expectations, rather than meekly succumb to them." Self-esteem has also been associated with the level of difficulty in setting and achieving goals. HSE people tend not only to choose more difficult goals (Pilegge & Holtz, 1997; Levy & Baumgardner, 1991), but also to achieve more when they strongly identify with their group (Pilegge & Holtz, 1997). In addition, HSE and LSE can influence task performance. HSE individuals are better at completing tasks that call for obvious solutions, while LSE individuals tend to be better at completing tasks that call for choosing from several alternative solutions (Weiss & Knight, 1980). Here LSE people are more likely to second-guess themselves while HSE individuals "seek less information before committing to a solution" (Rosenberg & Owens, 2001, p. 430).

NOTES ON SELF-ESTEEM AND SOCIETAL LIABILITIES

Self-esteem has been linked to a host of personal and societal ills and misfortunes. Indeed, most of the research on self-esteem has centered on its direct or indirect effect on, or ameliorative potential for, an array of negative psychological and behavioral outcomes (e.g., depression, anxiety, social isolation, teen pregnancy, and alcohol and drug abuse). Perhaps the most extreme manifestation of self-loathing is suicide. A number of studies have linked low self-esteem to both suicidal ideation (e.g., Dukes & Lorch, 1989) and attempted suicide (e.g., Hershberger, Pilkington, & D'Augelli, 1997; Tomori & Zalar, 2000). Two key themes running through these studies are unrealistic or especially negative social comparisons (especially among teens) and unfavorable reflected appraisals (especially direct reflections and perceived selves[4]). For example, in a large survey of Slovenian high school students, Tomori and Zalar (2000) found that male and female suicide attempters had significantly lower levels of self-esteem than did their nonattempter counterparts. Among the reasons offered is that low self-esteem may interfere with "constructive self-confirmation" while adversely affecting the establishment and maintenance of supportive interpersonal relations. These, in turn, help ameliorate the stressors that sometimes induce suicidal reactions (Tomori & Zalar, 2000, p. 232). In a study of gay, lesbian, and bisexual teenagers, Hershberger, Pilkington, and D'Augelli (1997) found that among the suicide attempters in their study (approximately 40%), low self-esteem was clearly a factor. Although causality could not be established in this cross-sectional survey, three prior factors that probably had an acute and negative impact on their self-esteems were age of awareness of homoerotic attractions, disclosure of sexual orientation to family and friends (resulting in real or perceived rejection), and victimization provoked by their sexual orientation (Hershberger, Pilkington, & D'Augelli, 1997). These three factors surely impacted their general desire to think well of themselves while also clearly conveying aspects of reflected appraisals, social comparisons, self-attributions, and psychological centrality (especially in the fear and confusion sometimes accompanying one's realization of and identification with being gay).

Self-esteem's role in deviance, especially juvenile delinquency, has had a spotty record. Some find little or no association (e.g., Scheff, Retzinger, & Ryan, 1989) while others have found modest associations (e.g., Owens, 1994; Rosenberg, Schooler, & Schoenbach, 1989). Kaplan's esteem-enhancement model of adolescent deviance specifically seeks to link low self-esteem (i.e., self-derogation) with juvenile delinquency (Kaplan, 1975, 2001). Briefly, Kaplan argues that youngsters are more likely to rebel against conventional group norms when their earlier participation in such groups has been experienced as self-derogatory. Using the self-esteem motive, he posits further that self-derogating youngsters may be attracted to deviance so long as the activity affords them self-enhancing experiences. One manifestation would be being "good at" being deviant (e.g., physically threatening others, skipping school, shoplifting).

Scheff (1994) makes a much broader argument by not only equating chronic low self-esteem with deep-seated shame, but also asserting the bold notion that some of history's most notorious despots and aggressors (e.g., Hitler) suffered from chronic, often unrecognized, shame and low self-esteem (Scheff, 2003). In his view, some despots' hatred of and aggression toward out-groups is a compensatory mechanism for their abysmal self-regard, no doubt a problem with their self-esteem motive and how they compare themselves with others.

In a somewhat different vein, Baumeister and associates (e.g., Baumeister, Bushman, & Campbell, 2000; Baumeister, Smart, & Boden, 1996) argue that crime, especially interpersonal violence, is not caused so much by low self-esteem but by overweening pride. Two basic mechanisms are at work: When individuals are confronted or challenged with discrepant negative information about the self, threatened egotism and an inflated and unstable belief in one's superiority (i.e., overweening pride) may induce a violent reaction in some people who believe they have been disrespected ("dissed") by another.

NOTES ON SELF-ESTEEM AND SOCIETAL BENEFITS

Most social and behavioral scientists place their professional focus on trying to understand and solve individual and social *problems*. While there are certainly enticing grant and publishing incentives for doing so, it almost seems as if we implicitly assume that if enough bad things are reduced or eliminated, good things will be able to shine through. Hence, there has been little research specifically linking self-esteem to societal triumphs. This need not be the case, nor is it universally so. We have already addressed self-esteem's positive role in decision-making, risk-taking, social movement participation, and involvement in the body politic. We turn now to some speculation on self-esteem's role in great artistic and scientific achievement. And for the present, it must remain speculative since we have no direct knowledge of Mozart's, Picasso's, and O'Keefe's self-esteem or that of Fermi, Marie Curie, and Freeman Dyson.

Addressing the issue of personality traits and creativity, Goldsmith and Matherly (1988) note that research consistently finds the following set of core personality traits associated with creativity: independence, self-confidence/self-esteem, and a belief that one is indeed creative. Creative people also tend to be self-assertive and self-sufficient, aggressive and dominant, and possess initiative (Stein, 1968 cited in Goldsmith and Matherly, 1988). Goldsmith and Matherly (1988) found a moderate correlation (r =.34, $p<.001$) between self-esteem (as measured on the Rosenberg Self-esteem Scale) and originality (*via* the Kirton Adaptation-Innovation Inventory) among a sample of American business students. A similar association was found between creativity (as measured on the Creative Motivation Scale) and Rosenberg's global self-esteem (r =.30, $p<.05$) (Goldsmith & Matherly, 1987).

Using an ideographic methodology, Scheff (1990) argues that high self-esteem is integral to creative genius. Examining the biographies of several noted scientific and artistic "geniuses" (i.e., people extremely successful at and widely recognized for their ability to innovate and create), Scheff found that highly innovative and creative individuals tend to possess some of the signal characteristics of high self-esteem people: the ability to withstand withering criticism and ridicule, take risks, and maintain single-minded devotion to one's work regardless of obstacles. To Scheff, this translates into an absence of the chronic shame and self-doubt that hobble most people's efforts to think and act far outside the established parameters of their field of artistic and scientific pursuits. According to our view, these highly creative individuals are no doubt imbued with innate talents and gifts, but they are also able to withstand negative reflected appraisals while relying on self-attributions of competence in their field of endeavor.

These observations seem to contradict the popular image of the suffering artist toiling at their art in misery and dejection. And there may be some seeds of truth to this image. However, if we return to self-esteem theory we can account for this seeming contradiction. First, we must recognize the difference between specific and global self-esteem (Rosenberg, Schoenbach, Schooler, & Rosenberg, 1995). Great artists persist because of their profound belief in their artistic vision and ability, an aspect of specific self-esteem. This says nothing about how they feel about their ability to sustain relationships with others, play sports, fit in with a peer group, or attract romantic partners. Second, if James (1890) is correct and self-esteem is borne from the ratio of success over pretensions, then their quest for artistic achievement (i.e., pretensions) may well outweigh their perceived success. If so, even a person with high self-esteem and high accomplishment could feel the sting of not measuring up to very high self-imposed standards and thus appear blue, moody or depressed. Last, we must note that every individual's self is composed of a hierarchy of identities and abilities. Those most important to one's self are held close to the center, others farther out. Highly creative people no doubt hold their "artist" or "scientist" identity close to the center and protect it. Other identities, such as being a good son, devoted mother, or obliging neighbor, may take a decidedly back seat in their constellation of identities. That being so, one could be a miserable human being in most areas of one's life, but unimpeachable as an artist or as a scientist.

Taken as a whole, and informed by Scheff (1990) and symbolic interactionism, society has as much of a role in creating genius as do an individual's genetic endowments. Our genes may make us *capable* of many things, but society shapes our self and thus our self-esteem. But high ability and high self-esteem are not sufficient. One also needs a nurturing environment, which, usually from an early age, is populated by highly competent and attentive teachers (both formal and informal) whom the budding genius interacts with and learns from (Scheff, 1990). A person's self-esteem may help them keep going in the face of adversity and facilitate risky though productive nonconformity. Self-esteem does not, in our view, cause great scientific or artistic achievement, but it certainly helps aid it, especially one's specific self-esteem as a very good artist or scientist.

CODA

Based upon the previous discussion, it is clear that self-esteem has very real implications for society, although not necessarily definitive ones. Low self-esteem may be associated with negative outcomes (although not always), such as social isolation, depression, and juvenile delinquency, while high self-esteem is generally associated with more positive outcomes, such as creativity and a proactive stance toward life in general. All of this points to the importance of the self-esteem motive for both the individual and society. However, at this time it cannot be definitively argued that one's level of self-esteem *causes* these outcomes. Still, empirical research and sound theory both point strongly to the proposition that self-esteem does indeed play a significant role in social and individual problems as well as in societal triumphs.

NOTES

1. The term "self-esteem entrepreneur" derives from Hewitt's (1998) idea of conceptual entrepreneurs: "Those who…seek to develop and promote ideas about the solution of individual and social problems. They typically focus on a single idea or concept—such as self-esteem—and seek to persuade others that it has singular powers to make individuals happier and the social world a better place" (p. 49). Since literally hundreds of books, pamphlets, newspaper and magazine articles, audiotapes, videos, CDs, and DVDs are available, which claim, rightly or wrongly, to teach people to understand and improve their own or another's self-esteem, we will use the more restrictive term "self-esteem entrepreneur."

2.   See, for example, Johnson's (1998) article in the science section of *The New York Times* entitled "Self-Image Is Suffering From Lack of Esteem" for one of the more egregious and ill-informed attacks on self-esteem from the mainstream press in recent years.

3.   We fully recognize that Swann's self-verification research has shown that some low self-esteem people prefer to have their negative self-views confirmed (e.g., Swann, Stein-Seroussi, & Giesler, 1992). However, this nuance is not central to the main thrust of the present argument.

4.   The literature generally discusses three kinds of reflected appraisals or feedback:
    (1)   *Direct reflections* are the actual and direct responses that alter has toward ego, regardless of how subjectively ego perceives and thus assesses them.
    (2)   *Perceived selves* are perhaps the most important aspect of reflected appraisals for the self. Here, ego simply speculates on how specific alters perceive him or her. As Rosenberg claims, "It is thus not others' attitudes toward us but our *perception* of their attitudes that is critical for self-concept formation" (1979, p. 65, emphasis in original).
    (3)   The *generalized other* is ego's composite sense of what others think of him or her.

REFERENCES

Allport, G. W. (1961). *Pattern and growth in personality*. New York: Holt, Rinehart and Winston.

Baumeister, R. F., Bushman, B. J., & Campbell, W. K. (2000). Self-esteem, narcissism, and aggression: Does violence result from low self-esteem or from threatened egotism? *Current Directions in Psychological Science, 9*, 26–29.

Baumeister, R. F., Smart, L., & Boden, J. M. (1996). Relation of threatened egotism to violence and aggression: The dark side of high self-esteem. *Psychological Review, 103*, 5–33.

Dukes, R. L., & Lorch, B. D. (1989). The effects of school, family, self-concept, and deviant behaviour on adolescent suicide ideation. *Journal of Adolescence, 12*, 239–251.

Gibson, J. L. (1981). Personality and elite political behavior: The influence of self-esteem on judicial decision making. *Journal of Politics, 43*, 104–125.

Goldsmith, R. E., & Matherly, T. A. (1987). Adaptation-innovation and self-esteem. *Journal of Social Psychology, 127*, 351–352.

Goldsmith, R. E., & Matherly, T. A. (1988). Creativity and self-esteem: A multiple operationalization. *Journal of Psychology, 122*, 47–56.

Goodwin, J., Jasper, J. M., & Polletta, F. (2001). *Passionate politics: Emotions and social movements*. Chicago: University of Chicago Press.

Hershberger, S. L., Pilkington, N. W., & D'Augelli, A. R. (1997). Predictors of suicide attempts among gay, lesbian, and bisexual youth. *Journal of Adolescent Research, 12*, 477–497.

Hewitt, J. P. (1998). *The myth of self-esteem: Finding happiness and solving problems in America*. New York: St. Martin's Press.

James, W. (1890). *The principles of psychology*. New York: Henry Holt.

Jasper, J. M. (1997). *The art of moral protest: Culture, biography, and creativity in social movements*. Chicago: University of Chicago Press.

Johnson, K. (1998 May). Self-image is suffering from lack of esteem. *New York Times*, p. B12.

Kaplan, H. B. (1975). *Self-attitudes and deviant behavior*. Pacific Palisades, CA: Goodyear.

Kaplan, H. B. (2001). Self-esteem and deviant behavior: A critical review and theoretical integration. In T. J. Owens, S. Stryker, & N. Goodman (Eds.), *Extending self-esteem theory and research: Sociological and psychological currents* (pp. 375–399). New York: Cambridge University.

Kaplan, H. B., & Liu, X. (2000). Social movements as collective coping with spoiled personal identities: Intimations from a panel study of changes in the life course between adolescence and adulthood. In S. Stryker, T. J. Owens, & R. W. White (Eds.), *Self, identity, and social movements* (pp. 215–238). Minneapolis, MN: University of Minnesota Press.

Levy, P. E., & Baumgardner, A. E. (1991). Effects of self-esteem and gender on goal choice. *Journal of Organizational Behavior, 12*, 529–541.

Owens, T. J. (1994). Two dimensions of self-esteem: Reciprocal effects of positive self-worth and self-deprecation on adolescent problems. *American Sociological Review, 59*, 391–407.

Owens, T. J., & Aronson, P. J. (2000). Self-concept as a force in social movement involvement. In S. Stryker, T. J. Owens, & R. W. White (Eds.), *Self, identity and social movements* (pp. 132–151). Minneapolis: University of Minnesota Press.

Owens, T. J., & Stryker, S. (2001). The future of self-esteem: An introduction. In T. J. Owens, S. Stryker, & N. Goodman (Eds.), *Extending self-esteem theory and research: Social and psychological currents* (pp. 1–9). New York: Cambridge University Press.

Peck, B. M., & Kaplan, H. B. (1995). Adolescent self-rejection and adult political activity: The mediating influence of achieved social status. *Social Psychology Quarterly, 58*, 284–297.

Pilegge, A. J., & Holtz, R. (1997). The effects of social identity on the self-set goals and task performance of high and low self-esteem individuals. *Organizational Behavior and Human Decision Processes, 70*, 17–26.

Rosenberg, M. (1979). *Conceiving the self*. New York: Basic Books.

Rosenberg, M., & Owens, T. J. (2001). Low self-esteem people: A collective portrait. In T. J. Owens, S. Stryker, & N. Goodman (Eds.), *Extending self-esteem theory and research: Sociological and psychological currents* (pp. 400–436). New York: Cambridge University Press.

Rosenberg, M., Schooler, C., & Schoenbach, C. (1989). Self-esteem and adolescent problems: Modeling reciprocal effects. *American Sociological Review, 54*, 1004–1018.

Rosenberg, M., Schooler, C., Schoenbach, C., & Rosenberg, F. (1995). Global self-esteem and specific self-esteem: Different concepts, different outcomes. *American Sociological Review, 60*, 141–156.

Scheff, T. J. (1990). *Microsociology: Discourse, emotion, and social structure*. Chicago: University of Chicago Press.

Scheff, T. J. (1994). *Bloody revenge: Emotions, nationalism, and war*. Boulder, CO: Westview.

Scheff, T. J. (2003). Shame in self and society. *Symbolic Interaction, 26*, 239–262.

Scheff, T. J., Retzinger, S. M., & Ryan, M. T. (1989). Crime, violence, and self-esteem: Review and proposals. In A. M. Mecca, N. J. Smelser, & J. Vasconcellos (Eds.), *The Social Importance of Self-Esteem* (pp. 165–199). Berkeley, CA: University of California Press.

Sniderman, P. M., & Citrin, J. (1971). Psychological sources of political belief: Self-esteem and isolationist attitudes. *American Political Science Review, 65*, 401–417.

Sullivan, J. L., Marcus, G. E., Feldman, S., & Piereson, J. E. (1981). The sources of political tolerance: A multivariate analysis. *American Political Science Review, 75*, 92–106.

Swann, W. B. Jr., Stein-Seroussi, A., & Giesler, R. B. (1992). Why people self-verify. *Journal of Personality and Social Psychology, 62*, 392–401.

Tomori, M., & Zalar, B. (2000). Characteristics of suicide attempters in a Slovenian high school population. *Suicide and Life-Threatening Behavior, 30*, 222–238.

Weiss, H. M., & Knight, P. A. (1980). The utility of humility: Self-esteem, information search, and problem-solving efficiency. *Organizational Behavior and Human Decision Processes, 25*, 216–223.

52

What Role Does Self-Esteem Play in the Ills and Triumphs of Society?

TOM PYSZCZYNSKI

To answer the question of what role self-esteem plays in society's ills and triumphs, we must first have a clear conception of what self-esteem is, what function it serves, and what role it plays in day-to-day human functioning. Given the enormous literature that has emerged on self-esteem and related phenomena over the last century, this is no simple task. Much of the controversy and confusion that currently exists in the self-esteem literature regarding the usefulness of self-esteem is a direct result of the absence of clear and widely agreed upon answers to these very basic questions—or in some cases, even clear statements of precisely what theorists are referring to when they use the term self-esteem.

THE NATURE AND FUNCTION OF SELF-ESTEEM

Although the concept of self-esteem is a multifaceted one that is used in different ways by different theorists, the term self-esteem typically refers to one's evaluation of, or attitude toward, oneself. Terror management theory (TMT; Greenberg, Pyszczynski, & Solomon, 1986) posits that self-esteem reflects one's assessment of the extent to which one is living up to the internalized standards of value of one's own individualized version of the cultural worldview. From this perspective, self-esteem is intimately tied to cultural values: Behavior that confers a positive self-evaluation in one cultural context might confer a very different self-evaluation in a different cultural milieu. One person's horrific mass murder is another person's courageous act of martyrdom for the good of his people. Although rooted in cultural values, self-esteem is also an individual construction that depends on the particular values that each of us has internalized from the panoply of cultural influences to which we have been exposed (cf. Pyszczynski, Greenberg, & Goldenberg, 2003); it is also the result of each individual's own subjective evaluation of his or her current standing relative to the standards of value that make up his or her worldview. Finally, self-esteem is a social construction that depends heavily on agreement from others that one is actually living up to the cultural standards in question. It is exceedingly difficult to believe that one is indeed kind, talented, beautiful, or more generally, a valuable person, if no one else agrees.

TMT posits that people are motivated to maintain self-esteem because self-esteem provides a buffer against the potential for anxiety that results from awareness of the inevitability of death in an animal with a strong propensity for continued existence. Research has provided converging support for this hypothesized anxiety-buffering function of self-esteem by showing that: (1) high levels of self-esteem reduce self-reports of anxiety and physiological arousal in response to threats and decrease anxiety-related defensive behavior; (2) reminders of one's mortality increase self-esteem striving and defense of self-esteem against threats across a wide variety of domains; (3) high levels of self-esteem, both dispositional and experimentally induced, eliminate the effect of reminders of mortality on both self-esteem striving and the accessibility of death-related thoughts; and (4) convincing people of the existence of an afterlife eliminates the effect of mortality salience on self-esteem striving. For a comprehensive review of the evidence regarding the anxiety-buffering function of self-esteem, see Pyszczynski, Greenberg, Solomon, Arndt, and Schimel (2004).

This analysis helps explain the great effort people put into living up to their internalized standards of value, the negative emotional reactions that result from falling short of these standards, and the multitude of defensive distortions that people employ to enable themselves to believe that they are meeting these standards when, in fact, they are not. It also fits well with contemporary theories of self-regulation that posit that people control their own behavior by comparing their current state with salient standards and then striving to reduce any discrepancies between self and standard that are detected (e.g., Carver & Scheier, 1981). From this perspective, the affect that results from falling short of one's standards reflects threats to self-esteem and provides the important function of signaling a need for behavior to restore self-esteem by engaging in behavior that brings one back in line with one's internalized standards of value. Put simply, people feel good about themselves, and derive self-esteem, when they are able to view themselves as living up to the cultural values to which they have committed themselves.

POSITIVE AND NEGATIVE CONSEQUENCES OF THE SELF-ESTEEM MOTIVE

This analysis implies that the human self-esteem motive is a "civilizing force" (Wicklund & Frey, 1980) that provides the motivational impetus to live up to the culture's standards for valued behavior by virtue of the protection against deeply rooted anxiety that it provides. The standards of value through which self-esteem is achieved typically function to meet the collective needs of the individual and society as a whole, and keep daily life running smoothly and with minimal conflict. Although there are certainly exceptions, to be discussed shortly, cultural worldviews typically laud behavior that facilitates the survival and prospering of the individual and collective and condemn behavior that undermines these goals. By linking self-esteem, and thus protection from the anxiety inherent in the human condition, to the meeting of cultural standards, the self-esteem motive provides the motivational impetus that keeps individuals on track in the pursuit of important personal goals and encourages behavior that is of use to the society at large. Whether one's self-esteem is rooted in being a successful hunter, farmer, parent, teacher, craftsman, scientist, artist, or entertainer, the behavior that confers self-esteem to the individual is, in most cases, functional for the society as a whole.

This is not to say that the pursuit of self-esteem is the *only* motivational force responsible for desirable behavior in any particular domain. Intrinsic motivation for creatively integrating new information and experiences with existing psychological structures, that results from the positive affect or exhilaration that such activity produces, is another important force that encourages creativity, exploration, and novel thought and behavior (Deci & Ryan, 2000; Greenberg, Pyszczynski, & Solomon, 1995). Because cultures tend to value creativity and risk-taking, such behavior also typically confers self-esteem—thus self-esteem striving and intrinsic motivation often work in concert to encourage novel or creative activities, such as works of art, music, literature, science, and the like. However, in some cases, the need to maintain self-esteem interferes with creativity by encouraging the individual to cling to old ideas or modes of thinking that have provided security or social approval in the past. In other cases, the need for self-esteem leads people to focus their creative efforts on pleasing the masses rather than creating the most original and stimulating innovations they might be capable of producing.

One factor that complicates matters considerably is the fact that, at least in most contemporary Western cultures (and increasingly in other parts of the world as well), self-esteem is often contingent on being the best, or at least one of the best, in whatever domain one is pursuing. The Western ideal is to stand out from, preferably towering above, the rest of the crowd. Although such contingencies of self-esteem can be highly motivating, and do indeed encourage excellence, they also have their drawbacks. First, they encourage competition, which can undermine the communal well-being and interfere with the joint pursuit of valued goals. This competitive desire to "be the best" is also likely to have detrimental effects on interpersonal relations. Tesser (1988) reviewed a considerable body of evidence suggesting that people minimize closeness to those who outperform them in domains in which their own self-esteem is based, and even go so far as to actively interfere with the goal striving of close others in such ego-relevant domains.

Another problem with the Western ideal of standing out above the crowd is that not everyone has the abilities, experiences, or opportunities to be "the best" at anything. To the extent that contemporary culture glorifies the values of physical appearance, wealth, material success, and "superstardom," many people inevitably will be left feeling inadequate, lacking the self-esteem needed to keep their anxiety in check. As much research has demonstrated, threats to self-esteem typically lead to a wide variety of defensive distortions of one's perceptions and beliefs that ultimately take people out of touch with the reality of their situation (for a review, see Greenberg et al., 1986). This interferes with their ability to learn from their failures and adjust their behavior to come closer to their goals. Threats to self-esteem can also lead to premature withdrawal of effort from activities where one might be able to eventually succeed (cf. Carver & Scheier, 1981) and attempts to compensate for one's shortcomings by investing one's self-esteem in socially destructive activities where success and recognition might be easier to come by.

Thus, as many have suggested over the years, difficulty attaining or maintaining self-esteem can lead to behavior that is maladaptive, for both the individual and society. Given the vital role that self-esteem plays in managing anxiety and regulating goal-directed behavior, people simply cannot live happy, successful, and productive lives without it. If people cannot obtain self-esteem in socially desirable ways, they are left unprotected from anxiety, which drives them to seek self-esteem in less desirable ways. The complex multi-faceted melting pot of ideas and values that constitute contemporary culture makes it possible for most people to find at least *something* they can use to derive self-esteem. People can be highly creative when it comes to finding ways of obtaining self-esteem, and the flexible nature of the system through which we come to know ourselves and the world around us provides much room for distortion and selectivity in the way we view ourselves. Unfortunately, many people turn to socially destructive groups and the values they espouse, such as gangs, intolerant political movements, and hate groups, as pathways to self-esteem. Others may invest their sources of self-worth that are less blatantly destructive but that are of little use to society, such as video games and beer chugging contests. The primary loss to society in such cases is that of unfulfilled potential rather than active harm-doing.

Another common way of dealing with an inability to maintain self-esteem is to blot out the resulting anxiety by chemical means or distractions. Alcohol and other drugs are one common way of numbing oneself to anxiety. Thrill-seeking, risk-taking, self-mutilation, or compulsive behaviors are other ways of reducing self-awareness so that anxiety is minimized. Besides reducing unpleasant levels of self-awareness, people may be attracted to the subcultures that surround the community of drug users and thrill-seekers because social acceptance from such communities often requires little other than that one keep engaging in the behavior that defines the subculture (e.g., consuming drugs, enaging in risky behavior). Although many people use drugs or engage in other distracting activities in moderation and enjoy the self-esteem provided by the camaraderie of the local bar or bungy-jumping group, the addictive qualities and physical dangers of drugs and such activities make this problematic for many others.

SUMMARY AND CONCLUSION

The pursuit of self-esteem is a deeply embedded feature of the human animal. To the extent that self-esteem provides a buffer against anxiety that is inherent in being human, and that self-esteem is a superordinate goal that unifies the pursuit of the many more concrete goals that people pursue in life, it is clear that people will not function well without it and will exert considerable effort to maintain it.

Whether the pursuit of self-esteem leads to socially productive or destructive behavior depends largely on the particular cultural standards that people pursue to obtain their sense of value. Although most cultural values facilitate effective functioning for both the individual and society, the fact that some people are unable to meet these standards makes it necessary for subcultures with alternative means of attaining self-esteem to emerge. Given the protection from anxiety that self-esteem provides, people will tend to gravitate toward whatever means of attaining self-esteem are likely to be effective for them.

The pursuit of self-esteem can lead to the best that humankind is capable of—kindness, caring, creativity, and hard work, which has led to great humanitarian, artistic, scientific, and other socially beneficial accomplishments. On the other hand, the pursuit of self-esteem can also lead to the worst of what our species can do—greed, selfishness, closed mindedness, and intolerance, which has led to such abominations and horrors as criminal activity, drug addiction, the Nazi Holocaust, the Ku Klux Klan, and the ongoing litany of wars that have plagued humankind since our species first emerged. In a sense, self-esteem is a lot like sex: It serves an important function, people will do just about anything to get it, and whether its pursuit leads to desirable or undesirable behavior depends on the opportunities and options one has at hand for getting it.

REFERENCES

Carver, C. S., & Scheier, M. F. (1981). *Attention and self-regulation: A control theory approach to human behavior*. New York: Springer.

Deci, E. L., & Ryan, R. M. (2000). The "what" and "why" of goal pursuits: Human needs and the self-determination of behavior. *Psychological Inquiry, 11*, 227–268.

Greenberg, J., Pyszczynski, T., & Solomon, S. (1986). The causes and consequences of a need for self-esteem: A terror management theory. In R. F. Baumeister (Ed.), *Public self and private self* (pp. 189–212). New York: Springer.

Greenberg, J., Pyszczynski, T., & Solomon, S. (1995). Toward a dual-motive depth psychology of self and human behavior. In M. H. Kernis (Ed.), *Efficacy, agency, and self-esteem* (pp. 73–99). New York: Plenum.

Pyszczynski, T., Greenberg, J., & Goldenberg, J. (2003). Fear versus freedom: On the defense, growth, and expansion of the self. In M. Leary & J. Tangney (Eds.), *Handbook of self and identity* (pp. 314–343). New York: Guilford Press.

Pyszczynski, T., Greenberg, J., Solomon, S., Arndt, J., & Schimel, J. (2004). Why do people need self-esteem? A theoretical and empirical review. *Psychological Bulletin, 130* (3), 435–468.

Tesser, A. (1988). Toward a self-evaluation maintenance model of social behavior. In L. Berkowitz (Ed.), *Advances in experimental social psychology* (Vol. 21, pp. 181–227). San Diego: Academic Press.

Wicklund, R., & Frey, D. (1980). How society uses self-awareness. In D. Wegner & R. Vallacher (Eds.), *Social psychological perspectives on the self*. Cary, NC: Oxford University Press.

53

How Self-Esteem Relates to the Ills and Triumphs of Society

DIANNE M. TICE and MATTHEW GAILLIOT

Most people would probably agree that having high self-esteem is desirable. It feels good to hold positive views of one's self and to feel like a valuable person. Indeed, some researchers have suggested that trying to maintain a positive view of the self is an important goal for most people in western cultures (Taylor & Brown, 1988). Likewise, there is a widespread belief among the general public as well as among educators, therapists, politicians, and other influential individuals that self-esteem is the cause of many of society's ills and triumphs (e.g., California Task Force, 1990). In 1986, California even appropriated a $245,000 annual budget to support a task force on self-esteem. California state legislators expressed hope that raising self-esteem would reduce crime, teen pregnancy, drug abuse, school underachievement, and even pollution. In this view, which is sometimes labeled the Self-Esteem Movement, high self-esteem causes people to develop superior social skills, intellect, and healthier lifestyles. People with low self-esteem are predicted to be less successful in their work and in their personal relationships, and are less productive citizens. The Self-Esteem Movement supports attempts to raise the self-esteem of people in the hope that higher self-esteem would lead to better personal and societal outcomes (California Task Force, 1990).

However, this popularly held view that self-esteem causes success has recently been challenged in a review article by Baumeister, Campbell, Krueger, and Vohs (2003). Baumeister et al. examined the most useful and empirically sound studies from over 15,000 articles dealing with self-esteem in order to determine if self-esteem leads to better life outcomes. They looked at the relationship between self-esteem and several important life domains: performance in school and work, interpersonal relationships, antisocial behavior, and mental and physical health. By analyzing almost every published article relating self-esteem to outcome variables, they were able to draw conclusions about how self-esteem affects life outcomes. In many cases, they found that high self-esteem neither causes positive outcomes nor prevents negative outcomes. The Baumeister et al. (2003) findings bear directly on the questions of how self-esteem relates to the ills and triumphs of society. If high self-esteem causes better performance, better relationships with others, less destructive behavior, and better health, then we could conclude that self-esteem is important for avoiding the ills and increasing the triumphs of society. If, however, self-esteem does not causally predict these positive and negative outcome variables, then the relationship between self-esteem and the ills and triumphs of society may be more complex than that suggested by the Self-Esteem Movement.

PERFORMANCE IN SCHOOL AND WORK

Proponents of the Self-Esteem Movement predict that having high self-esteem should cause students to get better grades (e.g., California Task Force, 1990). According to this view, a student with a better self-image might continue to work hard in classes despite initial failure and maintain confidence that ultimately fosters success. And in fact, several studies show a slight positive correlation between self-esteem and academic achievement (e.g., Davies & Brember, 1999; Hansford & Hattie, 1982). Students who feel better about themselves tend to earn higher grades. More detailed studies, however, have shown that the relationship between self-esteem and grades is caused by other factors, such as socioeconomic status and IQ (Bachman & O'Malley, 1977; Maruyama, Rubin, & Kingsbury, 1981). Students who come from wealthier families, for instance, have higher self-esteem and receive better grades, thus making it appear as if self-esteem is causing students to earn better grades.

Yet correlational data cannot demonstrate the causal direction of the relationship. While it is possible that self-esteem leads to receiving better grades, it is also possible that earning good grades causes one to feel better about oneself. And in fact, it appears that receiving better grades does lead to changes in self-esteem, rather than the reverse. Interventions and programs aimed at boosting self-esteem do not lead to improved grades (Scheirer & Kraut, 1979). Increases to a student's grades across time, however, do lead to higher self-esteem (Rosenberg, Schooler, & Schoenbach, 1989; Skaalvik & Hagtvet, 1990). After a thorough review of the evidence, Baumeister et al. (2003) concluded that self-esteem is probably affected by one's grades. Earning good grades increases self-esteem and earning bad grades decreases self-esteem. In this manner, self-esteem functions as a reward for hard work. Seeking to boost self-esteem artificially is probably a self-defeating strategy because it removes the incentive for hard work.

The relationship between self-esteem and work performance is similar to self-esteem and grades. Again, it might seem that high self-esteem should foster superior work performance. Work can sometimes be tedious and demanding, and perhaps feeling good about oneself would encourage one to continue in the face of discouragement. A few studies have shown a positive relationship between self-esteem and work performance (e.g., Brockner, 1983; Tharenou, 1979), which suggests that high self-esteem is related to better work performance. However, the direction of causality is unclear, so it is just as likely that doing well at work increases one's self-esteem as it is that having high self-esteem improves work performance. Studies in the laboratory demonstrate that high self-esteem does not lead to better performance.

For example, participants with high self-esteem do not do any better in solving math problems (Wallace & Baumeister, 2002) or playing video games (Baumeister, Heatherton, & Tice, 1993). If a relationship between performance at work and self-esteem does exist, then it seems likely that work performance affects self-esteem. People feel better about themselves after doing well at work.

In summary, it appears that there is positive correlation between self-esteem and performance at work or school, but an analysis of all studies suggests that the causal direction points to success increasing self-esteem rather than self-esteem predicting performance. Increasing a person's self-esteem may not increase performance, but improving performance is likely to boost self-esteem.

INTERPERSONAL RELATIONSHIPS

Another common belief in western cultures is the belief that you must love yourself before you can love someone else (e.g., Crooks & Baur, 1999). Even though it appears that high self-esteem does not facilitate school or work performance, it seems possible that self-esteem might foster better relationships. If a person feels good about himself or herself, then he or she might feel more positively towards others as well. In this manner, self-esteem could lead to better interpersonal functioning, which could be valuable in contributing to the triumphs and in avoiding the ills of society.

Another possibility, however, is that changes in self-esteem result from changes in the quality of a person's social relationships. This idea, proposed by Leary and colleagues (Leary, Tambor, Terdal, & Downs, 1995), is known as the sociometer theory of self-esteem. In this view, self-esteem acts to measure the quality of a person's social relationships. If someone meets a new friend, for instance, then self-esteem should increase; if a relationship with a friend suffers, then self-esteem should decrease.

Research on self-esteem and interpersonal relationships tends to support the sociometer theory of self-esteem, and not the view that self-esteem leads to better relationships. Even though people with high self-esteem believe they are more popular (Battistich, Solomon, & Delucchi, 1993) and have better quality relationships (Keefe & Berndt, 1996), objective tests show this to be false. When peers rate each other on various dimensions, people with high self-esteem are not better liked (Bishop & Inderbitzen, 1995), nor do they have superior social skills (Buhrmester, Furman, Wittenberg, & Reis, 1988). High self-esteem also does not lead to higher quality or longer lasting relationships. Although people with low self-esteem sometimes behave in ways harmful to relationships, such as being more likely to break up (S. S. Hendrick, Hendrick, & Adler, 1988) displaying distrust, or fearing abandonment (Murray, Rose, Bellavia, Holmes, & Kusche, 2002), high self-esteem can also be problematic. Relationship partners with high self-esteem, for instance, are more likely to leave a relationship when problems begin to develop (Rusbult, Morrow, & Johnson, 1987). Thus, it appears that having high self-esteem is not necessary for maintaining better relationships, despite what common sense might suggest. Rather, self-esteem may reflect the quantity and quality of one's relationships, such that increases in self-esteem result from improving one's relationships.

ANTISOCIAL BEHAVIOR

Even though self-esteem does not appear to contribute meaningfully to school and work performance or interpersonal relationships, the possibility that self-esteem could reduce anti-social behavior would help justify attempts of policy makers to boost self-esteem. If increasing people's self-esteem could reduce crime, drug abuse, and violence, for example, then it would be desirable to increase people's self-esteem through programs and interventions. Indeed, aggression has traditionally been viewed as stemming from low self-esteem. However, it seems that the opposite is actually true (Baumeister, Smart, & Boden, 1996). For instance, studies of bullying either have found that bullies are more sure of themselves than non-bullies (Olweus, 1990, 1994), or have found no relationship between bullying and self-esteem (Slee and Rigby, 1993).

Instead of people with low self-esteem being more aggressive, it is people who have high, but unstable self-esteem that are most likely to aggress (Kernis, Grannemann, & Barclay, 1989). Upon sensing a potential threat to their self-esteem, people with high but unstable or variable self-esteem act out aggressively in an attempt to prevent the threat to their fluctuating self-esteem. Kernis and Waschull (see Kernis & Waschull, 1995, for a review) suggest that it is a mistake to focus mainly on the level of self-esteem. In a comprehensive research program, Kernis and Waschull (1995) have shown that stability of self-esteem is more important in predicting hostility than is the level of self-esteem (see Kernis & Waschull, 1995, for a review). People with high but unstable self-esteem score higher on measures of hostility than do people with low self-esteem (whether stable or unstable), whereas people with high but stable self-esteem are the least hostile (Kernis, Grannemann, & Barclay, 1989). Lobel & Levanon (1998) suggest that other socially undesirable behaviors, such as cheating, interrupting, and annoying others, might also stem from high but unstable self-esteem.

Bushman and Baumeister (1998) found that narcissism, rather than self-esteem, predicted aggressive behavior. Although most narcissists have high self-esteem, the construct of narcissism involves overly inflated views of self as well as the belief that one is entitled to privileges and admiration by others (see American Psychiatric Association, 2000). Like the work by Kernis (Kernis & Waschull, 1995), Bushman and Baumeister's (1998) work suggests that a small subset of people with high self-esteem are the most aggressive.

Although low self-esteem does not lead to increased aggression, it is possible that low self-esteem would cause delinquency. Even though some studies show otherwise (e.g., Jang & Thornberry, 1998), there is some support for the idea that delinquency is caused by low self-esteem. For instance, ratings of self-esteem from parents, teachers, and children can predict rates of delinquent behavior 2 years later (Trzesniewski, Donnellan, Robins, Moffitt, & Caspi, 2002). Baumeister et al. (2003) report that correlations between self-esteem and delinquency vary among studies from nearly zero to around $-.30$, but are almost always negative, suggesting that the a relationship between low self-esteem and delinquency is present, although probably quite weak.

In summary, the relationship between self-esteem and some of the ills of society represented by antisocial behavior is complex. Low self-esteem does not appear to cause aggression and hostility, but the stability of self-esteem is related to aggressive behavior. People with high but unstable self-esteem are more hostile than people with low self-esteem or people with high but stable self-esteem. Narcissists are more aggressive than non-narcissists when their self-esteem is threatened. Juvenile delinquency may be more common among low self-esteem males than among high self-esteem males.

MENTAL AND PHYSICAL HEALTH

Perhaps the strongest benefit of having high self-esteem comes from greater happiness. People with high self-esteem describe themselves as being happier than those with low self-esteem (Diener & Diener, 1995). If self-esteem is an outcome of doing well in work, getting good grades, and having close friends, as suggested above, then it seems logical that rises in self-esteem would make people feel happier. Conversely, low self-esteem sometimes leads to depression (e.g., Murrell, Meeks, & Walker, 1991) and is a major contributor towards eating disorders (e.g., French et al., 2001). More research demonstrating a causal link between self-esteem and mental health is desirable, however. While the available data suggests that self-esteem affects one's happiness, evidence confirming such a causal relationship is lacking.

Although high self-esteem seems to beneficially influence mental health, the same cannot be said about self-esteem and physical health. Having high self-esteem does not prevent smoking, drinking, taking drugs, or engaging in early sex. In some cases, people with high self-esteem are more likely to have sex at an early age and experiment with drugs. Once again, more research is needed to demonstrate a clear relationship between self-esteem and physical health because the existing literature does not adequately demonstrate the nature of the relationship.

CONCLUSION

How does self-esteem relate to the triumphs and ills of society? Looking at a wide range of outcome variables, it seems that one's level of self-esteem does not cause many of the ills and triumphs of society. However, success does seem to raise self-esteem, and failure does seem to lower it. Certain subsets of people with high self-esteem (narcissists, and people with unstable high self-esteem) may be more aggressive, and young men with low self-esteem may be more prone to juvenile delinquency than young men with high self-esteem. Getting along well with others seems to increase self-esteem, and problems with relationships seem to lower self-esteem. Happiness is associated with high self-esteem, while depression and eating disorders are associated with low self-esteem.

For most people, maintaining a high level of self-esteem is important (Wills, 1981). Feelings about one's self usually fluctuate with one's successes and failures, so one may erroneously believe that the changes in self-esteem are causing one to succeed or fail. In this view, it seems possible that high self-esteem would prevent negative outcomes and foster positive outcomes. Indeed, many people promote this viewpoint and seek to increase self-esteem in the general public (e.g., California Task Force, 1990). After considering thousands of research articles on self-esteem, however, Baumeister et al. (2003) concluded that the ills and triumphs of society are usually not the result of having high or low self-esteem. Rather, self-esteem appears to reflect how well one is doing in school, work, and interpersonal relationships. Although some antisocial behaviors may be caused by low self-esteem (e.g., delinquency), others are caused by unstable, high self-esteem (e.g., aggression, cheating) and narcissism. High self-esteem may foster better mental health, but it does not seem to promote a healthier lifestyle.

Baumeister et al. (2003) concluded that self-esteem is only weakly related to most important life outcomes. As such, boosting self-esteem through school programs and other interventions is probably not a reasonable policy. Promoting self-control, which does lead to increases in the triumphs of society and decreases in the ills of society (Baumeister, Heatherton, and Tice, 1994), may be preferable to boosting self-esteem and have a more positive impact on society.

REFERENCES

American Psychiatric Association. (2000). *Diagnostic and statistical manual of mental disorders* (4th ed., text revision). Washington, DC: APA.

Bachman, J. G., & O'Malley, P. M. (1977). Self-esteem in young men: A longitudinal analysis of the impact of educational and occupational attainment. *Journal of Personality and Social Psychology, 35,* 365–380.

Battistich, V., Solomon, D., & Delucchi, K. (1993). Interaction processes and student outcomes in cooperative learning groups. *The Elementary School Journal, 94,* 19–32.

Baumeister, R. F., Campbell, J. D., Krueger, J. I., & Vohs, K. D. (2003). Does high self-esteem cause better performance, interpersonal success, happiness, or healthier lifestyles? *Psychological Science in the Public Interest, 4,* 1–44.

Baumeister, R. F., Heatherton, T. F., & Tice, D. M. (1993). When ego threats lead to self-regulation failure: Negative consequences of high self-esteem. *Journal of Personality and Social Psychology, 64,* 141–156.

Baumeister, R. F., Heatherton, T. F., & Tice, D. M. (1994). *Losing control: How and why people fail at self regulation.* San Diego, CA: Academic Press

Baumeister, R. F., Smart, L., & Boden, J. M. (1996). Relation of threatened egotism to violence and aggression: The dark side of high self-esteem. *Psychological Review, 103,* 5–33.

Bishop, J. A., & Inderbitzen, H. M. (1995). Peer acceptance and friendship: An investigation of their relation to self-esteem. *Journal of Early Adolescence, 15,* 476–489.

Brockner, J. (1983). Low self-esteem and behavioral plasticity: Some implications. In L. Wheeler & P. Shaver (Eds.), *Review of personality and social psychology* (Vol. 4, pp. 237–271). Beverly Hills, CA: Sage.

Buhrmester, D., Furman, W., Wittenberg, M. T., & Reis, H. T. (1988). Five domains of interpersonal competence in peer relationships. *Journal of Personality and Social Psychology, 55,* 991–1008.

Bushman, B. J., & Baumeister, R. F. (1998). Threatened egotism, narcissism, self-esteem, and direct and displaced aggression: Does self-love or self-hate lead to violence? *Journal of Personality and Social Psychology, 75,* 219–229.

California Task Force to Promote Self-Esteem and Personal and Social Responsibility. (1990). *Toward a state of self-esteem.* Sacramento: California State Department of Education.

Crooks, R., & Baur, K. (1999). *Our sexuality* (7th ed.). New York: Brooks/Cole.

Davies, J., & Brember, I. (1999). Reading and mathematics attainments and self-esteem in years 2 and 6—an eight-year cross-sectional study. *Educational Studies, 25,* 145–157.

Diener, E., & Diener, M. (1995). Cross-cultural correlates of life satisfaction and self-esteem. *Journal of Personality and Social Psychology, 68,* 653–663.

French, S. A., Leffert, N., Story, M., Neumark-Sztainer, D., Hannan, P., & Benson, P. L. (2001). Adolescent binge/purge and weight loss behaviors: Associations with developmental assets. *Journal of Adolescent Health, 28,* 211–221.

Hansford, B. C., & Hattie, J. A. (1982). The relationship between self and achievement/performance measures. *Review of Educational Research, 52,* 123–142.

Hendrick, S. S., Hendrick, C., & Adler, N. L. (1988). Romantic relationships: Love, satisfaction, and staying together. *Journal of Personality and Social Psychology, 54,* 980–988.

Jang, S. J., & Thornberry, T. P. (1998). Self-esteem, delinquent peers, and delinquency: A test of the self-enhancement hypothesis. *American Sociological Review, 63,* 586–598.

Keefe, K., & Berndt, T. J. (1996). Relations of friendship quality to self-esteem in early adolescence. *Journal of Early Adolescence, 16,* 110–129.

Kernis, M. H., Grannemann, B. D., & Barclay, L. C. (1989). Stability and level of self-esteem as predictors of anger arousal and hostility. *Journal of Personality and Social Psychology, 56,* 1013–1022.

Kernis, M. H., & Waschull, S. B. (1995). The interactive roles of stability and level of self-esteem: Research and theory. In M. P. Zanna (Ed.), *Advances in experimental social psychology* (Vol. 27, pp. 93–141). San Diego, CA: Academic Press.

Leary, M. R., Tambor, E. S., Terdal, S. K., & Downs, D. L. (1995). Self-esteem as an interpersonal monitor: The sociometer hypothesis. *Journal of Personality and Social Psychology, 68,* 518–530.

Lobel, T. E., & Levanon, I. (1988). Self-esteem, need for approval, and cheating behavior in children. *Journal of Educational Psychology, 80,* 122–123.

Maruyama, G., Rubin, R. A., & Kingsbury, G. G. (1981). Self-esteem and educational achievement: Independent constructs with a common cause? *Journal of Personality and Social Psychology, 40,* 962–975.

Murray, S. L., Rose, P., Bellavia, G., Holmes, J. G., & Kusche, A. (2002). When rejection stings: How self-esteem constrains relationship-enhancement processes. *Journal of Personality and Social Psychology, 83,* 556–573.

Murrell, S. A., Meeks, S., & Walker, J. (1991). Protective functions of health and self-esteem against depression in older adults facing illness or bereavement. *Psychology and Aging, 6,* 352–360.

Olweus, D. (1990). Bullying among school children. In K. Hurrelmann & F. Loesel (Eds.), *Health hazards in adolescence* (pp. 259–297). Berlin, Germany: Walter De Gruyter.

Olweus, D. (1994). Bullying at school: Long-term outcomes for the victims and an effective school-based intervention program. In R. Huesmann (Ed.), *Aggressive behavior: Current perspectives* (pp. 97–130). New York: Plenum Press.

Rosenberg, M., Schooler, C., & Schoenbach, C. (1989). Self-esteem and adolescent problems: Modeling reciprocal effects. *American Sociological Review, 54,* 1004–1018.

Rusbult, C. E., Morrow, G. D., & Johnson, D. J. (1987). Self-esteem and problem-solving behaviour in close relationships. *British Journal of Social Psychology, 26,* 293–303.

Scheirer, M. A., & Kraut, R. E. (1979). Increased educational achievement via self-concept change. *Review of Educational Research, 49,* 131–150.

Skaalvik, E. M., & Hagtvet, K. A. (1990). Academic achievement and self-concept: An analysis of causal predominance in a developmental perspective. *Journal of Personality and Social Psychology, 58,* 292–307.

Slee, P. T., & Rigby, K. (1993). Australian school children's self appraisal of interpersonal relations: The bullying experience. *Child Psychiatry and Human Development, 23,* 273–282.

Taylor, S. E., & Brown, J. D. (1988). Illusion and well-being: A social psychological perspective on mental health. *Psychological Bulletin, 103,* 193–210.

Tharenou, P. (1979). Employee self-esteem: A review of the literature. *Journal of Vocational Behavior, 15,* 316–346.

Trzesniewski, K. H., Donnellan, M. B., Robins, R. W., Moffitt, T. E., & Caspi, A. (2002, February). *Do juvenile delinquents have high or low self-esteem?* Paper presented at the annual meeting of the Society for Personality and Social Psychology, Savannah, GA.

Wallace, H. M., & Baumeister, R. F. (2002). The performance of narcissists rises and falls with perceived opportunity for glory. *Journal of Personality and Social Psychology, 82,* 819–834.

Wills, T. A. (1981). Downward comparison principles in social psychology. *Psychological Bulletin, 90,* 245–271.

Section V

Future Directions

Question 18

Where do we go from here?
What are the most pressing issues
facing researchers, practitioners, teachers,
and parents?

The essays in this section focus on the most pressing issues facing researchers, parents, teachers, and therapists. The authors who contributed to this section have widely varied backgrounds—Leary is a social/personality psychologist, Harter is a developmental psychologist, and Branden is a clinical psychologist—although each has focused extensively on self-esteem issues.

Leary focuses his comments primarily on the important issues facing researchers. He emphasizes the need for self-esteem researchers and practitioners to achieve a broader consensus on how precisely to conceptualize self-esteem and, until such time arrives, for them to be very explicit about their conceptualization. Moreover, Leary emphasizes how important it is that researchers ensure that the measures they use to assess self-esteem mirror their conceptualization. Another important challenge facing researchers, Leary asserts, is to go beyond simple lay explanations of the role of self-esteem and provide more complex and cogent theoretical explanations.

Harter raises issues pertinent to researchers, teachers, practitioners, and parents. Many of her comments for researchers emphasize developmental issues. Harter also writes that it is especially important to foster greater cross talk between developmental psychologists who study mainly children and social/personality psychologists who study mainly adults. For practitioners, Harter focuses on issues facing those who want to create interventions to promote higher and healthier self-esteem. One issue that Harter raises for teachers is the importance of identifying those children with violent or suicidal ideation who do not have histories of conduct disorders. Finally, Harter offers several important suggestions for parents.

Branden raises several major issues facing researchers that converge with those raised by Leary and Harter—agreeing on the definition of self-esteem, improving on the self-reported assessment of self-esteem, and operationalizing self-esteem in a way that allows for the real-life identification of those with healthy and unhealthy self-esteem. In addition, Branden emphasizes the need for better understanding of the behaviors of parents, teachers, and clinicians that can foster healthier self-esteem in children and in clients with self-esteem difficulties.

54

What Are the Most Pressing Issues Facing Researchers?

MARK R. LEARY

*U*pon learning that over 25,000 articles, chapters, and books have been published that deal with self-esteem, a naive observer might reasonably assume that most important questions about self-esteem have been answered by now and all that remains is for scholars to quibble over trivial and esoteric issues of interest only to them. As all researchers in the field know, however, this is far from the case and, despite the great amount of attention that has been devoted to the topic of self-esteem, experts continue to disagree about many fundamental issues.

The most pressing problem faced by scholars in the area—the one with the greatest implications for research, clinical practice, and applications by teachers and parents—involves the lack of a widely-accepted conceptualization of what self-esteem actually is. Importantly, the problem here is not that we have competing theoretical explanations of what self-esteem does or how it works. In fact, Feyerabend (1970), the noted philosopher of science, argued that science benefits by having competing theories. As he noted, a "plurality of theories must not be regarded as a preliminary stage of knowledge which will at some time in the future be replaced by the One True Theory" (p. 321). Having just one widely-accepted theory does not assure that the theory is a good one, and competing theories often generate new perspectives and creative research, as they clearly have in the case of self-esteem. The difficulty, then, is not that we have multiple theories on the table but rather that theorists and researchers do not agree on even their fundamental conceptualizations of self-esteem.

"Self-esteem" has been conceptualized in many different ways—as liking oneself, feeling good about oneself, believing that one has the ability to achieve one's goals, possessing a sense of worth, experiencing pride (as opposed to shame), holding a positive attitude toward oneself, feeling able to cope with threats and challenges, and so on. To make matters worse, many writers do not define how they use the term "self-esteem," seeming to assume that readers will know what they are talking about. Although one can see links among these various conceptualizations, they differ in ways that have important implications for understanding self-esteem. A belief in one's efficacy, a good feeling about oneself, and a judgment of one's worth are quite different things, for example, with different implications for theory, research, and application. The fact that the topic of self-esteem remains shrouded in confusion despite so much theoretical and empirical attention ought to give us pause and lead us to consider whether something about our conceptual approach to self-esteem is fundamentally flawed.

At minimum, we must maintain clearcut distinctions between beliefs about oneself (as captured by terms such as self-concept, self-representation, and self-efficacy), judgments of oneself as being low or high on particular attributes (e.g., viewing oneself as a good student or a poor athlete), and a generalized good or bad feeling about oneself (which is how most writers have regarded self-esteem). Self-relevant beliefs, judgments, and feelings are obviously related to one another, yet we create confusion by referring to all of them as "self-esteem."

The picture is complicated further by the fact that various measures and manipulations of self-esteem are used interchangeably even though they may actually reflect somewhat different constructs. In research on trait self-esteem, for example, the most widely used measure has been Rosenberg's (1965) scale, which primarily assesses people's judgments of themselves—being a "person of worth," having a "positive attitude" toward oneself, feeling "useless," thinking that one is "no good at all," and so on. However, another commonly-used measure (Coopersmith, 1967), consists of a hodgepodge of self-ratings—of one's emotions (e.g., worry, discouragement, happiness), confidence (e.g., being sure of oneself, taking care of oneself), reflected appraisals (e.g., popularity, likeability), relationships with parents and teachers (e.g., feeling understood), and behaviors (e.g., doing the right thing, being dependable). Yet another measure, the Texas Social Behavior Inventory, which Helmreich and Stapp (1974) described as an "objective measure of self-esteem" (p. 473), appears to assess primarily confidence in social situations. In an effort to distinguish between two basic dimensions of self-esteem, Taforodi and Swann (2001) offered a two-dimensional measure that assesses both self-competence ("I am very talented," "I am highly effective at doing things") and self-liking ("I am secure in my sense of self-worth;" "I feel good about who I am"). These two dimensions are clearly related to self-esteem (see Fleming & Courtney, 1984), but it is less clear that these self-judgments *are* self-esteem. And, given the variety of ways in which researchers and laypeople define self-esteem, one must wonder about how respondents answer single-item measures that simply ask them to rate the truth of the statement "I have high self-esteem" (Robins, Hendin, & Trzesniewski, 2001).

Similar confusions surround measures of state self-esteem. The only scale designed specifically to assess state self-esteem (Heatherton & Polivy, 1991) asks people to rate their beliefs and feelings about themselves at the moment. Although most of the statements are worded in terms of feelings (e.g., "I am worried...," "I feel frustrated..."), many of them actually assess beliefs. For example, "I feel as smart as others" could easily be reworded as "I *believe* that I am as smart as others," and "I feel confident about my abilities" seems to assess self-efficacy beliefs rather than "feelings" per se, raising the question of whether state self-esteem is a belief or a feeling. Other researchers have used affectively laden items, such as those from McFarland and Ross' (1982) factor analysis of mood-relevant adjectives (e.g., worthless, proud). The fact that researchers who have used more than one measure of state self-esteem in the same study sometimes obtain different patterns of results with the various measures suggests that they are not measuring precisely the same construct, again suggesting that we may have not successfully conceptualized the phenomenon before operationalizing it.

Likewise, in experimental studies of self-esteem, researchers have lowered and raised self-esteem in a variety of ways. Most commonly, participants have been provided with bogus feedback on tests of social skill, anagram-solving ability, general intelligence, dot estimation, or other abilities. Other manipulations of self-esteem have involved negative evaluations by other people, interpersonal rejection, or having people work on difficult (or unsolvable) problems without providing feedback. At present, we have little evidence that these various manipulations all target the same psychological process or that they are interchangeable.

Furthermore, these ambiguities with the conceptualization, measurement, and manipulation of self-esteem obscure other constructs that involve self-esteem—such as "self-esteem motivation" and "self-esteem threat." If we can not agree whether self-esteem is a judgment of self-worth, an attitude, a sense of efficacy, a belief, or a feeling, we can not talk meaningfully about what it means for people to be motivated to "protect their self-esteem" or for self-esteem to be "threatened."

No one would doubt that most of these various operationalizations do, in fact, measure or manipulate variables that are related to self-esteem, and some may even tap aspects of self-esteem itself. However, the fact that self-esteem has been measured and manipulated in so many diverse ways should make us wonder what it is we are trying to study. And, given the diversity of measures and manipulations, how certain are we that the findings obtained in one study are relevant to those obtained in another? As can be seen, the problem is not that we have competing theories about self-esteem but that we have not yet agreed on an answer to the more fundamental question of what self-esteem actually is. This state of affairs has created an impediment to theory, research, and application.

How did we arrive at this messy situation, and how might we find our way out of it? Let me suggest three sources of the problem and three corresponding solutions. (I must confess that I personally have been guilty of every offense that I describe in this section.)

First, the seemingly simple nature of self-esteem has seduced researchers into complacency regarding their conceptualizations and operationalizations. Self-esteem is such a part of everyday language that psychologists and laypeople alike think they know what it is, despite the fact that the term is often used very loosely. As a result, many researchers and writers have not been critical enough in how they have approached self-esteem. Perhaps we will someday arrive at a consensus regarding the best conceptualization of self-esteem, but until then, researchers must provide an explicit description of the conceptualization they are using and demonstrate that their operationalizations are consistent with it, being careful to distinguish self-esteem from empirically related constructs (such as self-efficacy and pride). Furthermore, psychologists must exercise greater care in how they talk about self-esteem to their clients and to the public at large. I recently heard the director of a community agency that helps disadvantaged children assert that, "All we have to do is give these kids self-esteem, and everything else will take care of itself." Such beliefs—whether held by parents, teachers, psychotherapists, or others—are not necessarily harmful (although they could be; see Crocker & Park, 2004), but they may focus our efforts in nonoptimal directions.

Second, we must go beyond simple-minded lay explanations of the effects of self-esteem to explanations that are based on cogent theories. For example, it should no longer be sufficient to simply assert that self-esteem causes aggression, delinquency, drug abuse, domestic violence, school difficulties, or other problems (Mecca, Smelser, & Vasconcellos, 1989) without offering one or more theoretical rationales for why such effects occur. Most importantly, researchers must resist the urge to view self-esteem as a causal variable unless its causal nature can be demonstrated. Too often, researchers have ignored the admonition not to infer causality from correlation and treated low and high self-esteem as if they caused various emotional, cognitive, and behavioral effects. Likewise, explanations of phenomena that rely on the notion that people are motivated to maintain their self-esteem must always take a step back to examine this motive rather than simply taking it as a given. Many of the theoretical advances regarding self-esteem during the past 15 years have suggested that self-esteem operates in the service of more fundamental psychological processes, such as terror management (Solomon, Greenberg, & Pyszczynski, 1991) or monitoring the social environment (Leary & Baumeister, 2000), yet many writers continue to assume that people are inherently motivated to seek self-esteem for its own sake.

Third, we should look for opportunities to go beyond the broad and abstract term, "self-esteem," to other, more precise constructs. My suspicion is that many effects of "self-esteem" are actually effects of other variables that either underlie self-esteem or that correlate highly with it. Because researchers have assumed that self-esteem is an important and powerful psychological entity in its own right, they have often not considered the possibility that the effects they obtain are not fundamentally due to self-esteem per se. This point is particularly true in counseling and psychotherapy in which many practitioners have assumed that raising self-esteem helps to solve an array of personal and interpersonal problems. Being careful to identify the actual effective agent in psychological change rather than attributing it to "self-esteem" will improve treatment effectiveness (see Leary, 1999; Leary, Schreindorfer, & Haupt, 1995).

To end on a promising note, one point around which agreement does seem to be emerging is that, contrary to popular opinion, self-esteem is not a panacea for personal or social problems. Not only does high self-esteem have certain downsides (Baumeister, Campbell, Krueger, & Vohs, 2003; Crocker & Park, 2004), but writers now question whether even the apparently positive effects of high self-esteem are actually due to self-esteem per se (Leary et al., 1995). Furthermore, we are beginning to see the logical error of assuming that, because people with naturally occurring high self-esteem sometimes have higher well-being than those with low self-esteem, pursuing higher self-esteem promotes well-being. These recent advances further highlight the conceptual morass that has impeded our understanding of self-esteem and demonstrate the benefits of conceptualizing self-esteem more carefully and critically.

REFERENCES

Baumeister, R. F., Campbell, J. D., Krueger, J. I., & Vohs, K. D. (2003). Does high self-esteem cause better performance, interpersonal success, happiness, or healthier lifestyles? *Psychological Science in the Public Interest, 4*, 1–44.

Coopersmith, S. (1967). *The antecedents of self-esteem.* San Francisco: W.H. Freeman.

Crocker, J., & Park, L. E. (2004). The costly pursuit of self-esteem. *Psychological Bulletin, 130*, 392–414.

Feyerabend, P. K. (1970). How to be a good empiricist: A plea for tolerance in matters epistemological. In B. Brody (Ed.), *Readings in the philosophy of science.* Englewood Cliffs, NJ: Prentice-Hall.

Fleming, J. S., & Courtney, B. E. (1984). The dimensionality of self-esteem II: Hierarchical facet model for revised measurement scales. *Journal of Personality and Social Psychology, 46*, 404–421.

Heatherton, T. F., & Polivy, J. (1991). Development and validation of a scale for measuring state self-esteem. *Journal of Personality and Social Psychology, 60*, 895–910.

Helmreich, R., & Stapp, J. (1974). Short form of the Texas Social Behavior Inventory (TSVI), an objective measure of self-esteem. *Bulletin of the Psychonomic Society, 4*, 473–475.

Leary, M. R. (1999). The social and psychological importance of self-esteem. In R. M. Kowalski & M. R. Leary (Eds.), *The social psychology of emotional and behavioral problems: Interfaces of social and clinical psychology* (pp. 197–221). Washington, DC: American Psychological Association.

Leary, M. R., & Baumeister, R. F. (2000). The nature and function of self-esteem: Sociometer theory. In M. P. Zanna (Ed.), *Advances in Experimental Social Psychology* (Vol. 32, pp. 1–62). San Diego: Academic Press.

Leary, M. R., Schreindorfer, L. S., & Haupt, A. L. (1995). The role of low self-esteem in emotional and behavioral problems: Why is low self-esteem dysfunctional? *Journal of Social and Clinical Psychology, 14*, 297–314.

McFarland, C., & Ross, M. (1982). Impact of causal attributions on affective reactions to success and failure. *Journal of Personality and Social Psychology, 43*, 937–946.

Mecca, A. M., Smelser, N. J., & Vasconcellos, J. (1989). *The social importance of self-esteem.* Berkeley: University of California Press.

Robins, R. W., Hendin, H. M., & Trzesniewski, K. H. (2001). Measuring global self-esteem: Construct validation of a single-item measure and the Rosenberg self-esteem scale. *Personality and Social Psychology Bulletin, 27*, 151–161.

Rosenberg, M. (1965). *Society and the adolescent self-image.* Princeton, NJ: Princeton University Press.

Solomon, S., Greenberg, J., & Pyszczynski, T. (1991). A terror management theory of social behavior: The psychological functions of self-esteem and cultural worldviews. In M. Zanna (Ed.), *Advances in experimental social psychology* (Vol. 24, pp. 91–159). Orlando, FL: Academic Press.

Tafarodi, R. W., & Swann, W. B. Jr. (2001). Two-dimensional self-esteem: Theory and measurement. *Personality and Individual Differences, 31*, 653–673.

55

Where Do We Go from Here?

SUSAN HARTER

W hat are the burning questions that we still face as *researchers*? First, there are demonstrated individual differences in the behaviorally manifest levels of self-esteem in young children and we do not yet fully appreciate the causes. How much of high or low self-esteem do children bring into the world by virtue of their temperament and talents, their genetic makeup, and how do these interact with parental responses to these clearly demonstrated tendencies? How can we get past the "blame-game" in which parents are made to feel guilty, if their children are manifesting deficiencies that are associated with low behaviorally manifest self-esteem. We also need more studies on how early child-rearing impacts young children's self-esteem since the manner in which parental figures socialize their children must also impact the early behavioral manifestations of self-esteem that adult observers reliably report.

Relatedly, we need to address the question of whether the earlier behavioral manifestations of self-esteem observed by teachers, parents, or others translate directly into the verbalizable self-esteem that emerges in middle childhood. Are those young children who manifest low self-esteem in the form of reticence, withdrawal, lack of curiosity and exploration, who are primarily onlookers on the fringes of the group, compromised in terms of learning, motivation, and social experiences? Will these behaviors prevent them from developing the kinds of competencies (cognitive, athletic, and social abilities) that form an importance basis for their sense of worth as a person in middle childhood? Here we will need careful longitudinal studies to determine if the behavioral manifestations of low self-esteem in early childhood translate into liabilities in later childhood when verbalizable domain-specific evaluations are being formed and will predict one's level of global self-worth or esteem as a person.

Secondly, we need to move in the direction of appreciating first and then documenting the *multiple pathways* to high and low self-esteem. Our own work has demonstrated, based on our model, six demonstrable pathways to high or low self-esteem (see Harter, 1999). To give but two examples, for some children and adolescents, self-evaluations in the domains of physical appearance, athletic competence, and peer acceptance, combined with level of *peer* support, are most predictive of level of self-esteem. However, for others, self-evaluations in the domains of scholastic competence, combined with *parent* support, are more predictive of self-esteem. There are other patterns as well. Thus, it will be important to identify the particular pathways for given individuals since *interventions* must be tailored to particular causes (see Harter, 1999), a point to which we shall return in the next section.

Third, we need to move beyond the position that self-esteem as a construct is equivocally a trait versus a state, by definition. The three strands of research presented indicate that for some individuals it is trait-like whereas for others it is more state-like. With that appreciation in mind, we now need to investigate the developmental origins leading to individual differences for those whose self-esteem seems to be more trait-like and for whom it appears more state-like, showing fluctuations across contexts as well as across time. Consistency versus variability in terms of how individuals are treated across contexts as well as time may be an initial promising avenue to pursue.

Fourth, it is essential that we address the inextricable link between perceived attractiveness and self-esteem. Here, societal issues abound. The punishing and narrow standards put forth by our culture that define attractiveness for women clearly take their psychological toll on females in our culture, beginning in childhood, since only a very small minority can achieve them. While this has historically been more of a challenge for women than men, during the past decade the same mentality has now been applied to males, beginning in childhood. That is, there are now rigid standards for how men should look, for example, muscular, great abs, calves, particular hair styles, etc. that now lead to males' preoccupation with their appearance. The societal focus is clearly on our worth as defined by the "outer" self as opposed to qualities that define our "inner" self. Our own research clearly demonstrates that the preoccupation with appearance, coupled with dissatisfaction with one's appearance, leads to low self-esteem, anxiety, depression, suicide, violence, as well as eating disorders. Research in this arena must necessarily address the role of society in promoting this mentality and its psychologically pernicious impact on both females and males.

Fifth, there is a contemporary movement suggesting that high self-esteem may not be the psychological commodity that many in the fields of psychology, education, and mental health have assumed it be. Arguments by Damon (1995) and Seligman (1993) have suggested that we have put too much attention on raising self-esteem (unrealistically). Educational efforts to raise self-esteem may be misguided, according to these authors, particularly if they are of the "you're OK" philosophy where one touts the skills of children unrealistically. Seligman further suggests that self-esteem may simply be an epiphenomenon, and not a useful construct as a mediator or outcomes. This is certainly a questionable assumption since there are numerous studies showing links between low self-esteem and mental health outcomes (depression and suicide, violence, teen pregnancy). What we do not know is why low self-esteem among our youth leads some to kill *themselves*, some to kill *others*, and yet leads some not to destroy but to *create* a life. Thus, our research needs to focus more clearly on the causes that differentiate these various outcomes.

The most recent challenge to the value of *high* self-esteem comes from Baumeister, Smart, and Boden (1996) suggesting that there is a dark side of high self-esteem, namely that it is associated with violence in the face of threats to the self (Baumeister et al., 1996). We need to thoughtfully examine such a contention. In Baumeister's model, high self-esteem associated with narcissism, low empathy, excessive need for approval, and unstable self-esteem combine to produce a tendency to violence. What we need to do is isolate the relevant, predictive variables in this constellation. Our own research (Harter, Low, & Whitesell, 2003) reveals that it is the low self-esteem individuals, also depressed, who are more likely to report violent ideation.

In order to examine Baumeister's contention concerning the dark side of high self-esteem more specifically, we have employed two different strategies. In the first, we have performed regressions where we have, for a sample of young adolescents, entered self-esteem, narcissism (including a sense of entitlement), empathy, and self-reported conduct, to predict violent ideation in the face of threats to the self. We find that the latter three variables do predict violent ideation; however, self-esteem does not contribute to the prediction of violent ideation (Harter & McCarley, 2003). This work also reveals that self-esteem and narcissism are very separate constructs both conceptually as well as empirically, correlated at −.01. As a second approach, we have identified those high and low in violent ideation, and then examined mean differences in self-esteem, narcissism, empathy, and conduct. Significant differences emerge for narcissism, empathy, and conduct, but not for self-esteem. Rather, differences were in the opposite direction in that the more violent group reported lower self-esteem. Further research is needed to address these issues including what levels of narcissism, empathy, and conduct put one at risk for acting on their violent ideation in the form of actual attacks on others.

As a sixth issue, considerably more attention must be paid to gender-bias criticisms that our schools are eroding the self-esteem of girls (see the AAUW, 1992 report on how schools are shortchanging girls, as well as similar contentions by Sadker and Sadker, 1994). More recently, Pollack (1998) has made a counter claim, namely that it is the boys that schools are shortchanging, leading to low self-esteem and negative emotional outcomes that cause them to stifle their true selves. Despite these controversial claims, that have received extensive media attention, there is no compelling empirical support for these contentions. Nor have there been studies documenting the potential *outcomes* that gender bias may engender. In an initial foray into this topic (Harter, Rienks, & McCarley, 2004) with middle school children, we documented that 75% of the students felt that teachers treated girls and boys equally and fairly. (It should be noted that most of the existing claims were based on observations and interviews that were conducted 10 to 20 years ago and thus cultural sensitivity to such issues may have had an impact).

With regard to outcomes, the minority who felt that teachers showed bias against their gender reported lower self-esteem as a student, lowered motivation for classroom learning, and lower levels of the expression of their opinions in the classroom. Many questions remain that require not only studies employing students' self-perceptions but actual observational studies that not only examine the level of potential teacher gender bias in the classroom but a broad range of possible outcomes. It would also be important to assess teacher perceptions. Finally, it will be critical to examine the *directionality* of the effects we obtained. Is it that perceived bias leads to negative psychological outcomes or might there be other determinants of low self-esteem as a student, lowered motivation, less expression of opinions that children and adolescents *bring* to the classroom (from home, from peers, from the media and popular culture) that in turn might lead this minority of students to see the teacher as biased?

Finally, as researchers examining these issues, we need to constantly keep in mind a developmental perspective (Harter, 1999). It is distressing that the sub-fields of developmental psychology and adult social psychology have not embraced the thinking of each discipline. We cannot merely take adult psychological paradigms and dumb them down to do work with children, changing the vocabulary of instruments, etc. Real progress could be made if developmentalists attempted to look at adult social psychological paradigms and think about how they might translate or not in developmental stages. At the same time, adult social psychologists need to become more aware of developmental stages in order to determine how the processes they have articulated might be similar or different, at different developmental levels. This is our mandate for the future.

Where do we go from here as *practitioners*? It is generally assumed that high self-esteem is a psychological commodity to be encouraged by practitioners, given the negative correlates of low self-esteem that have been extensively documented. Thus, how can practitioners such as psychologists, psychiatrics, social workers promote the development of high and healthy self-esteem? The intervention programs designed in the 1960s and 1970s had little effect in successfully enhancing self-esteem, particularly for any meaningful length of time. This left many discouraged about how to address this problem through future efforts.

Elsewhere, in a chapter on interventions to promote positive, adaptive self-evaluations (Harter, 1999), the usefulness of distinguishing between the *goal* of an intervention (e.g., enhanced self-esteem) and the *target* of the intervention, namely the strategies to be employed, was emphasized. For example, if self-esteem enhancement is the *goal*, an intervention strategy should be directed at its *determinants* (not at self-esteem itself as in the "I'm OK, You're OK" tradition). There are three critical corollaries to such an approach. First, one must have a *model* of the causes of self-esteem. For example, earlier in this essay our model, based on the formulations of James (1892) and Cooley (1902), was described. This model identified two general antecedents, perceived competence/adequacy in domains deemed important (from James) and perceived approval from significant others (from Cooley). The initial domains we included were Scholastic Competence, Behavioral Conduct, Physical Appearance, Peer Likability, and Athletic Competence. Sources of support have included Parents and Peers.

The model first specifies that perceived adequacy in the domains of Scholastic Competence and Behavioral Conduct were more highly related to parental support whereas perceived adequacy in the domains of Physical Appearance, Peer Likability, and Athletic Competence was more highly related to peer support. The strategy, therefore, would be to design an intervention to address these *determinants* that, if successful, should then enhance self-esteem as a result.

The second corollary builds upon our findings, described earlier, that there are *multiple* pathways to one's level of self-esteem for different individuals. Thus, interventions need to be tailored to the particular pattern of causes for a given individual. One intervention program will *not* fit all, although this has been the prevailing strategy in the field. Typically a program is designed that focuses on only one target (e.g., social skills training, cognitive-developmental interventions, conflict resolution, ropes courses, athletic skills, etc.) and that single-focused program is then administered to everyone in a group of low self-esteem individuals, a strategy that has not been successful. These programs have not been effective because each individual has a different pattern of pathways to low self-esteem. For some, it may be that poor scholastic self-concept leads to low parental support that in turn leads to low self-esteem. For another, negative perceptions of one's attractiveness may lead to low peer support that in turn leads to low self-esteem. For yet another, perceived athletic activity may be associated with low peer likability and peer rejection that results in low self-esteem. There are many other individual patterns of the pathways leading to low self-esteem for given individuals. Thus, for there to be self-esteem enhancement as the result of an intervention, it must target the particular psychological pathways as the focus of the intervention strategies.

The third corollary is that any intervention effort must have as its goal the promotion of *realistically* high self-esteem. Here Damon's (1995) argument is relevant in that he decries the efforts of those who have put too much attention on encouraging our children and adolescents to merely "feel good about themselves," telling they are "wonderful," which results in fragile, unrealistic self-esteem that leads children and adolescents to avoid challenging situations that would threaten such self-esteem. As a result, the avoidance of learning activities that may expose one's unrealistic self-esteem rob the individual of opportunities to master a variety of needed skills appropriate to their developmental level. Rather, interventions need to be tailored to domains where a given individual needs to improve (cognitive skills, conduct, athletic skills, social skills) and to relational niches (e.g., with parents, peers, or other significant others) where more support can be garnered (using our own model as an example). The philosophy here is that if the actual causes are addressed directly, improved skills and enhanced support should, in turn, improve self-esteem.

Where do we go from here if we are *classroom teachers*? Some of the suggestions in the preceding section may be apt, since often programs are developed for use within the school system. However, it is critical to appreciate that for many teachers self-esteem enhancement is not their primary job definition. Some resent what they view as the touchy-feely efforts to enhance the emotional and psychological health of their students, based on activities that they are supposed to initiate. They feel that it is more appropriate to refer students with problems to a school psychologist or social worker, to bring problems to the attention of school administrators and the students' parents. Other teachers are a bit more sanguine in terms of minor strategies they could employ in the classroom, either with small groups of children or individual students, efforts that might realistically enhance a child's self-esteem, more narrowly defined. For example, the focus might be on the child's self-concept as a student, where efforts to enhance learning skills in a given school subject may lead to enhanced self-concept in that arena.

On a larger societal scale, teachers have become saturated with indictments that they have been shortchanging girls in the classroom, and more recently they have been accused that they do not understand the emotional boy code under which male youth must operate (Pollack, 1998). Realistically, given the strength of the assault on teachers, some have become appropriately defensive about these accusations. Thus, what can teachers do rather than helplessly accept these psychological attacks? First, they can, by reading treatments of these issues such as our own, presented earlier, realize that there is virtually no research demonstrating these claims. The scant research that has been conducted, for example our own recent study (Harter, Rienks, & McCarley, 2004), reveals that in 2004, the vast majority of middle school students in our city do *not* see teacher bias against the genders. Rather, they feel that most teachers treat students equitably. Much has happened on the societal and educational scene in the last two decades that may make the old claims obsolete. Teachers have become more aware of bias issues and self-corrected some of their own behavior toward more egalitarian treatment.

It is also critical for teachers to appreciate the fact that gender *equity* is not synonymous with treating male and female students *equally*, namely, exactly the same. Rather, gender equity requires an appreciation for how male and female students have different needs, different learning styles, and different behavioral patterns in the classroom. Thus, if teachers are harsher in their discipline with boys, as our findings show in the perceptions of both male and female students, it is reasonable to assume, knowing from the gender literature that boys are more impulsive, aggressive, disruptive, that they require different treatment from the teachers. Similarly, different learning styles both across the two genders but also as revealed in individual differences within each gender, make lead to "unequal" or different treatment that may well be extremely equitable.

Teachers must also appreciate the fact (as most teachers do) that children and adolescents come to the classroom with considerable gender "baggage" that they bring from home, from the peer group, from societal messages about how they should look and behave according to the prevailing gender stereotypes in the culture. Their level of self-esteem can be the result of numerous factors independent of how they are treated by teachers. The problem, however, lies in the fact that school and the classroom represent a microcosm of the larger culture, an arena to which students bring their gendered experiences daily and act on them. It might be illuminating for interested and concerned teachers to work with educational and psychological researchers (such as myself) to assess as a teacher students' self-esteem and its causes during the first week of class to determine that there are major differences that cannot possibly be related to their behavior.

Finally, the issue of school violence has loomed its ugly head in the last 8 years, given the 11 high profile cases in which white males from predominantly middle class, suburban or small city environments have mercilessly shot other students within the school settings. What role should teachers play, here? Certain schools have initiated bullying programs, with various degrees of success. However, our own work on violent ideation among students reveals that there is a different breed of students who are engaged in violent *ideation* but who have not come to the attention of teachers and school officials because they are not the typical delinquent, conduct disordered, acting out student. The latter are well known to teachers. Interestingly, the actual school shooters were *not* students with histories of delinquent, conduct disordered behaviors. In fact, most had gone unrecognized by school personnel as potentially violent. In a recent study of ours, we found that of those students themselves, who self-reported violent ideation and conduct problems, teachers who also rated these same students on conduct reported that one-third had no conduct problems. Thus teachers are unaware of the fact that many students are aware of their conduct problems. This is not an indictment of teachers. Rather, it bolsters our contention that there are students sitting in classrooms keeping thoughts of violence as well as suicide strictly to themselves.

Why might such students be important to identify? The incidence of school shootings is so very low that this cannot be our focus. Yet, the student sitting in a class preoccupied with either violent or suicidal ideation who may not act on these thoughts is seriously compromised in other areas. He or she is not going to be invested in school learning, is not going to be motivated to perform, is likely, as a result, to get poor grades, miss classes, not turn in homework, and not engage in appropriate social behaviors with peers. Such students are also not likely to do well on the standardized tests that have unfortunately become the metric for evaluating teachers' competence, for providing funds, raises, etc. to schools. Such students need to be identified, in order that they can be referred to services to deal with psychological problems that should not be the teacher's responsibility. Once again, working with researchers who can help to identify such students would be one step toward progress in separating students' psychological problems from the teacher's role in the classroom.

Finally, where do we go from here if we are *parents*? It is a fact that most parents are well-meaning and want their children to feel good about themselves. Our investment in our children automatically leads to our wanting them to experience high self-esteem. The first thing a thinking parent should do is avoid those fluffy trade books that presume to put your child in some gendered category where it is assumed that he or she is like everyone else of the same gender. Avoid books that put you, as a parent, in a given gendered category, books that deign to claim that they know how you parent. (You know the books.) Try to get to sources such as this volume that explain the research in an objective and accessible manner that does not blame parents, teachers, or society, simplistically.

Realize that you *do* have an impact on your child's self-esteem through the values you encourage in terms of what you feel is important for your child to achieve. You also have an impact in terms of the support and approval you provide. With regard to your values for your child's successes, realize that your children want to please you and will adopt your values as their own. Their self-esteem will hinge, in part, on how successful they are in the domains they have come to value. If they have the skills and abilities to meet these goals, then high self-esteem will result. If they do not have the natural talents, but continue to attempt to meet these standards, low self-esteem will ensue. A touching Olympic story this year involved a young man who was diagnosed with dyslexia, a boy born to a family where academic success, nothing short of an Ivy League education would be acceptable. Obviously that was not in the cards, given his severe disability. One day a gym teacher introduced a running exercise, and this youth ran twice as fast as anyone in the school, students well beyond his age. Fast forward to the end of this story; he became one of the greatest Olympic runners of all times. The point of this vignette is that often parents have to give up their own dreams for their children, and shift to the areas of competence that are more natural to their children's talents and agendas. If the children experience success, then high self-esteem will result.

The second most important source of child self-esteem that emanates from parents involves genuine approval for the child's positive qualities, whatever they are. Children internalize parental approval such that they learn to approve of themselves, a process that leads to high self-esteem. There is another form of approval that is much less positive, in fact it is not perceived by children as approval at all. We (Harter, 1999) have labeled it "conditional approval," which refers to the fact that parents will communicate to their children that they will only approve or love them if they meet what are often very demanding if not impossible standards of competence or performance. Our findings reveal that children do not see this as approval at all, rather it specifies the psychological hoops through which children must jump in order to please their parents. Often they feel it is not within the realm of possibility. As a result they become hopeless and develop low self-esteem. Often parents' own parents exacted such a toll, yet it can be difficult breaking through the generational cycle.

Another very difficult task for parents is to counter the societal emphasis on physical attractiveness as the pathway to high self-esteem. For females, historically, and more currently for males, failure to meet the punishing standards of appearance clearly leads, in our own research, to body dissatisfaction, low self-esteem, depression and suicidal thinking in some, and eating disorders in others. It is difficult for parents to break through this societal mentality that one's outer self is more important than one's inner self, namely, qualities of kindness, decency, fairness, loyalty, support, and for parents to be able to communicate this to their children. In part, this is because we as parents are also victims of these societal messages specifying very narrow and unrealistic standards of appearance.

Finally, as parents we need to appreciate the distinction between genuinely high self-esteem, where one values oneself as a good person with positive qualities, and narcissism that includes a sense of entitlement. Well-meaning parents often inadvertently cross the line and encourage in their child a sense of entitlement and a somewhat egocentric view that he/she is "the greatest." Our own work indicates that narcissistic entitlement can compromise peer relationships, can interfere with learning, and when such fragile self-esteem is threatened, can lead to violence.

CONCLUSION

There are many new directions that can be pursued with regard to the study of self-esteem that involve the efforts of researchers, mental health practitioners, teachers in the classroom, and parents. Moreover, these efforts can dovetail, rather than representing separate endeavors. Interventions need to be based on meaningful research studies that not only meet stringent standards but are accessible to practitioners, teachers, and parents. It is toward this goal that we should all strive.

REFERENCES

American Association of University Women. (1992). *How schools shortchange girls.* Washington, DC: American Association of University Women Educational Foundation.

Baumeister, R. F., Smart, L., & Boden, J. M. (1996). Relation of threatened egotism to violence and aggression: The dark side of self-esteem. *Psychological Review, 103,* 5–33.

Cooley, C. H. (1902). *Human nature and the social order.* New York: Charles Scribner's Sons.

Damon, W. (1995). *Greater expectations: Overcoming the culture of indulgence in America's homes and schools.* New York: Free Press.

Harter, S. (1999). *The construction of the self.* New York: Guilford Press.

Harter, S., Low, S., & Whitesell, N. R. (2003). What have we learned from Columbine: The impact of the self-system on suicidal and violent ideation among adolescents. *Journal of Youth Violence, 2,* 3–26.

Harter, S., & McCarley, K. (2003). *Is there a dark side to high self-esteem leading to adolescent violence?* Poster presentation at the Biennial Society for Research in Child Development, Miami, Florida.

Harter, S., Rienks, S., & McCarley, K. (2004). *Do young adolescents perceive gender bias in the classroom?* Poster presented at APA convention, Honolulu, Hawaii.

James, W. (1892). *Psychology: The briefer course.* New York: Holt.

Pollack, W. (1998). *Real boys: Rescuing our sons from the myths of boyhood.* New York: Random House.

Sadker, M., & Sadker, D. (1994). *Failing at fairness: How America's schools cheat girls.* New York: Charles Scribner's Sons.

Seligman, M. E. P. (1993). *What you can change and what you can't.* New York: Fawcett Columbine.

56

What Needs to Be Done?

NATHANIEL BRANDEN

Some years ago, a number of professors, interested in self-esteem, were invited to contribute essays to a book entitled *The Social Importance of Self-Esteem*, edited by Andrew Mecca, Neil J. Smelser, and John Vasconcellos, and to be published by the University of California Press. I attended a self-esteem conference and found myself sitting next to one of the professors who would be contributing an essay.

I asked him what definition of self-esteem he was working for and if it was shared by the other contributors.

I was astonished to see him draw back tensely, glower at me suspiciously, and demand, "Why do you want to know?"

Astonished and fascinated by his response, I explained, as benevolently as I could, that if the research was to have value one would need to know what the writers meant by "self-esteem" and if all the writers were working with the same concept. Otherwise, it would be a Tower of Babel, and what merit could their conclusions have?

Still more angrily, he said, "Don't think you can trap *me* into a definition!" I was stunned (although I admit I was also amused). "Look," I said, "I don't know what you mean by 'trapped.' After all, we are colleagues. We are both interested in the subject of self-esteem. I have been working in this field for many years. Since you are working on a book about self-esteem, don't you think it's natural that I'd be interested in how you define the term? How can you possibly construe my question as a 'trap'?"

I do not remember how he answered. I only know his stance remained puzzlingly adversarial.

Unsurprisingly, the book was a disappointment. I do not know that it satisfied anyone.

If asked what I see as immediate challenges facing those who work in the field of self-esteem, either as researchers or as practitioners, I will answer—for reasons contained in the above story—that the first priority is to carve out a definition of self-esteem that researchers can agree on. No easy task, in my opinion.

Obviously, I must resist the temptation to argue for the definition of self-esteem that I have presented and elaborated on at length elsewhere (Branden, 1994). I see self-esteem as "the disposition to experience oneself as being competent to cope with the basic challenges of life and of being worthy of happiness." Whether one accepts this formulation or any variant of it, or something else entirely, I am persuaded that any definition of self-esteem needs to include both the issue of competence and that of worthiness, rather than just one of those constituents, and must be *reality-based,* not merely a matter of *feelings* (Mruk, 1995). And this means that our concept must be differentiated from narcissism or grandiosity. Otherwise, we will have the pleasure of reading in the newspapers that psychological studies now suggest that high self-esteem correlates with violent behavior more than low self-esteem does (Branden, 1997).

Another challenge to researchers and practitioners is the need to operationalize the concept of self-esteem so that we clarify what it looks like in action. How do we recognize a decent level of self-esteem? How do we recognize its absence?

And this is the doorway to yet another related challenge: that of creating a test that will measure levels of self-esteem. Everyone recognizes the limitations of self-reports. But how to improve on them is not obvious. Yet, in the absence of a reliable test, it is difficult to produce reliable research concerning self-esteem's effects. I see this as one of the toughest challenges we face.

A challenge that confronts not only researchers and practitioners, but also parents and teachers, is that of thinking through what behavior on the part of adults is likely to nurture self-esteem in young people, and what behavior is likely to accomplish the opposite, *and what are the grounds of their beliefs.*

Many clinicians, for instance, have discovered through experience that treating a client with acceptance and respect can support the client's struggle for a better self-esteem, while mere assurances of the client's worth are generally ineffective. Similarly, many parents and teachers have discovered—or learned from the late child psychologist Haim Ginott—that hyperbolic praise is likely to do more harm than good (Ginott, 1972). Many teachers have invited criticism for believing that a young person's self-esteem can be cultivated by having students sing or announce "I am unique." (It should hardly be necessary to point out that a hay sandwich is also "unique.")

I am sometimes asked for advice about selecting a psychotherapist who can helpfully address self-esteem issues. I suggest that people interview the therapist and ask these questions:

> What do you mean by "self-esteem"?
> What do you think self-esteem depends on?
> What will we do together that will have a positive effect on our self-esteem?
> *What are your reasons for thinking so?*

For many practitioners the ability to answer these questions will be their number one challenge. When we can answer them well, there is no end to the possibilities confronting us—taking our work into schools, prisons, the world of business, and the culture in general.

Some of the things we need to know about self-esteem can only be learned through controlled studies. But there is a great deal that can be learned by working with people and paying attention to the outcome of our interventions. Everyone knows that sometimes we have a pet "theory" about what *ought* to work and we keep repeating the favored move, ignoring the fact that it is not delivering the desired results. Over the years I have had to remind myself more than once of that wise observation that doing more of what doesn't work, doesn't work. And often I have learned more from my failures than from my successes—because failures stimulate new thinking (or should).

It is unrealistic to demand that we ought to use only those interventions that have been proven effective in controlled studies. A clinician cannot provide "data" for every move he or she makes. Practice is always ahead of research, and not only in psychology. But we can do our conscientious best to pay attention to outcome. For clinicians, parents, and teachers, that will be an unending challenge.

REFERENCES

Branden, N. (1994). *The six pillars of self-esteem*. New York: Bantam Books.
Branden, N. (1997). *The art of living consciously*. New York: Simon & Schuster.
Ginott, H. (1972). *Teacher and child*. New York: The Macmillan Company.
Mruk, C. (1995). *Self-esteem: Research, theory, and practice*. New York: Springer.

Author Index

Subject Index